A Birder's Guide to Washington

Second Edition

ABA Birdfinding Guide Series

2015

WASHINGTON'S ECOREGIONS

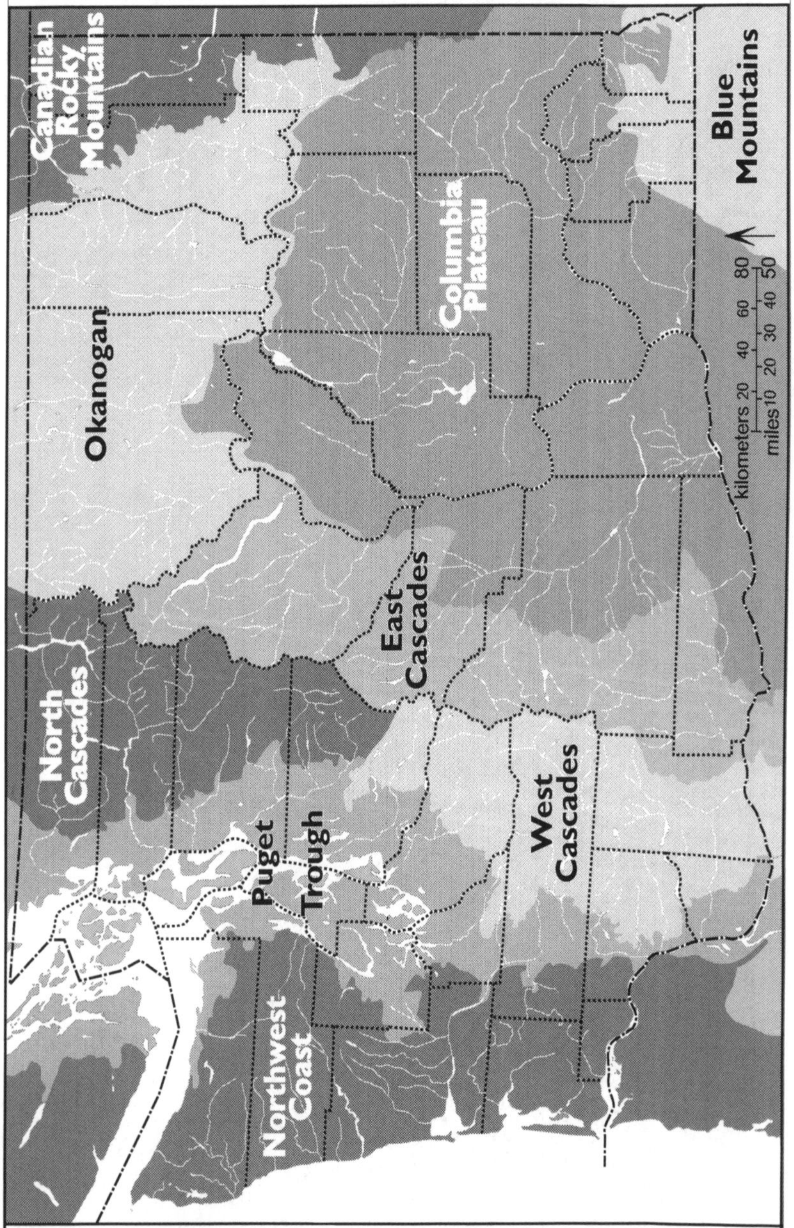

Canadian Rocky Mountains

Blue Mountains

Okanogan

Columbia Plateau

North Cascades

East Cascades

West Cascades

Puget Trough

Northwest Coast

kilometers 20   40   60   80
miles 10   20   30   40   50

Based on the boundaries adopted by the Washington Natural Heritage Program and The Nature Conservancy for use in ecoregional assessments and conservation planning.

A Birder's Guide
to
Washington

Second Edition

Jane Hadley, Editor

by the Members of the
Washington Ornithological Society

ABA Birdfinding Guide Series

2015

Copyright © 2015 by American Birding Association, Inc.
All rights reserved. No part of this publication may be reproduced, stored in a retrieval system, transmitted in any form or by any means, electronic, photocopying, or otherwise, without prior written permission of the publisher. Personal reproduction for recreational and educational purposes permitted.

Library of Congress Control Number: 2015940962

ISBN Number: 978-1-878788-40-5

Second Edition
1 2   3   4   5   6   7   8

Printed in the United States of America

Publisher
American Birding Association, Inc.

Editor
Jane Hadley

Maps and Layout
Cindy Lippincott using CorelDRAW and CorelVENTURA

Cover Photographs
©Paul Bannick/PaulBannick.com: Front Cover - Red-breasted Sapsucker
Back Cover - Sooty Grouse

Distributed by
American Birding Association
P.O. Box 744
93 Clinton Street, Suite ABA
Delaware City, DE 19706 USA
phone: 800-850-2473 or 302-838-3660
fax: 302-838-3651
web site: http://www.aba.org

For
TERRY AND DENNIS
AND HAL AND ANDY
and for the
FUTURE BIRDERS OF WASHINGTON

PREFACE AND ACKNOWLEDGMENTS

The present book is a revision and update of the first edition of *A Birder's Guide to Washington*, first published in 2003 by the American Birding Association, as a part of its series of birdfinding guides. Hal Opperman and Andy Stepniewski edited that book and also were major contributors of content along with some 30 members of the Washington Ornithological Society.

That guide was built upon *A Guide to Bird Finding in Washington*, by Terence R. Wahl and Dennis R. Paulson, first distributed in mimeographed form in 1971 and subsequently updated in numerous revisions, the last in 1991.

The 2003 first edition of *A Birder's Guide to Washington* has served as the bible of birdfinding in this state for more than a decade, relied upon by thousands of birders from inside and outside the state. It is regarded as one of the best, perhaps the best, of the state birdfinding guides.

Work on this second edition of *A Birder's Guide to Washington* began in 2013 and was completed in early 2015. We have retained the structure and organization of the first edition, but have made changes in content. The first edition contained 67 geographical sections; this second edition contains 65, having shed British Columbia sites. We made that decision mainly because Russell and Richard Cannings had recently published their excellent birdfinding guide for British Columbia; there no longer was a void needing to be filled by this guide.

We also decided to eliminate the annotated checklist for non-bird species, for space, time, and feasibility reasons.

The chief aim of the second edition was to bring the guide current, taking account of changes in names, habitat, birds, access, and other features of original sites in the 12 years since the first edition was published as well as adding worthwhile new birding sites. Some of the first edition authors returned in this edition to update their own sections, happily and importantly including Hal and Andy. But when original authors were unavailable for the task, we recruited new experts to revise and update the sections. Each of the revisers was given the freedom to decide to what extent he or she would revise the section, add new sites or delete old sites. In some cases, revisers found no need to change much of the original content; in other cases, the revisers made major changes.

Besides Hal and Andy, Bob Boekelheide, MerryLynn Denny, Scott Downes, Jon Isacoff, and Bob Kuntz deserve special mention for revising three or more sections. They truly stood tall.

Once the revisers submitted their work and the material was given an initial edit, some 60 volunteers dispersed around the state to "ground-truth" the routes, making sure that the directions and descriptions were accurate and easy to follow. Their findings, as they drove and walked the routes, were extremely valuable in improving the quality and accuracy of the content. Thanks go to these ground-truthers: Carlos Andersen, Gloria Baldi, Jeb Baldi, Timothy Barksdale, Kent Bassett, Elaine Bassett, Brian Bell, Blair Bernson, Robert Britschgi, Debbie Dain, Cathy Darracott, Jan Demorest, William Ehmann, Stephen Elston, Deborah Essman, Bob Flores, Carol Furry, John Gatchet, Helen Gilbert, Ruth Godding, Lindell Haggin, Eric Heisey, Ken Hemberry, Dick Johnson, Kurt Johnson, Mary Klein, Kay Lennartson, Jane Lester, Barry Levine, Laura Lippmann, Steve Loitz, Tom Mansfield, Teri Martine, Andrew McCormick, Steve Moore, Henry Mustin, Bob Myhr, Henry Noble, Ollie Oliver, Grace Oliver, Jim Owens, Amy Powell, Scott Ramos, Jo Reeves, Jeanelle Richardson, Randy Robinson, Penny Rose, Dave Slager, Margaret Snell, Jennifer Standish, Jack Stephens, Jerry Tangren, Rick Taylor, Tina Taylor, Jean Trent, Claire Waltman, Art Wang, Cricket Webb, and Matt Yawney.

Work on the new guide proceeded under three WOS presidents: Jack Stephens, Penny Rose, and Dan Stephens. Upon leaving office, Penny was designated the liaison between the project and the board; she has been a strong and helpful proponent throughout. I thank Penny, Jack, and Dan and the WOS board for their steadfast support.

WOS wishes to express its appreciation to the ABA and its president, Jeffrey Gordon, for their interest and partnership in publishing this revised edition. Our goals have been remarkably in synch, and the relationship trouble-free. Scott Flora, the ABA project manager, deserves our gratitude for his cooperative spirit and his capable shepherding of the project.

Cindy Lippincott, a contractor to the ABA, is a marvel of complementary talents who made my job so much easier than it could have been. Cindy, editor and graphic artist, also knows birds, geography, and a slew of other useful subjects. Always helpful, always friendly, always with a sense of humor, always competent, always conscientious, Cindy was a true pleasure to work with.

Bob Berman worked many technical wonders, including his signature bar graphs that convey so much information so gracefully.

Certain other individuals deserve special mention for their notable contributions. Hal provided me invaluable advice and encouragement throughout the two-year project. He was always available when I needed an ear, some wisdom, connections, or a bit of his extraordinary knowledge. I relied immensely upon him. And he contributed heavily to the content. I consulted Andy as well, drawing upon his knowledge of habitats and birding venues, and his many contacts. As in the original edition, Andy once again authored an exceptional number of sections—more than any other person. At his side was Ellen Quiring Stepniewski, who followed up on many of the details. All three have my profound gratitude. This revision simply would not have succeeded without them.

I also am greatly indebted to Randy Robinson, who helped to assemble and indicate the map changes needed for a number of the sections. Randy also ground-truthed several sections and revised others. In sum, he did whatever was needed and provided steady encouragement and support. The guide would have been significantly longer in preparation without his efforts.

Brian Bell must be designated ground-truther extraordinaire, having ground-truthed five territories. The birders of Washington owe special thanks to Matt Bartels, who updated the annotated checklist of birds, adding 32 species in the process, and Ryan Merrill, who updated the bar graphs of seasonal abundance. Matt and Ryan are among the most knowledgeable persons in the state about Washington's birds. As such, they are frequently called upon to share their knowledge, they have multiple responsibilities, and they spend much of their available time in the field. Lucky for us that they took what little spare time they have to update two of the most valuable features of this guide. Let us also thank the members of the Washington Bird Records Committee: without their conscientious and skilled consideration of rare bird reports, our picture of the birds of Washington—past, present and future—would be much the poorer.

Yet another set of individuals provided valuable assistance to the revisers or to me. This came in the form of helping to explore routes, sharing knowledge, answering questions, contributing maps or other documents, or reviewing text. Many thanks to these contributors: Jamie Acker, Steven Baker, Matt Bartels, Brian Bell, Joan Bird, Gary Bletsch, Wilson Cady, Sharon Cormier-Aagaard, Jim Danzenbaker, Mike Denny, Scott Downes, Jim Duemmel, Bob Flores, George Gerdts, Victor Glick, Bob Hansen, Dennis Hartmann, Randy Hill, Michael Hobbs, Mary Hrudkaj, Larry Hubbell, Stan Isley, Martha Jordan, Duane Karna, Kay Lennartson, Sheila McCartan, Ryan Merrill, Ann Musche, Glynnis Nakai, Dennis Paulson, Irene Perry, Steven Pink, Pam Pritzl, Jo Reeves, John Riegsecker, Randy Robinson, Douglas Schonewald, Michael Schramm, Libby Schreiner, Carol Schulz, Connie Sidles, Dan Stephens, Ruth Sullivan, Bill Tweit, Brad Waggoner, Andrea Warner, Diane Weber, Aaron Webster, Nancy Williams, Ann Marie Wood, Stan Wood, Charlie Wright, Matt Yawney, and Neil Zimmerman.

So many have contributed so much to this project. Washington's birders are fortunate indeed.

Jane Hadley
Seattle, Washington, May 2015

TABLE OF CONTENTS

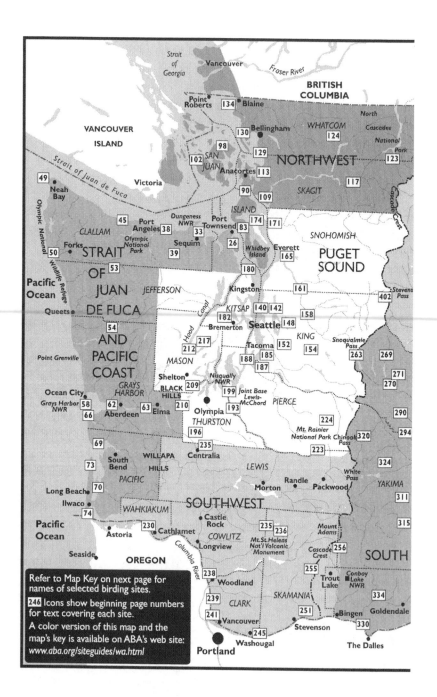

Strait of Georgia

Vancouver

Fraser River

BRITISH COLUMBIA

Point Roberts [134] Blaine

VANCOUVER ISLAND

[130] Bellingham

WHATCOM

North Cascades National Park

[124]

[98]

[102] SAN JUAN [129]

NORTHWEST

[123]

Anacortes [113]

[117]

[49]

Neah Bay

Strait of Juan de Fuca

Victoria

SKAGIT

[90] [109]

Olympic National Wildlife Refuge

[45] Port Angeles [38]

Dungeness NWR

ISLAND

Port Townsend [83] [174] [171]

SNOHOMISH

CLALLAM

[33]

Sequim

[26]

Whidbey Island

Everett [165]

PUGET SOUND

Olympic National Park

[50] Forks

STRAIT

[39]

[180]

OF [53]

JEFFERSON

Kingston

[161]

[402]

Stevens Pass

Pacific Ocean

JUAN

Hood Canal

KITSAP [140] [142]

[158]

Queets

DE FUCA

[182]

Bremerton

Seattle [148]

KING

[54]

Point Grenville

AND

[217]

[212]

MASON

Tacoma [152]

[154]

Snoqualmie Pass

[263]

[269]

Shelton [209]

Nisqually NWR

[188] [185]

[271]

[270]

Ocean City

GRAYS HARBOR

BLACK HILLS

[187]

PIERCE

Grays Harbor NWR [58] [62] [63]

[210]

[199] Joint Base Lewis-McChord

[290]

[66] Aberdeen Elma

Olympia [193]

THURSTON

[224]

[294]

[69]

[196]

Mt. Rainier National Park Chinook Pass [320]

[324]

[235]

[73]

South Bend

WILLAPA HILLS

Centralia

LEWIS

[223]

PACIFIC

White Pass

YAKIMA

Long Beach [70]

Morton

Randle

Packwood

[311]

Ilwaco

[74]

WAHKIAKUM

SOUTHWEST

Castle Rock

Mount Adams

[315]

Pacific Ocean

[230] Cathlamet

COWLITZ

[235] [236]

Cascade Crest [256]

Astoria

Longview

Mt. St. Helens Nat'l Volcanic Monument

SOUTH

Seaside

OREGON

Columbia River

[255]

Trout Lake

Conboy Lake NWR

[238]

Woodland

SKAMANIA

[334]

Refer to Map Key on next page for names of selected birding sites.

[239]

CLARK

[251]

Bingen

Goldendale

[246] Icons show beginning page numbers for text covering each site.

[241]

Vancouver

Stevenson

[330]

The Dalles

A color version of this map and the map's key is available on ABA's web site: www.aba.org/siteguides/wa.html

Portland

[245]

Washougal

REGIONS AND SELECTED SITES IN WASHINGTON

BRITISH COLUMBIA

IDAHO

Horseshoe Basin
439 Oroville • Chesaw 463 477
446 448 Metaline Falls
429 438 474
Tonasket 473 • Ione
445 Republic Sherman Pass Kettle Falls Pend Oreille River
422 Conconully 456 KETTLE RANGE SELKIRK MOUNTAINS PEND OREILLE
Rainy Pass Winthrop OKANOGAN Colville 471
418 Omak FERRY STEVENS • Usk 482
Twisp OKANOGAN 434 453 459 NORTHEAST 467 Newport •
426 Brewster 456 494
420 Grand Coulee
CHELAN Chelan Bridgeport 388 487
405 414 375 Wilbur 490
Leavenworth DOUGLAS Coulee City 391 Davenport 396 Spokane
412 384 Wilson Creek SPOKANE • Cheney
410 Wenatchee Soap Lake LINCOLN 495
Blewett Pass 370 369 Ephrata COLUMBIA Sprague
274 GRANT BASIN Ritzville
KITTITAS Moses Lake WHITMAN
277 351 THE PALOUSE
Ellensburg 281 350 Vantage ADAMS Colfax • 520
Yakima 285 354 Columbia NWR Pullman • Moscow
Naches Training 364 • Othello Washtucna 366
323 Center 367 GARFIELD
303 Hanford Reach National Mon. Snake River
Yakima • Moxee FRANKLIN SOUTHEAST
Toppenish NWR Sunnyside Richland • Pasco WALLA WALLA COLUMBIA Clarkston
CENTRAL 344 503 Dayton ASOTIN
Satus Pass 337 Kennewick McNary NWR Walla Walla BLUE MOUNTAINS 511 517
KLICKITAT 339 Umatilla NWR 505 507 515

OREGON

Columbia River

kilometers 20 40 60 80
miles 10 20 30 40 50

Strait of Juan de Fuca and Pacific Coast

- **26** Indian / Marrowstone Islands
- **33** Sequim Bay / Dungeness
- **38** Ediz Hook, Port Angeles
- **39** Hurricane Ridge / Deer Park
- **45** Clallam Bay / Sekiu
- **49** Cape Flattery
- **50** La Push
- **53** Hoh Rain Forest
- **54** Lake Quinault
- **58** Ocean Shores
- **62** Bowerman Basin
- **63** Chehalis River Valley
- **66** Westport
- **67** Tokeland
- **70** Willapa NWR
- **73** Leadbetter Point
- **74** Cape Disappointment SP

Northwest

- **83** Crockett Lake / Fort Casey
- **90** Deception Pass State Park
- **98** Orcas Island
- **102** San Juan Island
- **109** Fir Island / Skagit Flats
- **113** Samish Flats
- **117** Rockport / Marblemount
- **123** Colonial Creek Campground
- **124** Mount Baker
- **129** Larrabee State Park
- **130** Lummi Flats
- **134** Drayton Harbor

Puget Sound

- **140** Discovery Park
- **142** Montlake Fill / Union Bay
- **148** Lake Sammamish
- **152** Kent Valley
- **154** Rattlesnake Lake
- **158** Carnation Marsh
- **161** Crescent Lake Wildlife Area
- **165** Everett Ponds / Spencer Island
- **171** Stillaguamish River delta
- **174** Camano Island
- **180** Point No Point
- **182** Green Mountain State Forest
- **185** Saltwater SP / Dash Point SP
- **187** Gog-Le-Hi-Te Wetland
- **188** Point Defiance
- **193** JB Lewis-McChord Prairies

Puget Sound (continued)

- **196** Scatter Creek / Black River
- **199** Nisqually River delta
- **209** Totten Inlet / Kennedy Creek
- **210** Capitol State Forest
- **212** Great Bend / Annas Bay
- **217** Tahuya Peninsula
- **223** Mount Rainier - Paradise
- **224** Mount Rainier - Sunrise

Southwest

- **230** Julia Butler Hansen NWR
- **235** Coldwater Ridge
- **236** Windy Ridge
- **238** Woodland Bottoms
- **239** Ridgefield NWR
- **241** Vancouver Lowlands
- **245** Steigerwald Lake NWR
- **251** Skamania / Wind River
- **255** Indian Heaven / Mt Adams
- **256** Bird Creek Meadows

South Central

- **263** Commonwealth Basin / Hyak
- **269** Wish Poosh / Tucquala Lake
- **270** Cle Elum
- **271** Teanaway Road
- **274** Swauk Creek Basin
- **277** Kittitas Valley
- **281** Vantage Highway
- **285** Huntzinger Road
- **290** Buck Meadows
- **294** Wenas Campground
- **303** Cold Creek Road / YTC
- **311** Ahtanum Valley
- **315** Fort Simcoe State Park
- **320** Bumping Lake
- **323** Oak Creek Wildlife Area
- **324** Bethel Ridge
- **330** Lyle
- **334** Klickitat Wildlife Area
- **337** Rock Creek / Bickleton
- **339** Crow Butte Park
- **344** Yakima River delta

Columbia Basin

- **350** Frenchman Coulee
- **351** Potholes Wildlife Area
- **354** Lower Crab Creek
- **364** Saddle Mtns / White Bluffs
- **366** Washtucna
- **367** Palouse Falls SP, Lyons Ferry Pk
- **369** Beezley Hills

Columbia Basin (cont'd)

- **370** Moses Coulee
- **375** Waterville Plateau
- **384** Lower Grand Coulee
- **388** Steamboat Rock / Northrup Cyn
- **391** Swanson Lakes Wildlife Area
- **396** Reardan Ponds

Okanogan

- **402** Old Cascade Hwy / Union Gap
- **405** Lake Wenatchee / Fish Lake
- **410** Wenatchee Confluence SP
- **412** Swakane Canyon
- **414** Entiat River Basin
- **418** Stehekin
- **420** Chelan Ridge Hawkwatch
- **422** Methow Valley
- **429** Harts Pass
- **434** Timentwa Flats
- **438** Sinlahekin Wildlife Area
- **439** Similkameen River valley
- **445** Roger Lake / Freezeout Pass
- **446** Long Swamp
- **448** Okanogan Highlands
- **453** Nespelem

Northeast

- **456** Sanpoil River Valley
- **459** Silver Creek Road
- **463** Togo Mountain
- **467** Chewelah to Valley
- **471** Little Pend Oreille NWR
- **473** Big Meadow Lake
- **474** Sullivan Lake
- **477** Salmo Pass
- **482** Calispell Lake
- **487** Spokane Canyons
- **490** Spokane Valley
- **494** Mount Spokane State Park
- **495** Turnbull NWR

Southeast

- **503** Burbank Slough
- **505** Walla Walla River Delta
- **507** Biscuit Ridge / Lewis Peak
- **511** Wenatchee Guard Station
- **515** Chief Joseph Wildlife Area
- **517** Fields Spring State Park
- **520** Kamiak Butte County Park

SEE PREVIOUS PAGE

MAP KEY

INTRODUCTION

by *Hal Opperman and Andy Stepniewski*
revised by Hal Opperman, Jane Hadley, Josh Lawler, and Matt Bartels

Washington perches at the northwest corner of the conterminous United States—and birders know by instinct that corners are always good. Unlike the Southwestern borderlands, however, or South Florida, or or the bottom prong of the Lone Star State, Washington has no particular group of target species that occur nowhere else. Instead, our state is an ecological crossroads, offering year-round birding in settings of great natural beauty where an outstanding diversity of species can be found in a manageably small area.

Washington is the smallest of the 11 contiguous Western states, yet the state bird list stands at over 500 species, surpassing all but a few of the others. How can this be, for a state that covers just 3°20' of latitude? One answer is the great variation in relief across its 350-mile width. Another is the 3,000 miles of saltwater shoreline (thanks to Puget Sound and all those islands). Then, too, the state lies between the valleys of the Columbia and Fraser Rivers—two sea-level cuts across the Cascade Range that funnel birds between the interior and the coast. Both rivers have their origins in the British Columbia mountains and are among the largest on the continent.

Five of Washington's nine terrestrial ecoregions stretch north far into British Columbia, six extend south into Oregon or even California and Nevada, two reach eastward through the Rocky Mountains, while to the west lies the open Pacific. Have a look at the Ecoregions map on page ii and you will understand why 10 loons and grebes, 11 tubenoses, 12 woodpeckers, and 21 native sparrows and allies occur regularly every year in Washington, along with 42 species of shorebirds and 36 of waterfowl. Thirty-one species of gulls, terns, and their kin have been seen in the state, of which 20 occur regularly. What other state gives you a reasonable chance for 15 owls for your year list?

Equally revealing is a sampling of records of vagrants from the last half-dozen years: Baikal Teal, Common Eider, Hawaiian Petrel, Great Shearwater, Wedge-tailed Shearwater, Lesser Sand-Plover, Wilson's Plover, Mountain Plover, Wood Sandpiper, Long-billed Murrelet, Red-legged Kittiwake, Ross's Gull, Black-tailed Gull, Costa's Hummingbird, Eastern Wood-Pewee, Variegated Flycatcher, Bell's Vireo, Northern Wheatear, Smith's Longspur, McCown's Longspur, McKay's Bunting, Hooded Warbler, Summer Tanager, Painted Bunting, Dickcissel, Eastern Meadowlark, Orchard Oriole, Brambling, Lawrence's Goldfinch. These and many others arrive from all the compass points.

TOPOGRAPHY

Washington has a particularly complex, and fascinating, geological history. While you don't need to know your geology to bird the state successfully, an understanding of the basics can be helpful. Birds, after all, are tied to specific habitats, determined largely by climate. Climate is a function of topography—and topography is a consequence of geological events. Three great forces shaped the Washington landscape: plate tectonics, volcanism, and glaciation. Together they account for just about all of the distinctive birding regions of the state.

The western coastline of the primeval North American continent was once situated in Eastern Washington, not far from the present-day Idaho line. Moving gradually westward, the North American plate collided with two micro-continents. The Okanogan and Cascade terranes were successively annexed in this way. Tremendous pressures forced the ocean floor upward, tipping and folding the earth's crust into coastal mountain ranges that became the Selkirks and the Cascades. The Columbia Valley at Kettle Falls, the Okanogan Valley, and Puget Sound are remainders of the subduction trenches and former coastlines resulting from the meeting of these plates. Pushing westward, the continental plate next overrode an oceanic plate along a trench off the Washington coast, creating the Olympic Mountains and the Willapa Hills—a process that continues today at the rate of 2 or 3 inches a year. Raised up by subduction forces, the continental shelf slopes gradually to its edge 25–30 miles off the Olympic Peninsula—the destination of the Westport pelagic trips—before plunging steeply to the trench where the Juan de Fuca plate is slowly disappearing beneath the continent.

Plate collisions and crustal stresses have made Washington an area of intense volcanic activity for tens of millions of years. The most visible evidence is the High Cascades volcanoes—part of the "ring of fire" along the Pacific Rim—and the multiple outpourings of lavas in the Miocene epoch that left the Columbia Basin buried beneath basalt layers several thousand feet deep. Traces of volcanic activity are everywhere: pillow basalts, mudflows, layers of ash. The massive granite dome of the Okanogan Highlands results from an ancient volcanic event. Still farther back in time, the Blue Mountains trace their origins to an arc of volcanic islands off the coast of the old North American continent.

For the last two million years a succession of continental ice sheets advanced into Washington, then retreated. The most recent glaciation bulldozed its way across the northern third of the state beginning about 20,000 years ago, rounding off mountaintops, deepening valleys, gouging out future lake basins, and leaving behind great quantities of glacial debris when it withdrew 9,000 years later. The present physiognomy of Puget Sound is a textbook case of these processes at work. The glacial sheet was some 6,000 feet thick at the U.S.-Canada border; the site of Seattle lay beneath 3,000 feet of ice. Outwash from the melting glaciers created the gravelly soils of the South Sound Prairies at the southern extremity of glaciation, from Tacoma to Tenino. The Puget Basin is so filled with glacial crud (3,000 feet deep in places) that the nature of the underlying bedrock remains a matter of speculation for geologists.

On the Eastside, surges of glacial meltwater known as the Spokane Floods carved the Grand Coulee and many lesser but no less impressive channels, stripped topsoils to create the Channeled Scablands, steepened the Columbia Gorge, and deposited deep layers of silt in the beds of temporary lakes as far west as Vancouver/Portland. About 40 such floods occurred when periodic failures of ice dams released the impounded waters of Glacial Lake Missoula in western Montana.

Our book is organized into compact regions along county lines that artificially cut across the big topographic divisions more often than not. The following directory will help you to line up the topography with the associated birdfinding chapters (in plain italics).

Oceanic. Pelagic and inshore waters and coastline of Pacific Ocean and Strait of Juan de Fuca east to about Port Angeles. Since 2009, various Canadian, British Columbian, U.S. and Washington State geographic naming bodies have approved "Salish Sea" as an official designation for the inland marine waters of Washington and British Columbia. The Salish Sea extends from the north end of the Strait of Georgia and Desolation Sound to the south end of the Puget Sound and west to the mouth of the Strait of Juan de Fuca. *Strait of Juan de Fuca and Pacific Coast.*

Olympic Peninsula. North of the Chehalis River floodplain, bordered by Hood Canal, Strait of Juan de Fuca, Pacific Ocean. Dominated by Olympic Mountains. High-precipitation zone of western slopes contrasts markedly with rainshadowed northeastern portion. *Strait of Juan de Fuca and Pacific Coast, Puget Sound.*

Willapa Hills. Low coastal range south from the Olympic Peninsula to the Columbia River, including the Black Hills. *Strait of Juan de Fuca and Pacific Coast, Puget Sound, Southwest.*

Puget Trough/Willamette Valley/Georgia Depression. Lowlands between the coastal ranges and the Cascades. Includes the Georgia Depression northward from the San Juan Islands, inland marine waters eastward from Port Angeles and Victoria, Puget Sound, and a northern extension of the Willamette Valley of Oregon around Vancouver. (See description of "Salish Sea" in the Oceanic paragraph above.) The central Westside landform though not the largest, it figures in all four Westside chapters: *Strait of Juan de Fuca and Pacific Coast, Northwest, Puget Sound, Southwest.*

Cascade Range. High, wide mountainous belt separating Western from Eastern Washington. Wet west slopes, dry east slopes offer distinctively different habitats and birdlife, as do the Cascades north and south of Snoqualmie Pass. *Northwest, Puget Sound, Southwest, South Central, Okanogan.*

Columbia Basin. Central, dominant landform of Eastern Washington, relatively low-lying basin sloping from northeast to southwest and watered by the Columbia River and its tributaries. Core is in *Columbia Basin* chapter, periphery in all four of the other Eastside chapters: *South Central, Okanogan, Northeast, Southeast.*

Okanogan Highlands/Selkirk Mountains. Mountains and plateaus east of the Okanogan River and north of the Columbia Basin. *Okanogan, Northeast.*

Blue Mountains. South and east of the Columbia Basin, extending south into Oregon. Part of the Middle Rocky Mountains. *Southeast.*

WASHINGTON HABITATS

Few states show more dramatic contrasts in their environment than Washington. Elevations range from sea level to over 14,000 feet. Precipitation varies from over 200 inches annually on the Olympic Peninsula, nurturing a temperate rain forest and mountaintop glaciers, to a mere 6 inches in parts of the Columbia Basin, where near-desert conditions prevail. The primary reason for these contrasts is the Cascade Range, which runs from north to south the entire length of the state. Pacific storms slam into Western Washington for much of the year. The Wet Side is often cloudy and enjoys moderate temperatures at all seasons. East of the Cascades, Washington's Dry Side has a rainshadow climate. Summers are hot, winters cold; clear skies are the norm. Between these extremes, an array of precipitation and temperature regimes supports a remarkable variety of aquatic and terrestrial communities with a rich diversity of bird species. The most prevalent of these habitat types are summarized in the following pages.

Pelagic. Birding in Washington's pelagic zone is as good as anywhere in North America. Marine life of many kinds concentrates 25–30 miles offshore, near the edge of the continental shelf where upwellings are strongest. Typical birds include Black-footed Albatross, Northern Fulmar, Pink-footed, Buller's, and Sooty Shearwaters, Fork-tailed Storm-Petrel, Red-necked and Red Phalaropes, South Polar Skua, Pomarine, Parasitic, and Long-tailed Jaegers, Common Murre, Cassin's Auklet, Tufted Puffin, Black-legged Kittiwake, Sabine's Gull, and Arctic Tern.

Inshore Marine Waters. There is great variability in this habitat due to depth, bottom configuration and substrate, currents, and effects of tides on the water column and its animals. Thus all open salt water isn't equal when it comes to finding birds: different local conditions appeal to different species. The outer coast is exposed directly to the full power of the wind and waves of the Pacific Ocean; life here must be adapted to extremes, and many invertebrates are attached to the bottom. Eastward along the Strait of Juan de Fuca oceanic influences gradually diminish. The complex of protected basins and channels comprising greater Puget Sound is bathed twice daily through tidal action with an abundance of nutrients. Birds to expect in one place or another off Washington's coastlines include Surf, White-winged, and Black Scoters, Red-breasted Merganser, Red-throated, Pacific, and Common Loons, Horned, Red-necked, and Western Grebes, Sooty Shearwater (oceanic), Brandt's, Double-crested, and Pelagic Cormorants, Brown Pelican, Parasitic Jaeger, Common Murre, Pigeon Guillemot, Marbled and Ancient Murrelets, Rhinoceros Auklet, Tufted Puffin, Heermann's, Mew, Western, California, Thayer's, and Glaucous-winged Gulls, and Common Tern.

Sandy Beaches and Dunes. Sandy beaches backed by dunes characterize much of Washington's South Coast. Birds to look for near the water's edge include Brown Pelican, Black-bellied Plover, American and Pacific Golden-Plovers, Snowy and Semipalmated Plovers, Whimbrel, Ruddy and Black Turnstones, Red Knot, Sanderling, Dunlin, Baird's, Least, Pectoral, and Western Sandpipers, Heermann's, Western, California, Herring, and Glaucous-winged Gulls, and Caspian and Common Terns, Merlin, and Peregrine Falcon. Shorebirds feed on the abundant California Beach Fleas, a nocturnal crustacean, and on many other invertebrates. Huge numbers of shorebirds may roost along the beach at high tide. The unstabilized dunes closest to the beach are colonized mostly by introduced European Beachgrass. Birds seen here include Northern Harrier, American and Pacific Golden-Plovers, Snowy and Short-eared Owls, Horned Lark (*strigata*), Lapland Longspur, Snow Bunting, and Savannah Sparrow.

Rocky Shores. This habitat occurs mainly along the Outer Olympic Coast and the Straits of Juan de Fuca and Georgia, including the San Juan Islands. An exceptionally diverse fauna of marine organisms, including dozens of species of worms, snails, and other invertebrates, inhabits the intertidal zone. Sea stacks along the coast from Point Grenville north to Cape Flattery have large, but virtually inaccessible seabird colonies (Fork-tailed and Leach's Storm-Petrels, Common Murre, Cassin's Auklet, Tufted Puffin). Other typical birds of rocky shores include Harlequin Duck, Brandt's, Double-crested, and Pelagic Cormorants, Bald Eagle, Black Oystercatcher, Wandering Tattler, Black Turnstone, Surfbird, Rock Sandpiper, Heermann's, Western, and Glaucous-winged Gulls, Black-legged Kittiwake, Pigeon Guillemot, Peregrine Falcon, and Northwestern Crow.

Estuaries and Tidal Flats. The Puget Sound system is a giant estuary fed by numerous rivers, many with tidal flats. So, too, are two large, protected coastal bays—Grays Harbor and Willapa Bay. Rivers deposit sand and silt, providing an exceptionally rich substrate for burrowing invertebrates. Mudflats, salt marshes, tidal sloughs, and the littoral zone teem with loons, grebes, geese, dabbling ducks, shorebirds, gulls, and terns. Other typical birds found here include Double-crested and Pelagic Cormorants, Great Blue Heron, Osprey, Bald Eagle, Parasitic Jaeger, Pigeon Guillemot, Belted Kingfisher, Merlin,

Peregrine Falcon, Purple Martin, and American Pipit. The spring shorebird stopover at Grays Harbor National Wildlife Refuge is of international significance, especially for Black-bellied Plover, Dunlin, Western Sandpiper, and Short-billed Dowitcher.

Westside Ponds, Lakes, and Wetlands. This low- to mid-elevation family of freshwater habitats ranges from large, deep lakes to ponds, sewage lagoons, marshes (including brackish marshes), streambanks, and wet fields. Characteristic seasonal residents and migrants in environments with emergent vegetation and/or shallow edges include waterfowl (other than diving ducks), Pied-billed Grebe, Double-crested Cormorant, American Bittern, herons, Osprey, Bald Eagle, Northern Harrier, Virginia Rail, Sora, American Coot, Sandhill Crane, shorebirds (Killdeer and Spotted Sandpiper breed), gulls, Belted Kingfisher, falcons, Tree, Northern Rough-winged, and Cliff Swallows, Marsh Wren, Common Yellowthroat, and Red-winged Blackbird. Deeper, open waters attract loons, grebes, and diving ducks, although usually in lesser numbers than on salt water.

Westside Broadleaf Forests. Stands of hardwood trees blanket river floodplains, encircle ponds and wetlands, and crowd streambanks from the lowlands to the mountain passes. Red Alder and Bigleaf Maple dominate, with Black Cottonwood, Oregon Ash, Garry Oak, and various species of willows present locally. Broadleaf trees also appear following the removal of conifer forests by fire or clearcutting. The regenerating conifer forest eventually closes its canopy and shades them out, but small stands of hardwoods may persist even then in openings, near wet places, or on steep slopes. Bird species associated with broadleaf and mixed forest include Ruffed Grouse, Cooper's Hawk, Western Screech-Owl, Downy Woodpecker, Hutton's, Warbling, and Red-eyed Vireos, Black-capped Chickadee, Swainson's Thrush, Cedar Waxwing, Yellow, Black-throated Gray, and Wilson's Warblers, Black-headed Grosbeak, and Bullock's Oriole.

Westside Woodland/Prairie Mosaic. Pockets of grasslands dotted with brush and stands of Garry Oak, pines, and Douglas-fir occupy some of the driest parts of the Western Washington lowlands. Quite locally distributed, this unique habitat type occurs on the fast-draining glacial outwash soils of the South Sound Prairies and upper Chehalis River basin; south along the trough of the Cowlitz River to the plains around Vancouver; and in the lee of the Olympic Mountains from Sequim northeast to the San Juan Islands (the area of lowest rainfall in Washington west of the Cascades). Typical breeding species found much more commonly in one or more of these locales than elsewhere in Western Washington include Northern Harrier, Common Nighthawk, American Kestrel, Cassin's Vireo, Western Scrub-Jay, White-breasted Nuthatch (*aculeata*, now virtually extirpated), House Wren, Western Bluebird, Chipping and Vesper Sparrows, Western Meadowlark, and Purple Finch.

Westside Coniferous Forests. This is by far the largest habitat category, by area, in Western Washington. Forest types are differentiated into several zones by elevation and precipitation. All have been impacted in varying degrees by 150 years of commercial timber harvest.

Bathed in copious moisture, the luxuriant, moss-draped forest of the *Sitka Spruce zone* constitutes a narrow belt just up from the outer coastal beaches. Characteristic bird species of this rather uniform rain-forest habitat include Spotted Owl (scarce and declining), Rufous Hummingbird, Steller's Jay, Chestnut-backed Chickadee, Pacific Wren, Golden-crowned Kinglet, Varied Thrush, Townsend's Warbler, and Red Crossbill.

Farther east, in the rainshadow of the Olympic Mountains, the original forest of the low-lying Puget Sound *Douglas-fir zone* has been all but completely logged off. The present-day landscape away from the burgeoning cities is characterized by fragmented second-growth conifer forest interspersed with broadleaf woodlands, semi-rural residential development, farmlands, prairie, wetlands, and glacier-carved lakes. Avian diversity and numbers are higher in this varied landscape than in the Sitka Spruce zone. Familiar breeding species include Northern Flicker, Pacific-slope Flycatcher, American Crow, Violet-green and Barn Swallows, Black-capped Chickadee, Red-breasted Nuthatch, Swainson's Thrush, American Robin, European Starling, Orange-crowned and Wilson's Warblers, Spotted Towhee, Song and White-crowned Sparrows, Western Tanager, Brown-headed Cowbird, Purple Finch (declining), and American Goldfinch, along with several of the common coastal rain-forest species.

Forests of the *Western Hemlock zone* extend up the slopes of the Cascades and Olympics from just above the Sitka Spruce and Puget Sound Douglas-fir zones to mid-elevations, including all of the Willapa Hills. This is the most widespread forest type in Western Washington, dominated by Western Hemlock (the climax species), Douglas-fir, and Western Redcedar. Most of this zone is occupied by industrial tree farms, but significant stands of the original forests remain uncut—for example, in Mount Rainier National Park. Breeding birds more likely here than in the lower-elevation forest zones are Sharp-shinned Hawk, Band-tailed Pigeon, Northern Pygmy-, Barred (increasing), and Northern Saw-whet Owls, Vaux's Swift, Red-breasted Sapsucker, Hairy and Pileated Woodpeckers, Olive-sided and Hammond's Flycatchers, Common Raven, Brown Creeper, American Dipper, MacGillivray's and Yellow-rumped Warblers, Dark-eyed Junco, and Evening Grosbeak.

The *Silver Fir zone* occupies slopes of the Olympics and west Cascades at middle to high elevations. Silver Fir and Western Hemlock are the dominant tree species. These lichen-festooned forests receive abundant precipitation, much of it in the form of snow. Indicator bird species include Northern Goshawk, Gray Jay, Hermit and Varied Thrushes, Townsend's Warbler, and Pine Siskin.

Above the Silver Fir zone is the *Mountain Hemlock zone*, an excessively snowy subalpine belt extending to the upper limit of closed forests. The most typical breeding species—all of which also occur in lower-elevation forest zones—are Olive-sided Flycatcher, Gray Jay, Red-breasted Nuthatch, Pacific Wren, Golden-crowned Kinglet, Hermit Thrush, American Robin, Yellow-rumped Warbler, Dark-eyed Junco, Western Tanager, and Pine Siskin. Red-naped Sapsucker and several other Eastside species breed locally in small numbers in the Mountain Hemlock zone.

Alpine/Parkland. Clumps of Mountain Hemlock and Subalpine Fir, with some Whitebark Pine (drier sites), alternate with lush, herbaceous meadows. Sooty Grouse, Clark's Nutcracker, Common Raven, Mountain Chickadee, Mountain Bluebird, Hermit Thrush, American Robin, American Pipit, Slate-colored Fox Sparrow, Dark-eyed Junco, and Pine Siskin are the typical breeding birds. Dwarf alpine vegetation occupies a narrow, treeless strip between these subalpine parklands and the permanent ice and snow of the highest peaks. White-tailed Ptarmigan, Horned Lark (*alpina*), and Gray-crowned Rosy-Finch breed here. In late summer and early fall many raptors and passerines take advantage of the food resources of these high-elevation habitats.

Eastside Coniferous Forests. The *Subalpine Fir zone* is the interior complement of the Westside's Mountain Hemlock zone. Dominated by Subalpine Fir and Engelmann Spruce, it occurs mainly on the east slopes of the Cascades and eastwards, but also on high, east slopes of the Olympics and at the summits of some of the drier ranges in eastern Skagit and Whatcom Counties. Typical birds are much the same as for the Mountain Hemlock zone, with the addition of Spruce Grouse (mostly Okanogan and Northeast), Boreal Owl, American Three-toed Woodpecker, Boreal Chickadee (adjacent to the Canadian border), Ruby-crowned Kinglet, Townsend's Solitaire, Chipping Sparrow, Pine Grosbeak (mostly Northeast), Cassin's Finch, and White-winged Crossbill (irregular).

The *Interior Western Hemlock zone*, the wettest Eastern Washington forest habitat, has Western Hemlock and Western Redcedar as its principal tree species. It occurs mainly at mid- to upper elevations along the east slopes of the Cascades, and reappears at low to middle elevations of the Selkirk Mountains (the "Interior Wet Belt"). The typical birds are as for Western Washington wet forests.

The *Grand Fir zone* is a dense-forest type dominated by Grand Fir with a secondary component of Western Larch, Western White Pine, and Douglas-fir, often with an open understory. It occurs at lower middle elevations, below the Interior Western Hemlock and Subalpine Fir zones and above the drier forest habitats that edge the Columbia Basin. With few exceptions, the list of typical bird species resembles one for the Westside Western Hemlock and Silver Fir zones, e.g., Northern Goshawk, Spotted Owl, Hairy and Pileated Woodpeckers, Olive-sided Flycatcher, Gray and Steller's Jays, Mountain and Chestnut-backed Chickadees, Red-breasted Nuthatch,

Golden-crowned Kinglet, Hermit Thrush, American Robin, Yellow-rumped and Townsend's Warblers, Dark-eyed Junco, Western Tanager, Red Crossbill, Pine Siskin, and Evening Grosbeak.

Downslope from the Grand Fir forests, at the point where the Interior Douglas-fir zone begins, much of the moisture from Pacific storms has been wrung from the clouds. This rainshadow climate results in a relatively open forest characterized by Douglas-fir and some Western Larch and Grand Fir. Birds are much the same as those of the Grand Fir zone, with the addition of Calliope Hummingbird, Williamson's Sapsucker, Western Wood-Pewee, Hammond's Flycatcher, Cassin's Vireo, Townsend's Solitaire, Nashville Warbler, Chipping Sparrow, and Cassin's Finch.

An open forest dominated by Ponderosa Pine forms a broad ring around the Columbia Basin, with tongues up the Methow, Okanogan, and other river valleys. Fires are frequent in this tinder-dry habitat and are succeeded by extensive brushlands. This Ponderosa Pine zone has many birds of interest, including Flammulated Owl, Northern Pygmy-Owl, Common Poorwill, Lewis's, White-headed, and Black-backed (rare) Woodpeckers, Gray and Dusky Flycatchers, White-breasted and Pygmy Nuthatches, House Wren, Western and Mountain Bluebirds, Spotted Towhee, and Slate-colored Fox Sparrow. Several of the common species of the Interior Douglas-fir and Grand Fir zones can also be found here.

Eastside Oak/Pine Woodlands. This small zone characterized by savannahs and woodlands of Garry Oak and Ponderosa Pine with a bunchgrass understory occurs at low elevations in the Southeastern Cascades. Transitional between the Ponderosa Pine zone and steppe-sagebrush habitats, the Oak/Pine Woodlands zone represents the northern extension of an ecoregion that stretches along the eastern base of the Oregon Cascades to California's Modoc Plateau. Some of the typical bird species found here are Wild Turkey, Turkey Vulture, Golden Eagle, Anna's Hummingbird, Lewis's and Acorn (rare) Woodpeckers, Western Wood-Pewee, Say's Phoebe, Ash-throated Flycatcher, Western Scrub-Jay, House and Bewick's Wrens, Western Bluebird, Chipping and Vesper Sparrows, Black-headed Grosbeak, Lazuli Bunting, and Lesser Goldfinch.

Eastside Broadleaf Forests. Another bird-rich habitat is the fringe of Black Cottonwood, Quaking Aspen, White Alder, and other broadleaf trees along streams, ponds, lakes, and wetlands in the dry conifer-forest zones, reaching out into the shrub-steppe in places. Most of the species mentioned above for Westside broadleaf forests are also found in this Eastside riparian zone (Hutton's Vireo being a flagrant exception), together with Great Horned and Long-eared Owls, Black-chinned Hummingbird, Lewis's Woodpecker, Red-naped Sapsucker, Western Wood-Pewee, Pacific-slope Flycatcher, Eastern Kingbird, Bewick's Wren, Veery, Gray Catbird, Northern Waterthrush (boggy areas, Okanogan and Northeast), Nashville and MacGillivray's Warblers, American Redstart (mainly boggy areas, Northeast),

Yellow-breasted Chat, and Song Sparrow. Aspen groves—widely distributed across conifer-forest openings, bottomlands, and mountain slopes—appeal to cavity-nesting birds, especially woodpeckers.

Shrub-steppe. Shrub-steppe was once Eastern Washington's most extensive habitat type; it is now the most seriously threatened ecosystem in the state due to wholesale conversion for agricultural uses and to various other development pressures. Where it survives, the original landscape of the Columbia Basin might appear homogeneous to the passer-by, but this is hardly so. Grouped from wettest to driest are the following three major communities.

Almost all deep soils of the *Palouse and Blue Mountain Steppe* communities of Southeastern Washington have been converted to dryland wheat farming, hospitable to a limited range of species, including Gray Partridge and Horned Lark. The tiny remaining parcels of native vegetation are hillside Ponderosa Pine groves with scattered clumps of Quaking Aspen and thickets of Black Hawthorn, Common Snowberry, Nootka and Woods Roses, Western Serviceberry, Common Chokecherry, and Red-osier Dogwood, adjacent to grasslands with a high herbaceous cover. These harbor a riparian-like breeding avifauna including Northern Harrier, Eastern Kingbird, Black-billed Magpie, House Wren, Gray Catbird, MacGillivray's Warbler, Yellow-breasted Chat, Spotted Towhee, Vesper and Song Sparrows, and Bullock's Oriole. Most of the typical steppe birds have vanished along with their habitat.

Occurring mainly on higher, north- or northeast-facing ridges of the northern and eastern Columbia Basin, the *Three-tip Sagebrush/Idaho Fescue* communities are characterized by dwarfish mats of sagebrush with vigorous stands of Idaho Fescue and other tall bunchgrasses that attract shrub-steppe obligates such as Greater Sage-Grouse and Sharp-tailed Grouse (both rare, local), Swainson's Hawk, Short-eared Owl, Common Nighthawk, Say's Phoebe, Common Raven, Horned Lark, Sage Thrasher, Clay-colored (rare), Brewer's, Vesper, and Grasshopper Sparrows, and Western Meadowlark.

The *Central Arid Steppe* is situated in the lowest, hottest part of the Columbia Basin. In pristine form it is swathed with a combination of Big Sagebrush and Bluebunch Wheatgrass. Native grass cover is now much reduced through livestock grazing, however, and much of the area has been invaded by Cheatgrass, an exotic. Typical breeding birds include Greater Sage-Grouse, Red-tailed Hawk, Long-billed Curlew, Burrowing Owl, Common Nighthawk, American Kestrel, Say's Phoebe, Loggerhead Shrike, Common Raven, Horned Lark, Sage Thrasher, Brewer's, Lark, and Sagebrush Sparrows, and Western Meadowlark.

Eastside Cliffs and Talus Slopes. Coulees and canyons throughout the Channeled Scablands of the Columbia Basin and elsewhere at lower elevations in Eastern Washington provide a niche for nesting raptors and a host of other species. Among the most typical are Chukar, Red-tailed and

Ferruginous Hawks, Golden Eagle, Rock Pigeon, Barn and Great Horned Owls, Common Poorwill, White-throated Swift, American Kestrel, Prairie Falcon, Common Raven, Violet-green and Cliff Swallows, Rock and Canyon Wrens, European Starling, and Gray-crowned Rosy-Finch(winter night roosts).

Columbia Basin Wetlands. Widespread irrigation in the Columbia Basin has caused the water table to rise, expanding historical wetlands and creating new ones—a boon for many species of birds. A sample of the long list of breeding birds of Columbia Basin wetlands includes Canada Goose, dabbling ducks (several species), Redhead, Ruddy Duck, Eared, Western, and Clark's Grebes, Double-crested Cormorant, Great Blue Heron, Great Egret, Black-crowned Night-Heron, Virginia Rail, Sora, American Coot, Sandhill Crane (migration), Black-necked Stilt, American Avocet, Killdeer, Spotted Sandpiper, Wilson's Snipe, Wilson's Phalarope, Ring-billed and California Gulls, Caspian, Black, and Forster's Terns, Belted Kingfisher, Willow Flycatcher, Tree, Northern Rough-winged, and Bank Swallows, Marsh Wren, and Red-winged and Yellow-headed Blackbirds. Seep lakes, river deltas, ponds, and marshes offer excellent shorebirding, especially in fall migration.

Eastside Lakes and Reservoirs. Waterfowl, loons, grebes, and gulls have benefited greatly from the damming of the Columbia and Snake Rivers. Especially in fall, the migration of many species usually more associated with marine waters has been stopped in its tracks by the lure of the deep, wide reservoirs. Huge flocks of ducks remain as late into winter as ice-free conditions permit. Other Eastern Washington lakes and adjacent wetlands have a similar effect on a smaller scale. American White Pelicans now breed on two islands in Eastern Washington and are being seen in increasing numbers along the Columbia in all seasons. Bufflehead, Common and Barrow's Goldeneyes, Common Loon, Horned (rarely) and Red-necked Grebes, and Black Tern nest on natural lakes in forested parts of the Okanogan and Northeast.

Shrubby Thickets. This widespread family of habitats exists in a variety of situations at all elevations statewide—for example, forest edges and clearings (such as regenerating clearcuts); mountain slopes, including avalanche chutes; fencerows, dikes, and irrigation ditches; power-line and transportation corridors; free-standing patches of brush and small trees in open landscapes; and mature shrubbery in parks and gardens. Among the many birds that exploit these habitats for cover, nesting, or foraging are quails, Rufous Hummingbird, Willow Flycatcher (and other flycatchers), Black-capped Chickadee, Bushtit, House, Pacific and Bewick's Wrens, kinglets, Hermit Thrush, American Robin, Gray Catbird, Cedar Waxwing, Orange-crowned, Nashville, MacGillivray's, Yellow, and Wilson's Warblers, Common Yellowthroat, Yellow-breasted Chat, Green-tailed (rare, local) and Spotted Towhees, American Tree, Fox, Song, Lincoln's, Swamp, White-throated, Harris's, White-crowned, and Golden-crowned Sparrows, Dark-eyed Junco, Lazuli Bunting, House Finch, Lesser and American Goldfinches, and House Sparrow.

Farmlands. Washington contains large areas of pasture and agricultural land, often inhabited by species of native grasslands, although many of the latter are not able to switch to the simpler habitats produced by human endeavor. For example, extensive wheat fields are used by only one species, the Horned Lark, out of many that existed in the original grasslands. White-tailed Kite (Southwest and South Coast but currently rare), Northern Harrier, Red-tailed Hawk, and Barn, Great Horned, and Short-eared Owls are among the raptor species that exploit high rodent densities of hay fields and pasturelands at any season, joined by Rough-legged Hawk in winter. Swainson's and Ferruginous Hawks have adapted to hunting over Columbia Basin croplands in spring and summer. In Washington, Bobolinks nest only in irrigated hay fields in the Yakima Valley (declining), the Okanogan, and the Northeast. Dairies, feedlots, and grain-storage facilities may draw California Quail, Gray Partridge, Rock Pigeon, Mourning Dove, and thousands of starlings and blackbirds, along with the hawks and falcons that prey on them. Certain Westside and Eastside farmlands are famous for their large winter concentrations of waterfowl, raptors, cranes, and shorebirds, providing some of the best birding in the state. Orchards and vineyards, on the other hand, offer relatively few birds other than those species commonly associated with mankind.

CLIMATE CHANGE AND BIRDS IN WASHINGTON

by Josh Lawler

Climate change has the potential to affect many of the bird species in Washington. As temperatures increase and precipitation patterns change, we will likely see changes in habitat, food resources, species distributions, and the timing of migration, nesting, and hatching of many species. Vegetation models project the loss of many subalpine and alpine habitats, a shrinkage of the sagebrush steppe, and potential changes in Westside forests—some projections are for drier conditions and conversion to more Eastside-like forests, whereas other projections are for conversion to more northern California-like forests. Many bird species are already shifting their distributions poleward and upward in elevation, seemingly tracking increases in temperature. In some parts of the country, we are seeing earlier returns from migration and earlier breeding events. These changes in timing themselves are not a problem, but when shifts in the timing of flowering, insect emergence, and bird migration do not coincide, the resulting mismatches can negatively affect bird populations.

In addition to these more obvious impacts, climate change will also have more indirect effects on birds. For example, projected changes in temperature and precipitation are expected to result in larger and more frequent fires, particularly in Eastern Washington. These fires will benefit birds that make use of earlier successional habitats, but will negatively affect birds that inhabit more mature dry forests. In addition, ocean acidification—like climate change, also a result of increased greenhouse-gas concentrations—and warming seas are affecting marine and intertidal food webs. In conjunction with sea-level rise, these impacts have the potential to affect food resources and nesting habitat for shorebirds and pelagic species. Finally, as species move in response to climate change, we can expect to see new communities forming, and new interactions among species. Some birds may encounter new predators or new prey species and others may have to compete with birds with which they did not previously interact.

This is not to say that all bird species will be adversely affected by climate change. The most widespread species that inhabit many different environments will likely remain common because they are adapted to a wide range of climatic conditions. And some species in Washington will likely benefit from climate change, particularly those that are today uncommon in Washington but are much more common in Oregon and California. However, for some species that will be more adversely affected, management and conservation actions will be necessary to prevent declines. These include *mitigation actions* that work to reduce the amount of climate change we will likely experience (e.g., reducing fossil fuel use and decreasing forest loss) and *adaptation actions* that help species or ecological systems address the changes that will occur (things like managing forests with and for fire, restoring coastal habitats, and protecting and connecting lands across elevation and temperature gradients). It will take a combination of these actions to reduce the impacts of climate change on Washington's wild places and wild birds.

CONSERVATION

Throughout this guide, birding information intertwines with discussion of conservation concerns for birds and their habitats. By good fortune and foresight, large tracts of Washington lands are preserved in a natural or near-natural condition. However, economic pressures and the state's population growth are such that practically no land is 100 percent invulnerable to human exploitation, even when it has been set aside for wildlife. The future of birding as we know it depends on the continued protection of important breeding, foraging, and migratory bird areas and on the increasing awareness and activism of birders themselves. Volunteer opportunities abound where birders can put their birding skills to use at every level—from saving the local marsh or tidelands from development to participating in projects of hemispheric importance.

Washington has always been a conservation-minded state. Many parks and refuges have "friends of" membership groups. Consider supporting some of the state and regional organizations that unite people of diverse interests in a common cause, for example, Washington Environmental Council, Washington Wild, Kettle Range Conservation Group, Adopt-A-Stream Foundation, Conservation Northwest, and Audubon Societies throughout the state. For a true hands-on experience, join in the restoration of your neighborhood watershed: what's good for native vegetation is also good for water quality, spawning salmon, and birdlife. Most important, activities such as these build community understanding. Wherever you go, be an ambassador for birding. Wear your binoculars proudly. Patronize local businesses and tell people why you've come to their part of the state.

THE BIRDING YEAR

Washington is a year-round birding destination. However, most birds are strongly responsive to the seasonal cycle. Seasons are well marked, especially east of the Cascades. Precipitation is heavier in the winter and spring, summers generally being dry in all regions. In Western Washington winters are very wet, with overcast skies and light rain an almost constant condition in some years (before complaining, remember that overcast weather allows the best viewing because you do not have to contend with the low northern-latitude sun). This is interspersed with short periods of northeasterly winds that bring dry and cold air from the interior, resulting in clear skies and unsurpassed views of the mountains. Snowfall in the lowlands usually occurs at these times, when cold interior air meets moist coastal air. Above 1,000 feet in elevation, snow remains on the ground all winter, lasting at the 5,000-foot level into July or even August. Summers west of the Cascades are warm with the amount of rainfall variable from year to year; some summers are entirely dry and quite warm, others are cool and rainy. East of the mountains, winters are cold, and snow may stay on the ground throughout colder winters, even at the lowest elevations. In warmer winters, many ponds in the Columbia Basin remain open, and snow cover melts in a few days. Summers are very dry and hot in Eastern Washington. The desert areas remain green into June, but by July the general impression is one of death, many of the organisms having finished their annual life cycles and gone into a dormant state. Much of the vegetation is dry, and even birds are not particularly in evidence, except around water.

In four-month groupings, here are some of the highlights of the birding year. The bar graphs and the Annotated Checklist at the back of the book will help you fine-tune the specific destinations and the timing of your visits.

Spring and Early Summer (late March–early July). Spring shorebird migration is outstanding along the coasts, with highest numbers at Grays Harbor near the end of April (Red Knot, Western Sandpiper, Short-billed Dowitcher). In the Columbia Basin, Greater Sage-Grouse strut their leks in March–early April, about the same time that Sandhill Crane migration peaks. Forest owls are vocal and territorial. Prolonged and mostly low-key, spring passerine migration takes place over a broad front, with occasional weather-provoked fallouts and concentrations at headlands, along drainage corridors, or in riparian oases. May is the month of greatest species diversity. Westside Big Day record counts cluster toward the end of the first week of the month and about two weeks later east of the Cascades. June is the heart of the nesting season in most of the state's habitats—a good time to look for White-headed Woodpeckers and Gray Flycatchers in Ponderosa Pine woods; waterfowl, grebes, herons, rails, and terns in wetland habitats; or Pelagic Cormorants, Black Oystercatchers, Pigeon Guillemots, Rhinoceros Auklets, and a few Tufted Puffins on the Protection Island boat trip.

Late Summer and Early Fall (late July–early November). Roads in the Okanogan high country are snow-free—an invitation to look for Spruce Grouse, Great Gray and Boreal Owls, American Three-toed and Black-backed Woodpeckers, and Boreal Chickadee. This is also your window to look for White-tailed Ptarmigan and other species of alpine habitats. Or try the Blue Mountains for owls and woodpeckers. Midsummer to early fall, hawkwatching can be decent on clear days along Cascade ridges—for example, Red Top Mountain, Cooper Ridge, or Slate Peak. In late August–early September, passerine migrants concentrate in Eastside riparian corridors in open country. Hotspots such as Washtucna, Vantage, Tri-Cities parks, and Lyons Ferry and Palouse Falls State Parks are as close as Washington comes to true vagrant traps. Recently, Neah Bay, a coastal spot at the northwestern tip of the state, shows great promise and might prove to be the best of all. Late summer offers the greatest diversity on the Westport pelagic trips and the possibility of sought-after species such as Laysan Albatross, Flesh-footed Shearwater, and South Polar Skua. Shorebirding on the coast also peaks at this season, with American and Pacific Golden-Plovers, Bar-tailed Godwit, Ruff, and Sharp-tailed Sandpiper occurring regularly.

Late Fall and Winter (late November–early March). Southwesterly winter storms and timing of the tidal cycle severely limit pelagic birding possibilities, but protected marine waters welcome great numbers of waterfowl, loons, grebes, and other waterbirds. Chances are good for Ancient Murrelet (November–December best) and there's usually a Yellow-billed Loon around someplace. Black Oystercatchers, Black Turnstones, Surfbirds, and Rock Sandpipers patrol rocky shores, breakwaters, and jetties. Raptors and wintering waterfowl abound on Westside river floodplains, with prizes such as Emperor Goose, Gyrfalcon, and Snowy Owl. Raptors, including the last two named, work the snowy fields of Eastern Washington as well. Lapland Longspurs and Snow Buntings infiltrate Horned Lark flocks on the high plateaus. Northern Hawk Owls (rare), Bohemian Waxwings, Gray-crowned Rosy-Finches, and Common Redpolls visit Eastside cliffs, weedy roadsides, orchards, and ornamental plantings in towns. Sagebrush Sparrows and other shrub-steppe breeders return as early as February. On the Westside, Hutton's Vireos and Pacific Wrens are singing by early March.

GETTING AROUND

For better or worse, the only practical way to bird Washington is by automobile. All of our route descriptions presume that you will be traveling in a private vehicle. Mileages are point-to-point rather than cumulative. In other words, you must reset your trip-odometer to zero at each new mileage indication (or keep track mentally).

Maps. The Washington State Department of Transportation (WSDOT) no longer offers paper copies of its excellent highway map. On its web site at *http://www.wsdot.wa.gov*, the department has divided the state highway map into 18 small .pdfs that you can view or download for printing. Or buy a commercial map. Insets on any of these maps should be sufficient to steer you through all but the largest cities. For birding in and around Seattle, Spokane, or Tacoma, however, purchasing a detailed street map or using a digital map may save you time and anguish. Online maps often provide detail printed maps can't, but aren't always available in remote areas. For printed maps, the *Washington Atlas and Gazetteer* (DeLorme) is nearly indispensable if you are venturing off the main highways (but useless in cities). The *Washington Road and Recreation Atlas* (Benchmark Maps) covers the same ground at a smaller scale in attractive relief maps, with a few additional nuances such as regional climate information. These commercial maps and atlases are widely available at booksellers, convenience stores, and newsstands.

Some of the best birding in Washington is found in the six national forests: Olympic, Mount Baker-Snoqualmie, Gifford Pinchot, Okanogan-Wenatchee, Colville, and Umatilla. Forest Service maps that once were available free are now for sale either on-line or at forest service headquarters or ranger district stations. Somewhat detailed topographical maps are free for download from forest service web sites. (Type the name of the national forest and the word "topo map" into your preferred search engine or go to the web site for the individual forest and look for links to maps.) The downloadable topo maps have been divided into sections, which are easily viewable on a desktop computer. But the print is extremely small if you shrink these sections to fit onto 8.5 x 11-inch paper. National wildlife refuges often provide good maps on-line that you can print out, though you might have to search a bit for the link. Birders hiking in the Cascades or Olympics will appreciate the reliability and usefulness of the Green Trails maps, which can be purchased at outdoor and map stores: visit *www.greentrails.com* for specifics. Green Trails maps are now available for iPhones and starting to be available for Android.

Roads. Washington's extensive road system is administered by several jurisdictions. Many roads are numbered. We rely on these numerical designations wherever possible, with assorted abbreviations: "I" for the interstate highway system (example: I-90), "US" for federal highways (US-12), "SR" for state routes (SR-20), "FR" for U.S. Forest Service and certain other numbered forest roads (FR-25), "CR" for county roads (rarely used).

Forest Service nomenclature takes a little getting used to. Each national forest has its own numbering system, so the same road number may be used on different roads in different forests. (The Wenatchee and Okanogan National Forests merged in 2000, yet did not renumber the roads, so the same road number may show up on two different roads in this one national forest. The forest service distinguishes them by identifying the county.)

Trunk roads typically have two-digit designators (e.g., 25) and are wide, all-weather thoroughfares, hard-surfaced or well-graded gravel—easily passable by any passenger car unless closed by snow (few forest roads are plowed). As you drive along one of these roads, you may notice that it has suddenly acquired a couple of extra zeros (e.g., 2500). This means that although you are still on the main road it has now dropped to a lower standard of engineering and maintenance (unpaved for sure, more dips and curves, maybe narrower and rougher).

Secondary roads branching from trunk roads have four-digit numbers, the first two digits being those of the parent road (e.g., 2517). Generally speaking, all of these four-digit roads are suitable for regular passenger cars although you should be on the lookout for rocks, potholes, and severe washboarding in places.

The lowest category of forest roads consists of spurs, usually indicated by vertical brown signposts where they branch off. These signposts display three digits reading top to bottom (e.g., 063 or 228). The number of the road from which a spur branches also appears on the spur signpost in small print, and technically is part of the spur's designator (e.g., 2517-063)—but forest maps usually show just the three digits (and so do we in this guide). However, three-digit designators sometimes get reused within the same forest's road-numbering system, so only the full seven-digit number is guaranteed to be unique—important to consider for reporting a problem or for record keeping. Maintenance of spur roads varies from adequate to none, depending on their current use status. Many are for high-clearance vehicles only. Note, too, that forest roads of all categories are subject to washouts, so be prepared to stop with little warning. Be wary of log-truck traffic. It is always a good idea to inquire about logging activity and local road conditions at ranger district stations.

Some county roads in Washington used to be numbered, and you will still occasionally see old number signs on roadside posts. Today, however, counties have moved away from numbers in favor of road names. Naming systems and signage standards vary widely from county to county and are not without an element of whimsy. Moreover they seem to be constantly changing, so that names on the ground may not correspond to maps, printed or on-line. Road names in this guide usually are those visible on actual road signs. We try to point out naming disparities, but you may still encounter some and will need to rely on your instincts.

Ferries. The Washington State Ferries are part of the state highway system. Visit *http://www.wsdot.wa.gov/ferries* for full, up-to-date details of routes, fares, and schedules. Or download the handy WSDOT app to your digital device. It provides information on traffic delays, mountain pass conditions, and ferry schedules. If your itinerary involves travel by ferry, plan carefully to avoid delays.

Fees. "Pay to play" is increasingly a fact of life on many public lands in Washington. The sale of parking and user permits generates millions of dollars in revenues each year that are pumped directly back into maintaining wildlife habitat and providing public access—critical functions in these times of strapped state and federal budgets. Acquire the necessary permits before your birding visits (most government offices are closed on weekends). Patrolling is aggressive and the fines are substantial.

Fortunately, the federal government now issues a single pass good for access to lands of five agencies nationwide: the National Park Service, U.S. Forest Service, U.S. Fish and Wildlife Service, Bureau of Land Management, and Bureau of Reclamation. The America the Beautiful Pass (one of several "Interagency Annual Passes") covers entrance and standard amenity fees for a driver and all passengers in a personal vehicle at fee areas that charge by the vehicle (or up to four adults at sites that charge per person). Children age 15 or under are admitted free. You can get passes at forest service district and ranger offices, national parks and a few national wildlife refuges. You can also order them on-line or by phone (888-275-8747 Ext. 3). Day passes are usually available at most sites. More detailed information about the various passes and how to obtain them can be found at *http://www.nps.gov/findapark/passes.htm*.

As of 2015, an America the Beautiful Annual Pass available to everyone costs $80 per year. Other Interagency Annual Passes are available for seniors, the disabled, and the military. The Senior Pass, available to U.S. citizens or permanent residents age 62 or over, is $10 for a lifetime pass. Free passes are available for the permanently disabled, federal agency volunteers, and U.S. Military members and dependents. Golden Access and Golden Age Passports are no longer sold but are still honored. A Northwest Forest Pass, $30 a year, allows access to developed national forest sites in Washington and Oregon. Those who will also be visiting national forests outside Washington and Oregon, national wildlife refuges, national parks, and other federal recreation lands may be better off getting the more expensive America the Beautiful Pass, which covers all of these federal lands nationwide. (When this guide mentions that an America the Beautiful Pass is required, assume that the various Interagency Annual Passes mentioned above as well as day passes will also work.)

Many Washington State public lands also provide good to excellent birding. In 2011, the Legislature instituted a single pass, the Discover Pass, to park at or use public lands or water access points managed by the Washington State Parks, Washington Department of Fish and Wildlife (WDFW), and the

Department of Natural Resources (DNR). An annual Discover Pass costs $35 (including purchase fees); a daily Discover Pass is $11.50 (including purchase fees). The passes can be bought on-line, by phone (866-320-9933), or through license dealers such as sporting goods stores. Purchasers of hunting and fishing licenses are issued a free Vehicle Access Pass, which can be used at wildlife and water access sites in lieu of a Discover Pass. Full information about the Discover Pass is available at *http://www.discoverpass.wa.gov/*.

Winter birders may need more than the Discover Pass. The state Parks Department requires either daily ($20) or seasonal passes ($40) at winter sports Sno-Parks between December 1 and May 1. You may also need a special groomed-trails pass ($40) if you are in designated groomed-trails areas. If you have a current seasonal Sno-Park permit, you will not need to purchase a Discover Pass to use a designated Sno-Park for winter recreation activities. However, your Sno-Park permit may not be used to access other state recreation lands. More information is available at *http://www.parks.wa.gov/173/Winter-Recreation-Fees*.

Field Hazards. The only poisonous snake, the Western Rattlesnake, is confined to lower elevations east of the Cascades, usually in rocky terrain. Typically it is not aggressive. If you meet one, give it space and it will likely retreat. There are bugs in Washington, though the good news is there are no chiggers. Mosquitoes and biting flies can be bothersome in the warm months, especially in the mountains and wetlands. Repellent should make your visit tolerable. Wood Ticks abound in some of the drier forests and sagebrush areas of Eastern Washington. The best way to avoid them is not to brush up against vegetation, especially in spring. Tucking pantlegs into socks and dousing both with repellent may help. Poison Oak is locally abundant in interior southwestern parts of the state and eastward through the Columbia Gorge, and Poison Ivy is common in many parts of lowland Eastern Washington. It is a good idea to learn these plants ("leaves of three, let them be") before you head off into the bush. Black Bears can be met in forested regions. Heed the advice of "Bear Aware" pamphlets, particularly if you are in a campground. Out on the trail, troublesome encounters with either bears or Mountain Lions are very rare.

The summer sun can be intense, brutally so on snowfields and on the water. Protect yourself with broad-brimmed hat, long-sleeved shirt, long pants, and sunblock. If hiking at higher elevations, be alert for bad weather. A clear and calm morning can quickly change to cold rain and winds. Hypothermia is a definite hazard, even in summer. Carry the Ten Essentials (extra clothing, extra food, compass, map of the area, flashlight with spare bulb and batteries, knife, sunglasses, firestarter such as a candle stub, first-aid kit, matches in waterproof container). Water may not be available on high trails, especially late in the season. Assume all untreated water is contaminated.

Most areas open to hunters during hunting season should be avoided. Check dates at *http://wdfw.wa.gov/hunting/regulations/*.

Acronyms and Abbreviations used throughout the guide's text and maps include the following:

ACE – Army Corps of Engineers
aka – also known as
BLM – Bureau of Land Management
CG – Campground
CR – County Road
DNR – Department of Natural Resources (state)
FR – Forest Road. Roads within national forests.
HMU – Habitat Management Unit
NWR – National Wildlife Refuge
SR – State Route
USFS – United States Forest Service
WDFW – Washington Department of Fish and Wildlife (state)
WSDOT – Washington State Department of Transportation
USFWS – United States Fish and Wildlife Service

BIRDERS' INFORMATION NETWORK

The following resources are available to those planning a birding trip, looking for details on the current status of a particular species, seeking to report an interesting observation, or just generally interested in the birds of Washington.

Washington Ornithological Society. WOS publishes a bimonthly electronic newsletter (*WOSNews*) with birdfinding articles and other valuable features; a journal (*Washington Birds*); the *Field Card of Washington Birds*; and a membership directory. It sponsors numerous field trips to all corners of the state and hosts monthly meetings in Seattle and an annual conference at various locations. You can find a current, printable official checklist of Washington birds on-line on the WOS web site at *http://wos.org/*.

Washington Field Notes. This ongoing record of consequential bird observations is printed in the WOS newsletter about four times a year. The newsletters—and thus the field notes—can be searched on-line at the *http://wos.org*; look for the newsletter archives. Report your sightings by e-mail to *fieldnotes@wos.org*. The compiler, currently Ryan Merrill, is one of the Washington editors for *North American Birds*.

ABA members. Over 400 Washingtonians are members of the American Birding Association. Many of them have indicated that they are willing to guide visiting birders or respond to telephone or written queries. Codes used in ABA's on-line membership directory enable other ABA members to contact these generous people. The ABA web site *http://aba.org* features a lively blog, checklists of North American birds, content from *Birding* magazine, and access to birding listservs from around the country, including Washington's (click on "Birding News").

eBird. The *eBird.org* web site, launched in 2002 by Cornell Lab of Ornithology and National Audubon Society, has hugely affected the way birders report and get information about bird sightings, abundance, and distribution. Birders report multi-millions of sightings each year. You can easily learn what birds are found where in the state by going to the "Explore Data" section of the *eBird.org* web site. Another web site, *http://birdingwashington.info/dashboard/*, taps into eBird data to show notable sightings, sightings at hotspots, and sightings by species or for any location within the past 30 or fewer days. A Northwest region version of eBird is available at: *http://ebird.org/content/nw/*.

Audubon chapters. Washington has 25 chapters of the National Audubon Society. Visit *http://wa.audubon.org/* for links to chapter web sites, many of which offer detailed information on local birding areas. The web site also offers downloads of *The Great Washington State Birding Trail* maps, Audubon Washington's seven full-color maps with information about key birding spots around the state.

BirdWeb. This is Seattle Audubon Society's excellent on-line guide to the birds of Washington State. It provides handy seasonal abundance charts, range maps, and information about life history and migration and conservation status of Washington species. Ecoregion maps with checklists and birding sites can also be found here: *http://birdweb.org/*

Washington Birder. Washington Birder web site *http://www.wabirder.com/* offers well researched county checklists. You'll also find a spreadsheet, created using the county checklist abundance codes, that provides a quick county-by-county comparison of species in Washington. Inspired by Ken and Laurie Knittle, this is headquarters for the growing number of birders who compile county lists.

North American Birds. Bird observations of regional significance are documented in the quarterly *North American Birds*, published by the American Birding Association. These may be reported to the *Washington Field Notes* compiler (currently Ryan Merrill) or to one of the regional *NAB* editors (currently Brad Waggoner and Ryan Merrill, *fieldnotes@wos.org*)

Washington Bird Records Committee (WBRC). Observations of species on the Washington Review List (those with names italicized on the Annotated Checklist in the back of this guide or not listed there at all) should be reported to the WBRC with written details and any supporting evidence such as photographs and sound recordings. Go to *http://wos.org/records.html* for more information and to submit a report. Committee decisions are published in *Washington Birds*.

Tweeters. The Burke Museum at the University of Washington hosts this e-mail list on the birds of Cascadia. Some 3,200 subscribers make Tweeters a lively forum for discussion and a great place to learn about the latest interesting bird sightings. In fact, the Tweeters list has become the principal reporting venue for most Washington birders. Coverage centers on Washington—particularly Western Washington—but many postings concern Oregon and British Columbia. To subscribe, visit *www.scn.org/earth/tweeters*. Or you can read postings on-line in digest form at this same web site or on the ABA's Birding News web site: *http://birding.aba.org/*

Inland Northwest Birders. Here is an e-mail list devoted to birding in Eastern Washington and adjacent parts of Oregon and Idaho. To subscribe, visit *www.lists.uidaho.edu/mailman/listinfo/inland-nw-birders*.

Oregon Birders On-Line (OBOL). Washington-related bird observations and discussion occasionally figure on this e-mail list, especially in regard to the southwestern part of the state. Visit the web site at *http://www.orbirds.org/* for subscription information. Recent postings are also available at ABA's Birding News web site: *http://birding.aba.org/*

LOOKING AHEAD

Washington and its birding profile have changed with phenomenal rapidity. In the 40 years between 1970 and 2010, the state checklist of birds grew at a steady rate of more than three birds per year. The official state checklist, which can be found at *http://wos.org*, stands at 510 species, as of May 2015. However, the pace of the growth in the current decade beginning in 2010 has slowed to about two new birds per year. The growth in the earlier four decades was driven primarily by the fact that more and more people were looking for birds, spending more time in the field, and covering more territory. There still exist tantalizing possibilities for new species for the state. For example, seven birds have been recorded in British Columbia, Idaho, Oregon, and California, but not Washington, and 26 birds have been seen in three of those four states or provinces, but not Washington. Add in the potential new off-shore pelagic birds and you've got a rich pool of likely birds even without considering the surprises that pop up.

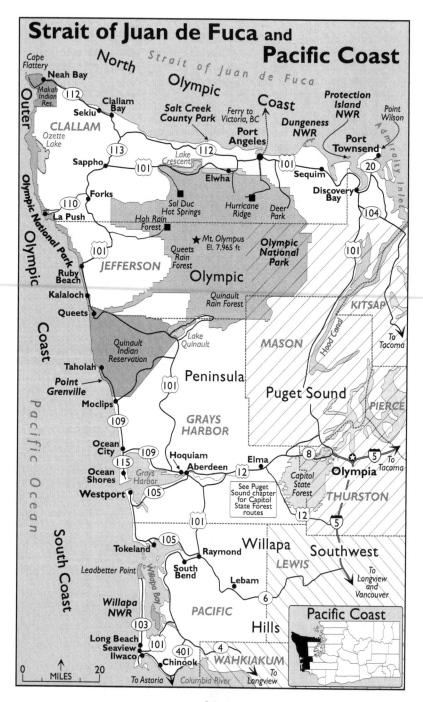

Strait of Juan de Fuca and Pacific Coast

North Olympic Coast

Strait of Juan de Fuca

Cape Flattery

Neah Bay

Makah Indian Res.

Outer

Sekiu

112

Clallam Bay

CLALLAM

Ozette Lake

113

Salt Creek County Park

Ferry to Victoria, BC

Protection Island NWR

Point Wilson

Sappho

101

Lake Crescent

112

Port Angeles

Dungeness NWR

Port Townsend

Admiralty Inlet

Olympic National Park

Forks

110

La Push

Elwha

101

Sequim

20

Discovery Bay

104

Sol Duc Hot Springs

Hoh Rain Forest

Hurricane Ridge

Deer Park

101

★ Mt. Olympus El. 7,965 ft

Olympic National Park

101

JEFFERSON

Queets Rain Forest

Olympic

Ruby Beach

Kalaloch

Quinault Rain Forest

KITSAP

Queets

Lake Quinault

MASON

Hood Canal

To Tacoma

Coast

Quinault Indian Reservation

Taholah

Point Grenville

101

Peninsula

Puget Sound

PIERCE

Moclips

109

GRAYS HARBOR

Pacific Ocean

Ocean City

109

Hoquiam

Elma

8

5

To Tacoma

Ocean Shores

115

Aberdeen

12

Olympia

Westport

Grays Harbor

105

Capitol State Forest

THURSTON

See Puget Sound chapter for Capitol State Forest routes

12

101

5

South Coast

105

Tokeland

Raymond

Willapa

Southwest

Leadbetter Point

Willapa Bay

South Bend

Lebam

LEWIS

To Longview and Vancouver

Willapa NWR

103

PACIFIC

6

Hills

Pacific Coast

Long Beach
Seaview
Ilwaco

101

401

Chinook

4

WAHKIAKUM

To Longview

0   MILES   20

To Astoria

Columbia River

STRAIT OF
JUAN DE FUCA
AND PACIFIC COAST

The seacoast of Washington stretches some 250 miles, from Point Wilson at the east end of the Strait of Juan de Fuca to Cape Flattery at the west end, then south along the Pacific Ocean to the Columbia River and the state of Oregon. The coast, including more than 800 offshore islands and rocky outcroppings, offers a variety of habitats and exciting birding opportunities in four rather different subregions: the interior of the Olympic Peninsula, the North Olympic Coast, the Outer Olympic Coast, and the South Coast. The whole area has a maritime climate. Winters are wet and relatively warm, but the damp air and a breeze can make it seem much colder than the thermometer indicates. It is wise to have raingear available. Summers frequently do not start until July and come close to drought with day after day of near-perfect weather through at least early September. Hot spells are infrequent.

The rugged, snow-capped peaks of the Olympic Mountains dominate the interior of the Olympic Peninsula, topped by 7,965-foot Mount Olympus. The mountains and the prevailing storm paths have created a rain-forest ecosystem on the west-facing slopes, with moderate temperatures, fog, and lots of rain—upwards of 200 inches per year. On the opposite side of the mountains, a rainshadow effect brings low rainfall to the area from Port Angeles to Port Townsend, which frequently enjoys blue sky on days when the rest of Western Washington is socked in. Dungeness, near Sequim on the North Olympic Coast, has just 15 inches of rainfall yearly. The South Coast has no high mountains to the east. Climate is similar to that of the Outer Olympic Coast, but rainfall is less abundant.

The North Pacific Ocean at this latitude tends to have a covering of stratocumulus clouds. With prevailing airflow from the west this leads to a lot of foggy mornings with the fog burning off during the day. It also means that it may be drizzling in the lowlands but bright sunshine on Hurricane Ridge in Olympic National Park at an elevation of 5,200 feet. Heavy snows are infrequent except in the high Olympics where they can be a problem. A more regular winter problem is light snow, freezing rain, or frost making the roads very slippery in the morning, especially on the North Olympic Coast.

Surface soils on the Olympic Peninsula are mainly composed of loose glacial debris. In exceptionally rainy years the earth slides in places, closing roads sometimes for long periods until repairs can be made. Large areas of subsidence may continue to move for months, but there is little danger of getting caught by a slide as it is usually more of a creep. Waterside bluff slides are more abrupt and do cause loss of life but present minimal danger to birders—the big ones mostly occur at night.

Information on road closures can be obtained by calling the Olympic National Park Visitor Center in Port Angeles (360-565-3130) or, for NF roads, the Pacific Ranger District Office in Forks (360-374-6522). For the western portion of the peninsula, also try the Visitor Information Center in Forks (360-374-2531), which has forest and park information and is open on weekends. (An America the Beautiful or Northwest Forest Pass is necessary to park at many trailheads. Car prowls do occur, even near towns. It is prudent to lock valuables in your trunk.

Campgrounds are numerous, but some are closed in the winter months and the most popular ones can be crowded during the short summer season. Restaurants, motels, gas stations, and other services are many and varied in larger communities such as Port Townsend, Sequim, Port Angeles, Forks, Ocean Shores, Hoquiam, Aberdeen, Westport, and the Long Beach-Seaview strip. Smaller communities also offer accommodations for travelers, although availability varies seasonally.

PORT TOWNSEND AND VICINITY

by Bob Norton

revised by Bob Boekelheide

Port Townsend lies at the mouth of Admiralty Inlet, where the relatively turbulent waters of the Strait of Juan de Fuca meet the protected waters of Puget Sound. Tidal fronts, or "tide rips," are most extreme where large tidal currents move through these entrances, concentrating fish and invertebrates for feeding flocks of birds and mammals. These feeding frenzies may occur throughout the year, attended by mergansers, loons, cormorants, alcids, gulls, and all other fish-eating birds in the area, including Marbled Murrelets all year, Ancient Murrelets in late fall and winter, and thousands of Rhinoceros Auklets during their nesting season. Tide rips flow relatively close to shore at Point Wilson and Marrowstone Point, making these locations especially attractive to birds and birders. Any saltwater rarity farther south in Puget Sound almost surely passed by here entering Puget Sound.

INDIAN AND MARROWSTONE ISLANDS

From the east end of the Hood Canal Bridge (page 178), follow SR-104 westward for 6.6 miles, then turn north toward Chimacum on SR-19. Continue

9.1 miles to a stop sign at Chimacum Road. Turn right here and travel 1.5 miles to the intersection with Oak Bay Road (SR-116). Turn right again. In 0.8 mile, where SR-116 turns left, continue straight ahead on Oak Bay Road, and in another 0.6 mile turn left onto Portage Way (*do not* make the sharper left turn onto Cleveland Street), which leads 0.2 mile to the lower part of **Oak Bay County Park**. The tidal lagoon and exposed mudflats are attractive for waterfowl, shorebirds, and gulls. Rocky shorebirds may be found on the jetty. The beach and offshore waters have good numbers of Brant, other waterfowl, loons, and grebes in winter months. Look for Red-throated and Yellow-billed among the Common Loons in Oak Bay.

Return to the intersection with SR-116 (Flagler Road) and go right toward Indian and Marrowstone Islands. In 0.6 mile a bridge crosses the channel to Indian Island. The island is U.S. Navy property and off-limits except for SR-116 and the shoreline of Oak Bay. Cross the bridge to a small public park immediately on the right; its few old apple trees and hedgerows of brambles can be productive for passerines. A good view of Oak Bay is available from **Indian Island County Park**, 0.8 mile beyond the bridge via a side road to the right. The park looks toward the jetty from a different angle, giving you another chance to pick up rocky shorebirds. Harlequin Ducks can be found here as well as the usual diving ducks, loons, grebes, and alcids. Check the beach, estuary, and marsh. A further 1.2 miles east on SR-116 brings you to the Indian Island-Marrowstone Island isthmus, with adequate parking on the right side of the highway. This low-lying land bridge often has dabbling ducks and shorebirds when the tide is too high for them elsewhere.

Continue on SR-116 for 1.3 miles onto Marrowstone Island and curve to the left at the fork to stay on SR-116. Go 2.5 miles to the **Nordland Store** and search adjacent shorelines of Mystery Bay for shorebirds and passerines. The upper end of Mystery Bay concentrates a surprising number of birds, particularly Greater Yellowlegs in winter. **Mystery Bay State Park**, 0.8 mile beyond the Nordland Store, offers a good viewpoint to scope the main portion of Kilisut Harbor, which often has impressive flocks of waterbirds in fall and winter.

Fort Flagler State Park is reached at the end of SR-116 in 1.9 miles. Enter the park and, at the intersection, turn left (west) and go 1.3 miles to the park's campground, where there's an excellent view of Port Townsend Bay and the entrance of Kilisut Harbor. A 600-yard spit extends west toward Rat Island, an island sandbar at the mouth of Kilisut Harbor. Here Brant, Harlequin Ducks, and other waterfowl congregate close to shore, three species of cormorants can be compared, and large flocks of shorebirds roost and forage on the beach and grass. Black Oystercatchers and Black Turnstones often feed here when the tide is low enough to expose the rocks at the tip of the spit.

Return to the main park intersection and turn left (north) 0.1 mile, then right (east) 0.6 mile to reach the old lighthouse at **Marrowstone Point**, just inside Admiralty Inlet. The road passes former barracks and leads downhill to

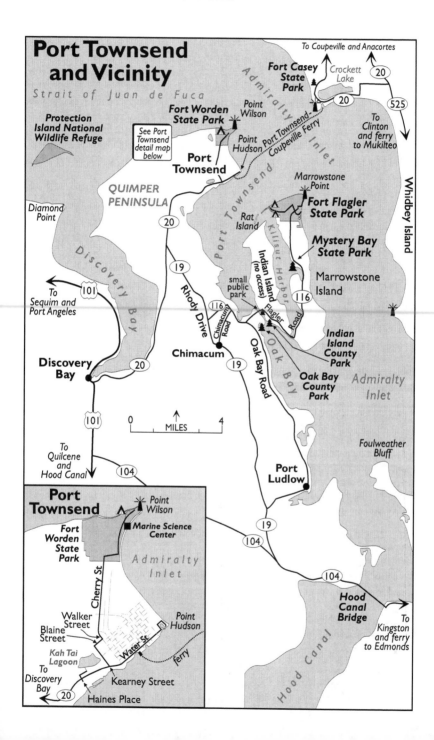

Port Townsend and Vicinity

Strait of Juan de Fuca

Protection Island National Wildlife Refuge

Diamond Point

QUIMPER PENINSULA

See Port Townsend detail map below

Fort Worden State Park

Point Wilson

Point Hudson

Port Townsend

Discovery Bay

To Sequim and Port Angeles

101

20

19

Rhody Drive

Chimacum

Chimacum Road

20

101

To Quilcene and Hood Canal

104

Discovery Bay

To Coupeville and Anacortes

Fort Casey State Park

Crockett Lake

20

20

525

To Clinton and ferry to Mukilteo

Port Townsend-Coupeville Ferry

Marrowstone Point

Fort Flagler State Park

Rat Island

Mystery Bay State Park

Marrowstone Island

Indian Island (no access)

small public park

116

116

Flagler

Oak Bay Road

Oak Bay

Indian Island County Park

Oak Bay County Park

Admiralty Inlet

Whidbey Island

Kilisut Harbor

Port Townsend Bay

Admiralty Inlet

0   MILES   4

Foulweather Bluff

Port Ludlow

19

104

Port Townsend

Fort Worden State Park

Point Wilson

Marine Science Center

Admiralty Inlet

Cherry St

Walker Street

Blaine Street

Kah Tai Lagoon

To Discovery Bay

20

Water St

Point Hudson

ferry

Kearney Street

Haines Place

Hood Canal Bridge

To Kingston and ferry to Edmonds

104

Hood Canal

the beach and lighthouse. Marrowstone Point is one of the best places to view feeding seabirds close to shore, including Marbled and Ancient Murrelets in November and December. A good tidal rip will usually have a wealth of feeding birds and is worth a thorough scan. In summer Pigeon Guillemots and Rhinoceros Auklets as well as gulls and terns fish here, and in winter ducks, loons, grebes, alcids, and gulls can be abundant. Search adjacent beaches and seasonal wetlands for shorebirds and passerines. Look offshore as well for Killer Whales, porpoises, seals, and sea lions.

PORT TOWNSEND

Retrace the route to the mainland, turning right on SR-116 at the stop sign at Oak Bay Road. Follow SR-116 for 2.0 miles from here to the junction with SR-19 (Rhody Drive), turn right (north), and continue on SR-19 as it flows into SR-20 in 3.4 miles. Another 4.3 miles north and east along SR-20 brings you to a traffic light at Kearney Street in Port Townsend. Turn left here and follow the signs to Fort Worden. The entrance is at the end of Cherry Street, in 1.8 miles.

Fort Worden State Park is a large park with many trails, open year round. The park's extensive forests contain typical Western Washington nesting and migrant species, although brushy areas on the park's east and west sides may produce interesting migrants. Follow the signs to the beach campground on the park's northeast side (0.8 mile). Walk the margins of the campground, looking for birds in brush at the base of the bluff. Check out the grass, dunes, and patches of windblown trees on **Point Wilson**, north of the campground. This sandy point of land has a concentrating effect on migrating landbirds. Also check the dunes and beaches for Horned Lark, American Pipit, and Snow Bunting.

From the parking lot at Point Wilson (0.3 mile), walk a short distance around the lighthouse to scan Admiralty Inlet. Feeding flocks containing sea ducks, cormorants, alcids, and gulls occur right off the point in nearby tide rips. Look for Ancient Murrelets in late fall and early winter, working the tide rips offshore. Ancients fly low in small groups of up to 20 birds, then dive into the water suddenly and simultaneously. Heermann's Gulls are common in summer and early fall, and migrating flocks of Bonaparte's Gulls in spring and fall may contain Parasitic Jaegers. Harlequin and Long-tailed Ducks are regular visitors, and Brandt's Cormorants can be seen year round. Look for the occasional Yellow-billed Loon. One of the spectacular bird shows in the state can be viewed at Point Wilson on summer evenings as Rhinoceros Auklets fly from Puget Sound to Protection Island, each carrying fish to feed to the chick in their burrow. Steller and California Sea Lions, Gray and Killer Whales, and Harbor Porpoises occur on occasion. Nearby, the Port Townsend Marine Science Center has an informative facility with touch-tanks and displays.

Follow signs to return to SR-20. At the traffic light at SR-20 (East Sims Way) and Kearney Street, turn left (northeast) onto East Sims Way. East Sims Way soon becomes Water Street, and in 0.5 mile the Washington State Ferry dock is on the right. The trip to Whidbey Island on the **Port Townsend-Coupeville Ferry** crosses Admiralty Inlet. When strong tidal currents are running, you may enjoy close-up views of feeding alcids and other waterbirds. The crossing takes about 30 minutes; you can return on the same boat or disembark to bird Fort Casey and Crockett Lake, both of which are within walking distance (page 81).

From the Port Townsend ferry dock, go northeast along Water Street—the center of the tourist district—to the **Point Hudson** marina at the northeast end (0.4 mile). Jog left for 0.1 mile on Monroe Street, right 0.1 mile on Jefferson Street, and right onto Hudson Street to parking areas near the Point Hudson RV park. At low tide, the gravelly spit here attracts Brant, shorebirds, and gulls, particularly Heermann's in summer. Search the breakwater pilings at the marina entrance for turnstones, Surfbirds, and occasional Rock Sandpipers, and offshore waters for loons, grebes, and alcids, particularly Marbled Murrelets.

On your way out of town on SR-20, visit **Kah Tai Lagoon**, the best place on the north Olympic Peninsula for Ruddy Ducks. From the traffic light at Kearney Street, proceed 0.5 mile on SR-20 and make a right turn onto Haines Place at the traffic light by the Safeway, followed by another right at the stop sign onto 12th Street, and finally a left turn onto the first gravel road into a small parking lot. The main lagoon is excellent for diving ducks, not only Ruddies, but also Lesser Scaup. Cattail marshes around the lagoon have rails and Marsh Wrens, and interesting shorebirds such as Buff-breasted Sandpiper have shown up at adjacent ponds.

From the Haines Place traffic light, continue west and south on SR-20 for 11.6 miles to the base of Discovery Bay at the junction with US-101. Turn right toward Sequim. (A left turn here will take you south along the west side of Hood Canal, page 214, or to SR-104 and east across the Hood Canal Bridge.)

DISCOVERY BAY TO PORT ANGELES

by Bob Norton

revised by Bob Boekelheide

The northeastern Olympic Peninsula, lying in the rainshadow of the Olympic Mountains, provides spectacular birding throughout the year. The wandering shoreline of the Strait of Juan de Fuca, with numerous bays, spits, and estuaries, has an abundance of rich coastal habitats for a wide variety of birds. Despite having the *driest climate in Western Washington, this region's focus for much of the year is waterbirds, particularly waterfowl, loons, grebes, shorebirds, alcids, and gulls. Terrestrial habitats on the coastal plain feature forests interspersed with agricultural areas, providing some of the greatest bird diversity in Western Washington and an abundance of unusual records in all seasons.*

Prior to the arrival of Euro-American settlers, the Sequim prairie had many open, grassy places due to low rainfall and frequent fires, likely set by Native Americans. (Sequim is pronounced Skwim, without the 'e.') Following settlement, fertile soils and available water from the Dungeness River led to extensive farming, changing much of the prairie into grazed pastures and hayfields. Birds typical of drier, sunny areas are attracted to this landscape, although some local nesting populations, such as Western Meadowlarks and Streaked Horned Larks, have been extirpated. The good weather is also a magnet for retirees. Over the last half-century the farmland has been rapidly replaced with suburban houses and the birds typically associated with and tolerant of humans.

DISCOVERY BAY AND PROTECTION ISLAND

From the junction with SR-20 at the foot of Discovery Bay, take US-101 toward Sequim. At 6.5 miles turn right onto Gardiner Beach Road and continue downhill, with a slight left jog, to **Gardiner Beach** on the shore of Discovery Bay (0.5 mile). Park here, where the road bends sharply to the left. An excellent tidal lagoon is on the right. Out on the bay scan for loons, grebes, alcids, and other waterbirds. Flocks of Pacific Loons work the bay during winter, as well as an occasional Yellow-billed Loon. Unusual species recently seen in this area include Emperor Goose. Gardiner Beach Road parallels the bay to a boat ramp, then heads west inland to a T-intersection with Diamond Point Road in 1.7 miles.

Turn right (north) on Diamond Point Road. It is 3.4 miles from here to the freshwater pond at **Diamond Point**. At the fork above the pond, stay right on Diamond Shore Lane South and drive counterclockwise around the pond. Search the pond for waterfowl such as Lesser Scaup and Ruddy Ducks. As you swing left onto Beach Drive (0.2 mile), look for some old pilings in Discovery Bay. This is the site of the quarantine station where sailing-ship passengers were made to wait before proceeding to Seattle. Cormorants and gulls use the pilings most of the year, as do Pigeon Guillemots during the nesting season. Continue along Beach Drive to a public viewpoint at Access Road (0.5 mile), looking north to Protection Island, two miles out in the Strait of Juan de Fuca. Back at the stop sign, turn right onto Diamond Shore Lane North and go to a small beach-club parking lot at the end (0.3 mile). Scope the waters offshore. In season, Rhinoceros Auklets and occasional puffins may be seen from these vantage points, along with many other coastal birds. On still, overcast days, you can make out marine mammals and larger birds such as eagles on Protection Island.

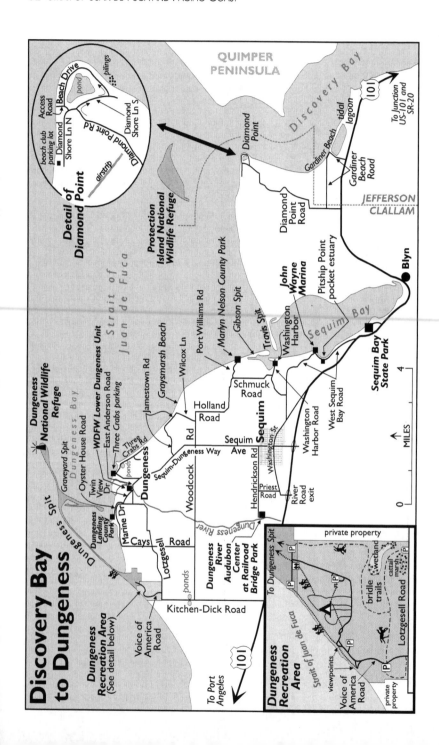

Discovery Bay to Dungeness

Dungeness Recreation Area (See detail below)

QUIMPER PENINSULA

Discovery Bay

To Junction US-101 and SR-20

Detail of Diamond Point

Access Road
Beach Drive
pilings
pond
Diamond Shore Ln N
beach club parking lot
Diamond Shore Ln S
Diamond Point Rd
airstrip

Gardiner Beach tidal lagoon

Gardiner Beach Road

Diamond Point

Diamond Point Road

JEFFERSON
CLALLAM

Protection Island National Wildlife Refuge

Strait of Juan de Fuca

Blyn

John Wayne Marina

Pitship Point pocket estuary

Sequim Bay

Dungeness Bay

Dungeness National Wildlife Refuge

Graveyard Spit

Dungeness Spit

Oyster House Road

WDFW Lower Dungeness Unit

East Anderson Road

Three Crabs parking

Jamestown Rd

Graysmarsh Beach

Wilcox Ln

Port Williams Rd

Marlyn Nelson County Park

Gibson Spit

Travis Spit

Washington Harbor

Schmuck Road

Holland Road

Sequim

Sequim Ave

Sequim St

West Sequim Bay Road

Sequim Bay State Park

Twin View Dr

Dungeness

ponds

Three Crabs Rd

Sequim-Dungeness Way

Woodcock Rd

Washington Harbor Road

Hendrickson Rd

Washington St

Priest Road

River Road exit

Marine Dr

Dungeness Landing County Park

Cays Road

Lotzgesell

Dungeness River Audubon Center at Railroad Bridge Park

Dungeness River

ponds

Voice of America Road

Kitchen-Dick Road

101

To Port Angeles

To Junction US-101 and SR-20

4

MILES

0

Dungeness Recreation Area

private property

To Dungeness Spit

P

wetland

cattail marsh

bridle trails

Lotzgesell Road

Strait of Juan de Fuca

viewpoints

Voice of America Road

private property

Protection Island, a 364-acre National Wildlife Refuge at the mouth of Discovery Bay, is one of the largest seabird nesting colonies in the state. Entry to this island refuge is strictly controlled to minimize disturbance, and boats circling the island must follow regulations that require vessels to stay at least 200 yards offshore. Primary nesting species include Pigeon Guillemots, Rhinoceros Auklets, and Glaucous-winged Gulls, along with fewer pairs of Pelagic Cormorants, Bald Eagles, Black Oystercatchers, and Tufted Puffins. Double-crested Cormorants formerly nested on the island, but eagle harassment likely caused them to desert their colony. The high, sandy bluffs at both ends of the island are pockmarked with Rhinoceros Auklet burrows, estimated in 2013 at about 36,000 breeding pairs. Large numbers of Rhinos can be seen feeding in Admiralty Inlet and other areas throughout the Salish Sea during spring and summer. Boat trips by Puget Sound Express (*www.pugetsoundexpress.com*) to view Protection Island birds, particularly to see puffins in summer, leave from Point Hudson Marina in Port Townsend and occasionally from John Wayne Marina in Sequim Bay. The trips may also explore other shorelines around Port Townsend Bay, including the area off Rat Island at the mouth of Kilisut Harbor.

SEQUIM BAY

Take Diamond Point Road back to US-101 (4.0 miles). Turn right toward Sequim and drive 5.5 miles to the entrance to **Sequim Bay State Park**. Drive through the campground and down to a boat ramp and parking, offering good scope views of the bay, particularly for diving ducks. Songbirds may be found in trees and scrubby growth in the campground and along park trails, including the Olympic Discovery Trail that bisects the state park. Hutton's Vireo and Townsend's Warbler can be found year round in adjacent forests.

Continue west 0.5 mile on US-101 and turn right on West Sequim Bay Road to **John Wayne Marina** in 1.2 miles. On the way, Pitship Point pocket estuary on the left at 1.0 mile frequently has Hooded Mergansers and other ducks as well as Marsh Wrens and wetland passerines. John Wayne Marina, built on property originally owned by the actor's family, has a north and a south parking lot. Both offer good scope-views of the bay and shoreline. Scan the south end where Johnson Creek empties into the bay for goldeneyes (both species), Hooded Mergansers, Horned Grebes, Black Oystercatchers, and guillemots. This is a favorite gull roost, with a mix of species during summer and fall. Drive past the main marina building to the north parking lot and walk to the farthest point overlooking the bay. This is the best vantage on Sequim Bay to see a variety of sea ducks and alcids. Pigeon Guillemots can be viewed year round, as well as Marbled Murrelets, Rhinoceros Auklets (less common in winter), and small numbers of Common Murres. Sequim Bay and nearby offshore waters between Dungeness Spit and Protection Island are some of the best locations for wintering Yellow-billed Loons in the state. In the fall and winter there is a good chance of close looks at Long-tailed Ducks,

Barrow's Goldeneyes, and Hooded Mergansers, along with the more common bay ducks.

Go back to the stop sign at the marina entrance and turn right on West Sequim Bay Road. Continue north and west for 2.0 miles, then right onto Washington Harbor Road. Continue straight at the bottom of the hill 1.2 miles to the back gate of Pacific Northwest National Laboratory (no visitors) at **Washington Harbor**. Park outside the gate in the small parking lot and scan the mudflats and adjacent habitat, which can be excellent for ducks, raptors, shorebirds, and gulls. Bald Eagles and Great Horned Owls have nested in the woods behind the parking area. Go back 0.4 mile to the stop sign and turn right onto Schmuck Road. Before climbing the bluff, turn left along the entrance road to the Sequim sewage treatment plant, park, and scan blackbird flocks at the dairy and adjacent fields for Yellow-headed and Rusty Blackbirds in season. After climbing the bluff, you will be in an agricultural area that may hold flocks of waterfowl and gulls; look, too, for Northern Shrike and Western Meadowlark in winter. Trumpeter Swan is regular; less predictable are Greater White-fronted Goose, Tundra Swan, and Sandhill Crane. In 1.2 miles Schmuck Road ends at a T-intersection with Port Williams Road. Turn right and go 0.5 mile to the end of the road at **Marlyn Nelson County Park**. Scan offshore for Brants, ducks (particularly Harlequin), loons, grebes, and alcids. This is a fairly dependable spot to find Eared Grebe, uncommon in Western Washington, and a great place to watch the social antics of Pigeon Guillemots that nest on adjacent cliffs.

One can walk along the beach either north or south, but be mindful that property owners restrict access to only the outer beach. Obey signs indicating restricted areas. Gibson Spit, to the south, produces more than its share of unusual sightings, and the 2.5-mile round-trip can be very rewarding. The tip of the spit provides a fine view of Travis Spit and the entrance of Sequim Bay. The bay's narrow outlet makes for strong tidal flows and is a favorite feeding spot for grebes, Pigeon Guillemots, and Rhinoceros Auklets. The tidal lagoon to the west, on private land, is attractive to ducks and shorebirds. During migration, shrubby habitats around the edges attract migrant passerines such as flycatchers and warblers.

DUNGENESS AND SEQUIM

The prairies, wetlands, coastline, and offshore waters between Sequim Bay and Dungeness Spit, on both sides of the Dungeness River, provide some of the best birding in Western Washington. Among areas of comparable size in the state, few can rival Dungeness in the number and variety of regularly occurring species and for its growing list of rarities. The Sequim-Dungeness Christmas Bird Count regularly tallies the greatest number of species for Washington (record 151 in 2011).

Leaving Marlyn Nelson Park, go west on Port Williams Road 0.8 mile and turn right onto Holland Road. This road winds north and west, and in 1.6 miles bears left to become Woodcock Road. The next road to the right (a further 0.2 mile) is Wilcox Lane. Turn right and follow Wilcox to its end at the Strait of Juan de Fuca (0.6 mile). There is parking for only two vehicles at the end of Wilcox, so it is available for few birders at a time. Walk to the water's edge and turn right to access **Graysmarsh Beach**. Graysmarsh is a large estate owned by the Simpson timber family, who allow public access to the first half-mile of beach but may close access at any time during hunting season. Read the signboard as you enter the beach, which gives current status and a map. This can be a very rewarding walk; be sure to check onshore and offshore for waterfowl, shorebirds, and gulls, and search the inland row of trees for migrant and nesting songbirds. Scan the marshes and adjacent ponds for raptors, shorebirds, shrikes, and sparrows.

Leaving Graysmarsh Beach, go northwest along the beachfront on Jamestown Road, which in a half-mile turns west away from the beach past some large dead cedars on the right (0.3 mile). These are the Jamestown Snags—a favorite roost for Bald Eagles and other raptors. At an intersection in 0.6 mile, turn right onto Sequim-Dungeness Way, which turns right in 1.2 miles to the small town of Dungeness. Continue north through town to the WDFW **Three Crabs** parking area near the water's edge (0.6 mile) and walk to the shoreline viewing area.

Dungeness Bay, framed by Dungeness Spit to the west and north, is one of the most important habitats on the Olympic Peninsula for waterfowl, shorebirds, and gulls. Eelgrass-associated waterfowl such as Brant and wigeons congregate by the thousands in season. Eurasian Wigeons can almost always be picked out of the American Wigeon flocks that gather near the beach. Depending on tides, shorebirds are often present on the beaches and using emergent shorelines along Meadowbrook Creek and adjacent ponds. This area has turned up many unusual shorebirds, such as Hudsonian Godwit, Ruff, and Red-necked Stint. Carefully scan nearby gull flocks, as they typically hold at least a half-dozen species and sometimes several more.

During the winter and migration, it is worth birding much of Three Crabs Road, which dead-ends at 1.3 miles. The land on the south side of the road is low-lying and marshy, providing excellent habitat for ducks, rails, shorebirds, and the raptors that eat them. Sharp-tailed and Stilt Sandpipers, along with Wilson's Phalarope, have been recorded several times during migration, along with regular sightings of Tropical Kingbirds and Yellow-headed Blackbirds.

Return along Sequim-Dungeness Way through Dungeness and turn right onto East Anderson Road at the stop sign (0.6 mile). Just west of the Dungeness River (0.3 mile) is the WDFW **Lower Dungeness Unit** of the North Olympic Wildlife Area (Discover Pass required) that accesses a 0.75-mile trail through grasses and marshland to the mudflats of Dungeness Bay, allowing very close views of shorebirds if you're careful not to disturb the birds. Make sure you remain on WDFW property, which is surrounded on both sides by private land, and avoid the area during hunting season.

Return to the parking area and turn right immediately onto Twin View Drive. At the next stop sign (0.5 mile), turn sharp right down Oyster House Road to **Dungeness Landing County Park** on the waterfront. The view of Dungeness Bay is superb from here, and shorebirding is often excellent on either a rising or falling tide. Scan the entire bay, including tidal islands and the south shoreline of Dungeness Spit. The mouth of the river may have large concentrations of ducks, shorebirds, gulls, and other birds, visible from the parking lot with a scope. Look for raptors, including falcons working the shorebird flocks and Snowy Owls during irruption years. Bald Eagles are abundant year round, including several nearby nesting pairs.

Return up Oyster House Road to the stop sign and turn sharp right onto Marine Drive. In 1.2 miles the road turns left and becomes Cays Road, which intersects Lotzgesell Road in another mile. Go right (west) on Lotzgesell 1.4 miles and turn right on Voice of America Road into the **Dungeness Recreation Area**, site of a large broadcasting facility during the Cold War. The recreation area is worth exploring for its mix of grasslands, ponds, and shrubby woods, particularly for raptors and passerines. A trail from a parking area 0.2 mile inside the entrance gate leads eastward to a grassy wetland with nesting ducks, rails, Marsh Wren, and Common Yellowthroat. Lapland Longspur and Palm Warbler have been seen here in winter. Farther along the road, turnouts on the left offer distant views over the Strait of Juan de Fuca from the high bluff, an excellent site to scope offshore for Black Scoters, Long-tailed Ducks, alcids, and Red-throated Loons in season. The waters between here and Port Angeles may hold hundreds of Red-necked Grebes from fall through spring.

Continue through the wooded campground to the parking lot of **Dungeness National Wildlife Refuge**, about a mile from the entrance gate. This beautiful 631-acre refuge includes Dungeness Spit, one of the longest natural sand spits in the world. Originally created to provide habitat for migrating Brant, which may number in the thousands, this refuge provides outstanding habitats for a wide variety of birds. The 10-mile round-trip out to the lighthouse is one of the best saltwater beach hikes in the state; however, human access is strictly limited to the outer (northside) beach to protect birds, marine mammals, and unique vegetation. The trail to the beach leaves from the parking lot (entrance fee or America the Beautiful Pass or equivalent required). The first half-mile is through coastal forest, then down a steep bluff trail to the beach. The 4.5-mile walk from here to the lighthouse on an exposed sand-and-pebble beach allows views of sea ducks, loons, grebes, alcids, and gulls. Some shorebirds use the outer beach, particularly Sanderlings, but all adjacent waters, beaches, and mudflats should be scanned for other species. This is one of the best places in the state to see Snowy Owls during irruption years. Be prepared for changing conditions during the walk; bring drinking water and protection against the elements, particularly wind.

Return to the Dungeness Recreation Area entrance on Lotzgesell Road and turn right (west). In 0.1 mile the road turns left (south) and becomes Kitchen-Dick Road. US-101 is reached in 3.1 miles. Turn right (west) for Port Angeles; turn right also to make a U-turn in 0.7 mile and head east for Sequim and the Dungeness River Audubon Center.

The **Dungeness River Audubon Center at Railroad Bridge Park**, northwest of the Sequim business district, offers informative displays and classes about the birds and natural history of the north Olympic Peninsula, as well as excellent birding through Dungeness River riparian forests. From US-101 on the west side of Sequim, take the River Road exit and drive north 0.2 mile, then turn right (east) at the roundabout onto Washington Street (the main street through Sequim). At the next intersection (0.1 mile) turn left (north) onto Priest Road and continue for another 0.6 mile to Hendrickson Road. Turn left (west) onto Hendrickson, and at the end of the road in 0.7 mile are Railroad Bridge Park and the Audubon Center (2151 West Hendrickson Road). The historic railroad bridge over the Dungeness River is the heart of the Olympic Discovery Trail, a superb bicycle/pedestrian trail across the north Olympic Peninsula, eventually reaching from Port Townsend to La Push. From Railroad Bridge, look for American Dippers throughout the year, and search riparian woodlands for diverse species of songbirds and woodpeckers. At peak nesting periods in May and June, these woods vibrate with the songs of Pacific-slope Flycatchers, Warbling Vireos, Swainson's Thrushes, Black-throated Gray and Wilson's Warblers, Western Tanagers, Black-headed Grosbeaks, and, in some years, Red-eyed Vireos. The Audubon Center is renowned for its superb collection of mounted bird specimens, allowing close examination of many species found in Western Washington. A guided bird-walk occurs every Wednesday morning, leaving from the Audubon Center at 8:30AM.

PORT ANGELES

From River Road and US-101 in Sequim, drive 15 miles west on US-101 to downtown Port Angeles (map on page 40). As you enter the downtown district on US-101 (aka Front Street), a moderate hill descends to an intersection where US-101 turns south (left) on Lincoln Street. Instead, turn right on Lincoln Street at this intersection, drive one block, and on the right enter the parking lot for the Port Angeles City Pier. This pier, right down the street from the Victoria ferry dock, provides an excellent viewing platform to scope **Port Angeles harbor**.

For even better looks, continue straight ahead on Front Street through the downtown district along the waterfront. Bear to the right on Front Street as it becomes Marine Drive and skirts the south side of the harbor. Worthwhile stops along Marine Drive include the Valley Creek Estuary Park (0.4 mile) and both the east and west ends of the Boat Haven (1.0 mile) to scan for waterbirds in the harbor.

At 2.1 miles from downtown, Marine Drive maneuvers through a large paper mill at the base of the spit and emerges at the west end of **Ediz Hook**. Ediz Hook is a natural sand spit created by the erosion of cliffs between Port Angeles and the Elwha River, forming the northern margin of Port Angeles Harbor. It is now "protected" by huge piles of boulders and other rip-rap to slow its own erosion. The Hook is an excellent location for waterfowl, shorebirds, and gulls most of the year, with many viewing pullouts. Harlequin Duck and Marbled Murrelet may be present at any time. Scan the north offshore side for sea ducks such as Black Scoter and Long-tailed Duck. Scope the old log booms and other floating structures in the harbor for shorebirds, especially at high tide, and search the beaches at low tide. In winter, Black Turnstone and Dunlin are most numerous, but, especially in migration, other rocky shorebirds like Surfbirds may be found. Look for Snow Buntings in winter along the logs and grasses on the south shorelines, and for Snowy Owls during irruption years.

The public road ends in two miles at the gate for the Coast Guard Air Station, off-limits to the public. A break in the seawall rocks just east of the public restrooms, near the end of the road, allows scans of the Strait of Juan de Fuca and access to the outer beach during low tide. Different species may be found on the north side, such as Black Scoter and Long-tailed Duck. Northern Fulmars, Sooty and Short-tailed Shearwaters, phalaropes, and Ancient Murrelets have been spotted here close to shore. The protective log boom under the Pilot House, on the harbor (south) side of the spit, is good for shorebirds, as is the adjacent cobble beach. In late fall and winter scan flocks within the harbor for loons, grebes, cormorants, and alcids, including wayward Thick-billed Murre and Ancient Murrelet. The harbor is an excellent place to see roosting Brandt's Cormorants mixed in with the more common Pelagics and Double-cresteds.

The **Coho Ferry** is a popular way to get to Victoria, British Columbia. Service is frequent in summer, less so in winter. Be sure to check schedules in advance, on-line at *http://cohoferry.com* or by phone at 360-457-4491. For additional cost, reservations during peak summer season may prevent long waits at the ferry line. The crossing takes about an hour and a half. The most windfree area—and also the best viewpoint for birds—is right at the bow. Of the many possible ferry trips in Washington, this one certainly has the greatest chance for pelagic species, but they are not assured. A trip during fall migration or following a storm out on the Pacific may feature ocean birds such as Northern Fulmar, Sooty or Short-tailed Shearwaters, Fork-tailed Storm-Petrel, phalaropes, Parasitic Jaeger, and Black-legged Kittiwake. The ferry terminal is located on Railroad Avenue, one block north and one block west of Front and Lincoln Streets in downtown Port Angeles.

THE HIGH OLYMPICS

by Bob Norton

revised by Bob Boekelheide

The Olympic Mountains stand out as a peninsula of snow-capped peaks surrounded on three sides by saltwater. The heart of the peninsula is Olympic National Park, one of the jewels of the national park system. Several roads follow river valleys up to mid-elevation trailheads around the perimeter of Olympic National Park, but the interior of the park is a roadless wilderness area. One of the most picturesque and accessible of these valleys is the Elwha River, the first large watershed west of Port Angeles. Only two roads in the park offer easy, extensive access to subalpine elevations, climbing the ridges above Port Angeles to Hurricane Ridge and Deer Park.

Olympic National Park is an excellent location to find Sooty Grouse. Sooty males are most evident in spring and early summer at mid-elevations when they are booming and displaying. Through the summer hens can be seen wandering with their chicks in subalpine meadows. Other montane species such as Northern Goshawk, Golden Eagle, Northern Spotted Owl, Black Swift, Clark's Nutcracker, Townsend's Solitaire, Gray-crowned Rosy-Finch, and Pine Grosbeak occur in the Olympics and are occasionally seen, but locating them may require extensive hiking.

During the ice ages, when the Strait of Juan de Fuca and Puget Trough were filled with Cordilleran glaciers, sections of the Olympic Mountains provided a refugium for plants and animals. Several forms unique to the Olympics evolved as a consequence of this isolation. One of the most obvious to visitors is the Olympic Marmot, a close relative of the more widely-distributed Hoary Marmot. The Olympic Arctic (Oeneis chryxus valerata), one of the most restricted-range butterflies in North America, can be found only on Hurricane Ridge and a few other high ridges close by. Several plant species unique to the windswept alpine zones are found only in these mountains.

Weather and road reports are available on the Olympic National Park visitor information tape (360-565-3131) and at the national park web site (http://www.nps.gov/olym). In summer, overcast skies in Port Angeles are not a reliable indicator of weather in the mountains, because the high country is usually above the stratocumulus layer. Conditions may change quickly in spring and fall, bringing blizzard conditions and whiteouts with little warning. From July through September, however, weather in the high country is often very pleasant, although mornings may be cool. Winters bring heavy snowfall; snow accumulation often continues through March and April.

HURRICANE RIDGE

Hurricane Ridge is the main tourist attraction in Olympic National Park, heavily used during the summer months. In the snow season, the road may be open Fridays through Sundays to allow access to the ski area, but it

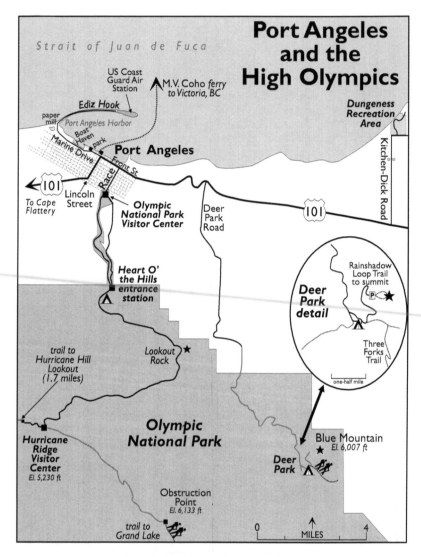

may also be closed for weeks on end in years when snowfall is too heavy for the plows to handle. Winter birds at higher elevations are usually limited to ravens and Gray Jays, but occasional winter reports include mountain finches such as Gray-crowned Rosy-Finch and Pine Grosbeak.

From US-101 in Port Angeles, turn south onto Race Street (seven blocks east of Lincoln Street) and follow the signs 1.0 mile to Olympic National Park Visitor Center, which provides information and a nice selection of books and maps for sale. Turn right as you leave the visitor center and in 0.1 mile bear right onto Heart O' the Hills Parkway, also known as Hurricane Ridge Road. Heart O' the Hills entrance station (fee or pass required) is another 5.2 miles ahead. The road is almost always open to this point even in winter. Just past the entrance station on the left is the **Heart O' the Hills campground**, where you can camp amidst massive old-growth Western Redcedars and Douglas-firs. Birding here is strong on Chestnut-backed Chickadee, Pacific Wren, and Golden-crowned Kinglet, with numbers of Varied Thrush most of the year. Marbled Murrelet and Vaux's Swift have been known to nest in the old-growth forest within the campground. Camp out in early summer and listen for calling murrelets as they fly overhead before dawn.

Hurricane Ridge Visitor Center is 11.7 miles farther up, at 5,230 feet elevation. Stop here to look over Big Meadow, nesting area for Horned Larks and American Pipits when snow-free patches open up in spring. A short hike on paved trails to nearby stands of Subalpine Fir may turn up Sooty Grouse. The road continues west another 1.4 miles to the **Hurricane Hill trail**. Gray Jays and juncos always seem to be around the picnic area along this road. The 1.7-mile walk to the summit of Hurricane Hill is recommended for subalpine breeders such as Horned Lark, Townsend's Solitaire, and American Pipit. Be vigilant for soaring Golden Eagles hunting these mountain meadows, and in late summer and fall watch for upslope migrant raptors like Northern Harriers and falcons.

Return to the Hurricane Ridge Visitor Center. At the east end of the parking lot the narrow gravel Obstruction Point road drops off to the right (southeast), ending in 7.8 miles at **Obstruction Point**. This road provides good access to subalpine and alpine habitats in the north Olympics, but in most years the Park Service does not plow the snow until July. In late spring and early summer, before it is open to cars, walk this road for subalpine nesting species such as Pine Grosbeak; a staff or ice axe may be helpful to get over the remaining snow banks. When open, an array of trails leave from the parking lot at Obstruction Point (elevation 6,133 feet). The trail along the ridge going south toward Grand Lake is good for Horned Lark and American Pipit. Look for Golden Eagles soaring over these ridges from their nest sites in the high Olympics, hunting for unwary Olympic Marmots. A backpacking trip from here to the peaks and glaciers of the northeastern Olympics may turn up Clark's Nutcracker and Gray-crowned Rosy-Finch.

DEER PARK

Deer Park is smaller than Hurricane Ridge, but offers similar birds with fewer people, no entrance fee, and at least as good a chance of seeing Sooty Grouse. It also has the only drive-in campground in the Olympic subalpine, on the south slope of Blue Mountain. Most years the road is open all the way to the top from about early July until the first major snowfall in early October. The rest of the year it may be closed to cars but can be walked, first through dense fir forests, then opening up into Subalpine Fir. From downtown Port Angeles, travel east on US-101 about 5.5 miles and turn right (south) on Deer Park Road. At the National Park boundary, 8.8 miles from US-101, the road turns to gravel. The road, though steep, curvy, and a bit rough, is suitable for ordinary autos. The undisturbed forests along most of the ascent are largely home to juncos, robins, and Varied Thrushes, until the trees begin to thin out in the subalpine. Look for grouse along the road. In 7.6 miles you reach a short loop road to the Deer Park Ranger Station; stay on the upper road, toward the campground and Blue Mountain. Bypass the campground, bear to the left, and continue uphill to a small parking lot on the northwest shoulder of Blue Mountain, 8.9 miles from the park boundary. Park here and walk the half-mile Rainshadow Loop Trail to the summit (elevation 6,007 feet). Clumps of trees near the summit are good for Sooty Grouse and migrants in season. During nesting, Horned Larks and American Pipits can be found on the exposed southern slopes all the way down to the campground. Walk or drive slowly through the campground to an old burn at the south edge. Another exposure to this burn may be obtained by hiking the first quarter-mile of the Three Forks Trail from the trailhead on the east side of the campground. This area has produced a nice selection of high-country forest birds.

ELWHA RIVER MOUTH TO THE WEST COAST

by Bob Norton and Bob Morse
revised by Bob Boekelheide

This is mostly a saltwater route, skirting bays and headlands along the Strait of Juan de Fuca. As you drive west, the terrain becomes increasingly rugged and the roads increasingly curvy. Oceanic influences increase, as does rainfall; forests are dense and fast-growing. At low to mid-elevations Douglas-fir, Western Hemlock, Western Redcedar, Red Alder, and Big-leaf Maple dominate. Sitka Spruce becomes increasingly noticeable west of Clallam Bay, eventually the dominant species of the coastal forest. Areas outside Olympic National Park are managed for timber production, and most have been cut over at least once. The usual low-elevation forest birds can be found wherever there are diverse forests and recent clear cuts, but even-aged stands of close-growing timber have relatively few birds.

ELWHA RIVER MOUTH

From Front and Lincoln Streets in downtown Port Angeles, drive 5.5 miles on US-101 to the intersection with SR-112, then turn right (west) on SR-112. In 2.1 miles, turn right (north) onto Place Road after crossing the Elwha River bridge. At 1.9 miles, turn right at the bottom of the hill and park at the end of the road to access the **Elwha River Mouth**. Follow the trail for about 175 feet, then continue left on the gravel levee 0.3 mile to the beach. A small lake on the west side of the levee often has a variety of ducks. This area has changed dramatically following removal of Elwha River dams upstream. Winter floods have carried huge amounts of sediments formerly deposited in slack water behind the dams, creating a new delta, tide channels, and sandbars at the river's mouth. The outer sand islands are a favorite roosting and bathing place for many species of gulls, particularly Thayer's in winter. Look for shorebirds using the new tidal channels and ponds. Although changing substrates may have made this area temporarily less favorable for diving birds, scan beyond the river mouth to offshore Freshwater Bay for coastal species such as sea ducks, loons, grebes, cormorants, and alcids.

ELWHA RIVER TO WHISKEY BEND

A side trip up the Elwha River into Olympic National Park (see map on next page) provides excellent birding from mid-April through mid-July, along with a look at one of the greatest ecological experiments of the early 21st century—the removal of two century-old dams on the Elwha River to restore salmon runs and benefit the entire river ecosystem. To get there from downtown Port Angeles, follow US-101 westbound 5.6 miles from the corner of Front and Lincoln Streets to the intersection with SR-112. Continue straight on US-101 for 3.0 miles, and turn south (left) onto Elwha River Road. The entrance booth for Olympic National Park (fee or pass required) is in 2.0 miles. Look for Harlequin Ducks, Northern Rough-winged Swallows, and American Dippers along the river, and search for flycatchers (particularly Hammond's), vireos, warblers, and other neotropical migrants in the deciduous trees around the entrance meadow. Continue past a campground and ranger station, and in 2.0 miles turn left onto **Whiskey Bend Road** (unpaved and narrow), which climbs about four miles up the east side of the Elwha Valley through magnificent forests to a trailhead parking lot (elevation 1,205 feet). In May and June hike the Humes Ranch Loop (4.3 miles) and its superb mixed forest trails to hear neotropical bird songs and occasional Northern Pygmy-Owl in the bottomlands between Goblin Gates and Humes Ranch.

SALT CREEK COUNTY PARK AND TONGUE POINT

Returning from the Elwha River mouth via Place Road, turn right (west) onto SR-112 and continue west for 5.0 miles to Camp Hayden Road. Turn right (north), and stay right at the fork in 3.4 miles to the entrance of **Salt Creek County Park**. This park contains a nice campground and Tongue Point, one of the best rocky tidepool areas in Washington. In warmer months with low daytime tides it may be very busy, but most of the year it is uncrowded. Where the road forks after the entrance booth (no fee for day use),

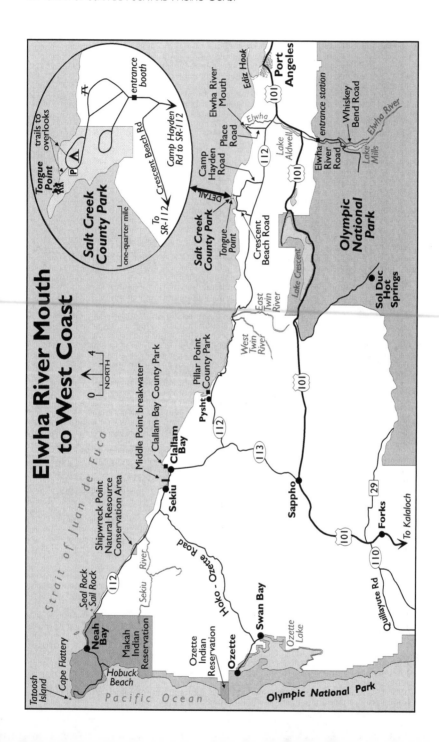

Elwha River Mouth to West Coast

stay right and drive north to the edge of the bluff. Park at the overlook to view the extensive kelp beds—a good place for Harlequin Duck and Marbled Murrelet. Other waterbirds may be present, so check offshore with a scope. In late September and early October, watch for kettles of Turkey Vultures crossing the strait from Vancouver Island, sometimes several thousand in a day. Continuing west through the wooded portion of the campground, you will arrive at small parking areas with stairs to Tongue Point, marked by interpretive displays. The point is worth exploring at low tide, especially if you have an interest in intertidal creatures. The algae can be very slippery, so a walking stick and rubber boots are recommended. Look for rocky shorebirds, including Black Oystercatchers, Black Turnstones, and occasional Surfbirds. River Otters are common. The more westerly overlook offers scope views of Crescent Bay. Long-tailed Ducks stay here surprisingly late into spring.

CLALLAM BAY AND SEKIU

Return to the park entrance and turn right onto Crescent Beach Road to return to SR-112. Turn right at the fork in 3.2 miles, and in another 0.3 mile resume traveling west on SR-112. The first sight of the Strait of Juan de Fuca after leaving Crescent Bay comes in 11.7 miles when the road winds downhill to the Twin Rivers. This north shore of the Olympic Peninsula is an important wintering area for sea ducks along with Horned and Red-necked Grebes. Marbled Murrelet surveys in summer reveal that a significant portion of the state's breeding population uses this coastline, likely nesting in Olympic National Park old-growth forests. In 9.2 miles, turn right to the entrance of **Pillar Point County Park**, another good access to scope for coastal birds. Continuing west on SR-112, in another 6.6 miles SR-112 meets SR-113, which leads south to US-101. Instead, turn right (north) on SR-112, to downtown Clallam Bay. Just as SR-112 makes a sharp left bend within the town of Clallam Bay (6.2 miles), turn right into a parking area (brown sign indicating *Clallam Bay Community Beach Entrance*). This is **Clallam Bay County Park**. Scoping the bay, lagoon, and river is frequently productive for waterfowl, alcids, and gulls, particularly Marbled Murrelets. Look along the river's edge for the occasional Green Heron. The park's bridge over the Clallam River lagoon, partly destroyed by beach erosion, is passable using a ramp placed by the Clallam County Parks Department from spring to fall, but the ramp is removed during winter. Regardless, the bridge makes a good scoping platform all year even if the beach is inaccessible.

Return to SR-112 and turn right (west). Halfway between Clallam Bay and the picturesque fishing village of **Sekiu** (pronounced *C-Q*) is Middle Point breakwater (1.2 miles), worth searching for rocky shorebirds, roosting gulls, and offshore birds. Continuing on SR-112, at 0.6 mile turn right (north) on Front Street into Sekiu, and from various vantage points check the bay and offshore waters for sea ducks, grebes, cormorants, and gulls. Return to SR-112 and turn right (west) toward Neah Bay. At 2.2 miles SR-112 intersects the Hoko-Ozette Road to **Lake Ozette**, a pristine area with trail access to wilderness beaches. Birders have turned up a surprising number of eastern vagrants (Eastern Phoebe, Northern Parula) near the Ozette campground and ranger station, and the lake is one of the few places in Western Washington with nesting Common Loons. SR-112 continues across the **Sekiu River** mouth 2.8 miles farther west, a good place to scope for gulls. From here to Neah Bay the scenic, winding road hugs the coast and travel is slow. In winter the waters hold diving ducks, loons, grebes, and alcids, but parking along this stretch of highway is limited, other than at **Shipwreck Point Natural Resource Conservation Area** (3.2 to 4.4 miles). Search the rocky intertidal there for Wandering Tattlers during spring and fall migration, along with Black Oystercatchers, Black Turnstones, and Surfbirds. Gray Whales summer along this portion of the strait. The best viewpoint for **Seal and Sail Rocks**, the only seabird nesting islands along this shore, is at 9.2 miles from the Sekiu River, on an outside curve just before the commercial sign for Snow Creek Resort. Scope the rocks and surrounding waters for marine mammals and a variety of birds, including all three cormorants and Tufted Puffin.

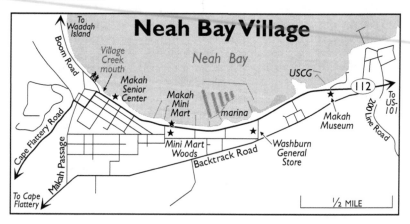

NEAH BAY

Continue west 3.2 miles to the community of **Neah Bay**, home of the Makah Tribe. Neah Bay and surrounding areas are a birding treasure, both for western migrants and vagrant species that funnel through this northwesternmost point of land in the Lower 48 States. But remember that you are a guest on the Makah Reservation. You must purchase a Makah Recreation Permit at the Makah Museum, Washburn's General Store, or the Makah Mini Mart as you enter town. The permit allows you access to trails, beaches, and designated visitor facilities, including at Waatch Valley, Hobuck Beach, and Cape Flattery.

Scan all of Neah Bay and its beaches for ducks, loons (including Yellow-billed), grebes, shorebirds, alcids, and gulls. Bald Eagles nest around the village and gather on the shorelines, visible year round. Pelagic birds sometimes seek shelter or wreck in the bay, including Northern Fulmars, phalaropes, Black-legged Kittiwakes, and, rarely, Fork-tailed Storm-Petrels. Search shrubby areas and shorelines in town for songbirds, which may form abundant flocks during migration. Across the street from the Makah Mini Mart is a scrubby alder forest known as **Mini Mart Woods**, where numerous vagrants have turned up in recent years. Search the gull roosts along the beaches and particularly at the mouth of Village Creek west of the Makah Senior Center (the last large building on the waterfront) for a variety of gulls, including Glaucous, Iceland/Kumlien's, and others. Beyond Village Creek and the monument for Fort Nuñez Ganoa, walk the Boom Road (aka Makah Passage) along the western edge of Neah Bay to the breakwater to Waadah Island, searching the brush and trees for migrant songbirds and the beaches and breakwater for ducks and shorebirds. Birding Neah Bay during migrant fallouts can be spectacular, with hundreds of birds everywhere. Realistically, vagrants could show up anywhere in town.

WAATCH VALLEY, HOBUCK BEACH, AND CAPE FLATTERY

After passing the Senior Center, follow the road signs to **Cape Flattery**. Cape Flattery Road continues south through alder woods and then curves west, paralleling the **Waatch River** (pronounced WY-*atch*), a short river system that forms a tidal grass estuary. As an island of open grass along the coast, the valley is attractive to many species unusual to wooded, wet Western Washington. Walk and drive both the paved Cape Flattery Road and unpaved Makah Passage, stopping at turnouts to scan the river and to search clumps of vegetation. All migrant flocks in the area should be searched closely for vagrants. At 2.0 miles from the Senior Center, a marsh on the right before the transfer station is a good spot for wintering Swamp Sparrow, and Rock Wrens have been found at the adjacent quarry/landfill. Search the power lines and fencepost perches for raptors, kingbirds (including Eastern and Tropical), shrikes, and bluebirds. Scan the marshes and riverbanks for geese, swans, herons, vagrant egrets, and shorebirds. Raptors circle overhead in April and May as they prepare for their flight north over the Strait of Juan de Fuca. In addition to the usual coastal migrants, search all soaring raptors overhead for Golden Eagles and buteos such as Swainson's and Broad-winged Hawks, which have been seen from nearby Bahokus Peak.

At 2.5 miles from the Senior Center, turn left onto Hobuck Road to cross the Waatch River bridge. Bear right in 0.1 mile, then continue 0.3 mile to **Hobuck Beach** (rental cabins and campground, daily use fee paid at entrance booth, or park at the far south end of the beach 0.8 mile farther). This is an extraordinary beach and dunes area known to concentrate vagrants. Walk to the north end of Hobuck Beach, at the Waatch River mouth, to view the

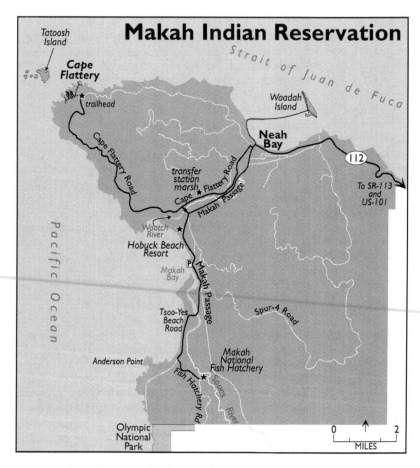

multi-species gull roost, which may contain thousands of migrant California Gulls in summer and fall, along with any possible gull species in Washington, including kittiwakes and Iceland/Kumlien's and Glaucous Gulls. Look for shorebirds along the beach and river mouth; Snowy Plover has been found here. Walk trails in the grassy dunes behind the beach to search for migrant and vagrant songbirds, which may hide in the stunted Sitka Spruce/willow forest. Many songbirds unusual to Western Washington have appeared here, along with incredible numbers of western species during migration fallouts. From the south end of Hobuck Beach, drive south in the next quarter-mile to view the mouth of the Tsoo-yess River (aka Sooes) and adjacent beaches. Continue south on Fish Hatchery Road 3.2 miles to the **Makah National Fish Hatchery**, where trails allow access to ponds and mixed woods that are attractive to Wood Ducks, mergansers, and migrant and nesting songbirds.

Return to the Waatch River bridge, but just before crossing the bridge turn right (east) onto Makah Passage Road, which parallels the river. The adjacent wetlands and islands of brush in the **Waatch Valley** have turned up an amazing variety of western migrants and vagrants; it is worth walking down and back to find birds. Return to and cross the Waatch River bridge and turn left (west) on Cape Flattery Road. Drive 5.2 miles to the **Cape Flattery** trailhead, traversing mixed forests and brushy spots. In late spring the songs of Pacific-slope Flycatchers, Swainson's Thrushes, and Wilson's Warblers, along with ever-present Pacific Wrens, resonate through these forests. Carry a scope down the three-quarter-mile Cape Flattery trail—well designed with boardwalks across the wet places—to viewing platforms overlooking the Pacific Ocean at the northwestern tip of the Lower 48. Seabird watching can vary from fair to excellent, depending on weather and visibility. Pigeon Guillemots nest immediately below the overlook in large caves at the base of the 100-foot cliffs. All three species of cormorants roost on the slopes below, with Pelagic Cormorants nesting on surrounding cliffs. Search for Brown Pelican, Black Oystercatcher, Rhinoceros Auklet, Black and Vaux's Swifts (late spring and summer; unpredictable), and Peregrine Falcon. Look for Rock Sandpipers in neighboring surge channels during migration. With a scope, search for shearwaters and their distinctive flight style coursing the waves beyond Tatoosh Island. Marine mammals include Sea Otter, Steller Sea Lion, Harbor Seal, Gray Whale, and Harbor Porpoise.

Tatoosh Island, one-half mile offshore and viewable with a spotting scope, supports several species of nesting seabirds, including Pelagic Cormorant, Common Murre, Pigeon Guillemot, Rhinoceros Auklet, Tufted Puffin, and Glaucous-winged and Olympic Gull (a hybrid of Glaucous-winged and Western). This is probably the easiest place in Washington to see puffins from shore, from May to August. Fork-tailed and Leach's Storm-Petrels, along with Cassin's Auklet, nest on Tatoosh as well, but these highly pelagic species visit their nest burrows only at night and are rarely seen from land during the day. A spectacular sight in spring is the evening gathering of thousands of Common Murres as they fly by cliffs and cluster on the water below. The number of murres nesting on Tatoosh Island has varied significantly over the last century, but recent nest predation by the burgeoning Bald Eagle population has become a significant threat. Tatoosh Island is also a landbird migrant trap. Numerous vagrants have been recorded by researchers, among them White-winged Dove, Brown Thrasher, Blackpoll Warbler, and Lark Bunting. The island is part of the Makah reservation and access is highly restricted. But the same vagrants could just as well show up at nearby coastal locations, and regular birding forays to this area could repay the effort.

To continue down the outer coast, return 26.8 miles from Neah Bay to the intersection of SR-112 and SR-113, then continue south another 10 miles via SR-113 to US-101. Turn right (south) on US-101 toward Forks, or left to return to Port Angeles.

OUTER OLYMPIC COAST

by Bob Morse

revised by Scott Horton

High, rocky bluffs and offshore islands that are home to over a dozen species of nesting seabirds dominate the Outer Olympic Coast from Cape Flattery to Point Grenville. *Storm-petrels, auklets, and puffins nest in burrows dug into grassy hillsides, while cormorants and murres nest on the high, open cliff ledges. The world's finest temperate rain forest stretches from the water's edge to the mountains of the Olympic National Park and is home to nesting Sooty Grouse, Marbled Murrelet, Varied Thrush, and Red Crossbill. Douglas-fir, Western Hemlock, Western Redcedar, Sitka Spruce, and Bigleaf Maple, luxuriantly draped with mosses and lichens, form a sensuous landscape with the richly carpeted forest floor. Populations of several characteristic birds of the western Olympic Peninsula have changed over the past 20 years. Since their dramatic recovery, Bald Eagles are nearly ubiquitous and the pressure they exert on prey species such as gull roosts is considerable; Spotted Owls have become nearly absent from the lower elevations, giving way to the colonizing Barred Owl that is now commonplace; Tufted Puffin populations have declined and they are much more difficult to view from shore. The following itinerary offers opportunities to sample the birds of the coast, rivers, and managed and old-growth forests at several spots, including the Hoh River country and Lake Quinault.*

LA PUSH

From US-101, turn west on SR-110. In 7.8 miles the Mora Road branches off on the right. Keep left on SR-110 toward the fishing village of La Push on the Quileute Indian Reservation. The road travels through Douglas-fir, Western Hemlock, and Sitka Spruce forests of varying ages and crosses into Olympic National Park as it nears La Push. The forested 1.3-mile Third Beach Trail, on the left in 3.8 miles, leads to a wilderness beach and the 17-mile beach trail south heading to the Hoh River. Pacific Wren, Varied Thrush, and Red Crossbill along with other forest birds are heard more often than seen here. Farther along (1.4 miles), Second Beach Trail, on the left, leads in 0.7 mile through spruce woods down to a picturesque beach where cormorants, Bald Eagles, Black Oystercatchers, Tufted Puffins, gulls, Harbor Seals and sometimes Sea Otters may be seen. Peregrine Falcons nest at Second Beach. Crossbill flocks are frequently seen in the beachfront forests from both beaches. The many small islands of the Quillayute Needles National Wildlife Refuge, just offshore, host thousands of nesting seabirds, including the state's largest colony of Leach's Storm-Petrels. The petrels are entirely nocturnal near their colonies and never visible during the day. Several of the beachfront islands at Second Beach offer excellent views of nesting seabirds including Pelagic Cormorant, Common Murre, Pigeon Guillemot, and others. It is possible

La Push and Vicinity

Olympic National Park

Pacific Ocean

overlook

Quillayute River

James Rd

River St.

dirt

Alder St.

La Push

First Beach

110

(500 feet)

Rialto Beach

Mora Campground

Little James Island

Mora Road

Soleduck River

Kohchaa Island

La Push

See detail of La Push, above right.

Quileute Indian Reservation

Slough Trail

James Island

First Beach

Quillayute River

To US-101 and Forks

Bogachiel River

110

Second Beach Trail

Quillayute Needles (sea-stacks)

Second Beach

Olympic National Park

CLALLAM

JEFFERSON

ONE MILE

Third Beach Trail

Third Beach

to approach too closely during low tide, so be sensitive and avoid disturbing the nesting birds.

On the outskirts of La Push, just after the La Push Ocean Park Resort cabins, turn right onto Alder Street and then immediately left onto River Street. At the T-intersection, go left onto Main Street (aka River Drive) and follow the road a short distance to a gravel parking area that provides a good overlook of the **Quillayute River** and First Beach to the south, with the Quillayute Needles and the open ocean beyond. The island at the river mouth is James Island with Little James Island at the far right. The larger of the two islands in the middle is called Kohchaa, which in the Quileute language means "gathering place for gull eggs and seafood." Peregrine Falcons nest on James Island, Bald Eagles on Little James Island. Gray Whales can be conspicuous off First Beach during their northward migration in April. If you accept Northwestern Crows as a distinct species, crows regularly seen at La Push and nearby beaches can probably be assigned to this species. During the summer salmon season, a charter fishing trip from La Push can encounter abundant and diverse seabirds including Northern Fulmar, Pink-footed and Sooty Shearwaters, Fork-tailed Storm-Petrel, Cassin's Auklet, Tufted Puffin, and other alcids, phalaropes, jaegers, Humpback Whales, and other marine mammals.

La Push has been notable for a seasonally large gull roost on the gravel bar near the Quillayute River mouth, easily viewable from the overlook. The dramatic increase in Bald Eagle numbers and their constant presence in the Quillayute estuary has diminished the size, but not the diversity of these gull flocks. Brown Pelicans and Heermann's Gulls arrive from Baja in summer, followed by Ring-billed and California Gulls from the interior. Pick out pure Western and Glaucous-winged Gulls among the far more common hybrids. In winter, check for Mew, Herring, Thayer's, and Glaucous (rare) Gulls. Also Bald Eagles, Black-legged Kittiwakes, and Peregrine Falcons regularly water and bathe here. Harlequin Ducks, all three scoters, Buffleheads, goldeneyes, and Common and Red-breasted Mergansers are often in the river mouth or channel. Crows (Northwestern) are common here. Check for Black Oystercatchers, Wandering Tattlers (spring and fall), and Black Turnstones (fall through spring) on the jetty and islands, and for loons and grebes in the boat basin. The area is attractive to unusual species, but underbirded. Mourning Dove, Western and Eastern Kingbirds, Sage Thrasher, Northern Mockingbird, Lapland Longspur, Snow Bunting, Palm Warbler, Western Meadowlark, Common Grackle, and Brambling are among the unusual migrant or wintering birds seen in this vicinity. Washington's only record of Great Knot is from La Push, and in 1996 an Emperor Goose spent the month of January here.

Retrace your route to Mora Road and turn left. The road enters Olympic National Park in 2.7 miles and winds through coastal old-growth forest, ending at the Rialto Beach parking area (2.2 miles). Several short hiking trails visit the Quillayute River or its sloughs, where birds of the forest, riverine growth, and river can be seen, including Spotted Sandpiper, Warbling Vireo, American Dipper, Swainson's and Varied Thrushes, and Yellow Warbler. Hooded Mergansers have raised their broods at the ponds across from the **Mora Campground** just inside the park entrance; Merlins have nested in the campground.

Rialto Beach is the departure point for beach hikers heading north. The picturesque Hole in the Wall, 1.5 miles north is a nice half-day hike. Twenty miles of wilderness beach trail leads to Cape Alava, where a three-mile trail connects to road access at Ozette Lake. To the south, a one-mile spit parallels the Quillayute River and ends at Little James Island.

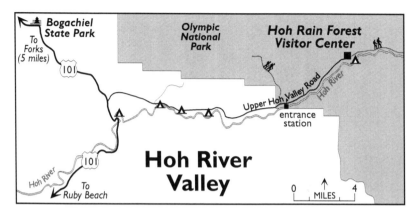

HOH RIVER VALLEY

Return to US-101 and turn right, continue through town to the Forks Visitor Information Center on the left (2.7 miles), which has national forest and national park information and maps. Summer hours: Monday–Saturday 10AM–5PM; Winter: Monday–Saturday 10AM–4PM; Sundays, year round: 11AM–4PM. Reset your trip-odometer to 0.0 here, travel 11.9 miles, and turn left onto the Upper Hoh Valley Road to reach the Olympic National Park's **Hoh Rain Forest**. The park entrance booth is 12.6 miles from US-101. The road passes through various stages of managed forests, from recent clearcuts to mature stands of Western Hemlock and Western Redcedar. There are many opportunities to pull over to look for species typical of these habitats, including Sooty Grouse, Northern Pygmy-Owl, Vaux's Swift (overhead, May through July), Hairy and Pileated Woodpeckers, Willow and Pacific-slope Flycatchers, Hutton's Vireo, Chestnut-backed Chickadee, Brown Creeper, Pacific Wren, Golden-crowned Kinglet, Swainson's and Varied Thrushes, and Orange-crowned and Wilson's Warblers. Stop at the alder grove at the parking lot on the right just before the entrance booth, where Downy Woodpecker, Hammond's Flycatcher, Warbling Vireo, Black-capped Chickadee, and Black-throated Gray Warbler are common from May through July. On the other side of the road, and a few hundred feet back west, a footbridge crosses a bog to a trail, good for birds of the coniferous forest from mid-May through mid-July. Barred Owls may be heard at night in the spring. Continue to the visitor center in about another six miles. Loop trails with interpretive signs lead through moss-draped maples, providing a good introduction to this classic temperate rain-forest ecosystem. In the nearby campground, watch for Gray and Steller's Jays. Crows here may also be thought of as "Northwestern"; these wide river valleys and coastal areas were its traditional range before development brought an end to their isolation from the widespread American Crow.

Return to US-101 and turn left. The road reaches the ocean at **Ruby Beach** (13.9 miles), and runs south through the coastal section of Olympic National Park for the next 10 miles. There are several well-signed access points to the beach, where Black Oystercatchers may be found in rocky places. Records of Tropical Kingbird and Tennessee and Black-throated Blue Warblers at Ruby Beach give a hint of the vagrant potential of this stretch of seldom-birded coastline. The Sooty Fox Sparrow can be conspicuous during breeding season here. The Destruction Island overlook, an unmarked, paved pullout (1.2 miles), can provide spectacular views, sometimes Gray Whales or Sea Otters (with scope) feeding just outside the surf line, and sometimes thousands of Sooty Shearwaters circling mysteriously just offshore. The island is a major seabird nesting site but at four miles offshore is too distant for viewing. Kalaloch Lodge is on the right in 6.2 miles.

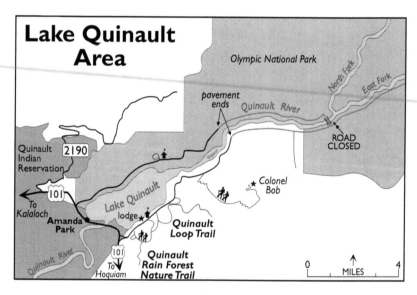

LAKE QUINAULT

After crossing the Queets River (5.0 miles south of Kalaloch Lodge), US-101 heads inland, running east and south through the Quinault Indian Reservation to Lake Quinault. This four-mile-long freshwater lake, fed by the Quinault River and other mountain streams, lies in the southwest corner of Olympic National Park. The adjoining dense conifers, lush broadleaf forests, and lakeside thickets provide a number of opportunities to sample the birds of this part of the Olympic Peninsula. Much of the better birding is along the south shore of the lake. Turn left about 26 miles from the Queets River bridge onto the Lake Quinault South Shore Road, then right in 1.4 miles into the **Quinault Rain Forest Nature Trail** parking lot (America the Beautiful or

Northwest Forest Pass required; available here from a self-service pay station). Take time to enjoy the half-mile, self-guided walk through magnificent old-growth temperate rain forest with its rich association of ferns, lichens, mosses, and Vine Maples. Colossal specimens of Douglas-fir, Western Redcedar, Western Hemlock, and Sitka Spruce dominate the trail and the gorge; you may see American Dippers in the cascades.

Continue on to the **Lake Quinault Lodge** in 0.7 mile. Built in 1926 in the heyday of the national-park style, the rustic lobby, expansive grounds, and dining room overlooking the lake are a "must see" for visiting birders. After staying here in 1937, President Franklin D. Roosevelt recommended that much of the north shore of the lake be included in Olympic National Park. The Quinault National Recreation Trail System, which starts across the road from the lodge, offers a series of hiking trails through the towering coniferous forests.

Birds of these habitats include Sooty Grouse, Barred and Northern Saw-whet Owls, Hairy and Pileated Woodpeckers, Gray and Steller's Jays, Common Raven, Chestnut-backed Chickadee, Red-breasted Nuthatch, Brown Creeper, Pacific Wren, Golden-crowned Kinglet, Varied Thrush, Townsend's Warbler, and Dark-eyed Junco. Check around the lodge, other lakeside buildings, gardens, and along the shoreline trail through broadleaf forests and shrubby thickets, for Red-breasted Sapsucker, Downy Woodpecker, Northern Flicker, Olive-sided and Pacific-slope Flycatchers, Hutton's and Warbling Vireos, swallows, American Dipper (in streams entering the lake, especially at the east end in winter), Swainson's Thrush, Orange-crowned, Yellow, Black-throated Gray, and Wilson's Warblers, Common Yellowthroat, Fox (winter), Song, and White-crowned Sparrows, Western Tanager, and Black-headed Grosbeak. The lake hosts wintering Trumpeter Swan, Hooded and Common Mergansers, Common Loon, and occasional Marbled Murrelets (summer), which nest in the old-growth trees in the hills. Around the lake, check for Osprey nests in snags, and Bald Eagles (especially in winter).

Just east of the lodge is the Quinault Ranger District Station, where you can obtain trail maps, a local bird list, and trailhead parking permits. The South Shore Road continues east, then leaves the lakeshore and meanders through open farmlands bordered by alders and maples to the **Upper Quinault Valley**. In winter, these fields may have herds of Elk. In 5.8 miles, the South Shore Road becomes a dirt road and parallels the Quinault River. Watch for Harlequin Duck (spring), and large numbers of Bald Eagles feeding on dead salmon in January along the river and creeks.

POINT GRENVILLE

Depending on tides, time of year, and weather, birding at Point Grenville can be outstanding or it can be dreary. May through early June is the best time, but other seasons can offer much. During migration and winter, seabirds and waterfowl pass the tip in good numbers. Point Grenville can be a great migrant trap and is almost always an excellent sea-watch location. Unusual birds such as Horned Puffin, Chestnut-collared Longspur, Palm Warbler, and Vesper, Lark, and Black-throated Sparrows have been seen here. Public access is restricted on much of the Quinault Indian Reservation, and non-tribal visitors to Point Grenville must have permission to bird there. Call the tribe at 360-276-8215.

Return to US-101 (stay left at the fork after the lodge) and go left (south). At 5.5 miles, turn right (west) onto the Moclips Highway, a 20-mile stretch of road through second-growth forest. At the T-intersection with SR-109, turn right (north) toward Taholah.

The paved road leads to abandoned buildings of the former Coast Guard station. Park here. During its use by the military, the area around the buildings was cleared and lawns planted. The facility was abandoned in the 1970s, and the fields have reverted to tall grass interspersed with shrubby thickets. Sooty Grouse nest in the narrow corridor of mixed coniferous and broadleaf forest habitat along the entrance road. Migrant songbirds use the California Wax-myrtle, other bushes, and forest edges. The Sooty Fox Sparrow has its southernmost known nesting location here, and is most abundant in the winter in bushes to the southwest of the buildings.

Walk north from the buildings, then west on a dirt track across an open field leading to an overlook facing west. In the past, Tufted Puffins have nested in the bluff just below the cliff face across from the offshore sea-stack. Pigeon Guillemots nest in the rock cliffs to the north and Pelagic Cormorants on the whitewashed, open cliff ledges to the south. On the offshore rock formations, Western and Glaucous-winged Gulls (and the more common hybrids of these two species) nest in the grassy areas near the top. Peregrine Falcons may be visible on these rocks or hunting nearby.

A second viewing area requires a short walk to the south side of the point. From the old buildings, follow a dirt road to the southwest. Where it appears to end, a small trail leads through thickets of alder, huckleberry, and Salal to a steep overlook. Black Oystercatchers are often seen below, on the rocky shoreline. Cormorants, puffins, and gulls nest on the second islet to the south. The waters below often have Surf and White-winged Scoters, loons, Western Grebes, and Common Murres.

The spectacular cliffs that characterize the Outer Olympic Coast end here, giving way to a broad coastal plain. Travel south on SR-109 to reach Ocean Shores and other birding sites of the South Coast.

SOUTH COAST

by Bob Morse

revised by Dianna Moore and Alan Richards

The South Coast has a gentler, more open terrain than the mountainous Olympic Peninsula. The seaboard consists of wide, sandy beaches, grasslands, intermittent timber stands, extensive rivers, tidal marshes, and two great estuaries—Grays Harbor and Willapa Bay. The backcountry stretches from the broad Chehalis Valley south over the rolling Willapa Hills to the lower reaches of the Columbia River. Nearly all of the ancient forests are gone, but trees grow quickly in this damp, mild climate (about 100 inches of rainfall annually). In some places, impressive second-growth stands with characteristics of the original forests are being nurtured through sound conservation management. These habitats attract a great diversity of avian species. Tens of thousands of shorebirds stop each spring to refuel on the 1,500 acres of mudflats at Grays Harbor National Wildlife Refuge. Nearby Ocean Shores—a magnet for rarities—is one of the premier birding hotspots in the state. Regularly scheduled boat trips out of Westport offer birders the opportunity to see albatrosses, shearwaters, petrels, jaegers, auklets, and other pelagic specialties. The 11,000-acre Willapa National Wildlife Refuge hosts a wide assortment and high numbers of wintering waterfowl. Willapa Bay is one of the most pristine, productive estuarine ecosystems in the United States.

OCEAN CITY

To reach the Grays Harbor area from Point Grenville, go south about 20 miles along SR-109 through Moclips, Pacific Beach, and Copalis Beach to the intersection with Second Avenue in Ocean City. Turn right to the seashore a few hundred yards ahead. Long stretches of the wide, hard-packed, **sandy ocean beach** can be driven between Ocean City and Point Brown at the south end of Ocean Shores. The next access point is four miles south, at the end of Damon Road—the first of five in Ocean Shores. The speed limit on the beach is 25 mph, and sections may be closed to vehicular traffic at certain times. It is illegal to drive over the razor-clam beds exposed at low tide. Stay on firm sand and keep an eye on incoming tides; careless motorists can easily get stranded. During spring and fall migration, large mixed-species flocks of shorebirds are common along the beach, especially at high tide. The beach is good for close studies of gulls including Heermann's (summer and fall), Mew (fall through spring), Ring-billed, Western, California (fall), Herring (fall through spring; uncommon), Thayer's (winter; rare), Glaucous-winged, Glaucous-winged X Western, and Glaucous (unusual). Scoters, loons, Brown Pelicans (late spring through fall), and gulls can be seen flying by offshore, and tens of thousands of Sooty Shearwaters streaming by in a seemingly endless line. They are actually moving in a five- to ten-mile-long oval loop; a scope can usually pick out the northbound and southbound "lanes." Here too Caspian Terns (spring and summer) can be seen among the gulls.

To reach Ocean Shores by conventional highway, continue south 1.9 miles on SR-109 from Ocean City and turn right onto SR-115. Be sure to check the trees along the east side of the highway; Bald Eagles often perch there, as does the occasional Red-tailed Hawk and Peregrine Falcon. The mixed forest and shrubs at **Ocean City State Park** (Discover Pass required), on the west side of the highway just north of Ocean Shores (0.8 mile), have a good selection of typical Western Washington lowland songbirds. Myrtle Yellow-rumped Warblers winter in good numbers in the California Wax-myrtle here and throughout Ocean Shores. Check the freshwater ponds along both sides of the entrance road for ducks, Pied-billed Grebe, Great Egret (rare, summer and fall), Green Heron (late spring and summer), Sora (summer), and yellowlegs (in migration). American Bittern and Virginia Rail have nested here, and Trumpeter Swans are present in winter.

OCEAN SHORES

Upon leaving the state park, turn right onto SR-115 and continue south. The road soon bends right (west). At 1.3 miles you can go straight ahead on Damon Road to a beach access. Otherwise, turn left (south) here and pass through the town gate on Point Brown Avenue, the main artery of Ocean Shores. If undisturbed by golfers, the **golf course** fairways on both sides of Point Brown Avenue south from the roundabout may host flocks of Cackling, Canada, and the occasional Greater White-fronted and Snow Geese, ducks, and shorebirds. Yellowlegs like the ponds that form on the greens during spring rains. Most of the golf course is easily viewed from neighboring roads. Two of the better vantage points are along Point Brown Avenue, from the rear of the Ocean Shores Cinema parking lot, and on Ocean Shores Boulevard, from the rear of the Ocean Shores Inn parking lot. Generally, golf-course birding is best early in the morning and at high tide. During stormy weather, this may be the best place in Ocean Shores to find various plovers, yellowlegs, and godwits.

Return on Point Brown Avenue to the roundabout, take the west or left exit to W Chance A La Mer, travel one long block, then turn left (south) onto Ocean Shores Boulevard to reach the **North Jetty** in 5.5 miles, best visited in the morning to avoid the glare of the afternoon sun. From the beach on the north side, scan the breakwater rocks for Wandering Tattler (mid-April through May, late July through mid-October), Black Turnstone (late July through May), Surfbird (late July through April), and Rock Sandpiper (early October through mid-April). Look also for Brandt's, Double-crested, and Pelagic Cormorants, and Mew (late August to May), Western, Herring (September to May), and Glaucous-winged Gulls. A scope is helpful. Walking out on the jumble of huge, tilted rocks that compose the jetty (treacherous) may be necessary to get good views of the rock birds, especially as the tattlers seem to prefer the outside face of the jetty. At high tides, or when big swells are coming in from the ocean, waves can break over the top. At such times, stay off the jetty altogether.

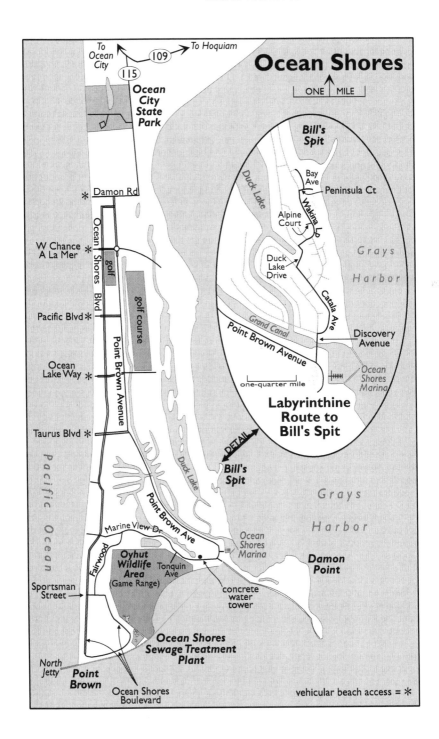

Ocean Shores

ONE | MILE

To Ocean City

To Hoquiam

109

115

Ocean City State Park

Damon Rd

Ocean Shores Blvd

W Chance A La Mer

golf

Pacific Blvd

golf course

Ocean Lake Way

Point Brown Avenue

Taurus Blvd

Pacific Ocean

Duck Lake

Point Brown Ave

Marine View Dr

Fairwood

Oyhut Wildlife Area
(Game Range)

Tonquin Ave

Sportsman Street

Ocean Shores Marina

concrete water tower

Damon Point

Grays

Harbor

North Jetty

Point Brown

Ocean Shores Boulevard

Ocean Shores Sewage Treatment Plant

Bill's Spit

Bill's Spit

Duck Lake

Bay Ave

Peninsula Ct

Wakina Ln

Alpine Court

Duck Lake Drive

Catala Ave

Grays

Harbor

Grand Canal

Point Brown Avenue

Discovery Avenue

Ocean Shores Marina

one-quarter mile

Labyrinthine Route to Bill's Spit

DETAIL

vehicular beach access = *

Weather permitting, the top of the jetty is a great place to set up a scope for a sea-watch, as far out toward the end as you feel comfortable scrambling. Wear warm clothing if you plan a prolonged stay during fall, winter, or spring. Scan south and west across the channel and ocean for passing birds of the same species mentioned for the ocean beach, plus Sooty Shearwaters (summer), Common Murre, Pigeon Guillemot, Rhinoceros Auklet, and Black-legged Kittiwake (fall through spring). Migrating flocks of Common Terns (May and mid-August through mid-September) often attract a Parasitic Jaeger. Harbor Seals and California Sea Lions are common in the waters south of the jetty. Gray Whales migrate off the coast and are sometimes visible from the jetty, especially from March through May. There are often a few whales right off the southern end of the jetty during the summer, feeding over the harbor bar.

The **Ocean Shores Sewage Treatment Plant**, located 0.8 mile farther on Ocean Shores Boulevard as it curves to the east, is open from 8:30AM to 4:30PM, Monday through Friday (please respect the hours of operation or we may lose this privilege); park in front of the office in the designated areas, or off Ocean Shores Boulevard near the fence. The three ponds provide shelter during storms as well as a high-tide refuge for ducks and gulls. Scope the edges closely for shorebirds, especially at high tide. Rarities such as a Temminck's Stint (November 2005), Wilson's Phalaropes (three in May 2008), or the occasional Ruff may show up again. Red-necked Phalaropes are regular in fall migration, and Red Phalaropes are possible after severe storms. Lapland Longspurs can usually be found from mid-September to mid-November in the short grasses between the fence and the jetty wall. Paths along the side fences provide access to the tidal mudflats and marshes of the Oyhut Wildlife Area (known as the **Game Range** to birders and natives alike). Each year seems to bring an interesting vagrant, such as the Smith's Longspur found here in August 2013, only the second record for the state. The best birding is one or two hours before or at high tide. Calf-high waterproof boots will increase your enjoyment of this habitat.

Continue on Ocean Shores Boulevard, which curves northward and becomes Sportsman Street. Go right on Fairwood Drive (0.8 mile), then right (east) onto Marine View Drive (1.1 mile). In 0.7 mile, turn right onto Tonquin Avenue, a dirt road that dead-ends at a state-regulated parking lot (Discover Pass required) near a radio facility. Walk around the gate, through an opening in the wax-myrtle to the right of the structure, and out into the salt marsh along the north edge of the Game Range. This access can be hazardous due to large logs piled there by high tides.

During fall migration, especially August, the birds that can be seen include Semipalmated Plover, Killdeer, Greater Yellowlegs, Dunlin, Baird's, Least, Buff-breasted, Pectoral, and Western Sandpipers, Semipalmated Plover, and dowitchers. This is also the best spot to find both American and Pacific Golden-Plovers (late August through early October) and is a magnet for the rarer migrants, such as the Eurasian Dotterel that spent two weeks in the fall of 1999, the Lesser Sand-Plover (formerly Mongolian Plover) that dropped by in August of 2010, and the Upland Sandpiper from early September of 2013. Merlins and/or Peregrine Falcons will most certainly strafe the large flocks of shorebirds, and Bald Eagles and Northern Harriers hunt this area, so be prepared to spend some time. Rubber boots are helpful. Be aware: the depth of water in the feeder stream can be deep, especially near high tide. Also, this is a waterfowl hunting area September through January.

Return to Marine View Drive and continue east (right). Across from the concrete water tower (0.4 mile), a small parking area leads to a path out to the beach, and an alternate way into the Game Range. In the open bay on the south side can be found Harlequin and Long-tailed Duck, scoters, Red-throated and Common Loons, Western Grebe, cormorants, Brown Pelican, and even a rarity such as the female King Eider that appeared in July of 2009 and stayed two years. Some summers Elegant Terns are numerous between here and the sewage treatment plant. Horned Lark, American Pipit; Lapland Longspur (fall) can also be seen on the sand.

Proceed east 0.3 mile along Marine View Drive to reach the parking area to Damon Point, a long sand spit extending east into Grays Harbor on the southeastern tip of the Ocean Shores peninsula. There are porta potties at the start of the trail, but this area is undergoing fairly rapid change with the winter storms eating away at what was once an asphalt road, and high tides and storm surges regularly overtopping the lowest parts on the way out to the end. Walk to the end of the asphalt, then east (left) up the south (right) side of the beach, approximately 1.5 miles to the tip. DNR now manages this spit and has asked that visitors obey the signage regarding off-limits areas.

The grassy area between the beach dunes and the treed area, about three-quarters of a mile from the parking area is where the Snowy Owls can be found during the irruption years, most recently the fall and winters of 2011 and 2012; this area is now breeding territory for the endangered Streaked Horned Lark (April through September).

Also from here, birders can get looks at Brant off the northeastern tip of Damon Point, as well as mergansers, loons (three records of Yellow-billed), grebes, cormorants, turnstones, and gulls, and sometimes Common Murre and other alcids. Birds may seek protection here from winter storms. Green Heron and Belted Kingfishers can be seen here in the summer. The Scot's Broom thickets around the intersection of Discovery Avenue and Point Brown Avenue, a little over 0.2 mile north, are one of the best spots in the state to find Palm Warbler in the fall and winter.

The best birding site on the North Bay of Grays Harbor is **Bill's Spit**, reached by a labyrinthine route one mile from the marina. (See inset map, page 59.) Geese, ducks, godwits, small sandpipers, and gulls congregate here, especially on a rising high tide. Bald Eagles, Northern Harriers, and Peregrine Falcons hunt the edges. Bill's Spit, Westport Marina, and Tokeland are probably the three most reliable places in the Lower 48 for Bar-tailed Godwit in the fall.

Go north on Discovery Avenue, turn right onto Catala Avenue, right onto Duck Lake Drive, right onto Wakina Loop, and right onto Peninsula Court where there is a poorly marked public easement between trees on the left just inside the cul-de-sac. The base of the spit can be approached on foot from here via a rough trail out to the beach; this area is also undergoing change from erosion. Please avoid flushing the resting birds, and be respectful of private property fronting the bay.

When you head back, check the area from the Ocean Shores Community Club on Catala Avenue southward to the marina for Tropical Kingbird (rare) and Palm Warbler in late fall. Turn right onto Point Brown Avenue, which will take you north through downtown Ocean Shores to the town gate in a bit more than five miles.

BOWERMAN BASIN

From Ocean Shores take SR-115 back to SR-109, reset your trip-odometer to 0.0, and turn right toward Hoquiam. In 14.6 miles, just before entering Hoquiam, take a right onto Paulson Road at the wildlife refuge and airport signs. At the T-junction (0.5 mile) go right on Airport Way along a sewage lagoon. Continue to the airport and park diagonally on the right. Walk around the gate, go west to the end of the pavement, then take the Sandpiper Trail on the right to the Grays Harbor National Wildlife Refuge shorebird-viewing areas.

The Grays Harbor estuary is one of eight sites in North America to be designated a Western Hemisphere Shorebird Reserve Network site of hemispheric importance. The extensive mudflats and the high concentration of invertebrates they support provide a rich resource for the tens of thousands of shorebirds that stop here to feed and rest before continuing their 7,000-mile journey from South America to their nesting grounds in the Arctic. The peak of spring migration occurs in late April and early May. At high tide 10,000 or 20,000 shorebirds may be feeding at your feet or swirling in vast clouds. Conversely, when the tide is out few birds remain as they spread out to feed in other parts of the estuary. The most prevalent species are Black-bellied and Semipalmated Plovers, Dunlin, and Western Sandpiper. Greater Yellowlegs, Red Knot, and Least Sandpiper are usually present but in much smaller numbers. Merlins and Peregrine Falcons regularly hunt here, providing a fascinating spectacle as flying balls of shorebirds maneuver to elude them. The annual Grays Harbor Shorebird Festival is timed to coincide with the peak of spring migration (information at http://shorebirdfestival.com). Bald Eagles, Red-tailed Hawks, and Northern Harriers also hunt the area, and a pair of Ospreys has a nest nearby and they are often seen during the late spring and summer. In fall, migrating shorebirds and waterfowl are present in lesser numbers, and the mudflats are sometimes visited by flocks of Sandhill Cranes for an overnight rest stop.

On the way out, drive around the sewage lagoon to check for waterfowl, grebes, phalaropes (Red can occur after winter storms), gulls (Franklin's is rare in migration), and three species of swallows. A Tufted Duck has appeared among the scaups several times just in time for the shorebird festival. South of the lagoon, the Chehalis River estuary mudflats are also worth a look.

CHEHALIS RIVER VALLEY

Return to SR-109, zero your trip-odometer, and turn right into Hoquiam. The highway flows into US-101 southbound, which will take you through Hoquiam to Aberdeen. At the east edge of downtown Aberdeen (5.4 miles) you can turn right with US-101 toward Westport (page 67). Or, you can opt for a side trip to explore the wooded and wetland habitats of the lower Chehalis River valley, in which case you should continue straight ahead (east) onto US-12 at this intersection. In 12.7 miles, turn right onto the Monte-Brady Road. At 0.8 mile, turn right again onto the **Brady Loop Road**. This seven-mile itinerary crosses open farmlands on the floodplain of the Chehalis River, where shallow ponds host good numbers of wintering waterfowl. Raptors regularly hunt these fields, including Bald Eagle, Cooper's, Red-tailed, and Rough-legged Hawks, American Kestrel, Gyrfalcon (rare), and Peregrine Falcon. Check the weeds, fencelines, and brushy patches along the road for Spotted Towhee, sparrows, American Goldfinches, and warblers in season. In 1.0 mile, the road takes a left turn beside thickets with large stands of alder (flycatchers and songbirds). At 0.7 mile there is a public fishing access to the Chehalis River. In another 0.5 mile the Brady Loop Road turns right while the Henry Foster Road continues straight ahead to meet the Monte-Brady Road a mile farther north. Drive part way up Foster Road, then turn around and come back to continue eastward along the Brady Loop, scanning ponds, bordering trees, and fields for waterfowl (swans on the larger ponds), raptors, and Western Meadowlarks. Short-eared Owls sometimes perch on fenceposts, and Western Scrub-Jays should be searched for around the farmhouses. After another 3.8 miles on Brady Loop Road E (including a final curving swing west), turn right at the Monte-Brady Road to return to US-12 100 yards ahead.

The 527-acre **Chehalis Wildlife Area** is a haven for waterfowl, shorebirds, and passerines in a mosaic of open wetland, riparian shrub, and meadow/field habitats, with some open water. However, the wildlife area is prone to flooding and may be inaccessible from late fall through spring. To reach it, turn right (east) onto US-12 and travel to the intersection with Schouweiler Road (3.3 miles). Turn right (south) here, then left at the stop sign at Allen Road S and follow the dirt road to the end at a metal gate (0.2 mile). Park out of the way, go around the gate, and walk straight ahead (south) on the dirt road. Birding the paths along weedy edges and thickets

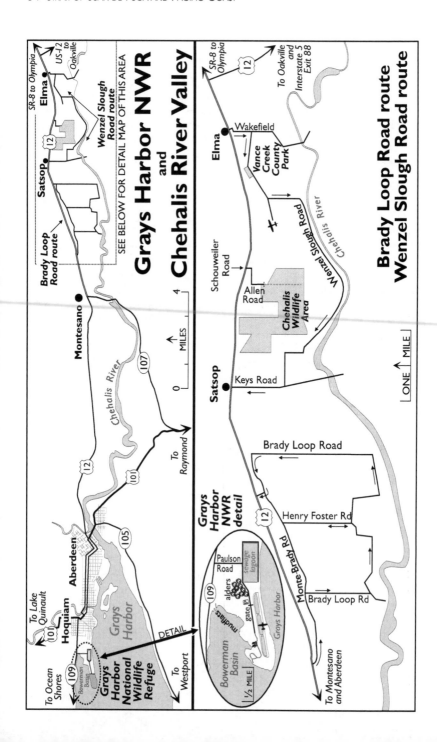

usually produces a good mixture of sparrows. Raptors hunt the fields, and geese and ducks, American Bitterns, and Virginia Rails can be found in the sloughs and ponds. Green Herons favor two larger ponds reached by walking east from the gate along a gravel berm.

Return to US-12, continue east 2.0 miles, and take the Third Street Elma exit. Turn right (south) at the stop sign onto Wakefield Road. In another 0.2 mile, turn right again at the county park and airport signs onto **Wenzel Slough Road**. A 10-mile loop westward from here through more fine floodplain habitat is at its best in winter and early spring when fields are flooded, but can be good in any season. Pull into the main parking lot of Vance Creek County Park, on the right in 0.5 mile, and bird the path across the footbridge, riparian habitat, and the long pond west of the parking lot for waterfowl, grebes, and gulls, as well as passerines (especially in migration). Fields near the airport, just ahead, sometimes have shorebirds in migration. Stop frequently anywhere along the route to check ponds, open fields, riparian vegetation, thickets, and brushy patches. Keep a watch for Bald Eagle, Northern Harrier, and Red-tailed Hawk. Swans and other waterfowl may winter in flooded fields and on small ponds. Waterfowl are skittish during hunting season, and you will get better views if you use your car as a blind. Do not enter fields without permission. At the intersection of Wenzel Slough Road and Keys Road, turn right to rejoin US-12. Turn right here and head east to bird Hood Canal (page 214), the Olympia area (page 206), or the South Sound Prairies (page 192). A left turn will take you back to Aberdeen and the road to Westport in about 17 miles.

GRAYS HARBOR SOUTH BAY

At the intersection with US-101 and SR-105 in Aberdeen, reset your trip-odometer to 0.0, turn left (south) toward Westport, and cross the high bridge over the Chehalis River. Just after the bridge, where the two highways divide, stay right on SR-105 toward Westport. In just under 11 miles, turn left to an unmarked parking area for the **Johns River State Wildlife Area** (Discover Pass required). Beyond the gate, trails lead for over a mile to coniferous and broadleaf forests, shrubby thickets, and fresh- and saltwater marshes. Look for Wood Ducks, other waterfowl, and Wilson's Snipe in the wetland habitats. Typical woodland and edge-loving species found here include Ruffed Grouse, Band-tailed Pigeon, Northern Flicker, Hutton's Vireo, Black-capped and Chestnut-backed Chickadees, Pacific and Bewick's Wrens, Golden-crowned and Ruby-crowned (winter) Kinglets, Yellow-rumped Warbler, Spotted Towhee, Golden-crowned Sparrow (winter, in brush along the dike trail), and Dark-eyed Junco.

To reach another portion of the wildlife area, continue southwest on SR-105 past the cranberry plant. In 0.7 mile, turn left onto Johns River Road just after the Johns River bridge. Bear left at the fork with the *Welcome to Johns*

River sign, left at the stop sign (0.1 mile), and right down the hill in 200 yards to a parking area (Discover Pass required). Habitats here include open farmlands and fresh- and saltwater marshes, adjoining the Johns River. A half-mile walk along the paved river-dike path to a blind should produce ducks, hawks, and occasionally a Short-eared Owl (at dawn); the trail continues unpaved for another mile or so past the blind. Elk sometimes browse in the open pastures.

Continue west on SR-105 for another 2.0 miles from Johns River Road to a sign on the right for **Bottle Beach State Park** (Discover Pass required). The 70-acre park has a parking area, a composting toilet, a covered blind, viewing platforms, and a trail along the creek. Shorebird viewing (including Red Knot) can be quite good during spring migration, especially two hours before incoming high tide, but it is good birding any time of the year. Continuing west on SR-105, Brady's Oysters at the west end of the Elk River bridge is worth a stop (turn right onto Oyster Place at 3.0 miles). Scan the river for ducks, loons, and grebes, and if the tide is out, shorebirds. Great Egret is regular in fall. Northern Saw-whet Owls may be calling from conifers to the west in the pre-dawn hours.

WESTPORT

One mile farther west, turn right and travel north on Montesano Street into Westport, the charter-boat fishing capital of the Pacific Northwest. In 3.0 miles, turn right on Wilson Avenue and park at the end of the road in front of Float 21. From the float, you can see Marbled Godwits in large numbers from fall through winter and the occasional Bar-tailed on the rock wall just east (right) of the float.

Go back on Wilson Avenue one block and turn right on Nyhus Street and follow it eight blocks to the bend to the right where it becomes Cove Avenue, then left onto Neddie Rose Drive at the stop sign (0.3 miles). Park at the end of the road (0.7 mile) and walk up onto the observation platform next to the public restroom. Gray Whales summer in the surrounding Grays Harbor channel. Throughout the year, scan for Surf and White-winged Scoters, Common Loon, Red-necked and Western Grebes, cormorants, and Black-legged Kittiwake (fall through spring). Parasitic Jaegers have been seen here, chasing kittiwakes and Common Terns during migration. When strong winds blow in from the ocean, Black Turnstones, Surfbirds, and Rock Sandpipers—normally out on the jetties—may seek protection on the leeward side of the rock groins to the west of the viewing platform. Wandering Tattler is also present in fall.

The nearby walkway next to the Harbor Resort leads to the docks of the Westport Marina and, at the end, to a fishing pier, which offers good views of grebes, cormorants, and gulls. The pier pilings sometimes host Black Turnstones and Surfbirds. Look around the docks for Long-tailed Duck, Barrow's Goldeneye, Red-throated, Common and Yellow-billed (rare; winter) Loons,

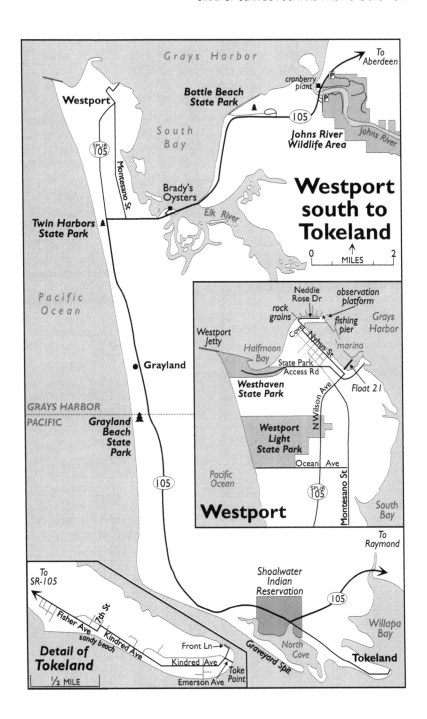

Grays Harbor

To Aberdeen

cranberry plant

Westport

Bottle Beach State Park

105

Johns River Wildlife Area

Johns River

South Bay

Brady's Oysters

Westport south to Tokeland

0 MILES 2

Montesano St.

Twin Harbors State Park

Elk River

Pacific Ocean

Grayland

GRAYS HARBOR

PACIFIC

Grayland Beach State Park

105

Neddie Rose Dr

observation platform

rock groins

fishing pier

Westport Jetty

Cove

Nyhus St

marina

Halfmoon Bay

State Park Access Rd

Grays Harbor

Westhaven State Park

Float 21

N Wilson Ave

Westport Light State Park

Ocean Ave

Pacific Ocean

SPUR 105

Montesano St

South Bay

Westport

To Raymond

Shoalwater Indian Reservation

105

To SR-105

Fisher Ave

7th St

3rd St

Kindred Ave

sandy beach

Detail of Tokeland

½ MILE

Front Ln

Kindred Ave

Emerson Ave

Toke Point

Graveyard Spit

North Cove

Willapa Bay

Tokeland

Western Grebe, Heermann's Gull (fall and winter), and California Sea Lion. In October of 2012, a Common Eider made a brief stop here, just outside the wall of the marina. Glaucous Gull is uncommon in winter; a scan of gulls on the roofs of the seafood processing plants or nearby fields may produce one.

Since the mid-1960s, **Westport Seabirds** has gone offshore to deep oceanic waters, looking for pelagic birds unlikely to be seen from shore. The Westport trips are well-known among birders for the reliability of Black-footed Albatross (seen on virtually every trip) and Fork-tailed Storm-Petrel (seen on almost all trips between May and October). Trips are run during all seasons, but most take place from late spring into early fall.

Probable for the July–October period are Laysan and Black-footed Albatrosses, Northern Fulmar, Pink-footed, Flesh-footed, Buller's, and Sooty Shearwaters, Fork-tailed and Leach's Storm-Petrels, Red-necked and Red Phalaropes, South Polar Skua, Pomarine, Parasitic, and Long-tailed Jaegers, Common Murre, Pigeon Guillemot, Marbled Murrelet, Cassin's and Rhinoceros Auklets, Black-legged Kittiwake, Sabine's Gull, and Arctic Tern. Tufted Puffin is possible. Most trips go about 30 miles offshore to the edge of the continental shelf, but as many as four trips annually head for oceanic waters 65–70 miles out, looking for *Pterodroma* petrels (Murphy's, Mottled) and other intriguing possibilities. Expert spotters accompany each trip. For current schedule and other details, check their web site at *http://www.westportseabirds.com* or leave a message at 360-268-9141.

The **Westport Jetty** offers similar birding possibilities to the Ocean Shores jetty across the channel, but the walk out is even more difficult and treacherous. The base of the jetty is accessible from Westhaven State Park (day use only, Discover Pass required). Turn right (west) at the park sign (obscured by a tree) onto Jetty Haul Road a short distance along Montesano Street as you head back south from town.

To head south toward Grayland and Tokeland, return to N Montesano Street, turn right and go 0.1 mile. Turn right onto N Wilson Avenue and continue on this road (which changes names several times) for 3.1 miles until it joins SR-105. Proceed straight ahead 11.7 miles to the sign for Tokeland, on the right.

TOKELAND

Tokeland, at the mouth of Willapa Bay south of Westport, is famous for long-legged shorebirds such as Greater Yellowlegs, Willet, Long-billed Curlew, and Bar-tailed (nearly annual in fall) and Marbled Godwits. Follow the signs from SR-105 through the Shoalwater Indian Reservation (map on previous page). Obey the 25-mph speed limit—it is strictly enforced. Where the arterial turns left 1.7 miles from the highway, continue straight ahead on Fisher Avenue and park by the rock wall where the road makes a left turn (0.2 mile). Walk out to the sandy beach and search the offshore sandspit and nearby beaches for Brown Pelican (late spring through fall), shorebirds, and gulls. This is one of the most reliable spots in the state for Willet and Long-billed Curlew in migration and winter. In late summer and fall, huge flocks of Sooty Shearwaters sometimes enter Willapa Bay and can be seen from this and other vantage points.

Continue left (north) on Seventh Street, then right in about 75 yards onto Kindred Avenue, which runs east into town. Take a right at Emerson Avenue (hidden street sign on left in 1.0 mile). This dirt road ends in a short distance at Toke Point. Scan the beach, rocks, and pilings for cormorants, Willet, Black Turnstone, Ring-billed, Western, California, Herring (winter), and Glaucous-winged Gulls. Scan the bay and marina for loons (Red-throated, Pacific, Common—and Yellow-billed occasionally in winter).

Return to Kindred Avenue, turn right, and continue a couple of hundred yards until the road ends at the Public Fishing Dock. Park and check the bay for seabirds, including Brant (winter, spring), or watch people tending their crab pots. Stretching west from here along Front Lane, the Tokeland Marina—and especially the long rock breakwater beyond the marina—are a favored high-tide godwit roost from late August through the winter. Very often one or more Bar-taileds can be picked out among 200–500 Marbleds, but the Bar-taileds usually disappear by early winter. Though much rarer, Hudsonian Godwit has been seen here, too. At low tide, the godwits can be anywhere in the Tokeland area including the shoreline at the marina or far out in the bay. Watch for Purple Martin (uncommon) in the marina from mid- to late summer.

For direct access to the rock breakwater and the surrounding saltwater marsh, drive west on Front Lane to My Suzie's Store and RV Park. Park out of the way and ask the managers for permission to bird the area (they are birder-friendly). Walk down the stairs at the west end of the RV park and on out to the marsh and breakwater. This is another good place to find Willet (winter).

Many rare landbird vagrants have appeared in Tokeland, among them Snowy Egret, White-winged Dove, Prairie Falcon, Tropical Kingbird, Chestnut-collared Longspur, Black-and-white Warbler, Northern Parula, Lark Bunting, and Hooded Oriole. Walk the short, dead-end residential streets in fall to see what you can see.

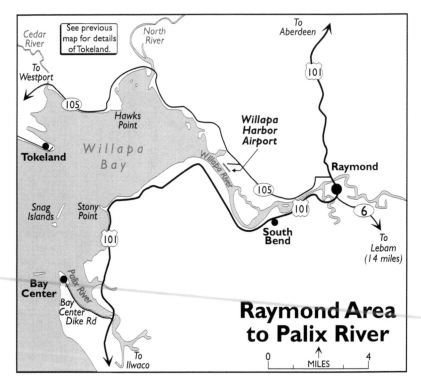

WILLAPA BAY

From Tokeland, SR-105 continues east along the north shore of Willapa Bay. The mouths of the Cedar (2.4 miles) and North (5.7 miles) Rivers can be checked for waterfowl in migration and winter. Turn west on Airport Road (5.9 miles) to the **Raymond Airport** (officially, Willapa Harbor Airport) on the floodplain at the mouth of the Willapa River. Occasionally, large Elk herds graze nearby. The fields and small freshwater ponds and sloughs along SR-105 near the airport support many wintering ducks and raptors. Watch for roosting shorebirds at high tide, and Palm Warbler in dense brush in fall and winter.

Continue east into the town of Raymond (watch for Western Scrub-Jays in residential areas). Turn right at the T-intersection with US-101 (4.5 miles). Drive southwest along the Willapa River toward South Bend, the "Oyster Capital of the World." Purple Martins can be found in season along the river. Beyond South Bend, Emperor Goose, Cattle Egret, and Tropical Kingbird have occurred (rarely), and Snow Goose uncommonly in the open farmlands from late fall to early winter. The road parallels the shoreline of Willapa Bay and crosses the Palix River in about 16 miles from Raymond. Turn west (right) onto the **Bay Center Dike Road**, just after the bridge. When flooded in winter, the fields to the south of the road have waterfowl (including Eurasian Wigeon among the flocks of

American Wigeon), shorebirds, and gulls. Large flocks of shorebirds, especially Black-bellied Plover, Dunlin, and dowitchers may be here during spring migration (late April). Loons, grebes, and diving ducks use the three-mile stretch of the river from its mouth to the bridge, and Virginia Rails are common along reedy banks and slough edges. Look for Great or even Snowy Egrets (rare in migration and winter). The best river birding is usually an hour or so before or after high tide.

Continue south on US-101 (map on next page), winding through managed forests interspersed with freshwater creeks that enter the saltwater marshes of Willapa Bay. At the stop sign for SR-4 in 13.5 miles, turn right with US-101 toward Long Beach. Here the road follows the Naselle River across open, expansive marshes. Headquarters for the **Willapa National Wildlife Refuge** are located on the left in 4.6 miles. Those with a boat can launch it across the road to gain access to nearby **Long Island**, the largest estuarine island along the Pacific Coast with 5,000 acres of saltgrass tidal marsh, intertidal mudflats, and mostly second-growth forest. (*Caution:* most low tides are too low for boating in this area.)

A 274-acre Western Redcedar grove is one of the last remnants of the old-growth coastal forest once prevalent in this area. Woods host Bald Eagle, Ruffed and Sooty Grouse, Red-breasted Sapsucker, and Pileated Woodpecker, as well as Elk, Mule Deer, Beaver, and a high concentration of Black Bears. Nesting Band-tailed Pigeons can usually be seen from May through September. Eelgrass beds off the west side of Long Island provide an important food source for large flocks of wintering and migrating Brant. Near the refuge headquarters, at dawn, Marbled Murrelets can be heard passing overhead during the breeding season (best during mid-June to mid-July).

The Lewis Unit of the Willapa NWR is now accessible only by small boat, using the Riekkola Unit entry, described in the following section. The habitat has been radically modified for the better by the recent removal of large dikes in the Porter's Point and Lewis units.

LONG BEACH PENINSULA

Continue west on US-101 toward Ilwaco (do not use Alternate-101). To reach the Long Beach Peninsula, turn right onto Sandridge Road in 4.7 miles (brown *Willapa National Wildlife Refuge* sign) and head north. A right turn onto 67th Place (1.6 miles) takes you past cranberry bogs and mixed forest to the parking area and gated entrance (open at some times of year) of the refuge's **Riekkola Unit**, in 2.3 miles. In winter, check the large flocks of both Cackling and Canada Geese for different subspecies. Among the two expected Cackling Goose subspecies of Ridgway's (*minima*) and Taverner's, look for the rare Aleutian during migration. A fair number of Dusky Canada Geese can be expected among the typical Canada Geese (*moffitti*), but Lesser Canada Geese (*parvipes*) may also be present, though rare.

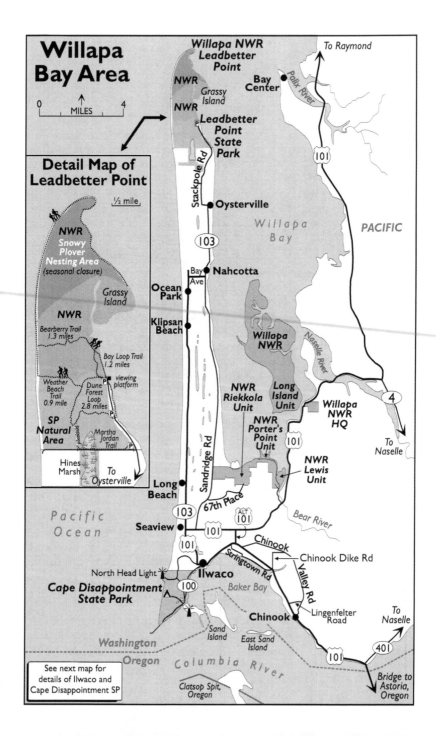

Willapa Bay Area

0 — MILES — 4

Detail Map of Leadbetter Point

½ mile

NWR
Snowy Plover Nesting Area
(seasonal closure)

NWR
Grassy Island

NWR
Bearberry Trail
1.3 miles

Bay Loop Trail
1.2 miles

viewing platform

Weather Beach Trail
0.9 mile

Dune Forest Loop
2.8 miles

P

P

SP Natural Area

Martha Jordan Trail

P

Hines Marsh

To Oysterville

Pacific Ocean

See next map for details of Ilwaco and Cape Disappointment SP

Willapa NWR Leadbetter Point

NWR
Grassy Island

NWR
Leadbetter Point State Park

Bay Center

Pallix River

To Raymond

101

Stackpole Rd

Oysterville

Willapa Bay

PACIFIC

103

Bay Ave
Nahcotta

Ocean Park

Klipsan Beach

Willapa NWR

Naselle River

NWR Riekkola Unit

Long Island Unit

Willapa NWR HQ

4

NWR Porter's Point Unit

101

To Naselle

NWR Lewis Unit

Long Beach

Sandridge Rd

103

67th Place

ALT 101

Seaview

101

Bear River

To Naselle

Chinook

Chinook Dike Rd

North Head Light

Cape Disappointment State Park

Ilwaco

100

Stringtown Rd

Valley Rd

Baker Bay

Chinook

Lingenfelter Road

To Naselle

401

Washington

Oregon

Sand Island

East Sand Island

Columbia River

Bridge to Astoria, Oregon

Clatsop Spit, Oregon

Return to Sandridge Road and turn north. Turn right at 273rd Street (10.5 miles) in **Nahcotta**, famous for its oysters: nearly 10 percent of oysters eaten in the U.S. come from Willapa Bay. Check the oyster-shell piles, marina, oyster plants, rock jetty, and nearby waters for Common Loon, Red-necked and Western Grebes, Ruddy and Black Turnstones, Surfbird, Herring Gull (winter), and Glaucous Gull (rare in winter). Also check the waters around the boat basin at the end of 275th Street. Farther north along Sandridge Road, bear right at Territory Road (3.0 miles) to visit the National Historic District of Oysterville with original houses from the 1860s and 1870s. Turn left onto the Oysterville Road (0.4 mile), which goes westward across the peninsula. At 0.4 mile turn north (right) onto Stackpole Road to reach the upper end of the peninsula.

Leadbetter Point State Park, a day-use natural area (Discover Pass required), begins at 2.9 miles north from Oysterville Road. Be bear-aware on all trails here. A small parking lot on the left near the state park entrance provides access to the new Martha Jordan Birding Trail, expected to be completed in 2015. The wheelchair-accessible portion of the trail follows a gravel easement road that reaches **Hines Marsh** in about a half-mile. This unusual interdunal wetland attracts Trumpeter Swans (winter; scope advised), waterfowl, raptors, and passerines. Jordan worked for years with several conservation organizations to restore and protect the wetland, adding some 240 acres to the state park. Farther along the easement road, the birding trail then turns north to connect with the state park's Dune Forest Loop trail.

The main parking lot for Leadbetter Point is 1.5 miles north of the park entrance, at the end of Stackpole Road. The land from here up to the end of the peninsula—part of the Willapa National Wildlife Refuge—is **Leadbetter Point**. Sandy trails lead westward, traversing an interesting succession of plant communities on the way to wide beaches fronting the Pacific Ocean. At the parking lot, mature Sitka Spruce forest with a dense and varied understory prevails; next comes a belt of Lodgepole Pine on sandy soils, and then a shrubby zone with many wax-myrtles—very attractive to wintering Myrtle Yellow-rumped Warblers. Approaching the ocean, introduced European Beachgrass grows in the unstable dunes, just above the high-tide zone. You may walk the outer beach northward all the way to the tip of the peninsula.

On the east side of the point, a rich salt marsh of Pickleweed and Arrowgrass floods and drains twice daily with the change of tides. The marsh and adjacent intertidal zone are an important feeding and resting habitat for Brant, especially during April and May when thousands stop here on their northward migration. There is no trail to **Grassy Island**, a thicket of willows, alders, and shrubs near the inner tip of Leadbetter Point that can have unusual passerines in migration. Walk the path to the beach on the east side of the point, then follow along the shore north to the tip and on to Grassy Island. It is a long trek. Attempting to take shortcuts may mean backtracks and futile detours to get around the tidal channels in the marshes. The area is prone to flooding at high tide, especially from October to April. Rubber boots are recommended.

While Leadbetter Point is an excellent site for shorebirds, long experience by birders has shown that Ocean Shores and Tokeland provide much easier access for viewing virtually all Washington shorebird species. However, if you want an opportunity to immerse yourself in a wilderness experience, Leadbetter Point is the place for you. With preparation, proper tides, and a willingness to walk, you may encounter shorebirds in great variety and number. Many records of state rarities come from here, including Gray-tailed Tattler, Upland Sandpiper, Little Curlew, Bristle-thighed Curlew, Hudsonian and Bar-tailed Godwits, and Curlew Sandpiper.

Two specific areas are worth mentioning: the salt marsh west of Grassy Island and the ocean beach and flats at the outer point and northwestern shore. In the salt marsh, you may see American and Pacific Golden-Plovers and Pectoral and Sharp-tailed Sandpipers. On the ocean beach and flats, look for Snow Buntings and Lapland Longspurs in winter; for Snowy Plover (but stay out of the clearly marked, restricted nesting area of this state-endangered species); and rarely, for Streaked Horned Lark, state-endangered subspecies. Impressive shorebird roosts may be encountered anywhere along the outer beach at high tide.

Return to Oysterville and continue south on Sandridge Road. Follow SR-103 where it turns westward on Bay Avenue (8.7 miles), then southward for about 20 miles through the towns of Ocean Park, Klipsan Beach, Long Beach, and Seaview, offering a profusion of motels, restaurants, galleries, and amusements. In Seaview, take US-101 south to the town of Ilwaco at the southern end of the Long Beach Peninsula (1.8 miles to the only traffic light in town, at Spruce Street).

COLUMBIA RIVER MOUTH

Go west from the traffic light at Spruce Street in Ilwaco and proceed counterclockwise on SR-100 Loop. In 2.1 miles turn right to the North Head Lighthouse. Park in the small lot (0.4 mile, Discover Pass required) and walk 350 yards to the scenic lighthouse. Migrant passerines are common, spring and fall, on the southwest-facing slope of shrubby thickets and mixed coniferous and deciduous woods. Gray Whales (spring), Sooty Shearwaters (fall and spring), American White Pelicans (rare, but increasing), and Brown Pelicans (late spring through fall) swim in offshore waters or fly by the lighthouse, along with scoters, other diving ducks, and Pigeon Guillemots. Black Oystercatchers and Surfbirds may be on nearby rocks.

Return to SR-100 Loop, turn right, then right again at the main entrance to **Cape Disappointment State Park** (1.1 mile). The 1,666-acre park, located at the mouth of the Columbia River, offers a wide variety of habitats

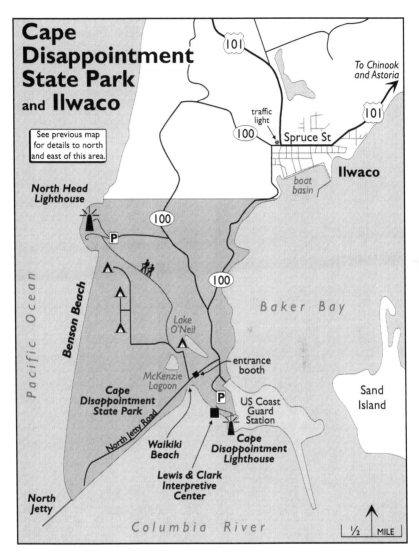

Cape Disappointment State Park and Ilwaco

See previous map for details to north and east of this area.

North Head Lighthouse

Pacific Ocean

Benson Beach

North Head Lighthouse

P

Lake O'Neil

McKenzie Lagoon

Cape Disappointment State Park

North Jetty Road

Waikiki Beach

Lewis & Clark Interpretive Center

North Jetty

traffic light

100

Spruce St

boat basin

Ilwaco

Baker Bay

entrance booth

P

US Coast Guard Station

Cape Disappointment Lighthouse

Sand Island

Columbia River

To Chinook and Astoria

½ MILE

including open salt water, rock jetty, rocky cliffs, sandy ocean beach, saltwater marsh, Sitka Spruce forest, freshwater lakes, Red Alder swamp, shrubby thickets, and park-like settings. (*Note:* A major project to shore up the jetties at the mouth of the Columbia River began in late 2014 and was expected to disrupt access to Cape Disappointment State Park for up to two years.) Drive ahead past the entrance booth, then follow signs into the campground. Freshwater Lake O'Neil and McKenzie Lagoon, in the center of the park, usually have Pied-billed Grebe, Green Heron (summer), and waterfowl (Trumpeter Swan in winter). Virginia Rails are numerous year round in the sedge marshes. Varied Thrushes patrol the lawns in winter. Check the trees and bushes here, and along the trail to the North Head Lighthouse (trailhead a bit farther along on the right) for passerines, including Orange-crowned, Black-throated Gray, and Wilson's Warblers from spring through fall, and Red Crossbill at any season. Brushy patches hold winter sparrow flocks. Come back out and drive right to the end of the North Jetty Road (0.8 mile). Along the way, isolated conifers on the south side often have interesting passerines during migration.

The **North Jetty** (under repair 2015–2016) of the Columbia River is subject to constant winter storms that change access, cut away beachfront, and deposit logs along access roads and parking lots. Pick your way out the rock jetty to view Pacific and Common Loons, long strings of passing Sooty Shearwaters in fall and spring, flying Surf and White-winged Scoters, and Black-legged Kittiwakes (uncommon). Search for Common and Arctic (rare) Terns during migration. Watch for jaegers, with Parasitic being the most likely, in fall and spring migration. Wandering Tattlers (spring and fall), Black Turnstones, Surfbirds, and Rock Sandpipers (rare) inhabit the jetty rocks. *Caution:* Stay off the jetty when winds and high or incoming tides create dangerous conditions with breaking swells, extreme spray, tidal wash, and treacherous footing.

Return toward the entrance booth. The parking lot for Waikiki Beach, near the campground entrance road, is an excellent place to observe the cliffs of **Cape Disappointment**, where Brandt's and Pelagic Cormorants, Glaucous-winged Gulls, and Pigeon Guillemots nest. Turn right at the stop sign after the booth to a parking lot for the Cape Disappointment Lighthouse (the oldest lighthouse still in use on the West Coast) and the Lewis and Clark Interpretive Center, reached by short, steep trails. Both offer great views of the huge swells as the Columbia River meets the Pacific Ocean. Use caution and stay behind the fence.

Return to the traffic light in Ilwaco and go east on Spruce Street (US-101 southbound). Before you leave town, the waters off the boat basin (three blocks south) are worth a look. Purple Martins nest in the pilings. **Stringtown Road** turns off to the right from US-101 in 2.0 miles from the stoplight in Ilwaco (easy-to-miss sign; see map on page 72). This road goes south past a small airport (Lapland Longspur fall and early winter), then turns east along the shore of Baker Bay. Here, on 18 November 1805, a member of the Lewis and Clark Expedition killed "a buzzard of the large kind" measuring 9.5 feet from wingtip to wingtip—an early record of the California Condor, once a regular visitor to the Columbia River.

Check roadside vegetation and feeders at houses for hummingbirds and passerines. In 2.6 miles Stringtown Road rejoins US-101. Turn right a short distance to the bridge over the Chinook River. The river mouth has shorebirds in fall and hundreds of ducks in fall and winter on an incoming tide, although they may be scarce during hunting season.

At the Stringtown Road intersection, drive cautiously straight across US-101 onto the Chinook Dike Road. Continue by open fields lined with brush (winter sparrows). At the T-intersection (1.2 miles), turn right onto **Chinook Valley Road.** This road is good for geese and ducks, especially during and after rainstorms, and is an important wintering area for raptors. In winter look for White-tailed Kite (rare), Bald Eagle, Red-tailed and Rough-legged Hawks, and Northern Shrike. At the next T-intersection (2.7 miles), turn left to stay on Chinook Valley Road (Lingenfelter Road, straight ahead, is also good).

In 0.8 mile Chinook Valley Road reaches an intersection with US-101 in Chinook. Turn left here. **East Sand Island** in the Columbia River (actually in Oregon, but visible to the southwest from the Port of Chinook turnoff a short distance ahead), hosts the largest nesting colony of Caspian Terns in the world. Also found on this island is the largest known Double-crested Cormorant breeding colony in Western North America. An increasing number of Brandt's Cormorants also nest at East Sand. Historically, Caspian Terns nested in Willapa Bay and Grays Harbor. But as the terns lost habitat to vegetation growth, predatory birds, erosion, and human actions, they settled at Rice Island, another dredge-spoil island 12 miles up the Columbia. There, terns devoured an estimated 11 million salmon smolts in 1998. In 1999 and 2000, the Army Corps of Engineers and wildlife agencies ordered vegetation cleared from East Sand Island in an attempt to draw the nesting terns away from high concentrations of migrating smolts at Rice Island. It worked, but the terns began nesting so densely at East Sand Island that the Corps proposed in 2014 to reduce their nesting habitat there. The cormorants consume even more juvenile salmon than do the terns, and the federal agencies are also proposing to shrink the size of their nesting colony. East Sand also serves as a spot for roosting or stopover by Brown Pelicans, Pelagic Cormorants, and several other species.

Four miles farther east, US-101 crosses the Columbia River to Astoria, Oregon, and SR-401 heads east and north along the Washington side of the river, cutting inland to Naselle 9.6 miles past the Astoria-Megler Bridge. At the T-intersection in Naselle (2.5 miles), turn right (east) on SR-4 toward Cathlamet (page 230), or turn left to head west back toward the coast on SR-4.

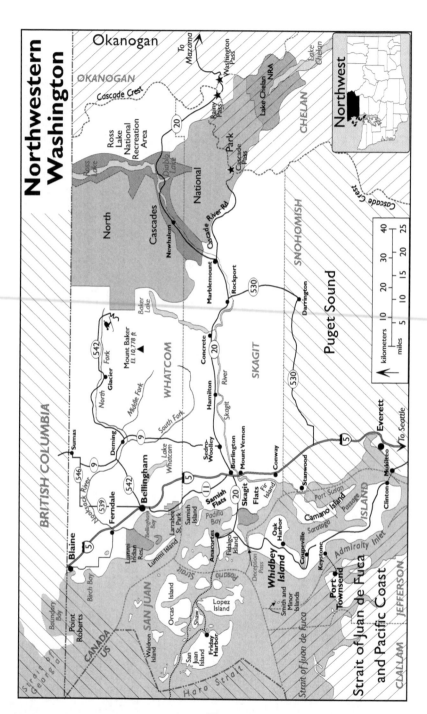

Northwestern Washington

Okanogan

OKANOGAN

Cascade Crest

To Mazama

Washington Pass

Lake Chelan

Ross Lake National Recreation Area

Ross Lake

Rainy Pass

Lake Chelan NRA

North

Diablo Lake

Cascade Pass

CHELAN

Cascades

Newhalem

National

Park

Cascade River Rd

SNOHOMISH

Cascade Crest

Marblemount

Rockport

530

Darrington

Puget Sound

Baker Lake

542

North Fork

Mount Baker El.10,778 ft

Glacier

Middle Fork

WHATCOM

Concrete

20

SKAGIT

kilometers

5   10   20   30   40

miles

5   10   15   20   25

South Fork

Hamilton

Skagit River

530

Sumas

Deming

9

Lake Whatcom

Sedro-Woolley

Burlington

Mount Vernon

Conway

Stanwood

Everett

5

To Seattle

BRITISH COLUMBIA

Nooksack River

546

9

542

Bellingham

11

Samish Flats

Skagit Flats

Port Susan

Mukilteo

539

Ferndale

Samish Island

Padilla Bay

Fir Island

Camano Island

Saratoga Passage

Clinton

CAMANO ISLAND

Blaine

5

Lummi Indian Res.

Larrabee St. Park

Bellingham Bay

Lummi Island

Anacortes

Fidalgo Island

Oak Harbor

Coupeville

Keystone

Admiralty Inlet

Birch Bay

Strait

Rosario Pass

Deception Pass

Whidbey Island

Port Townsend

Boundary Bay

SAN JUAN

Orcas Island

Shaw

Smith and Minor Islands

JEFFERSON

Point Roberts

Strait of Georgia

Waldron Island

San Juan Island

Friday Harbor

Lopez Island

Strait of Juan de Fuca

Strait of Juan de Fuca and Pacific Coast

CLALLAM

Haro Strait

CANADA
US

Northwest

NORTHWEST

Belying its size (the smallest of the nine regions in the book), Washington's Northwest enjoys an exceptional richness of birdlife in an exceptional geographic setting. Here the inland marine waters of Puget Sound, the Strait of Juan de Fuca, and the Strait of Georgia meet and mix. Here, too, are the deltas and estuaries of several rivers—the Skagit, the Samish, and the Nooksack/Lummi. Adding to the bounty, the state's best cross-mountain birding route ascends the Skagit Valley from floodplain through forested foothills to alpine meadows amidst the jagged, glacier-clad peaks of the North Cascades.

Tidal exchange between the Straits of Georgia and Juan de Fuca makes the San Juan Islands a choice seabird location. The coastal mainland and Whidbey and Fidalgo Islands offer numerous land- and waterbirding sites, from Drayton Harbor and Rosario Strait south to Puget Sound.

This region has the most important estuaries of the Puget Trough/Georgia Depression. The discharge of the Skagit is far greater than that of any other stream flowing into the basin south of Canada. The deltas of the Skagit, Samish, and Lummi Rivers are famous for wintering raptors and waterfowl. Gyrfalcon is dependable. So, usually, is Snowy Owl. Discrete subpopulations of Snow Goose and Brant winter here in their entirety. More Trumpeter Swans winter on the Skagit and Samish Flats than anywhere else in the conterminous United States. The estuaries attract shorebirds as well.

Vast, contiguous portions of the North Cascades are publicly owned and protected within North Cascades National Park, Mount Baker and Ross Lake National Recreation Areas, Mount Baker-Snoqualmie National Forest, and three designated wilderness areas. The North Cascades and Mount Baker Highways traverse several forest zones—Puget Sound Douglas-fir, Western Hemlock, Silver Fir, Mountain Hemlock, Interior Douglas-fir, and Subalpine Fir—on their way to trailheads for the Alpine/Parkland zone above treeline. High-elevation trails provide some of the best access in the state for alpine specialties such as White-tailed Ptarmigan and Gray-crowned Rosy-Finch.

Temperatures average two or three degrees cooler than farther south on Puget Sound (Bellingham mean temperature 37 degrees in January, 62 degrees in July). On the mainland coast, precipitation is about the same as in Seattle or Everett. Whidbey Island and the San Juans receive less precipitation due to the rainshadow effect of the Olympic Mountains. Eastward up the Cascade slopes annual precipitation increases approximately one inch per mile, reaching 92 inches at Newhalem.

Roads may be icy in the winter months; snow is infrequent. Of the two mountain highways, SR-542 is kept open all winter to the Mount Baker ski area, but SR-20 is closed most years above Newhalem from December into April.

The main line of communication is Interstate 5. Traffic is usually free-flowing, though ferry queues can be a serious bottleneck. Be sure to allow plenty of time for these in your travel planning.

Restaurants, lodging, gas, and other services are available in the larger communities and along the I-5 corridor. Campgrounds are fairly numerous in both lowlands and mountains, but demand for campsites often exceeds supply on weekends and in the summer season. Many campgrounds close for the winter. Whidbey Island and the San Juans are popular get-away destinations for mainlanders. Consequently, birders will find a wide selection of accommodations there, from basic motels to charming B&Bs and upmarket resorts, but these are often booked far in advance. Lodging reservations on the islands are highly recommended, especially during summer months.

Whidbey Island

by Kraig Kemper
revised by Steve Pink

Whidbey Island offers fine Western Washington birding in a magnificent setting at the top of Puget Sound, about 25 miles north of Seattle and 50 miles south of the U.S.-Canada border. With its many twists and kinks, the island has 148 miles of shoreline and stretches 50 road miles from end to end, but averages a mere three miles in width. From some vantage points it is possible to see at one time both bodies of water that flank it. The terrain is low and rolling, with the highest elevations reaching not much more than 550 feet above sea level.

The moderating effects of surrounding water and sheltering mountains provide a mild, temperate climate. Influenced by the Olympic Mountains' rainshadow, average annual rainfall varies from 18 inches at the central part of the island to 26 and 30 inches at the north and south ends—half to three-quarters the rainfall of Seattle or Everett.

Whidbey Island's rich saltwater habitats include open water bringing swells from the Pacific; sheltered passages and bays; rocky and sandy shoreline; and tidal mudflats and salt marsh. Early on, the island was commercially logged, then cleared for farming by settlers. Although little remains of the old-growth Douglas-fir forests that once cloaked the uplands, significant stands of mature second-growth coniferous and mixed forest can be found in some places. Other upland habitats include freshwater lakes, ponds, and wetlands; remnant prairies; pastures and croplands; parks and gardens; and shrubby thickets. This wide variety of habitats supports nearly 250 resident and migrant bird species.

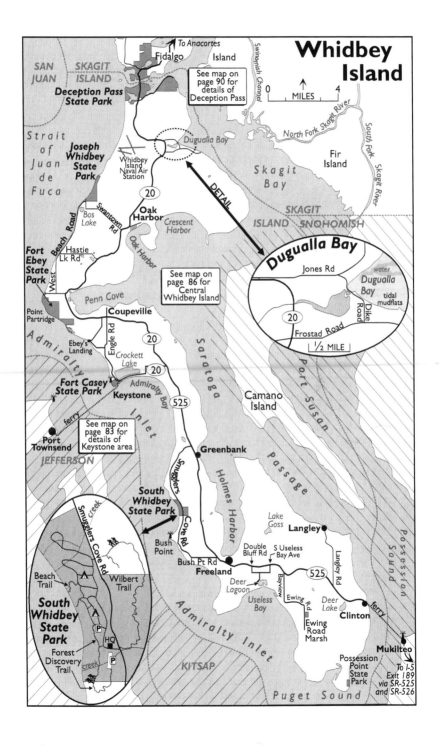

Whidbey Island

To Anacortes

Fidalgo Island

SAN JUAN

SKAGIT ISLAND

Deception Pass State Park

See map on page 90 for details of Deception Pass

0 — MILES — 4

Strait of Juan de Fuca

Joseph Whidbey State Park

North Fork Skagit River

South Fork Skagit River

Dugualla Bay

Whidbey Island Naval Air Station

Fir Island

Skagit Bay

DETAIL

20

Oak Harbor

Crescent Harbor

SKAGIT ISLAND · SNOHOMISH

Beach Road

Swantown Rd

Bos Lake

Hastie Lk Rd

Fort Ebey State Park

West

Oak Harbor

See map on page 86 for Central Whidbey Island

Dugualla Bay

Jones Rd

water

Dugualla Bay

tidal mudflats

20

Dike Road

Frostad Road

½ MILE

Penn Cove

Point Partridge

Coupeville

Admiralty

Engle Rd

Ebey's Landing

Crockett Lake

20

20

Fort Casey State Park

Keystone

Admiralty Bay

525

Saratoga

Port Susan

Camano Island

Passage

ferry

Port Townsend

JEFFERSON

See map on page 83 for details of Keystone area

Greenbank

Holmes Harbor

Smuggler's Cove Rd

South Whidbey State Park

Bush Point

Lake Goss

Langley

Possession Sound

Bush Pt Rd

Freeland

Double Bluff Rd

S Useless Bay Ave

Langley Rd

525

Smugglers Cove Rd

creek

Beach Trail

Wilbert Trail

South Whidbey State Park

P

HO

P

Forest Discovery Trail

creek

Admiralty Inlet

Deer Lagoon

Useless Bay

Bayview

Ewing

Ewing Rd

Deer Lake

Clinton

ferry

Ewing Road Marsh

KITSAP

Possession Point State Park

Mukilteo

To I-5 Exit 189 via SR-525 and SR-526

Puget Sound

The most productive times to bird are winter (November through mid-March) and during spring (late April through May) and fall (late July through September) migrations. Good shorebirds can be found in season. It would take more than a day to adequately bird all the locations in this section, so plan your route selectively. For shorebirds, focus on Deer Lagoon, Crockett Lake, and Swantown. For a winter trip, then look possibly to Penn Cove, Keystone Landing, Fort Casey State Park, and Dugualla Bay.

There are three means of automobile access: by ferry from Mukilteo (just south of Everett) to Clinton, by ferry from Port Townsend to the Coupeville Terminal (previously called Keystone Terminal; reservations strongly recommended during busy periods), or by highway over the Deception Pass bridge. The itinerary described here begins at the ferry terminal in Clinton, on the southeast side of the island. To get there from I-5, take Exit 189 and proceed west on SR-526 past the Boeing assembly plant, then right (north) on SR-525 to Mukilteo and the ferry landing; the route is well signed. The crossing of Possession Sound to Clinton takes 20 minutes and is usually not very birdy. The main highway from Clinton to the bridge at Deception Pass, going approximately north, starts as SR-525 and in 22 miles becomes SR-20.

DEER LAGOON

Deer Lagoon is one of the better shorebird destinations on Whidbey along with Crockett Lake and Swantown. From the Clinton Ferry, drive northwest 7.5 miles, then turn left on South Useless Bay Avenue, which, as the road curves to the right, becomes Millman Road. After 0.8 mile turn left into Deer Lagoon Road. Parking is limited. There is a locked gate at the end of the road, with a short access path to the left of the gate getting you onto the trail. Although signed *Private*, it does allow access. From here, walk south a short distance until you reach the dike. The area to the east is tidal, and if you catch the tide right, it can be spectacular for shorebirds. Previous rarities include both Hudsonian and Marbled Godwits, and also Stilt Sandpiper. Semipalmated Plovers, both yellowlegs, and Whimbrel are regular in season. On the west side of the dike is a large non-tidal lagoon that is good for ducks. There are several small islands that also attract shorebirds, particularly in fall.

SOUTH WHIDBEY STATE PARK

To return to SR-525, take Deer Lagoon Road to Millman Road, turn left, go 0.6 mile to Double Bluff Road, turn right, and proceed 0.6 mile to the highway. Turn left onto SR-525 and drive northwestward for just under two miles. Turn left (west) onto Bush Point Road (which becomes Smugglers Cove Road). Continue 4.9 miles to the **South Whidbey State Park** entrance on the left (Discover Pass required). This 348-acre park has heavily wooded uplands and an open, wave-washed beach with spectacular views across Admiralty Inlet to the Olympic Mountains. Trails through old Douglas-firs and

Western Redcedars are edged by ferns, Red Elderberry, Salmonberry, and Stinging Nettle. Year-round residents include Hutton's Vireo, Steller's Jay, Chestnut-backed Chickadee, Red-breasted Nuthatch, Brown Creeper, Pacific Wren, Golden-crowned Kinglet, and other Puget Lowlands forest species.

The Beach Trail from the former campground and parking area to the beach is steep. Look for sea ducks, loons, cormorants, and alcids on the open water, and check the beach for Great Blue Heron, Bald Eagle, Sanderling, and other shorebirds.

The mile-long Forest Discovery Trail, at the south end of the park, traces a pair of loops along the top of the bluff through Red Alder and conifers; bridges cross creeks and wet areas, bright with Skunk Cabbage in spring.

The Wilbert Trail, which begins on the east side of the highway opposite the park entrance, is a 1.5-mile loop through a 255-acre forest of old-growth Western Redcedar and Douglas-fir, with many snags where Osprey, Bald Eagle, and Pileated Woodpecker nest. If going north, continue on Smugglers Cove for 4.4 miles until you reach SR-525.

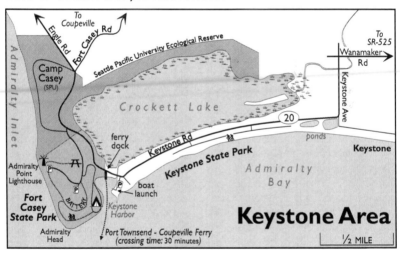

CROCKETT LAKE AND KEYSTONE HARBOR

Crockett Lake—a brackish 250-acre marsh and shallow lake formed by the long gravel bar of Keystone Spit—is located three miles south of Coupeville, adjacent to the Coupeville Ferry Terminal. The lake is noted for migrant shorebirds, gulls and terns, a good variety of ducks (many of which winter), raptors, and passerines around the marsh-edge habitat. Continue northwest (left) on SR-525 for 4.7 miles and then follow signs to the Port Townsend Ferry Landing. Turn left (west) onto SR-20 (West Wanamaker Road). Stay on SR-20 as it curves left then right toward the ferry landing.

SR-20 runs along Keystone Spit, paralleling the shores of Crockett Lake on the right (north) and Admiralty Bay on the left. For the next mile and a half you may park anywhere along the wide shoulder and walk out to bird the marsh and lake. Shorebirding is best when water levels are relatively low, exposing extensive mudflats. However, birds can then be a long way out, across wet grass and soft mud. You will need a spotting scope and rubber boots to bird effectively. Proceed with caution: the mud is deep and hazardous in places. Heat haze is often a problem in summer, so best be early.

Crockett Lake is outstanding for shorebirds in fall (mid-July through September). Common species include Black-bellied and Semipalmated Plovers, Killdeer, Spotted Sandpiper, both yellowlegs, Dunlin, Baird's (August), Least, Pectoral (September), Semipalmated (July–earlyAugust), and Western Sandpipers, both dowitchers, Wilson's Snipe, and Red-necked Phalarope. Whimbrel and Sanderling are fairly common. American Avocet (has nested), American and Pacific Golden-Plovers, Solitary Sandpiper, Black Turnstone, Red Knot, Ruff, Sharp-tailed and Stilt Sandpipers (August–September), Buff-breasted Sandpipers, and Wilson's Phalarope are uncommon to rare. Black-necked Stilt, Snowy Plover, Willet, Long-billed Curlew, Hudsonian Godwit, Curlew Sandpiper, and Red-necked Stint have each been recorded once. Grass and water edges may have American Pipit, Lapland Longspur, and Savannah Sparrow seasonally, or mega-rarities such as Snowy Egret, Little Blue Heron, Least Tern, or White Wagtail. Raptors frequent the whole area. A major portion of the spit, with freshwater ponds and a saltwater shoreline on Admiralty Bay, is open to the public (several parking lots at intervals on your left). Scope the ponds for ducks and shorebirds.

Just before the ferry terminal, turn left into a parking lot on the east shore of Keystone Harbor (1.6 miles). The state park boat launch (Discover Pass required) is one of the best on the island, with a good drop-off and excellent protection by breakwater and rock jetty. The jetty and pilings of the old Army quartermaster dock immediately to the east are now an underwater state park. Black Oystercatcher is sometimes seen on the rock jetty. Pigeon Guillemots nest and all three species of cormorants rest on the old platform and pilings. Heermann's Gulls may be here from July to September. Scan Admiralty Bay for Harlequin Duck, Red-throated and Common Loons, Horned and Red-necked Grebes, Pigeon Guillemot, and Rhinoceros Auklet.

The 30-minute ferry ride to Port Townsend (page 30) can be excellent for waterbirds. Marbled Murrelet, Rhinoceros Auklet, and other species are sometimes present in **Keystone Harbor** near the ferry slip.

FORT CASEY

From the ferry terminal and SR-20, continue northwest on Engle Road 0.4 mile to the **Fort Casey State Park** entrance on the left (Discover Pass required). Along with Fort Flagler and Fort Worden across Admiralty Inlet, Fort

Casey was part of a century-old coastal defense system that guarded the entrance to Puget Sound. These fixed-gun fortresses became obsolete after World War I, and the fort is now a 137-acre historic state park. Bird the wooded areas of the park (especially the picnic area) for species of the Puget Sound Douglas-fir zone, including summer visitors such as Pacific-slope Flycatcher and House Wren (local in Western Washington). Spring migrants may include Western Wood-Pewee and Yellow-rumped and Wilson's Warblers. Great Horned Owls are regular here. The campground (open year round) is another good vantage point for Keystone Harbor and the ferry dock. Walk out to the lighthouse on the bluff overlooking Admiralty Inlet. Nutrient-rich upwelling draws large numbers of Rhinoceros Auklets and gulls to feed offshore in summer and fall. Common Murres are often common from fall through spring.

From Fort Casey turn left onto South Engle Road, which eventually becomes Main Street, and continue 3.6 miles to the junction of US-20. At the junction either continue straight ahead for Coupeville and Penn Cove or if heading north, turn left onto SR-20.

PENN COVE

Follow Main Street into Coupeville. This is a popular tourist destination and in summer can be very busy. The **Coupeville Wharf**, located at the west end of Front Street, is worth a visit to take in the view of Penn Cove, a large bay that almost cuts across Whidbey Island from the east. Many loons, grebes, and other waterbirds winter on Penn Cove, including all three species of scoters (thousands of Surf and White-winged, just a few Black); some are present through summer. This is also an excellent location to observe both Common and Barrow's Goldeneyes.

From Front Street, go south a block to Coveland Street and turn right, then angle left onto Madrona Way. Follow Madrona Way westward along the edge of the high bluff. Places to park along this road are very limited; try to find a spot where you can safely scope the bay, particularly the floating mussel platforms (currently at 0.3 and 0.5 mile). Check the waters of the cove for scoters and other diving birds, including Harlequin Ducks. Black Turnstones, Dunlins, and other shorebirds often roost on the mussel platforms. The road swings north around the end of the cove. **Kennedy's Lagoon**, on the left side of Madrona Way 1.5 miles from the last pullout, may host ducks and a few shorebirds. Park at any of several pullouts on either side of the road for the next half-mile, north to the intersection with SR-20.

The west end of Penn Cove has a rocky and sandy shore that is one of the most accessible examples of this habitat type left within the inland marine waters of Washington. Rock-foraging shorebirds are present much of the year: Black Turnstone (most numerous) and Surfbird are common, Ruddy Turnstone is fairly common in migration, and Rock Sandpiper occurs most winters. Scoters and

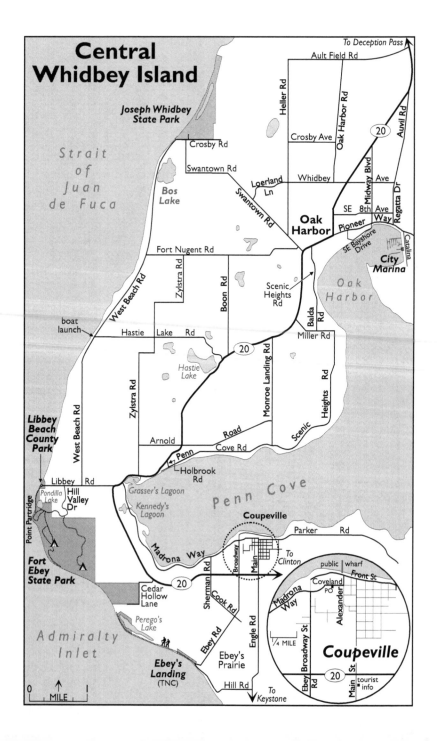

Central Whidbey Island

To Deception Pass

Ault Field Rd

Heller Rd

Joseph Whidbey State Park

Oak Harbor Rd

Crosby Rd

Crosby Ave

20

Auvil Rd

Swantown Rd

Strait of Juan de Fuca

Loerland Ln

Whidbey

Ave

Midway Blvd

Bos Lake

Swantown Rd

SE 8th Ave

Regatta Dr

Oak Harbor

Pioneer Way

Fort Nugent Rd

SE Bayshore Drive

Catalina

Zylstra Rd

Boon Rd

Scenic Heights Rd

City Marina

Oak Harbor

West Beach Rd

Balda Rd

boat launch

Hastie Lake Rd

Miller Rd

20

Hastie Lake

Monroe Landing Rd

Heights Rd

Zylstra Rd

Libbey Beach County Park

Arnold

Road

Cove Rd

Scenic

West Beach Rd

Penn

Holbrook Rd

Libbey Rd

Grasser's Lagoon

Pondilla Lake

Hill Valley Dr

Kennedy's Lagoon

Penn Cove

Point Partridge

Coupeville

Parker Rd

Fort Ebey State Park

Madrona Way

Broadway

Main

To Clinton

public wharf

Front St

Coveland

PO

20

Cedar Hollow Lane

Sherman Rd

Cook Rd

Madrona Way

Alexander

Perego's Lake

Engle Rd

1/4 MILE

Ebey Broadway St

Main St

Admiralty Inlet

Ebey Rd

Ebey's Prairie

Ebey Rd

20

Coupeville

tourist info

Ebey's Landing
(TNC)

Hill Rd

To Keystone

0   MILE   1

other waterbirds are often fairly close to shore. Small flocks of Eared Grebes, very local in Western Washington, are seen here throughout the winter.

Look for Greater Yellowlegs at **Grasser's Lagoon** at the northwest corner of Penn Cove. Migrating shorebirds sometimes shelter amidst the low vegetation on the pebbly spit that separates the lagoon from the bay. Turn right onto SR-20 from Madrona Way, then right again at a gravel pullout at the east end of the lagoon (0.2 mile) (also known as Zylstra Road), for another vantage point. Grasser's Hill, north of the highway, is popular with raptors, including Rough-legged Hawk (winter) and American Kestrel. Continue right 0.4 mile on SR-20 and turn right into a gravel lot beside the Penn Cove Pottery store. Walk across Penn Cove Road to the base of the pier (posted; stay off). The shoreline in both directions often hosts rocky shorebirds.

FORT EBEY AND POINT PARTRIDGE

Go back west on SR-20, which bends left at a junction 0.1 mile past the Madrona Way intersection. Turn right here onto Libbey Road. **Fort Ebey State Park** (Discover Pass required) is reached by turning south (left) onto Hill Valley Drive in 0.9 mile and following signs 0.7 mile to the entrance. Day-use facilities are open year round; the campground is closed November–February. The park offers excellent birding on 644 acres of coniferous and mixed woods, driftwood beach, grassy bluffs, and fresh- and saltwater habitats. Park near the restrooms and walk west 100 yards to the **Point Partridge** overlook. A panoramic view extends southeastward down Admiralty Inlet; south and southwest to Point Wilson, Port Townsend, and the snow-capped Olympic Mountains; west along the Strait of Juan de Fuca; northwest to Victoria and the southeast coast of Vancouver Island; and north to Vancouver and the San Juan Islands. A trail leads down from the bluff to a 1.5-mile sandy beach with shore- and marine birds. Black Oystercatchers forage on rocky outcroppings where the point meets the sea. This is also one of the island's best locations for Harlequin Duck.

From the other side of the restrooms, a short trail leads to Pondilla Lake, a depression left from the last ice age filled with fresh water. Dabbling ducks can be found here, and Bald Eagles often roost in nearby snags. Many resident and migrant forest birds are evident along the park's three miles of hiking trails. Five species of woodpeckers, and typical Westside songbirds such as Hutton's Vireo, Red-breasted Nuthatch, Pacific Wren, and Spotted Towhee, are here all year. Migrants and summer visitors include Olive-sided Flycatcher, Pacific-slope Flycatcher and several warblers (Orange-crowned, Black-throated Gray, Townsend's, Wilson's). This is the most reliable location for Red Crossbill on Whidbey Island, and good numbers of Varied Thrushes and Sooty Fox Sparrows can be found in winter.

The other side of Point Partridge is reached from **Libbey Beach County Park**. Return to Libbey Road, turn left, and go 0.3 mile to the road's end.

Many seabirds associated with the kelp-forest habitat of the open shoreline can be seen here—Harlequin Duck, Horned and Red-necked Grebes, Pelagic Cormorant, and Pigeon Guillemot. Surf and White-winged Scoters, Long-tailed Duck, Red-breasted Merganser, loons (Red-throated, Pacific, and Common), Black Oystercatcher, Common Murre, and Heermann's Gull also frequent these waters or the shoreline at the eastern end of the Strait of Juan de Fuca. A beach walk south around Point Partridge leads to connecting trails from Fort Ebey State Park, a half-mile away. To the north are six miles of public tidelands beneath 200-foot sandy bluffs. Don't get trapped by incoming tides.

WEST BEACH AND SWANTOWN

West Beach and Swantown attract marine ducks, shorebirds, and alcids. Return east 0.6 mile on Libbey Road, turn left onto West Beach Road, and proceed north 2.3 miles to the intersection with **Hastie Lake Road**. A parking area and boat launch on the left is another excellent point from which to view the eastern Strait of Juan de Fuca and the many seabirds associated with the Bull Kelp groves that thrive just beyond the low-tide line. Rarities such as Yellow-billed Loon and King Eider have been seen here. Black Oystercatchers and Harlequin Ducks are also regular here.

West Beach Road continues north and descends a hill to beach level at a spot called **Swantown**, with a small lake and salt marsh on the right. Park on the wide gravel shoulder on the left (beach) side of the road (2.5 miles) and look out over the eastern end of the Strait of Juan de Fuca. There is a high probability of seeing seabirds year round—especially large numbers of ducks (including Harlequin and Long-tailed), loons, and grebes. Gulls and alcids frequent the channel and feed near shore during the winter. Look for Sanderlings on the beach and Caspian Terns offshore.

Navigational lights on Smith and Minor Islands four miles to the west are important landmarks for boats traveling between Puget Sound and the San Juans. The two islands are part of a national wildlife refuge established in 1914 to protect Brant wintering on the neighboring eelgrass beds from slaughter by market hunters. Minor Island has a large breeding colony of Harbor Seals; Smith Island is an important nesting site for Pelagic Cormorant, Black Oystercatcher, Pigeon Guillemot, and Tufted Puffin. (Puffins are rarely seen from Whidbey Island.)

Bos Lake and the surrounding salt marsh (aka Swantown Lagoon), east of the road, are notable for migrating shorebirds, gulls, and terns, and for wintering waterfowl, waders, and raptors. In fall migration (mid-July through September) Bos Lake is an important shorebird stopover, second on the island only to Crockett Lake for numbers and species diversity. However, water levels vary throughout the year, and in fall the mudflats can be extensive and birds a long way out. You can scope from the edge of the road or, for closer views, pull on rubber boots and walk toward the exposed flats. Look for a log crossing over the slough, and beware of deep, sticky mud.

Continue on West Beach Road, turning right to the intersection of West Beach, Crosby, and Swantown Roads (1.0 mile). The entrance to 112-acre **Joseph Whidbey State Park** (Discover Pass required) is just ahead on the left (day use only; closed October–March). Paths lead from the picnic area to the broad sand and gravel beach. Expect the same waterbirds as at Point Partridge and the other Juan de Fuca overlooks.

Another access can be found next to the first residence on the south side of the park (on the left in 0.7 mile when coming from Bos Lake). Here is a graveled parking lot for a few cars and a trail that leads directly to the beach. Trails through the beach grass just above the driftwood line follow the beach north out of the park property. Just before leaving the park, a half-mile trail through a freshwater wetland offers good views of migrating and nesting waterfowl and marshbirds.

OAK HARBOR AND DUGUALLA BAY

Birding possibilities at **Oak Harbor** are similar to those at Penn Cove, including rocky shorebirds on the beach and the Oak Harbor City Marina. This is a good place to see gulls unusual elsewhere on the island (Thayer's, Glaucous). From Joseph Whidbey State Park, follow Swantown Road south and east 2.9 miles to an intersection with SR-20. Turn left onto SR-20 and continue east into the city of Oak Harbor. In 0.5 mile, where SR-20 turns north at a traffic light, stay straight ahead on SE Pioneer Way. Take the next right on SE City Beach Street (0.3 mile) and then turn left onto SE Bayshore Drive. Park anywhere along here to check the beaches for ducks, rocky shorebirds, and gulls.

If you still need to find rocky shorebirds, then the Oak Harbor City Marina is worth checking. Continue east along Bayshore Drive, turning right onto SE Pioneer Way, and continue a short distance before turning right onto SE Catalina Drive just before the entrance to the Naval Base. Look at the south end of the marina for the boat ramp; the shorebirds may be seen on marina docks and the logbooms.

Return to the light at SR-20. Drive north (right) on SR-20 to the intersection with Frostad Road (5.0 miles); turn right, continue 0.9 mile, and turn left onto Dike Road. (See inset map on page 81.) A gravel pullout on the right (0.3 mile) provides a view of Dugualla Bay, an indentation on the west side of Skagit Bay. Look for scaups, grebes, and cormorants on the bay, and herons, yellowlegs, dowitchers, and other shorebirds on the beach. The head of Dugualla Bay drains to a quarter-mile-long mudflat at low tide. Optimal viewing is on an incoming or receding tide.

Continue about 450 yards farther along the dike to another gravel pullout and viewpoint for bay and beach, on the right. Look also for waterfowl on the impounded lake and surrounding agricultural fields on the left (west) side of the road. This is the most reliable location for swans on Whidbey Island, and large numbers of Canvasbacks may be present in late winter. Watch for raptors, including Rough-legged Hawk and Peregrine Falcon, and for a variety of passerines in the hedgerows and brush along the dike. Continue 0.2 mile to Jones Road. Turn left to reach SR-20 in 1.0 mile.

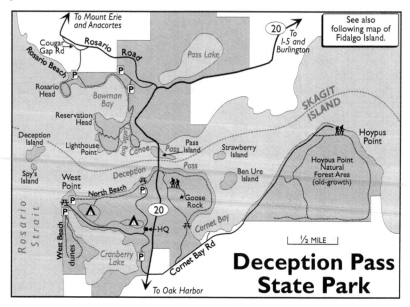

DECEPTION PASS STATE PARK

From Jones Road, continue north 3.4 miles on SR-20 and turn into the main entrance of picturesque Deception Pass State Park, on the left. Straddling the narrow, rocky channel separating Whidbey and Fidalgo Islands, the park offers 3,000 acres of old-growth Douglas-fir forest, saltwater beaches, tidepools, and freshwater lakes and marshes. A variety of overnight, day-use, recreational, and educational facilities are available at Cranberry Lake and West Beach, North Beach, Cornet Bay, and Rosario Beach. Most facilities are open year round, but some are closed in winter. Deception Pass State Park is the most heavily used state park in Washington. Because of high summer visitation, birding is best in early morning or evening or in the off-season.

Turn left at a fork in 0.4 mile, near the park office, following signs to the **West Beach** parking lot (0.8 mile). The largest of the park's freshwater lakes, Cranberry Lake, is on the left along the way. Wood Duck, Hooded Merganser, Pied-billed Grebe, and other waterbirds are sometimes present.

Also watch for the resident River Otters. Sand dunes separate the lake from West Beach, which has both rocky and sandy shoreline. Sea ducks, loons (especially Red-throated and Pacific), Horned and Red-necked Grebes, cormorants (all three species), and gulls may be seen offshore. Pigeon Guillemots and Marbled Murrelets are regular all year, and Rhinoceros Auklets are frequent in summer. Look for Black Oystercatcher, Black Turnstone, and Sanderling on the beach. The rest of the park is dominated by coniferous forest, and the large trees and edge habitat will yield a list of typical lowland species, including Varied Thrush in winter. The other branch at the fork near the park office leads to **North Beach** and excellent water-level views of the mouth of Deception Pass, where Red-throated Loons can be numerous in winter on the right tide.

Rosario Beach, another portion of the park, lies across Canoe Pass near the southern tip of Fidalgo Island. Take SR-20 north over the bridge. Turn left onto Rosario Road (1.0 mile from the south end of the bridge). Angle left onto Cougar Gap Road in 0.8 mile; at the bottom of the hill turn left onto the park entrance road (Discover Pass required). This can be a very busy place on summer weekends. Walk out to Rosario Head (a five-minute walk) for views of Bowman Bay—a fine place for alcids (Common Murre, Pigeon Guillemot, Marbled Murrelet, and Rhinoceros Auklet) at all seasons, although late fall through winter is the best time. Ancient Murrelets are often present from November through January.

In winter, huge numbers of Red-throated Loons may congregate here. Offshore rocks may have Harlequin Ducks as well as Brandt's Cormorants alongside Double-crested and Pelagic. Search the rocks to the north of the head for Black Oystercatchers and Black Turnstones, and keep an eye out for Wandering Tattlers (rare).

Return to SR-20 and drive north 5.1 miles to a major junction where SR-20 continues right (east) toward Burlington (I-5 Exit 230) and SR-20 Spur goes left to Anacortes and the San Juan Islands ferry terminal.

OTHER GOOD BIRDING SITES ON WHIDBEY ISLAND

See Whidbey Island map, page 81

Possession Point State Park

South of Clinton on Possession Road—forest trail and beach

Ewing Road Marsh

East of Clinton on Ewing Road—freshwater marsh

Ebey's Landing

South of Coupeville—prairie, cliffs, and beach

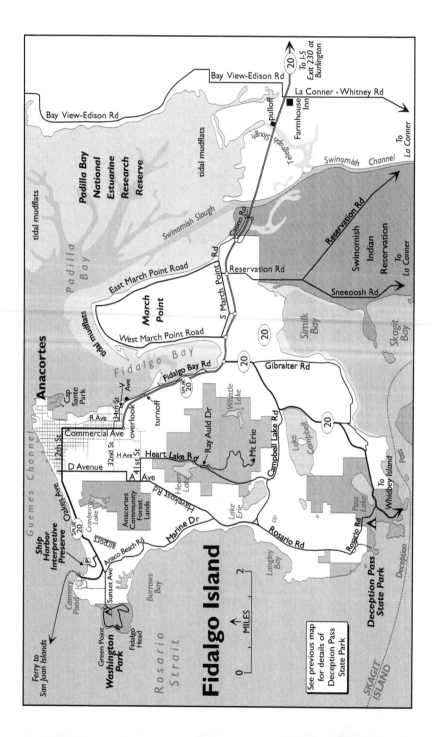

FIDALGO ISLAND

by Bob Kuntz

revised by Bob Kuntz

Fidalgo Island is perhaps best known as the home of the Anacortes Ferry Terminal—the jumping-off place for the San Juan Islands and Victoria, British Columbia. Birding cognoscenti, however, recognize the island as a fine and varied birding destination in its own right. Any or all of the sites described here are often included on a visit to Whidbey Island or to the Skagit and Samish Flats.

SWINOMISH SLOUGHS

Go 2.6 miles west on SR-20 from the traffic light at Bay View-Edison Road (north side of SR-20; south side is La Conner-Whitney Road). This intersection is also known as Farmhouse Inn corner. This will take you across the Swinomish (pronounced *SWIN-ih-mish*) Channel bridge onto Fidalgo Island. You are now on the Swinomish Indian Reservation. Turn right at the exit for March Point and then immediately right again onto Casino Road. At 0.1 mile you can pull off on the left (north) side of the road along **Swinomish Slough**, best viewed at low tide, to look for Semipalmated Plover, both species of yellowlegs, and other shorebirds. Return to a stop sign, turn right, and continue 0.8 mile to a sign reading *Casino Road*. Turn right onto this road (called East March Point Road on some maps), cross the railroad track, and pull off immediately on the right to check the several dredge-spoil islands, home to a colony of Glaucous-winged Gulls. Caspian Terns are regular summer visitors.

MARCH POINT AND FIDALGO BAY

A peninsula between Fidalgo and Padilla Bays, **March Point** is home to two major oil refineries. The tank farms and cracking towers at your back form an odd contrast with the spectacular natural scenery of Padilla Bay, Mount Baker, and the Cascades. Drive up the road along the eastern shoreline to the tip of the point, pulling off when there's an open view to scope the waters. Loons, grebes, cormorants, and several species of diving ducks are common here, especially from November through April. March Point is a good place to view Gray-bellied Brant (see also page 114). Check the refinery piers for Black Turnstones. Black Scoter is rare in **Fidalgo Bay**; Sanderling, American Pipit, and Snow Bunting are occasionally observed on the pebbly beaches. Continuing around the point, West March Point Road completes the loop back south to SR-20 in 5.7 miles.

Turn right and continue west about one-half mile. Here SR-20 turns left (south) toward Deception Pass and Whidbey Island. Stay straight onto SR-20 Spur, travel 2.7 miles, enter the roundabout, and turn right onto Commercial Avenue (SR-20 Spur). Continue into the Anacortes business district. At 1.2 miles, turn left with SR-20 Spur onto 12th Street.

MOUNT ERIE

If you are tempted by a panoramic view of the entire area covered by this chapter, with some good forest-birding possibilities thrown into the bargain, an excursion to Mount Erie will well repay the one-hour round trip. (To maximize your investment, choose a sunny day.) After heading west on 12th Street from Commercial Avenue, in 0.8 mile turn left onto D Avenue. This arterial jogs right, then left, becoming A Avenue. In 1.9 miles, turn left (east) from A Avenue onto 41st Street, then right in another 0.5 mile onto H Avenue, which continues south as Heart Lake Road. After passing Heart Lake on your right, turn left in 1.4 miles at the sign for *Mount Erie Viewpoint*. The 1.8-mile road through 1,400-acre **Mount Erie Park** ends at the 1,273-foot summit. Along the way, species to look for are similar to those for the wooded habitats of Washington Park (see below). There are four vista points, and by visiting each one you can see south the length of Whidbey Island and Puget Sound to Mount Rainier in the distance; southwest to the Olympic Mountains and the Strait of Juan de Fuca; northwest and north across Rosario Strait to the San Juan Islands, Vancouver Island, and the Coast Mountains of British Columbia; and east to the Cascades, Mount Baker, and the Skagit and Samish Flats.

WASHINGTON PARK

Return to the intersection of D Avenue and 12th Street, turning left onto 12th Street, which soon becomes Oakes Avenue. In 2.3 miles, at a right turn for the ferry terminal, continue straight ahead on Sunset Avenue to the entrance to **Washington Park** (0.6 mile), an excellent seabird viewing site from late September through mid-April. The one-way, two-mile loop road through this popular park starts just past the camping area. If you are driving, pull off on the left at Green Point, about 0.7 mile from the park entrance, to scope Rosario Strait and the west entrance to Guemes Channel. *Note:* the loop road is reserved for walkers, runners, and bicyclists up to 10AM, when it opens to automobile traffic. Naturally, the best viewing times are from early to mid-morning before the crowds arrive and with the sun at your back. At these times, the third-to-half-mile walk to Green Point from the parking area is worth the small effort. Take your scope. Three species of loons (Red-throated, Pacific, and Common) and three of grebes (Horned, Red-necked, and Western) are seasonally common, as are Common Murres, Pigeon Guillemots, and Marbled Murrelets. Rhinoceros Auklets are present in large numbers from July through October. In November and December, this is a good location to seek Ancient Murrelets. Harlequin Ducks and Black Oystercatchers are frequently seen along the rocky shoreline. At dawn, hundreds of Brandt's, Double-crested, and Pelagic Cormorants move up Rosario Strait to feeding areas.

Another good pullout is 0.2 mile ahead. Farther along the loop road (0.3 mile), a set of stairs leads to a rocky beach and more oystercatchers. The road weaves its way through a typical low-elevation forest of Western Hemlock, Douglas-fir, and Pacific Madrone—the beautiful understory tree with old, red peeling bark and young, smooth chartreuse bark. Stop often to walk the numerous trails, looking and listening for year-round resident species such as Red-breasted Sapsucker, Hutton's Vireo, Steller's Jay, Chestnut-backed Chickadee, Pacific and Bewick's Wrens, Golden-crowned Kinglet, Spotted Towhee, and Purple Finch. During migration and summer these may be joined by Rufous Hummingbird, Pacific-slope Flycatcher, Black-throated Gray and Townsend's Warblers, and Western Tanager. The loop road ends back at the main parking and picnic areas.

Ship Harbor Interpretive Preserve

From the end of the loop road, drive out of the park along Sunset Avenue 0.7 mile to a stop light (Sunset ends here). From the stop light continue straight ahead on Oakes Avenue (SR-20 Spur) for 0.5 mile and turn left onto Ship Harbor Boulevard (Glasgow Way on some maps). In 200 yards turn left at the T-intersection onto Clipper Drive, which becomes Edwards Way. Follow Edwards Way downhill 0.2 mile, where it dead-ends at a cul de sac parking area.

A paved section of the Guemes Channel trail extends east approximately one mile along Guemes Channel and provides opportunities to view loons, grebes, cormorants, a variety of waterfowl, and Pigeon Guillemot. This trail section is wheelchair accessible with trailside interpretive signs. Better birding can be experienced along the trail going west leading into Ship Harbor Interpretive Preserve. This trail leads to a boardwalk suspended over a wetland with multiple observation platforms and beach access. The trail ends at the ferry terminal, approximately 0.2 mile from where you parked.

Within the preserve you can see a seasonal variety of waterfowl (among others, Eurasian and American Wigeons, Cinnamon Teal, Long-tailed Duck, both goldeneyes, Hooded Merganser) and gulls (Bonaparte's, Heermann's, Mew, Thayer's, Glaucous-winged) as well as Virginia Rail, Sora, Anna's Hummingbird, Violet-green Swallow, Marsh Wren, and Common Yellowthroat. Look in the saltwater channel for scoters, loons (Yellow-billed recorded), grebes, cormorants, and Pigeon Guillemot. A highlight is a colony of Purple Martins that nest in the boxes provided; Osprey are also found nesting on the platforms at this site.

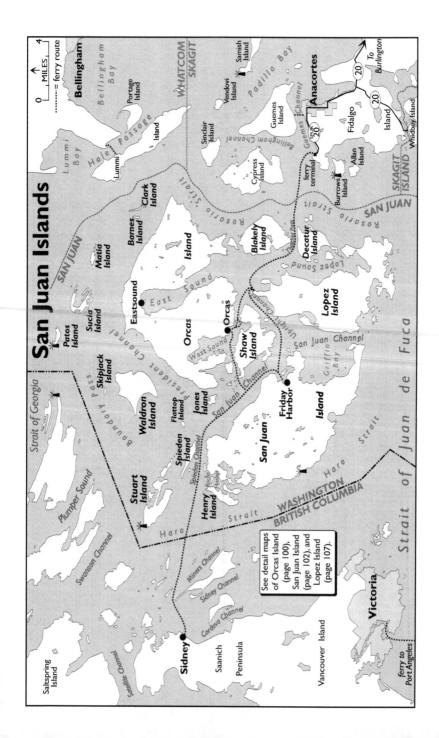

San Juan Islands

See detail maps of Orcas Island (page 100), San Juan Island (page 102), and Lopez Island (page 107).

SAN JUAN ISLANDS

by Barbara Jensen

revised by Barbara Jensen

The marine waters surrounding the San Juan Islands are the richest in the Puget Basin, abounding with plankton, the primary producers in the food chain. The many large bays, wide channels with fast-moving currents, and quiet harbors are prime locations to observe seabirds in winter and migration, Killer Whales, and Bald Eagles—whether by boat or from shore. On land, habitat variety is extensive, with forest, prairies, wetlands, rocky shoreline, and sheltered coves all in close proximity. Lying in the lee of the Olympic Mountains, the islands receive around 25 inches of rainfall a year, compared to 35–40 inches along the mainland to the east. The drier conditions exclude certain plant species common in the damp forests and valleys of Western Washington (for example, Vine Maple, Devil's Club, Deer Fern, Evergreen Huckleberry) while favoring other, more drought-resistant species such as Douglas Maple, Garry Oak, and Lodgepole Pine. House Wrens—more usually associated with the dry, open woodlands of Eastern Washington—breed abundantly. During migration, Lewis's Woodpeckers, Mountain Bluebirds, Townsend's Solitaires, and other species island-hop to and from Vancouver Island and the mainland.

The following accounts describe ferry birding possibilities as well as representative sites on Orcas, Lopez, and San Juan Islands. Allow a full day to bird each. If you have time for only one island, choose San Juan. Even without the small population of Sky Larks, which now appears to be extirpated, this is a major all-round birding destination with the most diverse array of upland and saltwater habitats in the archipelago. Island road systems are confusing at best, and it is helpful to stop by one of the many real estate offices for a free map.

Four of the islands are served by ferry from Anacortes. Some boats continue to Sidney, British Columbia, north of Victoria, and Sky Lark country. Contact Washington State Ferries (WSF) for schedules, fares, and information about travel to Canada. Spaces fill quickly and long waits for the next boat are common at certain days and times. Check the schedules carefully and arrive at the Anacortes terminal at least one hour or more before the scheduled departure time. WSF has proposed to begin taking vehicle reservations in 2015 for U.S. routes. If reservations are available, it is recommended you make one. Contact WSF at 800-843-3779 toll-free statewide, or on-line (the best) at http://www.wsdot.wa.gov/ferries.

From I-5 in Burlington, follow SR-20, then SR-20 Spur west through Anacortes to the ferry terminal; the route is clearly signed. Birding right around the terminal (previous page) will make the wait seem shorter.

SAN JUAN ISLANDS FERRY

Birding from the ferry is best in fall through spring. Most common marine species can be seen on this trip, though some are scarcer or absent in summer. Expected are Surf and White-winged Scoters, Long-tailed Duck, Red-breasted Merganser, Pacific and Common Loons, Horned, Red-necked, and Western Grebes, Brandt's, Double-crested, and Pelagic Cormorants, Common Murre, Pigeon Guillemot, Marbled and Ancient Murrelets (fairly common to common November–February), Rhinoceros Auklet (common March–September, common to uncommon fall–winter), and Mew and Glaucous-winged Gulls. Many other species occur in smaller numbers or less predictably, among them Red-throated and Yellow-billed Loons. Notable rarities recorded in these waters include King Eider (February and October), Thick-billed Murre (December), Kittlitz's Murrelet (January), Horned Puffin (July), and Black-headed Gull (September).

The ferry heads westward across broad Rosario Strait. Search here for diving birds, especially alcids. The route then passes among the islands, through narrow channels—sometimes with fast-moving water—and quiet bays. Check calm waters where birds shelter during windy weather. Look along tidal rips or lines on the water for concentrations of feeding birds or "bird balls," especially cormorants, Red-necked Phalaropes, alcids, and gulls in spring and fall. Steller and California Sea Lions and Harbor Seals fish these areas, too. Bald Eagles and Peregrine Falcons perch in the trees along the shoreline.

ORCAS ISLAND

Horseshoe-shaped Orcas Island is home to Moran State Park—the first state park in Washington—and to the highest point in the islands, Mount Constitution. The shoreline is mostly private, but there are a few public marine viewpoints. The routes take you through some of the best examples of forest, field, and wetland habitats. Woodland birding is good, especially in spring, for typical Puget Lowlands species such as Rufous Hummingbird, Olive-sided and Pacific-slope Flycatchers, Cassin's, Hutton's, and Warbling Vireos, Chestnut-backed Chickadee, Red-breasted Nuthatch, Black-throated Gray, Townsend's, and Wilson's Warblers, and Western Tanager. Black-capped Chickadee is notably absent, having thus far failed to colonize the San Juans. Trumpeter Swans and many ducks are common in winter. Bald Eagles are numerous all year. The island is overrun with Black-tailed (Mule) Deer, so drive cautiously, especially at night.

From the Orcas Island ferry landing turn right onto Killebrew Lake Road. Check forest and fields along the 2.2-mile drive to **Killebrew Lake**. Scan the lake for Wood Duck, mergansers, and Pied-billed Grebe. Nearby marshes are home to Virginia Rail, Sora, and MacGillivray's Warbler. At a junction at the end of the lake, stay left onto Dolphin Bay Road, which soon becomes gravel. Make another inspection in 1.2 miles at **Martin Lake**, then continue 3.6 miles to a T-intersection where Dolphin Bay Road turns right. Follow it right for 0.6 mile to Orcas Road. Follow Orcas north to Main Street in 2.9 miles and turn right into the town of Eastsound. After passing through town, Main Street becomes Crescent Beach Drive. Stop at **Crescent Beach Preserve**, just ahead, for waterfowl and for Bonaparte's, Mew, and Glaucous-winged Gulls or walk the wooded trail. At the stop sign in 1.2 miles, turn right onto Olga Road. The entrance archway to Moran State Park (Discover Pass required) is in 3.1 miles. Drive carefully through this popular park.

In 1.3 miles, turn left toward **Mount Constitution**. Stop at the Cascade Falls trailhead in 0.3 mile, on the right, and walk to a series of falls along the creek to look for American Dipper. From the Mountain Lake turnoff, on the right in another 0.6 mile, a level, 3.9-mile trail circles the lake (nesting mergansers and forest birds). Continue the winding, steep grade toward the summit. A turnout on a hairpin curve in 1.1 miles, on the left, and another on the right just around the bend, have magnificent views of the surrounding islands. The rocky south-facing slopes are open and grass-covered. Look for Sooty Grouse and Chipping Sparrow along the forest/grass edges. Similar habitat can be explored from two more turnouts 0.6 mile ahead, or from the parking area for Little Summit (elevation 2,040 feet), on the right in a further 0.1 mile. The road ends at the summit parking lot in 1.6 miles. Coniferous forests on the steep, north-facing slopes have Hairy and Pileated Woodpeckers, Golden-crowned Kinglet, Swainson's and Varied Thrushes, Yellow-rumped Warbler, Purple Finch, and Red Crossbill.

Climb the stone lookout tower, built in the 1930s by the Civilian Conservation Corps, for a 360-degree view of the San Juans, 130 miles south to Mount Rainier, east to the North Cascades, 50 miles north to Vancouver, British Columbia, west to Vancouver Island, and southwest to the Olympic Mountains. Look for Turkey Vultures, raptors, swifts, and Common Ravens. The 2,409-foot summit is at the north end of an exposed, stony plateau with subalpine-like vegetation dominated by Lodgepole Pines (one of the largest forests of this species in Western Washington). Brown Creepers and Townsend's Warblers may be seen close-up as they forage in the pines. Common Nighthawks nest on bare ground among the scrubby understory of Hairy Manzanita and Salal. Plants such as Rocky Mountain Woodsia, Rosy Pussy-toes, and Dwarf Mountain Daisy that grow here and nowhere else in the islands are outliers of populations in the Olympics and Cascades. To experience this unique habitat (and jaw-dropping views to the east across Rosario Strait and Bellingham Bay), walk the first half-mile of the ridgeline trail that leaves from behind the restrooms. The trail continues to Little Summit (2.2 miles from the parking lot), intersecting another trail that drops steeply down the mountain to Cascade Lake.

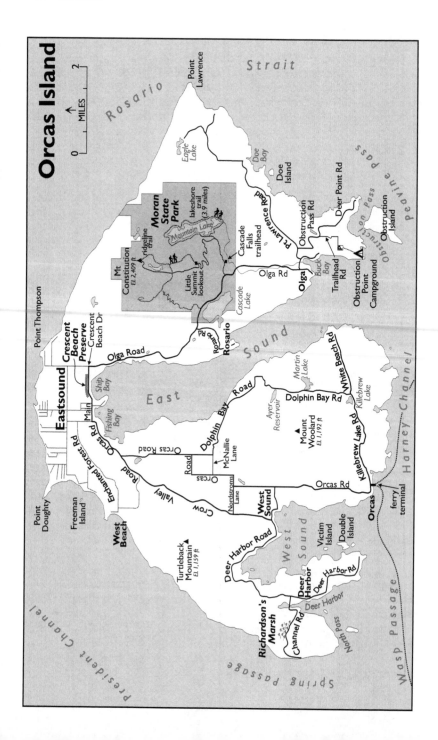

By car, return to Olga Road and turn left. The park's south boundary is in 0.4 mile, marked by an arch on a narrow bridge. Travel 1.5 miles to the intersection with Point Lawrence Road, on the left. Ahead, the road ends in 0.2 mile in the village of **Olga**, where a public dock provides a vantage point for waterbirds. Go east on Point Lawrence Road, which descends to the shoreline of **Buck Bay** in 0.2 mile. Gulls bathe in the freshwater outflow of a small creek that enters the bay, and feed on the bay or on the oyster beds and tideflats. Northwestern Crows are common along the shoreline. In migration, a few shorebirds may be present on the beach at high tide. About 0.3 mile after leaving Buck Bay, turn right from Point Lawrence Road onto Obstruction Pass Road, then bear right onto Trailhead Road at a junction in 0.8 mile. This potholed road passes through fine deciduous forest and a freshwater marsh (rails), ending in 0.8 mile at the trailhead parking lot for Obstruction Point Campground (Discover Pass required). A half-mile trail leads first through dense mixed woodlands, then open, dry forest of Douglas-fir and Pacific Madrone on steep slopes, to the campground and beach park. The site hosts a cohort of lowland forest birds including Hutton's Vireo, Steller's Jay (in the San Juans, found only on Orcas and Shaw), Chestnut-backed Chickadee, Red-breasted Nuthatch, Brown Creeper, Golden-crowned Kinglet, Dark-eyed Junco, and Black-headed Grosbeak. When the tide is running, Marbled Murrelets and other seabirds feed along the tidal rips where Obstruction Pass meets East Sound, affording good scope views from the beach.

Return to Eastsound and turn left from Main Street onto Orcas Road. In 1.1 miles turn right onto Crow Valley Road and continue 4.1 miles to the village of West Sound and a T-intersection with Deer Harbor Road, turning right. Travel 3.6 miles to Channel Road. Turn right and stop in 0.2 mile by the bridge across the channel between **Deer Harbor** and the lagoon on the right to check for wintering Common and Barrow's Goldeneyes, Black Oystercatcher, Black-bellied Plover, Black Turnstone, and Northwestern Crow. On the right in another 0.6 mile is the start of **Richardson's Marsh**, one of the most impressive freshwater marshes in the islands. Find a place to pull completely off. Walk the road for the next 500 yards, peeking through and over the bordering vegetation where you can. Though not very productive in winter, the open waters and extensive growth of cattails and other emergent vegetation can be excellent in spring and early summer. Look and listen for Wood Duck, teals, Hooded Merganser, Pied-billed Grebe, raptors, Virginia Rail, Sora, Rufous Hummingbird, Willow Flycatcher, Tree and Violet-green Swallows, Marsh Wren, Common Yellowthroat, and Red-winged Blackbird. Go back to Deer Harbor Road, turn left, and continue through West Sound to Orcas Road (0.8 mile past the junction with Crow Valley Road). Turn right; it is 2.4 miles to the Orcas ferry dock.

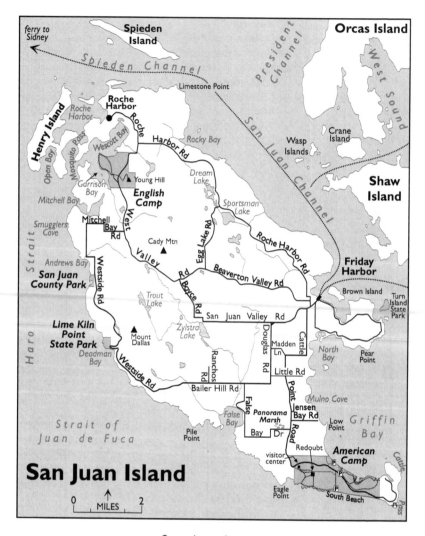

SAN JUAN ISLAND

Almost as large as Orcas but gentler in relief and less sprawling, San Juan Island offers a more complete set of habitats and excellent birding access. In one day of intense birding (two days is better), you may find a large variety of birds along dry, rocky coastlines with stands of Garry Oak and Pacific Madrone; in mixed forests of Douglas-fir, Bigleaf Maple, and other species that thrive in moister places; in extensive farmlands, open fields, freshwater marshes, and wetlands; in saltwater habitats of protected bays, mudflats, and channels with swift tidal currents; and on windswept grasslands overlooking the Strait of Juan de Fuca where Sky Larks once lived. Killer Whales and other marine mammals are easily seen from shore in the proper seasons. Numerous records of passerine rarities include Brown Thrasher, Red-throated Pipit, Tennessee Warbler, Indigo Bunting, and Lawrence's Goldfinch. With more consistent coverage, San Juan Island would probably be revealed as a standout songbird vagrant trap. The following itinerary visits a selection of sites in a clockwise loop from, and back to, Friday Harbor.

From the Friday Harbor ferry ramp, turn right onto Front Street, then left onto Spring Street, and continue through town. Spring Street becomes San Juan Valley Road, turning westward across the broad, open **San Juan Valley**. This is a productive area for raptors, but stopping along the narrow, busy road is dangerous. Park at a pullout on the left at Douglas Road (1.6 miles). Scan or walk carefully along San Juan Valley Road checking for Western Bluebirds in the summer. The wetlands and farmland can host Yellow-headed Blackbirds in summer and swans and ducks in winter. Drive 1.6 miles south along Douglas Road and scope from the corners of Madden Lane (0.7 mile), Little Road (another 0.7 mile), and Bailer Hill Road (0.2 mile farther) to check the fields and wetlands for Golden Eagle and many other species. Backtrack along Douglas and turn right onto Little Road. In 0.4 mile (check fences and oaks for Western Bluebirds), turn right onto Cattle Point Road, which passes through impressive stands of Garry Oak on dry, rocky outcroppings, intermixed with stands of Douglas-fir, open pastures, wetlands full of willows, and Pacific Madrone along the shoreline. Turn left at **Jensen Bay Road** (1.2 miles) and pull off occasionally to walk or scan these habitats. Olive-sided Flycatchers, Western Wood-Pewees, and Pacific-slope Flycatchers nest in the forests. The edge between pasture and forest can be good for Rufous Hummingbird, House Wren, and Orange-crowned and Black-throated Gray Warblers. The end of the road faces Griffin Bay and San Juan Channel, yielding scope views of ducks, loons, grebes, and alcids.

Return to Cattle Point Road and turn south. It is 1.5 miles to the visitor center entrance at **American Camp**, one unit of the San Juan Island National Historical Park. Drive in and park to bird woodlands and prairie. Bald Eagles nest within sight of the visitor center, and the nearby forest is good throughout the year for the usual flocks of chickadees, nuthatches, Brown Creepers, and wrens. Conifers here are gnarled from fierce winds that rip and snap off branches and treetops. This is a notable landfall for birds in migration. Possibilities in fall and spring are Lewis's Woodpecker, Red-breasted Sapsucker, Mountain Bluebird, Townsend's Solitaire, and MacGillivray's Warbler. Breeders include Rufous Hummingbird, Hutton's Vireo, Swainson's Thrush, Townsend's Warbler, and Red Crossbill. Water-stressed glacial soils are covered in extensive grasses. American Golden-Plovers, Whimbrels, and Snow Buntings can be here in the fall. Winter birding can be a challenge because of strong winds. Walk eastward to the top of the Redoubt, which overlooks the prairie. Spring flowers are abundant. Great Camas colors the area deep purple April to June. The bulb of this lily was an important food item of Native peoples, who regularly burned extensive areas of the islands to keep the woody plants in check and camas prairies open. Scan toward the water for Northern Harrier, Short-eared Owl, and Northern Shrike. European Rabbits introduced in the middle of the 19th century and farming have caused much disturbance, but the National Park Service is working on a major prairie restoration that will take many years to complete. Check the marked plots for progress.

Drive east on Cattle Point Road for 1.4 miles and turn right on Pickett's Lane. Park about 100 yards beyond the crest of the hill. A hundred Sky Larks once nested on these prairies. The colony has been eradicated by predation from introduced foxes and feral cats, but there are occasional reports of one. They could be anywhere; the area just west of this spot was once quite good. Listen for their high-pitched, trilled song and buzzy call-note, and watch for their towering courtship flight in the spring. A walk across the prairie may yield some hidden birds, but be mindful of the numerous rabbit holes.

Continue down to **South Beach** to look for Vesper Sparrows—the uncommon, local, and declining Westside subspecies (*affinis*)—in nearby dunes on the left. Dunes may be closed in summer (check for signs and fences) as it is habitat to the rare Island Marble Butterfly. The beach is made of smooth, surf-polished stones. The upper beach is piled high with driftwood thrown there during winter storms. The Olympic Mountains dominate the southern horizon 20 miles across the Strait of Juan de Fuca. Native peoples have used this area for 9,500 years as prime fishing grounds. Heat-shattered rocks can be found from the days of smoking salmon on the beaches. Look for Killer Whales fishing for salmon or possibly a filter-feeding Minke Whale. Scope the water from fall to spring for Surf and White-winged Scoters, Long-tailed Ducks, Common Goldeneyes, Red-breasted Merganser, Pacific Loon, Horned and Red-necked Grebes, Common Murre, Pigeon Guillemot, and Marbled Murrelet (usually found in pairs). Summer is a poor time for marine birds except for breeding Pigeon Guillemots and Rhinoceros Auklets. In late summer Cassin's Auklets can sometimes be seen, and there is even a small possibility of Tufted Puffins. In the fall look for Horned Larks and American Pipits in the dunes by the beach.

Return to Cattle Point Road, turn right, and drive 2.1 miles to the picnic area at **Cattle Point** (Discover Pass required). This is one of the best places in Washington for wintering seabirds. Turbulence resulting from the high-volume tidal exchanges (at times, 12 vertical feet in one tidal cycle) in the narrow (mile-wide) **Cattle Pass** keeps sediments suspended throughout the water column. This provides food to the abundant zooplankton, which in turn feeds the small fish upon which the seabirds prey. Harlequin Duck, Pelagic Cormorant, Black Oystercatcher, Black-bellied Plover, Black Turnstone, Surfbird, and Rock Sandpiper (uncommon) can be seen on the rocky shoreline and on Goose Island just offshore. Scope the rafts and single seabirds feeding mid-channel. Steller Sea Lions feed in the area and haul out on Whale Rocks to the southeast, where their golden-colored bodies are fairly easy to find with a scope. Listen for the roar of the 2,200-pound males from September to May. Nearby pocket beaches are places to find migrating sandpipers or birds trying to stay out of the wind. Raptors work the shoreline. Belted Kingfisher and Northern Rough-winged Swallow nest in the sandy cliffs. The rocky headland here is covered with deep glacial striations—a reminder of the massive, mile-thick ice sheet that passed over the islands during the last ice age. Go back along Cattle Point Road and turn left onto False Bay Drive, 1.2 miles past the visitor center entrance. On the right within a few hundred feet, **Panorama Marsh** is worth a look. Trumpeter Swans winter here, as do Gadwall, Northern Shoveler, Green-winged Teal, Ring-necked Duck, Bufflehead, and Hooded Merganser. Wood Duck and Pied-billed Grebe breed in the wetland, which is also good for breeding songbirds. Continue on through open farmland interspersed with mixed forests of Red Alder, Bigleaf Maple, and Douglas-fir, with views across the strait to the Olympics.

In 2.5 miles, stop at the head of **False Bay**, a University of Washington biological preserve and one of the few large, muddy bays in the islands. At low tide, when this shallow bay empties out for about a mile, the sulphur smell from algae can be powerful. High tide pushes the birds close to shore—even then, a spotting scope is useful. A freshwater stream from San Juan Valley enters the bay a couple of hundred yards to the west. Large numbers of American Wigeons (check for Eurasian Wigeons) feed here in the winter along with many other ducks. This is the most reliable place on the island for shorebirds in migration (Sharp-tailed Sandpiper has occurred in fall) and for Great Blue Herons and wintering Dunlins. Bald Eagles are numerous, as food is ample and nest sites are plentiful around the bay. Check willows along the shoreline for songbirds.

Continue north on False Bay Drive and turn left in 0.8 mile onto Bailer Hill Road. Long-eared Owl has been found in this lower end of San Juan Valley among the hedges and fields. Ranchos Road to the right in one mile is good for wintering raptors. Bailer Hill Road continues west, then swings north along the coast, becoming Westside Road. Turnouts provide spectacular views across **Haro Strait** to Vancouver Island and Victoria, British Columbia. The channel can be full of birds or seemingly empty, much depending on the wind direction and tides. From spring to fall, Killer Whales concentrate here to feed on salmon heading back to the Fraser River to spawn. **Lime Kiln Point State Park** (Discover Pass required), which is 4.8 miles from False Bay Road, and **San Juan County Park** (another 2.4 miles) are excellent whale watching points. Look also for marine birds and Black Oystercatchers. Harbor Seals feed in the Bull Kelp forests along the shore as does the occasional Steller Sea Lion or River Otter.

Drive north 1.8 miles from San Juan County Park, turn right onto Mitchell Bay Road, and in another 1.3 miles go left onto West Valley Road. Travel north 1.5 miles to the visitor entrance on the left for **English Camp,** the other unit of San Juan Island National Historical Park. The parking lot has mixed maple/coniferous forest on one side and Red Alder stands on the other. In the conifer woodlands, look for Pileated Woodpecker, Chestnut-backed Chickadee, Brown Creeper, Pacific and Bewick's Wrens, and Varied Thrush. The alder is productive for spring birds such as Rufous Hummingbird, Olive-sided and Pacific-slope Flycatchers, Hutton's Vireo, and Swainson's Thrush. Some of the oldest and largest known specimens of Bigleaf Maple grow near the barracks building. Check trees for a possible spring fallout of warblers—Orange-crowned, Yellow-rumped, and Townsend's are the most common species. Walk down to the blockhouse and turn around to see the Osprey nest perched on a snag at the top of the hill. Swallows work the parade grounds and Rocky Mountain Junipers (another botanical curiosity for Western Washington).

Sheltered **Garrison Bay** is good for wintering waterbirds, Black-bellied Plovers, and Black Turnstones. The trails here are easy and are sometimes productive for forest birds. From the parking lot, hike up **Young Hill.** Douglas Maple—a dry-site species—thrives here and elsewhere on the islands, where it replaces the ubiquitous Vine Maple of the damper mainland. The view from the 650-foot hilltop offers the overall essence of the San Juans: grassy hills and oak forest, narrow channels and quiet bays, with the immensity of Vancouver Island in the distance.

Turn left from English Camp and continue north on West Valley Road for 1.3 miles to Roche Harbor Road. Turn left and continue 2.2 miles to **Roche Harbor Resort** (pronounced *roach*, like the bug), an old company town turned resort in the 1950s. Some of the purest limestone west of the Mississippi was quarried and burned in the kilns here to produce lime. The highly groomed grounds are not highly productive for birding, but the flower gardens are beautiful and a good place for hummingbirds. It is fun to walk the docks where you may see all sorts of boats, from old wooden classics to the latest in ostentatious pleasure vessels. The bay has all three cormorants, Bald Eagles, and Pigeon Guillemots.

Walk trails through the fairly young second-growth forest around the resort periphery to find flycatchers, vireos, thrushes, warblers, and the Cooper's Hawks that chase them. Turning back, it is 10 miles to Friday Harbor via Roche Harbor Road (becomes Tucker Avenue in town), passing by more forests, fields, lakes, and wetlands. Finding a safe place to stop is difficult, but look for a possible flock of Trumpeter Swans in winter on Dream Lake at Lakedale Resort 5.1 miles from Roche Harbor. Keep an eye out for interesting species that might be found in these habitats on the way back to Friday Harbor.

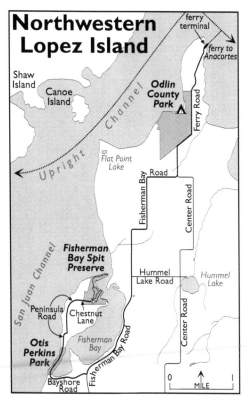

Northwestern Lopez Island

ferry terminal

ferry to Anacortes

Shaw Island

Canoe Island

Odlin County Park

Ferry Road

Upright Channel

Flat Point Lake

Fisherman Bay Road

Center Road

Fisherman Bay Spit Preserve

San Juan Channel

Peninsula Road

Chestnut Lane

Hummel Lake Road

Hummel Lake

Center Road

Otis Perkins Park

Fisherman Bay

Fisherman Bay Road

Bayshore Road

0 ↑ 1
MILE

LOPEZ ISLAND

Lopez is the third largest of the ferry-served islands, is fairly flat, and has amazing sites to view marine birds. Bring your scope for the best birding. From the ferry dock head south on Ferry Road 1.4 miles, turn right to **Odlin County Park**. Check the beach, overhanging trees, wetlands near the camp-ground, and Upright Channel.

Return to Ferry Road and turn south; the road becomes Fisherman Bay Road in 0.9 mile. Drive 3.8 miles to Bayshore Road, turn west, and go 0.6 mile to Otis Perkins Park on Fisherman Spit. Fisherman Bay is a shallow, muddy bay full of ducks, shorebirds, and more from fall to spring. Scan west to San Juan Channel for marine and rocky shorebirds. Walk or drive 0.8 mile of spit to Peninsula Road, turn left, and continue 0.8 mile (right at Chestnut) to **Fisherman Bay Spit Preserve**. This jewel faces the entrance to Fisherman Bay and overlooks San Juan Channel. Walk the trails through the mixed forest, meadows and pond, then to the beach. Retrace your route to the ferry.

SKAGIT FLATS

by Bob Kuntz

revised by Bob Kuntz

The Skagit Flats and the adjacent Samish Flats (page 112) form a floodplain where fertile soil and ample rainfall provide for a thriving farming industry. Potatoes, carrots, corn, winter wheat, barley, and a variety of other vegetables and grains grow bountifully. These farms are one of the world's largest producers of vegetable seeds and flower bulbs. A wide variety of habitats, mild temperatures, and a profusion of food make this area home to nearly 300 resident and migrant bird

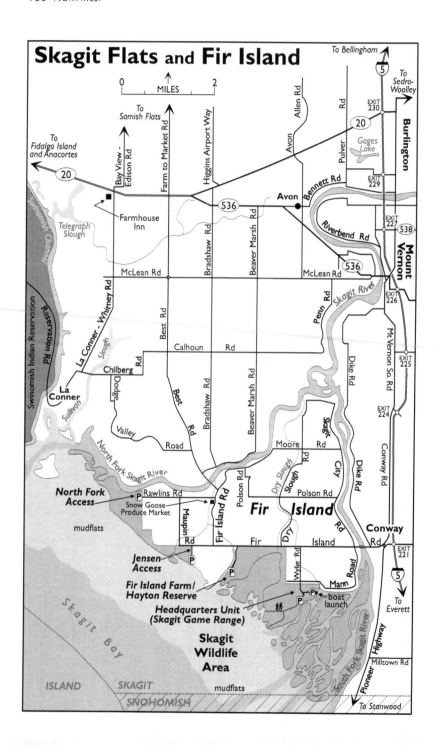

Skagit Flats and Fir Island

species. *Although birding is interesting all year, the best seasons are during spring (mid-March through May) and fall (mid-July through September) migrations and particularly winter (November through mid-March) when hundreds of thousands of swans, geese, ducks, and shorebirds can be found. The abundant waterfowl, small mammals, and salmon (spawning in the Skagit and Samish Rivers and their tributaries) attract raptors. Fifteen species of eagles, hawks, and falcons, and 13 species of owls, have been documented in the area—most of them annually.*

FIR ISLAND

Bounded by the North and South Forks of the Skagit River and ringed by dikes, low-lying Fir Island is the heart of the Skagit delta. From I-5 Exit 221 (Conway/La Conner), go west about 0.1 mile to the intersection of Pioneer Highway and Fir Island Road in Conway, and turn right onto Fir Island Road. A bridge in 0.5 mile crosses the South Fork onto the island. In winter, several hundred Trumpeter and Tundra Swans can usually be seen somewhere along the five-mile length of Fir Island Road between the South and North Fork bridges. This is a busy road, and the swans are a popular attraction, so be sure to pull completely off the roadway. Birders have been ticketed for blocking traffic and causing a road hazard. If you do not find the swans, try driving some of the other roads on Fir Island, particularly Dry Slough, Maupin, Moore, Polson, and Skagit City Roads. Fir Island and neighboring areas are also the winter home of 60,000 or more Snow Geese. The near-totality of a distinct nesting population of this species, from Wrangel Island in the northeastern Russian Arctic, winters on the Fraser and Skagit–Stillaguamish River deltas. On Fir Island, they may be seen foraging in the farm fields from late fall through April. The best viewing areas are along Fir Island Road, particularly at the Fir Island Farm/Hayton Reserve, at the Snow Goose Produce Market, and along Maupin Road. Fir Island is not a bad place to find Harlan's Hawk or even Gyrfalcon. Wetlands, brushy edges, and woodlots attract many other birds, including rarities, with one record each for Jack Snipe and Magnolia Warbler (September), and Yellow Rail and Vermilion Flycatcher (November). While still rare, Rusty Blackbird has been occasionally reported (late fall and winter).

SKAGIT GAME RANGE

The Skagit Wildlife Area, a 12,000-acre marsh, tideland, and estuarine preserve, offers several access points for viewing Skagit specialties. After crossing the South Fork from Conway, continue 1.3 miles along Fir Island Road and turn left (south) onto Wylie Road. In late fall and winter check for gulls, especially when farm fields have recently been plowed. Among the common Mew, Ring-billed, and Glaucous-winged Gulls you may find the occasional Western or California, and Glaucous Gull has been sighted here. In about a mile from Fir Island Road you come to the wildlife area's Headquarters Unit, locally known as the Skagit Game Range (Discover Pass required to park). From a fork just inside the boundary (check the treetops for a Merlin), the right branch leads to the office (no visitor center), a parking area, and usually very unclean toilets; the left branch goes to a boat launch and a second parking area with a new clean toilet.

The Game Range consists of a series of dikes and marshes intensively managed for salmon-rearing habitat and waterfowl. A trail follows the dikes from both parking areas, weaving though hedgerows and fresh- and saltwater marshes. Take the dike trail from the entrance to the headquarters parking area south for 0.4 mile to a fork. A new dike trail goes west (right) for approximately 0.5 mile or you can continue straight for up to one mile. Both sections are worth birding, as are the sloughs along the roads to the two parking areas.

In March, when the Red-flowering Currant and Salmonberry blossom, Rufous Hummingbirds return and set up territories over the densest patches of bloom. In April, Greater and Lesser Yellowlegs, Dunlins, Least and Western Sandpipers, and both dowitchers are common in the wet fields. Solitary, Baird's (fall), and Semipalmated Sandpipers are seen annually. Yellow-rumped Warblers return in late March; Myrtle may be as common as Audubon's through April.

May is a good month for migrants and residents. Look for Wood Duck, Cinnamon Teal, American Bittern, Green Heron, Virginia Rail, Sora, Solitary Sandpiper, Band-tailed Pigeon, Eurasian Collared-Dove, Bushtit, Swainson's Thrush, and several species of warblers and sparrows. The Game Range is good for migrant *Empidonax* flycatchers—mostly Willow and Pacific-slope, but Least, Hammond's, and Dusky are also possible. Fall passerine migration (mid-August to mid-September) is as good as anywhere in Western Washington. A dozen species of sparrows can be seen in winter—Spotted Towhee, American Tree (rare), Savannah, Sooty Fox, Song, Lincoln's, Swamp (uncommon to rare), White-throated (rare), Harris's (very rare), White-crowned, Golden-crowned, and Oregon Dark-eyed Junco. The best places to look for them are near the two parking areas and along the dike from the headquarters parking area to where the dike forks (first half-mile). Northern Waterthrush has been seen in fall and winter almost annually either along the slough to the north of the boat launch parking area or adjacent to the dike where it forks.

TIDELANDS ACCESS POINTS

Return to Fir Island Road, turn left (west), and go 1.5 miles to a public access road on the left. Turn onto the access road and drive south down the gravel road less than a half-mile to a parking area for the **Fir Island Farm/Hayton Reserve**, a unit of the Skagit Wildlife Area (Discover Pass required to park). This is an excellent place to view the wintering Snow Geese. A dike separates farm fields from salt marsh. Check the fields for Black-bellied Plover, American and Pacific Golden-Plovers (both rare), and the same assortment of sandpipers as can be seen at the Skagit Game Range.

Return to Fir Island Road and go left (west) for another 0.5 mile to where it makes a 90-degree right turn. Jog left here onto Maupin Road. Continue west 0.5 mile and turn left onto a gravel road leading to the **Jensen Access** of the Skagit Wildlife Area. Fields at this intersection, and along the access road, are excellent for shorebirds and American Pipits in spring (April–May) and fall (mid-July through September). Park by the dike at the end of the road (Discover Pass required), from which one can access the dike and salt marsh to the south. Among other species of shorebirds, Sharp-tailed (rare), Stilt (uncommon to rare), and Pectoral Sandpipers have been seen in the marsh. Optimal viewing is on an incoming or receding high tide. Otherwise, the exposed mudflats are extensive and birds can be a long way from the dike. Check the large driftwood for perched raptors (Bald Eagle, Northern Harrier, Merlin, Peregrine Falcon). Exercise caution if venturing into the marsh: the mud is deep and hazardous in places.

Back on Maupin Road, turn left and continue west and north for 1.3 miles to Rawlins Road. Turn left again and drive one mile to a dead end at a dike. Park along the edge of the road, making sure not to block other cars from leaving. You are now at the **North Fork Access**. This is an excellent place to look for Short-eared Owl (at dusk). Turn back, go 1.7 miles east to Fir Island Road, and turn right. Park at a pullout on the left in 0.1 mile, across from the **Snow Goose Produce Market**. Fields to the east often hold thousands of foraging Snow Geese and several hundred Trumpeter and Tundra Swans.

NORTHERN AND EASTERN FLATS

Swans, Snow Geese, and other waterfowl also winter in agricultural fields on the Skagit Flats north of Fir Island, as do many raptors, including Snowy Owls during flight years. From the produce market, turn back north and go 0.4 mile on Fir Island Road to the intersection with Best Road, on the left. Turn here and continue over the North Fork bridge for 4.5 miles to a roundabout at McLean Road. Bird the flats from a grid of roads east to Mount Vernon, north to SR-20, and west to La Conner and the Swinomish Channel. In April, enjoy the tulip fields with Mount Baker and the Cascades Range in the background. Turning left (west) from Best Road onto McLean Road, then right onto La Conner-Whitney Road (1.3 miles), brings you to the Farmhouse Inn and a Texaco station at the SR-20 intersection (1.8 miles). It is about six miles east on SR-20 to I-5 at Exit 230. Or you can turn west on SR-20 toward Fidalgo Island and Anacortes (page 92). Crossing over SR-20 and continuing north will bring you to the Samish Flats.

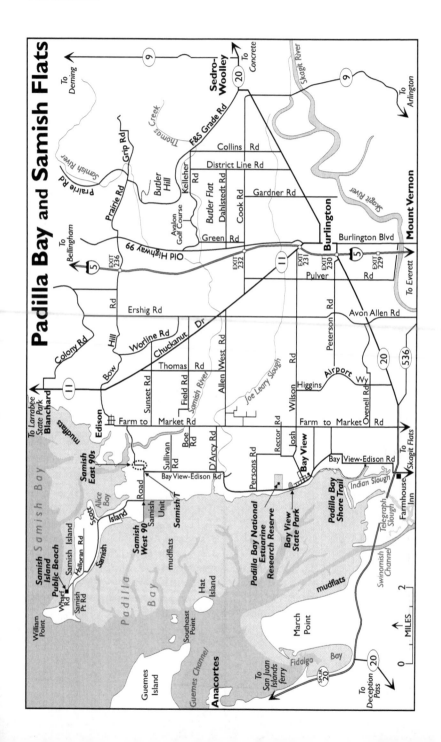

Padilla Bay and Samish Flats

SAMISH FLATS

by Bob Kuntz

revised by Bob Kuntz

The Samish Flats are one of the best locations in the state for winter raptor viewing. A dozen or more diurnal raptor species are recorded annually, the most common being Bald Eagle, Red-tailed Hawk (including Harlan's), Rough-legged Hawk (dark and light morphs), and Northern Harrier. Five falcon species occur here almost every winter (American Kestrel, Merlin, Gyrfalcon, Peregrine Falcon, and Prairie Falcon)—but just try finding all five on a single outing! Ten species of owls have been observed on the flats or in the adjacent forested foothills, including Barn, Great Horned, Barred, Great Gray (winter; rare), Long-eared (rare), Short-eared, and Northern Saw-whet. Snowy Owls can be common in a good flight year. Abundant winter rains form ephemeral pools in fallow fields, attracting shorebirds, Trumpeter and Tundra Swans, and 25 other species of waterfowl. Washington Department of Fish and Wildlife's "Barley for Birds" program provides food for thousands of ducks. Corn, potatoes, and carrots left from fall harvest also provide resources for waterfowl.

The area is intensively covered by birders, so it is no surprise that many unusual records have occurred here, including Falcated and Tufted Ducks, Iceland Gull, Tropical Kingbird, Clay-colored Sparrow, Rusty Blackbird, Orchard Oriole, and a Brambling in Sedro-Woolley. More records of Cattle Egret (fall–early winter) come from the Samish Flats than from any other Western Washington locality. In fall 1999 a Eurasian Kestrel hung out for a time near Blanchard, and a few ecstatic birders scored a six-falcon day.

The best way to bird the Samish Flats is to drive all the roads, looking for shallow pools with flocks of foraging or roosting birds, and checking fenceposts, power poles, the ground, and other perches for raptors. Several locations that seem to draw the birds more consistently, and that are on public property or provide adequate parking, are singled out below. Please make sure to pull your vehicle completely off the road when stopping, and observe private-property signs. Local residents are generally well-disposed toward birders. Good manners will further this rapport.

PADILLA BAY

The Samish Flats can be accessed directly from I-5 Exits 231 (Chuckanut Drive) or 232 (Cook Road), north of Burlington. However, if you are also visiting the Skagit Flats, as most birders do, a convenient connection is from SR-20 at the Farmhouse Inn corner (see page 108). At the traffic light there, go north across SR-20 and a railroad track and jog right, then left, onto Bay View-Edison Road. The south end of the **Padilla Bay Shore Trail** is on the left (west) in 0.9 mile (limited parking). The trail follows a dike northwestward along Little Indian Slough and the southeast shore of Padilla Bay to the north trailhead. (To park here, turn north from Bay View-Edison Road onto Second Street and go 0.1 mile north and park on left.) The 2.1-mile walk (one way) can be productive for waterfowl and shorebirds in migration and winter. The road distance between trailheads is also 2.1 miles.

Continue north on Bay View-Edison Road, respecting the speed limit through the town of Bay View, to the entrance to **Bay View State Park** (0.6 mile). Turn off right, then go immediately left and under the road to a beach and picnic area along the east shore of Padilla Bay. In winter, this is an excellent place to study Gray-bellied Brant, a form that nests on Melville Island in the Canadian High Arctic. The near-totality of the world population, estimated at perhaps 8,000 birds, winters on the rich eelgrass beds of Padilla and Samish Bays and the Fraser River delta; many come near shore here to preen and forage. Go back through the underpass and check the camping loop for lowland forest birds such as Band-tailed Pigeon, Barred Owl, Hutton's Vireo, Steller's Jay, Chestnut-backed Chickadee, Bewick's Wren, Spotted Towhee, and Red Crossbill.

Travel north another half-mile on Bay View-Edison Road and turn right into the visitor entrance of the Padilla Bay National Estuarine Research Reserve (360-428-1558). The 64-acre site provides a hiking trail through upland and forested habitats and a viewing platform overlooking Padilla Bay. Birds are similar to those found at Bay View State Park. The Breazeale Visitor Center, open 10AM to 5PM Wednesday through Sunday, has excellent interactive exhibits describing the estuary and its aquatic and terrestrial wildlife resources.

WEST 90 AND SAMISH ISLAND

The Samish Flats begin about two miles farther north, where Bay View-Edison Road meets D'Arcy Road. Continue north past D'Arcy Road for 2.0 miles to the spot known to birders as the **Samish T**, where Bay View-Edison Road turns right. Go left (west) here onto Samish Island Road, which provides excellent birding. Scan the power poles in winter for falcons (Gyr, Peregrine, Prairie). At dusk, look for Short-eared Owls. At 0.7 mile, where the road makes a right-angle turn to the right, is the Samish Unit of the Skagit Wildlife Area, long known to birders as the

Samish West 90 (Discover Pass required). In the fields southwest of this corner, state wildlife managers have created a series of shallow ponds that often attract shorebirds (spring and fall) and waterfowl (November–April). Walk west along the field edge, then south along a dike that provides views of some of the ponds and of Padilla Bay. From the West 90, continue north on Samish Island Road. For the next 1.5 miles, to an intersection with Scott Road, check the power lines and fenceposts for American Kestrel. Eurasian Wigeons reach their highest density in the contiguous United States in the fields to the west, between **Alice Bay** and Padilla Bay, where some American Wigeon flocks contain five percent or more of this species.

Turn right onto Scott Road and park in the church lot, on the left. You are now on **Samish Island**. The field to the west of the church has been productive for sparrows and other songbirds. Great Blue Herons fly back and forth between the bay and a rookery on the hill to the north. Check the treetops for a Merlin, particularly across the street from the church. You can also look into Alice Bay, one of the last corners of Samish Bay to fill at high tide. The hour before and after high tide is the best time to visit. At high slack tide, most birds roost or forage in the nearby farm fields. Black-bellied Plover and Dunlin are abundant in winter; Baird's (rare), Least, Pectoral (rare), and Western Sandpipers have all been seen during fall migration. Look for Semipalmated Plover in Alice Bay.

Go back to Samish Island Road, turn right, travel 1.6 miles, and turn left onto Halloran Road, which becomes Samish Point Road. In another 0.6 mile, turn right onto Wharf Road. **Samish Island Public Beach** is 0.2 mile ahead. This small park overlooking Samish Bay is excellent for viewing Brant, Harlequin Duck, all three scoters (Black is rare), Long-tailed Duck, Red-breasted Merganser, Pigeon Guillemot, Red-throated, Pacific (rare), and Common Loons, and Horned, Red-necked, Eared (occasional), and Western Grebes.

FARM TO MARKET ROAD

Return to the Samish T and go east (straight ahead) on Bay View-Edison Road. A right-angle turn to the left in 0.3 mile, followed by another to the right in 0.3 mile, have been dubbed the **Samish East 90s** by birders. This is another good place to look for Gyrfalcon, Peregrine Falcon, and Prairie Falcon. A further 0.6 mile brings you to the Samish River bridge. Cross, park on the left, and check the slough and adjacent fields on both sides of the road. In irruption years, this is a good location for Snowy Owl. Greater White-fronted Geese can sometimes be seen to the south in April.

The intersection with **Farm to Market Road** is 0.5 mile farther east along Bay View-Edison Road. Turn right (south) here. The next three miles offer unobstructed views of the flats on both sides. Be extra cautious when you stop; this is a busy road. Also drive the first two side roads to the east—Sunset Road (0.7 mile) and Field Road (0.7 mile)—over to Thomas Road, about a mile and a half east. In recent winters, this rectangle has been the most dependable place on the flats to find a Gyrfalcon, sitting on one of the posts in the middle of the fields or on a large dirt clod along a field edge. A good vantage point is the spot where Field Road makes a right-angle jog to the south. **Chuckanut Drive** (SR-11), though heavily traveled, goes through fields where swans can usually be seen. You will reach this road in a mile or less by continuing east across Thomas on either Sunset or Field. Turn south on Chuckanut (2.9 miles from Sunset or 1.8 miles from Thomas). Check the fencelines and treetops for raptors.

BUTLER FLAT

The **Butler Flat** area, isolated from the rest of the flats by the unnatural barrier of I-5, is too often neglected by birders. Many raptors winter here in fields along both sides of Cook Road, and side roads, from the freeway east to Sedro-Woolley. This is also an excellent place to look for Trumpeter and Tundra Swans from late November through early January when they are foraging in the cut corn fields. At the corner of Chuckanut Drive and Cook Road, turn left (east). Cross over I-5 at Exit 232 (1.3 miles). Then turn left from Cook onto Green Road, 0.1 mile after the interchange. Drive north 1.2 miles on Green Road. A wetland east of Green Road, managed by the Skagit Land Trust, offers fine viewing of marshland birds. In spring, all three teal species can be found here, as can American Bittern (rare), Virginia Rail, and Sora. The field west of the road may have a winter wigeon flock with several Eurasian Wigeons.

At the T-intersection a short distance ahead, turn right onto Kelleher Road. Go 0.4 mile to the entrance to Avalon Golf Course. Park on the north side of Kelleher where you can pull completely off. From here you can walk a short distance up the golf course entrance road for a closer look at the marsh, or east on Kelleher to bird the hillside and slough edge. About 250 yards east, a lane crosses the ditch to a good vantage point on a dike. The dike is now off-limits, but you can park at a wide spot in the road to scan the surroundings. Black and Vaux's Swifts have been seen here in early May. Alders on the hillside host a good assortment of spring migrants and summer residents, among them Rufous Hummingbird, Warbling Vireo, Bushtit, Swainson's Thrush, Orange-crowned and Wilson's Warblers, Black-headed Grosbeak, and Lazuli Bunting.

Drive east on Kelleher Road to an intersection in 1.9 miles where District Line Road comes in from the right. In late April and early May, migrating Whimbrels stop on Butler Flat to forage for insects in the freshly mowed winter wheat and hay fields. You can find a loose flock with as many as 300 Whimbrels anywhere inside the 0.5-by-1.5-mile rectangle bordered by District Line, Cook, Collins, and Kelleher Roads.

NORTH CASCADES HIGHWAY

by Bob Kuntz

revised by Bob Kuntz

From near sea level on the floodplain farmlands west of Sedro-Woolley, the North Cascades Highway (SR-20) follows the Skagit River eastward for 95 miles, ascending gradually to 5,477-foot Washington Pass. The route traverses several vegetation zones with a diverse and contrasting birdlife. Lower slopes are famous for damp, old-growth forests of Western Hemlock, Western Redcedar, and Douglas-fir that may reach heights of 200 to 300 feet. Broad swaths of luxuriant deciduous growth line the streams. Higher-elevation forests of Silver Fir give way to parklands with stands of Mountain Hemlock. Above treeline is an area of meadows and jagged, glacier-laden peaks that has been called North America's Alps.

The best times to visit are from May through October. During spring, summer, and fall, some of the many species to be found along the way are Barrow's Goldeneye, Sooty Grouse, Golden Eagle, Northern Pygmy-Owl, Black and Vaux's Swifts, Hammond's Flycatcher, Cassin's and Red-eyed Vireos, Gray Jay, Clark's Nutcracker, American Dipper, Mountain Bluebird, Townsend's Solitaire, MacGillivray's Warbler, American Redstart, Black-throated Gray and Townsend's Warblers, Slate-colored Fox and Lincoln's Sparrows, Lazuli Bunting, Gray-crowned Rosy-Finch, Pine Grosbeak, and Red and White-winged (irregular) Crossbills. In most years, the highway closes around the first of December and does not reopen until April. However, it is open year round below Newhalem. From mid-December through January, when Chum and Coho Salmon are spawning, the Skagit River between Rockport and Newhalem provides food and shelter to 300–500 Bald Eagles.

No gasoline or other services are available between Marblemount and Mazama, approximately 70 miles. For much of the itinerary described here the highway corridor passes through the North Cascades National Park. Park information is available on-line at www.nps.gov/noca. For updates on camping reservations, backcountry travel, and road closures, call 360-854-7200 or stop by any of several visitor centers and ranger stations along the route.

SEDRO-WOOLLEY TO MARBLEMOUNT

A stop at the National Park Service/U.S. Forest Service office in Sedro-Woolley to pick up maps and a North Cascades National Park bird checklist is an excellent way to begin your trip. From I-5 Exit 232 north of Burlington, follow Cook Road east 4.4 miles to its intersection with SR-20 (North Cascades Highway). Turn left and proceed 1.1 miles to the intersection with northbound SR-9. The office is on the left just before this intersection (open 8AM to 4:30PM Monday through Friday year round, and Saturday and Sunday from Memorial Day weekend at the end of May through Columbus Day in mid-October).

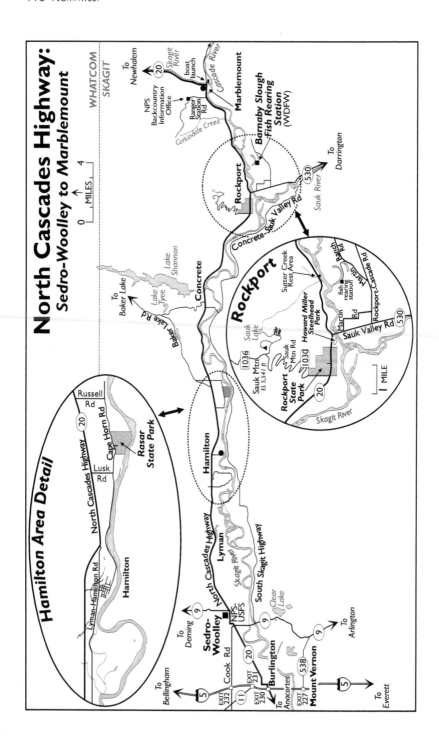

North Cascades Highway:
Sedro-Woolley to Marblemount

Hamilton Area Detail

Continue east for 14.7 miles on SR-20 and turn right onto Lusk Road just past the town of Hamilton. In 0.7 mile, turn left onto Cape Horn Road, then right in 0.8 mile into the **Rasar State Park** entrance. This 128-acre park, situated on the north bank of the Skagit River in a mixed-forest habitat, is best visited from May through September. Look for Northern Pygmy-Owl, Red-breasted Sapsucker, Downy and Hairy Woodpeckers, and resident/migrant passerines, including Pacific-slope Flycatcher and Cassin's Vireo. Turn right onto Cape Horn Road for 1.3 miles, then left (north) onto Russell Road to return to SR-20 in 0.8 mile.

The town of Concrete is about six miles farther east along SR-20. In another mile, east of Concrete where power lines cross to the Skagit River side of the road (0.8 mile past milepost 89), note the Osprey nest-platform on the south side (for the past two years this platform has hosted a pair of Canada Geese rather than Osprey). Continue east for 6.3 miles and turn left onto **Sauk Mountain Road** (FR-1030), an improved gravel road that winds upward to the Sauk Mountain Trailhead. At 1.6 miles, park at a gated logging landing and check the brushy hillside for Rufous Hummingbird, MacGillivray's Warbler, and Black-headed Grosbeak. In 1.4 miles, at milepost 3, stop to look for Townsend's Warbler. In 4.5 miles turn right onto FR-1036. In May and June, the last stretch of road to the trailhead (0.3 mile) is a good place to look for Gray Jay and Slate-colored Fox Sparrow. The 2.1-mile trail leads to alpine meadows on Sauk Mountain (summit 5,541 feet, elevation gain 1,040 feet). Watch for Sooty Grouse, Olive-sided Flycatcher, Hermit Thrush, and several species of warblers, sparrows, and finches. In July, the wildflower display is spectacular on these slopes.

Return to SR-20, turn left, go 1.6 miles, and turn right onto SR-530 (Sauk Valley Road). The entrance to **Howard Miller Steelhead Park**, along the north bank of the Skagit River, is on the right in 0.2 mile. You may find Ruffed Grouse (drumming in spring), Band-tailed Pigeon, and Vaux's and possibly Black Swifts flying overhead. At the west end of the campground, a footbridge will lead to trails that traverse swamps and woodlands along the river. Look for Osprey, Bald Eagle (winter), Red-breasted Sapsucker, flycatchers, warblers, and sparrows. The park can also be good for surprises, such as Iceland Gull, Dusky Flycatcher, Western Kingbird, and American Redstart. The past few years the campground has hosted several pairs of nesting Bullock's Orioles.

Cross the Skagit River on the SR-530 bridge and turn left onto **Martin Road** (0.3 mile from the park). At 0.2 mile is a small wetland with Willow Flycatchers, Warbling and Red-eyed Vireos, and an assortment of warblers, sparrows, and finches in spring and summer. A public river access 0.2 mile farther along Martin Road offers similar species. In the shrubby areas beside the road, look for Western and Eastern Kingbirds and Lazuli Bunting. Rarities are possible: Sage Thrasher and Yellow-breasted Chat have been found here. At a T-intersection in 1.3 miles, turn left onto Rockport-Cascade Road, then left again in 0.9 mile onto Martin Ranch Road. In 1.2 miles, turn left onto **Barnaby Slough Road** (rough graded) and drive a quarter-mile to a parking area and an interpretive display. If the gate is locked, park adjacent to the road; do not block the gate. Barnaby Slough (Discover Pass required) is a mosaic of habitats that provides excellent spring and summer birding. (Keep out November–February when the area is closed to provide sanctuary for waterfowl.) In addition to the usual lowland forest birds, the area has been good for vagrants, including Black-and-white and Chestnut-sided Warblers (one June record for each).

Retrace your route to SR-20 and turn right. **Sutter Creek Rest Area**, on the right in 2.4 miles (at milepost 100), is a great place to watch wintering Bald Eagles close-up (best before 10AM when they are foraging and interacting). The meadows between 2.5 and 3.0 miles farther east at **Corkindale Creek** often swarm with swallows (six species possible and the best place in Skagit County to find Bank Swallow). Watch also for Willow Flycatcher, Western and Eastern Kingbirds (rare but annual), Lazuli Bunting, and Bullock's Oriole.

Just over two miles from Corkindale Creek, turn left onto Ranger Station Road and continue 0.5 mile to the intersection with **Powerline Road**. Check along this road for a quarter-mile in both directions. Lazuli Buntings are dependable here. Ranger Station Road ends in 0.3 mile at the National Park Service's Backcountry Information Office. Return to SR-20 and turn left (east) toward Marblemount.

CASCADE RIVER TO WASHINGTON PASS

A side trip up the **Cascade River Road** to the Hidden Lake and Cascade Pass trailheads offers good birding in summer and fall, and magnificent scenery. Allow one full day for this trip. Note that the last few miles of the road are usually not clear of snow until the beginning of July. In Marblemount, where SR-20 makes a 90-degree turn to the left (north), stay straight onto Cascade River Road across the Skagit River bridge. Immediately turn right into the parking area for the Marblemount Boat Launch. This location is a good place to look for spring and fall migrant songbirds. To the north, across Cascade River Road, is a good place to look for Mountain Bluebird in spring. Back at the parking area take the trail that winds through a field along the Skagit and Cascade rivers, returning back to Cascade River Road 0.1 mile east of the parking area. Along the trail you may see Townsend's Solitaire and Nashville Warbler. Alder Flycatcher, Say's Phoebe, and Tennessee Warbler have all been observed here.

As you continue to drive the 23-mile road to the parking area at Cascade Pass Trailhead, watch for Barred Owl, Common Nighthawk, Red-breasted Sapsucker, Varied Thrush, Black-throated Gray Warbler, and other lowland forest species. Views from the trailhead are breathtaking. You are in a

U-shaped trough, glacially over-deepened, with steep valley walls, waterfalls, swift streams, and avalanche chutes grown to Sitka Alder thickets; similar terrain stretches north through the Coast Mountains of British Columbia and Southeast Alaska. Listen for the roar of falling ice as you view a series of hanging glaciers on Johannesburg Mountain.

Cascade Pass Trail winds along a series of switchbacks to Cascade Pass, a 3.7-mile hike that gains about 1,800 feet to an elevation of 5,392 feet. In summer near the trailhead you can find Sooty Grouse, Black and Vaux's Swifts, Olive-sided Flycatcher, Hermit Thrush, MacGillivray's, Yellow, Yellow-rumped, Townsend's, and Wilson's Warblers, and Slate-colored Fox Sparrow. At the pass, look for Clark's Nutcracker, as well as Hoary Marmot and Pika. To reach the alpine zone, cross the pass and continue down the other side for about 100 yards. Here the rough **Sahale Arm Trail** branches off to the left and goes north for about a mile and a half, following the ridgeline that marks the Cascade Crest (Columbia River drainage to the east, Skagit River to the west). The first mile is steep and rocky. The trail becomes gentler upon reaching Sahale Arm, a widening of the ridge, beginning at 6,300 feet elevation and ending at about 7,000 feet. "Sky gardens" along the way have many colorful wildflowers; Sooty Grouse are common in this habitat. Look for White-tailed Ptarmigan, American Pipit, and Gray-crowned Rosy-Finch on the broad, heather-covered slopes of Sahale Arm.

Another good place for Gray-crowned Rosy-Finch (and spectacular scenery) is **Sibley Pass**, reached by turning east from Cascade River Road onto Sibley Creek Road (FR-1540) about 10 miles above Marblemount (13-plus miles if coming down from Cascade Pass, on the right). Drive another 4.5 miles to the trailhead. Take the Hidden Lake Peak Trail, which for the first mile climbs through forest and then breaks out into the meadows of Sibley Creek basin. The saddle to the east is Sibley Pass. Take the switchbacks for about another mile until you reach an area where the trail straightens, traversing along a series of meadows and talus slopes. Leave the trail here and make your way a final mile up to the pass. In September, several hundred Gray-crowned Rosy-Finches have been observed foraging along the steep cliffs. Be watchful for Golden Eagle.

Six miles northeast of Marblemount, SR-20 enters the North Cascades National Park Service Complex. In about four more miles, look for the Whatcom County line sign (0.5 mile east of milepost 116). Park here, taking care not to block the gate, and walk south to the **Skagit/Whatcom County Line Ponds** and access to the Skagit River. This attractive riparian area consists of a mixture of deciduous (mostly Black Cottonwood and Red Alder) and conifer forest. In late spring and summer, Hammond's and Pacific-slope Flycatchers, Red-eyed Vireo, Swainson's Thrush, and Yellow-rumped, Black-throated Gray, and Townsend's Warblers can be heard and seen. American Redstarts nest here—their only confirmed breeding site in Western Washington. In winter, Bald Eagles congregate along the river and ponds

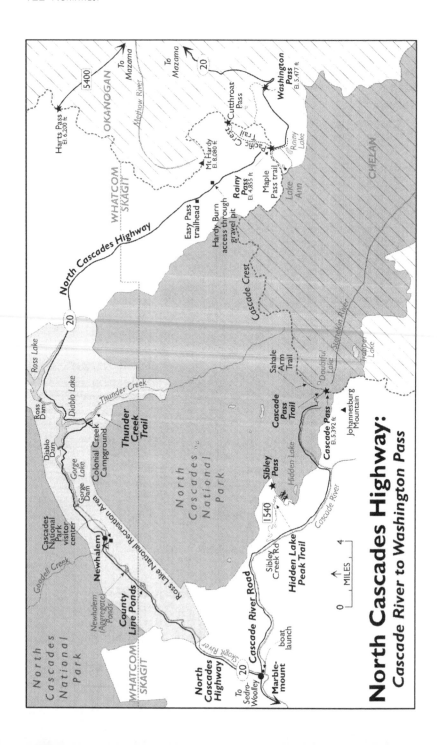

North Cascades Highway:
Cascade River to Washington Pass

to feed on salmon that have spawned and are dying. Check the ponds for Hooded Mergansers and other waterfowl. This is a good place to compare Common and Barrow's Goldeneyes. American Dippers can be seen swimming under water, plucking salmon eggs off the bottom of the pond and bobbing to the surface to swallow them, then submerging again to repeat the process.

Drive another 1.7 miles and turn off right onto a gravel service road (0.1 mile east of milepost 118). Park here, again making sure not to block the gate. (Do not drive through the gate even if it is open; you might get locked in.) The **Newhalem (Aggregate) Ponds** can be reached by walking west along the road until it crosses a spawning channel. Go left, then right to get to the main pond, a second pond, and the Skagit River, or continue straight to the north edge of the main pond. Waterfowl and Bald Eagles use the ponds in winter. During the breeding season, woodpeckers, flycatchers, vireos, thrushes (including Veery), warblers (including American Redstart), Western Tanagers, and finches are abundant in the riparian growth between the spawning channel and SR-20.

East on SR-20, stop in 1.7 miles at the Goodell Creek bridge for American Dippers (present all year). On the right in another 0.1 mile is Newhalem Campground and the main visitor center for the park complex, well worth a visit. Back on SR-20, turn right and in another 0.5 mile enter the town of **Newhalem** (no services, except for a general store). Check the steep hillside and brushy area on the left for Violet-green Swallow, Orange-crowned, Nashville, MacGillivray's, and Wilson's Warblers, Western Tanager, Pine Siskin, and Evening Grosbeak.

Colonial Creek Campground, on Diablo Lake, is 10 miles east of Newhalem on SR-20. Turn right into the south unit of the campground and drive the one-way loop to the amphitheater and the Thunder Creek Trailhead. MacGillivray's Warblers nest in the shrubs near the amphitheater, and a pair of Barred Owls is resident here. Hike the first mile of trail along the lake to the bridge over Thunder Creek. Check the excellent riparian habitat at the creek mouth for Red-breasted Sapsucker, Olive-sided Flycatcher, Western Wood-Pewee, and a variety of songbirds. Barrow's Goldeneyes nest here, and Harlequin Ducks are seen occasionally.

For the next 29 miles the highway climbs steadily through superb alpine scenery to Rainy Pass. Stop often at the many pullouts to look and listen for Sooty Grouse, Black Swift, Hammond's Flycatcher, Townsend's Solitaire, Hermit Thrush, Yellow-rumped and Townsend's Warblers, Lincoln's Sparrow, and Western Tanager. In about 21 miles (0.5 mile past milepost 151), Red-naped Sapsucker, Pine Grosbeak, and White-winged Crossbill (erratic) are often seen at the Easy Pass Trailhead. In another 1.6 miles (0.1 mile past milepost 153), turn left into a gravel pit and park so as not to block truck access. Walk to the uppermost edge of the gravel pit, and follow a steep, poorly marked trail uphill through the woods. Spruce Grouse are occasionally seen along the edge where the trail emerges from the trees at the lower end of the **Hardy Burn**, below Mount Hardy. The burn has been good for Northern Goshawk, Golden Eagle (flying along the ridge above), woodpeckers (although the burn now appears to be too old for American Three-toed and Black-backed), Clark's Nutcracker, Mountain Bluebird, Townsend's Solitaire, and Red Crossbill. Calliope Hummingbird, Red-naped Sapsucker, Dusky Flycatcher, and Lincoln's Sparrow have been seen by the edge of the gravel pit near SR-20.

The picnic-area parking lot at 4,855-foot **Rainy Pass** (4.6 miles) is a good place to look for Northern Pygmy-Owl. Gray Jays, both species of crossbills, and other mountain finches may be present along the easy first section of Maple Pass Loop Trail 740 and the side trail to Lake Ann (1.8 miles, 700 feet elevation gain). Trail 740 continues steeply after that for 2.2 miles to Maple Pass (6,600 feet); White-tailed Ptarmigan have been found on the slopes above the pass. The trail loops back to Rainy Pass (7.5 miles total). The five-mile hike north along the Pacific Crest Trail to Cutthroat Pass offers the possibility of Spruce Grouse, Mountain Chickadee, Bohemian Waxwing (late summer–early fall), Pine Grosbeak, and crossbills, as well as other mountain species.

It is another 4.8 miles to **Washington Pass** on the divide between the Methow and Stehekin River drainages—the highest point on the North Cascades Highway (5,477 feet). Turn left into the rest stop entrance road 0.3 mile east of milepost 162. The meadow north of the highway is a good place to look for Spotted Sandpiper, Mountain Bluebird, American Pipit, and other alpine nesters. A short, paved trail leads to a scenic overlook of the upper Methow Valley. Look here for Gray Jay, Clark's Nutcracker, Red Crossbill, and an occasional Pine Grosbeak. The highway descends along the east slope of the Cascade Range, giving access to birding sites on the Dry Side (page 424).

MOUNT BAKER HIGHWAY

by Bob Kuntz

revised by Randy Robinson and Fanter Lane

Mount Baker is the northernmost volcano in Washington and, at 10,778 feet, the highest peak in the North Cascades Range. A good highway to the 5,000-foot elevation, and numerous trails reaching alpine habitats around 6,000 feet, make this one of the state's most accessible locations for White-tailed Ptarmigan and Gray-crowned Rosy-Finch. Mount Baker is popular with hikers and campers (four Forest Service campgrounds along the highway) on summer and fall weekends. Consult the Washington Trails Association web site (WTA.org) for detailed information about the hikes. Hit the road and trails early in the morning to beat the crowds. Be prepared for any kind of weather at any season. Ninety-five feet of snow fell on Mount Baker in the winter of 1998–1999, setting a world record. In a normal *year, upper-elevation trails are snow-free by the middle or end of July, and the birding season extends to early October. The road to the ski area is kept open all winter but you will not find many birds at this season.*

The Mount Baker Highway (SR-542) runs east from I-5 Exit 255 in Bellingham to its end in about 60 miles. During migration, check in appropriate habitat along the road for Eastside species such as Least Flycatcher, Western and Eastern Kingbirds, Nashville Warbler, and Lazuli Bunting, which have all been reported in the area.

From December to February, one of the best eagle-viewing areas in Washington is east of Deming. From the SR-9 intersection at the east edge of Deming turn right from SR-542 in a half-mile onto Truck Road (no sign at the intersection). Drive 0.6 mile on Truck Road and turn right into **Deming Homestead Eagle Park**. The park encompasses 100 acres of braided channels of the Nooksack River. To see the eagles, turn left (east) at the gravel path, then look for paths which lead east through the small cottonwoods and brush to the river (rubber boots advised). The edge habitat of the park yields passerines in season. Least Flycatcher has been reported here. From the park, or along Truck Road, look for Black Swifts over the river in June and July.

Continue 1.7 miles on Truck Road to **Mosquito Lake Road**. Turn right and immediately come to a bridge crossing the North Fork Nooksack River. As many as 50–60 Bald Eagles can be seen at one time on the exposed gravel bars or in the trees lining the river, where they congregate to feed on spawning and dying salmon. Continue south from the bridge 0.1 mile and turn left onto North Fork Road. This less traveled road has excellent eagle watching too. Return to SR-542 via Mosquito Lake Road.

The Glacier Ranger Station, run jointly by the National Park Service and U.S. Forest Service, is located 17 miles east of Mosquito Lake Road on SR-542 or 19 miles east of the SR-9 intersection on SR-542. (An America the Beautiful or Northwest Forest Pass is required to park at trailheads beyond this point and you may purchase one here.) Shortly after you leave the ranger station (0.6 mile), turn right onto Glacier Creek Road (FR-39), then almost immediately left onto FR-37, which winds upward 12 miles to the Skyline Divide Trailhead (elevation 4,000 feet). The three-mile **Skyline Divide Trail** brings you to superb subalpine meadows (elevation 6,000 feet) that in July are carpeted with wildflowers. Here you may find species such as Golden Eagle, Clark's Nutcracker, American Pipit, and Gray-crowned Rosy-Finch (fall).

Twelve miles farther east on SR-542, on the left, is a Washington Department of Transportation facility. At the east end of the facility is a sign for Twin Lakes Road (FR-3065), which leads to the **Yellow Aster Butte trailhead** in just over four miles (elevation 3,700 feet). This hike starts in forest where American Three-toed Woodpecker has nested next to the trail. In 1.8 miles, the trail breaks out of the forest near the intersection with the Tomyhoi Lakes Trail. Stay left at the intersection and look and listen for

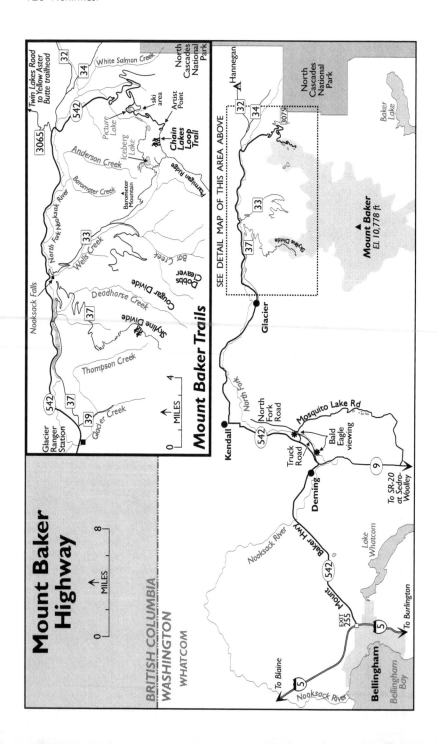

Mount Baker Highway

Sooty Grouse. In another 1.8 miles (elevation 5,600 feet) a rock and heather basin below the trail holds some snow until late in the season. Ptarmigan nest in this basin. The trail splits here, the left branch leading down into the basin and the right branch up to Yellow Aster Butte. Climb the butte (elevation 6,180 feet) scanning the steep snowfields on the flanks of the butte for Gray-crowned Rosy-Finch.

Continue on SR-542. When you come to a fork in 7.8 miles at **Picture Lake**, stay right. There are many areas to park along this much-photographed lake, rimmed with Mountain Hemlock and with Mount Shuksan in the background. Check the Sitka Mountain Ash thickets for Pine Grosbeak and migrant songbirds, especially in fall. At 0.5 mile from the fork, turn right just before Chair #1 and drive another 1.7 miles to reach Artist Point (elevation 5,100 feet) near timberline. From here several trails traverse the northeast side of Mount Baker. Ptarmigan breed in the rock slabs and heather at the top of Table Mountain. The trail is only one mile long, but in places it is steep and exposed. It can also be very crowded.

The **Chain Lakes Loop Trail** is an easy five-mile hike (out and back) across alpine meadows past a chain of six lakes, including Iceberg Lake. (The loop is nine miles.) **Ptarmigan Ridge Trail** follows the Chain Lakes Loop Trail for one mile, then veers left onto Ptarmigan Ridge, reaching Camp Kiser in a little more than three additional miles. Parts of this trail may be under snow until early August. The best place for finding White-tailed Ptarmigan is the first two to three miles of Ptarmigan Ridge. To improve your chances, get up the trail early, before other hikers have spooked the birds. Other alpine species seen along these trails include Golden Eagle, Black and Vaux's Swifts, Horned Lark, Mountain Bluebird (uncommon), American Pipit (more likely on the Chain Lakes Trail), Lapland Longspur (rare in fall), and Gray-crowned Rosy-Finch. Hoary Marmots and Pikas are common. Pay attention to whistling marmots, as they may signal the approach of a Golden Eagle. Mountain Goats are fairly common and often seen along the southeast side of Ptarmigan Ridge.

BELLINGHAM AND VICINITY

by Bob Kuntz

revised by Bob Kuntz

The port city of Bellingham is situated some 90 miles north of Seattle and 20 miles south of the U.S.-Canada border, between the Strait of Georgia and the North Cascades foothills. Nearby protected bays, deltas of the Nooksack River and several lesser streams, lowland lakes, and fragmented patches of forestland offer numerous birding opportunities. Migration (late April through May, late July through September) and winter are the most productive seasons. Influenced by outflows of arctic air from Canada's Fraser River valley, the area has several winter records of Northern Hawk Owl and Great Gray Owl. Black Scoter and Snow Bunting are more

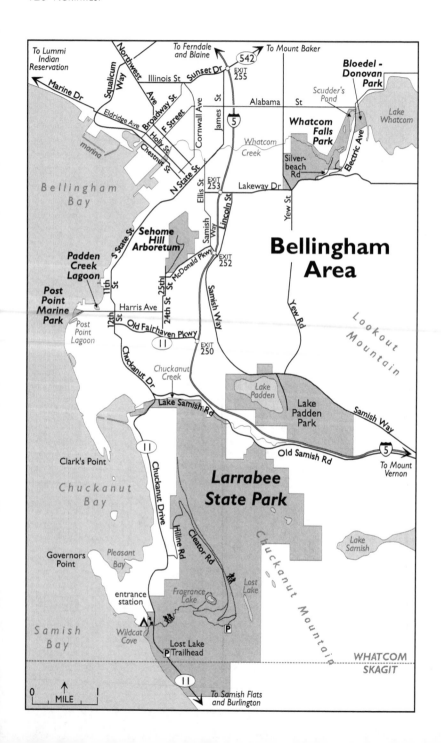

To Lummi
Indian
Reservation

To Ferndale
and Blaine

To Mount Baker

Bloedel -
Donovan
Park

Marine Dr

Northwest Ave

Squalicum Way

Illinois St

Sunset Dr

542

EXIT
255

Scudder's
Pond

Lake
Whatcom

Eldridge Ave

Broadway St

F Street

Holly St

Cornwall Ave

James St

Alabama St

Whatcom
Falls
Park

Electric Ave

Chestnut St

marina

Whatcom
Creek

Silver-
beach
Rd

Bellingham
Bay

N State St

Ellis St

Lincoln St

5

EXIT
253

Lakeway Dr

Yew St

Bellingham
Area

Sehome
Hill
Arboretum

Samish Way

McDonald Pkwy

EXIT
252

Padden
Creek
Lagoon

11th St

25th St

Post
Point
Marine
Park

12th St

Harris Ave

24th St

Old Fairhaven Pkwy

S State St

Samish Way

EXIT
250

Yew Rd

Lookout
Mountain

Post
Point
Lagoon

11

Chuckanut Dr

Chuckanut
Creek

Lake
Padden

Lake
Padden
Park

Samish Way

5

Lake Samish Rd

Old Samish Rd

To Mount
Vernon

Clark's Point

11

Chuckanut Drive

Chuckanut
Bay

Larrabee
State Park

Chuckanut Mountain

Lake
Samish

Governors
Point

Pleasant
Bay

Hiline Rd

Cleator Rd

Lost Lake

entrance
station

Fragrance
Lake

Samish
Bay

Wildcat
Cove

P

Lost Lake
P Trailhead

WHATCOM
SKAGIT

0 MILE 1

11

To Samish Flats
and Burlington

easily found here than farther south in Puget Sound. Notable records of northern rarities include King Eider (Birch Bay; Bellingham Bay; Drayton Harbor), Hudsonian and Bar-tailed Godwits (Semiahmoo Bay), Thick-billed Murre (Drayton Harbor), and Brambling (Lummi Flats, January).

LARRABEE STATE PARK

Encompassing 2,700 acres of conifer forest with a sprinkling of Pacific Madrone and other broadleaf trees, Larrabee State Park (Discover Pass required) clings to the slopes of Chuckanut Mountain along the rocky shore of Samish Bay. Coming from the south on SR-11 (Chuckanut Drive), the park is about five miles north of the Samish Flats (page 112). Coming from I-5, take Exit 250 on the south edge of Bellingham, go west on SR-11 (Old Fairhaven Parkway) 1.3 miles to 12th Street and turn left to stay on SR-11. The road then veers left in about 200 yards onto Chuckanut Drive. The main park entrance is about five miles south, on the right. After the entrance station, swing left to the parking lot and short trail for the beach. In winter this is a good place to look for Harlequin and Long-tailed Ducks, Barrow's Goldeneye, loons, Western Grebe, and cormorants (all three species). Occasionally Black Turnstone and Surfbird can be seen on the offshore rocks. At any season you may find Band-tailed Pigeon, Hutton's Vireo, and an assortment of other Westside lowland forest species. Across the highway from the park entrance, a stiff hike up the Fragrance Lake Trail will give you additional exposure to forest habitats.

Travel south 0.5 mile on Chuckanut Drive and turn left into Larrabee State Park Lost Lake Trailhead parking area. The parking area, as well as the trails in the surrounding area are very good for woodpeckers, and spring flycatchers, vireos, warblers, and finches. To drive up the side of **Chuckanut Mountain**, return north 1.7 miles on Chuckanut Drive and turn right onto Hiline (Cleator) Road, which ends in 3.7 miles at an overlook from which you can see soaring Bald Eagles or other raptors when winds are favorable. This road, which turns into a dirt road with potholes and some rough spots, can be good all year but is best in spring and early summer. Much of the forest has been logged at different times in the past, and habitats are in various stages of succession. Stop often to look for Northern Pygmy-Owl, Barred Owl, Band-tailed Pigeon, and nesting flycatchers, vireos, chickadees, thrushes, warblers, sparrows, and finches.

BELLINGHAM

From the corner of Old Fairhaven Parkway and 12th Street, where SR-11 goes east to I-5 and south to Larrabee State Park, drive north three blocks, then turn west onto Harris Avenue. On the right in 0.2 mile, **Padden Creek Lagoon** is a good place in winter to look for saltwater ducks and gulls. In spring and summer, Green Heron can be found here. Continue another quarter-mile through the historic Fairhaven business district and turn left onto Post Point Road, which ends at **Post Point Marine Park**. Check the waters of **Bellingham Bay** for Harlequin and Long-tailed Ducks, scoters, both goldeneyes, Red-throated, Common, and even Yellow-billed (several records) Loons, Red-necked and Western Grebes, cormorants, Common Murre, Pigeon Guillemot, Marbled Murrelet, Ancient Murrelet (December and January), and Rhinoceros Auklet (well offshore).

For **Lake Padden**, leave I-5 at Exit 252 northbound and turn right (south) onto Samish Way. Continue 1.8 miles to the west entrance of the park. From southbound I-5 Exit 252, turn left at the light off the exit ramp. Cross the overpass while moving into the right lane, turn right onto Samish Way, and proceed 2.0 miles to the park entrance. Parking is plentiful. Lake Padden is a 148-acre park with good facilities and a well maintained primary 2.6-mile loop trail around the lake. There are an additional 5.1 miles of secondary trails veering off the primary loop trail. Habitats include mixed deciduous/coniferous forest, a lake, and open fields around the lake. Birding on the lake from the main trail is best during winter, spring, and fall. The lake attracts many waterfowl in winter and spring, including Ring-necked Duck, Common Merganser, and Ruddy Duck, and an occasional Redhead or Canvasback. Spring songbird migrants are numerous and more abundant on the quieter secondary trails. Osprey, Bald Eagle, and Barred Owl frequent this park and can be viewed from the main trail. No permits are required.

For **Whatcom Falls Park**, leave I-5 at Exit 253. Travel east 1.5 miles on Lakeway Drive and turn left onto Silverbeach Road (just past the Bayview Cemetery). An entrance to the park is about 0.2 mile from this intersection, on the left. A second entrance is reached by continuing on Lakeway Drive about 0.2 mile past Silverbeach Road to Electric Avenue. Turn left onto Electric Avenue and left again at the entrance in about 300 yards. Birding is good year round in the woods and along Whatcom Creek, which bisects the park with several wetlands. Look for American Dippers below Whatcom Falls. Nearby **Bloedel-Donovan Park**, at the northwest end of Lake Whatcom, is 0.8 mile north of Lakeway Drive on Electric Avenue. During winter, look for waterfowl and gulls. In spring, Wood Ducks, Hooded Mergansers, and Virginia Rails nest at Scudder's Pond, on the west side of Electric Avenue 0.1 mile farther north. Watch for Beavers and signs of their activities. These and many other Bellingham parks are interconnected by an excellent series of trails, which birders will enjoy exploring.

LUMMI INDIAN RESERVATION

The birding sites described in this section are within the boundaries of the Lummi Indian Reservation and subject to the laws of the Lummi Nation. A Letter of Permission, good for one year, is required to bird on tribal lands (other than paved county roads). This letter is free and may be applied for, in person, during weekday business hours through the Lummi Planning Department, Lummi Business Council Building, 2665 Kwina Road, east of Haxton Way. Call well ahead for details and to arrange Letter of Permission pick-up (360-384-2307). Be respectful of private property; bird from the roadside. No foot or vehicle access is allowed on the Aquaculture Dike or on the tidelands.

Drive west on Slater Road from I-5 Exit 260, crossing the Nooksack River in 1.6 miles. Continue another 0.6 mile to the intersection with Ferndale Road, the northeast corner of the reservation. Go left (south) 1.9 miles on Ferndale, then turn right onto Marine Drive. After 0.8 mile, veer to the left from Marine Drive onto **Lummi Shore Drive**. The road soon approaches Bellingham Bay and bends a bit to the right, with a view of the Nooksack River delta on the left. Over the next few miles, Lummi Shore Drive follows the northwest shore of the bay. Stop at the many pullouts to look out over the delta and the river mouth. Geese, swans, herons, and Bald Eagles are often abundant, but you will need a scope to get good views. Loons, grebes, saltwater ducks, and gulls are common in Bellingham Bay. At 6.4 miles from Marine Drive, Lummi Shore Drive makes a right and becomes Lummi View Drive, and for the next 1.7 miles follows the shoreline of **Hale Passage** with Lummi Island across the channel. Check along the channel, particularly at Gooseberry Point near the ferry terminal, for Brant, loons, Red-necked Grebe, Greater Scaup, scoters (including Black), Common Murre, Pigeon Guillemot, Marbled Murrelet, and Rhinoceros Auklet. This is also a good location to look for jaegers (usually Parasitic) during fall migration.

Lummi View Drive curves right, past the ferry terminal and becomes Haxton Way. Short-eared Owl is regularly seen along Haxton Way, between Kwina Road and South Red River Road. Continuing north, in 5.9 miles you reach South Red River Road and the edge of the **Lummi Flats**. These low-lying, fertile fields on both sides of the Lummi River—part of the Nooksack delta system—are among the best birding areas around Bellingham. Swans, hawks, owls, falcons, and shrikes and other passerines, are abundant on the flats in winter (the best season). Drive any of the roads to check wet spots for shorebirds (spring) and blackbirds (Rusty possible fall–winter). South Red River Road, with a low volume of traffic, is the most leisurely road for birding. In late evening, Harlan's Hawks can found here. Winter sparrows use the hedgerows bordering the slough; check finches feeding on the alder cone crop for redpolls (one record of Brambling). Areas of open ground such as those at the west end of Kwina Road can be productive for American Pipits, Lapland Longspurs, and there is one November record of McKay's Bunting.

From South Red River Road, go north on Haxton Way for 0.6 mile to Slater Road. Turn left (west), drive 3.6 miles, and turn left onto Beach Way. In 1.3 miles, after curving right onto S Beach Way, turn left onto Sucia Drive. Drive one mile, turn left onto Thetis Way. When you come to the T, turn right onto Salt Spring Drive to Sandy Point, a gravel spit at the northwest end of Lummi Bay. Look for scoters, loons, grebes, and shorebirds. An Osprey pair nests on

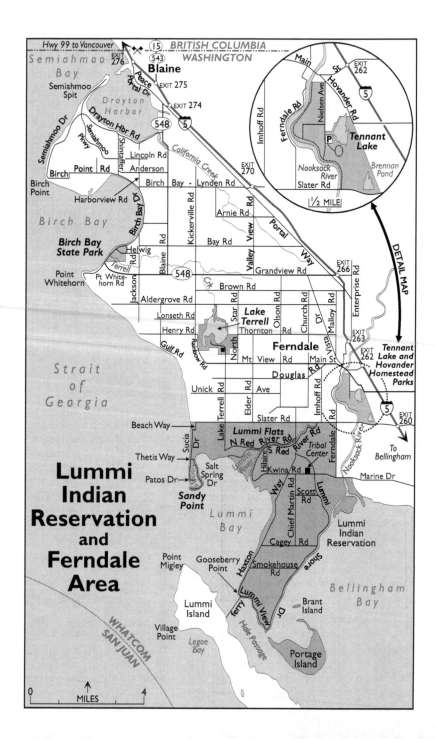

a platform in the bay to the west. Jaegers have been observed here, as well as Snowy Owl during irruption years.

TENNANT LAKE AND LAKE TERRELL

Tennant Lake, along the Nooksack River south of Ferndale, is at the heart of a 720-acre tract jointly administered as a county park and a state wildlife area. Varied habitats make this an excellent birding site at any time of year. An observation tower and a boardwalk through a cattail marsh to the lake provide opportunities to view Green Herons, waterfowl, and raptors. Other trails run south and west through grasslands, wetlands, and deciduous forest. The boardwalk and the area around the lake are off-limits to all but hunters from mid-September into January. From I-5 Exit 262, go west 0.5 mile on Main Street to Hovander Road. Turn left, drive 200 yards, then take the second right onto Nielsen Avenue and continue 0.9 mile to the parking area for the visitor center, on the left (the first right from Hovander goes to a WDFW boat-launch area on the river). From the Lummi Flats the site is easily reached by following Slater, Imhoff, and Douglas Roads to Main Street.

Lake Terrell Wildlife Area, established in 1947, offers 1,500 acres of open water, marshlands, grasslands, and mixed deciduous/coniferous forest. Hunting is allowed here, so the best times to visit are spring into September when you will find a good variety of waterfowl, marshbirds, swallows, and other songbirds. From Ferndale, head west on Main Street, which becomes Mountain View Road. In 4.5 miles, turn right onto Lake Terrell Road. Continue 0.8 mile to the parking lot (Discover Pass required to park). Or go north from Slater Road on Lake Terrell Road (2.4 miles west of Haxton Way) to reach the parking lot in about three miles. Common Loons nested at Lake Terrell through 1987, and alternate-plumaged individuals are still occasionally observed during the breeding season. Look for Trumpeter Swan, Wood Duck (nesting), Canvasback, Redhead (late winter and spring), Hooded Merganser, and Ruddy Duck. Lake Terrell regularly attracts unusual passerines in spring and fall, among them Least Flycatcher (one record), Bank Swallow, House Wren, American Redstart, and White-throated Sparrow.

BIRCH BAY

From I-5 Exit 266, follow the signs for **Birch Bay State Park** west along Grandview Road for eight miles, turn right onto Point Whitehorn Road. Continue 0.6 mile north to Birch Bay Drive. If you wish to bird the forested area above the waterfront, turn right 0.1 mile after entering the park and walk the half-mile Terrell Marsh Trail through some of the park's 193 acres of lowland forest, looking and listening for the usual woodpeckers and passerines. Wood Ducks and Hooded Mergansers can often be found in the fresh- and saltwater marsh habitats at the estuary of Terrell Creek. Otherwise, for the next 1.4 miles you are in the state park (Discover Pass required). The best waterbirds are found beginning at the south end of the park and continuing up Birch Bay Drive to the picnic area across from the public restrooms. This is an excellent winter viewing area for Brant, Harlequin Duck, scoters (all three species), Long-tailed and Ruddy Ducks, Red-throated and Common Loons, Horned, Red-necked, Eared (uncommon), and Western Grebes, alcids, gulls, and terns (especially on the beaches in town). Western Sandpipers and other shorebirds occur in spring migration along the shoreline, and Dunlins winter in good numbers.

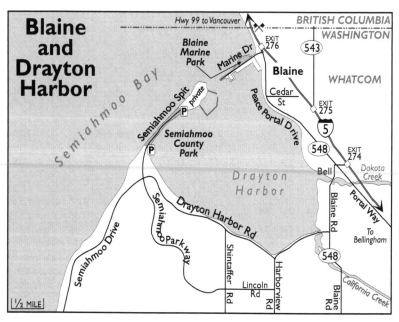

DRAYTON HARBOR AND SEMIAHMOO BAY

Drayton Harbor, a large estuarine bay isolated from Semiahmoo Bay by Semiahmoo Spit, is one of the most important winter waterbird sites in the state. If you are coming from I-5, take Exit 270 and go west on Birch Bay-Lynden Road for about four miles, then turn right (north) onto Harborview Road, which intersects Lincoln Road in 1.0 mile. Turn left and follow Lincoln (becomes Semiahmoo Parkway at Shintaffer Road) to the end to access the spit. If you are coming from Birch Bay, turn right from Birch Bay Drive at the north end of the bay onto Shintaffer Road (3.5 miles from the intersection of Birch Bay Road and the state park road). In 0.6 mile, follow the Semiahmoo sign by turning left onto Semiahmoo Parkway.

A resort occupies the tip of **Semiahmoo Spit**; however, a county park extends about two-thirds of the length of the spit from the base, giving good views of **Drayton Harbor** on the inside and of **Semiahmoo Bay** to the north. There is convenient parking at both ends of the park. In winter this is an excellent place to view Brant, dabbling and diving ducks (including all three species of scoters), loons, grebes, cormorants, Black Oystercatchers, Sanderlings, Dunlins, alcids, and gulls. Ospreys, Bald Eagles, and Peregrine Falcons use the spit. Lapland Longspurs and Snow Buntings also are occasionally sighted here.

At the opposite corner of Drayton Harbor, look through the many ducks at the mouth of California Creek for an occasional Eurasian Wigeon. To get there, leave Semiahmoo Spit by turning left at the top of the hill onto Drayton Harbor Road. Stay left for 3.1 miles around Drayton Harbor to a small gravel lot on the left before the bridge which affords a view of the mouth of California Creek. A variety of waterfowl can be observed here, along with resident Belted Kingfishers. Continue on Drayton Harbor Road for 0.1 mile and turn left onto Blaine Road. Go north for 0.9 mile to Peace Portal Drive. Turn left here and drive 1.4 miles to the intersection with Cedar Street in Blaine. Park and cross the road. A bluff above the railroad tracks provides a panoramic view of the harbor. Look for Brant and diving birds. Whimbrels (late April–May), Marbled Godwits, Caspian Terns, and other shorebirds may be present on an incoming tide. Another good viewpoint is the parking lot behind the Red Caboose, a few blocks farther north.

Blaine Marine Park, at the mouth of Drayton Harbor within sight of the Peace Arch and the U.S.-Canada border, affords closer views of the same species as at Semiahmoo Spit. Continue north through the four-way stop to the first traffic light on Peace Portal Drive and drive three-fourths of the way through the roundabout, exiting onto Marine Drive. (From I-5 northbound, take Exit 276, cross under the freeway, and continue halfway through the roundabout, exiting onto Marine Drive. Southbound from Canada, take the Blaine City exit and follow the roundabout to Marine Drive.) Marine Drive goes out a spit for two-thirds of a mile, terminating at a fishing pier at the entrance to Drayton Harbor. The pier is a good spot for observing Harlequin Duck, Barrow's Goldeneye, cormorants, and (in spring and fall) Caspian and Common Terns. Across the channel, Harbor Seals haul out onto the concrete breakwater at the end of Semiahmoo Spit. Waterbird viewing from the fishing pier is good at any tide level.

The tideflats on the north (Semiahmoo Bay) side of Marine Drive often have impressive numbers of shorebirds, conveniently viewed from a paved promenade atop the low bluff along the edge of the bay. Shorebirding is best near the base of the spit as the incoming tide pushes the feeding birds toward shore. Besides the species expected for Washington's inland marine shorelines, uncommon species and even rarities have turned up here during spring and fall migration, including Whimbrel, Hudsonian (rare), Bar-tailed (rare), and Marbled Godwits, and Red Knot.

Puget Sound

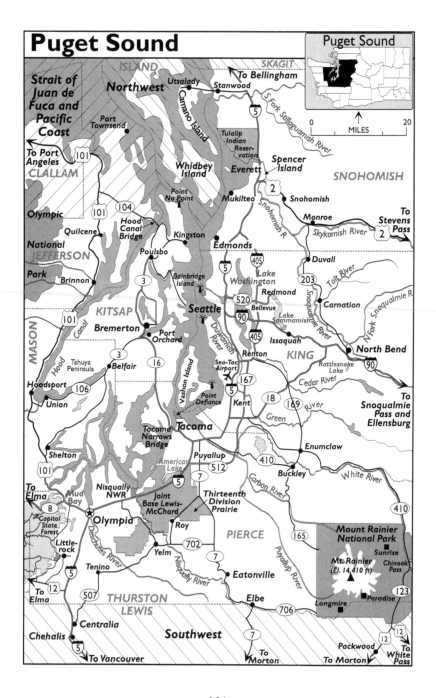

Puget Sound

Strait of Juan de Fuca and Pacific Coast

Northwest

To Bellingham

To Port Angeles

CLALLAM

Port Townsend

Utsalady

Stanwood

Tulalip Indian Reservation

Spencer Island

Everett

Mukilteo

SNOHOMISH

Snohomish

Monroe

To Stevens Pass

Olympic

Quilcene

National

JEFFERSON

Park

Brinnon

Hood Canal Bridge

Kingston

Poulsbo

Edmonds

Duvall

Tolt River

Skykomish River

Whidbey Island

Point No Point

Bainbridge Island

Lake Washington

Redmond

Carnation

KITSAP

Bremerton

Port Orchard

Seattle

Bellevue

Lake Sammamish

MASON

Hood Canal

Tahuya Peninsula

Belfair

Vashon Island

Duwamish River

Issaquah

Renton

KING

Rattlesnake Lake

North Bend

Hoodsport

Union

Sea-Tac Airport

Cedar River

To Snoqualmie Pass and Ellensburg

Point Defiance

Kent

Green River

Tacoma Narrows Bridge

Tacoma

Shelton

Puyallup

American Lake

Enumclaw

Buckley

White River

To Elma

Mud Bay

Nisqually NWR

Joint Base Lewis-McChord

Thirteenth Division Prairie

Capitol State Forest

Olympia

Roy

PIERCE

Mount Rainier National Park

Sunrise

Mt. Rainier (El. 14,410 ft)

Chinook Pass

Little-rock

Yelm

Nisqually River

Eatonville

Longmire

Paradise

Tenino

THURSTON

LEWIS

Elbe

Carbon River

Puyallup River

Centralia

Southwest

Chehalis

To Vancouver

To Morton

To Morton

Packwood

To White Pass

MILES

SKAGIT

ISLAND

Camano Island

S Fork Stillaguamish River

N Fork Snoqualmie R.

Snoqualmie River

Deschutes River

Nisqually River

PUGET SOUND

Puget Sound is that portion of the Salish Sea stretching east from the Strait of Juan De Fuca through Admiralty Inlet and south from Rosario Strait and Deception Pass. Puget Sound is a region of strong contrasts surrounding the inland marine water body of the same name. More than 50 percent of the state's population lives along the east shore of the Sound from Everett to Tacoma, in a narrow, crowded, 70-mile strip undergoing the trials of rapid growth. At the other extreme lie some 1,400 square miles of roadless, uninhabited wilderness, including all or parts of 11 designated Wilderness Areas and two National Parks. In little more than an hour one can move from monumental urban traffic snarls to "difficult hiking over steep forested slopes and along exposed ridges through tangles of huckleberry and thimbleberry . . . a wilderness experience seldom surpassed in primitive solitude and exertion."* Truly there is something here for every birding taste!

The region's greatest glory is the Sound itself, plied by Washington's famous ferries. The open waters and shorelines of the deep Main Basin from Point No Point past Seattle and Tacoma to The Narrows, and of the South Sound, Hood Canal, and the many lesser bays, inlets, and passages, harbor some of the largest populations of marine birds in the U.S. Five major rivers drain into the Sound from the West Central Cascades. The estuaries of the Duwamish (Seattle) and the Puyallup (Tacoma) have been converted to pure industrial landscapes, but the Snohomish estuary at Everett, although much reduced, still has some fine bird habitat. The Stillaguamish and the Nisqually—the smallest of the five estuaries and the least disturbed—are among the state's best birding sites. While both have been partially drained and diked for agriculture, the Nisqually has undergone estuary restoration reconnecting tidelands and floodplain to the Sound and lower river.

The low-elevation Puget Sound Douglas-fir zone surrounds the Sound, ringed successively by the Western Hemlock, Silver Fir, Mountain Hemlock, and Alpine/Parkland zones as one moves up the slopes to the permanent ice and snow of Mount Rainier—at 14,410 feet, the highest peak in Washington. Set into the lowland Douglas-fir south of the Sound is the unique Woodland/Prairie Mosaic zone, a landscape of dry grasslands and Garry Oaks. Significant parts of the higher-elevation zones are in protected status, but those at lower elevations are greatly altered. The Puget Sound Douglas-fir forest is

---

* *Wonder Mountain Wilderness Area web site:* http://www.wilderness.net/NWPS/wildView?WID=657

mostly gone, and the oak prairies are sadly reduced. The Western Hemlock zone now consists largely of managed forests. And yet, thanks to a good system of urban, suburban, and rural parks and natural areas, each of these zones still retains its characteristic birdlife.

The Sound enjoys a favorable climate for birds and for those who wish to find them. At the Seattle-Tacoma airport, the average annual precipitation is 38 inches (the same as Indianapolis, Tulsa, and Washington, DC); 158 days have some precipitation (like Pittsburgh and Cleveland); winters are mild (January average temperature 39 degrees, the same as Raleigh and Little Rock) and summers cool (July average temperature 65 degrees, as at Duluth and Caribou, Maine). Annual precipitation increases as one moves eastward up the Cascade slopes (105 inches at Snoqualmie Pass) or southwestward around the Olympics toward the coast (52 inches in Olympia). Most of the winter precipitation in the mountains falls in the form of snow. Snoqualmie Pass on I-90 is open most of the time, but ice and snow are a common hazard and traction devices may be required. Stevens Pass on US-2 is frequently closed for snow clearance, and Chinook Pass on SR-410 is closed for the entire winter season. Snow is infrequent in the lowlands, but a couple of inches that stick can cause a real mess. Traffic is always a mess in the urban agglomeration, even in nice weather. Monster tie-ups on I-5, I-90, and other major thoroughfares are becoming routine. Drive smart. Try not to be a returning weekender on Sundays or holidays. You'll do fine if you avoid morning and evening rush hours and check traffic reports.

SEATTLE AND VICINITY

by Hal Opperman
revised by Hal Opperman

Seattle is built around Elliott Bay, at the estuary of the Duwamish River. Two miles east, Lake Washington gathers the flow of the Sammamish and Cedar Rivers from the Cascades and foothills. When the first settlers arrived, the surrounding lands were covered with an ancient forest of Douglas-fir and other conifers. The outlet of Lake Washington was the Black River, at its southern end. The Green River, draining the Cascades to the southeast and flowing northward from present-day Kent across a wide floodplain, joined the Black River in Tukwila to form the Duwamish. Vast tidelands occupied the southern end of Elliott Bay at the mouth of the Duwamish, some 10 miles farther north.

Today one sees a radically altered landscape. Long ago, the ancient forests found their way to the sawmill. The Duwamish was dredged to deepen and straighten it for port facilities. Railroad yards—more recently replaced by sports stadiums—were built on fill where the tidelands used to be. The opening of the Ship Canal to Puget Sound (1916) lowered the level of Lake Washington 10 feet, and the Black River ceased to flow. The flat floodplain valley of the Green River, with its rich alluvial soils, was first cleared for farming, and then succumbed to industrial and commercial development.

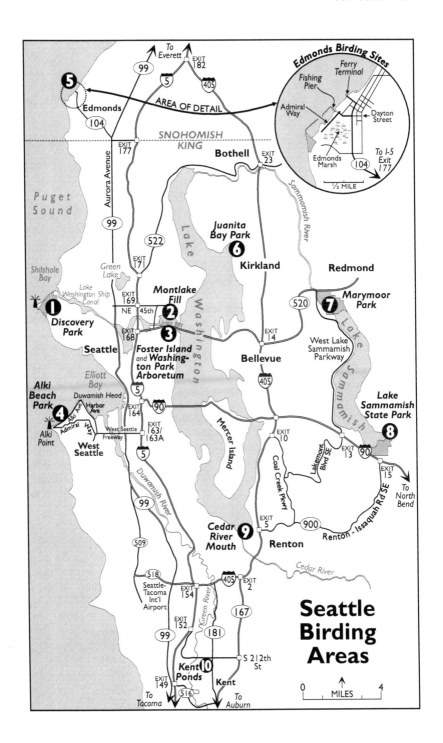

To Everett

99

EXIT 182

5

405

5

Edmonds Birding Sites

Ferry Terminal

Fishing Pier

Admiral Way

Dayton Street

AREA OF DETAIL

Edmonds

104

SNOHOMISH

KING

Edmonds Marsh

To I-5 Exit 177

104

½ MILE

Aurora Avenue

EXIT 177

Bothell

EXIT 23

Sammamish River

Puget Sound

99

522

Juanita Bay Park

6

Kirkland

Redmond

Green Lake

EXIT 171

Shilshole Bay

Lake Washington Ship Canal

EXIT 169

Montlake Fill

2

520

7

Marymoor Park

Lake Washington

Discovery Park

1

NE 45th

Union Bay

3

EXIT 168

EXIT 14

West Lake Sammamish Parkway

Seattle

Foster Island and Washington Park Arboretum

Bellevue

Lake Sammamish

Elliott Bay

Duwamish Head

Harbor Ave

5

90

405

Alki Beach Park

4

Alki Way

Admiral

West Seattle Freeway

EXIT 164

EXIT 163/163A

Lake Sammamish State Park

8

Alki Point

West Seattle

5

Mercer Island

EXIT 10

Lakemont Blvd SE

EXIT 13

90

EXIT 15

To North Bend

Duwamish River

99

Coal Creek Pkwy

EXIT 5

900

Renton - Issaquah Rd SE

Cedar River Mouth

9

Renton

509

Cedar River

518

EXIT 154

EXIT 2

405

Seattle-Tacoma Int'l Airport

Green River

167

Seattle Birding Areas

EXIT 152

99

181

S 212th St

Kent Ponds

10

Kent

0   MILES   4

EXIT 149

516

To Tacoma

To Auburn

Despite the changes, nearly all of the typical Puget Lowlands avian species can still be found easily and enjoyably without leaving the Seattle metropolitan area. Described below are several fine birding sites right in the city. Numerous others in the surrounding suburbs are presented in clockwise order from north to south, all of them within a 30-minute drive by freeway from the city center.

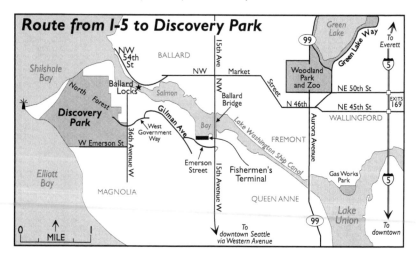

Discovery Park

Seattle's best one-stop birding venue, Discovery Park can be exciting at any season. More than 250 bird species have been recorded in the park—half the number for the whole state. Scattered throughout its 534 acres are representative fragments of most of the habitat types that can be found in the immediate Seattle area, with saltwater, beaches, meadows, and mixed forest being the most important. Sixty-six species of birds breed here, and 80 species might be found on a good day during migration.

From I-5 Exit 169, go west on NE 45th Street through the Wallingford business district. Follow the arterial as it slants right to 46th, passes under the SR-99 viaduct, shortly bends right again to become NW Market Street, and descends Phinney Ridge into Ballard. Continue west on Market to 15th Avenue NW, turn left (south) and cross the bridge over the Ship Canal, then go right on Emerson Street (becomes W Emerson Place) past the Fishermen's Terminal and railroad yard to the stop sign at Gilman Avenue W. Turn right onto Gilman, following this arterial as it becomes W Government Way and winds its way to the park's east entrance, a bit more than five miles from I-5. (*From downtown Seattle* take Western Avenue northwestward along the waterfront, staying with the arterial as it merges into Elliott Avenue and turns north onto 15th Avenue W; exit right to loop across 15th onto Emerson Street and proceed west as above.)

A short distance inside the park (see map on next page), turn left into the east parking lot by the visitor center (open 8:30AM–5PM except Mondays and holidays). Here you may pick up maps and a bird list, and ask the naturalist about current bird-sightings information, birdwalks, and other programs. Permits are available for senior citizens and those with disabilities to drive down to West Point and park. Otherwise you may leave your car here, or continue along the main park road 0.5 mile to the north parking lot, or drive south from the east entrance on 36th Avenue W, then west on W Emerson Street, to the south entrance and parking lot.

The moderately level **Loop Trail**, 2.8 miles, circles the park, passing through woods, thickets, and grasslands. This circuit takes two hours at a leisurely pace; many side trails lead to beach and wetland habitats. Listen for the insect-like "song" of male Anna's Hummingbirds in clearings. Hutton's Vireo is easy to find in early spring by its monotonous zwee...zwee song. Owls may surprise you at any location or season. Bald Eagles survey the shoreline, and sometimes nest in the park. Pigeon Guillemots have nested in the South Bluff.

South Meadow has nesting Savannah Sparrows in summer, and occasionally a few Western Meadowlarks in winter. Raptors are often seen here, especially in fall. Look for Anna's and Rufous Hummingbirds, Willow Flycatcher, Orange-crowned Warbler, and Black-headed Grosbeak in brush or trees around the edges. Parts of the meadow have recently been cleared of

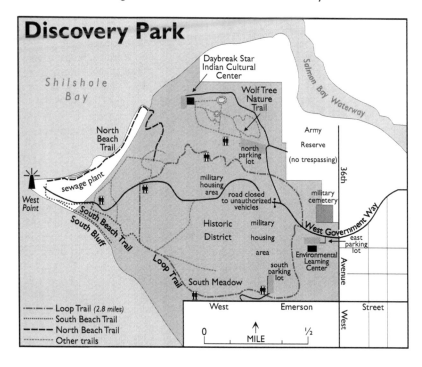

Discovery Park

Daybreak Star
Indian Cultural
Center

Salmon Bay Waterway

Shilshole
Bay

Wolf Tree
Nature
Trail

Army
Reserve
(no trespassing)

North
Beach
Trail

north
parking
lot

sewage plant

military
housing
area

road closed
to unauthorized
vehicles

military
cemetery

West
Point

South Beach Trail

South Bluff

Historic
District

military

housing

area

military

West Government Way

36th

east
parking
lot

Environmental
Learning
Center

south
parking
lot

Loop Trail

South Meadow

Avenue

West Government Way

West   Emerson   Street

West

------- Loop Trail (2.8 miles)
·········· South Beach Trail
- - - - North Beach Trail
·········· Other trails

0   ½
|_____|_____|
          MILE

Scot's Broom and other invasive growth, and replaced by new plantings of Salal, snowberry, huckleberry, Cascade Oregon-grape, and other natives, providing excellent habitat for birds. Remnant Scot's Broom and blackberry tangles are good for sparrows, including Lincoln's and Golden-crowned in fall.

North Forest is a thick belt of mixed woodland with clearings, extending from the visitor center across the north side of the park. In winter, look for a Hutton's Vireo or a warbler in the numerous flocks of small passerines. Accipiters are fairly common. Red-breasted Sapsucker is an uncommon visitor, usually around the beginning of the year. **Wolf Tree Nature Trail** leaves from the northwest corner of the north parking lot, and is a good place in summer for Cassin's and Warbling Vireos, Pacific Wren, Swainson's Thrush, and Black-throated Gray Warbler. A spur trail leads west to three small ponds where you may find herons, swallows, waxwings, and small numbers of ducks.

West Point, jutting out into Puget Sound, is an outstanding birding spot, with sandy and rocky shorelines and an historic lighthouse (1881). North Beach Trail (prone to mud-slide closure: check at the visitor center) descends the bluff to a rip-rap retaining wall. Loons, grebes, and ducks, including an occasional Long-tailed or Harlequin Duck, can be found on Shilshole Bay, while a long freshwater pond above the beach attracts dabbling ducks and other waterfowl. Look for Wandering Tattler (fall) and Whimbrel (fall or spring) on rocky outcrops exposed at low tide. Songbirds frequent the fringe of small trees, especially in migration. Both the north and south sandy beaches are good for shorebirds. Merlin and Peregrine Falcon are possible. Migrating Brant use the eelgrass beds offshore (January–April). West Point itself is a fine lookout for alcids, gulls, terns, and other waterbirds. Small numbers of Ancient Murrelets are likely in fall (November is best). Careful observation of fall flocks of Bonaparte's Gulls may result in a sighting of a rare Little or Sabine's Gull, or a dashing Parasitic Jaeger. Franklin's (rare), Heermann's (uncommon), and Thayer's Gulls may be seen close in. During stormy periods of strong southwest winds there is even a chance of a Sooty or a Short-tailed Shearwater well offshore, especially in late fall. South Beach Trail leads back up to the Loop Trail and South Meadow.

MONTLAKE FILL AND UNION BAY

The Montlake Fill ("the Fill" for short; officially, **Union Bay Natural Area**) is a popular, productive birding destination on Lake Washington. When the lake was lowered, an extensive peat-bottomed marsh emerged from the shallows of Union Bay at the mouth of Ravenna Creek. Much of the marsh was gradually filled with garbage, debris, and rubble over the next 50 years, and converted to shopping malls, athletic fields, and parking lots. When dumping ceased, the most recent fill was covered with soil, graded, seeded, and left to nature. The tract grew up to grass and scattered brush with some stands of broadleaf trees, a swamp at the eastern end, and remnants of marsh

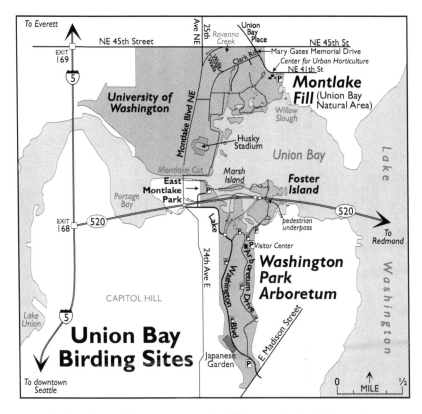

To Everett
NE 45th Street
EXIT 169
5
University of Washington
Montlake Blvd NE
Ave NE
25th
Wells Wells
Ravenna Creek
Clark Rd
Union Bay Place
NE 45th St
Mary Gates Memorial Drive
Center for Urban Horticulture
NE 41th St
P
Montlake Fill (Union Bay Natural Area)
Willow Slough
Husky Stadium
Montlake Cut
Union Bay
East Montlake Park
Marsh Island
P
Foster Island
Lake
Portage Bay
EXIT 168
520
520
pedestrian underpass
To Redmond
P
P Visitor Center
P
Washington Park Arboretum
24th Ave E
Washington
Arboretum Drive
Blvd
CAPITOL HILL
Lake Union
5
Union Bay Birding Sites
Japanese Garden
P
E Madison Street
L a k e   W a s h i n g t o n
To downtown Seattle
0   MILE   ½

around the edges. Almost at once, this 75-acre island of habitat became a magnet for birds.

To reach the Fill, go east from I-5 Exit 169 onto NE 45th Street, through the University District, along the north edge of the University of Washington campus, and down a viaduct across 25th Avenue NE to a traffic light. Bear left here, and at the second light go right onto Mary Gates Memorial Drive. The entrance to the Fill is on the right in 0.2 mile, at the University of Washington Center for Urban Horticulture (free visitor parking). Find someplace else to go birding on football Saturdays.

Over 250 species of birds have been recorded, including state rarities such as Scissor-tailed Flycatcher, Blue-headed Vireo, Brown Thrasher, Chestnut-collared and McCown's Longspurs, and Indigo Bunting. Species more commonly associated with Eastern Washington stray regularly, for example, Black-necked Stilt, American Avocet, American Kestrel, Say's Phoebe, both kingbirds, Loggerhead Shrike, Mountain Bluebird, Vesper and Sagebrush Sparrows, Lazuli Bunting, Bobolink, Western Meadowlark, and Yellow-headed Blackbird. American Bittern, Green Heron, Virginia Rail, and Sora are in the marsh much of the year (uncommon to absent in winter). In summer and migration, Vaux's Swifts are common, and Black Swifts may forage over the Fill on overcast days.

Several shallow ponds at the Fill (formed in depressions where the garbage settled unevenly) and adjacent Union Bay host many ducks, including Blue-winged and Cinnamon Teal in summer. The ponds help compensate for Seattle's poverty of shorebird habitat, attracting a great diversity of species in spring and fall migration—albeit in small numbers. In addition to the usual yellowlegs, dowitchers, and peeps there are records for many scarcer species, including Solitary, Upland, Sharp-tailed, and Stilt Sandpipers, and Ruff.

The Fill is actively managed as a mix of habitats, with open grassland, native shrubs, and ponds bordered by plantings or left with open edges. Invasive Scot's Broom, Himalayan Blackberry, and Purple Loosestrife are being brought under control. However, rampant woody growth around pond edges in recent years has increasingly diminished shorebird habitat and viewing access. Hope remains that the will can be mustered to reverse this unfortunate development. When you visit, please stay on the paths.

FOSTER ISLAND AND WASHINGTON PARK ARBORETUM

[Note: Access to Foster Island and the Arboretum will be disrupted and in some cases permanently altered by construction for the realignment of the western end of SR-520, currently underway.]

To explore the other side of Union Bay, you can walk from the Fill around the east end of Husky Stadium, along the Montlake Cut, left over the drawbridge, then left again down the steps and back east on the other side of the canal to East Montlake Park; you can also drive to the park as described in the next paragraph. Walk east across a footbridge onto the path (often wet) across **Marsh Island**, just north of SR-520. Tree Swallow, Marsh Wren, Common Yellowthroat, and other species nest along the path. Another footbridge brings you to the north end of **Foster Island**, where a pair of Bald Eagles often hunts from a cottonwood. In winter, Union Bay can be packed with waterbirds (Trumpeter Swan, wigeons, Bufflehead, Hooded and Common Mergansers, Double-crested Cormorant, American Coot, many others), and this is an excellent vantage point for scoping.

Continue south through the pedestrian underpass to reach the main part of the island (see map). Or you may drive there from the Fill by returning along Mary Gates Memorial Drive to NE 45th Street and turning left (west). Stay in the left lane and follow the road as it curves south, joining Montlake Boulevard NE. You will pass Husky Stadium and cross the bridge over the Montlake Cut. Immediately after the SR-520 overpass, turn left onto Lake Washington Boulevard E. (A short distance ahead on the left, 24th Avenue E is the entrance road to East Montlake Park, with parking for the Marsh Island footpath; see preceding paragraph). Lake Washington Boulevard curves right (south), then left, to a stop sign. Turn left at the next stop sign a few hundred feet ahead onto E Foster Island Road, which ends in about 0.2 mile, near the south footbridge to the island.

Foster Island woodlands and nearby backwaters of Union Bay are good for small songbirds, including mixed winter foraging flocks of chickadees, nuthatches, and kinglets. Rare vagrants such as Blue-gray Gnatcatcher and Black-and-white, Tennessee, and Chestnut-sided Warblers have been found here. Wood Duck, Gadwall, Mallard, Great Blue Heron, Green Heron (summer), Belted Kingfisher, Northern Flicker, and Pileated Woodpecker are often seen around the island. Cliff Swallows nest nearby most years on the sides of the SR-520 bridge.

The neighboring **Washington Park Arboretum** was designed and installed as part of John C. Olmsted's plan for Seattle parks and boulevards (1903–1936). Extending south from Foster Island for about a mile to Madison Street, the 230-acre public park holds the second-largest collection of temperate woody plants in North America. eBird reports 145 species for the park, including a good assortment of summer and year-round resident edge-loving and forest birds. You may walk into the Arboretum from Foster Island. You may also drive along Lake Washington Boulevard as described above, but rather than turning left onto E Foster Island Road, bear right with the boulevard and on into the park.

WEST SEATTLE

Alki Beach Park in West Seattle (see map on page 139) is a fairly consistent place for Black Turnstone and Surfbird in winter, especially at Duwamish Head on the north end and around Alki Point to the south, and is also a good seabird overlook. Take Exit 163A from I-5 southbound, or Exit 163 if northbound, onto the West Seattle Freeway, then exit onto Harbor Avenue SW, birding the shoreline parks on Harbor and Alki Avenue SW, ending at Alki Point.

EDMONDS

The 22.5-acre **Edmonds Marsh** has birds of brackish marsh and tidally influenced mudflats, a rare habitat type for the Seattle area. (See inset map on page 139.) To get there, take SR-104 west from I-5 Exit 177 to the Edmonds ferry dock; do not get in the ferry lanes but turn left onto Dayton Street, then left into a parking lot just before the railroad crossing; the marsh is at the back. An interpretive walkway provides good viewing for waterfowl, rails, shorebirds, and passerines. The **Edmonds Fishing Pier**, at the north end of the marina, is excellent for seabird viewing. From the Edmonds Marsh, cross the railroad tracks on Dayton Street, park, and walk out.

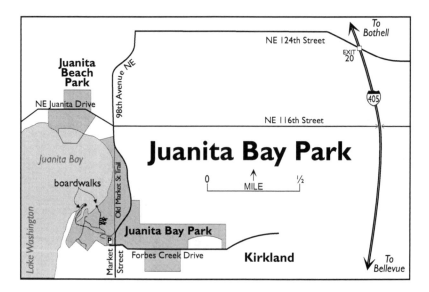

JUANITA BAY PARK

Despite its modest size (110 acres), extensive groomed lawns, and proximity to a busy commercial district, this little jewel of an urban park is an enjoyable and productive birding destination in any season. Two boardwalks and a causeway provide elevated platforms for viewing and photography of a fine variety of wetland habitats, including wet meadow, cattail marsh, a beaver pond, alder/willow swamp, and the shallow embayment where Forbes Creek joins Lake Washington.

Resident wetland birds include Wood Duck, Pied-billed Grebe, Bald Eagle, Virginia Rail, Red-breasted Sapsucker, Downy and Hairy Woodpeckers, Marsh Wren, and Red-winged Blackbird, joined in summer by Green Heron (irregular, has nested), Osprey, Western Wood-Pewee, Willow Flycatcher, Purple Martin, Common Yellowthroat, Yellow Warbler, and Bullock's Oriole. Winter brings an increased variety of waterfowl, including swans in recent years. Check the muddy edge of the lake at the north end of the bay for Wilson's Snipe (September–April). The rest of the park, including the undeveloped half east of Market Street, contains just enough mature conifers and shrubs to round out one's bird list with woodland and backyard species.

The park is located 1.4 miles north of downtown Kirkland on Market Street. Coming from farther afield, the fastest access is from I-405 Exit 20 (20B if northbound). Go west on NE 124th Street to the traffic light at 100th Avenue NE (1.1 mile). Turn left (south) here and follow the curving arterial (name changes to 98th Avenue NE). At the Forbes Creek Drive traffic light (1.2 mile), turn right (west) into the parking lot for the park.

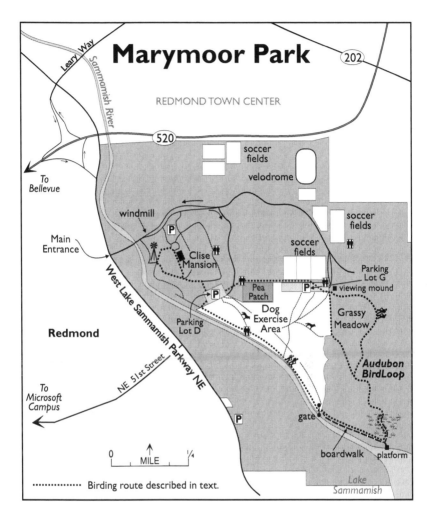

Birding route described in text.

MARYMOOR PARK

Despite heavy use (over three million visitors a year), 640-acre **Marymoor Park** offers good birding in all seasons, with a list of over 220 species, and is a notable migrant trap. Early morning on a weekday is the best time to visit.

Travel east from Seattle on SR-520 to the W Lake Sammamish Parkway NE exit. Turn right. The park entrance is 0.2 mile south of the offramp, on the left. Obtain a parking ticket at automated pay stations ($1 bill; good all day). In about 0.4 mile, at the third stop sign, turn right and continue south to Parking Lot D. From the far left corner of the lot take the Audubon BirdLoop trail to the left, a 1.4-mile walk through most of the park habitats. An informative trail brochure is available at interpretive kiosks and the park office.

For the first half-mile the trail follows the Sammamish River through riparian habitat inside the dog-exercise area. Swallows and Common Yellowthroats abound in summer. Search the riverbanks for Green Heron, Spotted Sandpiper, and Wilson's Snipe. Willow Flycatchers nest along the river; Wilson's Warblers and Western Tanagers pass through in migration; Ruby-crowned Kinglets and Fox Sparrows are numerous in winter. Look for the nesting colony of Great Blue Herons in tall trees right beside the trail.

Passing through a gate at the other end of the dog area, the BirdLoop trail continues on a boardwalk through forest to a platform at the north end of Lake Sammamish, at the outlet of the Sammamish River. Western Wood-Pewee, Warbling Vireo, Swainson's Thrush, and Black-headed Grosbeak nest in the forest. Watch for Wood Ducks on the river. Gourds installed near the platform attract nesting Purple Martins and Tree Swallows. Black Swifts regularly forage over the lake on cloudy summer days.

Bending sharply left, the boardwalk goes through a cattail marsh (Virginia Rail) followed by a small deciduous woodland and finally wet grasslands lined by willows. You should find Rufous Hummingbird and Yellow Warbler in summer; Orange-crowned Warbler and other migrants; and Black-capped Chickadee, Marsh and Bewick's Wrens, and American Goldfinch year round.

The trail splits upon emerging from the thickets to offer a choice between the east and west sides of an extensive meadow. Savannah Sparrow nests here in summer; Short-eared Owl, Northern Shrike, and Western Meadowlark are seen in winter; spring passage brings the occasional Say's Phoebe, Mountain Bluebird, or Lazuli Bunting. The two branches converge at a kiosk. The nearby viewing mound is an excellent vantage for scoping the meadow.

Walk back west to the starting point on a path between the soccer fields and Parking Lot G. Sparrows gather along shrubby edges in fall and winter. The grass playing fields here and elsewhere in the park host American Pipits in fall, and gulls, shorebirds, and large flocks of geese (mostly Cackling and Canada, with sometimes a few Greater White-fronted and Snow) in winter.

A 0.4-mile side loop of the trail takes you from the back right corner of Parking Lot D through a grove of conifers to the park office and historic Clise Mansion. Barn Owls nest in the old windmill.

LAKE SAMMAMISH STATE PARK

Lake Sammamish State Park occupies 512 acres at the south end of the lake, at I-90 Exit 15. At a traffic light north of the interchange, turn left onto NW Sammamish Road. In 0.4 mile, turn right into the park entrance (Discover Pass required). The park can be crowded, especially on summer weekends. Birding is best at the back, away from the beaches and freeway, on

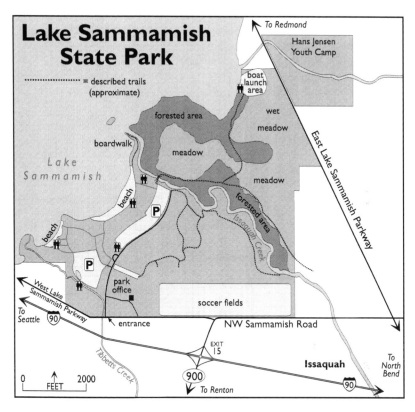

Lake Sammamish State Park

weekday mornings. Unsurfaced park trails are predictably soggy in winter months (mud boots advisable).

Drive in to the farthest parking lot (when gated in winter, park in the first lot and walk). The paved path along the two beaches is good for a seasonal variety of ducks, gulls, other waterbirds, and mixed-forest species. At the footbridge over Issaquah Creek, just north of the parking lot, look for Wood Ducks, mergansers, and returning salmon (fall). Walk left next to the fence without crossing the bridge, peering in at creekside logs and low branches, to the barrier-free boardwalk leading to the mouth of the creek. Green Heron, Spotted Sandpiper, Tree Swallow, Swainson's Thrush, and Black-headed Grosbeak are found here in breeding season.

Backtrack and continue across the north end of the parking lot, keeping the creek on your left. A path through large cottonwoods opens into a grassy clearing with old fruit trees. Red-breasted Sapsucker, Western Wood-Pewee, Willow and Pacific-slope Flycatchers, Warbling and Red-eyed Vireos, Cedar Waxwing, Yellow Warbler, Bullock's Oriole, and Purple Finch nest here. Keep left along the edge of the clearing across a small footbridge. The trail follows the creek (nesting Belted Kingfisher and Northern Rough-winged

Swallow), with a large wet meadow on the right (Northern Shrike in winter, Marsh Wren year round), to a Douglas-fir forest (Hutton's Vireo year round, Pacific Wren in winter, Black-throated Gray Warbler in migration).

A 1.3-mile hike to the park's boat launch starts from the parking lot. Cross the footbridge, go right on the mowed trail, then left at a fork in about half a mile. Rufous Hummingbird, Common Yellowthroat, and Savannah Sparrow nest along the way. Look up for Black Swifts on cloudy summer days and north for the Great Blue Heron nesting colony across the meadow in tall trees.

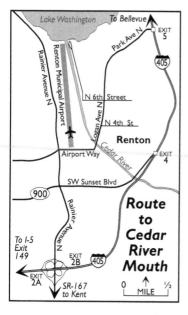

CEDAR RIVER MOUTH

Located in an industrial zone at the south end of Lake Washington, this is the Seattle area's finest site for gulls outside the breeding season (especially late November–early March). Herring Gull (very local around Seattle) is fairly common, as is Thayer's. Glaucous is annual, though rare; Slaty-backed has occurred several times. The only state record of Great Black-backed Gull is from here (Jan–Feb 2004). The common gulls occur in large numbers, providing good comparative studies of plumage cycles. Winter also brings a nice variety of diving ducks.

Take I-405 Exit 2 (2B if southbound) for Rainier Avenue S/Renton. Go north 1.2 miles on Rainier Avenue S and turn right (east) onto Airport Way S, continuing to its end in 0.4 mile. Bend left here onto Logan Avenue S (becomes Logan Avenue N), and in 0.5 mile turn left (west) at the traffic light onto N 6th Street. At the stop sign (0.2 mile), continue straight ahead into the park entrance (gated at sunset), and right onto Nishiwaki Lane (formerly N Riverside Drive). A narrow park (toilets) follows the channelized river north to its mouth (0.6 mile), between the runway of the Renton Municipal Airport on the west and a Boeing plant on the east. Ample parking can be found along Nishiwaki Lane.

Walk out onto the decks at the City of Renton Boathouse at the north end of the park. Gull-watching is best approaching nightfall, as birds return to roost and bathe after spending the day upriver at the Cedar Hills Regional Landfill. Old logs and stumps washed out from the river provide perches; some mud- and gravel bars emerge when water levels are down. Migrant songbirds use the small trees and brush all through the riverside park. Palm Warblers have wintered here more than once.

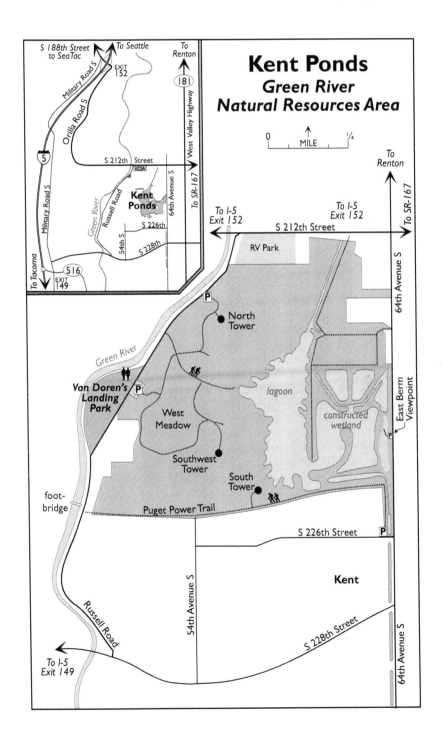

Kent Ponds
Green River
Natural Resources Area

S 188th Street to SeaTac

To Seattle

To Renton

Military Road S

EXIT 152

Orilla Road S

181

West Valley Highway

5

S 212th Street

KOA

Kent Ponds

Green River

Russell Road

64th Avenue S

To SR-167

S 226th

54th S

S 228th

To Tacoma

516

EXIT 149

0 — MILE — ¼

To Renton

To SR-167

To I-5 Exit 152

To I-5 Exit 152

S 212th Street

64th Avenue S

RV Park

P

North Tower

Green River

Van Doren's Landing Park

P

lagoon

West Meadow

constructed wetland

East Berm Viewpoint

P

Southwest Tower

South Tower

foot-bridge

Puget Power Trail

S 226th Street

P

Kent

54th Avenue S

Russell Road

S 228th Street

64th Avenue S

To I-5 Exit 149

KENT VALLEY

The Kent Valley, the alluvial plain along the Green River south of Seattle, was once a vast area of wetlands and open fields famous for raptors, waterfowl, and migrating shorebirds—much like the Skagit and Samish Flats farther north. Although overtaken by industry, warehouses, and suburban growth in recent decades, the valley still harbors remnant patches of habitat. Favorite birding spots come and go; the following is perhaps the most stable and reliable of these.

The itinerary described here (map on previous page) proceeds in a clockwise loop from the corner of S 212th Street and 64th Avenue S, northwest of downtown Kent. To reach the starting point from I-5, take Exit 152 and go east on curving Orillia Road, which becomes S 212th Street upon reaching the valley floor. In 2.7 miles, turn right (south) onto 64th Avenue S. *(Coming from SR-167, take the S 212th Street exit, travel west 1.5 miles, and turn left onto 64th.)*

The **Green River Natural Resources Area** (GRNRA; familiarly, **Kent Ponds**) has transformed the former settlement ponds of a wastewater treatment facility into a 304-acre wildlife sanctuary and enhanced wetland for stormwater retention. What you will be mostly doing is scanning the wetlands from the periphery for waterbirds (Wood Duck, Gadwall, Mallard, American Bittern, Great Blue Heron year round; in winter, wigeons, Northern Shoveler, Northern Pintail, Green-winged Teal, Ring-necked Duck, Hooded Merganser, Ruddy Duck; Baikal Teal recorded); and for raptors perched or in flight (nesting Cooper's and Red-tailed Hawks; Osprey, Bald Eagle, Northern Harrier, Peregrine Falcon, Short-eared Owl; American Kestrel irregular; Red-shouldered Hawk recorded). A trail following the south edge, and other trails in the western meadows, provide passerine birding (nesting Willow Flycatcher, swallows, Marsh and Bewick's Wrens, Common Yellowthroat, Savannah Sparrow, Lazuli Bunting; Yellow-breasted Chat recorded; winter sparrows). Parking is limited along the east and south sides, usually plentiful along the west side.

Go south on 64th to a small turn-in on the right marked by a GRNRA sign (0.5 mile). Walk up a short path onto the **East Berm**, an overlook to the west across a pond. Continue driving south 0.3 mile, turn right onto S 226th Street, then immediately right into a small parking area. A broad, paved, non-motorized, barrier-free trail goes north, connecting in about 350 yards to the **Puget Power Trail**, which runs west from here nearly a mile along the south edge of GRNRA.

Drive west on 226th from the trailhead parking spot to a T-intersection in 0.5 mile. Parking is allowed to the right, along the stub of 54th Avenue S that ends at the Puget Power Trail in a short distance. Walk 350 yards back east to a side trail into the **South Tower** (700 yards if coming from the east end). Climb the tower for decent scope views northeast to the largest of the three GRNRA ponds.

Go south on 54th to the T-intersection with S 228th Street (0.4 mile). Turn right here, and in 0.2 mile angle off right onto Russell Road. In 0.9 mile, find a GRNRA parking lot on the right with an entry gate into the meadows and access to the Southwest Tower. You also may park on the other side of the road at Van Doren's Park (public toilets). Another parking area and gate with access to the North Tower and trails is 0.4 mile farther north. From here it is 0.2 mile north to S 212th Street.

SNOQUALMIE VALLEY TO EVERETT

by Hal Opperman
revised by Hal Opperman

At the end of the last ice age, impounded waters burst from a glacial lake east of the present site of North Bend, scouring out a lowland valley extending some 40 miles to Puget Sound. Today, three forks of the Snoqualmie River come down from the Cascades to unite at the head of this valley. After plunging over Snoqualmie Falls a few miles downstream, the river meanders across a broad floodplain with ancient oxbows, ponds, marshes, wet meadows, and patches of woods. The Tolt River flows in from the east at Carnation, and the Skykomish joins the Snoqualmie near Monroe to form the Snohomish, with its estuary 15 miles farther on at Everett. Converted to farmland by early settlers, the valley has largely preserved its bucolic character despite intense development pressures. From foothills to tidelands, this riverine ecosystem offers the best all-round birding in the Seattle/Everett metropolitan area.

The route described below follows the river closely, with a representative selection of good birding spots. However, the enterprising will find the same birds practically anyplace in the valley where there is a bit of habitat. Those inclined to leave their cars will enjoy walking or biking along the Snoqualmie Valley Trail, an abandoned railroad grade between Cedar Falls and Duvall that provides many birding opportunities. For the most part the birds mentioned are those that can be found in migration or the breeding season.

Winter birding out in open country is also excellent, although access is regularly disrupted by flooding, and dense morning fog does enshroud the Snohomish Flats occasionally. Look for raptors perched or hunting—a Golden Eagle or a Gyrfalcon is not an impossibility. Be on the alert for unusual species in winter sparrow flocks along brushy ditches and fencerows, blackberry tangles, and thicket edges. American Tree, Clay-colored, Swamp, White-throated, and Harris's Sparrows are possible among the numerous Spotted Towhees, Fox, Song, Lincoln's, White-crowned, and Golden-crowned Sparrows, and Dark-eyed Juncos. Windbreaks and pine plantations may harbor roosting owls. In wooded tracts, foraging flocks in conifers or among bare branches may include Downy Woodpecker, Hutton's Vireo, and Yellow-rumped or Townsend's Warblers along with Black-capped and Chestnut-backed Chickadees, Bushtit, Red-breasted Nuthatch, Brown Creeper, Bewick's Wren, Golden-crowned and Ruby-crowned Kinglets, and various finches. Pacific Wrens frequent the understory, and now and then you may pick up the call-note of a skulking Hermit Thrush.

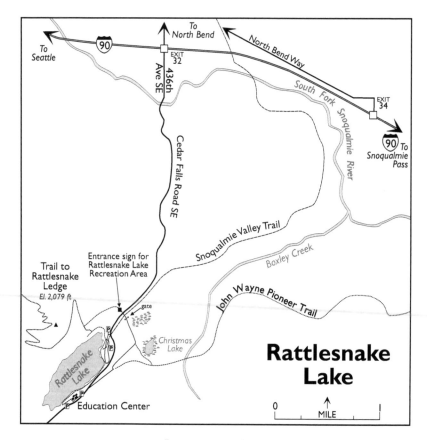

RATTLESNAKE LAKE

The itinerary begins at the foot of the Cascades at Rattlesnake Lake, southeast of North Bend at an elevation of 900 feet. From I-90, go south at Exit 32 on 436th Avenue SE, which crosses the South Fork Snoqualmie River and changes name to Cedar Falls Road SE, arriving in 2.7 miles at the sign for the **Rattlesnake Lake Recreation Area.** (Despite the name, there are no rattlesnakes in Western Washington.) The first of several parking lots is 0.2 mile ahead, on the right (toilets here and elsewhere). Ospreys patrol the lake in summer; Western Screech-Owls and Barred Owls nest in the surroundings. The John Wayne Pioneer Trail climbs across the Cascades from here to Eastern Washington, following the old Milwaukee Road railway grade (Discover Pass required in designated parking lots). Local trails lead along the lakeshore and through the woods to Rattlesnake Ledge, with a fine overlook. Conifer-forest specialties on the way up may include Hairy Woodpecker, Varied Thrush, and Townsend's Warbler. Peregrine Falcons have nested on the rock face.

The principal source of Seattle's drinking water, the 141-square-mile watershed is managed as an ecological reserve, closed to the public. Common Loons—rare breeders in Washington—nest on the reservoir, but except for tours (inquire at the Education Center) you are limited to exploring the watershed around the edges. For one productive spot, go back to the recreation area sign, turn right (east) onto an unmarked gravel road, and continue straight about 150 yards to a closed gate. Park out of the way and walk around the gate. In 50 yards, turn off left and follow a track through mixed forest, primarily big old Red Alders with some second-growth conifers and Black Cottonwoods, with a large wetland on your left. In about a quarter-mile stay right where the track forks and continue a short distance to **Christmas Lake**, a shallow lake with much emergent vegetation and drowned-out snags where Tree Swallows nest. Woods and shoreline offer a fine selection of birds of the Westside lowlands in migration and summer, including Band-tailed Pigeon, Vaux's Swift, Rufous Hummingbird, Red-breasted Sapsucker, Pileated Woodpecker, Western Wood-Pewee, Willow, Hammond's, and Pacific-slope Flycatchers, Hutton's and Warbling Vireos, Steller's Jay, Red-breasted Nuthatch, Pacific Wren, Swainson's Thrush, Cedar Waxwing, Common Yellowthroat, Yellow, Black-throated Gray, and Wilson's Warblers, Spotted Towhee, Song Sparrow, Dark-eyed Junco, Black-headed Grosbeak, Purple Finch, and Evening Grosbeak.

NORTH BEND TO FALL CITY

King County's **Three Forks Natural Area** is a discontinuous, 2.5-mile string of parcels along the Snoqualmie River and its forks between North Bend and Snoqualmie. From I-90 Exit 31, take SR-202 north 0.6 mile to a traffic light in the center of the North Bend business district. Turn right here onto North Bend Way, then left in two blocks (0.1 mile) onto Ballarat Avenue NE. Stay on this main road as it changes name and turns right (0.6 mile) toward Mount Si, then left (0.5 mile) in a rural setting where it becomes 428th Avenue SE. The road soon crosses the Middle and North Fork Snoqualmie Rivers a few hundred yards apart. In 1.4 miles turn left (west) onto SE Reinig Road. Parking for the natural area is immediately on the left (seasonal toilet; if gate is closed in winter, park across the road in a small pullout).

From here you may walk a short distance to the foot of the North Fork bridge, or take a wide trail to the right through broadleaf and mixed forest, reaching the river in about a quarter-mile. A pullout 0.2 farther west on the left side of Reinig Road offers quicker access to the best birding habitat, but parking is limited. Take the trail through gallery forest and willow thickets to the union of North and Middle Forks; the South Fork flows in half a mile downstream. Red-eyed Vireo, locally distributed in Washington and a Snoqualmie Valley specialty, can be found in mature riparian vegetation here and elsewhere along the river, along with several other nesting passerines such as Pacific-slope Flycatcher, Swainson's Thrush, and Black-throated Gray

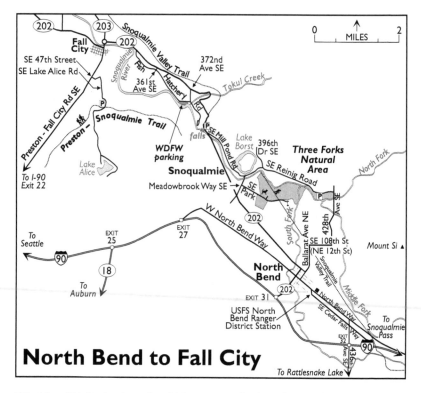

North Bend to Fall City

Warbler. Walk the broad cobble margins looking for swallows and swifts overhead, Spotted Sandpiper on gravel bars, Green Heron in overhanging streamside branches, and Common Merganser on the river.

Continue driving west beside the river on Reinig Road. At the stop sign in 1.5 miles, where 396th Drive SE comes in from the right, bear left with Reinig Road and at the fork in 0.3 mile stay left onto Meadowbrook Way SE, crossing the Snoqualmie River bridge. In 0.2 mile, go left onto SE Park Street. Turn left at the entrance to the Three Forks Off-Leash Dog Area (0.3 mile; additional parking and restrooms available across the road at Centennial Fields Park). Walk through the double gates into the dog-exercise area, a fenced lawn bordered by trees and brush. Walk right, birding the edge habitat, reaching a gate and the Snoqualmie Valley Trail at the far end. Cross over the trail into another piece of the Three Forks Natural Area. A large, open willow- and shrub-lined field occupies most of the acreage between the trail and the river, together with stands of tall cottonwoods, with Mount Si as a backdrop. The field can be difficult to walk, even when freshly cut; a well-trodden trail on the left is the most practical route to the back, but walking the edge on the right side of the field can be productive. Expected breeding species include Rufous Hummingbird, Red-breasted Sapsucker, Western Wood-Pewee, Willow Flycatcher, Warbling and Red-eyed Vireos, Cedar Waxwing, Common Yellowthroat, Yellow Warbler, Savannah Sparrow, Black-headed Grosbeak, and American Goldfinch. Lazuli Bunting is found regularly although not annually (Indigo Bunting in 2009).

For an interesting, only barely longer return route, walk left (south) on the Snoqualmie Valley Trail through broadleaf forest with a wide slough on the right, emerging at the entrance to Mount Si Golf Course (public). Exit right onto SE Park Street. The right shoulder affords close views of the tops of riparian willows and associated birdlife along the slough on the way back to the dog-area parking entrance.

Return to Meadowbrook Road, turn left, go 0.5 mile, passing Mt. Si High School, to the intersection with SR-202 (Railroad Avenue). Turn right, and in 1.8 miles find the visitor center for 272-foot-high **Snoqualmie Falls**, a popular day-trip destination for residents of Pugetopolis. The falls in full flow are a spectacular sensory experience, but if water is being diverted for power generation, they can be reduced to a trickle. Peregrine Falcons nest beside the falls on rock ledges.

Continue along SR-202 and turn left onto 372nd Avenue SE (1.4 miles). In 0.2 mile, turn right onto SE Fish Hatchery Road, then immediately left into the WDFW parking lot (Discover Pass required). Scramble down the short trail to the Snoqualmie River where it emerges from the gorge below the falls; **Tokul Creek** flows into the river just upstream on the left (also viewable from the creek bridge by walking back along Fish Hatchery Road from the parking lot). This is a good place to find American Dipper.

Continue downriver along **Fish Hatchery Road**, pulling off frequently to bird streamside trees, open fields, and scattered wetlands. Black and Vaux's Swifts can sometimes be seen overhead. In 0.6 mile, an oxbow on the right supports an extensive marsh, home to Hooded Merganser, Virginia Rail, Wilson's Snipe, and Marsh Wren. Continue ahead to 361st Avenue SE (0.3 mile) and turn right to rejoin SR-202 in 0.1 mile. Turn left here to the traffic circle north of the Snoqualmie River and Fall City (1.6 miles).

Follow SR-202 around the traffic circle, exiting across the bridge. Do not turn right with SR-202 (0.1 mile), but instead swing left onto Preston-Fall City Road SE. In 0.6 mile, turn left (east) onto SE 47th Street, which in 0.2 mile bends south and becomes SE Lake Alice Road. In another 0.6 mile, turn right into a parking lot (portable toilet) where the road intersects the **Preston-Snoqualmie Trail**, a former railroad grade. Park and cross back over the road. The wide, blacktopped, non-motorized, barrier-free trail goes east along a wooded hillside, ending in about two miles at an overlook high above Snoqualmie Falls. On an early morning in June the trees are alive with songbirds. A Pileated Woodpecker may surprise you, or even a Barred Owl.

CARNATION AND VICINITY

From the bridge in Fall City, drive west on SR-202, the Fall City-Redmond Road to a junction with 324th Avenue NE (1.0 mile). Turn right and follow the paved road down the broad, flat valley as it jogs and changes names several times, eventually turning north and becoming West Snoqualmie River Road NE. Breeding species of this open landscape include Savannah and White-crowned Sparrows, Red-winged and Brewer's Blackbirds, House Finch, and American Goldfinch. In winter scan the sodden fields for ducks and other waterfowl, American Pipit, Western Meadowlark, and perhaps a Northern Shrike. Check brushy patches for winter sparrow flocks.

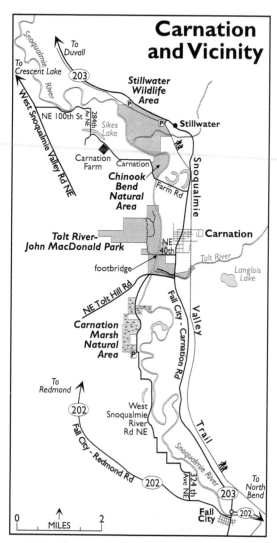

Continue to a turnout on the left (4.0 miles from SR-202). Here an overgrown trail gives access to one corner of the **Carnation Marsh Natural Area**, an unimproved tract extending northward for over a mile. This former river course is impenetrably vegetated and mostly flooded (with help from Beavers), and the road shoulders are narrow, so park at this spot and bird along the road on foot. Close to 100 species have been recorded in the breeding season, including 10 species of ducks, Ruffed Grouse, American Bittern, Osprey, Virginia Rail, Wilson's Snipe, five species of woodpeckers (Red-breasted Sapsucker, Downy, Hairy, Northern Flicker, Pileated), Olive-sided, Willow, and Pacific-slope Flycatchers, four species of vireos, six of swallows, Marsh Wren, and most of the other Puget Lowlands songbird species.

Continue driving north to the intersection with NE Tolt Hill Road in 1.7 miles and turn right (east) onto a bridge over the Snoqualmie River. In 0.6 mile turn left again at the junction with Fall City-Carnation Road (SR-203), and drive north across the Tolt River into the town of Carnation. The main entrance to **Tolt River-John MacDonald Park** is reached by turning left onto NE 40th Street (0.5 mile). Go straight in to the parking lots (toilets, picnic shelters). You can walk south through the campground to the Tolt River at the point where it joins the Snoqualmie, birding the tall riparian trees, but the best birding is on the west bank of the Snoqualmie, reached by a suspension footbridge. This area of diverse habitats (forest, grasslands, brushy edges, riparian) is served by an extensive trail system. Expect almost any Western Washington lowland species including Hammond's and Pacific-slope Flycatchers, Cassin's, Hutton's, Warbling, and Red-eyed Vireos, Steller's Jay, Black-capped and Chestnut-backed Chickadees, Orange-crowned, MacGillivray's, Black-throated Gray, and Wilson's Warblers, Western Tanager, Black-headed Grosbeak, and Bullock's Oriole. As elsewhere along the Snoqualmie, swifts often forage overhead. Belted Kingfisher and many swallows can be seen from the bridge.

Return to SR-203. Turn left (north). In 3.3 miles, about 300 yards past the Stillwater store, turn left into the **Stillwater Unit** of the Snoqualmie Wildlife Area and park (Discover Pass required here and at a second parking area 0.7 mile farther north). Bordered on the northeast by the highway and on the southwest by the river, this section of the Snoqualmie floodplain extends about a mile and a half as the river flows and three-quarters of a mile across. It is managed for hunting, with numerous open fields where grain crops are left to ripen for feed, framed by ditches, dikes, and sloughs. Maples, cottonwoods, alders, and willows flourish along watercourses; blackberries and other dense brush provide winter sparrow cover along field borders; cattails and sedges dominate the marshy places. Birds typical of these habitats can be found readily in the appropriate seasons. Avoid the area during the hunting season (September to January with some variation—the current year's regulations are usually posted at the parking lots). In the non-hunting months of the year you may wander the area freely.

The **Snoqualmie Valley Trail** passes the back side of both parking lots. A good cross-section of habitats can be sampled by walking right (northwest) along the trail from the south parking lot. A marshy pond between trail and highway has herons and other waterbirds. In about 400 yards, a service road descends the embankment on your left. Follow this road toward the southwest. It turns left along a dike, right to follow a slough, left across the slough, then right again toward the river. A pair or two of Lazuli Buntings have nested here some years. At the back of the last field turn right when you reach a row of tall trees, then bear left across a grassy stretch to the high river bank, home to a colony of Northern Rough-winged and Bank Swallows.

Walking south along the trail from the south parking lot for a half-mile or so, to the second of two bridges, takes you through fine riparian and wetland habitat. The elevated trail embankment provides exceptional access and viewing for common breeding species such as Red-breasted Sapsucker, Willow Flycatcher, Swainson's Thrush, and Common Yellowthroat. American Bittern is also here, although difficult to see. Yellow-breasted Chat has been recorded.

Return to your car and head back toward Carnation. In 1.9 miles, turn right (west) onto Carnation Farm Road, which soon crosses the Snoqualmie River (0.8 mile). In an elbow of the river on the right, the 59-acre **Chinook Bend Natural Area**—a former pasture successfully restored to native floodplain, riparian, and wetland vegetation—offers some of the same birding possibilities as in similar habitats at Stillwater and elsewhere in the valley. Turn in to parking just west of the bridge, or at a larger lot about 500 yards farther ahead. The imposing **Carnation Farm** (2.3 miles), once a model dairy farm for "contented cows", is now the home of Camp Korey, a non-profit organization supporting children with serious medical conditions.

Long, narrow **Sikes Lake**, lying in the valley just below the westernmost farm buildings, is good for ducks in winter. In 0.5 mile, 284th Avenue NE turns off to the right (north). A bridge across Sikes Lake is a fine vantage point. Along this and other valley roads, hay fields saturated by winter rains host flocks of Gadwall, American Wigeon, Mallard, Northern Pintail, Green-winged Teal, and other ducks; Eurasian Wigeon can usually be picked out with a scope. Continue along 284th Avenue as it turns left and morphs into NE 100th Street, a lightly-used road with many places to stop to bird the fields and the river.

Turn right (north) onto West Snoqualmie Valley Road NE (1.9 miles). It is imprudent to poke along on this far busier road, but there are a few places where you can safely pull off to scan the valley (swans in winter). At the Snohomish County line in 6.7 miles the name changes to High Bridge Road. Turn right (east) in another 1.9 miles onto Crescent Lake Road and recross the Snoqualmie River.

CRESCENT LAKE

On the left in 0.4 mile from High Bridge Road is the south entrance to the **Crescent Lake Unit** of the Snoqualmie Wildlife Area (Discover Pass required). The lake is a broken O of water in an old river oxbow, bordered by trees and tangled vegetation. The 360-acre wildlife area includes the land inside the oxbow and west to the Snoqualmie River. About a third of the total area is sharecropped with a part of the grain left standing for wildlife. From the parking lot, a wide track follows the edge of the lake northwestward. Blackberries and other brush provide winter cover for sparrows, and the trees are attractive to woodpeckers, Pine Siskin, and other species (avoid the open fields and lake edges in fall if hunters are present). Farther north, where the lake ends, a path on the right enters an extensive tract of mature maples, alders, willows, and other hardwoods, crisscrossed by a maze of often-muddy trails. This is probably the best chunk of relatively little-disturbed floodplain forest left in the region. In spring and summer, look and listen for Red-breasted Sapsucker, Pacific-slope Flycatcher, Warbling and Red-eyed Vireos, Black-capped Chickadee, Swainson's Thrush, Purple Finch, and other woodland species.

Exiting the parking lot, turn left onto Crescent Lake Road, which follows the lake (walking this stretch gives good viewing) to a pullout on the left in 0.3 mile by a closed gate. Here you can walk into the wildlife area across a filled-in piece of the lake; in summer, expect Green Heron, Willow Flycatcher, Common Yellowthroat, Yellow Warbler, and Bullock's Oriole. At a three-way junction in 0.3 mile turn right (east) onto 203rd Street SE, which traverses the site of a former state honor farm. On the left, an extensive wet meadow swells in winter into a long, shallow pond—still known to birders as the **Monroe Prison Farm Pond**—that has attracted well over 100 bird species. A small concrete pad at 0.1 mile from the intersection affords convenient parking. The land is part of a private waterfowl hunting club; please do not trespass. Bird from the pad or on foot elsewhere along the road with a scope. The pond is about 200 yards out.

Backtrack to the three-way intersection and turn right onto Tualco Road. Keep straight 0.2 mile and go left onto Tualco Loop Road. The north entrance to the wildlife area is 500 feet ahead on the left. Park in the lot (Discover Pass required) and walk in along the service road that continues the entrance road, turning left to cross the lake on a culvert. You are now in the hole of the doughnut. Dense trees and blackberries on the perimeter screen the lake from view but offer excellent cover for wintering sparrows (Rusty Blackbird in 2015). Go either way around the cornfields. By following paths through the hardwood forest at the west end of the second field you can reach the south parking lot and walk a complete loop.

North from the parking lot, Tualco Loop Road crosses Riley Slough, bordered by tall broadleaf trees and blackberries, then continues on through

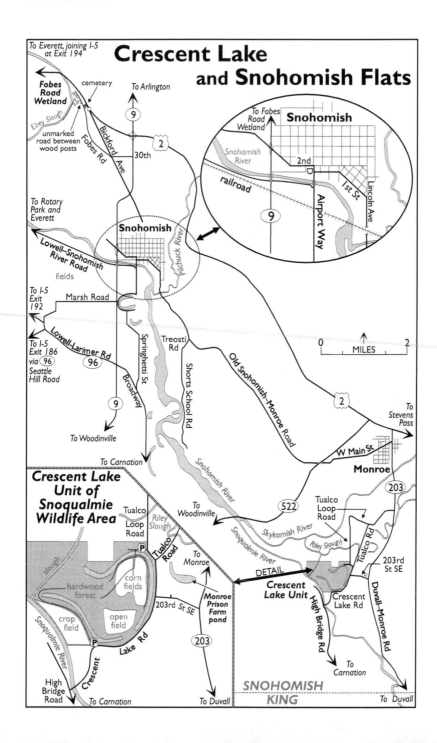

Crescent Lake
and Snohomish Flats

To Everett, joining I-5 at Exit 194

Fobes Road Wetland

cemetery

To Arlington

Ebey Slough

unmarked road between wood posts

Bickford Ave

Fobes Rd

30th

9

2

To Rotary Park and Everett

Lowell-Snohomish River Road

Snohomish

fields

Pilchuck River

To I-5 Exit 192

Marsh Road

To I-5 Exit 186 via 96 Seattle Hill Road

Lowell-Larimer Rd

96

Springhetti St

Broadway

Treosti Rd

Shorts School Rd

Old Snohomish-Monroe Road

9

To Woodinville

To Carnation

Snohomish River

Snohomish

To Fobes Road Wetland

Snohomish River

railroad

2nd

9

Airport Way

1st St

Lincoln Ave

0   MILES   2

2

To Stevens Pass

W Main St

Monroe

203

Crescent Lake Unit of Snoqualmie Wildlife Area

Tualco Loop Road

Riley Slough

Tualco Road

slough

hardwood forest

corn fields

crop field

open field

P

P

203rd St SE

Lake Rd

High Bridge Road

To Carnation

Crescent

To Woodinville

To Monroe

Monroe Prison Farm pond

203

To Duvall

Snohomish River

Skykomish River

522

Snoqualmie River

Riley Slough

DETAIL

Crescent Lake Unit

Crescent Lake Rd

High Bridge Rd

Tualco Loop Road

Tualco Rd

203rd St SE

Duvall-Monroe Rd

To Carnation

SNOHOMISH
KING

To Duvall

farmland (winter raptors, gulls, blackbird flocks). At the intersection in 1.4 miles go straight ahead onto Tualco Road, then left in 0.7 mile onto SR-203 (Duvall-Monroe Road), which crosses the Skykomish River in another 0.8 mile and enters the city of Monroe. At a traffic light in downtown Monroe in 0.6 mile, turn left onto W Main Street to continue to the Snohomish Flats. (If you go straight and cross the railroad tracks, the next light is at US-2; turn left here to join I-5 at Everett, or right for the Cascades and Stevens Pass, page 404).

SNOHOMISH FLATS

Headed west through downtown Monroe from SR-203, Main Street passes under SR-522 (1.8 miles), continues west as the Old Snohomish-Monroe Road, and in about 3.5 miles drops down onto the **Snohomish Flats**. This open farm country is home to a large population of raptors in winter, including one or two Gyrfalcons in recent years. Along the stretch from here to the Pilchuck River bridge (1.9 miles), scan isolated treetops, fencerows, utility poles, and the ground. Make sure you pull safely off the road; shoulders are narrow in most places. A side trip down Treosti Road/Shorts School Road and back can also be productive.

Soon after the bridge and a railway underpass, the road—now Lincoln Avenue—enters the old river town of Snohomish. A short way past the city limits, turn left onto First Street. Public restrooms are on the left in six blocks, at Avenue B. In two more blocks, go left (south) at Avenue D across the Snohomish River bridge, following Airport Way south and west to a traffic light at SR-9 (1.1 miles from the bridge). A two-mile-wide band of fields between the river on the north and Lowell-Larimer Road on the south, stretching westward from SR-9 for about five miles, is worth scanning in winter. There are several informal pullouts along both of these roads, and also along Marsh Road, which continues west from the Airport Way/SR-9 intersection to Lowell-Larimer Road at Larimers Corner (2.0 miles). Raptors and swans can be of interest, as can shorebirds when the fields are partially flooded.

The **Fobes Road Wetland**, northwest of Snohomish, is one of the best pieces of accessible wet meadows and freshwater marsh in the river bottoms. Take SR-9 north from Second Street in Snohomish to the intersection with 30th Street/56th Street SE (2.2 miles; traffic light). Turn left (west) to a stop sign at Bickford Avenue (0.4 mile). Continue straight across the intersection onto Fobes Road. Drive past a wooded hillside cemetery on the right (1.3 miles from Bickford). Just ahead, turn off left between two wood posts, drive down an unmarked lane until the way is barred by a gate (about 75 yards), and park without blocking access. Walk around the gate and down the path toward an arm of the river (Ebey Slough). Walk the dike upstream (left) for about half a mile, until the marshy habitat peters out, birding the wetlands (scope desirable) and riparian trees and shrubs.

Regular in breeding season are Canada Goose, Wood Duck, Gadwall, Mallard, Cinnamon Teal (a few Blue-winged briefly in May–June), Pied-billed Grebe, Great Blue Heron, Osprey, Bald Eagle, Red-tailed Hawk, Virginia Rail, American Coot, Killdeer, Mourning Dove, Vaux's Swift, Rufous Humming-bird, Belted Kingfisher, Western Wood-Pewee, Willow Flycatcher, Eastern Kingbird (nests regularly), swallows, Marsh Wren, Common Yellowthroat, Yellow Warbler, Song Sparrow, Red-winged Blackbird, Bullock's Oriole, Pur-ple Finch, and American Goldfinch. Many other waterbirds and passerines may be found in migration. Before leaving, a walk north to the end of Fobes Road (0.3 mile) and a visit to the cemetery will doubtless produce a few more species, such as Swainson's Thrush, Cedar Waxwing, and Black-headed Gros-beak, that shun wide-open wetland habitats.

Running west from the south end of the Avenue D/Airport Way bridge in Snohomish (but not accessible from SR-9), Lowell-Snohomish River Road lies between the diked river and a high railway embankment, eventually con-verging with Lowell-Larimer Road at the east edge of Everett. It is possible to get a view of the flats in a few places, but *stay off the railroad tracks!* In 5.6 miles, on the right, **Rotary Park** (restrooms) has fine broadleaf riparian habitat along a well-traveled passerine migration corridor. The paved, wheelchair-ac-cessible **Lowell Riverfront Trail** begins here and continues downstream for about a mile and a half, with a side loop through restored wetland and forest.

The next stops are downriver on the Snohomish delta. To get there from Lowell-Snohomish River Road, cross the railroad tracks 0.2 mile west of the entrance to Rotary Park; continue west two blocks (name changes to Lenora Street); and turn right onto S Second Avenue (Lowell-Larimer Road), reaching the Exit 192 interchange with I-5 at 41st Street SE in 1.2 miles. Or you can travel about five miles westbound on US-2 from the inter-change with SR-9 north of Snohomish. In both cases, take I-5 northbound when you reach it.

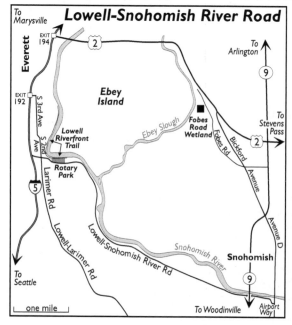

EVERETT SEWAGE TREATMENT PONDS

The strategically located Everett sewage ponds function as part of the Snohomish estuary ecosystem, attracting a good number and variety of birds in all seasons. Birders are welcome, but must remain outside the fences. The ponds are reached from Exit 195 on northbound I-5. Turn left at the end of the offramp onto E Marine View Drive. At the interchange in 1.5 miles, turn left for the onramp to SR-529 (Pacific Highway) northbound and cross the Snohomish River. Stay in the right lane and turn right at the first road, 28th Place NE, 0.2 mile from the north end of the bridge, indicated by signs for the marina and for Langus Riverfront Park. Immediately after turning off, turn right again onto 35th Avenue NE. At the next intersection (0.3 mile from SR-529) turn left onto Ross Avenue. Continue past Dagmars Landing (marina), staying right where 12th Street NE branches off in 0.9 mile (do not cross over I-5). Ross Avenue becomes Smith Island Road at this intersection. You soon come to Langus Riverfront Park along the Snohomish River on your right (restrooms). Pass under I-5. The entrance to the wastewater facility is reached in 1.1 miles from 12th.

(From I-5 southbound, take Exit 198 *North Broadway-Port of Everett* onto SR-529 southbound; cross the Steamboat Slough/Union Slough bridges, and watch for the sign to Langus Riverfront Park; exit right at 0.5 mile onto Frontage Road, which turns left in 0.7 mile and passes under SR-529. At the stop sign with 35th Avenue NE, bear right onto Ross Avenue and continue past the marina, as above.)

Drive east through the treatment complex to a parking lot on the right (0.3 mile). Park here and continue on foot another 350 yards to the southeast corner of the large oxidation lagoon, on the left. A crushed-rock track runs northward next to the fence for nearly a mile, providing excellent viewing of the lagoon and the smaller polishing pond north of it. (Birds of the saltwater marshland east of the track are similar to those of Spencer Island, described below.)

In migration and winter, the ponds may be crowded with freshwater ducks or they may be nearly empty. High tides often drive waterfowl to take refuge here, as does hunting pressure during the open season (October–January). The ponds are large, so if you are careful, the birds will usually swim away from you rather than taking flight. You will not regret toting your scope.

Canada Goose, Gadwall, Mallard, Northern Shoveler, and Ruddy Duck are resident. Cinnamon Teal is uncommon spring through fall, along with a very few Blue-winged Teal (May–June). From fall to winter Wood Duck, American Wigeon, Northern Pintail, Green-winged Teal, Canvasback, Ring-necked Duck, both scaups, Bufflehead, Common Goldeneye, Hooded Merganser, and Horned Grebe are present in varying numbers; look carefully also for the odd Eurasian Wigeon, Redhead, Surf Scoter or other sea duck, Barrow's Goldeneye, or Eared Grebe.

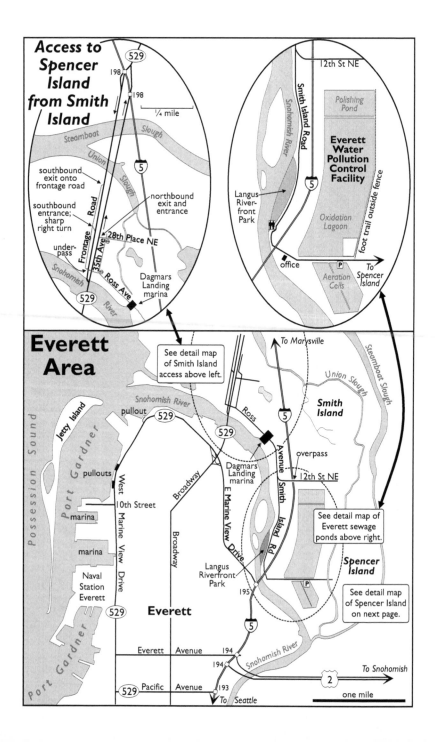

Access to Spencer Island from Smith Island

529
198
198
¼ mile
Steamboat Slough
Union Slough
5
southbound exit onto frontage road
southbound entrance; sharp right turn
Frontage Road
underpass
35th Ave
28th Place NE
northbound exit and entrance
Snohomish River
529
Ross Ave
Dagmars Landing marina

12th St NE
Smith Island Road
Snohomish River
Polishing Pond
Everett Water Pollution Control Facility
foot trail outside fence
Langus Riverfront Park
Oxidation Lagoon
5
office
Aeration Cells
P
To Spencer Island

Everett Area

See detail map of Smith Island access above left.

To Marysville
Snohomish River
pullout
529
Ross
5
Union Slough
Smith Island
Steamboat Slough

Jetty Island
Possession Sound
Port Gardner
pullouts
West Marine Drive
10th Street
marina
marina
Naval Station Everett
529
Everett
Broadway
Broadway
E Marine View Drive
529
Dagmars Landing marina
Avenue
overpass
12th St NE
See detail map of Everett sewage ponds above right.
Langus Riverfront Park
195
Smith Island Rd
P
Spencer Island
See detail map of Spencer Island on next page.
5
Everett Avenue 194
194
Snohomish River
To Snohomish
2
Port Gardner
529 Pacific Avenue 193
To Seattle
one mile

The ponds attract many gulls. Glaucous-winged is present all year (common except in summer). Bonaparte's is common October–November. Ring-billed and California are fairly common to uncommon in migration, uncommon to rare in winter. Herring and Thayer's can usually be found in winter. Western occurs annually (winter). Ranks of Mew (winter) and other species often line the border of the lagoon. Winter high tides may drive Black-bellied Plover and Dunlin to roost around the pond edges.

Directions for returning to I-5 follow the Spencer Island account.

SPENCER ISLAND

The Snohomish estuary consists of numerous low-lying islands separated by sloughs. Across Union Slough to the east of Smith Island (where the Everett sewage ponds are situated) is 412-acre Spencer Island, diked and converted to farmland around 1930 but now managed for wildlife and non-motorized recreation. The north end is owned by the

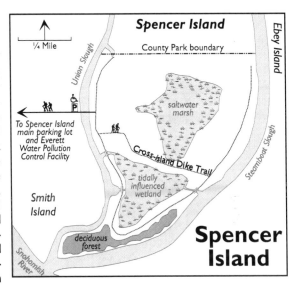

Washington Department of Fish and Wildlife, while the southern half is a county park. Most birders visit just this southern part, along a loop trail (not handicap accessible) atop dikes that have been breached in several places, creating tidally influenced wetlands in the interior of the island.

Park at the lot 0.3 mile east of the sewage plant entrance, as described above. Walk east from the parking lot along the road for 700 yards and cross the old iron bridge to Spencer Island. Take the trail right from the end of the bridge, then walk left onto the dike that crosses the island. A right turn at the far end of this cross-island trail will take you along Steamboat Slough and back around the south end of the island to the iron bridge, with woodland birding opportunities.

Wetlands host Virginia Rail year round, nesting Spotted Sandpiper, and modest numbers of other shorebirds in migration—mostly yellowlegs, Least Sandpiper, dowitchers, and Wilson's Snipe (fall). Tree, Violet-green, Northern Rough-winged, Cliff, and Barn Swallows are abundant (March–August);

Purple Martin and Bank Swallow have been recorded. Present in marshlands and bordering woods in nesting season are Vaux's Swift, Anna's and Rufous Hummingbirds, Downy, Hairy, and Pileated Woodpeckers, Western Wood-Pewee, Willow Flycatcher, Black-capped Chickadee, Marsh and Bewick's Wrens, Swainson's Thrush, Cedar Waxwing, Common Yellowthroat, Yellow Warbler, Black-headed Grosbeak, Red-winged Blackbird, Purple Finch, and American Goldfinch. Raptors at various seasons include Osprey, Bald Eagle, Northern Harrier, Sharp-shinned, Cooper's, and Red-tailed Hawks, and Peregrine Falcon. In winter, Fox, Song, Lincoln's, and Golden-crowned Sparrows flock together with Dark-eyed Juncos along slough edges and in brushy places. Eastern Kingbird has nested on the island for many years. On certain June mornings when cold, cloudy weather forces them down from the mountains, hundreds of Black Swifts may forage at eye level over the wetlands and nearby sewage lagoons.

To reach I-5 *northbound* (see *Access* inset map, page 166), retrace your route past Langus Riverfront Park and the marina to the intersection with 35th. Turn right here and continue 0.3 mile to 28th Place NE, turn left, then immediately right onto SR-529. The northbound I-5 onramp exits left in 1.3 miles, after the highway divides.

To return to Everett and I-5 *southbound,* retrace your route as above, but at the Ross/35th intersection stay left beneath the overpass and follow Frontage Road north. In 0.5 mile a sharp right puts you onto SR-529 southbound and over the Snohomish River bridge to an exit for Marine View Drive, on the right (0.9 mile). Get off here. At the traffic light at the end of the offramp loop, you can turn left with SR-529 to the Everett waterfront (see below). A right turn will take you south on Marine View Drive to a southbound I-5 onramp in 1.5 miles.

EVERETT WATERFRONT

A visit to the Everett waterfront is a good way to round out your day list. (See map on page 166.) Turn left at the aforementioned traffic light and follow SR-529 as it swings west onto Marine View Drive. In 0.9 mile, after descending a bridge across the railroad tracks, turn immediately right to a shoreline access at the mouth of the Snohomish River. Scan for Ospreys (numerous nests on pilings), various waterbirds, and shorebirds on the flats exposed at low tide. In 0.4 mile farther south on W Marine View Drive, a pullout on the right offers great views of the harbor. In a another 0.4 mile, turn right onto 10th Street (signs for Port of Everett) to the public boat launch (restrooms), another good viewing spot. The parking area ($3 fee from May through September) often has a lot of gulls in winter. Purple Martins from the colony across the estuary at Priest Point sometimes forage here. Just offshore to the west is **Jetty Island**, a dredge-spoil barrier separating Port Gardner—the natural harbor at the river's mouth—from Possession Sound. The two-mile-long,

200-yard-wide island is served by a passenger ferry operated daily from July 5 through Labor Day. Sandy beaches and a lagoon provide nesting habitat for gulls; shorebird migration beginning in July is another attraction.

To reach I-5 northbound, continue south on SR-529 past the marina, then left onto Everett Avenue. For I-5 southbound, go four blocks farther south and turn left onto Pacific Avenue.

TULALIP BAY

To reach Tulalip Bay, west of Marysville on the Tulalip Indian Reservation, take Exit 199 from I-5 and drive west 4.7 miles on Marine Drive NE (Tulalip Road) to a traffic light at 64th Street NW. Turn left here, then right (0.3 mile) onto Totem Beach Road. In 0.7 mile, park at the Tulalip Marina (restrooms). In winter, scope the sheltered bay for seabirds. White-winged Scoter—comparatively scarce in the southern Salish Sea—is regular here. Black Turnstones rest on rock jetties and log booms; American and Pacific Golden-Plovers and Bar-tailed Godwit have been seen in fall and winter among commoner shorebirds on the distant spit toward the southwest.

For closer views of the spit, go back along Totem Beach Road to 64th (reset to 0.0 mile). Continue ahead, following Mission Beach Road onto the peninsula on the south side of the bay, reaching the base of the spit in 1.2 miles. Scope from here and from a couple of other viewpoints on the way in. Birding is best an hour or two on either side of the high-tide mark, when birds are pushed in to roost on the narrowed spit. Note that Marine Beach Road serves private residential property. Shoulders are narrow, and no designated public parking is provided. Make sure to pull off only where possible to do so completely out of traffic and without blocking access to driveways; out of courtesy to residents, remain close to your vehicle and be ready to move it if asked.

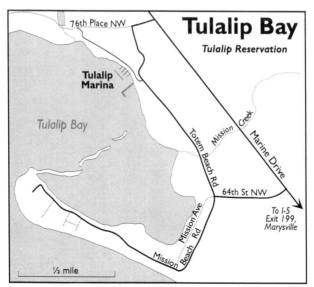

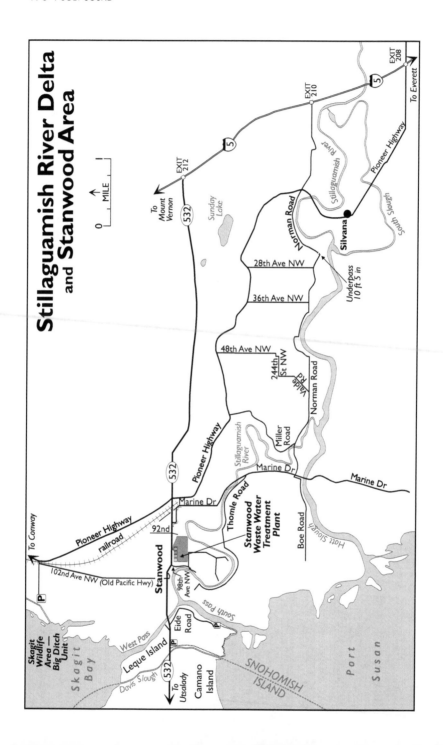

Stillaguamish River Delta and Stanwood Area

STANWOOD AND CAMANO ISLAND

by Hal Opperman

revised by Hal Opperman

The Stillaguamish River discharges into two tidal channels south of Stanwood: West Pass, joining Skagit Bay, and South Pass, joining Port Susan. Like a miniature version of the Snohomish estuary, the sloughs and alluvial deposits at the mouth of the river have been diked to create dry land for crops and dairying. Taken as a whole, this is a major site for waterfowl and shorebirds from late fall to early spring, and supports a large population of wintering raptors. It is an area of hemispheric significance for Snow Geese and Dunlins. To the west lies Camano Island, reached by a high bridge over West Pass. The Camano shoreline offers several fine viewpoints for scoping Skagit Bay, Saratoga Passage, and Livingston Bay—highly productive waters for waterfowl, loons, grebes, and alcids, especially in the colder months.

STILLAGUAMISH DELTA

For a tour of the Stillaguamish delta, go west from I-5 Exit 208 toward Silvana on Pioneer Highway. The road turns northwest, enters the town of Silvana, turns north, and crosses the Stillaguamish. Immediately after the bridge, turn left onto **Norman Road** (3.6 miles from I-5). When partially flooded in spring, open fields on the right can attract migrating shorebirds; look them over from Norman Road or from any of the connecting roads running north to Pioneer Highway. At the junction with Miller Road, stay left on Norman, which crosses the river once more, to a stop sign at Marine Drive (4.7 miles from the beginning of Norman Road). Go straight across onto **Boe Road**, with the Hatt Slough dike on your left. The main attraction along this road is waterfowl (sometimes thousands of Snow Geese) and shorebirds in the fields, especially on high tides. Look, too, for Merlin and Peregrine Falcon. In winter, Short-eared Owl may be seen here or elsewhere on the delta—primarily at daybreak or in late afternoon—and Snowy Owl at any time of day during an invasion year. Boe Road dead-ends in 1.4 miles at the levee along Port Susan. The Nature Conservancy owns 4,000 acres across the levee, including a formerly diked tract recently reconverted to tidal inundation. Visits to this Port Susan Bay Preserve are by advance permission only. (See details at the entrance sign, or visit *www.nature.org/washington*.)

Go back to Marine Drive and turn left. In 0.9 mile turn left onto **Thomle Road**, which ends in 1.9 miles at a food-processing plant. The winter possibilities are similar to those along Boe Road, including American Pipit and Western Meadowlark in the fields and a good diversity of sparrows in brushy spots. Permission to enter the fields is sometimes granted at the plant office; otherwise, scan or scope from the roadway.

Return to Marine Drive. Turn left (north), cross the river again, then, just before the SR-532 underpass, turn left with Marine Drive onto what older maps call 267th Street NW, and continue to the traffic light (1.4 miles from the Thomle Road junction). Go left onto SR-532, and in another 0.2 mile turn left onto the stub end of 92nd Avenue NW and park. This is presently the only publicly accessible spot to scope any part of the **Stanwood Waste Water Treatment Plant**—one corner of one pond. Freshwater ducks (dabblers plus scaups and other *Aythya* species) are the most numerous inhabitants, but you may also find an interesting gull or shorebird (phalaropes in migration). Unusual passerines have been found along the weedy dikes and fencerows. Swallows can be abundant in migration.

Turn left onto SR-532 and head west out of Stanwood, up and over the high bridge. Part way down the embankment on the other side of the bridge (1.1 miles), note the turnoff to **Eide Road** on the left, but *keep driving, because left turns are not permitted here*. Turn around farther on at a less hazardous spot and approach this turnoff from the west. Eide Road follows the levee along the east side of Leque (pronounced *LEK-wee*) Island, formed between Camano Island and the mainland by sediment from the outwash of the Stillaguamish and now constituting the **Leque Island Unit** of the WDFW's Skagit Wildlife Area (Discover Pass required). Park in the first parking lot (0.6 mile) or the second, larger one a bit farther in, and walk on ahead. Rubber boots will serve you well from fall through spring, even sometimes in summer.

Dikes protecting this former farmland from flooding have not been maintained for years and have a history of failing. A major breach in 2010, shored up provisionally with a makeshift patch, left behind several shallow ponds just past the parking lots. Replenished regularly by high-tide seepage, these ponds have proven hospitable to shorebirds. Black-bellied Plover, Killdeer (breeds), Greater Yellowlegs, Dunlin, and Western Sandpiper can be found nearly year round. Semipalmated Plover, Solitary Sandpiper (uncommon, mostly August), Lesser Yellowlegs, Whimbrel (mostly May), Baird's, Least, Pectoral, Semipalmated, and Western Sandpipers, Short-billed and Long-billed Dowitchers, Wilson's Snipe, and Wilson's and Red-necked Phalaropes are regular in decent numbers in migration, and Spotted Sandpiper in breeding season only. The list of rare, casual, and accidental visitors includes Black-necked Stilt, American Avocet, American and Pacific Golden-Plovers, Willet, Hudsonian and Marbled Godwits, Red Knot, Ruff, Sharp-tailed and Stilt Sandpipers, Red-necked Stint, and Sanderling. No one knows how much longer this shorebird bonanza will last. A long-term management plan for the wildlife area, which may or may not include preservation and enhancement of shorebird habitat, is under development.

In winter, Short-eared Owls can be numerous at dusk. Although much rarer, Long-eared Owls have roosted here regularly in recent winters. Snowy Owls are often in the area in a good flight year—look for them on low perches such as fenceposts, driftwood and other detritus along dikes, or on the ground. Barn Owls shelter in dense shrubbery but are rarely abroad in daylight. Bald Eagle, Northern Harrier, and Red-tailed and Rough-legged Hawks are present in winter—sometimes in high numbers—along with less common raptors such as Merlin and Peregrine Falcon. Leque Island provides excellent habitat for sparrows and other wintering passerines. Small trees and brush sometimes have flocks of Yellow-rumped Warbler and Purple Finch, and many unusual species have been found here over the years, including Say's Phoebe and Northern Mockingbird.

Walk on out along the dike where you can, but blackberry growth makes this difficult or impossible in most places. Three easily recognizable access points before and between the two parking lots allow views across the channel to the dike on the Thomle Road side (Snowy Owls some winters). Another way is to proceed south from the ponds along the east edge of the field to its end (look for wintering Western Meadowlarks), then clamber up onto the dike at a promontory overlooking **Port Susan**. This shallow bay is great for shorebirds an hour or two before and after high tide, when a relatively narrow zone is exposed between land and water's edge. At low tides the birds disperse over vast areas of mudflats extending almost farther than the eye can see. At high tide, viewing can be good for shallows-loving waterbirds. A Snow Goose flock is often at Port Susan in winter, and if something puts them up, 20,000 geese create an impressive snowstorm to the south. From here, you can continue to walk the perimeter of the island clockwise on the dike, in the fields, or along Davis Slough, to another WDFW parking area on the south side of SR-532. Stay out of the fields when waterfowl and pheasant hunters are present (roughly, October–January; current regulations are usually posted in parking lots).

To continue west toward Camano Island on SR-532, you must first go right from Eide Road, then turn around in Stanwood and head back west across the high bridge. Pull off quickly on the right at the foot of the bridge (0.1 mile past Eide Road). A dike at this north end of Leque Island was left unrepaired after its collapse several years ago, and the land is now flooded or at least extremely wet most of the time. Wintering Black-bellied Plovers may roost or feed here; dowitchers and sometimes other shorebirds may appear in migration. Flocks of Snow Goose, Trumpeter Swan, and other species of waterfowl fly freely back and forth between Port Susan and Skagit Bay, especially on an incoming tide. Dunlins rise up in large balls when displaced by the tide or by the Merlins and Peregrine Falcons that pursue them. Up to 50,000 Dunlins winter on Port Susan/Skagit Bay, one of the largest concentrations in North America.

Another pullout on the right in 0.3 mile, on Camano Island just across the Davis Slough bridge, offers similar possibilities. Land west of the dike on both sides of SR-532 is private and posted. In winter, many raptors patrol the fields and the salt marsh or avail themselves of handy perches. Bald Eagle, Northern Harrier, and Red-tailed and Rough-legged Hawks are common. Sharp-shinned and Cooper's Hawks are fairly common, and Harlan's Red-tailed Hawk and Gyrfalcon have occurred.

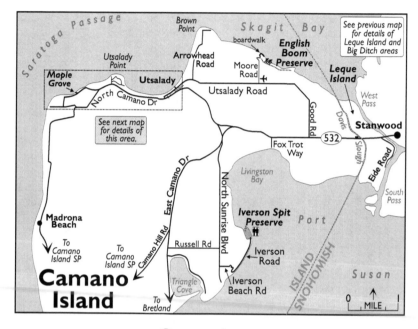

CAMANO ISLAND

Seven miles across at its north end and tapering 15 miles to its south point, Camano Island was completely logged over between 1855 and 1920. Conforming to the typical pattern of Puget Lowlands land-use succession, the level ground was then cleared of stumps and used for agriculture for many decades. Today, the last farm fields and second-growth forest are disappearing beneath a wave of residential development. Most of the shoreline is private. However, a few publicly accessible points provide an opportunity to view the marine environment and its rich birdlife, while remnant woods and other upland habitats can be sampled along the quiet roadsides and in parks. Breeding has been documented for 80 species on the north part of the island, and over 130 species have been found there on the Skagit Bay Christmas Bird Count.

From the pullout at Davis Slough on SR-532, travel west 0.9 mile and turn right onto Good Road, which bends west and becomes Utsalady Road. In 1.8 miles, just past the airport, turn right (north) and follow Moore Road to its end in 0.6 mile, staying right to a parking area, picnic shelter, and interpretive signage near the beach. This is **English Boom Preserve**, a county park on the southwest edge of Skagit Bay. All that remains of the boom (log-sorting and rafting facility) of the English Logging Company is the forest of pilings offshore, now fitted out with Purple Martin nest boxes. The shoreline to the west is private. To the east a muddy beach stretches all the way to Davis Slough; a small salt marsh cut across by tidal channels lies between it and the bluffs. You may bird this area from a beachside boardwalk (flooded at winter high tides) or along the trail across logs and channels on private land closer to the bluff, generally passable at any season (1.0 mile round trip).

In winter, Green-winged Teal and other dabbling ducks use this habitat, as do shorebirds (mostly Dunlins). Among the resident songbirds, listen for three species of wren (Pacific, Marsh, Bewick's). This part of the bay is shallow, and probably best birded on an outgoing tide. Depending on tides, wind direction, and where the hunters happen to be pushing them on a given day, thousands of ducks may be present. Diving birds feed along a deep channel offshore, among them Greater Scaup, scoters, Bufflehead, Common Goldeneye, Red-breasted Merganser, loons, and grebes (mostly Horned and Red-necked). When the Snow Goose flock is resident on the Fir Island tidelands, you will see a white mass like a snowbank four or five miles across Skagit Bay to the northeast.

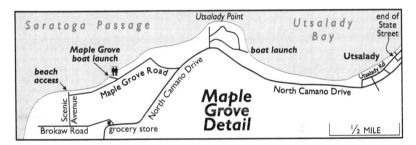

Go back out to Utsalady Road, turn right, and drive over to Utsalady. In the heyday of logging, Utsalady could boast of the busiest port and one of the largest mills on Puget Sound, but today it is a sleepy retirement community without so much as a convenience store. Three open lots on the right side of the road offer lookouts onto **Utsalady Bay**. The first one is in 1.8 miles, opposite the end of State Street. On the leeward side of the island from the prevailing southwest winds, the sheltered bay harbors scoters, Buffleheads, dozens of goldeneyes (including many Barrow's), Red-throated and Common Loons, and sometimes one or two Eared Grebes or a Thayer's Gull. In calm weather you may see birds of deeper waters farther out on Saratoga Passage. Utsalady Road continues another 0.3 mile, past the other two lots, and bends left to a stop sign at North Camano Drive. Turn right here. In 1.1 miles, turn right onto Utsalady Point Road, which doubles back and drops down to a public boat launch (0.3 mile) where you can scope the west side of Utsalady Bay.

Come back up and turn right onto North Camano Drive. In 0.2 mile take another right onto Maple Grove Road and drive down to the **Maple Grove Boat Launch** (0.4 mile; toilets). Saratoga Passage is at its narrowest here—three miles from Whidbey Island—and the deep channel is close to shore. Many birds feed here, and others fly up and down the channel. Practically any Washington gull species is possible. Specialties include Harlequin

Duck; loons (especially Pacific— there are a few records of Yellow-billed); all three cormorants (Brandt's is rare); and alcids (Common Murre irregular fall to spring, Pigeon Guillemot year round, Marbled Murrelet fairly common in winter, Rhinoceros Auklet in summer). In winter, Western Grebes can often be found far out in the channel. This is an excellent place to set up a scope and do a sea-watch when there is activity.

Continue right from the parking lot rather than going back uphill to the left the way you came. Maple Grove Road ends at Scenic Avenue in 0.4 mile. Park out of the way. The right stub of Scenic Avenue is a beach access. The sand-and-cobble beach may have Sanderlings—local on Camano Island due to limited habitat. Scan the waters; Marbled Murrelets are often here, especially to the left (northwest). Drive a couple of blocks up Scenic Avenue away from the beach to its end at Brokaw Road. Turn left and go to the stop sign at Huntington's Grocery corner (0.3 mile), and left onto North Camano Drive. In 3.6 miles, stay right at the fork onto Sunrise Boulevard to a traffic light with East Camano Drive in 0.2 mile, and continue straight ahead on Sunrise. In 2.6 miles, turn left onto Iverson Beach Road, which meanders 0.4 mile to Iverson Road. A left turn brings you to the road-end parking lot in 0.5 mile.

Iverson Spit Preserve, a popular 120-acre county park (toilets), enjoys a splendid setting at the mouth of Livingston Bay. A well-marked 0.9-mile loop trail takes you through several different habitats—salt marsh, tidal channels, freshwater marsh, woods, brushy edges, cultivated field, beach, tide flats, open bay—with their typical birds. You may also walk northward along the beach and the salt marsh behind it. Over 150 species of birds are recorded at Iverson Spit, including a wide selection of dabbling and diving ducks, loons, grebes, and other waterbirds; Bald Eagle, Virginia Rail, Caspian Tern, Mourning Dove; and the expected flycatchers, swallows, and woodland, marsh, and grassland songbirds.

Go back to East Camano Drive and turn right onto SR-532. In 1.1 miles, turn right onto Fox Trot Way, which dead-ends in 0.2 mile. **Livingston Bay**, to the south, can hold thousands of ducks. This is a good vantage point, but the tide runs *waaay* out, so time your visit for a three- or four-hour bracket centered on peak high tide. On sunny days, try for early morning or late afternoon to avoid the glare. You may walk out to the shoreline here. However, beach and tidelands to the east and west are private. Drive east on SR-532 to reach Stanwood.

BIG DITCH

From SR-532 on the west side of Stanwood, turn north onto 102nd Avenue NW. (See map on page 170.) The name changes to Old Pacific Highway as you travel north out of town. In 2.4 miles, just as the road swings right and is about to cross the railroad track, turn left (west) onto a dirt road signed *Big Ditch Access*, which ends in 0.6 mile at a parking lot on the right (Discover Pass required). One of several developed access points to the Skagit Wildlife Area, the **Big Ditch Unit** is located about a mile south of the mouth of the South Fork Skagit River. Walk up onto the dike above the parking lot, across the big drainage ditch that ends at a tide gate on your left, and through a turnstile beside a steel-pipe gate. You are on a high levee with the ditch on the inside. A vast salt marsh covered with cattails and cut through with sloughs extends to the tidelands of Skagit Bay to the west. This is primarily a winter birding site. The levee for a mile northward provides a privileged post from which to scan for raptors, including Peregrine Falcon, which hunts over the marsh and mudflats. In a good flight year there is usually a Snowy Owl or two at Big Ditch. A wintering Snow Goose flock is sometimes out on the intertidal zone.

Drive back out and cross the railroad track to the stop sign at Pioneer Highway. To reach birding sites to the north, turn left and go 4.4 miles to the junction with Fir Island Road in Conway (page 108). If you turn south (right), it is 2.6 miles to SR-532 in Stanwood, and 4.8 miles east from there to I-5.

ACROSS THE SOUND (KITSAP COUNTY)

by Hal Opperman

revised by Hal Opperman

Bainbridge Island and the Kitsap Peninsula, joined together by a highway bridge over Agate Passage, lie between Puget Sound on the east and Hood Canal on the west. Once completely covered by towering lowland forests of the Puget Sound Douglas-fir zone, this area has been 99+ percent logged off and is now a mosaic of second-growth forest, agricultural land, light to medium development (single-family dwellings with parks and other open spaces), and heavy urban/industrial development (around Bremerton). The landscape is endowed with small lakes, ponds, streams, and wetlands (but no large rivers)—and plenty of saltwater shoreline. The area is relatively lightly birded except for one outstanding site—Point No Point—and, incidentally, a few lesser spots along the standard route from Seattle to the North Olympic Coast.

Not that there are few birds! On the contrary, 115 species breed here, and 120 or more are routinely found on Christmas Bird Counts—impressive numbers, considering the county's small size and comparatively uniform habitat. The rural setting offers a good chance to observe the regular Puget Trough landbirds, including Band-tailed Pigeon, Rufous Hummingbird, Red-breasted Sapsucker, Pileated Woodpecker, Olive-sided and Pacific-slope Flycatchers, Hutton's Vireo, Violet-green Swallow, Chestnut-backed Chickadee, Bewick's Wren, Swainson's Thrush, Black-throated Gray and Wilson's Warblers, Spotted Towhee, Western Tanager, Black-headed Grosbeak, and Purple Finch. Owls find the mixture of open forest and clearings to their liking: Great Horned, Northern Pygmy- (uncommon), Barred, and Northern Saw-whet all nest.

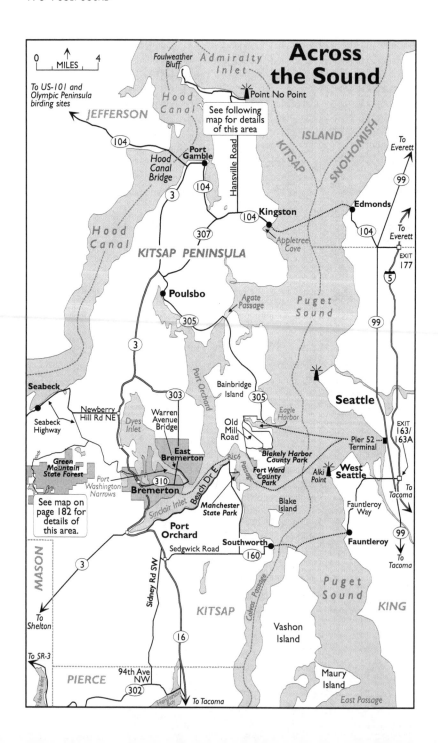

Across the Sound

See following map for details of this area

See map on page 182 for details of this area.

Most visitors arrive by one of the four cross-sound ferry routes. Truth be told, ferry birding is usually dull. Out in the channels you may see alcids, scoters, and gulls as fly-bys or feeding in tidal rips, but birds are far more numerous in protected waters near the terminals where they may readily be seen from shore. Amazing sightings do occur, especially in migration or a day or two after a major storm along the outer coast.

If you should find yourself docking in Kitsap County on a fine early morning in May, June, or July, drive off the ferry, pick up a map, and take some time to go prospecting for birds on your own. Landbirds tend not to be concentrated at a few favored areas, but instead are widely and rather evenly distributed. You are just as likely to find them along the many quiet roadsides as in the public parks. Although most of the shoreline is privately owned, there are numerous spots to get a peek at bays, coves, inlets, and passages. Waterbirding can be good at any season. Pigeon Guillemots nest in sandbank burrows at several places along the shoreline, and the Warren Avenue Bridge across the Port Washington Narrows in Bremerton has a nesting colony of Pelagic Cormorants.

Here are a few suggestions to get you started. If you arrive on the Kingston ferry, check the viewpoints on the west side of Appletree Cove, opposite the ferry dock. On Bainbridge Island, go around the west end of Eagle Harbor (where the ferry arrives) and bird your way south through woods and orchards along Old Mill Road NE to Blakely Harbor County Park—an abandoned mill site with rocky shoreline, salt marsh, meadow, and forest, now under restoration (trails and plantings of native vegetation)—and on to Fort Ward County Park. Seabeck, on Hood Canal about a 15-mile drive from the Bremerton ferry dock, offers mixed woodlands, a saltwater bay, and the productive estuary of Seabeck Creek. Not far from the Southworth ferry landing is forested Manchester State Park (Discover Pass needed to park), north of Manchester on Rich Passage. From here you can follow Beach Drive E along the shoreline to Port Orchard, with seabird and shorebird possibilities.

Ferries to Bremerton and to Bainbridge Island leave from the Pier 52 terminal at the foot of Madison Street in downtown Seattle. The ferry to Kingston leaves from Edmonds (take Exit 177 from I-5 about 13 miles north of downtown Seattle and follow the signs along SR-104 to the dock). The ferry to Southworth—perhaps the most picturesque of the four routes, and often the birdiest—sails from the Fauntleroy terminal in West Seattle. (Take the West Seattle Freeway exit from I-5 about 2.5 miles south of downtown Seattle, then follow the signs along Fauntleroy Way.) Crossing time varies from 30 to 60 minutes, depending on the route. Service is frequent, but waits for auto boarding can be long during commuting hours and on holidays and summer weekends. For automated fare and schedule information, phone 206-464-6400 in Seattle or 800-843-3779 toll-free statewide, or visit http://www.wsdot.wa.gov/ferries on-line.

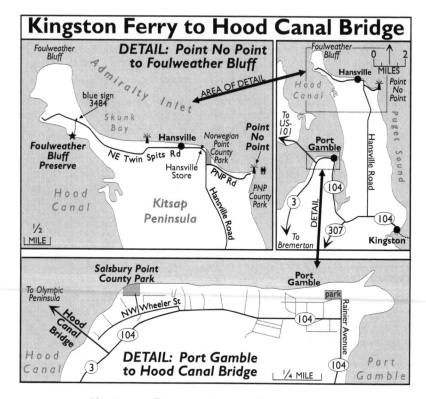

Kingston Ferry to Hood Canal Bridge

DETAIL: Point No Point to Foulweather Bluff

Foulweather Bluff

Admiralty Inlet

AREA OF DETAIL

blue sign 3484

Skunk Bay

Hansville

Norwegian Point County Park

Point No Point

Foulweather Bluff Preserve

Hood Canal

NE Twin Spits Rd

Hansville Store

PNP Rd

Kitsap Peninsula

Hansville Road

PNP County Park

½ MILE

DETAIL: Port Gamble to Hood Canal Bridge

Foulweather Bluff

Hood Canal

Hansville

Point No Point

0 2 MILES

Puget Sound

To US-101

Port Gamble

Hansville Road

104

3

DETAIL

307

104

To Bremerton

Kingston

Salsbury Point County Park

Port Gamble

To Olympic Peninsula

Hood Canal Bridge

NW Wheeler St

park

Rainier Avenue

Hood Canal

3

104

104

104

Port Gamble

¼ MILE

KINGSTON FERRY TO HOOD CANAL BRIDGE

Kitsap County's destination birding site, **Point No Point** is conveniently accessed by the ferry from Edmonds. Drive west on SR-104 from the Kingston ferry ramp to the traffic light at Hansville Road (2.5 miles) and turn right (north). Turn right again in 7.4 miles onto Point No Point Road. The small parking lot at the lighthouse (0.9 mile; toilets) may be full; if so, come back 0.2 mile to a grassy overflow parking strip along the right shoulder or to the adjacent, paved WDFW parking lot and boat launch (ADA accessible; restrooms; Discover Pass required). Walk past the lighthouse along the sandy beach to the point. Admiralty Inlet, on the left, brings oceanic waters to the entrance of Puget Sound, on the right. Strong currents churn up plankton and small invertebrates when tides are running. Large concentrations of Pacific Sand Lance and Pacific Herring gather in the tidal rips at these rich feeding areas, in turn attracting high numbers of marine birds. Until the dramatic decline of the salmon runs, Point No Point was renowned for its sport fishery, for the same reason.

In fall migration, Parasitic Jaegers attend flocks of Common Terns that sometimes number in several dozens. Many hundreds or even thousands of

Bonaparte's Gulls work the rip tides in fall and winter. Rarities such as Black-legged Kittiwake and Sabine's, Black-headed, Little, Laughing, and Franklin's Gulls are sometimes among them. All the regular Washington alcids occur here seasonally (Ancient Murrelet, mostly in November; Cassin's Auklet and Tufted Puffin, rare; single records of Thick-billed Murre, Long-billed Murrelet, and Horned Puffin). Western Washington's first record of Arctic Loon was at Point No Point in the winter of 2000–2001, and Yellow-billed Loon has been seen more than once. When tides go slack, the feeding frenzy ends and most of these birds disappear, but be sure to check the calmer waters back west toward the boat ramp and around the point to the south, which usually have a sprinkling of birds at any tide stage.

To the south and west a cattail marsh, edged by brush, is well worth checking, as is the driftwood-lined beach to the south. Point No Point is something of a songbird migrant trap. High flight numbers sometimes pile up here, among them record counts of Western Kingbird, Cedar Waxwing, Western Tanager, and Black-headed Grosbeak. "Dryside" sparrows (Brewer's, Vesper, Lark, Black-throated) have shown up. Notable vagrant records include Blue-gray Gnatcatcher, White Wagtail (twice), and Indigo Bunting. The uplands to the south—cloaked in mature second-growth forest—are in Point No Point County Park, accessible by a trail that starts where the bluff meets the beach.

Return to Hansville Road and turn right. The road bends left at the Hansville Store (0.1 mile), becoming NE Twin Spits Road. Just before the store, the beach at Norwegian Point County Park, on the right, provides another spot to scope Admiralty Inlet waters and sometimes serves as a high-tide shorebird roost (mostly Black-bellied Plovers).

Continue westward on NE Twin Spits Road. At 2.7 miles from the store, look for a blue address sign numbered 3484, on the right, followed by a pulloff and hidden trailhead in the trees on the left. Park here; this is the access point for The Nature Conservancy's **Foulweather Bluff Preserve**. A short trail leads through mature hardwoods and conifers, with an understory of Sword Fern, Salal, Evergreen Huckleberry, and Cascade Oregon-grape, past a quiet lagoon to the beach on Hood Canal. Hutton's Vireo and other lowland forest birds can be found here. The road ends in another 0.7 mile along the waterfront at Twin Spits, with a view across the mouth of Hood Canal.

Go back to Hansville Road and south to the traffic light at SR-104. Turn right. Follow SR-104 as it turns right at the next traffic light (1.4 miles) and reaches **Port Gamble** in another 3.5 miles. Pay attention to the speed limit in town. Where the highway takes a 90-degree turn to the left (approximately 0.2 mile) go straight ahead a couple of blocks on Rainier Avenue to a small park in the center of this well-preserved old mill town, founded in 1853 by the Puget Mill Company (later Pope & Talbot), once the dominant lumber company on the Sound. At the time of its closing in 1995, the Port Gamble mill was the oldest continuously operated sawmill in the U.S. You can scope the waters of Hood Canal from the overlook, but the log dumps are off-limits. The park's trees may hold passerines in migration. Return to SR-104 and turn right. Just after leaving town turn right onto Wheeler Street (0.8 mile), then right again in 0.2 mile into **Salsbury Point County Park**. The boat-ramp parking lot offers water-level views of Hood Canal, with good seabird possibilities.

Back at the highway, a right turn leads in 0.4 mile to the east end of the Hood Canal Bridge. Here you may turn right with SR-104 to reach Port Townsend and the coast (page 58), or the west shore of Hood Canal (page 214). Continuing straight ahead on SR-3 rather than crossing the bridge will take you down the Kitsap Peninsula toward Bainbridge Island, Bremerton, and points south.

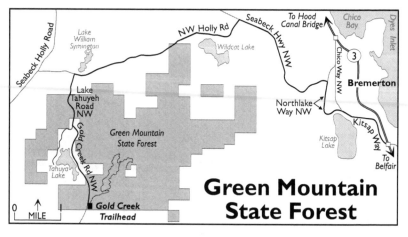

SOUTHERN KITSAP COUNTY

If you are attempting to find Mountain Quail, your itinerary may well point you across the Sound via the Bremerton or Southworth ferries. Introduced long ago and once widespread in Western Washington, this elusive species hangs on in a few scattered populations from the Kitsap Peninsula south and west toward Shelton and Elma. Locations may not be predictable from one year to the next, but Mountain Quail sightings are almost always reported, so it is worth monitoring eBird and Tweeters in advance of your visit. Even if there are current reports, however, your chances of ticking this bird are only fair.

Recently, birders have tended to zero in on the Tahuya Peninsula, in the hook of Hood Canal west of Belfair in Mason County (page 219). However, Mountain Quail appear to be no less numerous in far more lightly birded Kitsap County just north of there. Most of this area is covered by commercial tree farms, with tracts harvested in rotation leaving a few standing trees, stumps, and bare ground, soon colonized by a patchwork of low, scruffy growth. This is ideal Mountain Quail habitat for the decade or so it takes re-planted trees to crowd out the open understory. Forest roads are gated to exclude vehicles but are open to foot traffic. Time spent exploring these roads in the proper early-successional habitat likely will pay off. The quail are far easier to find in the first two or three hours after dawn. The best season is from March to early May when males are calling. They can be heard from a great distance and sometimes come in to recordings. You may hear family groups clucking in the brush, but they are adept at racing away under cover. Count yourself lucky if you get a brief glimpse.

One productive Kitsap County site is **Green Mountain State Forest**. A hike to the summit of Green Mountain through various ages of forest and some meadows (about five miles round trip, 1,200 feet elevation gain) has yielded numerous Mountain Quail observations, as well as Ruffed (near the bottom) and Sooty Grouse. Green Mountain is also the most accessible place in this predominantly low-lying county to find species such as Northern Pygmy-Owl, Hammond's Flycatcher, Cassin's Vireo, Gray Jay (summit), Townsend's Warbler, and Townsend's/Hermit hybrid types.

The best birding route to the summit departs from the Gold Creek trailhead. Exit from SR-3 at Kitsap Way in Bremerton and turn west (east from this exit, SR-310 leads to the Bremerton ferry landing). At a Y-intersection in 1.4 miles, take the left fork (Northlake Way NW). In 1.0 mile, turn left onto Seabeck Highway NW, then left in another 3.0 miles onto NW Holly Road. Continue 4.2 miles to the intersection with Tahuyeh Lake Road NW (aka Lake Tahuyeh Road NW) and turn left. In 1.2 miles, stay to the left onto Gold Creek Road NW. The trailhead parking lot is in 1.8 miles on your left (restrooms; Discover Pass required). Be aware that parts of the forest may be closed during logging operations, and that this popular trail is used by motor-cycles, ATVs, horses, and mountain bikes as well as by hikers. Weekday mornings are usually the most peaceful time for birding.

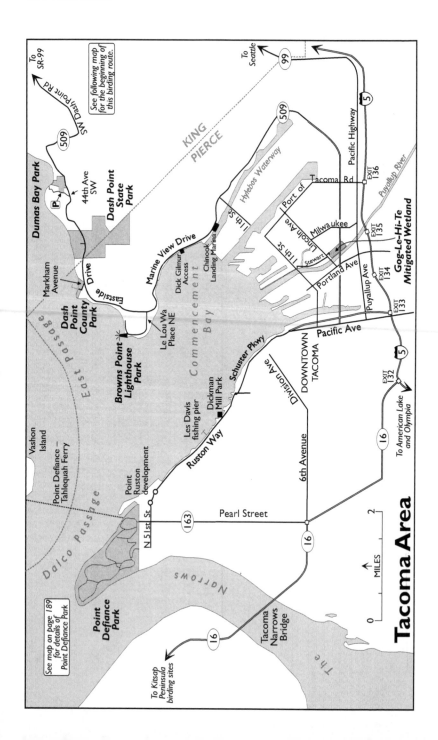

Tacoma Area

TACOMA AND VICINITY

by Bill Shelmerdine and Thais Bock

revised by Bruce LaBar and Art Wang

The logging, shipping, and manufacturing center of Tacoma lies at the southeast corner of the main basin of Puget Sound. Here the Puyallup River (pronounced pew-AHL-up), with its tributaries the Carbon and the White, delivers Mount Rainier's glacial meltwaters to Commencement Bay. Like Seattle, the city is built where ancient forests once stood, and the tideflats and estuary have been dredged, channeled, and filled to create the deepwater port and rail yards. In this intensively urbanized setting, a necklace of viewpoints strung along the shoreline on both sides of Commencement Bay offers fine saltwater birding in fall, winter, and spring. Christmas Bird Count data show that White-winged Scoter, Pacific Loon, Brandt's and Pelagic Cormorants, Common Murre, Pigeon Guillemot, Rhinoceros Auklet, and Bonaparte's and Thayer's Gulls are all many times more abundant in Tacoma than in Seattle (but Seattle is far stronger in Brant, Harlequin Duck, and Black Scoter). Point Defiance Park, at the west end of this chain of viewpoints, is the birding gem of the metropolitan area. Here the waters of the South Sound and those of the Main Basin mix at The Narrows, creating optimal seabird foraging conditions. A splendid swatch of the original forest subsists in the uplands of the park. American Lake, in the nearby suburbs, is worth checking for wintering waterfowl and for gulls in fall and winter when large flocks of Bonaparte's Gulls are sometimes present.

DES MOINES MARINA TO COMMENCEMENT BAY

A tour of saltwater parks begins at the **Des Moines Marina**. (See map on next page.) Go west from I-5 Exit 149 (Exit 149B, if northbound), following SR-516 (aka Kent Des Moines Road) to its end in 1.9 miles. Curve right (north) onto SR-509 (aka Marine View Drive) and drive 0.3 mile to S 223rd Street. Turn left for five blocks to a right curve where S 223rd becomes Cliff Avenue S. A left at the stop sign takes you to the marina's long fishing pier and breakwater; go straight ahead to reach adjacent Beach Park where Des Moines Creek empties into Puget Sound. Gulls line the pier's railings; wintering wigeons, Harlequin Duck, all three scoters, both goldeneyes, and grebes provide close-up viewing. Return to Marine View Drive and continue south 1.7 miles. Turn right onto South 251st Street, then immediately left onto 8th Place S to the entrance of **Saltwater State Park** (Discover Pass required), just ahead. Look for Black Scoter in winter, Brant in spring, and a variety of landbirds on forested bluffs.

Return to Marine View Drive and continue south to its end (1.0 mile), then double back to the left with the arterial, which becomes Woodmont Drive S. At the traffic light (0.6 mile), turn right (south) onto 16th Avenue S to the next traffic light at S 272nd Street (0.7 mile). Go right here, winding your way downhill (street names change several times) to Redondo Beach Drive S (0.9

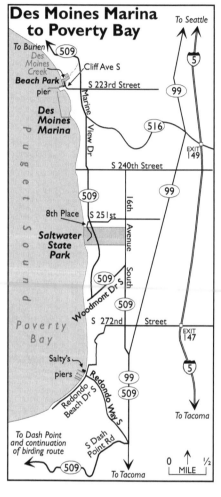

Des Moines Marina to Poverty Bay

To Seattle

To Burien
509
Des Moines Creek
Cliff Ave S
S 223rd Street
99
5

Beach Park
pier

Des Moines Marina
Marine View Dr
516
EXIT 149

S 240th Street

509
16th Avenue
99

8th Place
S 251st

Saltwater State Park
South Avenue

509
Woodmont Dr S
509

S 272nd Street
EXIT 147

Poverty Bay

Salty's
piers
99
509
5

Redondo Beach Dr S
Redondo Way S

To Tacoma

To Dash Point and continuation of birding route
S Dash Point Rd
509

To Tacoma

0 — ½ MILE

Puget Sound

mile). Turn left to a fishing pier, boat launch, and boardwalk on Poverty Bay (0.1 mile). Pigeon Guillemots and Rhinoceros Auklets favor this area.

From Salty's Restaurant, take Redondo Way S uphill (southeast) 1.0 mile to the intersection with S Dash Point Road (SR-509). Turn right and stay on SR-509 and SW Dash Point Road for 5.0 miles, with many sharp turns, including a right at a traffic light at mile 3.1 and a left at mile 4.0, past a sewage treatment plant and Dumas Bay Centre to 44th Avenue SW. Turn right (north) and go 0.2 mile to a parking lot on the right for **Dumas Bay Park**. (Turn back to page 184 to follow route on map.) Walk downhill through the woods for five minutes, looking for Pileated Woodpeckers and wintering Varied Thrushes, to the beach and the large, shallow bay fed by three streams. Loons, rafts of wigeons, and shorebirds are among the seasonal features. Virginia Rail and Sora are summer residents in the freshwater marsh. A few Great Blue Heron nests may be glimpsed through trees lining the road.

Return to SR-509, continue west 0.9 mile, and turn right into **Dash Point State Park** (Discover Pass required). Trails and campgrounds are good for woodland birds such as Hutton's Vireo and Townsend's Warbler. Along the saltwater shore and wide beach look for loons and alcids.

Return to SR-509 (now called East Side Drive NE), continue west, and after crossing into Pierce County turn right at Markham Avenue NE (0.6 mile). The short road winds down into **Dash Point County Park**. The fishing pier can be productive for alcids. Ancient Murrelets (November–December) are difficult to find nowadays, although Pigeon Guillemots are usual. Parasitic Jaegers appear in September when Common Terns are in migration.

Go back to SR-509/East Side Drive NE and continue west, then south, 1.5 miles to Brown's Point Shopping Center on the right. Angle right (west) here onto Le Lou Wa Place NE (becomes Tok A Lou Avenue NE) and go 0.6 mile to **Browns Point Lighthouse Park**. Marbled Murrelets have become rare in South Puget Sound, but are still fairly reliable here; in May and June they can be seen in breeding plumage. Titlow Beach at the south end of the Narrows, Point Defiance, and the ferry to Vashon Island may be better spots to search.

Return to SR-509 and continue downhill (southeast) to **Commencement Bay** (1.2 miles), at the eastern margin of what used to be the tideflats at the mouth of the Puyallup River. Stop at the first large turnout past the Marina at Browns Point (at sea level) and also a little bit farther along at the well-signed Dick Gilmur Memorial Shoreline Public Access pullout to scan log booms for dozens of herons and large flocks of gulls at high tide. Rarities such as Black-tailed, Slaty-backed, and Franklin's Gulls have been found in this area. Any of the numerous pullouts can be productive, especially the one just past the Chinook Landing Marina, as SR-509 continues southeastward along Hylebos Waterway. Look for Least and Western Sandpipers (migration), Black Turnstones on log booms (winter), and rafts of ducks during migration. Beginning at 0.2 mile past the Chinook Landing pullout, you can begin to see Purple Martin nest boxes on pilings to your right. To get a good view, however, turn right at E 11th Street and park at a small weedy, graveled area on the right less than 0.1 mile from SR-509.

Return to SR-509 and turn right. SR-509 bends south and west around the end of Hylebos Waterway. Exit SR-509 at Port of Tacoma Road (offramp 5.1 miles from Dick Gilmur Access) and turn left (south) to Pacific Highway East (SR-99) (0.3 mile). Turn right on Pacific Highway East, cross the Puyallup River, then turn right on E Portland Avenue (1.2 miles), drive 0.5 mile, and turn right at the light on Lincoln Avenue. Recross the Puyallup River and turn right in 0.3 mile to the **Gog-Le-Hi-Te Mitigated Wetland** (aka Lincoln Avenue Marsh). *(For a direct route from I-5 to Gog-Le-Hi-Te, take Exit 135 to Portland Avenue and go north 0.7 mile on E Portland Avenue toward the Port of Tacoma, then turn right at the light on Lincoln Avenue.)* This rehabilitated garbage dump in the vast wasteland of industrial Tacoma has hosted a number of surprising species since 1990 (a Bar-tailed Godwit visited the new marsh upon its completion). More than 120 species have been photographed here since 2009. Green Herons nest here. Two openings to the river allow daily tidal action on the mudflats, which feature two ponds, one close to Lincoln Avenue and the other farther east up river. Both are good for shorebirds during spring and fall. More recently this area has proven to be a hotspot for large gulls in winter. Thayer's occurs in nearly pure flocks, Glaucous is regular, Slaty-backed has appeared almost annually, a Lesser Black-backed Gull was a one-day bird in January 2014, and a Kumlien's Iceland Gull stayed for over two weeks in January 2000. When searching for gulls, check also the roof of the meat-rendering plant just to the east and other roofs in the vicinity.

On leaving the wetland, turn left on Lincoln Avenue, then right onto Stewart Street (0.1 mile). Drive down Stewart through the industrial area along the Puyallup River, stopping to check for gulls bathing in the river, then staying to the left of a guard gate and going under the bridge. Park where the road ends (0.8 mile). A trail next to a chain-link fence leads to the mouth of the river and Commencement Bay. At certain tide stages you may find many more gulls along the river here than at Gog-Le-Hi-Te.

Return to Lincoln Avenue and drive southwest across the Puyallup River bridge, turning right (northwest) onto East Portland Avenue right after the bridge. Travel 0.8 mile on Portland to E 11th Street and park at the closed bridge on the right. Walk up to the top for a different view of the bathing gulls in the river. This has been a great spot for Slaty-backed Gull and other uncommon gulls. Be sure to check the nearby roof tops for resting gulls.

Turn left (southwest) on 11th Street and cross over the Thea Foss Waterway on the Murray Morgan Bridge into the heart of Tacoma. Turn right on Pacific Avenue and continue west 0.3 mile to the Schuster Parkway. Follow the parkway as it curves northwestward along the shoreline. Move into the left lane, and in 1.4 miles take the overpass across the railroad tracks onto **Ruston Way**, lined by a two-mile scenic waterfront park. Several turnouts with parking provide good access. Look for gulls and other waterbirds, and sometimes Black Turnstone. Barrow's Goldeneyes are often present in winter; check around pilings and dilapidated piers, such as at Dickman Mill Park. The **Les Davis Fishing Pier** (1.4 mile) provides sheltered viewing and restrooms. Purple Martins and Pigeon Guillemots are present at several spots along the waterfront in summer. Waterfront access by vehicle ends at the new Point Ruston development, but there is a paved trail behind this development that connects with the beginning of Point Defiance Park. This is another great area to view Commencement Bay for waterbirds. Continue on Ruston Way as it bends westward and, at the second roundabout, becomes N 51st Street. Turn right in 0.3 mile onto Pearl Street (SR-163) to the east entrance to Point Defiance Park (0.2 mile).

POINT DEFIANCE AND THE NARROWS

A thumb of land projecting into Puget Sound at a mile-wide constriction called The Narrows, Point Defiance is Tacoma's destination birding site. Large volumes of water flow though the passage from the South Sound to the main basin of Puget Sound and back again, across a shallow sill, creating strong currents and tidal rips. Mixing of deep and surface waters here brings an upwelling of nutrients, and consequently ideal feeding conditions for marine birds as well as seals, sea lions, and salmon. The seasonal seabird occurrence at Point Defiance ranks as one of the best in the state. From fall through spring large numbers of Bonaparte's, Mew, and other gulls, and alcids and other diving birds, feed in The Narrows and surrounding saltwater areas.

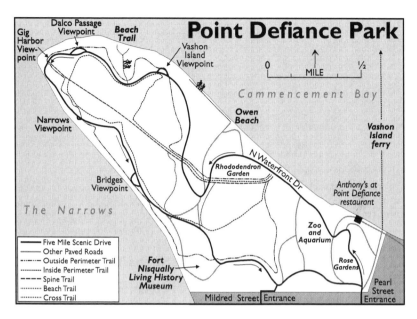

All of the birding sites and viewpoints are contained within 765-acre **Point Defiance Park**. Around the end of the point are high bluffs from which you can look down upon the water. Beach trails—especially at the northeast base of the point—allow water-level viewing. Several walking trails in the upland portion lead through beautiful remnants of the Puget Sound Douglas-fir forest. The Point Defiance Zoo and Aquarium, Rhododendron Garden, and Fort Nisqually Living History Museum provide additional attractions for birders and non-birders alike.

The information kiosk (free maps) just inside the Pearl Street entrance is a good place to start. The wintering wigeon flock on the nearby lawns and pond almost always includes Eurasian Wigeon. Drive the Five-Mile Scenic Drive loop road counterclockwise. Turnoffs near the beginning take you to the boathouse and public marina and (farther ahead) to **Owen Beach**, providing views of the calm waters of outer Commencement Bay. Scan here for a variety of waterbirds. You can also backtrack along the waterfront to the Point Defiance ferry terminal for additional views. From Owen Beach, walk the beach path northwestward. The strata exposed in the bluffs tell the story of the last great advance and retreat of the Puget Lobe of the continental ice sheets (17,000–13,000 years BP).

Return to Five Mile Scenic Drive and continue the loop. Walk the trails to explore old-growth conifer forest with the typical suite of tree species of the Puget Lowlands. Many of the massive trees and snags show signs of active woodpecker work. The common bird species include Steller's Jay, Black-capped and Chestnut-backed Chickadees, Red-breasted Nuthatch, Brown

Creeper, Pacific Wren, and Golden-crowned Kinglet. Hutton's Vireo (year round) and Townsend's Warbler (winter) are frequently present as are Hairy and Pileated Woodpeckers and many other species. Listen for flocks of Red Crossbills and Pine Siskins overhead. In summer, add Pacific-slope Flycatcher and Swainson's Thrush. In winter, a few Hermit and Varied Thrushes are present.

Scope the water from each of several bluff viewpoints, all the way around the point to Fort Nisqually. The outer portion of the loop road is sometimes gated and requires a walk that is well worth the effort. Try to check at least **Vashon Island, Dalco Passage,** and **Gig Harbor Viewpoints**. Take the secondary beach trail about a quarter-mile past the Vashon Island Viewpoint for water-level viewing. A few Pigeon Guillemots nest in the north bluff. From fall through spring, Double-crested and Pelagic Cormorants, Common Murres, and Rhinoceros Auklets are common in The Narrows; search also for the occasional Parasitic Jaeger in September (when Common Terns or Bonaparte's Gulls are here in numbers). This is a great place to search for Little Gull among the Bonaparte's and other rare species, as well.

SR-163 (N Pearl Street) southbound from the park entrance brings you to the northbound onramp to SR-16, on the right, in 3.0 miles. Turn right here for the Narrows Bridge and Kitsap County (page 178). The southbound SR-16 onramp—on the left in 0.3 mile, after the underpass—will take you to the I-5 interchange at Exit 132 (3.5 miles).

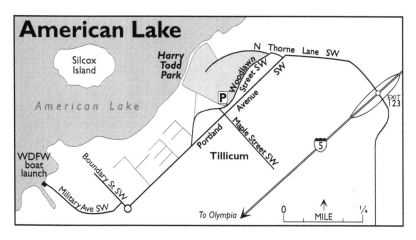

AMERICAN LAKE

A large lake southwest of Tacoma at the north edge of Joint Base Lewis-McChord, American Lake gained attention from birders primarily because of a Little Gull present among Bonaparte's Gulls every winter during the 1990s. But the Little Gull has not been seen in many years. Even though gulls are not always there (presumably they spend a fair amount of time on Puget Sound), potential for a variety of waterfowl and easy access from I-5 make this a popular stop.

Take Exit 123 (Thorne Lane) from I-5. At the traffic light, follow the signs to Tillicum/American Lake and turn northwestward onto North Thorne Lane SW. Follow the signs to Harry Todd Park in Lakewood, the traditional Little Gull spot. (Turn right to stay on Thorne in 0.3 mile, then left onto Woodlawn Street SW in 150 yards, and right into the parking lot 0.2 mile ahead.) Bring a scope; the gull flock can be quite far out.

Another vantage point is from the **WDFW boat ramp** (Discover Pass required) a bit farther west. Turn right out of the parking lot, then immediately left onto Maple Street for one block and right again onto Portland Avenue SW. Go straight 0.5 mile to a roundabout at the entrance to the National Guard's Camp Murray, turn right onto Boundary Street for one block, and then left onto Military Avenue SW (a gravel road through a gate), which is the entrance to the boat ramp area (0.3 mile ahead; Discover Pass required). This is a wonderful spot for wintering waterfowl such as Canvasback (uncommon in Pierce County), possible Redhead, Ring-necked Duck, Greater and Lesser Scaups, Bufflehead, and Common and Barrow's Goldeneyes.

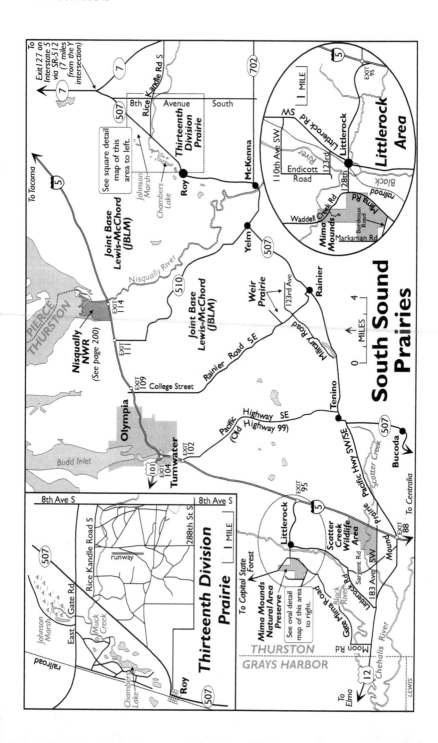

South Sound Prairies

Littlerock Area

Thirteenth Division Prairie

SOUTH SOUND PRAIRIES

by Bill Shelmerdine

revised by Kathy Slettebak, Arn Slettebak, and Denis DeSilvis

A unique (and shrinking) ecosystem of grasslands, oaks, and conifer woodlands stretches westward across Joint Base Lewis-McChord (JBLM), southwest of Tacoma, to Littlerock, south of Olympia, marking the southern edge of the Puget Lobe of the last glaciation. Between about 14,000 and 13,200 BP, the ice sheet gradually withdrew. Dammed by the retreating glacier and hemmed in east and west by the Cascades and the Olympics, meltwaters formed a huge lake. Runoff was directed westward from the lake's south end into the Chehalis River, depositing gravelly, excessively drained, nutrient-poor soils in plains, channels, and terraces. The prairies that later developed on the glacial outwash occupy the driest spots within the Puget Sound Douglas-fir vegetation zone that surrounds them. The suggested birding route follows the glacial meltwater drainage plain from east to west, through excellent examples of these native prairies.

This Woodland/Prairie Mosaic zone has several habitat types. The dry, treeless grasslands are blanketed with clumps of Idaho Fescue separated by a tight layer of moss and other low herbaceous plants. Bordering forest stands include Lodgepole Pine, Western White Pine, and relict Ponderosa Pine, but are mostly of Douglas-fir and Garry Oak. Salal, Common Snowberry, Indian-plum, and Western Serviceberry are typical of the understory. Numerous swamp and bog communities exist in spots where drainage is poor. Oregon Ash and Garry Oak dominate the riparian areas.

Bird species resident within the South Sound Prairies, but uncommon or highly local elsewhere in Western Washington, include Northern Bobwhite (introduced), Mourning Dove, Common Nighthawk, Horned Lark, House Wren, Western Bluebird, Chipping and Vesper Sparrows, Lazuli Bunting, and Western Meadowlark. Distinctive races of several butterflies are near-endemic to this zone, among them Great Spangled and Zerene Fritillaries, the state-endangered Mardon Skipper, and Edith's Checkerspot. These glacial outwash prairies are also home to the state-threatened Western Gray Squirrel and the seriously declining Mazama Pocket Gopher.

About 4,000 acres of grasslands remain of an estimated 150,000 acres historically. Agriculture and suburban sprawl account for most of the loss. Garry Oak and Douglas-fir are encroaching on much of the rest—an unintended consequence of fire suppression. Prior to white settlement, openings were maintained by fires, including deliberate burning by Native Americans. Modern management interventions such as controlled burns, brush clearing, and selective logging take place periodically on some of the remaining portions.

JOINT BASE LEWIS-MCCHORD PRAIRIES

Joint Base Lewis-McChord (JBLM) Range Complex, a U.S. military training facility, offers several prairie sites worth birding. JBLM is a closed installation. To get access to JBLM, go to the Visitor Center for JBLM-Lewis Main and Lewis North at Exit 120 off I-5 near the Liberty Gate. Hours are 5AM to 10PM daily. You will need your driver's license, current vehicle registration, and proof of insurance in order to obtain a visitor vehicle pass. After you get your vehicle pass, you will need to obtain an area access permit—good for 24 months—and map issued by Range Control. The Area Access office is located in Building 4074 at the intersection of Stryker and Kaufman Avenues, JBLM Main (253-967-6371). JBLM has numerous training areas, each designated by a number (indicated here by TA and then the number). Areas where training is occurring are closed to the public. To avoid disappointment, call ahead for closure information (253-967-6277). The web site is at http://www.lewis-mcchord.army.mil/DPTMS/training/range/range.htm. Make sure you know the numbers of the areas you want to visit. Hunting (especially for upland birds) is a popular activity in many areas, so use caution.

JBLM birding is best in May. Prairie wildflowers are at their peak then, too, among them Henderson's Shooting Star, Common Camas, Chocolate Lily, Blue-eyed Grass, and Puget Balsamroot. Dry Douglas-fir forest edges are particularly good in spring for a variety of bird species favoring lowland conifer forests. In the early 1980s, JBLM began a bluebird nest-box program. There are now about 160 nesting pairs of Western Bluebirds scattered about the training and range areas. In winter, things are usually pretty quiet; Northern Shrike can often be found, and Short-eared Owl, Merlin, and other raptors less reliably.

Armed with a valid area-access permit and current access information, drive east on SR-512 from I-5 Exit 127. In about two miles, turn right (south) onto SR-7, and, at the fork in 5.1 miles, stay right onto SR-507. Two excellent areas—Johnson Marsh (TA 10) and Chambers Lake (TA 12)—are well worth visiting if they are open. Travel 3.9 miles on SR-507 and turn right at the light onto East Gate Road. Just past a small outlet creek, go right at 1.0 mile onto an unmarked gravel road (small yellow sign) that runs through Douglas-fir forest along the west side of **Johnson Marsh** for well over a mile, with many vistas and access points. The zone where the forest meets the marsh supports a great diversity of passerines, including flycatchers, four species of wrens (House, Pacific, Marsh, Bewick's), and warblers. Wood Duck, Hooded Merganser, and Purple Martin nest at Johnson Marsh, which is also one of the few places in Western Washington where Yellow-headed Blackbird occurs occasionally (has nested).

Return to East Gate Road, turn right (west), and continue another 1.0 mile west on East Gate Road. Turn left onto the first asphalt road at the Roy Gate road sign just before the railroad crossing. This road runs south along the west edge of a large prairie with scattered Ponderosa Pines to a closed gate on the northern outskirts of Roy. A good graded road turns off to the left in 0.4 mile, crossing the north end of the tract. Look and listen for House Wren, Western Bluebird, and Chipping Sparrows. Six-tenths of a mile south of this intersection, another paved road branches off to the southeast, crosses the prairie, and runs along the west side of **Chambers Lake**, which is fringed with brush and open stands of Ponderosa Pine, Douglas-fir, and Garry Oak—good for passerines. The lake itself may have Wood Duck, Ring-necked Duck, and Lesser Scaup among other ducks, and Virginia Rail. After the lake, the pavement ends and the dirt road swings back north through the forested eastern part of the area.

To access TA 4 and TA 5, two of the best birding areas on JBLM, go back to East Gate Road, turn left, cross the railroad tracks, and continue past the gun ranges. At 2.2 miles turn left onto a paved road. Travel 0.6 mile and take the right fork. TA 5 is on the right. On the left is an artillery impact area, the 91st Division Prairie, which is the largest prairie in western Washington. This is a restricted area. Watch for bluebird boxes along the road. At 2.1 miles from the fork, just before the OP 8 sign, make a right turn uphill to an overlook of this huge prairie. MacGillivray's Warbler and Lazuli Bunting have nested in the immediate area, and American Kestrel, and Yellow and other warblers, nearby.

Return to the main road and turn right (west). At 1.6 miles from the overlook, bear right (north) at the fork. **TA 5** is on the right and **TA 4** is on the left. Good birding areas are accessible at various pullouts on either side of this road. The area along the tree line to the west (TA 4) is a migrant trap, especially for warblers in the spring. Various flycatchers, Purple Martin, Tree Swallow, House Wren, Western Tanager, and Purple Finch may be found here regularly.

Retrace your route to East Gate Road. Turn right and cross SR-507. Continue east 2.0 miles to the intersection with Eighth Avenue S, and turn right. Thirteenth Division Prairie (only TA 13 is accessible)—a vast prairie bordered by open, dry Douglas-fir forest and a few scrubby clearcuts—begins just south of Rice Kandle Road S, 2.5 miles from the SR-507 intersection (about half a mile south of East Gate Road). Turn off to the west and drive Rice Kandle Road (dirt road) to likely habitat. **TA 13** is west of the first major dirt road that goes south from Rice Kandle Road. Muck Creek runs through the site in a corridor of Oregon Ash. Short-eared Owl, Common Nighthawk, Western Kingbird, Horned Lark, and Vesper Sparrow are among the birds seen at least occasionally. The vegetation along the creek can be good for migrant passerines and riparian species.

Travel south on Eighth Avenue S. Once you cross 288th Street S (2.5 miles from Rice Kandle Road S) you are off the military reservation. Continue 4.0 miles south and turn right onto SR-702. Weir Prairie (TA 21; Tenalquot Prairie on some maps), near Rainier, can be reached by turning left (south) on

SR-507 in McKenna. Continue to Yelm and take a left onto First Street to follow SR-507 to Rainier. In Rainier, take the first right turn after Centre Street onto Minnesota Street, unsigned. The road bends left, then right, becoming 138th Street SE and finally Rainier Road SE. In 2.1 miles, turn right (northeast) onto Military Road SE, which in 0.6 mile bends right (east) onto 123rd Avenue SE. Where the road bends, take an immediate sharp left turn and then a quick right into the access road for **Weir Prairie** (TA 21), which is surrounded by a chain-link fence topped with barbed wire. This is normally a good place for Western Bluebird and Western Meadowlark. In early spring, look also for Mountain Bluebird (rare). Unusual birds, including Acorn Woodpecker, have been found here in recent years. The Garry Oaks along much of the west edge of the prairie are a good place to search for passerines, including House Wren.

Go back to Rainier Road SE and turn right (northwest). This stretch of Rainier Road bisects **Lower Weir Prairie**, with well-maintained gravel roads leading off in several directions. The prairie has Northern Bobwhite, Vesper and Savannah Sparrows, and Western Meadowlark. For one reasonably consistent location for Northern Bobwhite, go right from Rainier Road onto a road at the northwest edge of the prairie (0.6 mile from the Military Road intersection); follow this paved-though-potholed road 0.8 mile to an intersection with a gravel road. Park here and walk southeastward (right) toward some snags, a rise (glacial terrace edge), and shrubby cover in the center of the prairie. House Wren and Western Bluebird are here as well. Roadside forest edges may hold Hammond's Flycatcher, MacGillivray's Warbler, Chipping Sparrow, Western Tanager, and several others.

SCATTER CREEK AND BLACK RIVER

Return to the town of Rainier and turn right (southwest) onto SR-507, continuing to Tenino (city limits sign 6.8 miles). If you explore side streets and residential areas north from the main drag, you should be able to find Western Scrub-Jay on phone lines or other perches. At the other edge of Tenino (about two miles), turn right (west) onto Pacific Highway SE (Old Highway 99), then bear right (west) onto 183rd Avenue SW (5.2 miles). Soon after crossing over I-5, turn right onto Guava Street (0.4 mile) and continue straight to the large gravel parking lot near the end, on the left (Discover Pass required). This is the main entrance to **Scatter Creek Wildlife Area** at the north edge of Mound Prairie. The site is popular with upland bird hunters and dog trainers and should be avoided in the hunting season, which is not a hardship since the best period for birding is late April though early June. (Game bird releases occur—don't assume California Quail, Northern Bobwhite, or Ring-necked Pheasant are wild or established, and certainly the occasional Chukar is not part of the countable avifauna.)

This is a great place for an early morning walk in spring. Take the trail westward from the parking lot, between the barn and the creek—and for the more ambitious, all the way around the oak grove, fields, edges, and over-grown areas to the west and south. There is a fine riparian area of Oregon Ash with surrounding Garry Oak and understory shrubs. Across the creek are co-nifers of the typical lowland Douglas-fir association. These varied habitats will produce an excellent list of Western Washington lowland species, in addition to many of the local prairie specialties. When restoration efforts have kept the invasive Scot's Broom at bay, Scatter Creek can be a fabulous spot for prairie wildflowers from May into the summer.

From the parking lot at Scatter Creek Wildlife Area, go back south to 183rd Avenue SW, turn right, and travel west 1.6 miles to Sargent Road SW. Go right (north) to the intersection with Littlerock Road SW in 2.0 miles, and turn right again. The road follows the **Black River**, on the left, which flows south into the Chehalis. The valley's breadth is a reminder of the tremendous volume of glacial meltwater that coursed through this area for centuries, as the last ice age came to an end. There is not much river access on foot, but birding is excellent from a canoe or kayak. A gravel pullout 2.2 miles ahead is a good place to launch. To reach other access points, drive north to Littlerock (4.3 miles from Sargent Road), jog right onto 128th Avenue SW, then left, continuing north on Littlerock Road for another 0.5 mile. Turn left onto 123rd Avenue SW to a river crossing. An open wetland here has resident wa-terfowl, rails, and other marsh birds, and a few shorebirds in migration. Turn right 0.2 mile past the bridge and go north on Endicott Road SW. Mima Prairie is on your left. Watch for Elk. In 1.3 miles from 123rd, the road turns right and becomes 110th Avenue SW.

Another canoe launch is located near the river bridge (0.7 mile). A five-mile stretch of the river upstream from Littlerock to the south end of Black Lake, near Olympia, is the backbone of the Black River unit managed by Nisqually National Wildlife Refuge. The slow-flowing river and dense riparian vegetation, with Oregon Ash, Black Cottonwood, Red-osier Dogwood, wil-lows, and other trees, has been described as having a character reminiscent of rivers in the southeastern United States. Expect Green Heron (common), Bullock's Oriole, and other typical riparian species, including a few small concentrations of Red-eyed Vireos.

MIMA MOUNDS

Birders should not miss visiting the nearby Mima (pronounced MY-muh) Prairie, west and south of Littlerock, to ponder the elusive origins of the strange mounded surface of the ground. Interpretive displays at the 445-acre Mima Mounds Natural Area Preserve will help get you started with some of the explanations that have been proposed. Prehistoric pocket gophers are among the more intriguing hypotheses. From the intersection with Littlerock

Road in Littlerock, go west on 128th Avenue SW. At the intersection in 0.8 mile, go right (north) onto Waddell Creek Road SW. Proceed 0.8 mile and turn left into the entrance to Mima Mounds Natural Area Preserve (brown sign). Continue to the parking and picnic area, where nature trails lead from conifer woods to the prairie edge. Western Meadowlarks are common on the grasslands. Return to Waddell Creek Road. A left turn brings you in 1.6 miles to the Waddell Creek Entrance to the Capitol State Forest (page 211).

Backtrack on Waddell Creek Road SW until it becomes Mima Road SW at the junction with 128th Avenue SW. Continue south for 0.9 mile, where the forest edge thins. This part of the preserve can be viewed from Mima Road SW on the east, Bordeaux Road SW on the south, and Marksman Road SW on the west (map on page 192). Pullouts are few and traffic presents a hazard. One wide pullout with a sign noting prairie restoration efforts is located a quarter-mile down Bordeaux Road SW. This area is actively managed to control Scot's Broom and other invasives. Species abundance and distribution, and ease of birding, shift with the vegetation.

Return to 128th Avenue SW and turn right (east) to I-5 Exit 95 in 3.7 miles. Take I-5 northbound for Olympia (page 208), or southbound to Centralia, Chehalis, and birding sites of Southwestern Washington (page 226). Or continue down Mima Road to Gate Road SW, then left onto Moon Road SW to reach US-12 (about eight miles).

OLYMPIA AND VICINITY

by Bill Shelmerdine

revised by Bill Shelmerdine and Shep Thorp

Main routes between Puget Sound (Salish Sea), southwestern Washington, the outer coast, and the Olympic Peninsula meet in Olympia, at the southernmost extent of Puget Sound. A few miles east is the Nisqually River delta, the most pristine of the Sound's large estuaries and a significant birding site. The South Sound splits into several inlets with many interesting birding opportunities, including at the end of Budd Inlet in downtown Olympia. Western Scrub-Jays now nest regularly in the city, following recent range expansion. Watershed Park, near the city center, is a fine place to look for lowland forest birds.

NISQUALLY NATIONAL WILDLIFE REFUGE

Nisqually NWR is a birding jewel in the South Sound, offering thousands of acres of freshwater marsh, saltwater marsh, and tidally influenced estuary of the Nisqually River and McAllister Creek. Tidally influenced sloughs and channels within the estuary, and deciduous and mixed riparian forest are the hallmark of habitat restoration, providing an essential nursery for juvenile salmon as they make their way from their birthplace in creeks and rivers to the Sound and ocean where they'll grow into mature adults. Well over 200 species of birds have been seen in these diverse habitats, over 175 expected annually. In winter, the refuge supports thousands of waterfowl and dozens of raptors. Winter is also good for passerines such as woodpeckers, Northern Shrike, sparrows, and finches. Although thousands of Dunlins winter on the Nisqually Reach, providing an important food source for Peregrine Falcons, high numbers of shorebirds stop to feed in the spring, mid-April through mid-May.

The steady trickle of autumnal shorebird migration begins at the end of June and runs through November. Passerine migration can be excellent in the riparian woodlands during April, May, and August. Summer is the slow season, but even then the refuge is alive with good numbers of nesting Rufous Hummingbirds, Western Wood-Pewees, Willow Flycatchers, Tree, Cliff, and Barn Swallows, Yellow Warblers, American Goldfinches, and the songs of Swainson's Thrushes. A scope will be helpful on both the Nisqually Estuary Trail and the Nisqually Estuary Boardwalk Trail.

On I-5, just east of Olympia, take Exit 114 and follow the signs a short distance into the refuge (entrance fee at visitor center kiosk or America the Beautiful Pass required). After 12 years of planning, in 2009 the refuge began a major restoration project to remove dikes and reestablish estuarine salt marsh to 762 acres of 1,000 that had been diked for agriculture at the beginning of the 20th century. Extensive renovations since 1999 include: the new Norm Dicks Visitor Center with Nature Shop, interpretive exhibits, auditorium, and parking; Environmental Educational Center for formal programs; upgraded and

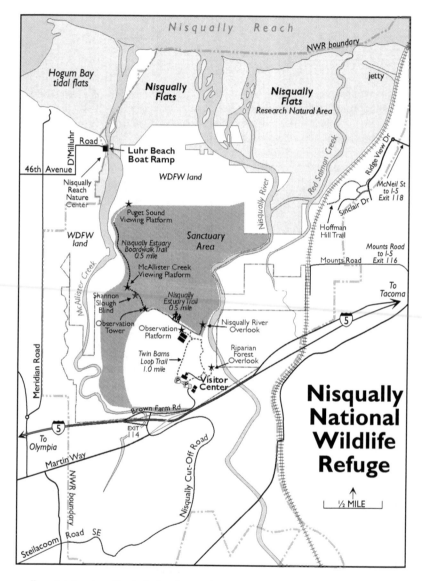

well-maintained trails and viewing areas; a one-mile barrier-free boardwalk loop trail through riparian habitat; a half-mile dike adjacent to the Nisqually River surge plain; freshwater wetlands; saltwater marsh; and a one-mile-long boardwalk which courses over tidal flats, channels, and marsh plain. A gravel road atop the old dike system remains between the Riparian Forest Overlook cutoff and the Nisqually River Overlook, running parallel to the east side of the Twin Barns Loop Trail. A new dike, which includes the Nisqually Estuary Trail, was built in 2009 to preserve 250 acres freshwater marsh and riparian forest adjacent to the visitor center. The Nisqually Estuary Boardwalk Trail was opened in 2011 and extends beyond the new dike over 762 acres of the recovering estuary, providing overlooks of Shannon Slough, McAllister Creek, and Puget Sound from atop the farthest reaches of the old historic dike. The last 700 feet of the new boardwalk are closed during hunting season (mid-October to late January) to provide distance between hunters and nature watchers. The historic Twin Barns are permanently closed due to earthquake damage. The walk along the Nisqually Estuary Trail and Nisqually Estuary Boardwalk Trail (four miles round trip from the visitor center) provides opportunities to observe all the habitats the refuge has to offer.

Immediately west from the visitor center, at the old McAllister Creek access road, a green gate protects the sanctuary of freshwater wetlands. In winter, thousands of Cackling Geese—mostly *minima* subspecies, but often Taverner's, and, rarely, Aleutian—can be found. Most winters a small number of Greater White-fronted Geese reside here, as well as hundreds of American Wigeons, Mallards, Northern Shovelers, Northern Pintails, and Green-winged Teals. Fox, Song, and Golden-crowned Sparrows, and Spotted Towhees utilize the edge habitat during the winter, and there are reports of uncommon White-throated and Harris's Sparrows as well. Refuge staff manage water levels and vegetation in the freshwater wetlands to provide winter habitat for waterfowl and summer habitat for passerines. From May through June, American Bittern, Sora, Wilson's Snipe, Common Yellowthroat, and Savannah Sparrow are present.

The **Visitor Center Pond** in winter is a good place to find Gadwall, Ring-necked Duck, Pied-billed Grebe, and American Coot. During spring and summer, the pond hosts Wood Duck, Cinnamon Teal, Hooded Merganser, and American Bittern. The Twin Barns Loop Trail encircles riparian forest with ponds and sloughs. Along the boardwalk during the winter look for Downy Woodpecker, Black-capped Chickadee, Brown Creeper, Golden- and Ruby-crowned Kinglets, Audubon's Yellow-rumped Warbler, and Pine Siskin (during an irruption year). During spring and summer, Cliff and Barn Swallows nest at the visitor center, and many Tree Swallows nest in the snags. Female Rufous Hummingbirds build their nests in leaf-covered overhangs, most often over water, while males zealously guard blossoming Osoberry and Salmonberry. Western Wood-Pewee, Willow Flycatcher, Marsh and Bewick's Wrens, American Robin, Common Yellowthroat, Yellow Warbler, Song Sparrow, and American Goldfinch have all been observed nesting along the loop trail. Nashville and Black-throated Gray Warblers can be seen during migration in April and May.

The cutoff for the Twin Barns is a good place to check for Virginia Rail and Swamp Sparrow in winter. **Twin Barns**, in fact, is one of the refuge's most productive birding areas. A half-mile from the visitor center, it features a large wheelchair-accessible viewing platform. Scan for waterfowl, raptors, and Northern Shrike (October–April). The slough between the Twin Barns Observation Platform and the Nisqually Estuary Trail, or new dike, is the historic head of Leschi Slough, which channels through the very heart of the refuge and empties into Puget Sound at the northern extent of Nisqually Reach. The freshwater slough provides winter sanctuary for Lincoln's Sparrow and late spring stopovers for Lazuli Bunting. Barn Owls inhabit the barns but are rarely seen due to resident, nesting Great Horned Owls in the large Black Cottonwood trees in the riparian forest. Red-breasted Sapsuckers frequent the Bigleaf Maples east of the Twin Barns. Bullock's Orioles nest in the large cottonwood trees at the edge of forest near the Twin Barns cutoff and around the parking lot.

Between the start of the **Nisqually Estuary Trail** and west to where historic Leschi Slough runs under the dike, you can bird edge habitat of boggy freshwater marsh and bramble to the south, and brackish marsh, riparian forest, and surge plain to the north. During winter, check the tall trees for Bald Eagle, Red-tailed Hawk, and Peregrine Falcon. Tides nine feet and higher will push waterfowl and shorebirds closer to the dike, providing nice opportunities to observe American Wigeon, Northern Shoveler, Northern Pintail, Green-winged Teal, Bufflehead, Greater Yellowlegs, Dunlin, Long-billed Dowitcher, and Mew and Ring-billed Gulls. Annually, there are two or three Eurasian Wigeons seen and, rarely, Common (Eurasian) Teal and Iceland (Kumlien's) Gull.

The entire Nisqually Estuary Trail provides an excellent opportunity to see predators of many species, as traveling voles and insects come to the surface while looking for a way around the dike. American Bittern, Great Blue Heron, Northern Harrier, Rough-legged Hawk (rare), Short-eared Owl (rare), American Kestrel (uncommon), and Northern Shrike all hunt the edges of the dike. During spring and fall migration, the mudflat is a great area to scope for shorebirds like Black-bellied Plover, Pacific Golden-Plover (rare), Semipalmated Plover, Lesser Yellowlegs, Whimbrel, Marbled Godwit, Ruff, Pectoral Sandpiper, and Long-billed Dowitcher. American Pipits migrate through in large flocks for one to two weeks in the spring and fall, occasionally including a Lapland Longspur.

West of Leschi Slough, the inside of the Nisqually Estuary Trail is freshwater cattail marsh. In winter, this may be the best area for observing American Bittern, Virginia Rail, and Lincoln's and Swamp (rare) Sparrows. During spring and summer, this freshwater marsh provides habitat for breeding Blue-winged, Cinnamon, and Green-winged Teal, Northern Shoveler, American Coot, Wilson's Phalarope (rare), Marsh Wren, Common Yellowthroat, and Red-winged Blackbird. During migration, Solitary (annual) and Buff-breasted (rare) Sandpipers have been observed where flooded fields meet freshwater marsh. Occasionally, Yellow-headed Blackbirds are seen, and nest-building behavior has been observed. During stormy spring days with low cloud cover, scan the skies for Black Swifts.

The entrance to the **Nisqually Estuary Boardwalk Trail** starts at the end of the Nisqually Estuary Trail, where the **Observation Tower** provides an excellent platform to scan the Shannon Slough area. Historic channels remain despite diking for nearly 100 years. Bivalves have returned, and, in winter, Surf Scoter and Common Goldeneye can be observed foraging. West of the observation tower is the Shannon Slough Blind, a good place to photograph winter residents like Greater Yellowlegs, Dunlin, and Least and Western Sandpipers (rare).

The next covered platform is the McAllister Creek Viewing Platform, which overlooks the confluence of Shannon Slough and McAllister Creek. In winter, this is an excellent place to scope for dabbling ducks, Bufflehead, Common Goldeneye, Red-breasted Merganser, Red-throated and Common Loons, Horned Grebe, Great Blue Heron, Great Egret (uncommon), Spotted Sandpiper, Greater Yellowlegs, Dunlin, Least Sandpiper, and Mew, Ring-billed, California, and Glaucous-winged Gulls. In spring, there is an active Bald Eagle nest just south of the confluence along the west bank of McAllister Creek. Belted Kingfishers and Northern Rough-winged Swallows nest in tunnels along the clay banks of McAllister Creek. Rarely, Black-necked Stilt and American Avocet have been seen in migration feeding in the mudflats. You can occasionally see Baird's and Semipalmated Sandpipers during fall migration.

Starting in February and ending in October, the Nisqually Delta is visited by upwards of seven swallow species. Tree, Northern Rough-winged, Cliff, and Barn Swallows all nest on the refuge. There are Purple Martin nest boxes on an aging pier that is now closed to access (page 205) on the west side of McAllister Creek across from the end of the boardwalk, and this species is often seen and heard foraging over the refuge. High numbers of Violet-green Swallows migrate through, foraging on the swarms of midges and sandflies from March through May. Bank Swallow is seen each year during spring and fall migrations. As you walk along the boardwalk toward the **Puget Sound Viewing Platform** at the end, listen to the sounds coming from the coniferous forest on the west bank of McAllister Creek. This is the most reliable area to add Pileated Woodpecker, Steller's Jay, and Red-breasted Nuthatch to your refuge species count. Occasionally, Common Raven is seen flying from one hillside to the other over the delta. At the viewing platform, you can appreciate the expanse of the delta and Nisqually Reach. In winter, this is the best place to observe Brant, Greater Scaup, White-winged Scoter, Red-throated, Pacific, and Common Loons, Horned and Eared Grebes, Brandt's, Double-crested, and Pelagic Cormorants, Northern Harrier, Pigeon Guillemot, Rhinoceros Auklet, Bonaparte's and Glaucous Gulls, Snowy Owl (irruption years), Short-eared Owl (mouth of Nisqually River), Merlin, Peregrine Falcon, Harbor Seal, California Sea Lion, and Killer Whale (rare). A second pair of nesting Bald Eagles can be observed directly west on the west-bank hillside of McAllister Creek in spring. In summer, Caspian Terns are frequently heard and seen foraging. Scope the marsh plain for unexpected visitors like Pacific Golden-Plover, Whimbrel, Franklin's Gull, and Black and Common Terns.

The **Nisqually River Overlook** can be the best place to observe Common Merganser in late winter. The river also is a good spot for observing Mallard, Common and Barrow's (uncommon) Goldeneyes, and, occasionally, Spotted Sandpiper. In August, this can be a good place to pick up Green Heron during juvenile dispersal. The recently restored habitat just north of the overlook has yielded visits by MacGillivray's Warbler during spring migration. Along the east side of the Twin Barns Loop Trail, larger-diameter tall trees can host Hairy and Pileated Woodpeckers and Brown Creeper. Where the forest opens up and elderberry is available, Band-tailed Pigeon, Swainson's Thrush, and Cedar Waxwing feast on berries. In winter, the resident Great Horned Owl occasionally can be seen. Pine Siskins frequently are found feeding on Red Alder catkins. Red Crossbills and Evening Grosbeaks are heard most often as they fly over. Chestnut-backed Chickadees can be difficult to find due to the lack of coniferous trees, but the mature deciduous trees in the southeast section of the Twin Barns Loop Trail near the Riparian Forest Overlook cutoff have been productive for this species in winter. In spring, this habitat is very good for Western Wood-Pewee, Hutton's and Warbling Vireos, Swainson's Thrush, Black-throated Gray Warbler, Western Tanager, and Black-headed Grosbeak.

In spring the section of forest surrounding the **Riparian Forest Overlook** is a good spot to see Pacific-slope Flycatcher, Red-eyed Vireo (rare), and Pacific Wren. The understory provides nice habitat for breeding Wilson's Warblers; wherever the forest opens up exposing bramble, you may find Orange-crowned Warbler year round. The orchard next to the Education Center is a good place for Red-breasted Sapsucker, Northern Flicker, Varied Thrush (winter), Orange-crowned Warbler, and White-crowned and Golden-crowned Sparrows (winter).

The area east of the Nisqually River can be viewed from **Mounts Road** and from the Hoffman Hill Trail. Take Exit 116 (Mounts Road) from I-5, head west, and follow the road for 1.6 miles to the turnaround near the end of the road. Walking this quarter-mile section of road provides a good view of estuary saltwater marsh.

Hoffman Hill Trail is accessible from I-5 Exit 118 (Center Street in Dupont). Proceed west on Center Street, then take a left onto McNeil Street. Follow this road for nearly two miles to a rotary T-intersection with Ridge View Drive and take a left. Follow Ridge View for a half-mile; park on the right side of the road across from the basketball court in the local park. The gravel path behind the homes on Sinclair Drive leads to the refuge's **Hoffman Hill Trail**, which provides mixed-forest habitat and views of the Nisqually River mouth, Red Salmon Creek, and the northeast side of the Nisqually Reach.

LUHR BEACH

Several side trips near the Nisqually NWR often are worthwhile. The open fields and agricultural lands along Nisqually Cut-Off Road SE, just south and on the other side of I-5, are often good in fall and winter, attracting large flocks of waterfowl, gulls and blackbirds—and at times shorebirds, raptors, and locally uncommon birds.

Another worthwhile nearby birding destination is **Luhr Beach**. To reach it, go right (west) 1.1 miles on Martin Way E up the hill from the Nisqually interchange immediately south of I-5. (See map on page 200.) Turn right (north) onto Meridian Road and go a half-mile to a traffic circle; exit the traffic circle on the first spur to the right, remaining on Meridian Road. Continue north 2.1 miles to 46th Ave NE and turn right. In 0.2 mile turn left onto D'Milluhr Road NE and follow it around a half-mile to a boat ramp and parking area for the **Nisqually Reach Nature Center**. To the east is the Nisqually Delta and the outer edge of the Nisqually National Wildlife Refuge. To the north are the open waters of the Nisqually Reach of the Salish Sea. Birds are often plentiful here, but distances are often long—a scope is a must for birding this site. The nature center has an aging dock that is now closed to access. Birding is from the edge of the parking lot or the adjacent shoreline. Look for Purple Martins, which nest here. This is a popular location for kayaking, fishing, and duck hunting. Those wishing to bird by kayak are advised to avoid the waterfowl hunting season (October–January).

The distance across the mouth of McAllister Creek—a popular high-tide roost for gulls and sometimes waterfowl—to the edge of the delta is 1,500 to 2,000 feet. This site has produced a number of remarkable sightings over the years and is worth checking, particularly near high tide. It is a mile north to the deep waters of the Reach where wayward seabirds are sometimes sighted.

Waterfowl, loons, and grebes are often abundant here. It is perhaps the most reliable spot in the county to find Brant, as well as Harlequin and Long-tailed Ducks, Black Scoter, and Eared Grebe (all local rarities and not found every year). In September–October you have a reasonable chance of spotting a Parasitic Jaeger out on the Reach when numbers of Bonaparte's Gulls or Common Terns (uncommon) are moving through. In Snowy Owl invasion years this is often the best place in the South Sound to find one (or three) hanging out on the outer part of the delta.

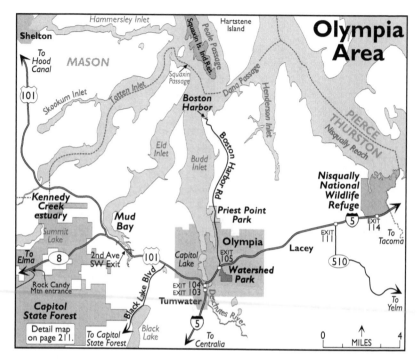

OLYMPIA AND BUDD INLET

Washington's capital offers a variety of waterbirds and passerines right in the center of town. From I-5, turn off at Exit 105 and follow the signs for the Port of Olympia. The exit will deposit you onto Plum Street. Head north and in 0.7 mile turn left onto Olympia Avenue NE. Park on Olympia or turn left onto Chestnut or Jefferson Streets for parking and walk back to the head of East Bay to check an outfall pipe there where gulls and diving ducks often feed. Mudflats exposed at low tide attract small flocks of shorebirds in spring and fall, and Purple Martins use the nest boxes on pilings in the bay. You may follow the footpath along the west side of the bay as far as the marina, or drive, pulling off where shoulders and views allow. If driving, head north on Marine Drive along the shoreline of East Bay, bearing right at the intersection in 0.4 mile toward Swantown Marina. This deeper (dredged) part of the bay is good in winter for bay ducks, loons, and grebes. A raised parking area just past the marina and boat launch offers the best vantage point of lower Budd Inlet. Park here and walk along the path, or continue driving, bearing right, and park between Anthony's Hearthfire Grill and KGY radio station, at the tip of the point between East and West Bays, called Northpoint. Bonaparte's and Mew Gulls, and Caspian Terns (summer) are sometimes here in numbers, along with diving birds, including three species of cormorants and Rhinoceros

Auklet. Shorebirds are not common, but a few unusual species have turned up here, and this is your best bet in the downtown area.

Backtrack on Marine Drive, turn right onto Market Street NE, and go 0.2 mile to the roundabout at Olympia's Farmers Market. Directly across the circle and ahead one block is a marina and parking. Viewing is from the boardwalk along the water or from the observation tower to the north. The water is deeper than in East Bay and may have a different assortment of waterbirds. Check sailboat rigging for Purple Martins. Return to the circle, turn right, take Capitol Way N seven blocks south (toward downtown), and turn right onto Fifth Avenue. In four blocks, at Simmons Street, park in the lot on the left to go birding on foot along **Capitol Lake**—noted for diving ducks and a large gull flock that roosts there in the afternoon. Cross 5th Avenue at the traffic light and then head west (left) two blocks. At low tide, the footbridge across the 5th Avenue dam is a great spot to view the schools of Chinook Salmon that stage at the mouth of Capitol Lake in August, awaiting entry to the Deschutes River.

There are two options for birding Capitol Lake. Birding on foot is from the paved (barrier-free) footpath that makes a 1.5-mile loop around the lower (north) lake and goes down the west side of the upper (south) lake. The less green approach is to drive west two blocks on Fifth Avenue and bear left at the fork onto Deschutes Parkway, which parallels the shoreline with many places to park. Marathon Park is a convenient parking area between the lower (north) and upper (south) pools. Check both lakes and Percival Cove for a good variety of waterfowl; the species composition varies between these three impoundments. Virginia Rail, Marsh Wren, and Red-winged Blackbird nest in the small marshes at the south end. American Dipper is a regular wintering species at Tumwater Falls about a mile farther upstream.

Boston Harbor, about seven miles north of Olympia at the confluence of Budd and Eld Inlets, is a good place to view birds of the deeper, more open waters of Puget Sound (Salish Sea). Go back east on Fourth Avenue through the business district and turn left (north) onto Plum Street, which soon becomes East Bay Drive NE. A sidewalk provides a good place from which to look for birds on East Bay. Priest Point Park, at 1.5 miles from the Fourth Avenue intersection, is good for waterbirds and birds of the wet conifer forest.

Continue on north 5.5 miles (name change to Boston Harbor Road), then go left 350 yards on 73rd Avenue NE to the harbor. Scope the inlet from the vicinity of the boat ramp. Saltwater ducks, loons, grebes, cormorants, alcids, gulls, and terns, fly above the channel or feed along current lines when tides are changing, sometimes in good numbers. Oddities may appear after large winter storms.

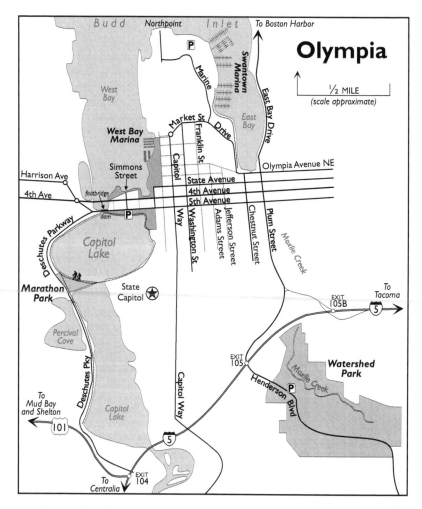

Watershed Park is a 115-acre wooded ravine a mile south of downtown Olympia. Go south on Plum Street, and at the traffic light just before the
I-5 onramps bear right toward the southbound onramp but then stay left and
go under the freeway onto Henderson Boulevard SE. A 1.5-mile loop trail begins at a gravel parking area on the left shoulder 0.3 mile ahead. Douglas-fir,
Western Hemlock, Bigleaf Maple, and other large trees shade a lush and varied understory. Snags are numerous. Red-breasted Sapsucker and Hairy and
Pileated Woodpeckers have nested. Vaux's Swifts are often overhead. Barred
Owls are sometimes found roosting along the creek. Many forest birds nest
here or are year-round residents; others can be found in spring migration.
This is a decent spot to look for Hutton's and Cassin's (spring) Vireos.

ELD AND TOTTEN INLETS

At the upper end of Eld Inlet a few miles west of Olympia, (map on page 206) Mud Bay is one of the last areas to be flooded by a rising tide. One to two hours before peak high tide, shorebirds and small gulls often concentrate close to the road for excellent viewing. At low tide, birds disperse up or down the bay. Take the Second Avenue SW exit from US-101 (just across the bridge over the bay, if you are coming from Olympia). Turn east (right if coming from Olympia, left if from Shelton) onto Mud Bay Road and park at either end of the concrete bridge spanning Mud Bay (0.2 mile). A good variety of gulls can be found here. Franklin's has been seen with the large Bonaparte's flock in September and October. Shorebirding is good in fall and spring, with all of the typical migrants occurring at least occasionally. Dunlins winter in good numbers, along with the occasional Black-bellied Plover, Spotted Sandpiper, Greater Yellowlegs, or Willet (rare). Sometimes there are large numbers of Hooded Mergansers in fall.

Also be sure to check **Perry Creek**. Two viewing spots are available. From the US-101, 2nd Avenue (Mud Bay Road) exit, cross south over US-101 and go 0.3 mile to Old Highway 410 SW, turn right and proceed to the concrete bridge over Perry Creek (0.4 mi.). This is a great place to view migrating Chum Salmon late November through December. The site excels for gull watching with flocks of 500–1,000 birds at times, mostly of the large species. Lower Perry Creek is reached from Madrona Beach Road, on the north side of US-101, 0.6 mile from the 2nd Avenue exit.

The rich estuary of **Kennedy Creek** at the end of Totten Inlet is particu-

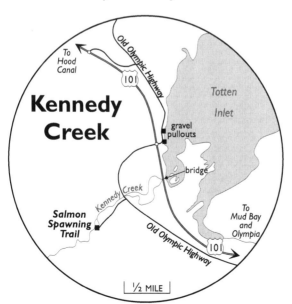

larly good for shorebirds and gulls. Extensive mudflats at low tide make for difficult viewing, but incoming tides often push birds in close. Visiting within an hour or two of high tide should do the trick. Continue west on US-101 from Mud Bay. In 1.0 mile, where SR-8 goes straight ahead, bear right with US-101 (appears as an exit), following signs toward Shelton and Port Angeles. In 5.5

miles, turn off right onto Old Olympic Highway, just after the Kennedy Creek bridge (traffic is heavy; be careful). A gravel parking area just off the highway, on the right, gives a view of the innermost part of the estuary.

The mouth of Kennedy Creek is an important wintering site for Black-bellied Plover and Dunlin. In spring and fall migration, these species as well as Greater Yellowlegs, Least and Western Sandpipers, and Long-billed Dowitcher are common. In September, high numbers of the smaller gulls stage here, mostly Bonaparte's, Mew, and Ring-billed. Kennedy Creek has one of the largest remaining Chum Salmon runs in the South Sound, attracting the larger gulls (and fishermen) from late October into December to feed on the spent carcasses. The outer part of the estuary can be seen well from a second gravel pullout about 0.1 mile ahead on Old Olympic Highway. Birds often roost just across the creek at high tide. If visiting on a weekend from the first of November through the first weekend in December, check out the salmon spawning trail about one mile upstream. Drive across US-101 and go 0.7 mile on Old Olympic Highway. Turn right onto a gravel road and drive an additional 0.5 mile to the **Salmon Spawning Trail** and interpretive site.

To reach Chehalis River valley and South Coast birding sites (page 64), return south to SR-8 and turn west. Continuing north on US-101 will take you to Hood Canal.

CAPITOL STATE FOREST

The 90,000-acre Capitol State Forest, at the heart of the Black Hills southwest of Olympia, is probably the most reliable, readily accessible place in Washington to look for Hermit Warbler (especially higher-elevation areas along ridges). Also found here are Mountain Quail (uncommon to rare) and a lowland population of Gray Jay. This is a working forest—in other words, intensively managed by the DNR for timber harvest. Vegetation is generally young to middle-aged conifers dominated by Douglas-fir and Western Hemlock interspersed with clearcuts in various stages of regrowth. Few large, old forest stands remain. The network of logging roads can be confusing. Some areas are poorly signed; road numbers change; closures may spring up unexpectedly. It is essential that you pick up a map ($9) at the Olympic National Forest headquarters at 1835 Black Lake Boulevard immediately southwest of US-101 (phone: 360-956-2300), open Monday–Friday. An alternative is to check the DNR web site for downloadable maps (*http://www.dnr.wa.gov/*). Roads are aggregate-surfaced and usually suitable for passenger vehicles, but beware of logging-truck traffic, especially on weekdays.

Convenient access points are the Rock Candy Mountain Entrance from SR-8 on the north side of the forest (4.5 miles west of the US-101 intersection with SR-8), the Delphi Entrance on the east side, and the C-Line Entrance one mile southeast of Porter on US-12. To reach the Delphi Entrance, take the Black Lake Boulevard exit from US-101 (the first exit west of I-5 in Olympia) and head south

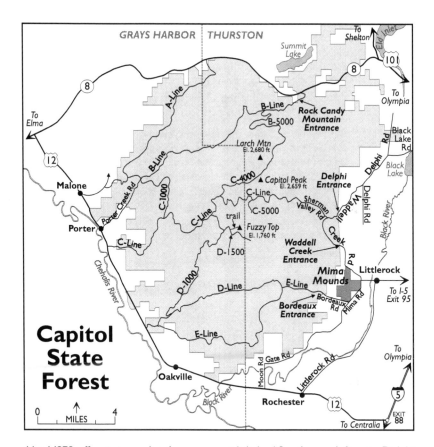

GRAYS HARBOR | THURSTON

Capitol State Forest

0 — MILES — 4

(the USFS office is immediately on your right). In 4.3 miles, go left onto Delphi Road. At a fork in 2.1 miles, turn right onto Waddell Creek Road to reach the Delphi Entrance at Sherman Valley Road in 2.7 miles. Another option is to continue west from Mima Mounds Natural Area Preserve (page 192) on Waddell Creek Road for 1.6 miles to the Waddell Creek Entrance. A good through route starting at the Rock Candy Mountain Entrance follows the B-Line to Road B-5000, which turns into C-4000, thence to the C-Line and out the Delphi or Waddell Creek Entrance.

An alternate route runs E-W (or W-E) along the length of the C-Line. From the west, enter from US-12 at the C-Line Entrance one mile southeast of Porter. Near the top of the ridge, a short detour south on the D-1000, then the D-1500 toward Fuzzy Top can be productive. A similar detour to the north on C-4000 toward Capitol Peak is worthwhile. Continuing on the C-Line will bring you to the Delphi Entrance. This latter route covers more Grays Harbor County territory and is of interest to county listers.

Some worthwhile areas to search for Gray Jay and Hermit Warbler include along Road C-4000 between Larch Mountain and Capitol Peak (the two highest points in the Black Hills), the trail at Fuzzy Top (accessed from the west on Road D-1500), and along the C-Line between the junctions with Roads C-4000 and C-5000. Mountain Quail have been seen in spring along Road C-4000 near Larch Mountain.

Other species of interest in these wet conifer-forest habitats include Sooty Grouse (uncommon and heard in spring more often than seen), Band-tailed Pigeon, Northern Pygmy-Owl (uncommon), Hammond's Flycatcher, Hutton's Vireo, and Black-throated Gray (alder patches) and Townsend's Warblers. Search brushy clearcuts and margins for Olive-sided Flycatcher, MacGillivray's Warbler, and Western Tanager. The most common species encountered will likely be Chestnut-backed Chickadee, Pacific Wren, and Golden-crowned Kinglet; Varied Thrush is common in fall and winter.

HOOD CANAL AND EAST OLYMPICS

by Bill Shelmerdine

revised by Diane Yorgason-Quinn, Faye McAdams Hands,
and Bill Shelmerdine

Hood Canal—a beautiful, sheltered arm of Puget Sound—is one of only a few true fjords in the conterminous United States. Its deep waters, steep sides, and narrow, rocky shoreline support comparatively smaller numbers of wintering waterbirds than the rest of the Sound. Birding is primarily from along the edge of US-101, which clings to the west rim of Hood Canal. There are few places to get out and walk, and the shoreline is either not accommodating to foot travel or is privately owned. However, birding can be quite productive at the modest deltas, salt marshes, and shallow waters at the mouths of the principal rivers (from east to west, then south to north, Union, Skokomish, Hamma Hamma, Duckabush, Dosewallips, and Big and Little Quilcene) and a few smaller creeks. Such estuarine habitats draw waterfowl and gulls, and most have salmon runs that attract birds in season (usually October–November). Numerous forest roads and wilderness trails reach into the eastern Olympics from US-101. Birders may wish to sample lower-elevation forest habitats on an easy drive up 2,800-foot Mount Walker, or hike through upper-elevation forest zones to alpine parkland at the 6,200-foot summit of Mount Townsend.

GREAT BEND AND ANNAS BAY

From the intersection with SR-8 west of Mud Bay (page 206), proceed north on US-101 21.3 miles to the Purdy Cutoff Road north of Shelton. Turn right here, opposite the George Adams National Fish Hatchery (a spot for

American Dipper), and descend the lower Skokomish River Valley to the junction with SR-106 (2.8 miles). Turn right toward Union. After another two miles you will reach the south end of Hood Canal and the mouth of the river at **Annas Bay**. There is one small pullout on the left. This area offers extensive excellent saltwater habitat and high concentrations of birds, especially in winter. Bald Eagles are numerous at all times, especially when the salmon are running in early winter. The main drawback is access. Much of the lower Skokomish River lies within the Skokomish Indian Reservation or is in private ownership. Generally, birding—though productive—will be from the edge of the road and a long-distance affair. Find a wide spot along the shoulder and scan the salt water, shoreline, and delta.

Common wintering waterfowl include Mallard, Northern Pintail, Red-breasted Merganser, and large flocks of American Wigeons. Farther out in the bay Canvasback (uncommon) and Common Goldeneye are found along with flocks of Surf, White-winged, and Black Scoters (uncommon to rare). This is a favorite area for loons and grebes. Yellow-billed Loon has been seen here, and Clark's Grebe has been found among the Westerns. Continue 1.7 miles to **Union**, where Hood Canal makes its Great Bend to the east. Pull out on the left, across from Union Country Store, and scan the open salt water. This is a good spot for birds that prefer deeper, more open waters than those of Annas Bay. In August, Purple Martins may be seen on pilings or boats at the small marina.

Turn around and retrace SR-106 west to US-101 (5.2 miles from the Union Country Store), and turn right (north) to **Potlatch State Park** (1.9 miles) at the northwest corner of Annas Bay (Discover Pass required). The waters here are quite productive from fall into spring. Horned, Red-necked, and Western Grebes are common, as are Red-throated and Common Loons. Scaups, scoters, and goldeneyes also winter here in good numbers.

A half-mile north of the state park on US-101 is Skokomish Park at Potlatch (formerly Tacoma Power's Saltwater Park). A large parking lot with boat ramp is on the right, across from the powerhouse. The penstocks and power canal discharge a large volume of cold, fresh water that has been diverted from the North Fork Skokomish River and the Lake Cushman hydroelectric project. Conditions here attract a variety of waterbirds, including Harlequin Duck (occasional) and Barrow's Goldeneye.

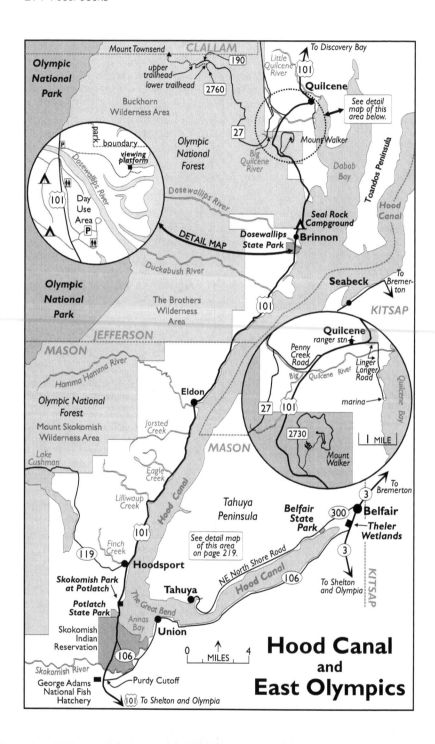

Hood Canal
and
East Olympics

HOODSPORT TO QUILCENE BAY

The fish hatchery on Finch Creek, on the right at the north end of the town of **Hoodsport** (2.8 miles), is also good for waterbirds. Park at the hatchery (portable toilet available) and walk through the complex to the creek mouth. Continuing north on US-101, you will pass over bridges at the mouths of Lilliwaup Creek (4.3 miles with a WDFW pullout 0.5 mile past bridge), Eagle Creek (2.5 miles), and Jorsted Creek (3.2 miles), which can have concentrations of waterbirds in fall and winter. There is a small pullout just past the Eagle Creek bridge on the right. All three cormorants (Brandt's uncommon) roost on the pilings of the former log dump and decking area just north of Jorsted Creek, and Purple Martins sometimes use them in late August and early September.

The **Hamma Hamma River** (1.5 miles) is a large stream with an estuary and salt marsh. There is one pullout 0.25 mile past the bridge. Brant, bay ducks, gulls, and sometimes shorebirds may be seen from a spot on the south side of the Hamma Hamma Oyster Company at the south end of the estuary. When salmon are running (October–November), look for Bald Eagles in the trees just upstream of the bridge on the far side of the estuary. There is a Great Blue Heron rookery nearby. The **Duckabush River estuary** (9.9 miles) was once known for its small wintering population of Trumpeter Swans, but they have been absent in recent years. Pullouts are narrow and the traffic unforgiving, so be careful.

Dosewallips State Park (3.1 miles), at the mouth of the Dosewallips River just south of Brinnon, offers some of the best and most accessible birding on Hood Canal (Discover Pass required). Diverse habitats include conifer forest in and around the campground, a Red Alder-dominated riparian zone along the river, and thickets, openings, and salt marsh leading to the open shoreline and sloughs at the river's mouth. Turn right off the highway into the day-use area (restrooms), or left to the campground.

For the best birding, drive 0.4 mile north across the river on the highway bridge to the beach-trail parking lot on the right just past the bridge (not well signed), and walk to the beach through mixed riparian vegetation beneath some large cottonwoods. Vireos, chickadees, kinglets, and warblers may be here in good numbers during migration; Hutton's Vireo and Townsend's Warbler are usually somewhere in the vicinity during fall or winter. The area around the viewing platform can be good for sparrows, with Savannah, Song, Lincoln's, White-crowned, and Golden-crowned Sparrows present seasonally. From the platform itself, the shoreline, salt marsh, and open-water habitats beyond can be scanned (best at high tide). Harbor Seals haul out at the river mouth, and gulls can be abundant. If you walk across the bridge, scan upstream and down. Harlequin Duck (rare), Common Merganser, and American Dipper have all been seen here. Around the end of September you may be treated to the sight of spawning salmon. Seal Rock Campground (1.2 miles), just off US-101, has many of the same birds and is also a delightful place to camp, although it closes for the winter in September.

Quilcene Bay is a rich winter area for waterbirds. From the Olympic National Forest Hood Canal Ranger District office at the south edge of the town of Quilcene (10.2 miles; maps, road and trail information), continue 0.3 mile to a fork where US-101 northbound bends left. Go straight ahead (east) onto Linger Longer Road. The road soon turns right. About 1.1 miles from US-101, turn left into Indian George Creek access. There is poor signage here, but look for a sign at the far end of the parking area for Quilcene Bay State Tidelands (Discover Pass required), then drive out to the shore of the bay. Return to Linger Longer Road and turn left, continuing 0.6 mile to where the road dead-ends at the Herb Beck Marina. This is a good place to scope the bay and shoreline at any tide stage. There are picnic tables and toilets when the port office is open.

MOUNT WALKER AND MOUNT TOWNSEND

The short trip up **Mount Walker** is an excellent way to see birds of the conifer forest. Head northbound from Seal Rock Campground on US-101 for 5.6 miles, turn right onto FR-2730 at the sign for the Mount Walker View Point. (Southbound from Quilcene, this turnoff is on the left 4.6 miles from the ranger station.) The four-mile road is suitable for passenger vehicles, but not recommended for trailers. It is gated from October through March, a time when bird activity is at a lull. Both Townsend's and Hermit Warblers are found here (and a range of intergrades between the two). The steep side slopes allow for views into the canopy, which greatly simplifies finding these and other frequently-encountered species such as Hammond's and Pacific-slope Flycatchers, Gray and Steller's Jays, Chestnut-backed Chickadee, Brown Creeper, Pacific Wren, Golden-crowned Kinglet, and Varied Thrush. Watch for Sooty Grouse crossing the road with young in the late summer. Northern Goshawk and Northern Pygmy-Owl are sometimes seen. Birds can be found anywhere from the Mount Walker trailhead, a quarter-mile from the highway, to the summit (elevation 2,804 feet) with spectacular views of Puget Sound, Mount Rainier, and Seattle to the east, and the Olympic Mountains to the west. Those who crave exercise may park at the trailhead and walk the two-mile trail to the top (roughly 2,000 feet elevation gain). The trail climbs steeply through hundred-year-old Douglas-fir forest with Pacific Rhododendron, Salal, and Cascade Oregon-grape understory.

If you enjoy hiking, consider an outing to **Mount Townsend**, about 15 miles north and west of Quilcene. From US-101, turn west (right) onto Penny Creek Road (0.9 mile south from the ranger station in Quilcene). After 1.4 miles, turn left onto FR-27 (Big Quilcene River Road) and continue 12.4 miles to FR-2760, then left another 0.7 mile to the lower trailhead. Park here at a wide spot in the road (America the Beautiful or Northwest Forest Pass required). To save a mile of hiking each way and 500 feet of elevation gain (but also skipping deep woods and views of Sink Lake), do not turn off at the lower trailhead but instead continue up FR-27 for another 1.2 miles, then go left on FR-190 to the upper trailhead (0.7 mile). The moderately difficult but well-maintained Trail 839 climbs 3,350 feet over 5.5 miles to the Alpine/Parkland vegetation zone, traversing the Olympic Douglas-fir and Subalpine Fir zones on the way. The 6,200-foot broadly rounded summit—densely carpeted with Common Juniper, Shrubby Cinquefoil, and boreal lichens—is in the Buckhorn Wilderness Area. Snowfall is relatively light on the dry northeast side of the Olympics, so the trail is usually snow-free by June. The summer wildflower show can be fantastic. Birding possibilities are similar to those for Deer Park (page 40), but without the cars and people. Look for Sooty Grouse in the open subalpine forest and Townsend's and Hermit Warblers near the trailhead.

BELFAIR AND THE TAHUYA PENINSULA

On SR-3 in Belfair, 0.5 mile north of the junction with SR-106, is **Theler Wetlands**, the estuary complex at the mouth of the Union River. Turn left off of SR-3 into the Mary E. Theler Community Center and park south of the building where you will see the entrance to the wetlands. There are a number of examples of bird-related public art to be seen, as well as a native plant area with labels. A pit toilet is at the parking lot and another at the farthest end of the trails. About two miles (3.8 out and back) of trails access riparian areas, an alder/cedar swamp, salt marsh, and tidelands. Trails are level and wheelchair friendly. Rock Wall Trail, Alder/Cedar Swamp Trail, and South Tidal Marsh Trails are short with easy return to the parking lot. River Estuary Trail is the longest and most diverse. In 2013 the dikes along the River Estuary Trail were breached in two locations to restore 29 acres of pasture to salt marsh.

If one includes the adjacent Pacific Salmon Center/WDFW lands, there are 135 acres of area protected from development. A good variety of habitats are found here, home to over 200 species of plants and many species of insects; as many as 176 species of birds have been seen here including a number of rarities. Rock Wall Trail is good for warblers and flycatchers in the spring and summer, as well as year-round Barred Owl. Alder/Cedar Swamp trail has mixed riparian forest and has had Red-breasted Sapsucker, Downy, Hairy and Pileated Woodpeckers, Hutton's Vireo, Pacific Wren, and Cedar Waxwing in any season. In spring and summer, look for Orange-crowned, Black-throated Gray, and Wilson's Warblers, and Western Tanager. This trail can be closed in the winter due to slippery boardwalks. South Tidal Marsh Trail is an elevated trail that leads nearly to the tideflats. The marsh and alder thicket can be good for Willow Flycatcher, Warbling Vireo, Marsh Wren, and Yellow Warbler. Waterfowl, a variety of gulls, and a few Caspian Terns can be seen along the shoreline. In spring, the rails of the boardwalk are lined with Tree, Violet-green, and Barn Swallows. Watch for Anna's and Rufous Hummingbirds and Great Blue Herons anywhere.

River Estuary Trail has ponds and sloughs where River Otters are frequently seen; Virginia Rails and Belted Kingfishers nest here. This trail is partly on dikes that have been breached to allow the marsh to return to historical estuary for salmon and wildlife enhancement. The restored tidal marsh hosts a good variety of waterfowl including Northern Pintail, Green-winged Teal, and Common Merganser, as well as Black-bellied and Semipalmated Plovers, Killdeer, Dunlin, and Spotted, Sharp-tailed, Least, Pectoral, and Western Sandpipers, dowitchers, Wilson's Snipe, and Bonaparte's Gull. The crabapple trees, blackberry bushes, and other shrubs have Cedar Waxwings, House and Purple Finches, Red Crossbills, and a good variety of winter sparrows. American Pipit (migration), Savannah Sparrow, and American Goldfinch are in former pastures near the Salmon Center, which are also good for Greater White-fronted, Cackling, and Canada Geese. Raptors have included Bald Eagle (reliable), Northern Harrier, Cooper's and Red-tailed Hawks, American Kestrel, Merlin, and Peregrine Falcon. Northern Shrikes are seen in winter.

Turn left out of the Theler parking lot onto northbound SR-3, go 1.1 miles, and turn left onto SR-300 (aka NE Clifton Lane). It's 3.1 miles to **Belfair State Park**, on the left. Good restrooms are available here. A Discover Pass is required, and rangers are often there to sell them. After the gate, turn left and curve toward the water on the southeast, which is the outlet of Mission Creek into Hood Canal. This is a good marine bird spot and sometimes hosts rarities such as Eared Grebe, Willet, and Semipalmated Sandpiper. The campground is in the southwest beach area at the outlet of Little Mission Creek, which trails through the campground to the beach and has most woodland species in appropriate seasons as well as Mountain Quail historically.

To find Mountain Quail, familiarize yourself with their calls and try to do this route in March through May. At other seasons, playback of calls may be helpful. Turn left out of Belfair State Park onto SR-300 and head west. Continue on SR-300 as it becomes North Shore Road. In 7.8 miles at the 11000 block, turn right onto Canyon Drive into Belfair View Estates and continue upwards on this winding road. In 0.5 mile at the top of the hill, Canyon Drive becomes Hurd Road. Continue on **Hurd Road**, stopping at several intersections with dead-end roads where the roadway widens next to open scrubby areas. Listen for Mountain Quail. Hurd Road changes to gravel at Belfair View Road. Continue another 0.5 mile north on Hurd Road to a pullout on the right by a yellow gate, the unsigned entrance to state forest land. You may enter on foot. This is the best spot for Mountain Quail and also provides great views of the Olympic Mountains on the left (west) side of the road. Listen as well for Hermit and Townsend's Warblers in springtime.

Backtrack down Hurd Road to the intersection with North Shore Road (SR-300), then turn right. In 3.1 miles, cross the Tahuya River Bridge, then in 0.1 mile turn right onto **NE Belfair-Tahuya Road**. In 0.4 mile, veer left to stay on Belfair-Tahuya Road. Proceed 4.8 miles to **NE Tahuya-Blacksmith Road**. Turn left here and begin looking and listening for Mountain Quail.

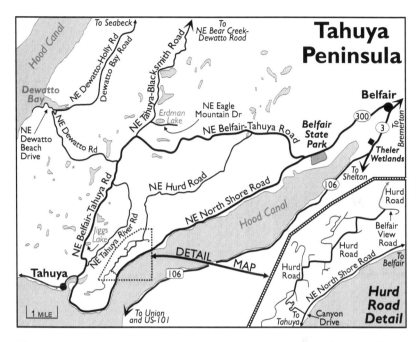

They've been seen in recent years between this turnoff and NE Eagle Mountain Drive (0.7 mile), especially a little more than half way along this stretch.
Mountain Quail do move around, and many of the roads in this general area
have good shrubby habitat. One promising possibility is to continue north on
Tahuya-Blacksmith Road, giving special attention to the gravel portion of the
road between Eagle Mountain Drive and NE Bear Creek-Dewatto Road.

Other worthwhile stops reachable from the western end of the
Belfair-Tahuya Road include **Harvey Rendsland Park at Jiggs Lake** on
Belfair-Tahuya Road (1.3 miles from North Shore Road) and **Dewatto Bay**,
where cliffs next to you host Pigeon Guillemot nest holes. Guillemots can be
seen in the water there at all times of the year, as can other waterfowl including loons and grebes in migration and in winter. To reach this bay, travel 4.0
miles from North Shore Road on Belfair-Tahuya Road and turn left onto NE
Dewatto Road. It's 3.6 miles to NE Dewatto Beach Drive, where you turn left,
go 0.7 mile and park before the *End of County Road* sign. To return to Belfair
from the Tahuya-Blacksmith Road, go back to Belfair-Tahuya Road, turn left,
and proceed 6.5 miles to North Shore Road. This is the eastern end of the
Belfair-Tahuya Road, and you are just a half-mile west of Belfair State Park.
Turn left to get to the park and to Belfair.

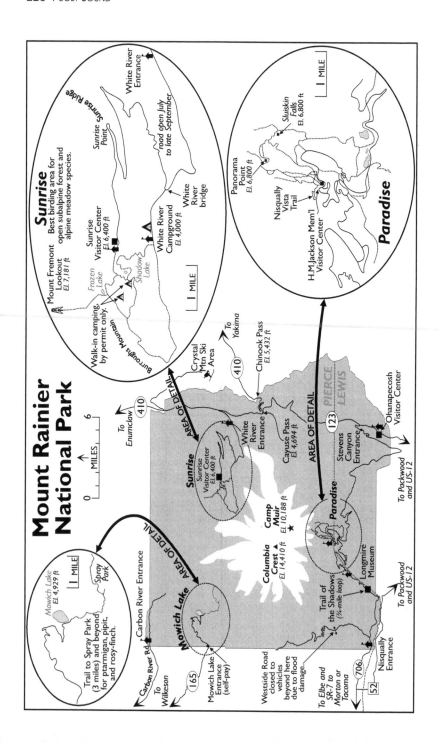

MOUNT RAINIER

by Bill Shelmerdine
revised by Bill Shelmerdine

Many sought-after bird species nest on, or visit, the upper west slopes of the Cascades above Puget Sound, but much of this country is accessible only by backpacking. The three trans-mountain highways run through cut-over forests at relatively low elevations most of the way to the crest, and the species that live in these habitats can usually be found just as well in the lowlands. The best birding these roads have to offer is at the actual summits: Snoqualmie Pass on I-90 (page 262), Chinook Pass on SR-410 (page 318), and Stevens Pass on US-2 (page 404). By visiting these places birders can readily find the common and even some of the uncommon mountain species, but chances of finding any of the true alpine specialties are remote. Fortunately, one high-elevation Puget Sound site has both good birds and ready access. You will have to set aside at least one full day to go there, but even if you miss a target bird or two, you will not regret a trip to Mount Rainier. (Fee or America the Beautiful Pass required.)

A striking feature and major landmark, Mount Rainier is readily visible from many locations around Western and Eastern Washington. It is a composite volcano of massive proportions with an extensive system of glaciers covering roughly 37 square miles—the largest single-peak glacial system in the Lower 48. Currently considered dormant, it has had a history of intense volcanism. One can only imagine the incredible bulk and height of the 16,000-foot ancestral summit, reduced to its present 14,410 feet by violent eruptions, mudflows, and thousands of years of glacial erosion. The mountain and surrounding lush, old-growth forests are included within 235,625-acre **Mount Rainier National Park**, famous for spectacular scenery and subalpine wildflowers (July–August). The fall color change can be just as impressive.

The park is a good place to look for the typical birds of wet conifer forests, but the big treat is easy birding access to subalpine forest and alpine areas. Gray Jay, Clark's Nutcracker, Mountain Chickadee, Hermit Thrush, Cassin's Finch, and Evening Grosbeak are common in the subalpine. Sooty Grouse, Golden Eagle, Mountain Bluebird, and Townsend's Solitaire are fairly common, while Black Swift (rare) and Pine Grosbeak are seen occasionally. The most sought-after specialties—White-tailed Ptarmigan, Boreal Owl, Gray-crowned Rosy-Finch—are present at certain times and places, but finding them may require intensive searching (and luck). The late season (mid-August–October) is often productive for these species.

Mount Rainier is popular with tourists from around the world and also with local day-trippers. Spring and summer—overall, the best seasons to visit—are also the most crowded. Visitor pressure declines after Labor Day, but even then, finding a spot in a designated pullout or parking area is much easier on weekdays and early in the morning. The park receives a lot of snow.

Average annual snowfall at Paradise, on the south side of the park, exceeds 50 feet. In typical years, trailheads and trails to alpine habitats will be snow-free and accessible from July into October. The road to Paradise from the Nisqually Entrance is kept open year round (bring tire chains in winter). All other roads are subject to snow closures, especially between late October and early May. If planning a visit early or late in the season, call ahead (360-569-2211) to check access, snow levels, and trail conditions.

There are five summer entrance points. Most visitors—birders in-cluded—go in either via the Nisqually Entrance (on the southwest side) to Longmire and Paradise, or via the White River Entrance (on the northeast side) to Sunrise. A loop trip connecting these two entrances around the southeast side of the park is possible, too, but time-consuming. Birders with only a day to spend should consider focusing their efforts at Sunrise, especially if pursuing the higher-elevation species. The **Sunrise Visitor Center** is about 75 road miles from Tacoma, 90 from Yakima, or 95 from Seattle, mostly on two-lane roads that can be slow going, so count on a long day. Better still, take a couple of days and camp at one of the many campgrounds (reservations essential at the height of the season). In addition to Sunrise, there are visitor centers at Paradise, Longmire, and Ohanapecosh, offering interpretive dis-plays, books, maps, and snacks. Basic maps and information can also be ob-tained at kiosks where entrance fees are paid. Gasoline is not available inside the park, so gas up before you go in.

Large portions of the park are covered by dense, wet conifer forest. For-ests at lower elevations around the park's perimeter are in the Western Hemlock zone. Douglas-fir, Western Hemlock, Western Redcedar, and Grand Fir are the primary large tree species. Several stands of old growth have massive trees over 200 feet tall, and a complex, multi-storied structure. The interiors of these stands are dark, have variable understory vegetation, and are typically covered with downed logs and mosses. Pacific Wren is the most conspicuous member of the bird community here, and possibly the only one you will actually see. Other species spend most of their time up in the can-opy, where you can best find them from overlooks. Forests become more open above 5,500 feet, transitioning into subalpine parklands and alpine meadows. Bird-viewing is much easier in these habitats.

While some of the bird species change with the forest type, many remain the same. Characteristic species of lower-elevation forests include Ruffed Grouse, Northern Pygmy-Owl (uncommon), Red-breasted Sapsucker (fairly common), Hairy Woodpecker, Pacific-slope Flycatcher, Pacific Wren, Swainson's Thrush, and Western Tanager. Species that may be found in both lower- and higher-elevation forest zones include Sooty Grouse, Olive-sided Flycatcher (fairly common), Gray and Steller's Jays, Chestnut-backed Chick-adee, Red-breasted Nuthatch, Brown Creeper, Golden-crowned Kinglet, Varied Thrush, Townsend's and Wilson's Warblers, Dark-eyed Junco, Red Crossbill, and Evening Grosbeak. Pine Grosbeak, a much sought-after and uncommon species, is occasionally reported from higher-elevation forests and trails above Paradise, near Sunrise, on the trails around Reflection Lakes, and at Chinook Pass. Vaux's Swifts nest and roost in the larger tree stands and can often be seen flying above the canopy or river valleys. American Dippers are fairly common throughout the park from forest zones up to the edge of the snowfields, along clear-running rivers, lakes, and alpine streams.

LONGMIRE AND PARADISE

The Nisqually Entrance (elevation 2,003 feet) is 14 miles east of Elbe on SR-706. The 23-mile road from there to Paradise (elevation 5,560 feet) offers an excellent elevational transect of the park's forest types and their associated birdlife. Especially impressive old-growth stands can be found about five miles inside the entrance, as one approaches **Longmire**. Across the road from the National Park Inn (6.4 miles), the Trail of the Shadows offers birds of open, lowland habitats—meadows, Beaver pond, cattail marsh, alder thickets—along a three-quarter-mile loop rimmed by forest. At **Paradise**, trailheads provide easy access into open subalpine parkland and meadows, with fine wildflower displays, plenty of Hoary Marmots, and nesting Horned Larks and American Pipits. White-tailed Ptarmigans are sometimes seen above Paradise Park at elevations ranging from 6,300 to 7,000 feet, but Sunrise is usually a better bet for this species. Gray-crowned Rosy-Finches also occur in the area, but during the summer they often haunt crags and cliffs high on the mountain, for example at Camp Muir (elevation 10,188 feet)—definitely within the realm of alpine wilderness travel and not for the inexperienced or unprepared. Weather on the mountain changes suddenly and can be fierce.

MOWICH LAKE

If you are tempted by subalpine meadows on a par with Paradise but without the crowds, head for the Mowich Lake Entrance on Mount Rainier's remote northwest side. Depending on snowpack, the road may not open until late July. Facilities are minimal, and reaching the alpine zone requires an invigorating hike. From SR-410 at the south edge of Buckley, turn south onto SR-165. Keep left at the fork in 1.7 miles, and continue 2.9 miles to Wilkeson. In 5.9 miles, take the right branch at another fork and go 11.2 miles through managed forests to the park boundary and self-pay fee station. It is another 5.6 miles to the end of the road at Mowich Lake (elevation 4,929 feet). American Dippers are sometimes seen at the lake's outlet. Hike the trail three miles to Spray Park, where the meadows begin. At the high point in the trail, roughly a mile later, an unmarked trail goes south and uphill, traversing extensive alpine habitats. In this landscape of heather and fell field, look for White-tailed Ptarmigan, American Pipit, and Gray-crowned Rosy-Finch, the latter especially higher on the trail near the permanent snowfields and cliffs.

SUNRISE

The White River Entrance (elevation 3,500 feet) is reached by turning west from SR-410 onto a side road 4.6 miles inside the park's north boundary and 3.6 miles north of the SR-123 intersection at Cayuse Pass. The ranger station and entrance kiosk are 1.4 miles ahead. This is big-conifer habitat of the Western Hemlock zone, with birds characteristic of wet lowland forests. Varied Thrush is often found in these lower-elevation areas. The road to the White River Campground (elevation 4,000 feet) branches off to the left in 3.9 miles, just after the White River bridge. Just beyond is the gate for winter closure. Nightly closures can occur anytime after early September—call ahead for status. From the gate the road climbs steeply, and Alaska Yellowcedar, Silver Fir, and Mountain Hemlock become increasing components of the forest stands. Bird species characteristic of these upper-elevation forests include Ruby-crowned Kinglet, Hermit Thrush, and Yellow-rumped Warbler. In 7.8 miles, a large pullout at **Sunrise Point** (elevation 6,100 feet) provides a fabulous viewpoint, and trailheads to some interesting areas away from roads and crowds. In late summer and fall, Elk bugle from the forest edges.

For the next three miles the road traverses large meadows with dense clusters of subalpine tree species. Sooty Grouse, Red-tailed Hawk, American Kestrel, Clark's Nutcracker, Common Raven, and Mountain Bluebird are seen along this stretch. The road ends at the **Sunrise Visitor Center** (elevation 6,400 feet), perhaps the single best birding area in the park for species of open subalpine forests and alpine meadows. Trees and edges right around the visitor center have Chestnut-backed Chickadee, Red-breasted Nuthatch, both kinglet species, Chipping Sparrow, Dark-eyed Junco, and Pine Siskin; Gray Jay and Clark's Nutcracker should be nearby, as should Cascade Golden-mantled Ground Squirrel, Yellow-pine Chipmunk, and Hoary Marmot. In September, look for mixed-species flocks including flycatchers, vireos, warblers, and sparrows.

There is a noticeable passage of raptors in the fall; the Sunrise Area and Chinook Pass to the east are some of the best places in the park to search. Golden Eagle and Prairie Falcon are fairly regular while Northern Goshawk is occasionally sighted. Boreal Owls have been found in September and October in subalpine stands extending west from Sunrise Point to the walk-in Sunrise Camp beyond the visitor center (between about 5,800 and 6,400 feet elevation). Please do not torment them with excessive tape-playing.

To get the most out of Sunrise birding, obtain a map and hike some of the trails beginning at the visitor center. The high trail to Frozen Lake is the best bet for Townsend's Solitaire and Cassin's Finch, whereas the trail west toward Sunrise Camp and Shadow Lake is better for Sooty Grouse (also try the adjacent trails) and Gray Jay. Mountain Chickadees are found throughout the area. Frozen Lake (elevation 6,750 feet), reached in about a mile, is the minimum distance one must go to find some of the true alpine species. Horned

Lark and American Pipit are often here, while Baird's Sandpiper and other shorebirds have been seen along the margins of the lake during fall migration. From this point and above is the summer range of the White-tailed Ptarmigan. The most reliable location in the park over the last few years has been along the 1.8-mile trail from Frozen Lake to the **Mount Fremont Lookout**. The birds have been found around scree and loose, rocky slopes, and within heather clumps and other low alpine vegetation—especially on the ridge right by the lookout (elevation 7,181 feet). Another traditional though less reliable location for ptarmigan is **Burroughs Mountain** (in similar habitat, elevation 7,100 to 7,400 feet) west of Frozen Lake. Gray-crowned Rosy-Finches nest higher on Rainier, well above the areas that hikers and birders usually visit, but they are given to substantial up-and-down movements each day. In summer, you may detect them about late-lingering snowfields near areas of rocks, cliffs, or seeps. They are more conspicuous in fall when they gather in post-breeding flocks.

South of the road to Sunrise, SR-410 has a few places to pull off and look out over the forest and valley below. These can be good for Vaux's Swift (often foraging at eye level) and birds of the canopy. From the intersection at Cayuse Pass, you may continue eastward on SR-410 to bird Chinook Pass (page 318) and sites in South Central Washington. SR-123 runs south to the Stevens Canyon Entrance (11 miles), where you may turn west on the road to Paradise (21 miles). SR-123 continues south past the Ohanapecosh Visitor Center to the park boundary in three miles and joins US-12 in another 2.5 miles. A left (east) turn here will take you in about 13 miles to White Pass—another South Central access point. Westbound, US-12 goes to Packwood and southwestern Washington birding sites, including the "back door" route to Mount Saint Helens (page 236).

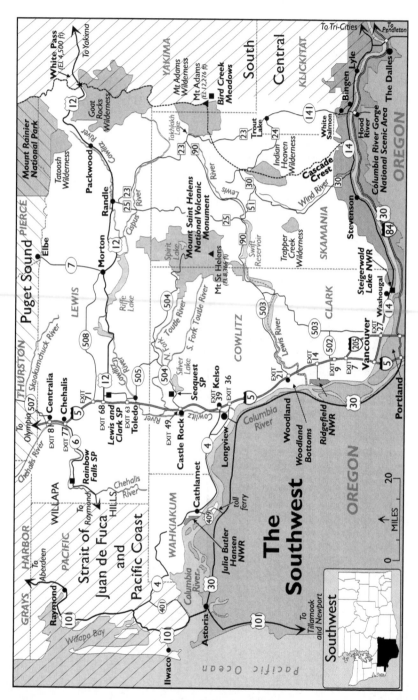

SOUTHWEST

Put simply, southwestern Washington is the Westside's Columbia Basin. Although its northwest and northeast corners are drained by the Chehalis and Nisqually Rivers, all the rest is in the Columbia River watershed. Culturally and economically, this region looks more to Portland/Vancouver than to the Puget Sound megalopolis—especially south of Centralia and Chehalis. Good birds are often reported to the Portland Rare Bird Alert (RBA) and the OBOL email list before they show up on Tweeters.

The Southwest was one of the first parts of Washington to be explored and settled by Euro-Americans. Lewis and Clark found few bird species new to science on their 4,100-mile Voyage of Discovery (1804–1806), and none in what is now Washington, even though they obtained several first state records. Fort Vancouver (which you can visit in Vancouver) played a prominent role in the area's early ornithological history. While based here between 1834 and 1836, John Kirk Townsend identified eight new bird species and several other distinct forms, including Vaux's Swift, Chestnut-backed Chickadee, Bushtit, Western Bluebird, MacGillivray's, Audubon's Yellow-rumped, Black-throated Gray, Townsend's, and Hermit Warblers, and Oregon Dark-eyed Junco. John James Audubon depicted all of these, from Townsend's specimens, in his *Birds of America*. No California Condor is better known than the one that served for Audubon's plate, a specimen taken by Townsend near the mouth of the Columbia.

The Southwest is differentiated into five subareas by its topography. On the west are the Willapa Hills, a low coastal range with few summits above 2,500 feet. On the east is the Cascade Range, rugged and remote, topped by Mount Adams at 12,276 feet. Another massive volcano, Mount Saint Helens, sits many miles west of the crest. Interstate 5 runs north and south down the middle of the third subarea—the lowlands between the coastal hills and the Cascades. The fourth subarea is the Columbia River bottomlands, especially those around Vancouver, and the last is the Columbia Gorge east to the Cascade divide.

The Willapa Hills are seldom visited by birders. Abundant rainfall blessed these hills with magnificent forests, but only scattered fragments of old growth have escaped the loggers. Nearly all of these lands belong to timber companies (with a few state forests) and are managed as tree farms, which limits bird species diversity. Gray Jay and Hermit Warbler are among the more interesting species to be found here if one takes the time to explore the hundreds of miles of logging roads.

The central lowlands—unglaciated, in contrast to glacially overriden Puget Sound to the north—consist of level ground or low hills, with few lakes. Much of this area was originally covered with Douglas-fir forests, but the deep alluvial soils prompted early clearing for agricultural use. In the northern part, from Chehalis south to Toledo, prairies and stands of Garry Oak still occupy patches of sandy, gravelly soils deposited by outwash from the melting glaciers farther north. Farther south, the Cowlitz River flows down to Longview, and the Columbia flows up to meet it, through a relatively narrow trough. Miles of tree farms extend to the east and west.

The plains around Vancouver are a northward continuation of Oregon's Willamette Valley. As the last ice age came to a close (15,000–13,000 Before Present), each release from the failed ice dams on Glacial Lake Missoula created large, temporary lakes in low-lying basins along the Columbia. The Willamette Valley was thus flooded dozens of times, depositing rich lacustrine soils that grew to prairies when the flooding ended. The original vegetation of these prairies is long gone, plowed under by settlers who arrived on the Oregon Trail. Large tracts of floodplain forest—Black Cottonwood, Oregon Ash, Bigleaf Maple, Garry Oak—still thrive adjacent to the Columbia, notably at Ridgefield National Wildlife Refuge. Diked fields at this refuge and elsewhere in the lowlands support high numbers of waterfowl, raptors, and Sandhill Cranes in migration and winter.

The Cascade Range occupies the eastern half of the area. Most of this territory, with typical Wet Side forests, is in the Gifford Pinchot and Mount Baker-Snoqualmie National Forests and the Mount Saint Helens National Volcanic Monument. Many of the national forest lands are subject to timber sales, but significant parts are permanently preserved in wilderness areas. Other stands of old growth survive on Forest Service lands—for example, along the Lewis River above Swift Reservoir. Numerous sites around Mount Adams and Mount Saint Helens provide forest birding as good as any in Western Washington.

The ancestral Columbia River maintained its course westward to the Pacific as the Cascades were slowly uplifted, carving the deep Columbia Gorge. The gorge was further widened as powerful floodwater torrents swept through the constriction following the repeated failures of ice dams on Glacial Lake Missoula. The flood crest averaged 1,000 feet high at the east end of the gorge, lessening to 500 feet at the west end. Today the Columbia Gorge is a notable migration corridor for birds and for remnants of the once-epic salmon runs. It is also an important site for wintering waterbirds.

Precipitation varies greatly within the region. Cathlamet, near the ocean, receives an average of 80 inches annually. The central lowlands receive 45–60 inches, rising to 70 inches at higher elevations of the Cascade foothills.

Vancouver receives just 39 inches (the same as Seattle), but in the heart of the Columbia Gorge 46 miles east, Stevenson averages 84 inches annually. Eastward through the gorge precipitation gradually drops off.

Marine low-pressure systems moving east bring heavy winter rains to the west end of the gorge. High pressure east of the Cascades drives gale-force winds westward through the gorge, bringing hot, dry air in summer and cold, continental air in winter. Sometimes the two opposing systems meet in winter, and when this happens, the west end of the gorge can see ice storms and blowing snow. Strong, steady winds in summer and fall make the gorge a renowned windsurfing site. But they can also hamper birding.

Temperatures are much the same as elsewhere in Western Washington. Means for Centralia and Vancouver are 39–40 degrees in January and 65–66 degrees in July.

The two trans-Cascades highways are open all year, although US-12 across White Pass is subject to snow-clearance closures (usually brief). SR-14 through the Columbia Gorge, and other lowland roads, may be made hazardous by ice and snowfall.

Accommodations and services may be found in the Vancouver/Portland metropolitan area, in cities and towns north along the I-5 corridor, and also in a few communities along US-12 and the Columbia.

FINDING SOUTHWESTERN SPECIALTIES

by Hal Opperman and Andy Stepniewski
revised by Randy Hill, Russ Koppendrayer, Wilson Cady,
Matt Bartels, and Ryan Merrill

Five bird species are closely associated with southwestern Washington. Three of these—Red-shouldered Hawk, Black Phoebe, and Western Scrub-Jay—are expanding their ranges into the state from western Oregon. White-tailed Kite is now very rarely seen, while Hermit Warbler is retreating southward as it loses ground to Townsend's Warbler.

RED-SHOULDERED HAWK

Although Red-shouldered Hawks have wintered recently in widely scattered parts of the state, this species is dependable only along the lower Columbia River. A Red-shouldered Hawk first wintered at **Ridgefield National Wildlife Refuge** in 1991, and others (sometimes two or three) have wintered there each year since then. Individuals are now being found at Ridgefield NWR with increasing regularity in breeding season as well. Although nesting is suspected, it has not been confirmed.

There are also both winter and summer records for Red-shouldered Hawk downstream at **Julia Butler Hansen National Wildlife Refuge**, near Cathlamet. This refuge was established in 1972 specifically to protect and manage the endangered Columbian White-tailed Deer. Although distant from other sites described in this chapter, the refuge is definitely worth a visit if you are on your way to or from the coast. Habitats include tideland Sitka Spruce

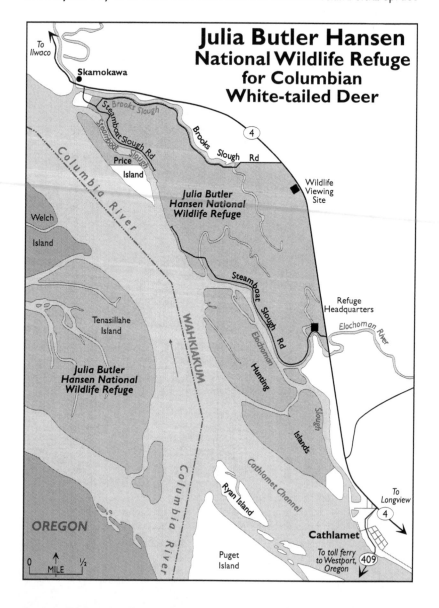

Julia Butler Hansen National Wildlife Refuge for Columbian White-tailed Deer

forest, riparian woodland, tidal and freshwater wetlands, and open fields, making for a diverse and abundant birdlife.

Two miles north of Cathlamet, turn west from SR-4 onto Steamboat Slough Road. This road has been undercut by the Columbia River after 2.7 miles where it now dead ends. A new dike is being constructed farther from the river that will provide tidal habitat. Especially numerous are Cackling and Canada Geese (various subspecies) and other waterfowl. A variety of raptors are conspicuous. The riparian woodlands have the usual assortment of wet-forest passerines. Return to SR-4 and go two miles northwest to Brooks Slough Road. Turn left and in 2.6 miles left again on the other end of Steamboat Slough Road to its terminus. There is excellent birding in all seasons along this route.

BLACK PHOEBE

At the time *Birds of Washington* was published in 2005, only six records of Black Phoebe in Washington had been accepted, mostly found during the winter. Since that time, the population has expanded greatly northward into Washington, with breeding first documented in 2011 and annually since. Although all three phoebe species found in the U.S. are migratory and the first flycatchers to arrive in late winter or early spring, the Black Phoebe is mainly a resident species across its range. The mild yearlong climate of the Pacific coast is conducive to post-breeding dispersal to the north, with increased winter occurrence likely a result of climate change.

While this species occurs somewhat randomly in counties west of the Cascades with five to ten records annually since 2010, by far the most likely areas are along the lower Columbia River in Clark, Cowlitz, and Wahkiakum Counties. Nesting was documented in closed areas of Ridgefield NWR from 2011–2013 with young fledged from two different nests each year (including 20 nestlings that were banded in 2012 and 2013). "Resident birds" were seen from October 2010 to February 2014 before they disappeared from that location after a period of harsh weather. Coincidentally, a suspected breeding pair was found across the Columbia River in St. Helens, Oregon during the spring of 2014. Nesting also was documented near the office at Julia Butler Hansen NWR in 2014, and nesting was assumed the year before. All nests were found on man-made structures. With increased spring sightings recently in the Puget Trough, this breeding expansion north is likely to continue.

Post-breeding movement seems associated with the presence of open water, with running water probably a key factor in winter survival where insects can be found even with ponds frozen. Some likely areas are at the two refuges where nesting is documented, especially along channels where tide gates are present or water is pumped from drainage ditches in diked lowland areas. Places with access and suitable habitats near the Columbia River include: **River S Unit of Ridgefield NWR** along Bower Slough, Julia Butler Hansen

NWR near headquarters and the Columbia River levee, Puget Island south of Cathlamet, Woodland Bottoms along Dike Road, Vancouver Lake and lowlands along Lower River Road, and the Willow Grove area west of Longview south of SR-4.

WESTERN SCRUB-JAY

Western Scrub-Jay is the most widespread of the five species, though rarely numerous. Once confined to the Vancouver Lowlands, for the last 60 years it has been pushing slowly, inexorably northward up the lower Cowlitz Valley and up and down the Columbia. Western Scrub-Jays are now fairly common year-round residents at lower elevations in relatively open landscapes (towns, open woods, edges) throughout southwestern Washington, north to Tacoma, west to the coast, and into the eastern Columbia Gorge and up to Yakima. They are breeding north to Bellingham. Western Scrub-Jays favor Garry Oaks when available—for example, at Ridgefield National Wildlife Refuge (page 240)—but are not tied to them. These jays are still enough of a novelty that Washington birders look for them when visiting the Southwest.

WHITE-TAILED KITE

White-tailed Kites were steadily increasing in numbers through the mid-2000s. They nested locally in the interior Southwest as well as along the South Coast. The first nesting record was in Raymond in 1988. Up until the mid-2000s, they were seen, most commonly in winter, hunting the rank grasslands at Julia Butler Hansen National Wildlife Refuge, and also as far up the Columbia as Steigerwald Lake National Wildlife Refuge. Farther north, they were occasionally seen on some of the glacial outwash prairies that dot the lowlands between the Chehalis and the Cowlitz Rivers, from Centralia to Toledo. However, since 2010, the White-tailed Kite is notable mostly for its absence: they have nearly disappeared from the state. Two consecutive harsh winters are suspected as the reason. Whether the species will make a return is unclear.

HERMIT WARBLER

Hermit Warblers inhabit Douglas-fir forests on the east and south slopes of the Olympic Mountains, on the west slopes of the Cascade Range south of the Cowlitz River, and southward and westward through the Willapa Hills. Their range is contracting as they are being displaced by the competitively superior Townsend's Warbler, which is advancing from the north and east. The two species meet along narrow, moving hybrid zones in the eastern Olympics—for example, near Quilcene (page 216)—and the southwestern Cascades. During the nesting season, use caution in identifying either species anywhere along the west slopes of the Cascades between White Pass and

Mount Adams—for example, around Takhlakh Lake (page 256) and Indian Heaven (page 255). Hybrids may be seen farther afield in post-breeding dispersal or fall and spring migration, but rarely east of the Cascade Crest or north of Puget Sound.

Most hybrids have yellow faces and therefore are mistaken for Hermits, while the smaller share of hybrids that have black masks are usually called Townsend's. It is important to check multiple characteristics. "Good" Hermits have gray (not green) backs and pure-white underparts with no yellow below the bib, no streaking on the flanks (a touch on the lower flanks is OK), and a white gap between the bib and the back. "Good" Townsend's have a solid-black crown (yellow in Hermits except for a small amount of black approaching the nape), heavily streaked flanks, and a bright yellow breast; the black bib corners reach the green back. Hybrids cannot confidently be separated from either parent species by song.

If you want an identification challenge, drive some of the forest roads north, east, and south of Packwood, on US-12 about 20 miles below White Pass. This is smack in the middle of the hybrid zone, and you may see Townsend's, Hermits, and everything in between. Singing birds often come down to taped playbacks of their songs, affording close looks.

Phenotypically pure Hermit Warblers can reliably be found on the south side of Mount Saint Helens (page 216) and also in the Willapa Hills—for example, at Capitol State Forest near Olympia (page 211). Go exploring for Hermits on your own in the lightly birded hills farther south. They have been reported singing high in the canopy in the mature Douglas-fir, Western Hemlock, and Western Redcedar forest at Rainbow Falls State Park. From Exit 77 on I-5, take SR-6 west about 16 miles to the park entrance (Discover Pass required). The rushing waters of the Chehalis River provide good habitat for American Dippers and a scenic spot to picnic.

MOUNT SAINT HELENS

by Wilson Cady and Andy Stepniewski
revised by Russ Koppendrayer

In May of 1980, the eruption of Mount Saint Helens transformed 230 square miles of forest lands into a barren moonscape now mostly contained within the 110,000-acre Mount Saint Helens National Volcanic Monument. The devastation sent an ash cloud northeast across the continent, blew megatons of logs and avalanche debris into lakes and rivers, and in the process created a laboratory for the study of recolonization by flora and fauna. Vegetation is recovering rapidly as nature rushes to heal this massive insult. As plant communities evolve, so do the bird populations that depend on them. Inside the monument the landscape was left to regenerate unaided, and over 80 species of birds have already been found nesting. By

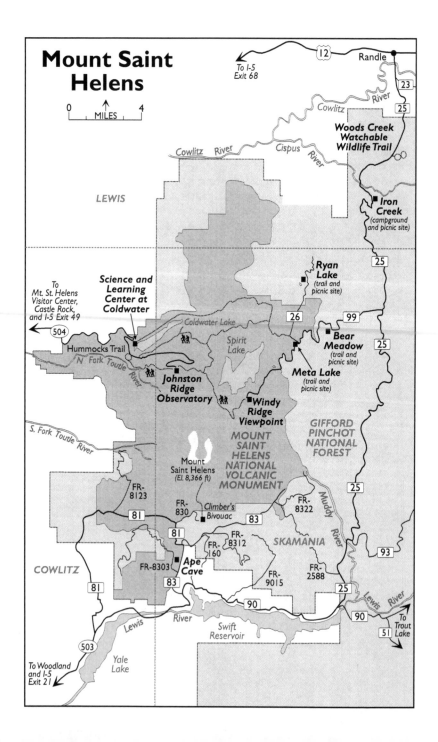

Mount Saint Helens

0 ▲ MILES 4

To I-5
Exit 68

12   Randle

23

25

Cowlitz   River

**Woods Creek
Watchable
Wildlife Trail**

LEWIS

Cowlitz   River

Cispus   River

**Iron
Creek**
*(campground
and picnic site)*

25

To
Mt. St. Helens
Visitor Center,
Castle Rock,
and I-5 Exit 49

**Science and
Learning
Center at
Coldwater**

**Ryan
Lake**
*(trail and
picnic site)*

26   99

25

504

Coldwater Lake

Spirit
Lake

**Bear
Meadow**
*(trail and
picnic site)*

Hummocks Trail

N. Fork Toutle River

**Johnston
Ridge
Observatory**

**Windy
Ridge
Viewpoint**

Meta Lake
*(trail and
picnic site)*

S. Fork Toutle River

*MOUNT
SAINT
HELENS
NATIONAL
VOLCANIC
MONUMENT*

*GIFFORD
PINCHOT
NATIONAL
FOREST*

25

Mount
Saint Helens
(El. 8,366 ft)

FR-
8123

FR-
830   Climber's
Bivouac

81

81

FR-
8303   **Ape
Cave**

83

83

FR-
8312

FR-
160

FR-
8322

SKAMANIA

FR-
9015

Muddy   River

FR-
2588

25

93

COWLITZ

90

Lewis   River

Swift
Reservoir

25   Lewis   River

90

To
Trout
Lake

51

503

Yale
Lake

To Woodland
and I-5
Exit 21

contrast, dead timber outside the boundaries was salvaged and the area replanted, creating an even-aged stand of young trees with little avian diversity.

Within the monument you must stay on the maintained trails, which limits the number of places you can search for birds. Some of the trails are up to 30 miles in length and are designed for backcountry hiking and camping trips. A federal day or annual pass is required to park at trailheads and other designated areas in the monument and the surrounding Gifford Pinchot National Forest. Higher-elevation roads are closed to auto traffic in winter, usually from late November until sometime in June. Call monument headquarters (360-449-7800) for access information if you are contemplating an early- or late-season visit.

NORTHWEST SIDE (TOUTLE RIVER)

Most of the visitor amenities are found on the western side of the volcano. Take Exit 49 from I-5 at Castle Rock and go east five miles on SR-504 to the **Mount Saint Helens Visitor Center**, where you can pick up maps and other information. This state-owned visitor center is on Silver Lake, a large, shallow body of water formed by a mudflow from a previous eruption that blocked small streams. Along the 0.5-mile Silver Lake Wetlands Trail you can search for Wood Duck, American Bittern, Virginia Rail, and Sora, among many other species. Other spots around the lake have fewer people and can be birded from roadside.

Located across SR-504 from the visitor center, **Seaquest State Park** has old-growth forests of the type that existed before these lowlands were converted to tree farms. Spotted Owls once nested here but have been replaced by Barred Owls. Red-breasted Sapsucker, Hutton's Vireo, Brown Creeper, and other denizens of old-growth conifers are still fairly common.

Operating as a visitor center on weekends only, the **Science and Learning Center at Coldwater** is located about 38 miles east of the previous stop on SR-504, within the national volcanic monument, where trees and other debris were blown down into the Toutle River. Regrowth of herbaceous plants is rapidly changing these areas. There are many trails in the recovering forests, and some of the better birding is found here due to the variety of plants and insects providing food sources. Orange-crowned, MacGillivray's, Yellow, and Wilson's Warblers nest here, and Common Yellowthroats are found in the riparian growth along the creeks. Different, forest-loving species can be found in patches of standing dead trees and in those sheltered areas where ridges blocked the blast and there are still living trees. Western and Mountain Bluebirds nest in stubs, which also are home to Vaux's Swifts and several species of woodpeckers.

The 2.3-mile-long **Hummocks Trail** at the south end of Coldwater Lake loops through a landscape pockmarked by cattail marshes, small ponds, and tree-lined lakes. This is one of the better birding spots, with many passerines nesting in the maturing alder forest. Mallards, Ring-necked Ducks, Ruffed and Sooty Grouse, Pied-billed Grebes, Soras, American Coots, and Red-winged Blackbirds also nest in the wetlands. Bank Swallows use the cliffs formed of volcanic ash.

The open pumice plains north of the mountain were created by landslides and both pyroclastic and mudflows. Due to depth of the pumice and ash, this habitat is recovering slowly. Birds that may be found here include Common Nighthawk, Prairie Falcon, Horned Lark, Rock Wren, and Western Meadowlark. Trails starting from the **Johnston Ridge Observatory**, where the road ends, lead to Windy Ridge on the southeast side of Spirit Lake. Be sure to carry water when hiking in this desert-like landscape.

NORTHEAST SIDE (WINDY RIDGE)

To reach the less frequently visited, but no less spectacular, east side of the monument (closed in winter), drive east from I-5, Exit 68 on US-12 for 48 miles to Randle. Turn south onto SR-131 (aka Cispus Road, becomes FR-25) and continue 5.8 miles to the parking area for the 1.5-mile **Woods Creek Watchable Wildlife Trail**, which goes through mixed hardwood and conifer forest to Woods Creek Beaver Pond. Many typical Westside lowland species can be found on this loop, including Ruffed Grouse, Red-breasted Sapsucker, Downy, Hairy, and Pileated Woodpeckers, Western Wood-Pewee, Willow, Hammond's, and Pacific-slope Flycatchers, Warbling Vireo, Tree Swallow, Black-capped and Chestnut-backed Chickadees, Pacific and Marsh Wrens, Swainson's Thrush, Orange-crowned, MacGillivray's, Yellow, and Black-throated Gray Warblers, Common Yellowthroat, Song Sparrow, Purple Finch, and Pine Siskin. Just past the pond, the **Old-growth Loop Trail** takes off, returning to this point in one mile. This aptly named trail is excellent for woodpeckers, Varied Thrush, and Townsend's (or Townsend's X Hermit) Warbler. Northern Goshawk occurs, but is infrequently seen.

Another 3.9 miles south along FR-25 is **Iron Creek Campground**, situated in an impressive old-growth forest along the Cispus River. Two-tenths of a mile farther on FR-25, a short interpretive trail at the Iron Creek Picnic Site goes through giant Douglas-firs, Western Hemlocks, and Bigleaf Maples reminiscent of the Olympic rain forests. Another trail follows the river downstream to the campground through similar forest. Birds are not numerous or conspicuous in this habitat, but you should find Chestnut-backed Chickadee, Pacific Wren, Golden-crowned Kinglet, and Swainson's and Varied Thrushes.

FR-25 winds south from here, alternating between old-growth and second-growth forests for 10.1 miles to FR-99, gateway to the northeast side of Mount Saint Helens. Climb this paved but twisting road 4.7 miles to **Bear Meadow**, at the edge of the blast zone. One can gain a clearer appreciation of the pre-eruption forest by walking up Boundary Trail 1, which begins north of the picnic site and ascends a sidehill, in a few hundred yards entering dense, old-growth Western Hemlock, Silver Fir, and Noble Fir forest where Hermit and Varied Thrushes and Townsend's (or Townsend's X Hermit) Warblers are common. A quite different habitat and birdlife can be found in the blast zone, below the picnic area.

Continue along FR-99 and turn right in 4.4 miles onto FR-26, reaching **Ryan Lake** in 5.0 miles. Walk the 0.6-mile interpretive trail with signage that explains the near-complete recovery of the lake's waters since the eruption. Return to FR-99, turn right, and drive the 0.2 mile to **Meta Lake**. Birding along the short trail to this small lake should reveal many birds typical of the recovering forest, among them Sooty Grouse, Rufous Hummingbird, Hairy Woodpecker, Northern Flicker, Willow Flycatcher, Warbling Vireo, Tree Swallow, Pacific Wren, Swainson's and Hermit Thrushes, American Robin, Orange-crowned, MacGillivray's, and Yellow Warblers, Fox, Song, Lincoln's, and White-crowned Sparrows, Dark-eyed Junco, and Pine Siskin.

Windy Ridge lies 6.8 miles ahead. En route, watch for Dusky Flycatchers on the brushy slopes and Townsend's Solitaires in steep, rocky areas by the roadside. At the parking lot, the long series of steps ascends steeply about 200 feet to a superb viewpoint of Mount Saint Helens and Spirit Lake. Canada Geese have found the recovering Spirit Lake and migrating waterfowl are possible here as well. Other species you may see in this area include Bald and Golden Eagles, Horned Lark, and Mountain Bluebird.

SOUTH SIDE (LEWIS RIVER)

Take Exit 21 from I-5 at Woodland and travel east up the Lewis River valley on SR-503 (becomes FR-90). Obtain a map of the Gifford Pinchot National Forest and drive some of the roads on the south and southeast sides of the mountain, to the intersection with SR-25 at the east end of Swift Reservoir. Lush vegetation and old-growth forest in this area were spared as the volcano blew to the northwest. Pure-looking Hermit Warblers can be found in these woods, which lie west of the hybrid zone. **Ape Cave**, the longest lava tube in the Lower 48, is worth a visit. Turn north from FR-90 onto FR-83 at the west end of Swift Reservoir. In about a mile and a half stay left onto FR-8303 and continue to the cave entrance in another mile and a half. Lanterns are available for rent.

You can go north on FR-25 to Randle (turning off along the way on FR-99 to visit Windy Ridge), and complete a loop around the mountain by returning to I-5 on US-12. For those who enjoy backcountry exploration, FR-90 follows the Lewis River upstream from Swift Reservoir for many miles (old-growth forest, waterfalls, forest service campgrounds), eventually reaching FR-23 at the edge of the Mount Adams Wilderness Area near Takhlakh Lake (page 256). You can take FR-23 south to Trout Lake or north to US-12 at Randle.

VANCOUVER AND VICINITY

by Wilson Cady

revised by Wilson Cady

The Columbia River bottomlands north and east of Vancouver, though mostly diked, offer vast freshwater marshes, grasslands, shallow lakes, and some of the densest remaining high-quality floodplain forest in Washington. The mile-wide Columbia is tidal here, and the shoreline is just a few feet above sea level, conveying an estuarine feeling. The most important sites are the Lewis River delta, near Woodland; alluvial deposits from the outwash of the Willamette River, near Vancouver; and the mouth of the Columbia Gorge, near Washougal. Birders come here principally to find waterfowl, raptors, Sandhill Cranes, and gulls, in migration and winter. Birding is also good for typical passerines in all seasons, and the area has had its share of rarities.

WOODLAND BOTTOMS

The Woodland Bottoms are a diked remnant of the former floodplain at the confluence of the Columbia and Lewis Rivers. Nearly all of the land inside the dike has been converted to agricultural use; crops are rotated yearly. In migration and winter, geese, ducks, and Sandhill Cranes move from field to field depending on what foods are available. The best way to bird this area is by

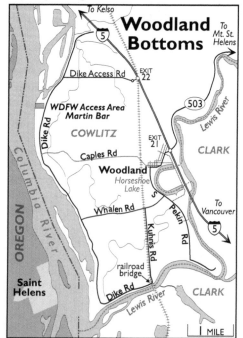

scanning the fields as you drive the road on top of the encircling dike, looking for signs of bird activity. When you see something interesting, drive the crossroads to get closer. The dike road also gives access to riparian forest, beaches, and sandbars along the Columbia River. Bald Eagle, Rough-legged Hawk, and other raptors can be plentiful here, feeding on birds or on salmon and smelt in the Lewis River. In years when there is a smelt run, loons, grebes, and thousands of gulls gather at the river's mouth in March.

Take Exit 22 west from I-5, go around two round-abouts and onto Dike Access Road, and continue for 1.6 miles to the dike. To the right,

Dike Road dead-ends in 1.3 miles after paralleling a shallow slough bordered by an extensive willow forest on the far shore. Shorebirds and wading birds use the mudflats exposed when water levels are low. Purple Martins sit on the power lines around the pumping station.

Return to the intersection with Dike Access Road and continue south on Dike Road for 0.7 mile to the WDFW Access Area at Martin Bar, on the Columbia River. (A daily fee or Discover Pass required; the Port of Woodland owns the surrounding land and is seeking to buy the WDFW site; a port pass will be required if the sale occurs.) The wave-protected waters around the offshore sandbars here and for the next four miles harbor loons, grebes, and waterfowl, while geese and gulls roost on the sandbars.

In 4.7 miles from Martin Bar, the dike-top road makes a 90-degree turn to the east, following the Lewis River. Check for birds on the pilings. Barrow's Goldeneyes winter near the railroad bridge (1.0 mile). From here, drive north on Kuhnis Road 1.6 miles to an intersection. Turn right on Whalen Road, then bear left on South Pekin Road (which will become Fifth Street as it enters Woodland), skirting Horseshoe Lake and reaching Davidson Avenue in 1.3 miles. Turn right and follow the main road through Woodland to I-5 Exit 21 in 0.6 mile.

RIDGEFIELD NATIONAL WILDLIFE REFUGE

This 5,150-acre refuge was created in 1965 to protect the Dusky Canada Goose, a dark-breasted subspecies that nests mainly on the Copper River delta in south central Alaska. A daily fee or an America the Beautiful Pass is required and is good at both units of the refuge that are open to the public. Oak woodland, extensive areas of marsh, and wet fields attract a great diversity of other bird species, including Sandhill Cranes. Much of the refuge is closed to provide sanctuary for Bald Eagles and other nesting species. Two units that are open to the public can be reached by taking Exit 14 from I-5 and driving west on SR-501 (Pioneer Street). Turn left at S Ninth Avenue in Ridgefield (2.5 miles) and drive 0.6 mile to the entrance to the **River "S" Unit**, on the right. The entrance road goes steeply down through a ravine forested with Douglas-fir, Western Redcedar, and Bigleaf Maple where you may find Hutton's Vireo, Varied Thrush (winter), and other passerines. Across Lake River, the refuge is diked and managed through agricultural practices to provide winter food and resting areas for up to 25,000 geese and 40,000 ducks. Tundra Swans are abundant from fall to mid-March.

Between October 1 and April 30, you must remain in your vehicle as you travel the 4.0-mile auto tour route. The only exceptions are the entrance parking lot and the observation blind at **Rest Lake**. Birds become accustomed to vehicles and remain close to the roads without flushing, allowing observation and photography. During the rest of the year you may get out and walk anywhere along the tour route. Wheelchair-accessible Kiwa Trail, just past

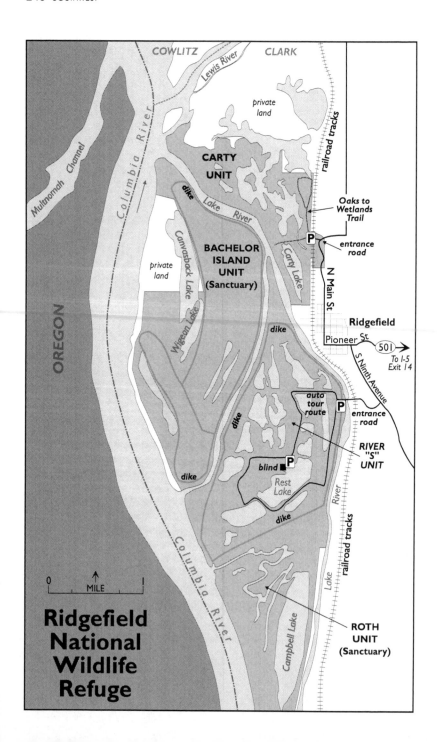

COWLITZ

CLARK

Lewis River

Columbia River

Multnomah Channel

private land

CARTY UNIT

dike

Lake River

Oaks to Wetlands Trail

Carty Lake

entrance road

Canvasback Lake

private land

BACHELOR ISLAND UNIT (Sanctuary)

Wigeon Lake

N Main St

Ridgefield

dike

Pioneer St

501

To I-5 Exit 14

S Ninth Avenue

auto tour route

entrance road

dike

RIVER "S" UNIT

blind

Rest Lake

dike

OREGON

dike

Columbia River

0   MILE

Lake River

railroad tracks

Campbell Lake

ROTH UNIT (Sanctuary)

Ridgefield National Wildlife Refuge

the observation blind, loops through wetlands with nesting rails. Yellow-headed Blackbirds nest in cattail patches on several of the lakes along the auto tour.

The water level of the many lakes on this unit is controlled to optimize the growth of aquatic plants upon which the waterfowl feed. American Bitterns, Virginia Rails, and Soras are common in these habitats. Recently, Black Phoebes have nested and wintered here and may be encountered along the Auto Tour Route. In late summer some of the lakes become mudflats, attracting up to a dozen species of shorebirds. The stands of Oregon Ash, Black Cottonwood, and willows on both this and the Carty Unit are the best place in the state to look for Red-shouldered Hawks, which have wintered here annually for more than two decades.

To visit the **Carty Unit** return to Ridgefield and turn left onto Pioneer Street, then right in 0.4 mile onto Main Avenue, which leaves town and drops down to cross Gee Creek (brush and trees worth checking for winter sparrow flocks) on its way to the refuge entrance, on the left (1.0 mile). This undiked, non-hunting unit—open year round—preserves a Columbia River floodplain in much the same condition as in 1806, when Lewis and Clark visited the Chinook village of Cathlapotle and its 900 inhabitants near this spot. A cedar plankhouse has been built here with help from the Chinooks to provide visitors with information about the people and their connection to the land.

Two trails await you on the other side of the footbridge spanning the railroad tracks. The one to the left goes down a hill and along an old road skirting Carty Lake, through cottonwood and willow stands. In winter, Merlins and Peregrine Falcons prey on ducks, snipe, and other birds in the open meadows. The **Oaks to Wetlands Trail**, to the right, is a nearly-level, two-mile loop that starts under majestic Garry Oaks. Western Scrub-Jays are common here. The hardwood forests of Clark County are perhaps the only place in the state where one can still reliably see White-breasted Nuthatches of the subspecies *aculeata*, which once nested fairly commonly from the Vancouver Lowlands north to the Fort Lewis Prairies. This coastal form is still widespread in western Oregon, but the Washington population is close to extirpation. The trail continues over basalt outcroppings forested with Oregon Ash, Garry Oak, and Douglas-fir, with places where you have good views of ponds and wetlands. Many bird species use these mixed habitats.

VANCOUVER LOWLANDS

A diked remnant of the vast floodplain at the confluence of the Columbia and Willamette Rivers, west of the city of Vancouver, the Vancouver Lowlands attract many of the same species as the adjacent Ridgefield National Wildlife Refuge to the north. Birding is best here from early fall through late spring, when wintering species congregate. The large flocks of Cackling and Canada Geese may contain five or more subspecies and should be carefully

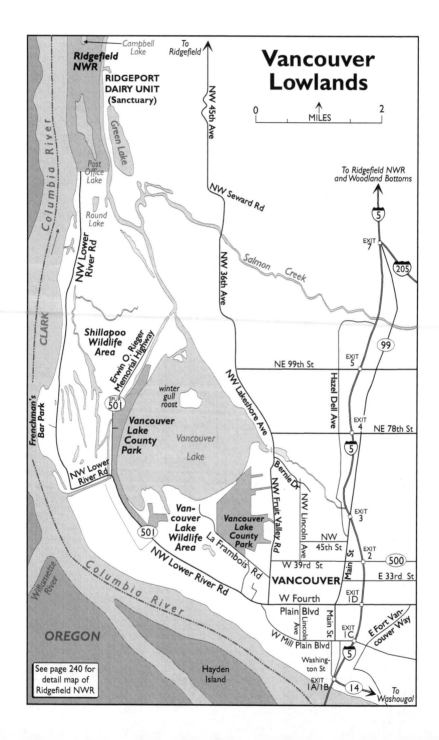

Vancouver Lowlands

Ridgefield NWR

RIDGEPORT DAIRY UNIT (Sanctuary)

Campbell Lake

To Ridgefield

Green Lake

Post Office Lake

Round Lake

NW 45th Ave

NW Seward Rd

NW 36th Ave

Salmon Creek

To Ridgefield NWR and Woodland Bottoms

5

EXIT 7

205

0   MILES   2

Columbia River

NW Lower River Rd

Shillapoo Wildlife Area

Erwin O. Rieger Memorial Highway

CLARK

Frenchman's Bar Park

winter gull roost

SPUR 501

Vancouver Lake County Park

Vancouver Lake

NW Lower River Rd

NW Lakeshore Ave

NE 99th St

EXIT 5

99

Hazel Dell Ave

EXIT 4   NE 78th St

5

Van-couver Lake Wildlife Area

501

Vancouver Lake County Park

La Frambois Rd

Bernie Dr

NW Fruit Valley Rd

NW Lincoln Ave

EXIT 3

NW Lower River Rd

W 39th St

VANCOUVER

NW 45th St

EXIT 2   500

E 33rd St

Willamette River

Columbia River

OREGON

W Fourth

EXIT 1D

Plain Blvd

Lincoln Ave

Main St

W Mill Plain Blvd

EXIT 1C

E Fort Van-couver Way

See page 240 for detail map of Ridgefield NWR

Hayden Island

Washing-ton St

EXIT 1A/1B   14

To Washougal

5

checked for other geese—Greater White-fronted, Emperor (casual), Snow, Ross's (rare), and Brant.

Take Exit 1D from I-5 and drive west on Fourth Plain Boulevard (SR-501). In 1.5 miles, at the Fruit Valley Road intersection, stay straight ahead onto NW Lower River Road.

Continue west, checking the ponds and fields for geese, ducks, Great Egrets, and Sandhill Cranes. In 3.3 miles, stop on the right at the parking lot for the flushing channel that brings water from the Columbia River into **Vancouver Lake**. The influx of fresh water attracts fish and the birds that feed on them. Loons, Western Grebes, and Double-crested Cormorants winter here. Occasionally a Red-necked or Clark's Grebe can be spotted among them. During late summer and at low tide, mudflats in a bay on the right (south) side of the flushing channel attract shorebirds. With a surface area of 2,800 acres, Vancouver Lake was less than three feet deep until it was dredged and the flushing channel constructed. The dredge spoils were used to make an island in the center of the lake that serves as a night-time roost for over 5,000 gulls during the winter months. Check them when they depart at dawn, or at dusk as they are returning.

Just ahead is an intersection where NW Lower River Road turns left. Stay straight ahead onto SR-501 Spur/Erwin O. Rieger Memorial Highway and continue 0.6 mile to the entrance to **Vancouver Lake County Park**, on the right. Ornamental trees and thick plantings of shrubs throughout the park attract migrant and wintering passerines. At the north end of the park is a trail lined with roses and other thick brush that harbors many sparrows. The trail leads to an Oregon Ash forest that may produce roosting owls or hawks.

Turn right from the park entrance and continue north. For the next 1.7 miles, until it ends, the road parallels the shore of Vancouver Lake. The land on the right side of the road is owned by Clark County Parks, and access to the lake is available in several spots. On the left side, the road follows one edge of the **Shillapoo Wildlife Area** (WDFW permit or Discover Pass required to park), approximately 1,000 acres of grasslands and wetlands around the bed of a seasonal lake used as a pheasant-release site for hunting purposes. In winter, Short-eared Owls are found in the open fields. Geese, Tundra Swans, and Sandhill Cranes can be numerous here when hunters are not present.

Return to Lower River Road and turn right (west). The fields on both sides of the road in 1.5 miles are one of the better spots in the lowlands to find Sandhill Cranes and goose flocks. Opposite the entrance to Frenchman's Bar Park (0.3 mile) is a Great Blue Heron rookery. Continue scanning the fields and ponds as you drive to **Post Office Lake** (4.5 miles), in the south section of Ridgefield National Wildlife Refuge. The fields and lake here, which are closed to hunting, are often swarming with geese and ducks in winter. From the parking lot at the end of Lower River Road you can walk the old road on top of the failing dike for about a mile. (*Note:* There is a plan to close the road

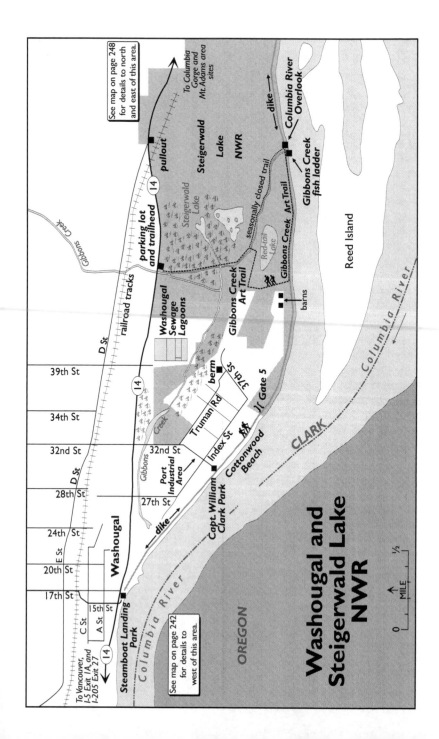

See map on page 248 for details to north and east of this area.

To Columbia Gorge and Mt. Adams area sites

Columbia River Overlook

dike

Gibbons Creek fish ladder

Steigerwald Lake NWR

pullout

(14)

Steigerwald Lake

Gibbons Creek Art Trail

seasonally closed trail

Red-tail Lake

parking lot and trailhead

Gibbons Creek Art Trail

Reed Island

Gibbons Creek

Columbia River

barns

railroad tracks

D St

Washougal Sewage Lagoons

39th St

(14)

Gibbons Creek

berm

37th St

34th St

Truman Rd

Gate 5

Index St

CLARK

32nd St

32nd St

Port Industrial Area

27th St

Cottonwood Beach

D St

28th St

Capt. William Clark Park

dike

24th St

Washougal

Columbia River

20th St

E St

17th St

15th St

Steamboat Landing Park

OREGON

C St

A St

To Vancouver, I-5 Exit 1A, and I-205 Exit 27

(14)

See map on page 242 for details to west of this area.

Washougal and Steigerwald Lake NWR

0   ½
    MILE

1.3 miles short of Post Office Lake that could take effect in 2016 or 2017. If the road is closed, try nearby Frenchman's Bar Regional Park, which has trails and access to the river.)

Return toward Vancouver and turn left (north) onto NW Fruit Valley Road. In 0.4 mile, at the intersection with La Frambois Road, check the **Fruit Valley Sewage Treatment Plant** ponds for diving ducks—mostly Ring-neckeds and Lesser Scaup, with some Canvasbacks and Ruddies. With a spotting scope you may be able to find a few Greater Scaup and possibly a Redhead or even a Tufted Duck (casual). La Frambois Road continues north to a parking area and boat launch in the **Vancouver Lake Wildlife Area**—some 500 acres of brush and fields and a stretch of shoreline at the south end of the lake (Discover Pass required). During hunting season, when the fields are a pheasant-release site and the boat launch is used by duck hunters, bird from the road.

WASHOUGAL AND STEIGERWALD LAKE

Upriver from Vancouver, a productive stretch of Columbia River bottomland—now diked and drained—extends eastward for about four miles from the town of Washougal to Point Vancouver, at the mouth of the Columbia Gorge. This is a migration crossroads, as birds following along the Cascade foothills or traveling through the gorge stop to use the ponds, marshes, pastures, riparian woodlands, river beaches, and offshore waters. Over 200 species have been recorded here, including numerous unusual species such as Tufted Duck, Surf Scoter, White-faced Ibis, White-tailed Kite, Red-shouldered Hawk, Black-necked Stilt, American Avocet, Gyrfalcon, Gray Flycatcher, Black Phoebe, Sage Thrasher, and Palm Warbler. A substantial part of these lands is within the 1,049-acre **Steigerwald Lake National Wildlife Refuge**, established in 1984 and featuring a walking trail opened to the public in 2009.

Take Exit 1A from I-5 (or Exit 27 from I-205), drive east on SR-14 to Washougal, and at the stoplight at 15th Street turn right to **Steamboat Landing Park** (10 miles east of I-205). From the floating fishing dock, scan the Columbia River for diving ducks, loons, and grebes over the rocky reef just downstream. The park is the west access to the dike separating the Columbia from its former floodplain around Steigerwald Lake. The Columbia River Dike Trail extends east for about 3.5 miles; do not cross any fences onto refuge or private property.

To shorten the walk to the best birding places, return to SR-14 and drive east to the S 32nd Street entrance to the Port Industrial Area, on the right (1.0 mile). Just after turning off, stop at a pullout on the right side of S 32nd Street that affords views of a remnant channel of Gibbons Creek. To the west, the creek is lined with trees and brush, good for Wood Ducks and Green Herons.

East across the road, the creek goes through a large marsh where bitterns and rails are common.

Continue south on S 32nd Street to Index Street and the Captain William Clark Park parking lot by the dike (0.5 mile). A trail over the dike leads to sandy **Cottonwood Beach** through an extensive riparian forest of cottonwood, ash, and willow—excellent in migration for passerines. Bullock's Oriole is a conspicuous nester here.

If you plan on walking the dike, use the parking lots farther east on Index Street. From there, a path leads into the forest at Cottonwood Beach farther away from most beach activities, and the Columbia River Dike Trail, which is open to jogging, bicycling, horseback riding and dog walking. Note **Reed Island** out in the Columbia River, the southernmost spot in the state and accessible only by boat. This undeveloped state park has a Great Blue Heron rookery. Check the shallow, protected waters between the island and the dike for diving ducks, loons, and grebes, and the open fields for geese, raptors, and cranes. There is a series of Purple Martin nesting colonies along the dike, and some Purple Martins nest in the cottonwood snags on the refuge.

Along the dike, note the white posts with mileage marks. The barns at mile 1.25 often have wintering sparrows around them. Shallow Red-tail Lake, just past these barns, at the refuge boundary, is good for wintering waterfowl and nesting American Bitterns. Here one can access the Steigerwald Lake NWR via the south end of the Gibbons Creek Art Trail, and walk the trail north two miles to the visitor parking lot on SR-14.

At mile 2.0 is the **Gibbons Creek fish ladder**, installed to allow salmon and Steelhead to return to the creek after a 20-year absence. Long rows of cottonwoods parallel to the river mark what were the tops of sandbars when this area flooded annually, before construction of the dike. Here you may find nesting White-breasted Nuthatches (the declining Westside race), House Wrens, and Lazuli Buntings. And here is the east entrance to the Gibbons Creek Art Trail; this segment of the trail is closed from 1 October to 1 May to protect a wintering wildlife feeding area. Before walking back to your vehicle, you can continue out the Dike Trail for another half-mile to where a fence marking private property crosses the dike.

Go back to S 32nd Street. Drive north to SR-14, turn right, and drive east. On the right in 0.5 mile, the **Washougal Sewage Lagoons** are viewable from the entrance road or from the highway shoulder a few yards ahead. Wood Ducks are numerous here in spring and summer.

As you travel east you can safely stop on the wide, paved highway shoulder to view the refuge. A pullout on the right, at the entry to the Columbia Gorge National Scenic Area, marks the entrance to the Steigerwald Lake NWR visitor parking lot (0.5 mile). From here a 2.75 mile round-trip trail leads through the wetlands and cottonwood forest and connects to the Columbia River Dike Trail. The plantings around this parking lot attract many birds including nesting Lazuli Buntings. This trail forms a loop, but one section of the trail is closed between October 1 and May 1, to prevent disturbance to wintering waterfowl. During that time, you will need to return on the same trail you walked out. The U.S. Fish and Wildlife Service has enlarged what remained of the lake, and volunteers have planted native shrubs, ash and willow trees along the creek and wetlands. Cattail patches have reappeared and Yellow-headed Blackbirds, a species that formerly nested here, are being seen again. Thousands of geese and ducks use these fields and the ponds during winter. After returning to SR-14 and turning right, you will need a spotting scope at the last viewing spot, just past the railroad overpass (0.6 mile).

Western Columbia Gorge:
Washougal to Bonneville Dam

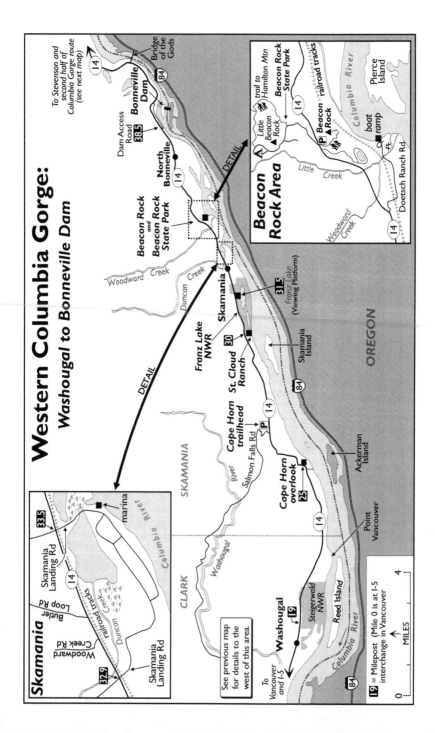

To Stevenson and second half of Columbia Gorge route (see next map)

Bridge of the Gods

14

84

Bonneville Dam

Dam Access Road **38.5**

North Bonneville

14

Beacon Rock and Beacon Rock State Park

DETAIL

Woodward Creek

Duncan Creek

Skamania

31.5 Franz Lake (Viewing Platform)

Franz Lake NWR

St. Cloud Ranch **30**

Skamania Island

DETAIL

OREGON

Cape Horn trailhead

Salmon Falls Rd

14

Cape Horn overlook **25**

Ackerman Island

84

SKAMANIA

CLARK

Washougal River

Point Vancouver

See previous map for details to the west of this area.

Washougal **19**

Steigerwald NWR

Reed Island

To Vancouver and I-5

Columbia River

84

19 = Milepost (Mile 0 is at I-5 interchange in Vancouver)

← MILES

0   4

Beacon Rock Area

trail to Hamilton Mtn

Little Beacon Rock

Beacon Rock State Park

railroad tracks

Columbia River

Pierce Island

14

Beacon Rock

P ▲ Rock

boat ramp

Little Creek

Woodward Creek

Doetsch Ranch Rd

14

Skamania

32.9

Woodward Creek Rd

Butler Loop Rd

Skamania Landing Rd

railroad tracks

Duncan Creek

14

Skamania Landing Rd

33.5

marina

Columbia River

WESTERN COLUMBIA GORGE

by Wilson Cady

revised by Wilson Cady

The Columbia River Gorge National Scenic Area is a place of outstanding natural, cultural, and scenic interest. Traveling east through this near-sea-level break in the mountains for some 80 miles, SR-14 provides a striking wet-to-dry transect, from Western Hemlock and Douglas-fir forests on the west to Garry Oak and Ponderosa Pine toward the east, and finally grasslands and shrub-steppe. Fifteen species of plants that grow in the gorge are found nowhere else in the world. The streams and rivers in the gorge flow from the mountains south to the Columbia River creating a south side to the Cascade Mountains. This and the sea-level break through the mountains makes for a lack of physical barriers that allows plants and animals from both sides of the Cascade Mountains to populate pockets of suitable habitats throughout the gorge.

Floodwaters released periodically from Glacial Lake Missoula rushed through the narrow gorge, creating the oversteepening of its sides one sees today. One result is the many waterfalls (mainly on the Oregon side). Another is slope instability, provoking large-scale landslides over the millennia since the floods subsided. In some places on the Washington side the road is built atop slide debris. The sites and trails in the National Scenic Area managed by the Forest Service require a Northwest Forest Pass or an America the Beautiful Pass; Beacon Rock State Park requires a Discover Pass.

Prominent mileposts line SR-14 (mile zero is at the I-5 interchange in Vancouver). These offer the most convenient reference points through the gorge. The route begins at milepost 19, just past the easternmost viewing pullout at Steigerwald Lake. From here, it is about 45 miles to the town of Bingen and south central Washington.

At milepost 25 is the Cape Horn Overlook, with one of the best views in the gorge. Peregrine Falcons nest below you on the cliff face formed by at least five separate volcanic flows, while Turkey Vultures and Cliff Swallows cruise by at eye level. The seven-mile-long Cape Horn Trail loop starts from a parking lot at milepost 26.3. The first half-mile of the upper trail passes through a mixed hardwood forest with a nice mix of birds and native plants.

The only remnant of the **Saint Cloud Ranch**, on the right at milepost 29.9, is the century-old apple orchard on the banks of the Columbia River. The trees while in bloom can be filled with migrant birds feeding on nectar and insects. During fall and winter the fruit attracts many species, and Red-breasted Sapsuckers bore sap wells in the ancient limbs.

Franz Lake National Wildlife Refuge is closed to the public, but there is a viewing platform above the lake at milepost 31.5. This large, shallow backwater of the Columbia River is completely covered with Wapato (also known as Indian Potato) in summer. This plant was a food staple of Native Americans and the starchy roots are a favorite food of swans. In winter, if the

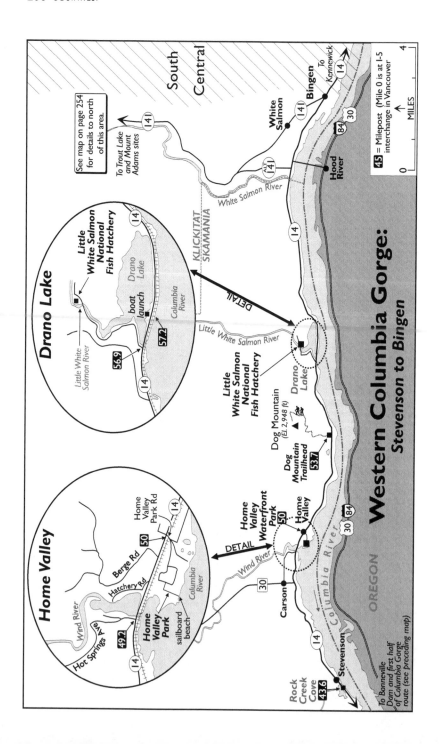

Western Columbia Gorge:
Stevenson to Bingen

Home Valley

Drano Lake

See map on page 254 for details to north of this area.

45 = Milepost (Mile 0 is at I-5 interchange in Vancouver

water level is low enough for them to be able to reach these tubers, over 1,000 Tundra Swans may gather here.

As you enter Skamania at milepost 32.9, exit to your right onto **Skamania Landing Road**. This one-mile loop crosses the railroad tracks and circles a small impoundment on Duncan Creek. The dam is opened and the lake drained during fall and winter to allow passage for spawning salmon and Steelhead. This creates a rare habitat type in the gorge—mudflats that attract shorebirds. Wooden pilings in the Columbia River at the private marina on the east end of the loop are used by Purple Martins.

Continue east 1.1 miles and turn right on the Doetsch Ranch Road railroad overpass and down to the picnic area and boat ramp at the base of **Beacon Rock State Park**, a prominent landmark (Discover Pass required). Watch for the Peregrine Falcons that nest on the southeast side of this monolithic volcanic plug. Return to SR-14 and continue east 0.8 mile to the parking lot for the trail that leads to the top of the rock, 840 feet above the river. The trail is steep but guarded by railings at all exposed points, and the views are great. Occasionally, one can hear Canyon Wrens calling from the rock. Across the road is the entrance to Beacon Rock State Park (camping and picnic areas). Trails from here go through the forest to Hamilton Mountain on the north rim of the gorge. Lazuli Buntings nest on the open, shrubby slopes. Use caution, as one of the most common shrubs on the exposed hillsides in the gorge is Poison Oak.

At milepost 38.5 is Dam Access Road. After leaving the highway, turn left at the stop sign and follow the road to **Bonneville Dam**, where an underwater viewing room allows you to observe American Shad, salmon, Steelhead, and other species as they travel through the fish ladder. Walk up the short trail from the upstream end of the visitor parking lot to the viewpoint. Look for loons, grebes, gulls, and rafts of ducks on the calm waters above the dam in the winter. A right turn after coming off the highway leads to Strawberry Island (aka Hamilton Island) with open grasslands, a pond and river views. Return to SR-14, turn right and continue east.

As you enter the town of Stevenson (see map on next page), stop at the pullout on the south side of the road at milepost 43.6, just before crossing the bridge over Rock Creek, to scan **Rock Creek Cove**. This shallow, weedy, wind-protected backwater is closed to hunting. Large flocks of waterfowl feed here, including both dabbling and diving ducks. Canvasbacks and Redheads are regular. The mudflat at the mouth of Rock Creek is one of the few spots in Skamania County where shorebirds can be found in migration. At the county fairgrounds across the cove, geese and ducks can be observed closely as they feed on the lawn or come for handouts.

Stop at the mouth of the **Wind River** at milepost 49.2. Harlequin Ducks nest higher up the river but may be seen near the mouth in spring and early summer. **Home Valley Waterfront Park** is on your right at milepost 50.

As you enter the park take the road to the right toward the sailboard beach, where a small wetland and thick riparian woods are worth a check in migration. There are a few primitive camping spots at the east end of the park, past the ball fields. In fall and winter, the bay upstream holds diving ducks—best observed from the highway shoulder just past the park.

Park at the **Dog Mountain Trailhead** at milepost 53.7 and check the rafts of Ring-necked Ducks and Lesser Scaup for Canvasback, Redhead, and Greater Scaup. The trail to the top of Dog Mountain takes you to one of the most spectacular wildflower displays in the gorge. Differences in soil depth, slope, and aspect, and the 3,000-foot elevation gain, create an extended bloom time. Lazuli Buntings nest in brushy patches near the top. Watch for Poison Oak along this trail, which also marks the western limit in the gorge for rattlesnakes.

On the west end of Drano Lake at milepost 56.9 is the one-mile spur to the **Little White Salmon National Fish Hatchery**. Common and Barrow's Goldeneyes winter where the Little White Salmon River enters the lake, along with Hooded and Common Mergansers. The falls at the hatchery are a good spot to find American Dippers, and Harlequin Ducks nest just upstream from the hatchery building. At the end of the fall salmon run, Bald Eagles and gulls gather on the sandbars to feed on the spawned-out fish. Drive back to SR-14, turn left, and park on the wide shoulder on the south side of the highway opposite the boat launch (milepost 57.2). Drano Lake—the wind-sheltered impoundment north of the road—usually has Canvasbacks and Redheads in the mixed flocks of ducks. Scan the lake from the shoulder.

When you reach the White Salmon River bridge and Alternate SR-141 in about six miles you are entering South Central Washington. See page 328 for the continuation of the Columbia Gorge route on the Dry Side.

MOUNT ADAMS

by Andy Stepniewski
revised by Andy Stepniewski

M ount Adams, Washington's second-highest peak (12,276 feet), is a dormant volcano with numerous glaciers and snowfields. The summit is on the Cascade Crest at the west edge of the Yakama Indian Reservation, roughly 30 miles north of the Columbia Gorge, 30 miles south of White Pass, and 30 miles east of Mount Saint Helens. This remote region has been little explored by birders, even though it is scenic, birdy, and eminently birdable with a bit of preparation and care. Make sure you have a Gifford Pinchot National Forest map and an America the Beautiful or Northwest Forest Pass. Overnight camping expands the possibilities, as there are no motels between US-12 and SR-14, and it is a long drive in and out. Expect birds of wetlands, moist and transitional Wet Side–Dry Side forests, and meadows ranging from lower-elevation zones up to the subalpine. Alpine species such as White-tailed Ptarmigan, American Pipit, and Gray-crowned Rosy-Finch are documented on Mount Adams, but reaching their habitat requires serious hiking, which few birders attempt.

TROUT LAKE

The best access point for the Mount Adams area, and a good base for exploring all parts of it, is the unincorporated town of Trout Lake, which lies in a broad valley between the Indian Heaven Wilderness Area on the west and the mountain on the north. Basic services are available here (gas, cafe, general store). Eastbound on SR-14 in the Columbia Gorge, turn left just after crossing the White Salmon River bridge onto Alternate SR-141, joining the main trunk of the highway in 2.1 miles. From SR-14 westbound, turn right onto SR-141 in Bingen and drive through White Salmon, reaching the intersection with Alternate SR-141 in 4.8 miles. It is about 19 miles north from this corner to the junction with the Mount Adams Recreation Highway in Trout Lake. If you are traveling between Trout Lake and birding sites in the upper Klickitat country (page 335), your connector is Sunnyside Road, which heads east from Mount Adams Recreation Highway 0.3 mile north of SR-141. At an intersection in 3.9 miles, where Sunnyside Road turns right (south), stay straight ahead onto Trout Lake Highway, reaching Glenwood in about 12 miles.

SR-141 continues west through Trout Lake, passing in 0.8 mile the USFS Mount Adams Ranger District station (information, maps, passes). In another 0.8 mile, turn north onto Trout Lake Creek Road. Elk Meadows RV Park (0.9 mile) is a heavily forested campground with excellent facilities for tent and vehicle campers, where birders are welcome. From the northeast end of the campground a wide trail goes east and downstream for about a mile along the edge of marshy **Trout Lake** (elevation 1,950 feet). Fifty or sixty species can be observed here on an early-morning walk in June, including Hooded Merganser (uncommon), Pied-billed Grebe, American Bittern, Osprey, Virginia

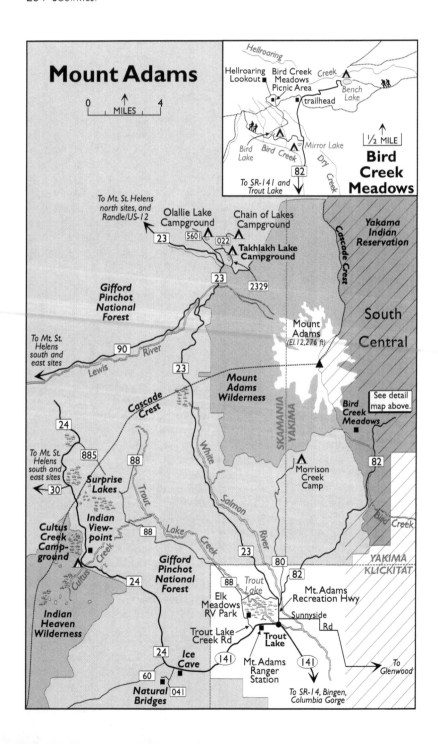

Mount Adams

0 |‚—‚—‚—| 4
  MILES

Bird Creek Meadows

Hellroaring Lookout ■
Hellroaring
Bird Creek Meadows Picnic Area
■ trailhead
Bird Creek Creek
Bench Lake
Mirror Lake
Bird Lake
½ MILE
82
To SR-141 and Trout Lake

To Mt. St. Helens north sites, and Randle/US-12

Olallie Lake Campground
Chain of Lakes Campground

23
5601
022
Takhlakh Lake Campground

Cascade Crest

Yakama Indian Reservation

23
2329

Gifford Pinchot National Forest

To Mt. St. Helens south and east sites

90
Lewis River

23

Mount Adams
(El. 12,276 ft)

South Central

Mount Adams Wilderness

SKAMANIA
YAKIMA

See detail map above.

Bird Creek Meadows ■

24

To Mt. St. Helens south and east sites

885

88

30

Surprise Lakes

Indian View-point

88

Morrison Creek Camp

82

Bird Creek

Cultus Creek Camp-ground

Cultus Creek

Trout Lake Creek

Salmon River

23

80

82

YAKIMA
KLICKITAT

Gifford Pinchot National Forest

24

88
Trout Lake

Mt. Adams Recreation Hwy

Elk Meadows RV Park ■
Sunnyside Rd

Indian Heaven Wilderness

Trout Lake Creek Rd
■ **Trout Lake**

24
Ice Cave
141
Mt. Adams Ranger Station
141

60

Natural Bridges 041

To SR-14, Bingen, Columbia Gorge

To Glenwood

Rail, Band-tailed Pigeon, Common Nighthawk, Belted Kingfisher, Red-breasted Sapsucker, Downy, Hairy, and Black-backed (rare) Woodpeckers, Western Wood-Pewee, Willow and Hammond's Flycatchers, Cassin's and Warbling Vireos, Tree, Violet-green, and Northern Rough-winged Swallows, Swainson's Thrush, Gray Catbird, Orange-crowned, Nashville, Yellow-rumped, Townsend's, Hermit (uncommon), and MacGillivray's Warblers, Common Yellowthroat, and Western Tanager, Purple Finch, and Evening Grosbeak. Veery can also be found here, but if missed, return to Trout Creek Road, turn right (north), and check streamside thickets where the road passes close to the creek over the next 2.5 miles.

INDIAN HEAVEN

The Indian Heaven area is reached by going west from Trout Lake on SR-141, which becomes FR-24 upon entering the Gifford Pinchot National Forest (about four miles past the Trout Lake Creek Road turnoff). In another mile, take time to visit the **Ice Cave**. It is a bizarre experience to leave balmy summer weather and singing Hammond's Flycatchers, Hermit Thrushes, and Townsend's Warblers to descend a ladder 30 feet into winter temperatures and snow. Heed the signs advising you to dress up. **Natural Bridges**, just ahead, is another attraction worth a few minutes' detour to visit. Returning to FR-24 from the Ice Caves, turn left and continue west 0.8 mile. Turn left onto FR-041, then right in 0.3 mile onto FR-050. Vine Maples line the lava-tube ravine, with a couple of natural bridges adding a delightful architectural touch.

Another 0.8 mile west on FR-24, keep right at its junction with FR-60. In nine miles, stop at Cultus Creek Campground, on the left, where you may find good-looking Hermit Warblers (but you are still in the Hermit-Townsend's hybrid zone). The **Indian Heaven Wilderness Area** (20,650 acres) lies just west of the campground. A trail network visits a few of the 175 small lakes in this plateau landscape, where wet meadows fringed by fir and spruce forests alternate with brushy terrain. Mosquitoes can be fierce, so you may prefer to visit at the end of summer after they have disappeared. Singing will have ceased by then for many bird species, but the huckleberry picking is great. In years of White-winged Crossbill invasions, Indian Heaven often has its share of this enigmatic species. Stop at **Indian Viewpoint** 0.5 mile farther north on FR-24 to enjoy the superb view of Mount Adams and to look for mountain birds in the treetops without having to crane your neck.

The terrain around the **Surprise Lakes**, 2.9 miles ahead, includes numerous boggy ponds and large brush fields (maintained by burning in the past, less so in recent times) of huckleberries, Mountain Ash, and Beargrass, with extensive forest typical of the Mountain Hemlock and Silver Fir zones. Birds of the meadows and bogs include Mountain Bluebird, Hermit Thrush, and Fox, Lincoln's, and White-crowned Sparrows. Forest birds include Black-backed Woodpecker, Gray and Steller's Jays, Mountain and Chestnut-backed Chickadees, Varied Thrush, and Townsend's and Hermit Warblers (and inter-grades). Mosquitoes are very bad in the early season. Starting in late July, large flocks of warblers, sparrows, and other small passerines can be found around the meadows; Nashville Warblers are common at that time. Native Americans camp here in August and September to pick huckleberries.

To reach the south and east sides of Mount Saint Helens, you can turn left from FR-24 onto FR-30 at a fork 0.6 mile farther on, then right onto Curly Creek Road (Ape Cave-Mount Saint Helens) FR-51 in another 10.6 miles. In five miles this road joins FR-90 along the Lewis River, about four miles east of Swift Reservoir (page 237).

TAKHLAKH LAKE

The west side of Mount Adams, with several trailheads for the Mount Adams Wilderness, is accessed by taking the Mount Adams Recreation Highway north from Trout Lake, keeping left in 1.4 miles onto FR-23 (to Randle). This road runs upstream (north) along the White Salmon River, crosses the headwaters area of the Lewis River, and enters the Cowlitz River watershed on the northwest side of the mountain. In about 23 miles, where FR-23 goes left, keep right onto FR-2329, which goes right again in 0.7 mile and reaches Takhlakh Lake Campground in another 0.7 mile. Takhlakh Lake (elevation 4,385 feet), amidst tall firs, affords awesome views of the north face of Mount Adams. Many species typical of the higher mountain forests can be found here and at other nearby campgrounds (Chain of Lakes, Olallie Lake), including Gray Jay, Pacific Wren, and Varied Thrush. Be sure to look carefully at any Townsend's or Hermit Warblers; this is the heart of the hybrid zone. Spruce Grouse are now proved a very uncommon resident in the forests north and east of Takhlakh Lake, especially in areas of sandy soils thick with Lodgepole Pine and a groundcover of Dwarf Huckleberries. Drive forest roads in fall for best results.

BIRD CREEK MEADOWS

Near timberline on the southeast slopes of Mount Adams, Bird Creek Meadows have good subalpine forest birding and beautiful displays of wild-flowers. The area is open from 1 July through 30 September (fee, collected by the Yakama Nation; in years of heavy snow the road may not open until later). Go north from SR-141 in Trout Lake on the Mount Adams Recreation Highway. At an intersection with FR-23 in 1.4 miles, keep right onto FR-82. In 0.6 mile, at another fork where FR-80 (the road to Morrison Creek Camp, the base camp for mountain climbers) goes straight ahead, stay right again with FR-82. At the next five-way junction (2.6 miles), make sure to keep easterly on FR-82 (clearly marked). In 5.8 miles, you cross the divide (elevation 4,000 feet) into the Klickitat River watershed and the Yakama Indian Reservation (stay left). Extensive forest fires have altered the landscape along this route. Check for woodpeckers in areas of snags. Williamson's Sapsucker is also regular here. Mirror Lake is another 4.4 miles over a rough and bumpy dirt road (large trailers not advised). Just beyond the lake (0.1 mile), turn left onto a road that leads in one mile to **Bird Lake** and a primitive campground in a forested setting where Gray Jay, Varied Thrush, and Townsend's Warbler are common.

Although a trail to the mountain meadows begins here, perhaps a shorter alternative is to return to the main road and drive north (toward Bench Lake) another 1.1 miles to a trailhead signed *Bird Creek Meadows*, on the left. Park and begin a 2.5-mile loop, returning to this spot. Birds along the way include Gray and Steller's Jays, Clark's Nutcracker (attracted to Whitebark Pines), Mountain Chickadee, Townsend's Solitaire, Hermit Thrush, Yellow-rumped and Townsend's Warblers, and Cassin's Finch. Flocks of migrant warblers and sparrows appear in late summer, along with many other scattered up-mountain migrants. The trail reaches the Bird Creek Meadows Picnic Area (elevation 6,100 feet) in less than a mile. The subalpine meadows to the west are a peaceful alternative to the crowds at Paradise on Mount Rainier.

Find a trail leading north from the picnic area up the side of a ridge. Stay right at a junction, and continue up a sandy, bouldery gully for 0.5 mile to Hellroaring Lookout (6,350 feet), with spectacular views of the south ridges of Mount Adams and the rocky and meadowed valley below. Look for Mountain Goats on the meadows across the valley. Views to the southeast extend downslope to Glenwood and Conboy Lake National Wildlife Refuge (page 335)—a reminder that you are already in Eastern Washington. To return to your car, follow the steep trail that descends the ridgeline to the east.

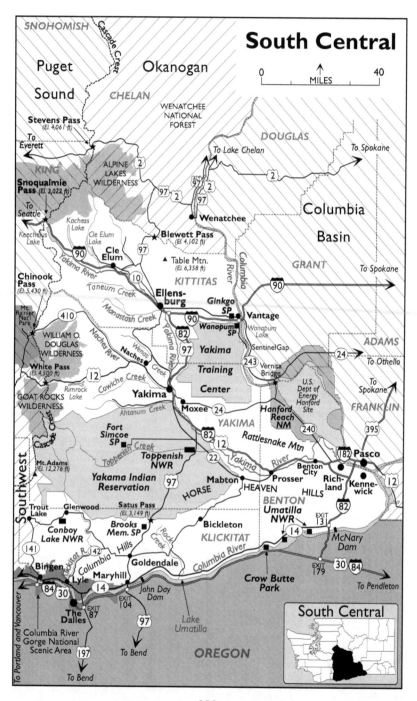

South Central

0 ↑ MILES 40

SNOHOMISH

Puget
Sound

Okanogan

CHELAN

WENATCHEE
NATIONAL
FOREST

DOUGLAS

To Lake Chelan

To Spokane

Stevens Pass
(El. 4,061 ft)
To
Everett

KING

ALPINE
LAKES
WILDERNESS

Cascade Crest

2

**Snoqualmie
Pass** *(El. 3,022 ft)*

To
Seattle

97 2

97 2

97

Columbia

Basin

Kachess
Lake

Cle Elum
Lake

Wenatchee

*Keechelus
Lake*

**Cle
Elum**

97

Blewett Pass
(El. 4,102 ft)

Columbia River

GRANT

To Spokane

**Chinook
Pass**
(El. 5,430 ft)

Yakima River

10

▲ Table Mtn.
(El. 6,358 ft)

KITTITAS

**Ellens-
burg**

**Ginkgo
SP**

90

Vantage

90

Mt.
Rainier Nat'l
Park

410

Taneum Creek

Manastash Creek

82

**Wanapum
SP**

Wanapum
Lake

ADAMS

24

To Othello

**WILLIAM O.
DOUGLAS
WILDERNESS**

Naches River

Naches

97

Yakima

SentinelGap

243

Vernita
Bridge

To
Spokane

White Pass
(El. 4,500 ft)

12

Wenas
Creek

Training

U.S.
Dept of
Energy
Hanford
Site

FRANKLIN

Rimrock
Lake

Cowiche Creek

Center

395

**GOAT ROCKS
WILDERNESS**

Yakima

Moxee

24

**Hanford
Reach
NM**

240

Ahtanum Creek

YAKIMA

Cascade Crest

Mt.Adams
(El. 12,276 ft)

**Fort
Simcoe
SP**

Toppenish Creek

82

12

Rattlesnake Mtn

182 **Pasco**

Southwest

**Toppenish
NWR**

22

Yakima River

**Benton
City**

Richland

**Kenne-
wick**

12

**Yakama Indian
Reservation**

97

Mabton

HEAVEN

Prosser

BENTON

HILLS

82

**Trout
Lake**

Glenwood

Satus Pass
(El. 3,149 ft)

HORSE

**Umatilla
NWR**

EXIT
13

141

**Conboy
Lake NWR**

**Brooks
Mem. SP**

Rock Creek

Bickleton

KLICKITAT

14

McNary
Dam

Bingen

Columbia Hills

Goldendale

Columbia River

EXIT
179

30 84

To Pendleton

Klickitat R.

42

Lyle **Maryhill**

84 30

14

John Day
Dam

**Crow Butte
Park**

EXIT
87

EXIT
104

**The
Dalles**

**Columbia River
Gorge National
Scenic Area**

197

To Portland and Vancouver

97

OREGON

Lake
Umatilla

To Bend

To Bend

South Central

SOUTH CENTRAL

One of the two largest regions of the nine in this book, South Central Washington is also one of the most varied in topography, climate, vegetation, and wildlife. Much of the region is within day-trip distance of Puget Sound (one hour to Snoqualmie Pass, two to Ellensburg, two and a half to Vantage or Yakima). Hence, for most birders, this is the gateway to the Dry Side of the state.

Pacific storms drench the west slopes of the Cascades, resulting in the great conifer forests that characterize the Pacific Northwest in the popular imagination. East of the crest, however, precipitation declines. Forests become more open, and instead of firs and hemlocks, there are many Ponderosa Pines. Farther down, precipitation is lower still—too low for any tree growth except along streams. A belt of shrub- and grasslands begins at the lower forest edge. This arid shrub-steppe zone extends across the Columbia River all the way to the eastern boundary of the state.

The region's dominant physical features are the Cascade Range on the west and north, and the Columbia River on the east and south. Secondary in importance is the so-called Yakima Fold Belt—a series of west-east trending basalt ridges emanating from the Cascades and dividing the region into numerous valleys. The many elevations, aspects, slopes, soils, and microclimates of this ridge-and-valley system support a wealth of plant communities and a corresponding diversity of animal life.

About three-quarters of South Central Washington is drained by the Yakima River. Gathering waters from the mountains to the west and north, this stream carves through several high ridges via the Yakima Canyon, then flows south and east across the farms and orchards of the broad Yakima Valley to join the Columbia River at Richland. Numerous minor streams drain the fringe of shrub-steppe on the east and south directly to the Columbia. East of Mount Adams, the Klickitat River waters a unique landscape of meadows, parklands, cliffs, and Garry Oaks, cutting its canyon down to the Columbia Gorge at Lyle.

What do birders come here to find? The perennial draw for Wet Siders is breeding birds of the lower forest zone and adjacent shrub-steppe: Common Poorwill, Calliope Hummingbird, White-headed Woodpecker, Gray Flycatcher, Say's Phoebe, Loggerhead Shrike, Sage Thrasher, and Brewer's, Lark, Black-throated, and Sagebrush Sparrows. But there is much more than that.

The "proven" route for a Washington Big Day record (208 species) spends fully half the day in this region: from White Pass east down through Toppenish and west over Satus Pass to Lyle. The Garry Oak habitats of the Columbia Gorge and Klickitat country are the only place in the state to find Acorn Woodpecker and the best place for Ash-throated Flycatcher. Chickens are good: Chukar, Gray Partridge, Greater Sage-Grouse, Sooty Grouse. So are owls: Flammulated, Burrowing, Spotted (sadly, much reduced), and Northern Saw-whet. Parks in Richland and Kennewick are great passerine migrant traps. Waterbirds crowd Columbia River reservoirs in migration and winter, and the Yakima River delta is one of the interior Northwest's best fall shorebird spots.

Temperature and precipitation follow a gradient from northwest (coolest, wettest) to southeast (warmest, driest). July average maximum temperature is 81 degrees in Cle Elum (in the lower mixed-forest zone southeast of Snoqualmie Pass) and 87 degrees in Yakima (in the shrub-steppe zone 50 miles farther southeast). Cle Elum receives 22 inches of precipitation annually, Yakima just eight. Winter temperature is about the same in both places (January average minimum 20 degrees), but it snows a lot more in Cle Elum (81 inches compared to 24 inches in Yakima). These are only examples. Weather patterns are strongly influenced by the region's complex topography, and local variation can be great.

Snowfall is heavy in the mountain passes. Chinook Pass (SR-410) closes for the winter, but Snoqualmie Pass (I-90) and White Pass (US-12) are kept open. So is US-97 across Blewett Pass and Satus Pass. When conditions merit, traction devices may be required on any of these passes, so be prepared. Forest roads on the east slopes of the Cascades close by default when snow accumulates. Snowfall is light in the lowlands, and roads (including SR-14 through the Columbia Gorge) stay open all winter long, except for the occasional storm. Watch for ice, however. In spring, wind may hamper birding in open country. (The Kittitas Valley is notorious for this.) Strong, steady winds are characteristic of the Columbia Gorge in any season.

There are numerous motels, restaurants, gas stations, and other services in Cle Elum, Ellensburg, Yakima, Toppenish, the Tri-Cities, and across the Columbia in Hood River and The Dalles, Oregon, as well as (less reliably) in smaller communities, especially along the I-90 and I-82 corridors. Campgrounds are plentiful along the various routes traversing national forest lands; elsewhere they are few and far between.

SNOQUALMIE PASS AND VICINITY

by Hal Opperman and Andy Stepniewski
revised by Hal Opperman

Fifty miles east of Seattle on Interstate 90, Snoqualmie Pass is the most traveled and accessible crossing of the Cascades. The pass is super wet, with about 100 inches of precipitation annually, including an average of 450 inches of snow. Wet, mild conditions prevail eastward from the crest for many miles along the upper east-slope Cascades, favoring development of a once-impressive conifer forest, much of which was clearcut in the final decades of the last century. One hundred and fifty years ago, Congress granted alternate one-square-mile sections of land to the Northern Pacific Railroad in a wide corridor on each side of the proposed right-of-way. The railroad was built up the Yakima River valley from the Tri-Cities to the crest at Stampede Pass, then down the Green River drainage on the west slope, reaching its terminus at Tacoma in 1887. The checkerboard of remote, rugged timberlands remaining in railroad ownership was left largely unexploited until the 1980s, when a massive logging program was initiated. Even the Spotted Owl crisis of those years could not slow the rush to "get the cut out." Fortunately, the sections in public ownership have been managed less aggressively, while the forests on the logged-off land-grant sections are now slowly regenerating. Under the visionary leadership of the Mountains to Sound Greenway Trust, land exchanges have consolidated ownership in public hands—largely erasing the checkerboard pattern and ensuring that areas of beauty and ecological diversity with thriving birdlife will remain even near I-90. The higher elevations to the north on both slopes of the Cascades are formally protected in the Alpine Lakes Wilderness Area.

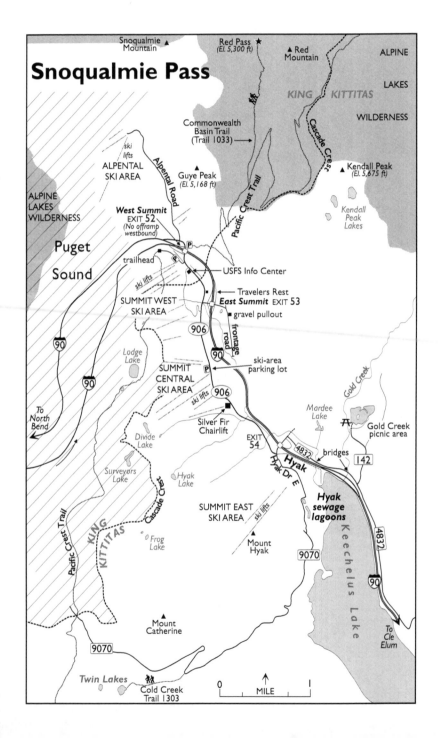

Snoqualmie Pass

Snoqualmie ▲
Mountain

Red Pass ★
(El. 5,300 ft)

▲ Red
Mountain

ALPINE

KING   KITTITAS

LAKES

WILDERNESS

Commonwealth
Basin Trail
(Trail 1033) →

Kendall Peak
(El. 5,675 ft) ▲

ski
lifts
ALPENTAL
SKI AREA

Alpental Road

Guye Peak
(El. 5,168 ft) ▲

Pacific Crest Trail

Cascade Crest

Kendall
Peak
Lakes

ALPINE
LAKES
WILDERNESS

West Summit
EXIT 52
(No offramp
westbound)

P

Puget

trailhead

P

Sound

ski lifts

USFS Info Center

SUMMIT WEST
SKI AREA

Travelers Rest
East Summit EXIT 53

906

gravel pullout

frontage road

90

ski-area
parking lot

Lodge
Lake

P

Gold Creek

90

SUMMIT
CENTRAL
SKI AREA

906

Mardee
Lake

Gold Creek
picnic area

To
North
Bend

ski lifts

Silver Fir
Chairlift

EXIT
54

4832

bridges

142

Divide
Lake

Hyak

Surveyors
Lake

Hyak
Lake

Cascade Crest

SUMMIT EAST
SKI AREA

ski lifts

Hyak Dr E

**Hyak
sewage
lagoons**

Keechelus Lake

4832

Frog
Lake

Pacific Crest Trail

KING

KITTITAS

Mount
Hyak ▲

9070

90

Mount
Catherine ▲

9070

To
Cle
Elum

Twin Lakes

Cold Creek
Trail 1303

0   MILE   1

SNOQUALMIE PASS

Snoqualmie Pass (elevation 3,022 feet) is not high enough to reach the subalpine, but the combination of forests, fake "meadows" of ski slopes, and some clearcuts has produced varied habitats. The summit area can be reached from any of three I-90 exits. Coming from the Seattle side the first is Exit 52, signed *West Summit*. (However, there is no offramp for westbound traffic at this exit, so those coming from the Ellensburg side should use Exit 54 or Exit 53 instead.)

If you have time for a hike, the **Commonwealth Basin Trail** goes through an uncut forest of Silver Fir on the west slope of the Cascades, out of range of traffic noise, with decent birding possibilities. Go left from the West Summit offramp onto Alpental Road, passing under the interstate. In 100 yards, turn right and drive a short distance to the large trailhead parking lot for the northbound Pacific Crest Trail (America the Beautiful or Northwest Forest Pass required). Follow this trail as it climbs into the Alpine Lakes Wilderness. In 2.5 miles (elevation 4,000 feet), Trail 1033 branches off to the left and drops down into the basin of Commonwealth Creek, then climbs into the subalpine, with a series of switchbacks, to **Red Pass** (2.5 miles, elevation 5,300 feet). Sooty Grouse, Hammond's Flycatcher, Gray Jay, Townsend's Solitaire, and Hermit and Varied Thrushes nest here, along with most of the familiar species of Puget Lowlands forests. From Red Pass, high crags of the Cascades can be seen across the deep valley of the Middle Fork of the Snoqualmie River, to the north, with Mount Baker in the distance. Gray-crowned Rosy-Finches nest in rock clefts along steep, treeless slopes in the high country here and throughout the wilderness area, usually well away from trails. For experienced off-trail hikers, a challenging traverse westward from Red Pass to Lundin Peak (elevation 6,067 feet) and Snoqualmie Mountain (elevation 6,278 feet) may turn up a few, but there are far more comfortable ways to see this species.

Many mountain birds can be found closer to the interstate, although traffic noise can be an unpleasant distraction. A couple of hundred feet right (south) from the West Summit offramp is an entrance sign for The Summit at Snoqualmie, on the right. Turn in, then go straight ahead into the upper parking lot for the Summit West chairlifts. Slate-colored Fox and Lincoln's Sparrows sometimes breed here in wet, brushy spots at the edge of the ski slopes, as do Willow Flycatchers and White-crowned Sparrows. A gravel road out the far end of the parking lot swings left and up to a parking area for the **Pacific Crest Trail** southbound (0.3 mile; Northwest Forest Pass required). A two-mile hike to Lodge Lake in the lower subalpine runs through intact forest, brushy ski slopes, and marshes (high point 3,600 feet), offering more chances to find Fox and Lincoln's Sparrows. Red-breasted Sapsuckers nest in snags along the crest (sometimes in mixed pairs with Red-naped).

Turn right from the Summit West entrance and proceed along SR-906 (the old highway) through the small commercial district. The **USFS Information Center** on the right (0.1 mile; open seasonally) has maps and parking permits. On the right in another 0.2 mile, scan the trees near the entrance to Village at the Summit, across the road from the WSDOT restrooms, for Band-tailed Pigeons that are seen regularly in spring, sometimes in sizable flocks.

Return to SR-906 and continue south. Roadside brush may have singing MacGillivray's and Yellow Warblers and White-crowned Sparrows. In 0.1 mile, turn left and go under I-90 (this is Exit 53, **East Summit**). In 0.2 mile, swing right onto the frontage road on the other side of the interstate and park at a gravel pullout on the left in 0.1 mile. Walk the road both ways. The forest is dense, with houses tucked among big conifers. Sooty Grouse, Varied Thrush, Townsend's Warbler, and Pine Siskin are usually here in late spring and summer.

Much of the wide, flat saddle of the pass was originally occupied by forest with broken-topped old trees, small pools, and patches of wet meadow. A remnant of this interesting habitat survives between the old highway and Interstate 90, laced with cross-country ski tracks. Red-breasted Sapsucker, Pacific Wren, Varied Thrush, and MacGillivray's, Yellow-rumped, Townsend's, and Wilson's Warblers are typical of the species found here in May–June. An entrance track heads off left from SR-906, 0.8 mile south of the East Summit interchange; park in the ski-area lot on the right side of the road and walk back across. Or drive another 0.5 mile and park at the **Silver Fir Chairlift**, on the right. The overflow parking lot on the opposite side of the road affords access to several tracks into the forest.

HYAK AND GOLD CREEK

Continue along SR-906 for 0.8 mile from the Silver Fir Chairlift to a 90-degree right turn, then a 90-degree left turn in 200 feet, alongside the **Hyak sewage lagoons**—worth a look for ducks (Barrow's Goldeneye in summer), migrating shorebirds, and flocks of swallows. The pavement ends in 0.1 mile at the start of FR-9070, a good gravel road into the forests and clearcuts of the backcountry. From a trailhead in a switchback on the left 2.6 miles ahead, the easy, though rocky, **Cold Creek Trail 1303** ascends initially through an old clearcut, then into old-growth forest (mostly Western Hemlock and Silver Fir), to the first of the Twin Lakes (0.8 mile, 100 feet elevation gain). Look for Barrow's Goldeneye, Spotted Sandpiper, American Dipper, and the usual songbirds associated with wet forest, especially Varied Thrush.

Return to the old highway and cross under I-90 to the other side of the Hyak interchange. Beginning on the left in another 0.6 mile, a stretch of gravel flats with willows is a good place for nesting Fox Sparrows. Small trees for the next 0.2 mile, up to the **Gold Creek** bridge, are often aswarm with

Yellow-rumped Warblers in migration, and Barrow's Goldeneyes are sometimes spotted upstream from the bridge. In another 0.2 mile, potholed FR-142 (144 on older maps) turns off to the left. Travel 0.4 mile to the entrance of the Gold Creek picnic area, on the left (America the Beautiful or Northwest Forest Pass required). A short, paved, barrier-free interpretive trail leads to several ponds. Look for Barrow's Goldeneye and other waterfowl, Black and Vaux's Swifts, Willow Flycatcher, Warbling Vireo, Yellow Warbler, and Fox Sparrow (in willow growth on streamside gravel deposits). In fall, neotropical migrant songbirds move along Gold Creek; altitudinal migrants such as Ruby-crowned Kinglet and Dark-eyed Junco stage here on the way to lower-elevation wintering grounds. By scanning the ridgetops you might spy a Mountain Goat.

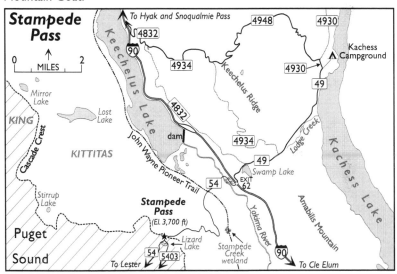

STAMPEDE PASS

East of Snoqualmie Pass, the road to Stampede Pass (FR-54) starts from the south side of I-90 at Exit 62. In 0.2 mile a snag-filled swamp, on both sides of the road, is excellent in summer for Red-breasted Sapsucker (be alert for Red-naped and hybrids as well), Black and Vaux's Swifts, Willow Flycatcher, Tree Swallow, and MacGillivray's Warbler. Forest in the vicinity of the Yakima River bridge another 0.2 mile ahead, has nesting Osprey, Barred Owl, Pileated Woodpecker, American Dipper, and Yellow and Townsend's Warblers. Proceed on FR-54. In 0.6 mile the road changes from asphalt to gravel and in another 0.2 mile intersects the John Wayne Pioneer Trail (Iron Horse State Park, the trackbed of the former Milwaukee Road transcontinental rail line). Just past the crossing, leave your vehicle at a wide turnout on the left. Eastward (to the left when approaching from I-90), this smooth, level, non-motorized trail (elevation 2,500 feet) passes through mostly third-growth forest, opening up in 1.0 mile to an extensive wetland of shrubby willows and snags as the trail crosses **Stampede Creek** on an elevated embankment. Woodpeckers, flycatchers, many songbirds, and various other species forage or reside seasonally in the swamp.

FR-54 and numerous other roads that branch from it give access to mountain forests on both sides of the crest, most of them in various stages of post-logging regeneration. **Stampede Pass** (elevation 3,700 feet) is reached in about 4.5 miles from I-90. Lizard Lake, just across the pass, attracts a variety of birds. Vaux's Swifts sometimes afford close-up views below eye level as they pursue insects near the water surface. The road forks here; keep right on FR-54 (also signed 5400). The wide, well-maintained gravel road drops down into the basin at the head of the Green River drainage, to the site of the old railroad town of Lester (elevation 1,600 feet). Birding possibilities are much the same as at Snoqualmie Pass and elsewhere on the Cascade west slopes.

CLE ELUM AND VICINITY

by Andy Stepniewski and Hal Opperman
revised by Scott Downes

Twenty-five miles east of Snoqualmie Pass and a thousand feet lower in elevation, precipitation plummets to roughly 25 percent of that at the crest. Ponderosa Pine and Douglas Maple—both indicators of drier habitats—are increasingly common from Easton to Cle Elum, and the birdlife changes as well. Exploring the Yakima River valley along this stretch, and the Cle Elum River valley from its confluence with the Yakima northward past Cle Elum Lake, allows one to observe a mix of bird species—some characteristic of the Wet Side, several others of the Dry Side, and many that are equally at home in both. An America the Beautiful or Northwest Forest Pass is required for trailheads mentioned in this section and to park in many areas of the national forest.

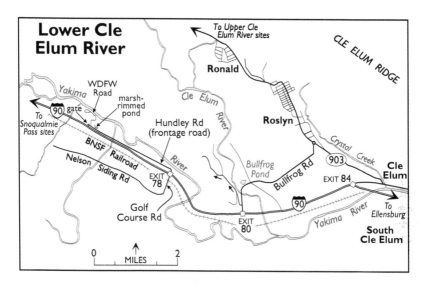

LOWER CLE ELUM RIVER

For a first taste of these Eastside habitats, take I-90 Exit 78, marked Golf Course Road. On the north side of the interchange, go left (west) onto the frontage road (Hundley Road). After 2.1 miles, note the marsh-rimmed pond below the road on the right. Waterfowl such as Wood and Ring-necked Ducks may be found here, and the willows should have a Yellow Warbler or two. In another 0.1 mile, just before the road ends at a church-camp gate, turn right onto a fishing access road. Continue through more marsh and riparian habitat—birding gets better as you leave the freeway noise behind. The road ends in 0.5 mile at the Yakima River (Discover Pass required). The floodplain gallery forest of mature Black Cottonwoods may have Warbling and Red-eyed Vireos, and Nashville, MacGillivray's, and Yellow Warblers.

Return to I-90 and go east a couple of miles to Exit 80. Head north toward Roslyn on Bullfrog Road. Intermingling of habitats here allows many species of birds to nest in a very small area. Birding is sure to be rewarding in and around the open Ponderosa Pine forests, mixed forests (Douglas-fir and Grand Fir with an understory of Douglas Maple, alders, and willows), brushy thickets, lakes, and marshes—particularly from May through July.

Cross over the Cle Elum River on Bullfrog Road. In 0.1 mile, Bullfrog Pond is on the left, behind a guard rail. Pull off on the right 50 yards ahead at a turnoff for a private road, taking care not to obstruct traffic. Walk back and hop over the guard rail. Hooded Merganser, Vaux's Swift, and Common Yellowthroat may be found around the pond. Walk along the old road that goes south through wet woodlands to the river. Look for Warbling and Red-eyed (in the tall Black Cottonwoods) Vireos, Black-capped Chickadee, Veery, and Yellow

Warblers. There are a couple of records of American Redstart here. Both sides of Bullfrog Road north and east from the pond to the intersection with SR-903 (a roundabout in 2.1 miles) are open Ponderosa Pine woods, good for Hairy Woodpecker, Mountain Chickadee, Red-breasted Nuthatch, Western Bluebird, Chipping Sparrow, Western Tanager, and Purple and Cassin's Finches.

Take the second exit from the roundabout onto northbound SR-903 to the the former coal-mining town of Roslyn. Often, feeders are found in town, though the locations may change. All three *Carpodacus* finches (Purple, Cassin's, House) are regular around Roslyn, and these feeders have proven to be a great place to study this sometimes confusing group, along with Red Crossbill, Pine Siskin, American Goldfinch, and Evening Grosbeak.

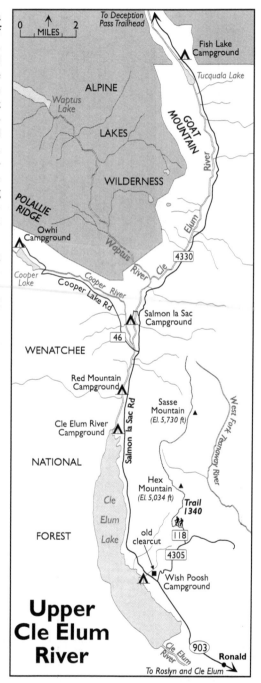

Upper Cle Elum River

UPPER CLE ELUM RIVER

Return to SR-903 in Roslyn and turn north. Travel through the town of Ronald and continue north for another 3.9 miles (name changes to Salmon la Sac Road after entering the Okanogan-Wenatchee National Forest). On the left is the entrance to **Wish Poosh Campground** (fee). There is usually a pair of Pileated Woodpeckers in the campground, and the mixed Douglas-fir and Douglas Maple forests around the edges have Black-throated Gray Warbler. You'll note many other birds on a June or July walk about the marshy terrain toward Cle Elum Lake.

Another 7.9 miles north on Salmon la Sac Road brings you to the Cooper Lake Road (FR-46), which immediately crosses the Cle Elum River, on the left. In the afternoon and early evening in summer, the bridge is a good vantage point from which to scan the skies for Black and Vaux's Swifts. Vaux's nest nearby, usually in tall snags among the Black Cottonwoods along the river. Black Swifts likely breed in the Cle Elum Valley. Continuing on this road five miles you will come to Owhi Campground, set in moist forest on Cooper Lake, and access to the high-country hiking trails of the Alpine Lakes Wilderness.

Back on Salmon la Sac Road and headed upriver, you reach **Salmon la Sac Campground** by turning left at a fork in 1.2 miles and crossing a bridge. Black Swifts forage over the river and campground at treetop level in late afternoon. Trails up Polallie Ridge and the Waptus River valley into the wilderness area leave from here.

More good hiking opportunities are available if you take the right branch at the fork onto FR-4330 (unpaved; be prepared for clouds of dust as cars stir up the glacial flour) and travel about 10 miles to **Tucquala Lake**. Common Nighthawks, swifts, and swallows often forage above this shallow lake and marshy meadow. Continue 2.5 miles to the end of the road. From here a gentle trail follows the Cle Elum River about five miles into the Alpine Lakes Wilderness through old-growth forest, then climbs 900 feet in a final mile to join the Pacific Crest Trail at Deception Pass (elevation 4,500 feet). In these lakes, open meadows, and wetter forests you may find most of the same species as lower down the valley, plus Barrow's Goldeneye, Golden Eagle, Gray Jay, Clark's Nutcracker, American Pipit, and Fox and Lincoln's Sparrows. In years when spruces are producing a large cone crop, both Red and White-winged Crossbills should be looked for.

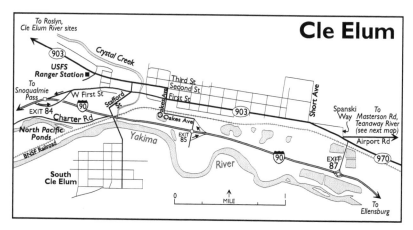

AROUND CLE ELUM

Headng south from Roslyn on SR-903, take the second exit from the roundabout to continue on SR-903 toward Cle Elum. The USFS Cle Elum District Ranger Station (509-674-4411) is on the right, 1.5 miles ahead—a good place to pick up a map and inquire about road and trail conditions. Continue east 0.4 mile to Stafford Street, turn right, cross First Street (0.1 mile), and continue ahead. (If you are coming from the west on I-90, take Exit 84, which enters Cle Elum on First Street; go past the Safeway and turn right onto Stafford at the foot of the hill, following signs for South Cle Elum.) Go 0.4 mile on Stafford to the I-90 underpass, then make an immediate right (west) turn onto Charter Road next to the railroad tracks (one-way traffic regulated by a signal), to the **Northern Pacific Ponds** (0.2 mile). Occupying more than a mile of former streambed cut off when the railroad embankment was built across the floodplain, diverting the Yakima River into a new channel, these ponds have a good fringe of marsh vegetation and sizable cottonwoods. Wood Duck, Hooded Merganser, Ruffed Grouse, Osprey, Virginia Rail, Eastern Kingbird, Tree Swallow, Gray Catbird, and Nashville Warbler all nest.

Return to First Street, turn right, and drive east through the business district. (Many homes on residential streets north of First Street and parallel to it have feeders and ornamental plantings that attract Bohemian Waxwings and various finches in winter.) In 1.6 miles turn left, then jog immediately right onto **Airport Road**, which continues east, then south. At the intersection with Masterson Road (2.4 miles) check the pines to the southeast for Pygmy Nuthatch and Red Crossbill.

Continue south on Airport Road 0.8 mile to SR-970. Drive straight across the highway into a fishing access at the Yakima River (0.3 mile; Discover Pass required). Here, amidst tall Black Cottonwoods and thick understory vegetation, you might find Warbling and Red-eyed Vireos, Yellow Warblers, and other riparian birds. In winter, American Dipper is often found here.

Return to SR-970 and go right to its junction with SR-10 (0.1 mile). Turn right (east) onto SR-10 and drive one mile to the bridge that crosses the Teanaway River just upstream from its confluence with the Yakima River—a popular rafting put-in spot. Look for American Dipper nesting under the bridge. Red-naped Sapsucker, Western Wood-Pewee, Red-eyed Vireo, Veery, Gray Catbird, Nashville and Yellow Warblers, and Western Tanager are found in the riparian areas during the summer. Wood Duck, Cinnamon Teal, Hooded Merganser, and Common Yellowthroat are regular on the small pond and marsh just west of the bridge on the north side of the highway. Scenic SR-10 continues on, following the canyon along the Yakima River toward Ellensburg and Kittitas Valley birding sites (page 277).

TEANAWAY RIVER AND SWAUK CREEK

by Andy Stepniewski and Hal Opperman

revised by Scott Downes

The Blewett Pass Highway (US-97 from Ellensburg, joined by SR-970 from Cle Elum) provides easy access to the basins of two streams draining the south slope of the Wenatchee Mountains. Sasse Ridge divides the Cle Elum River drainage, to the west, from the Teanaway Basin. The Swauk Basin is the next one east, across Teanaway Ridge; Table Mountain separates it from the Naneum Basin still farther east. Lower elevations have birds of dry Ponderosa Pine forests and riparian habitats. Mixed-conifer forests in the middle elevations are known for their owls. Fall hawkwatching can be good on some of the higher ridges. Upper elevations have birds of subalpine forests and mountain meadows. An America the Beautiful pass or Northwest Forest Pass is needed to park in many areas listed in this section.

TEANAWAY RIVER BASIN

About seven miles east of Cle Elum, Teanaway Road turns off to the northwest from SR-970, midway between its junctions with SR-10 and US-97.

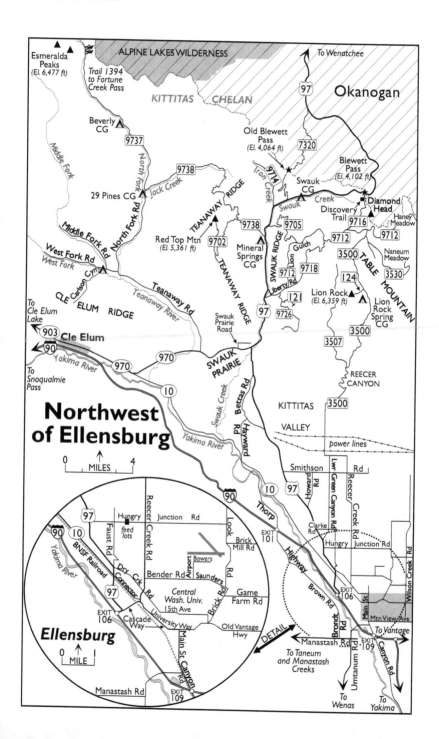

Esmeralda Peaks (El. 6,477 ft)

ALPINE LAKES WILDERNESS

Trail 1394 to Fortune Creek Pass

KITTITAS   CHELAN

To Wenatchee

97   Okanogan

Middle Fork

Beverly CG
9737

North fork

9738

Old Blewett Pass (El. 4,064 ft)   7320

Iron Creek

9714

Blewett Pass (El. 4,102 ft)

Swauk CG

Diamond Head

Haney Meadow

29 Pines CG   Jack Creek

TEANAWAY RIDGE

Swauk   Creek

Discovery Trail   9716   9712

Middle Fork Rd

North Fork Rd

Red Top Mtn (El. 5,361 ft)   9702

9738

9705

9712   9712

3500   TABLE MOUNTAIN

Naneum Meadow   3530

West Fork Rd
West Fork

Carbon Cyn

CLE   ELUM   RIDGE

Teanaway River

Teanaway Rd

TEANAWAY RIDGE

Mineral Springs CG

SWAUK RIDGE

Lion Gulch

9712
Liberty Rd

9718

124

Lion Rock (El. 6,359 ft)

Lion Rock Spring CG

To Cle Elum Lake

903   Cle Elum

90
Yakima River

970   970

Swauk Prairie Road

97

121

9726

3500

3507

To Snoqualmie Pass

10

SWAUK PRAIRIE

Swauk Creek

Bettas Rd

Hayward Rd

Yakima River

REECER CANYON

KITTITAS

VALLEY   3500

Northwest
of Ellensburg

0   MILES   4

power lines

Smithson   Lwr Green Canyon Rd   Reecer Creek Rd   Rd

10   97

Howard Rd

Thorp

97

90   10

Hungry   Junction   Rd

feed lots

Faust Rd

Reecer Creek Rd

Look Rd

Brick Mill Rd

EXIT 101

Clarke Rd

Hungry   Junction Rd

Wilson Creek Rd

BNSF Railroad

Yakima River

97

Dry Crk Connector Rd

Bender Rd

Airport

Bowers

Saunders

Brick Rd

Central Wash. Univ. 15th Ave

University Way

Game Farm Rd

Old Vantage Hwy

Highway

Brown Rd

EXIT 106

Main St

Mtn View Ave

To Vantage

EXIT 106

Cascade Way

Main St Canyon Rd

Ellensburg

0   MILE   1

DETAIL

Manastash Rd

Brandt Rd

Umtanum Rd

EXIT 109

Canyon Rd

Manastash Rd

EXIT 109

To Taneum and Manastash Creeks

To Wenas

To Yakima

For the next seven miles, up to the intersection where it splits into West Fork Road (left) and North Fork Road (straight ahead), Teanaway Road goes through farmlands in the broad **Teanaway River valley**, flanked by areas of riparian growth and Ponderosa Pine forest. Although this is mostly private land, there are places along the way to pull off the road to bird. In spring and summer, look for Turkey Vulture, Osprey (nests along the river), Wilson's Snipe, Common Nighthawk, Vaux's Swift, Eastern Kingbird, swallows, Western and Mountain Bluebirds, MacGillivray's and Yellow Warblers, Savannah and Song Sparrows, Red-winged Blackbird, Western Meadowlark, Brewer's Blackbird, and Brown-headed Cowbird around buildings, open fields, brushy fencerows, and ditches and other wet spots. In the winter, look for Bohemian and Cedar Waxwings in the riparian areas and for Common Redpoll during years when the species invades the area. Red-tailed and Rough-legged Hawks hunt the area in fall and winter.

More than 50,000 acres of the north, west, and middle forks make up the new Teanaway Community Forest, bought by DNR in 2013 and managed cooperatively with WDFW and a community advisory committee. Public ownership will allow more access to lands than previous private ownership, but recreation passes such as Discover Pass may be required in the future within the forest.

To bird the West Fork Road, go west 0.6 mile and park near the intersection where Middle Fork Road turns off to the right. Bird on foot for a half-mile north along Middle Fork Road, then a half-mile west along **West Fork Road** to a gate on the left. Check the bridge over the Teanaway River for Harlequin Duck and American Dipper in spring and summer. Bird the campground on the south side of the road before the bridge for a good selection of Ponderosa Pine birds and riparian birds along the river. In an hour's birding of this sampler of habitats you may find Ruffed Grouse, Rufous and Calliope Hummingbirds, Red-naped Sapsucker, Hairy and Pileated Woodpeckers, Western Wood-Pewee, Dusky Flycatcher, Cassin's and Warbling Vireos, Black-capped and Mountain Chickadees, Red-breasted Nuthatch, Brown Creeper, House Wren, Golden-crowned Kinglet, Townsend's Solitaire, Veery, Swainson's and Hermit Thrushes, Cedar Waxwing, Nashville Warbler, Spotted Towhee, Chipping Sparrow, Dark-eyed Junco, Western Tanager, Black-headed Grosbeak, Purple and Cassin's Finches, Red Crossbill, Pine Siskin, and Evening Grosbeak. West Fork road ends in 0.4 mile, but continues as a dirt track, not recommended during wet weather. A good selection of forest habitats occurs along this stretch, and Northern Pygmy-Owl is often encountered. The **Middle Fork Road** is good for Wild Turkeys and offers a similar mix of forest birds to that encountered on the West Fork Road. Pavement ends in 2.7 miles, but you can continue on the USFS road through habitat that supports all three nuthatch species and other common forest birds.

As you continue north on **North Fork Road**, the surrounding forests, especially where unlogged, used to be home to a few Spotted Owls, but they now appear to be gone, replaced by Barred Owls. FR-9738 branches off to the right in 5.5 miles and runs east up Jack Creek, flanked by extensive tracts of old-growth forest. Northern Goshawks are seen fairly regularly along this route. A prime area for Flammulated Owls is at 4.5 miles up FR-9738 on a sidehill to your left where Douglas-fir and Ponderosa Pine provide suitable habitat. For the next four miles, you pass through mature forest. Remember that calling for Spotted Owls, a federally Threatened and state Endangered species, is prohibited. After crossing Teanaway Ridge, FR-9738 descends the Blue Creek drainage, reaching US-97 in about 15 miles from North Fork Road.

North from the intersection with FR-9738, North Fork Road becomes FR-9737. There are several branches—be sure you stay on FR-9737. It is nearly 10 miles to the end of the road at the trailhead (elevation 4,200 feet) for **Esmeralda Basin Trail 1394**. This popular trail traverses forest, subalpine meadows, and the rugged high country of the Wenatchee Mountains—famous for its July wildflowers. Most of the birds can be seen in the first two miles in the lower, lusher part of the basin. An additional 1.5 miles on a rockier tread brings you to Fortune Creek Pass (elevation 6,000 feet), and views to the west of glacier-mantled Mounts Daniel and Hinman at the Cascade Crest. Birds that might be seen along this trail include Rufous Hummingbird, Hairy Woodpecker, Hammond's Flycatcher, Warbling Vireo, Gray Jay, Clark's Nutcracker, Mountain and Chestnut-backed Chickadees, Pacific Wren, American Dipper, Golden-crowned and Ruby-crowned Kinglets, Townsend's Solitaire, Hermit and Varied Thrushes, Yellow-rumped and Townsend's Warblers, Chipping, Fox, and Lincoln's Sparrows, Dark-eyed Junco, Western Tanager, Cassin's Finch, and Red Crossbill. Pikas and Hoary Marmots are frequently encountered mammals.

SWAUK CREEK BASIN

Although fragmentation resulting from logging has affected some species, this forested basin retains its well-deserved reputation for owls— Flammulated, Great Horned, Northern Pygmy-, Barred, and Northern Saw-whet. March through early May is best, as calling by most species diminishes later in the season. Other bird species of mountain forests may be found here as well, including Northern Goshawk and Williamson's Sapsucker.

To reach one good owling spot, go north three miles on US-97 from the SR-970 intersection. Turn right (east) onto Liberty Road (FR-9718), then right again in 0.7 mile onto FR-9726. Keep on the main road 0.8 mile to Pine Gulch Road (FR-121). Go left here for another 0.7 mile to a sharp bend where the road is blocked. The mature Grand Fir forest in this area is good for owls, including Barred and Northern Saw-whet Owls.

For another owling route, go back to Liberty Road (FR-9718) and turn right. In 0.7 mile, keep left onto FR-9712 as it goes up Lion Gulch. In three miles, keep left onto FR-9705. Beginning in one mile and thereafter for another mile, listen for Flammulated Owls as this road switchbacks up a south-facing slope grown to Ponderosa Pine and Douglas-fir. Another suitable spot for this species is at about three miles from FR-9712. Then the road begins a descent into north-facing ravines with moister forest—habitat for Northern Saw-whet Owls—and rejoins US-97 in about 2.5 miles.

Just north of Mineral Springs Campground on US-97 (3.6 miles north of Liberty Road and 0.8 mile south of FR-9705), FR-9738 turns off and follows Blue Creek to the west. At a fork in 2.6 miles, keep left onto FR-9702 (staying right with FR-9738 brings you to the North Fork Teanaway Road in about 12 miles). FR-9702 ends at a small parking lot in 4.7 miles. Take the graded, but steep, half-mile trail to the lookout tower on **Red Top Mountain** (elevation 5,361 feet). Hawkwatching can be good here from mid-August through October, especially on clear days with winds from the north or east. Sharp-shinned, Cooper's, and Red-tailed Hawks are the most common species. Less common, but still regular, are Bald Eagle, Northern Goshawk, Rough-legged Hawk (late fall), Golden Eagle, American Kestrel, and Merlin. You may also see small parties of Turkey Vultures. The occasional Broad-winged Hawk may pass through these areas in fall migration. If you hit the wrong conditions for raptors, the view from Red Top northwest to the granitic ramparts of the Enchantments may be compensation enough.

Continue north on US-97 and in 2.9 miles turn left onto FR-7320 (aka FR-9715), a winding section of highway across the Wenatchee Mountains that was decommissioned when US-97 was rerouted. The open, forested slopes and meadows up to and around Old Blewett Pass (4.0 miles; elevation 4,064 feet) are known for owls (particularly Flammulated and Northern Saw-whet), Common Poorwill, Williamson's Sapsucker, and Red Crossbill. Half a mile north on US-97 from the FR-7320 turnoff, **Swauk Campground** is in a birdy area with riparian, forested, and meadow habitats all close by. Look for Hammond's Flycatcher, Swainson's and Hermit Thrushes, Nashville, MacGillivray's, and Townsend's Warblers, Pine Siskins, and wandering flocks of Evening Grosbeaks.

Climb 4.1 miles on US-97 to **Blewett Pass** (elevation 4,102 feet; called Swauk Pass on older maps), gateway to birding routes in the Okanogan (page 404). From here, in summer, one can take FR-9716 south 0.5 mile to the **Discovery Trail**, a graded, 2.7-mile interpretive loop through forest habitats in varying states of regeneration after logging. A good selection of montane forest birds should be encountered, including Rufous Hummingbird, Hairy Woodpecker, Olive-sided and Hammond's Flycatchers, Warbling Vireo, Gray Jay, Mountain Chickadee, Red-breasted Nuthatch, Golden-crowned Kinglet, Townsend's Solitaire, Hermit and Varied Thrushes, Yellow-rumped and Townsend's Warblers, Western Tanager, Cassin's Finch, and Evening Grosbeak. Wildflowers are an added bonus. You can shave a mile off by bearing left just after marker 16. However, going the extra mile will reward you with the best views and the largest and oldest trees.

TABLE MOUNTAIN

Continue on FR-9716 for 3.2 miles and turn left onto FR-9712, which follows a valley between the talus-strewn slopes of Diamond Head to the north and Table Mountain to the south. The western edge of Diamond Head is also a place to watch for migrating raptors, with a similar species composition to Red Top Mountain. Large, spring-green Western Larches (golden in fall) cling to the steep slopes. In 1.6 miles, at the junction with FR-3500 (FR-35 on some maps), keep straight on FR-9712. As the road climbs, subalpine tree species such as Subalpine Fir, Lodgepole Pine, and Engelmann Spruce become common. Williamson's Sapsucker is common, especially in the Western Larch zones. Mountain species such as Gray Jay and Hermit Thrush are common.

A large fire swept through Table Mountain the fall of 2012. The fire burned most of the habitat on top of Table Mountain while creating a mosaic of burned and unburned vegetation farther down the slopes. The burned areas should produce various woodpecker species and other species favoring these burns such as Mountain Bluebird. Northern Goshawk and Northern Pygmy-Owl are often encountered in this area, though goshawk habitat was reduced by the 2012 fire.

Haney Meadow is reached in another 3.2 miles at about 5,500 feet elevation. Boreal Owl has been noted in this general area; the best time to look for this reclusive species is September and October. The 2012 fire burned most of the habitat around Haney Meadows, but small patches of unburned forest remain. The status of Boreal Owl after the fire remains uncertain. Back at FR-3500, you can continue on FR-9712 and retrace your route back to US-97 at Blewett Pass. Alternatively, turn left onto FR-3500 for a memorable drive across Table Mountain to Ellensburg. The roadbed is rough for the first four miles, to a four-way junction. Here the even rougher FR-124 turns off right to Lion Rock—0.8 mile; elevation 6,359 feet; on the west side of Table Mountain—another fall hawkwatching site, similar to Red Top Mountain.

Continue south on FR-3500. In 2.1 miles, the road (now paved) begins a spectacular, seven-mile descent to the Kittitas Valley, with numerous switchbacks and expansive views. The subalpine forest is soon left behind, replaced briefly with a mixed-conifer association, then Ponderosa Pines (fine wildflower show in late spring and early summer), and eventually riparian habitat along Reecer Creek Road (page 279). The patches of Mountain Big Sage host breeding Vesper Sparrows and the wet meadows breeding Lincoln's Sparrows.

If you are traveling from Blewett Pass to Ellensburg via US-97—the conventional route—two slight variants enlarge the birding possibilities. The first is **Swauk Prairie**; from the junction of US-97 and SR-970, travel 0.6 mile on SR-970 and turn right onto Swauk Prairie Road. The birding here features raptors in the winter, including Rough-legged Hawk, and open-country birds in the spring and summer, including both Western and Mountain Bluebirds.

For the second diversion, return to the intersection of US-97 and SR-970, turn right onto US-97, proceed 1.7 miles, and and turn right onto Bettas Road. Western and Mountain Bluebirds are often numerous around these ranchlands. In 2.7 miles, turn right onto graveled Hayward Road (not plowed in winter), which crosses shrub-steppe habitat. Vesper Sparrows inhabit the grassier parts. In 2.8 miles from Bettas Road you reach SR-10 where you can turn east to Ellensburg or west to Cle Elum. Crossing SR-10 and continuing straight ahead onto N Thorp Highway will take you across the Yakima River and through the town of Thorp to I-90 Exit 101 in about five miles, with road-side wetland and riparian birding possibilities along the way.

KITTITAS VALLEY

by Andy Stepniewski and Hal Opperman
revised by Scott Downes

Ellensburg is an agricultural and college town in the midst of the Kittitas Valley. Irrigated farmlands here grow high-quality Timothy hay of worldwide renown. Raptors, including owls, are beneficiaries of hay farming, as these fields support high rodent populations.

The Kittitas Valley is a notable wintering raptor area. Red-tailed Hawk is the most common species, usually with several Harlan's in the local contingent. Northern Harrier, Rough-legged Hawk, and American Kestrel can also be numerous. Prairie Falcons hunt the fields and shrub-steppe edges. Merlins can be spotted perched atop tall conifers either in town or about farmhouses. Golden Eagles sometimes descend to the valley from the surrounding canyons where they nest, especially when snow cover is heavy. Bald Eagles are opportunists. There are usually a few along the Yakima River all winter, but look for them especially in the late winter and spring calving season, when they are attracted to afterbirth and perhaps stillborn calves. Barn Owls are common farmland residents, where they feed over the fields at night and roost in barns during the day. Great Horned Owls are residents of riparian areas and windbreaks. Short-eared Owls can be found in areas of high grass cover, especially around the Ellensburg Airport. Check livestock ponds for Cinnamon Teal and Wilson's Phalarope in spring and summer. Though migratory shorebirds are not numerous in the county, checking flooded fields and livestock ponds are your best chance for finding this group. Northern Harriers, Long-billed Curlews, and Short-eared Owls attempt to nest each year in hay fields and grasslands, and some succeed, despite predation and adverse harvest schedules. A few pairs of Swainson's Hawks nest, at the western edge of their Washington range, in the intensively farmed area east of I-82 and south of I-90. A Discover Pass is required to bird state-owned lands mentioned here.

ELLENSBURG

To bird Ellensburg, take Exit 109 from I-90 and proceed north on Canyon Road to the first pull-in on the right. (See inset map on page 272.) A large pond behind the **Bar 14 Restaurant** attracts waterfowl in spring and fall and can have Cackling Goose, Canada Goose, the occasional swan in winter (Trumpeter and Tundra both possible), and a variety of dabbling and diving ducks. If the fields surrounding the pond are flooded, check them for migrant shorebirds. Unusual geese such as Greater White-fronted and Snow have been noted.

Continue north (becomes Main Street) about a mile and a half to the Ellensburg business district. To the east lies a residential area and the Central Washington University campus. From December through February, ornamental plantings in these areas can host irruptive species such as Bohemian Waxwing and Common Redpoll. Both Blue Jay and Western Scrub-Jay have been recorded in this area. A Hoary Redpoll was found during the winter of 2002 amongst a large flock of Common Redpolls.

From Main Street, turn right (east) onto University Way; follow this road for 1.0 mile and turn left onto Brick Road, which eventually becomes Sanders Road after a sharp left curve. In 0.1 mile from the curve, turn right (north) onto Look Road and check open fields for raptors. The east end of the airport is on your left in less than a mile.

NORTHWEST KITTITAS VALLEY

The Kittitas Valley north and west of Ellensburg is known for its raptor diversity. Songbird diversity and breeding Long-billed Curlews are also a draw for birders in spring and summer. Continue north on Look Road to **Hungry Junction Road** (1.8 miles from the start of Look Road). Check the stock pond just before the intersection for waterfowl and migrating shorebirds, then turn left onto Hungry Junction Road, which runs west to an intersection with US-97. The entire 4.2-mile stretch is worth exploring. The airport is on the south for over a mile—an excellent place for wintering raptors, including Northern Harrier and Red-tailed and Rough-legged Hawks. During the winter, Short-eared Owls frequent the western end of the airport near dawn and dusk.

From Hungry Junction Road, search areas south of the road at the west end of the airport for owls. American Tree Sparrows winter on airport grounds. Special permission is needed to go onto the airport grounds, but occasionally you can find birds along the north margin of the airport on Hungry Junction Road. Small numbers of Gray Partridge may be found in this area; previously common, the species is now declining.

At 2.3 miles, there is a small pond on your right (north) that can host a good variety of geese in migration, including Greater White-fronted and Snow Goose, both unusual. Slightly farther west, the intersection with Reecer

Creek Road is a possible spot for Gray Partridge. West of this intersection, spilled grain at a big livestock-feeding operation attracts California Quail and Gray Partridge, especially when snow cover limits foraging opportunities in the farmlands. Blackbirds abound in the feedlots; search through these flocks for unusual species such as Yellow-headed Blackbird and, on rare occasions, Rusty Blackbird.

Roads to the north of Hungry Junction Road such as Faust, Clarke, and Reecer Creek Road have Gray Partridges in low concentrations. Search along the road, particularly in grassy areas and during dawn and dusk. If you find yourself in these areas during times of recent snowfall, Gray Partridges can be attracted to the road in search of grit. In spring, Long-billed Curlews are possible in the last two miles of the road, particularly on the north side.

Return to the intersection of Hungry Junction Road and **Reecer Creek Road** and turn left (north). Travel up Reecer Creek Road for 4.4 miles, reaching the intersection with Smithson Road. Smithson Road provides similar birding to Hungry Junction Road, but with a greater chance of seeing nesting Long-billed Curlews, particularly in the first mile east of US-97. Turn left onto Smithson Road and search the fields for the entire 3.8 miles to US-97. From January to March, concentrations of Bald Eagles can be found along this road.

Return to the intersection of Smithson and Reecer Creek Road. Turn left (north) and follow the road for two 90-degree turns as the road heads north, leaving the Kittitas Valley bottom and passing under several sets of power lines in the next mile. Wilson's Snipes winnow above the wet fields east of the road in spring. Check the power lines for Golden Eagles and Prairie Falcons. After passing a couple of ponds on the right (scope them from the road) and a ranchette development, the road narrows to a single, paved lane (FR-3500), bends toward the northeast, and enters the small canyon of Reecer Creek. For about two miles until it hits the hill, switches back, and starts to ascend steeply, the road follows the creek in an area of brush, grassy slopes, and small deciduous trees that can be fantastically birdy. In the riparian zone expect Warbling Vireo, Veery, Nashville, MacGillivray's, and Yellow Warblers, and Lazuli Bunting; Gray Catbird is possible. To the left of the road, look for Vesper Sparrows in the mixed grassland and shrub-steppe. Bohemian Waxwings have been seen here in fall, feeding on the fruits of various berry-producing shrubs and trees (wild rose, Bitter Cherry, Common Chokecherry, Black Hawthorn, Red-osier Dogwood)—a natural habitat that birders too seldom search for this winter visitor. Northern Shrikes can be found here in the fall and winter. Upon climbing the hill, watch for dry-forest species such as Cassin's Vireo and Western Tanager in the conifers at the head of the canyon; and Common Poorwill at night. By continuing north up Table Mountain on FR-3500, you can reach Lion Rock, Liberty, and Blewett Pass (page 404).

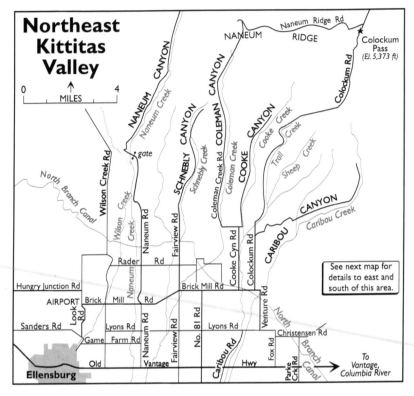

Northeast Kittitas Valley

0 ———↑——— 4
MILES

NORTHEAST KITTITAS VALLEY

From the intersection of Hungry Junction Road and Look Road, drive south 0.5 mile on Look Road and turn left (east) onto Brick Mill Road to bird the northeast part of the valley. In winter, raptors should be in evidence in the numerous fields. In 5.1 miles, **Number 81 Road** turns off to the right and runs south 3.0 miles through similar habitat to the Old Vantage Highway. Go left (east) here to reach Vantage and the Columbia River. At least one pair of Swainson's Hawks typically nests along Number 81 Road. Watch fields in these areas, as well as the corner of Parke Creek Road and Christensen Road, farther east, for Long-billed Curlews.

A series of canyons coming down into the valley from Naneum Ridge—the eastern extremity of the Wenatchee Mountains—can be reached by driving north a few miles from Brick Mill Road. Distances below are from intersection of Look and Brick Mill Roads. Once they leave farm and ranch country, these canyon roads are minimally maintained and recommended only for high-clearance vehicles. Areas above 5,000 feet may be snowed in until June or in some years, July. There are many spur roads in these areas; stay on the "Green Dot" roads as shown on the *Naneum Ridge Forest "Green Dot"*

Roads map. If you are considering exploring these lands, download a copy of it at *dnr.wa.gov* or pick up a copy at the district office in Ellensburg (713 Bowers Road, 509-925-8510) if you are there on a weekday.

To reach *Naneum Canyon* (gated at its mouth but you may walk or bike in), turn north on Naneum Road (2.3 miles from Look Road). *Schnebly Canyon* can be reached via Fairview Road (4.0 miles from Look). To reach *Coleman and Cooke Canyons*, turn north on Cooke Canyon Road (6.4 miles from Look); when the road reaches a T, go left to Coleman Creek Road for Coleman Canyon and right for Cooke Canyon. Take *Colockum Road* (7.2 miles east of Look), the old stage road to Wenatchee, up Trail Creek and over 5,373-foot Colockum Pass. Any of these canyons offers fine birding of the shrub-steppe/Ponderosa Pine ecotone, and for the adventurous, a transect of other forest habitats as one moves up, reaching the Subalpine Fir and Engelmann Spruce zones in several places. Colockum Road and Coleman Creek Roads are the most traveled and birded.

The best birding is along **Naneum Ridge Road**, accessed at the top of Cooke Canyon Road or by turning left just north of Colockum Pass on Colockum Road. Along this ridge, you can find Dusky Grouse, small populations of Spruce Grouse, and American Three-toed Woodpecker. Fall records of Boreal Owl exist. Riparian patches along either Cooke Canyon Road or Colockum Road are worth exploring for a diverse suite of riparian species.

THE COLUMBIA SLOPE: VANTAGE TO SENTINEL GAP

by Andy Stepniewski

revised by Scott Downes

This is a scenic, lightly traveled, 28-mile alternate route from Ellensburg to the Columbia River. Prior to the completion of I-90, this road was known as US-10; today many call it the Old Vantage Highway. This popular birding route offers access to good-quality shrub-steppe habitat, where many of the shrub-steppe obligates of the Columbia Basin can be found. A Discover Pass is needed for many sites, including the Quilomene Unit and spots along the Columbia River.

VANTAGE HIGHWAY

You can reach this road from either Ellensburg or Kittitas. From Ellensburg, go east on University Way from the corner of Main Street at the north end of the Ellensburg business district. Stay on this main road as it heads out of town into farmland and becomes the Vantage Highway east of Ellensburg. To reach this highway from Kittitas, take eastbound I-90 Exit 115 (the last interchange before the Columbia River). Turn north over I-90 and follow Main Street through downtown Kittitas. Turn right on Patrick Avenue

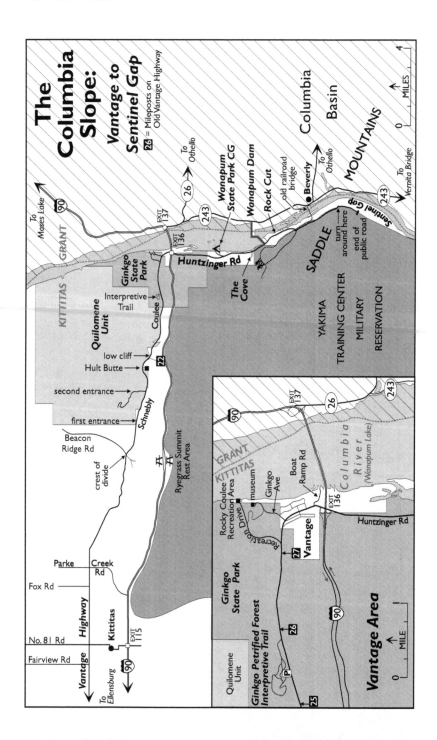

The Columbia Slope: Vantage to Sentinel Gap

26 = Mileposts on Old Vantage Highway

To Othello

26

Wanapum State Park CG
Wanapum Dam
Rock Cut
old railroad bridge
To Othello
Beverly
243
To Vernita Bridge

Columbia Basin

MOUNTAINS

0   MILES   4

To Moses Lake

90

GRANT

KITTITAS

EXIT 137

243

EXIT 136

Huntzinger Rd

Ginkgo State Park

Interpretive Trail

Quilomene Unit

Coulee

The Cove

SADDLE

turn around here
end of public road

Sentinel Gap

YAKIMA TRAINING CENTER

MILITARY RESERVATION

low cliff
Hult Butte
22

second entrance

first entrance

Schnebly

Beacon Ridge Rd

crest of divide

Ryegrass Summit Rest Area

EXIT 137

26

243

90

GRANT
KITTITAS

Columbia River (Wanapum Lake)

Boat Ramp Rd

Rocky Coulee Recreation Area

museum

Ginkgo Ave

EXIT 136

Huntzinger Rd

Parke Creek Rd

Fox Rd

Highway

Vantage

Kittitas

EXIT 115

No. 81 Rd

Fairview Rd

90

To Ellensburg

Recreation Drive

27 Vantage

Ginkgo State Park

Quilomene Unit

Ginkgo Petrified Forest Interpretive Trail

P

26

90

25

Vantage Area

0   MILE   1

for 0.2 mile and then take a left to Number 81 Road. This will take you to the Vantage Highway in one mile.

The highway continues east through irrigated fields. Long-billed Curlews are often found in the spring and early summer in the eastern irrigated fields, particularly those near Parke Creek Road (about four miles east of Number 81 Road). About a half-mile farther, at milepost 11, the road leaves the irrigated fields and enters unfarmed shrub-steppe habitat. Watch for Burrowing Owls on both sides of the Vantage Highway near Sunset Road. In recent years, owls have nested in this area; adults in the spring and young birds in the summer may be found sitting along the highway. In spring and summer, look for shrub-steppe species such as Loggerhead Shrike, Mountain Bluebird, Sage Thrasher, and Sagebrush Sparrow as the winding highway continues to climb for 5.8 miles to a divide.

The highway begins a gradual descent along **Schnebly Coulee** toward the Columbia River. In 1.8 miles, pull off to the left at a sign for the **Quilomene Wildlife Area**. In spring this is a great spot for Mountain Bluebird and Sage Thrasher. From the parking area, a rough road leads into a vast expanse of largely wild country, stretching north for 22 miles and east eight miles to the sheer basalt cliffs of the Columbia. Most of this land—some 134,000 acres—lies within two state wildlife areas, Colockum and the L.T. Murray, which can also be accessed off the Colockum Road. (Quilomene and Whiskey Dick now are units of L.T. Murray.) These lands are open from April 1 through November 30 and require a Discover Pass. Birding is excellent in varied habitats of rimrock, shrub-steppe, riparian vegetation along several creeks, and Ponderosa Pine at the upper edge. Motorists should not attempt to enter this country except in a high-clearance, four-wheel-drive vehicle and with emergency equipment, including a spare tire.

Another entrance to the wildlife unit is 1.7 miles farther east. Just inside is a dense stand of Bitterbrush and Big Sagebrush with deep Bluebunch Wheatgrass, prime habitat for Sage Thrasher and Brewer's and Sagebrush Sparrows. In April and May, the wildflower display can be quite beautiful. Winds are frequently fierce, especially during spring months. These lands have a small population of Gray Flycatchers along with other shrub-steppe birds. The roads can be good for Common Poorwill just after sunset.

Winter birding can produce Rough-legged Hawk, Golden Eagle, and Prairie Falcon, among other interesting raptors. Gyrfalcon has been noted on this highway. Be sure to look through winter Horned Lark flocks for Lapland Longspur and Snow Bunting. Winter birding is best when there is some snow cover on the surrounding lands. Northern Shrikes are often found along this stretch during the winter, but a few Loggerhead Shrikes may linger into winter months, so careful observation of shrikes is needed.

The highway soon begins a sweeping curve to the left, dropping down and swinging back to the east around the north base of **Hult Butte** through excellent Sagebrush Sparrow habitat. In 1.9 miles, at milepost 22, Schnebly Coulee narrows and starts to descend more steeply. Stop at a pullout on the right in 0.2 mile at a low cliff with lichen- and moss-encrusted basalt columns. Great Horned Owls frequently nest in this band of basalt columns. Brush patches in the moister spots harbor songbirds, especially in migration. Chukars are common in this area and may be seen or heard along the rimrock in early morning and near sunset. Checks of the scattered patches of riparian vegetation about two miles beyond MP 22 can turn up migrant songbirds. Before a 2004 fire, a pair of Ash-throated Flycatchers bred here and may once again return once the vegetation matures.

In 3.5 miles, the **Ginkgo Petrified Forest Interpretive Trail** entrance is on the left. During spring and fall migration, you might find a few migrants in the small collection of trees at the parking lot, which constitutes a micro migrant-trap. During the winter, the few juniper trees often host a Townsend's Solitaire or two. In 1.7 miles, turn left onto Recreation Drive. On the left in 0.3 mile, there is a small white gate that leads to state park lands to the north. Most summers a Black-throated Sparrow or two can be found singing on the slopes here. Continue to the end of the road where a small grove of trees serves as a good area to search for spring and fall migrants and where the waters of the Columbia can be scoped. This area, known as Rocky Coulee Recreation Area and managed by Grant County PUD, has picnic tables and a restroom.

Returning up Recreation Drive, take a left and wind up the road to the **Ginkgo Petrified Forest State Park Interpretive Museum**. Here you can scan the waters of the Columbia River. The wide expanse of the river has been dammed to create Wanapum Lake. Ducks, loons, and grebes are found from fall through spring. With careful scanning you may pick out unusual birds such as scoters and Pacific Loon. White-throated Swifts nest in the cliff face below and Chukars are often heard in the rimrock during the early morning and late evening. The trees here often produce an array of migrants, with some potential for vagrants: American Redstart and Blackpoll Warbler, for example, have been found here. Take Ginkgo Avenue to Main Street in Vantage and turn left. In 0.5 mile you can get onto I-90 (Exit 136) for points to the east or continue south to Huntzinger Road destinations below.

Just north of I-90, take a left at Boat Ramp Road and follow it to a parking area on the north side of I-90 at the Columbia. From October through April, a mix of wintering waterbirds including ducks, loons, and grebes can be found. If water levels are low, gulls may roost on the shore here, and terns can be found from spring through fall. Unusual species such as Black Scoter, Pacific Loon, and Mew Gull have been noted here.

HUNTZINGER ROAD

The I-90 interchange in Vantage is at the west end of the Columbia River bridge. Winds can be fierce in the Vantage area, especially during the spring. During windy periods, morning birding is the best. Go south from the interchange onto Huntzinger Road, which follows the river through several excellent sites for birds of the arid shrub-steppe and rocky cliffs.

Drive south on Huntzinger Road and turn left into the **Wanapum State Park Campground** (2.5 miles). The trees in the camping area and trees and edge habitat in the day-use areas can host a diversity of spring and fall migrants and wintering birds. Numerous vagrants have been found here, so check the flocks carefully. Be sure to scope the waters of the Columbia. Large rafts of ducks are found from October through April, with uncommon birds such as scoters, Long-tailed Duck, and Red-breasted Merganser occasionally noted. Tufted Duck has been reported here a couple of times, so scan through the scaup flocks carefully. In summer the campground is crowded and noisy, especially on weekends and during the Gorge Amphitheatre concert season. At such times try to visit early in the morning or during the weekdays. Labor Day weekend is especially busy.

Watch for Chukars along Huntzinger Road. Listen for their raucous calls, and keep an eye open for them along the roadside or standing motionless on the rimrock. Chukars are most active in early morning and late evening. Check the slopes of Huntzinger Road for Black-throated Sparrows. Most years at least one singing male can be found along this road and during years of influx, multiple birds have been noted.

Once again driving south, stop along the road, on the right, by a gate in a rocky bowl with sparse shrub-steppe vegetation (0.7 mile). This spot has been reliable for Black-throated Sparrows some years (late May through early July). Farther south on Huntzinger Road is **The Cove**, (formerly called Getty's Cove), a day-use area managed by Grant County PUD and Washington State Parks and requiring a Discover Pass (0.7 mile). The pullout on the river side allows you to scope the Columbia River.

As at Wanapum State Park, large flocks of waterbirds can be found between October and April and unusual birds such as scoters, Long-tailed Duck, and loons may be found among the more common scaup (both Greater and Lesser), Common Goldeneye, and grebes. The impoundment on the right side of the road is worth checking for waterfowl (look closely for Eurasian Wigeon). Walk the grounds of the day-use area during migration. These trees and shrubs can host a diversity of migrants, and vagrants have been reported here. A Bald Eagle nest is located within the day-use area; the area around it is closed off during nesting months.

The west end of **Wanapum Dam** is in 0.8 mile. Continue another 0.4 mile beyond that and turn left below the dam onto a track that leads to the

Columbia, at a Grant County PUD site called **Huntzinger Boat Launch**—a good place from which to scope for waterbirds in winter. Facilities here include a restroom and parking lot. Barrow's Goldeneye is regular here in the winter. Red-breasted Merganser is possible among the more numerous Common Mergansers during fall and winter months. Most winters a Pacific Loon can be found here, and Yellow-billed and Red-throated Loons, both rare in the Columbia Basin, have been noted.

In 0.6 mile from Huntzinger Boat Launch access, Huntzinger Road goes through a rock cut and crosses a short fill; pull off on the right at either end of the embankment to look for Say's Phoebe, Rock Wren, and Canyon Wren. Canyon Wrens are resident here, and Rock Wrens often are found during winter. This area often hosts Gray-crowned Rosy-Finches in winter, and they occasionally roost along the rimrock. Scope the gravel islands in the Columbia for American White Pelican, gulls (mostly Ring-billed and California, but, in fall and winter, also Herring and Glaucous-winged), and Caspian and Forster's Terns, plus Common Terns in migration. Unusual gulls, including Mew, Thayer's, and Glaucous, have been noted. Barrow's Goldeneye and unusual loons are possible along this stretch. Gulls are most evident when water levels on the river are low, exposing large areas of gravel.

South from the rock cut, Huntzinger Road approaches the base of the towering cliffs where the Columbia cuts through the Saddle Mountains at **Sentinel Gap**. Near the gap, an old railroad bridge crosses the river. A pull-out on the left allows you to scope the waters around the bridge. Watch for Great Egrets from spring through fall—a good variety of waterbirds can be found, including loons, grebes, and American White Pelican. From the bridge, drive south along the cliffs, scanning them for Chukar, Golden Eagle, White-throated Swift, and Peregrine and Prairie Falcons.

Turn around when the road leaves the cliffs and retrace your route to Vantage. You can take I-90 eastbound to birding sites of the Columbia Basin (page 348). If you are traveling I-90 back to Ellensburg, stop at the **Ryegrass Summit** rest area at the top of the 10-mile grade west of Vantage. In spring and early summer, this is a good spot for Sage Thrasher and Brewer's Sparrow.

TANEUM CREEK AND MANASTASH CREEK

by Hal Opperman and Andy Stepniewski
revised by Scott Ramos

Southwest of the Kittitas Valley, the east slopes of the Cascades are dissected by ravines and canyons with innumerable variations in slope and aspect, creating niches for a wide array of breeding species. The best time to visit is from late May through July; winter snow closes most of the higher elevations. A fine loop through this area goes up Taneum Creek, then south over Taneum Ridge to Buck Meadows, and back out to the east following South Fork Manastash Creek. Coming from the west, take I-90 Exit 93 (Elk Heights). Turn left across the interstate, then right at the next stop sign onto Thorp Prairie Road. At a stop sign in 3.5 miles, turn right onto the I-90 overpass to a junction (0.2 mile), then right onto W Taneum Road.

Exit 101 (Thorp) is your access if coming from the east. Go left (south) across the interstate, and in 0.6 mile turn right onto Thorp Cemetery Road, which will take you in 4.8 miles to the foot of the I-90 overpass; continue straight ahead here onto W Taneum Road. No gas or services are available along this loop.

TANEUM CREEK

The valley quickly narrows, as South Cle Elum Ridge rises up on the right and Taneum Ridge closes in from the left. Pull off at a small, inconspicuous rock quarry on the right in 1.3 miles, across from a mailbox numbered 6680. Calliope Hummingbird, Vesper Sparrow, and Lazuli Bunting inhabit the brushy, grassy slopes; look for Vaux's Swift overhead. The county road ends, and FR-33 begins, in 0.8 mile. Steep rock faces overhang the road on the right (nesting Cliff Swallows).

In 0.7 mile is a sign marking the entrance of the **L.T. Murray Wildlife Area**. A track on the left a couple of hundred yards ahead leads down to tall trees along Taneum Creek (Warbling Vireo, Evening Grosbeak). The road then runs beside wet meadows and a cattail marsh, accessible on foot in several places. An excellent riparian area can be found in another 0.9 mile. Park and walk toward Taneum Creek; logs have been placed over the stream to create shaded fish habitat. Brush and tall trees along the stream for several hundred yards in both directions have nesting Mourning Dove, Western Screech-Owl, Red-naped Sapsucker, Western Wood-Pewee, Pacific-slope Flycatcher, Warbling Vireo, House Wren, Veery, Swainson's Thrush, Cedar Waxwing, Nashville, MacGillivray's, and Yellow Warblers, Spotted Towhee, Western Tanager, Black-headed Grosbeak, and Bullock's Oriole.

In 1.4 miles, primitive Moonlight Canyon Road (high-clearance vehicle advised) leads up the ridge to the right, where the open, south-facing Ponderosa Pine forest offers Williamson's Sapsucker (higher up), Dusky Flycatcher, Cassin's Vireo, Mountain Chickadee, Yellow-rumped and Townsend's Warblers, Chipping Sparrow, Lazuli Bunting, Cassin's Finch, and Red Crossbill.

Back on FR-33, **Taneum Campground** (elevation 2,400 feet), across the stream on a footbridge in 0.8 mile, has a small stand of old-growth Ponderosa Pines. At the back of the campground, look for Hermit Thrush and Nashville Warbler.

In another 1.4 miles, primitive Cedar Creek Road turns up the ridge to the right; in 0.2 mile, check the small meadow for Gray and Dusky Flycatchers, Warbling Vireo, Nashville, MacGillivray's, and Wilson's Warblers, Chipping and White-crowned Sparrows, Western Tanager, and Cassin's

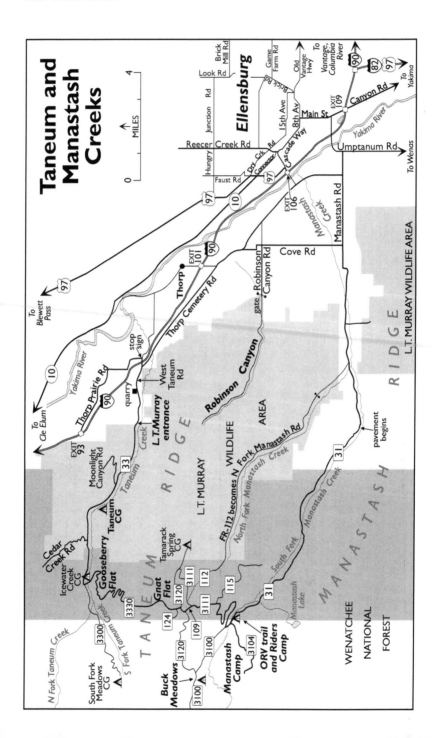

Taneum and Manastash Creeks

Finch. In another 1.2 miles is **Icewater Creek Campground** with a good mix of vegetation. Expect Ruffed Grouse, Downy and Pileated Woodpeckers, Cassin's and Warbling Vireos, Swainson's and Hermit Thrushes, Nashville, MacGillivray's, Yellow, Yellow-rumped, and Townsend's Warblers, plus Western Tanager, Black-headed Grosbeak, Purple Finch, and Evening Grosbeak.

TANEUM RIDGE

As you continue up FR-33, forests gradually become denser. Ponderosa Pine yields ground to Douglas-fir, and Hermit Thrush replaces Veery. At a fork in 0.2 mile, where FR-33 continues straight, bear left onto FR-3330 (well-maintained gravel), which drops down to cross Taneum Creek, then immediately begins to climb the cooler, wetter, north-facing slope of Taneum Ridge, with many pullouts, side roads, and informal trails. Most of the forest is second-growth, with some recent clearcuts and a few big old trees. Western Larch begins to appear. Note that on June 15 trails are opened to ORVs in this area.

After 2.9 miles of steady rise, the road levels out temporarily at Gooseberry Flat (elevation 3,500 feet), then twists and turns its way upward for another 3.7 miles to **Gnat Flat** (elevation 4,800 feet), an area of open steppes, aspen groves, and isolated conifer stands. Characteristic species of the habitats here and on the way up include Sooty Grouse, Turkey Vulture, Northern Goshawk, Flammulated Owl (local), Rufous Hummingbird, Williamson's and Red-naped Sapsuckers, Hairy, American Three-toed, and Black-backed Woodpeckers (the last two rare), Olive-sided and Dusky Flycatchers, Gray Jay, Mountain Chickadee, Red-breasted Nuthatch, House Wren, Mountain Bluebird, Townsend's Solitaire, Hermit Thrush, Nashville, Yellow-rumped, and Townsend's Warblers, Chipping Sparrow, Western Tanager, and Cassin's Finch. Mixed-conifer forests on these flats are logged in rotation, and the various successional stages attract different sets of birds.

Farther south, the flats have large patches of sagebrush, and in 1.5 miles the road reaches its high point of 4,900 feet at an intersection with FR-124 on the right (signboard with map of road system). Follow FR-124 for 0.2 mile to a grand overlook of the Frost Creek valley with a clearcut below, but a nice lunch spot, nevertheless. Look for Northern Goshawk, Common Raven, House Wren, Mountain Bluebird, Townsend's Solitaire, Yellow-rumped Warbler, Chipping Sparrow, Western Tanager, Cassin's Finch, and Evening Grosbeak.

Return to FR-3330, then, at a junction in 0.4 mile, where FR-3330 ends, take FR-3120 to the right (signed for Buck Meadows). Go left in 0.3 mile onto FR-109, a cutoff road that descends through second growth and clearcuts on a drier, south-facing slope with areas of meadow and sagebrush (Yellow-rumped and Townsend's Warblers and Chipping Sparrow). FR-109 ends at another junction in 0.5 mile; bear right here onto FR-3111. In 1.2 miles, where FR-115 turns off to the left, stay straight ahead on FR-3111.

BUCK MEADOWS

For the next 3.7 miles, the road winds down through dry, open forests (Mountain Chickadee, Red-breasted Nuthatch, Pine Siskin), meeting FR-31 at Buck Meadows (elevation 4,300 feet). Turn left here onto FR-31 across South Fork Manastash Creek, and in 0.3 mile turn right onto FR-3104. In the first half-mile, meadows open up on the left. Park and walk down to aspen groves and a small stream to look for Williamson's and Red-naped Sapsuckers, War-bling Vireo, MacGillivray's and Yellow Warblers, Dark-eyed Junco, Black-headed Grosbeak, and other nesting species of these mid-elevation forest wetland openings.

A similar area is reached by returning to FR-31 and going right 0.5 mile. Park across from an ORV trail (4W311) and walk around a rail fence on the right side of the road. A meadow extends back for a considerable distance. Ruby-crowned Kinglet, Wilson's Warbler, and Lincoln's Sparrow may be present in trees and brush along the wetland edges on the left. Stands of Lodgepole Pine, Western Larch, and Engelmann Spruce here and on the other side of FR-31, in Riders Camp, may have Hammond's and Dusky Flycatchers, Gray Jay, Townsend's Solitaire, Hermit Thrush, Yellow-rumped and Townsend's Warblers, Western Tanager, Red Crossbill, and Pine Siskin.

MANASTASH CREEK

The drive down the Manastash drainage is a recapitulation in reverse of the birding possibilities along Taneum Creek, but on a grander scale. For the next 6.5 miles FR-31 descends smartly in a canyon with steep basalt cliffs, rockslides, and scattered Ponderosa Pines. Stop from time to time to look for Golden Eagle, White-throated Swift (uncommon), American Kestrel, Prairie Falcon, Common Raven, and Rock and Canyon Wrens. Then the valley broad-ens out somewhat into a generous riparian zone. For about the next six miles, you may find Ruffed Grouse, Calliope Hummingbird, Lewis's Woodpecker, Red-naped Sapsucker, Cassin's Vireo, Northern Rough-winged Swallow, Black-capped and Mountain Chickadees, Red-breasted and White- breasted Nuthatches, House Wren, Nashville, MacGillivray's, and Yellow Warblers, Laz-uli Bunting, Purple and Cassin's Finches, and typical riparian species.

The paved county road begins at 9.7 miles from Riders Camp at Buck Meadows. From here, it is 7.4 miles on Manastash Road to the intersesction with Cove Road in the southwest corner of the Kittitas Valley and another 3.6 miles east from there to an intersection with Umptanum Road, where you can turn left to Ellensburg (easy access to I-90 Exit 109) or right to Wenas.

ROBINSON CANYON

For an interesting side trip from Manastash Road, go north 2.9 miles on Cove Road and turn left onto Robinson Canyon Road. A gate marks the entrance to the L.T. Murray Wildlife Area in 3.1 miles, at the mouth of Robinson Canyon. Park here, or pass through the gate and park in another 0.3 mile. This small drainage has Gray Flycatchers and most of the other characteristic species of the lower Ponderosa Pine zone, although in lesser numbers than the Wenas Creek region to the south. One or more of Flammulated, Western Screech-, Northern Pygmy-, and Northern Saw-whet Owls can usually be found somewhere along the canyon, and Common Poorwills forage from the road at night. The trail that leads up the canyon has recently been washed out, but a scramble across the creek leads to another trail on the south side; you can walk along it up the gulch for about four miles (mind the rattlesnakes).

Cove Road ends at S Thorp Highway (1.2 miles); a left turn brings you to the intersection with Thorp Cemetery Road (1.4 miles) where another left turn takes you back to Taneum Creek and the start of this loop; going straight on S Thorp Highway, the I-90 interchange at Exit 101 is 0.6 mile ahead.

WENAS CREEK LOOP

by Andy Stepniewski and Hal Opperman

revised by Andy Stepniewski

The Wenas Creek region, often simply referred to as "Wenas," is situated at the lower forest/shrub-steppe margin. Well known to naturalists, Wenas is an excellent place to observe a wide range of breeding birds within a short distance. Habitats range from arid, low-elevation shrub-steppe to park-like Ponderosa Pine forests and higher-elevation mixed-conifer communities. An added bonus is the presence of several riparian-zone environments along permanent streams draining the Cascades' east slopes. Birding is best from late April into July, with mid-May through June being the peak time.

Camping at Wenas Campground is a popular way to experience the region. Since 1963, Audubon Society members from throughout Washington have gathered here over Memorial Day weekend at the height of the spring wildflower and birding seasons, when from 130–150 species of birds are recorded.

The loop begins just off I-90 at Exit 109 (the east Ellensburg exit). Total driving distance is about 90 miles. Allow one day to complete the whole loop comfortably. It is described in four segments: 1) from Ellensburg via Umtanum Creek to Wenas Campground; 2) the campground and vicinity; 3) down the Wenas Valley to Selah, just north of Yakima; and 4) three options for the return leg to Ellensburg, described in the following section. A portion of the first and second segments is on gravel roads, parts of which may not be passable in winter or during the spring thaw. Once you leave Ellensburg there are no facilities on the loop until you reach Selah. Make sure you have topped up your fuel tank and have all provisions.

Much of the Wenas Creek Loop falls into the Wenas Cooperative Road Management Area. Roads open to public motor-vehicle travel are posted with a round green reflector on white route markers. These are the so-called "green-dot roads." All other roads are closed to motor vehicles, but you may walk on them. Many roads are gated from December 1 to May 1. A Discover Pass is required to park or walk on lands surrounding the main road.

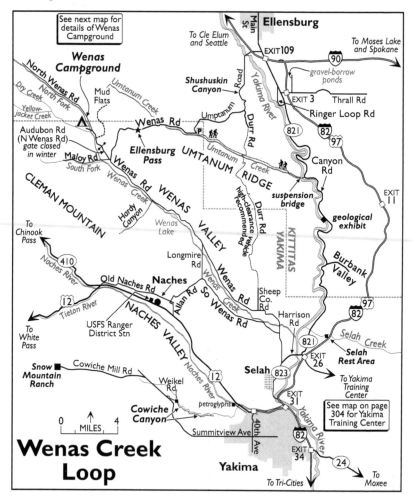

UMPTANUM ROAD

From I-90 Exit 109 (Canyon Road) in Ellensburg, go north 0.5 mile on Canyon Road. At the McDonald's restaurant, turn left (west) onto Umptanum Road. The road crosses the Yakima River (1.0 mile), turns south, passes through flat agricultural fields, and then begins a steep ascent into **Shushuskin Canyon**. A riparian area that attracts migrants is on the left part way through the canyon (2.3 miles from the Yakima River). At the top of the canyon, the pavement ends at the junction where Durr Road goes left (1.7 miles); keep straight on Umptanum Road, which bends west almost at once. The landscape is mainly shrub-steppe vegetation. Mountain and a few Western Bluebirds nest in the boxes set out by the Yakima Valley Audubon Society along the roadside. Farther west along Umptanum Road, you enter the **L.T. Murray Wildlife Area** (2.8 miles; sign) and shrub-steppe habitat, composed of Big Sagebrush (grayish-hued shrubs) and Bitterbrush (brownish-green-hued shrubs). In this area, from April through July, look for Loggerhead Shrike, Horned Lark, Sage Thrasher, and Brewer's and Vesper Sparrows. In winter, there are few birds in the shrub-steppe, but the farmland may have Red-tailed and Rough-legged Hawks and an occasional Prairie Falcon or Northern Shrike.

The road continues west, then turns south and crosses into Yakima County, where the road name changes to North Wenas Road. The edge of the Ponderosa Pine zone is reached at a mixed pine and riparian area on the right (1.7 miles). There are often many birds here in spring and early summer, including Great Horned Owl and Lewis's Woodpecker. Migrant flycatchers, vireos, kinglets, and warblers may be common in April and May. Continue to a WDFW parking area on the left side of the road (0.3 mile). A trail follows Umtanum Creek downstream eight miles or so, all the way to the Yakima River. Even a short walk along this stream can be good for migrants. You reach picturesque Umtanum Falls in less than a mile.

The road bends sharply westward as you leave the parking lot. A brushy stretch along the road in 1.1 miles is a good place to look for Ash-throated Flycatchers, a rare breeder this far north. They sometimes nest in the bluebird boxes; in the past, a good spot for these flycatchers has been in the neighborhood of box 63. As the road continues west and higher into the foothills of the Cascade Range, the Ponderosa Pine forest becomes more continuous (1.5 miles), reflecting an increase in precipitation. The open pine woods along this stretch have Gray Flycatchers, first noted in 1970 in the Wenas Campground, now widespread and fairly common in lower elevation Ponderosa Pine forests in Eastern Washington. Look and listen also for White-headed Woodpecker and Red Crossbill. In areas with pines, the nest boxes along the Umptanum/Wenas Road bluebird trail have many Western Bluebirds and House Wrens with the occasional White-breasted Nuthatch and Yellow-pine Chipmunk. Hundreds (one year over 1,000) of Western and Mountain Bluebirds fledge from this and several other trails in the Wenas region each year.

Ellensburg Pass (2.2 miles) in the pines marks the high point on the road. From the pass the road continues west, leaving the Umtanum Creek drainage and descending into the Wenas Creek drainage through Ponderosa Pines and a brushy riparian area flanking the road (1.5 miles). This habitat is good for Lazuli Bunting. At dusk on warm spring or summer nights, Common Poorwills call from the bordering slopes and are often seen on the road. Drive slowly to avoid hitting these remarkable birds. (Road gated in winter.)

The pavement begins again at a three-way junction (2.1 miles). Turn right from the main road onto an unpaved road that forks immediately. Stay right onto **Audubon Road** (North Wenas Road on some maps). A gate at the end of the county road in 1.4 miles is locked winter through spring, usually opening in early May. Initially, this bumpy road traverses shrub-steppe composed mainly of Bitterbrush and scattered Ponderosa Pines. Lewis's Woodpecker, Western Bluebird, Spotted Towhee, Brewer's (a few) and Vesper Sparrows, and Cassin's Finch should be found along this stretch. As you proceed northwestward, the road gets rougher (but is usually passable to standard automobiles), and soon meets North Fork Wenas Creek (0.3 mile). Water flows over the road in spring, but the bottom is good and one can usually drive through easily. However, go slowly and be especially cautious if the water is high.

You'll skirt fine riparian habitat here, with tall cottonwoods, willow and alder thickets, and aspen glades. This area has many birds—Vaux's Swift, Red-naped Sapsucker, Western Wood-Pewee, Black-capped Chickadee, Veery, Cedar Waxwing, Yellow Warbler, and Black-headed Grosbeak are common. Turkey Vultures may nest along the steep escarpment above the road. Keep left at a junction (0.5 mile) with a dirt track leading to Mud Flats (four-wheel drive only). The road leaves the riparian zone and continues west through grassy fields and open pine woods to a junction (0.5 mile). Turn left here, across the bridge over North Fork Wenas Creek. A few yards ahead is a large sign marking the entrance to the campground.

WENAS CAMPGROUND

The **Wenas Campground** is well known for its variety of breeding species. It is also a popular destination and therefore best visited on weekdays. On weekends during spring and summer you will likely encounter throngs of campers, horseback riders, dirt-bikers, and archery groups from the Yakima area. The campground is primitive and unpatrolled, with no piped water, toilets, hookups, or telephone; if you plan to stay here, bring all your own supplies. It's a good place to find birds of the lower Ponderosa Pine zone.

Four different habitats, each with a distinct complement of breeding birds, occur in proximity. Along the North Fork, in the campground, is a lush riparian community; Vaux's Swift, Red-naped Sapsucker, Downy Woodpecker, Western Wood-Pewee, Pacific-slope Flycatcher, Warbling Vireo, House Wren, Veery, Nashville, MacGillivray's, and Yellow Warblers, and Black-headed Grosbeak are common. The Ponderosa Pine woods in and around the campground have White-headed Woodpecker (scarce in some years), Gray Flycatcher, Mountain Chickadee, White-breasted and Pygmy Nuthatches, Townsend's Solitaire (usually nesting near a steep bank), Chipping Sparrow, Cassin's Finch, and Red Crossbill (irregular, depending on pine seed crops). Brushy slopes mixed with young pines surrounding the area are excellent for Sooty Grouse, Calliope Hummingbird, Dusky Flycatcher, Nashville Warbler, and Fox Sparrow. Finally, moister forest is en-

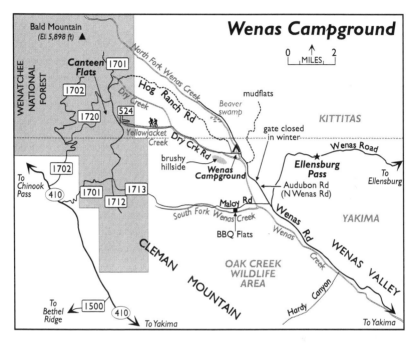

countered a mile or so north from the campground, along with nearby riparian vegetation. Hammond's Flycatcher and Yellow-rumped Warbler are found here.

The campground proper is best visited on foot. Adjacent areas, described below, are partially accessible by car, but hiking is the most rewarding way to experience them if you have the time and the inclination.

From the south entrance sign, a dirt road heads west along the north side of **Dry Creek**. A short walk or drive up this track leads to three good areas for birds. In 400 yards, at the intersection with Hog Ranch Road on the right, continue straight ahead on Dry Creek Road for another 250 yards and drive or hop across the creek—usually not difficult, but pay attention when the creek is full in early spring. Immediately after crossing, explore the brushy hillside to your left. Calliope Hummingbird, Dusky Flycatcher, Townsend's Solitaire, Nashville Warbler, and Fox Sparrow should be encountered from May through July in the Deerbrush, which creates a brush field reminiscent of the chaparral found in the mountains from Oregon south through California. Sooty Grouse are often heard booming on the slopes above. Look also for Prairie Falcon, which nests in the Yakima Canyon and commutes to these Cascade foothills to forage.

From the parking area at the end of Dry Creek Road, hikers may wish to continue westward beyond the berm, along the decommissioned road that follows Dry Creek, a fine riparian corridor with occasional rock outcrops, bordered by drier slopes with Ponderosa Pine habitats and open, grassy ridges. In 2.5 miles, watch for **Yellowjacket Creek** coming in from the left. Turn onto the trail that follows it, and continue another 1.5 miles to a section-line fence. (A short spur road switchbacks steeply from this point to FR-1701 at Canteen Flats, page 319.) This four-mile (each way) hike with a gentle, 1,300-foot elevation gain, offers an excellent transect of east-slope habitats, ending in moister, mixed-conifer forest at 3,900 feet. Among many other species, look for Ruffed Grouse, Western Screech-Owl, Common Nighthawk, Calliope Hummingbird, Pileated Woodpecker, Hammond's and Dusky Flycatchers, Cassin's and Warbling Vireos, Mountain Chickadee, Red-breasted Nuthatch, Brown Creeper, House and Pacific Wrens, Veery, Swainson's and Hermit Thrushes, MacGillivray's, Yellow-rumped, and Townsend's Warblers, Western Tanager, Black-headed Grosbeak, Purple and Cassin's Finches, Red Crossbill, Pine Siskin, and Evening Grosbeak.

Return to the spot where Dry Creek Road crosses the creek, backtrack the 250 yards east to the intersection, and turn left (north) onto the green-dot road (unmarked **Hog Ranch Road**). This is an easy drive for ordinary vehicles for 1.5 to 2 miles with a few parking areas for exploration on foot. Walk north along this dirt track for a few hundred yards. The brushy, willow-lined hillside to the west is another good area for Calliope Hummingbird, Dusky Flycatcher, Nashville Warbler, and Fox Sparrow. The open pine forests on this bench, with little or no undergrowth except Pinegrass, are the favored habitat for Gray Flycatcher, first recorded in the state in 1970 at Wenas Campground. White-headed Woodpecker, Pygmy Nuthatch, and Cassin's Finch may also be found here.

Those with a four-wheel-drive vehicle may drive beyond this bench and uphill on Hog Ranch Road, through open pine and Douglas-fir forests interspersed with rocky, treeless balds. Flammulated Owl (local), Common Poorwill (dusk), White-headed Woodpecker, and Western and Mountain Bluebirds can be found along this road, which eventually reaches higher-elevation mixed-conifer and subalpine forests on Bald Mountain. However, the rough jeep track is difficult even with four-wheel drive. Access to this area is much easier from the southwest, off SR-410 via FR-1701 (Benson Creek) and FR-1702 (Rock Creek). These graded roads are suitable for ordinary vehicles (page 319).

To explore moister habitats, return to and cross the bridge below the campground entrance. Turn left onto **North Wenas Road**, which leads to habitats with Douglas-fir, Grand Fir, and tall riparian vegetation. The road is easily traveled by ordinary vehicle, and there are several places to park and explore the riparian area by foot.

WENAS VALLEY

Back at the junction just off Wenas Road, where Audubon Road begins, take the other branch and head west on **Maloy Road**. This gravel road passes hay fields at first, then enters fine riparian habitats of cottonwoods and aspens at the crossing with North Fork Wenas Creek (0.7 mile). This is private land and you must bird from the road. Veery and Swainson's Thrush occur in the woodlands here. Look also for House Wren, Yellow Warbler, and Black-headed Grosbeak. The agricultural edge habitat is attractive to Purple Finch, a local nester east of the Cascade Crest. A number of "eastern" vagrants or spring overshoots have occurred in this area from early June through mid-July, among them Least Flycatcher (regular; may breed), Ovenbird, American Redstart, and Rose-breasted Grosbeak.

Farther west on Maloy Road, you reach a fork (0.3 mile). DNR closed the road here while it negotiated to acquire land to provide public access to BBQ Flats (to the west). The department said it would add toilets, fencing, gates, and road extensions; it expected access and facilities to be ready by July 2015. Explore the open pine forest in this area, looking (and listening) for White-headed Woodpecker, Gray Flycatcher, White-breasted and Pygmy Nuthatches, Cassin's Finch, and Red Crossbill.

Return to the pavement on Wenas Road. Take a right (southeast) and drive down the Wenas Valley, a mosaic of hay and grain fields and riparian habitats. The **Hardy Canyon** entrance to the Oak Creek Wildlife Area is on the right in 4.0 miles, at a pipe gate that is usually locked. Park, walk through the pedestrian access (locked December 1 to May 1), cross Wenas Creek on a wooden bridge, and go exploring on foot. This beautiful area is filled with birds associated with riparian, field, and shrub-steppe habitats. In the breeding season look for Ruffed Grouse, Cooper's Hawk, Least and Pacific-slope Flycatchers (along Wenas Creek), Ash-throated Flycatcher (some years present near brush on the sidehill south of the creek), Eastern Kingbird, Warbling Vireo, Tree Swallow, Gray Catbird (a few), Nashville and Yellow Warblers, Yellow-breasted Chat, Spotted Towhee, Black-headed Grosbeak, and Lazuli Bunting. Spring migration (end of April through mid-May) can be impressive. Depending on weather conditions, flycatchers, vireos, warblers, and tanagers can be found in good numbers then. Early May is a good time to look for Golden-crowned Sparrows, after the main northbound push of White-crowneds (race *gambelii*) has gone through.

A five-minute walk south from the bridge brings you to the upper edge of aspen woodlands. From here a rough, seven-mile road heads up Hardy Canyon to the 4,700-foot summit of Cleman Mountain (the ridge between the Naches River and Wenas Creek). Shrub-steppe vegetation in the lower part of the canyon is attractive to Vesper Sparrows. If you continue to climb you will notice a gradual change to coniferous forest.

Return to Wenas Road and turn right (southeast). Look for a sign indicating Public Fishing Access on your right (1.5 miles). Take this down to **Wenas Lake** (0.1 mile; poorly maintained pit toilets). High water and hordes of anglers often make Wenas Lake unattractive to birds during spring and early summer. However, lower water levels expose a wide area of mud by late July or August in many years. If and when this happens, Wenas Lake can be good for shorebirding. Common fall migrants include both yellowlegs species, Solitary, Least, Semipalmated, and Western Sandpipers, Long-billed Dowitcher, and Red-necked Phalarope. A number of rarities have been encountered here, including Wandering Tattler (one record), Willet, and Stilt Sandpiper. A fine riparian area can be reached by walking upstream from the parking area along a trail bordering Wenas Creek. From May through July, look for Eastern Kingbird, Bank Swallow, Gray Catbird, Yellow Warbler, Black-headed Grosbeak, Lazuli Bunting, and Bullock's Oriole.

Continue southeast on Wenas Road. At Longmire Road (3.8 miles), stay left on Wenas Road. Anywhere along this stretch of agricultural land keep an eye out for Swainson's Hawk (spring and summer). At **Sheep Company Road** (6.3 miles), turn left (north) and continue to the entrance of the L.T. Murray Wildlife Area (1.3 mile), a large reserve of shrub-steppe and stony ridges. Just south of the entrance sign, look for a pair of Burrowing Owls on the east side of the road. Long-billed Curlews are occasionally seen in spring on the grasslands here.

Three choices for returning to Ellensburg are described in the following section. One of them, Durr Road, goes north across the wildlife area from this spot, but is recommended only for high-clearance vehicles. To access the other two, return along Sheep Company Road to Wenas Road, turn left, and continue east and south to a junction with SR-823 (4.8 miles). Straight ahead, SR-823 (Wenas Road) soon reaches Selah. A left turn at this intersection onto SR-823 (Harrison Road) brings you to SR-821 (1.8 miles). Turn left to follow the Yakima Canyon route to Ellensburg, or turn right to the Exit 26 interchange with I-82. Here you may go south to Yakima, north to Ellensburg, or straight ahead to the Yakima Training Center (page 304).

FROM YAKIMA TO ELLENSBURG

by Andy Stepniewski and Hal Opperman

revised by Andy Stepniewski

Take your pick of three routes between these county seats. (Refer to map on page 292.) All three are about 30 miles long, but the time required to travel them differs greatly. Unimproved Durr Road, the oldest, slowest, and most difficult, goes over the top of a high ridge through extensive shrub-steppe with a touch of riparian habitat. The Yakima Canyon—the leisurely, paved, water-level route, featuring steep cliffs and a fine riparian zone—has the most varied year-round birding possibilities. The interstate has some birding potential, too, despite limited access, and of course it's the newest, fastest, and easiest route.

DURR ROAD

Durr Road—the stage road from Yakima to Ellensburg in the late 1800s—begins where Sheep Company Road ends, at the entrance to the L.T. Murray Wildlife Area north of Selah (previous page). (Ignore the *Dead End* sign at E Huntzinger Road.) This gravel and bare-rock road through Wild West scenery reaches Umptanum Road southwest of Ellensburg in about 15 miles. *Do not attempt to drive it except in a high-clearance vehicle with sturdy tires (including a full-sized spare), extra drinking water, and emergency supplies.* A four-wheel drive is advisable in wet conditions. If you are properly equipped, you can expect to find shrub-steppe species such as Loggerhead Shrike and Sage Thrasher. Brewer's, Vesper, and Sagebrush Sparrows occur commonly in suitable sagebrush stands. A few Greater Sage-Grouse may survive on this side of the Yakima River, but are seldom reported. Horned Lark and Mountain Bluebird are common on the high barrens, where you might also see Bighorn Sheep. A variety of raptors such as Northern Harrier, Red-tailed, Ferruginous (rare), and Rough-legged (winter) Hawks, Golden Eagle, American Kestrel, and Prairie Falcon should be looked for in this huge area.

The road climbs steadily. Stay right at 2.8 miles (past Bell Telephone Road), then left in 0.1 mile, to reach the top of Umtanum Ridge (5.2 miles, go right at the fork, away from the towers). The view from the 3,500-foot summit is spectacular, with Ellensburg to the north and Yakima to the south, framed by the snowy Cascade volcanoes to the west and the vast Columbia Basin to the east.

Descending northward from the summit (350 feet from the previous fork, stay left), Durr Road reaches Umtanum Creek in about three miles. The creek offers great birding for riparian species on rough trails for the adventuresome hiker, west (upstream) three and one-half miles to Umptanum Road or east (downstream) four and one-half miles to the Yakima River. After fording the creek, Durr Road climbs out of the canyon and continues north about four more miles to Umptanum Road. Look for Lark Sparrow in overgrazed shrub-steppe, before the wheat fields start. Follow Umptanum Road across the Yakima River and into Ellensburg.

YAKIMA CANYON

If you have at least two or three hours and it's not midday on a summer weekend (when all of Yakima, or so it seems, floats the river on rafts or roars along it on jet skis), by all means take the Yakima Canyon route. This old highway, formerly part of US-97 but since supplanted by the interstate, was built through the canyon in parallel to the historic Northern Pacific Railroad. The river winds along a magnificent gorge cut through three basalt ridges that host a dense breeding population of raptors. Chukar, White-throated Swift (summer), and Canyon Wren are also common. Access to riparian areas along lower Umtanum Creek is another highlight.

Go north onto SR-821 from I-82 Exit 26, four miles north of Yakima. At the intersection with SR-823 a short distance ahead, reset your trip-odometer to 0.0 and continue straight on SR-821 (aka Canyon Road). Pull off on the right at the first major wide spot after entering the canyon (3.3 miles). From March through June, watch for Red-tailed Hawk, American Kestrel, and Prairie Falcon, all of which nest on the towering basalt cliffs here and elsewhere in the canyon. In winter, Bald Eagles patrol the river for whitefish and carrion (fish or mammalian).

The next pullout (0.5 mile) is around a sharp, blind curve, so slow down and signal as you approach it. Golden Eagle and other raptors nest on the cliffs across the river to the west. Listen for White-throated Swift and Canyon Wren, both of which are common here. In winter, survey the waters and banks of the river below for Common Goldeneye, Common Merganser, and Bald Eagle. Farther up the canyon, a side road comes in from Burbank Valley on the right (3.4 miles). Recreational access points along this stretch allow you to pull off beside the river. After sunset, listen for Common Poorwill on the open slopes and Western Screech-Owl in the riparian groves.

From Burbank Creek Road, stay on SR-821 as it twists and turns along the Yakima until you come to a geological exhibit (4.7 miles) on the left that explains the antecedent nature of the river here. Prior to the regional uplifting of the various east-west trending ridges in the canyon, the Yakima River likely was a mature stream, meandering across a fairly level, low landscape. Uplift of the basalt ridges apparently took place very slowly, permitting the erosive, down-cutting powers of the river to keep pace. Thus, the ancient bends and loops in the river course remain. Looking west across the river, the striking whitish ash layer from the huge Mount Mazama eruption in south-central Oregon 6,600 years ago is visible just above the river. The collapse of Mount Mazama created Crater Lake. The explosion sent 116 cubic kilometers of ash across all the western states and three Canadian provinces, as far eastward as Nebraska. Another favored nest cliff for Golden Eagle is visible from here, high on the shoulder of Baldy Mountain (the highest mountain to the southeast—left, downriver). Look for it to the right of the summit below the west shoulder, on the largest, lichen-coated cliff.

From the exhibit, drive on up the canyon to the Umtanum Recreation Site (3.8 miles). Turn left off the highway and swing right to a parking area (America the Beautiful or daily pass required). A suspension footbridge crosses the Yakima River to the mouth of Umtanum Creek. A trail parallels the creek for eight miles all the way to Umptanum Road (page 292). However, the trail becomes difficult to find after about 2.75 miles, and at 3.5 miles, it is closed to the public for nearly 0.8 mile between February 1 and July 15 to protect nesting raptors.

The lower end of this trail is a favorite in spring for birders and hikers. You may encounter a local population of Bushtits—as yet an uncommon species east of the Cascade Crest. Yellow-breasted Chats are also present. Cooper's and Red-tailed Hawks, Golden Eagle, American Kestrel, and Prairie Falcon nest on the canyon walls or in the trees along the creek. Rock and Canyon Wrens are also common. You can't miss Spotted Towhee, except in mid-winter. From mid-April through the end of May a wide array of neotropical migrants (flycatchers, vireos, warblers, Western Tanager, Bullock's Oriole) should be looked for in the riparian zone.

In the warmer months keep an eye out for Western Rattlesnakes, which are frequently encountered along this trail. Watch them from a distance but do not harm them. In general, this species is not aggressive and would rather avoid you, too. Watch the steep slopes for Bighorn Sheep. A sizable herd (nearly 300 in 2005) resides in this area. Your first clue to their presence might be the sound of dislodged rocks clattering down the talus slopes. Watch also for Yellow-bellied Marmots, the western equivalent of the Woodchuck.

Continue north toward Ellensburg, pulling off along the river at a widening in the shoulder just before a pine grove (4.3 miles). The road embankment has lots of Prickly Pear Cactus. The cliffs across the river should be scanned for Red-tailed Hawk, American Kestrel, Prairie Falcon, and Common Raven. The small caves not far above the river may harbor Great Horned Owls. In winter you are sure to see Bald Eagles along this stretch.

Turn left from SR-821 at Ringer Loop Road (4.1 miles), go west over the railway track, and drive this road toward the Yakima River. Shortly before the road turns north, a fishing access on the left (0.3 mile) offers a place to park and wander along the tall cottonwoods and other streamside growth (Discover Pass required). Birds of the riparian zone are a feature here. At night listen for Western Screech- and Long-eared Owls. Ospreys nest in the area, too. Follow Ringer Loop Road as it turns north and crosses a small wetland before rejoining the highway (0.9 mile),

Drive north 1.4 miles to Tjossem Road, and turn right. Go 0.1 mile east to Berry Road, turn left onto Berry, and **Tjossem Pond** (aka Sorenson Pond) is 0.1 mile ahead on the right. The waters and grassy shoreline of the pond, a private game reserve, often host a good assortment of ducks and geese fall through spring. The pond is generally frozen in late December and January, but is often one of the last in the area to freeze, likely because it's deeper. In fall, look for Greater White-fronted and Snow Geese among Cackling and Canada Geese. Fall also has produced records of Surf and White-winged Scoters, Long-tailed Duck, and Pacific Loon, though all are rare here. Unusual shorebirds are possible here as well with records of Black-necked Stilt and American Avocet, both rare for the county.

To reach I-90 from Tjossem Pond, continue north on Berry for 0.6 mile, turn left with Berry, and go 0.4 mile to Canyon Road. Turn right—it's a quarter-mile to I-90.

INTERSTATE 82

Much of the arid rainshadow landscape in the river valleys of South Central Washington has been converted to irrigated agriculture. Little natural vegetation survives except along the riparian corridors of rivers and major creeks. However, a significant tract of the original shrub-steppe ecosystem occurs along I-82 between Yakima and Ellensburg, much of it within the Yakima Training Center.

Start at I-82 Exit 26 north of Yakima (there is a Great Blue Heron rookery in the large Black Cottonwood grove to the west of the freeway). As you head north on I-82 toward Ellensburg, the Redmon Bridge crosses the deep gorge of Selah Creek in about two and one-half miles. Unfortunately, there is no place to pull off from the northbound lanes, but if you are traveling south toward Yakima, stop at the Selah Rest Area (13 miles south of Exit 11). The overlook beyond the restrooms provides a dramatic view of Selah Creek. Especially between April and July, check the basalt cliff at the north end of the parking area for nesting Ferruginous Hawk (rare or absent in recent years), Prairie Falcon, White-throated Swift (which apparently nests in openings in the concrete arches of the freeway bridge), and Violet-green and Cliff Swallows. Say's Phoebe and Rock Wren should also be looked for here. Red-tailed Hawk and American Kestrel are hard to miss.

At Exit 11, signed *Military Area*, shrub-steppe birds such as Sage Thrasher and Brewer's, Vesper, and Sagebrush Sparrows can sometimes be observed beyond the fences on both sides of the interstate (easier to find in early morning when traffic is still relatively light). A pair of Common Ravens often nests under the freeway overpass.

In eight miles, take Exit 3 (Thrall Road) and go east less than 0.1 mile to Number 6 Road. Turn left (north) and travel 1.3 miles to a gravel road on the left (signed *Public Fishing*) that leads to two gravel-borrow ponds (Discover Pass required). These ponds (a large one on the north and a smaller one to the south) can have many ducks in migration and winter when they are not being used by anglers. In fall, scoters and Long-tailed Ducks regularly visit en route to the ocean. One can also walk the east bank for birds of scrub and marsh.

Back on I-82, it is three more miles to the I-90 junction, and a mile west from there to the east Ellensburg exit.

YAKIMA TRAINING CENTER

by Andy Stepniewski
revised by Andy Stepniewski

The Yakima Training Center comprises the largest remaining contiguous block of shrub-steppe habitat in Washington—365,000 acres stretching from the Columbia River west to I-82 and from I-90 south to the outskirts of Yakima. This U.S. Army subinstallation (of Joint Base Lewis-McChord) is one of the few areas of the state where the shrub-steppe ecosystem continues to function on a landscape scale. Nearly all bird species characteristic of this zone can be found here, including the declining Greater Sage-Grouse. Birding is superb in riparian areas during migration.

GREATER SAGE-GROUSE LEK TOURS

The Yakima Training Center is one of two sites in Washington where Greater Sage-Grouse still occur in significant numbers. Your best chance to observe them is on one of the organized tours conducted during the peak courtship period in March, offered by center biologists in conjunction with the Yakima Valley Audubon Society (P.O. Box 2823, Yakima, WA 98901 or http://yakimaaudubon.org) and the Seattle Audubon Society (206-523-4483). At other seasons, you are unlikely to get more than a brief view as birds flush in the distance. The tour will take you to a lek where females gather to observe displaying males, starting well before sunrise. While at the lek site, look for other shrub-steppe species such as Horned Lark, Sage Thrasher, and Vesper and Sagebrush Sparrows.

BIRDING THE CENTER ON YOUR OWN

You may enter the center on your own in any month, although access to some parts of it may be restricted from time to time due to military exercises, changes in rules, or closures to protect sage-grouse. It is illegal to come and go any direction other than the MP Station on the west side of the training center; you cannot exit by the East Gate.

Take Exit 26 from I-82 just north of Yakima. You will need a Recreation Card ($10 in 2015). To obtain this card (and a good map), get instructions from the entrance checkpoint (0.7 mile), as the process to obtain this card changes from time to time. You will need your current vehicle registration, driver's license, and proof of insurance. You will also be asked to state the purpose of your visit (birdwatching) and your destination. Allow 35–45 minutes for the check-in process. While birding can be productive in many parts of this huge installation, birders are advised to stick to the Cold Creek Road (aka Firing Center Road), described below. Access to this area is usually granted. The route goes east from the MP station to East Gate and passes

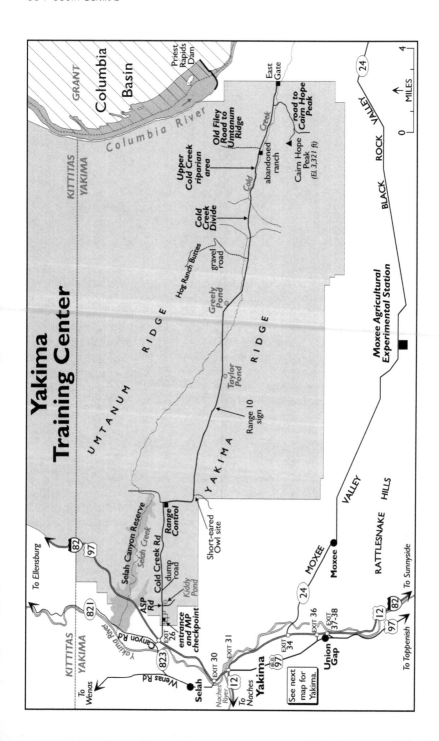

through a variety of shrub-steppe and riparian vegetation communities, giving an opportunity to see many bird species of these habitats. Military activity may be evident year round, but most tracked-vehicles remain on a side road paralleling the main road. The round trip from Exit 26 is about 60 road miles; excursions to and from Hog Ranch Buttes, Umtanum Ridge, Cairn Hope Peak, and Selah Creek will add another 15 miles. The Cold Creek Road provides a very full day of birding, especially if you take advantage of the hiking possibilities.

Depending on the timing of your visit, the center may be crawling with soldiers and military machinery or it may be a deserted wilderness. In either case it is potentially a hazardous place. Some precautions are in order:

It is wise to carry a cell phone and make sure you have the MP's phone number. Get the current number when you check in (this number has a curious way of changing). The MP will assist you in an emergency.

You will fare better if you drive a high-clearance vehicle (with six-ply tires if possible) and carry a shovel. Make sure your spare tire is in good shape.

Drive gravel roads slowly, especially on curves (to minimize risk of sidewalls of your tires coming in contact with sharp rocks).

Carry extra food and water, especially in summer, and emergency clothing in winter. Be aware that there is often an extreme fire hazard on the installation in summer. Do not drive a low-clearance vehicle over Cheatgrass or other weedy or grassy terrain. A Cheatgrass fire can outpace a vehicle in motion!

Wearing hunter orange, at least a vest, is usually required.

COLD CREEK ROAD

From the MP station, continue east onto Cold Creek Road. You soon pass ASP Road (unsigned, 0.7). The Kiddy Pond behind a grove of introduced Black Locust trees at this corner has birds of the riparian zone in migration. East on Cold Creek Road, at a road marked *Refuse Collection Site* (0.7 mile), turn right (south) and drive a short distance toward the dump, a good area for Sagebrush Sparrow. Return to Cold Creek Road and turn right.

From here to Range Control (4.0 miles) is fine shrub-steppe habitat, especially on the south side of the road. If conditions are noisy due to tactical vehicles and other traffic, hurry along. If not, stop occasionally to look and listen for Sage Thrasher and Brewer's, Vesper, and Sagebrush Sparrows. Sagelands along this stretch are home to many Black-tailed and a few White-tailed Jack Rabbits—one of the few sites in Washington where these rabbits can still be found. Because of the high rodent and Jack Rabbit population, this is a good area in which to look for raptors such as Northern Harrier, Red-tailed Hawk, Golden Eagle, and American Kestrel. At Range Control (now closed, but buildings still there), Sagebrush Sparrows are common in the sagebrush on the north side of Cold Creek Road. Grasshopper Sparrows may sometimes be found in the weedy, grassy terrain uphill and south from here.

From the east side of the Range Control complex, turn right (south) and keep on the paved road. Short-eared Owls are often seen on the slopes just to the south of a major bend in the road (1.5 miles), particularly at dawn and dusk. Stop to search for Sagebrush Sparrow, which becomes less numerous eastward from this spot to well beyond the Cold Creek Divide, as increasing moisture induces a grass cover higher than its liking. Continue east to the Range 10 sign (5.0 miles), where the sagebrush is good for Greater Sage-Grouse, Northern Harrier, Short-eared Owl, Prairie Falcon, Sage Thrasher, and Brewer's and Vesper Sparrows.

Taylor Pond is on the right (south) in another 2.7 miles—not visible from the road but marked by the first riparian-zone vegetation east of Range Control. This sensitive area, protected by fencing, is a magnet for many birds. Enter on foot through an unlocked gate. Northern Harriers are common. Look also for Long-eared Owls and migrant passerines in the trees. An extensive Greater Sage-Grouse conservation area, off-limits to military activity, lies between Taylor Pond and the following site.

Greely Pond (2.6 miles), an isolated stand of riparian habitat, offers excellent birding for migrants in spring and fall. To enter, walk to the east side of the fenced area and downstream. The small pond may have nesting Soras. Great Horned Owls nest here, as do Bullock's Orioles. Dense Big Sagebrush east of the pond once hosted a summering Clay-colored Sparrow. Passerines are often thick in migration.

Continue east from Greely Pond to a well-maintained gravel road (1.7 miles), turn left, and climb four miles to the summit of Hog Ranch Buttes, former site of several communication towers. Do not attempt this side trip if there is mud or snow on the road. Chukar, Gray Partridge, migrant raptors (including Northern Goshawk and Gyrfalcon), Snow Buntings (late fall), and Gray-crowned Rosy-Finches (winter) have all been seen on this route, and good-quality lithosol plant communities attract Horned Larks. The view from the summit (elevation 4,100 feet) extends from Mount Jefferson in Oregon north to Mount Stuart.

Return to the Cold Creek Road, turn left, and climb 1.2 miles to a broad pass, the Cold Creek Divide, at an elevation of nearly 3,000 feet. Here you leave the Selah Creek drainage and enter that of Cold Creek. The extensive Three-tip Sagebrush/Bluebunch Wheatgrass habitat is a prime foraging ground for nesting raptors such as Northern Harrier, Swainson's and Red-tailed Hawks, and American Kestrel. Watch for Short-eared Owl at dusk and dawn. Fall raptor migration (late August–October) can be exciting, too. Watch for Northern Harrier (61 one September day), Sharp-shinned, Cooper's, Swainson's, Red-tailed, and Rough-legged (beginning in October)

Hawks, Golden Eagle, American Kestrel, and Prairie Falcon, as they circle and sail south from Umtanum Ridge. Common Ravens also migrate south in large numbers. In fall, listen and look for Lapland Longspur and Snow Bunting. Gray Partridge occurs in these grasslands, but is difficult to spot.

The shrub-steppe community along the north slope of Yakima Ridge (to the south), from the divide east along Upper Cold Creek, is in excellent condition. A hike up one of the fire-break roads should produce Sage Thrasher and Brewer's and Vesper Sparrows. In 1.1 miles from the divide, riparian areas with thickets of Black Hawthorn, wild rose, Coyote Willow, and Blue Elderberry, and groves of Black Cottonwood, Peach-leaf Willow, and Quaking Aspen, offer sensational birding for migrants. From late April through early June, and again from late July through September (and even October), the area can be alive in early morning with migrant flycatchers, vireos, kinglets, warblers, tanagers, and sparrows. This is especially so in the fall when hundreds, even thousands of birds can be viewed each hour winging their way west and up the valley on any given morning. In the brushy thickets, abundant fruit attracts Lewis's Woodpecker (early September), Townsend's Solitaire, American Robin, Varied Thrush, and Sage Thrasher. Some species occur in stunning numbers (e.g., 65 Hammond's Flycatchers and 675 Ruby-crowned Kinglets tallied in one two-hour period). Sharp-shinned Hawks (as many as 20 one morning) provide an escort.

Unusual migrants noted here include Barred Owl, Gray Flycatcher, Pine Grosbeak, and Purple and Cassin's Finches. Black Swift—almost unknown as a migrant east of the Cascades away from its breeding haunts—has been noted twice in early September. The abrupt eastward bend in the Columbia River at Priest Rapids (five miles north), and the availability of food and shelter along Cold Creek, may prompt many southbound passerines to strike south and west on a direct overland route rather than detouring east around the White Bluffs along the Hanford Reach. This area is recovering from fire, but there is regrowth here, and similar, unburnt areas are accessible downstream.

Continue downstream 2.2 miles and turn right to an abandoned ranch, where riparian habitat hosts many nesting and migrant birds. Continue east on Cold Creek Road. On the left in 0.2 mile, Old Filey Road (gravel) leads to the crest of Umtanum Ridge. En route, Greater Sage-Grouse, Sage Thrasher, and Brewer's and Vesper Sparrows may be found in the excellent Three-tip Sagebrush habitat. The view from the crest is vast. Directly below is Priest Rapids Lake, to the north are the Saddle Mountains and the Stuart Range, and to the east are the many nuclear reactors on the Hanford Site, with Rattlesnake Mountain rising in the southeast.

Return to the Cold Creek Road and turn left (east). Turn right in 2.1 miles onto a road that descends and crosses Cold Creek, then steeply climbs the north flank of Yakima Ridge below Cairn Hope Peak (1.0 mile). The Nature Conservancy and the Washington Natural Heritage Program recognize the plant communities on this slope as some of the finest remaining Big

Sagebrush/Bluebunch Wheatgrass shrub-steppe vegetation in the state. All of the regularly occurring shrub-steppe passerines can be found here readily. (Grasshopper Sparrow is uncommon.)

Return to Cold Creek Road and continue downstream to East Gate (1.2 miles). In addition to the plants mentioned for Upper Cold Creek, Water Birch (copper-colored trunk and branches) is abundant along these lower stretches; the buds are an important winter food source for the now extirpated Sharp-tailed Grouse. Taken in conjunction with the high-quality shrub-steppe vegetation along the ridges south of Cold Creek, this is potentially excellent habitat for Sharp-taileds and a prime site for a reintroduction effort.

Return to the major intersection at Range Control and turn right (north) to a crossing of Selah Creek (0.5 mile). A hike downstream on the dirt track on the south side of the stream leads past riparian habitats and, farther on, to cliffs. Many raptors nest in this area—Northern Harrier, Swainson's, Red-tailed, and Ferruginous (at least formerly) Hawks, Golden Eagle, Great Horned, Long-eared, and Short-eared Owls, American Kestrel, and Prairie Falcon. The lower part of the canyon has no trails and reaching it involves a rigorous hike. Watch out for rattlesnakes in the warm months. White-throated Swift, many Violet-green and Cliff Swallows, Rock and Canyon Wrens, Lazuli Bunting, and Bullock's Oriole may also be found along the creek.

Turn in your visitor pass at the MP checkpost on the way out.

YAKIMA AND VICINITY

by Andy Stepniewski

revised by Andy Stepniewski

Yakima is situated at the head of the richly productive Yakima Valley and the foot of the Cascades. This thriving center for light manufacturing, forest products, and (especially) agriculture has 93,000 residents. Parks on the edges of the city offer birding of wetland and riparian habitats in any season. The agricultural land and shrub-steppe of the Moxee and Black Rock Valleys east of the city are known for raptors and for migrating and wintering songbirds. To the south, lower Toppenish Creek hosts species of wet fields and marshes in all seasons, while Fort Simcoe in the upper Toppenish drainage has Lewis's Woodpeckers and other birds of Garry Oak habitats. The lower Naches Valley west of Yakima features birds of cliffs and streamside vegetation.

YAKIMA

Fine birding is available right within the city, principally along the Yakima Greenway—a wide, paved path paralleling the Yakima River for nine miles that passes through riparian, marsh, and open-field habitats. There are four main access points, one from US-12 and three from I-82.

At the 16th Avenue exit on US-12 (one mile west from Exit 31 on I-82), go north and immediately find the parking area for the western part of the Yakima Greenway. Walk the path east (downstream), to the base of the railway-bridge abutments. American Dippers descend to winter here from their summer haunts in the Cascades.

From Exit 33 or 33B on I-82 (Yakima Avenue/Terrace Heights), drive east on E Yakima Avenue 0.3 mile to S 18th Street. Turn right (south) and continue 0.1 mile to the **Sarg Hubbard Park** entrance and parking. You can go either north or south from here. The path to the south soon reaches a small, marshy area where Virginia Rail and Wilson's Snipe might be found. Dabbling ducks such as Green-winged Teal are frequent. Farther south is Buchanan Lake, on the west side of the path. In winter, this large, deep lake is attractive to diving ducks and grebes. Ring-billed Gulls are common in summer. The Yakima River lies east of the path. Bald Eagles are common here in winter, as are Common Goldeneyes and Common Mergansers.

From Exit 34 on I-82, go east on Nob Hill Boulevard (SR-24) 0.1 mile to the first traffic light. Turn left (north), then immediately left onto W Birchfield Road, which becomes Arboretum Drive as you curve north to reach the **Yakima Area Arboretum** and Jewett Interpretive Center (0.3 mile). Many trails connect here, including the Noel Pathway to Sherman Park. To the east are Black Cottonwood and mature riparian woodlands of the William Schroeder Memorial Wetland. This habitat is good in migration and winter for a variety of passerines. Western Screech-Owl is possible here, as are Downy Woodpecker and Bewick's Wren. To reach brush piles that are excellent in winter for sparrows, walk left on a small path at the *William Schroeder Memorial Wetland* sign about 200 feet to an opening surrounded by brush. Lots of seed is put out here by the Yakima Valley Audubon Society, attracting Fox, Song, Lincoln's, White-throated, Harris's (rare), White-crowned, and Golden-crowned Sparrows. Extensive ornamental plantings are another feature of the arboretum. In fall and winter, American Robins, Varied Thrushes, and waxwings feed in the hawthorns just to the north of the center. To reach the Yakima Greenway, head back south on Arboretum Drive and then east on Birchfield, continue straight, past the parking for the southern end of the Noel Pathway, 0.2 mile to the Robertson Landing parking area. From here, walk north or south on the greenway trail.

Yakima Sportsman State Park can also be reached from Exit 34. From the traffic light 0.1 mile east of I-82, drive east on SR-24 to University

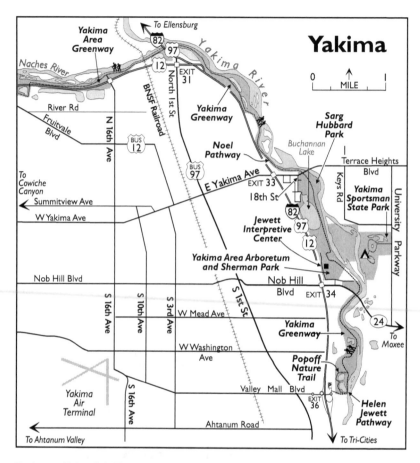

Parkway (1.0 mile). Turn left (north) and go 0.9 mile to the park entrance. The duck pond in the park is good for Wood Ducks—often more than 100 may be found here. Western Screech-Owl is possible and Great Horned Owl is common. The riparian woodlands on the west side of the park can be birdy: look for Downy Woodpecker, Black-capped Chickadee, and Bewick's Wren.

From Exit 36 on I-82, pull into the parking area on the north side of the roundabout on the east side of the freeway for the southernmost access to the Yakima Greenway. From the parking area, walk southeast to the **Bob and Helen Popoff Nature Trail** (gravel). The trail makes a short loop north through a cattail marsh where Common Yellowthroat is sometimes found, then past several ponds, and finally groves of Russian Olive trees, swarming in winter with berry-eating birds such as American Robin, Varied Thrush, and Evening Grosbeak (and clouds of European Starlings). The Helen Jewett Pathway begins another few hundred feet to the east. This has proven to be a very popular local birding trail. First comes riparian woodland, then a tree-rimmed pond attractive to Ring-necked Duck, Hooded Merganser, and other diving ducks from fall through spring (except when frozen). Western Screech-Owl and Bewick's Wrens are expected year round in the riparian woodland. In summer the cast swells, including Eastern Kingbird and Gray Catbird.

MOXEE AND EAST

East of Yakima on SR-24 is the **Moxee Agricultural Experiment Station**, 16.5 miles from I-82 Exit 34. (See map on page 304.) This USDA research facility features 10 long rows of conifers and some deciduous trees planted as windbreaks to shelter field crops, and appears as a wooded island in the midst of wide-open country. Long-eared Owls have nested here. Barn, Great Horned, Short-eared, and other owls roost in the trees in winter. Swainson's Hawks also nest. You will see lots of Black-billed Magpies and California Quail, which attract Cooper's Hawk and Northern Goshawk in winter. Migrant passerines use this oasis, too. Pull off and park near the caretaker's house between the road and the rows of trees, and obtain permission to enter. The gate may be closed on weekends. Don't neglect the westernmost row of trees that has many ash trees where Purple Finches winter erratically.

In some winters, good hawkwatching can be had along SR-24 in the **Black Rock Valley**, for example, in an area of mostly abandoned wheat fields 1.8 miles east of the experimental station. Short-eared Owls forage in these fields, especially in winter, and sometimes roost in the trees. In addition to raptors, look for Gray Partridge (fairly common but elusive resident of the valley) and Long-billed Curlew (April through July). Beginning 2.5 miles farther east on SR-24 and continuing for the next six miles, scan the open country for Northern Harrier, Red-tailed, Ferruginous (mainly March through May), and Rough-legged (November through April) Hawks, Golden Eagle (especially February through April when migrants are moving north), American Kestrel, and Prairie Falcon. Though rare, Gyrfalcon is regularly found here; most records span December through mid-March. Horned Larks by the thousands gather grit on the roadway in winter. Pick through these large flocks carefully for Lapland Longspur and Snow Bunting. If you stop, make sure to park your vehicle completely off the pavement. Traffic moves very fast.

AHTANUM VALLEY TO DARLAND MOUNTAIN

For mountain birding offering a chance at Spruce Grouse, woodpeckers, and Boreal Owl, head west on Ahtanum Road; it's 40 miles to the end at Darland Mountain. Take Exit 36 from I-82, go west 0.3 mile, through two roundabouts, to Main Street. Turn left (south) onto Main and go 0.4 mile to Ahtanum Road. Go right (west) 13.7 miles to **St. Joseph Mission at Ahtanum**, where a fine stand of Oregon White Oaks attract Lewis's Woodpeckers and many migrants, especially in spring migration. In another 5.3 miles

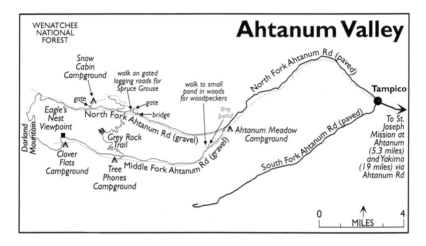

WENATCHEE NATIONAL FOREST

Ahtanum Valley

Snow Cabin Campground
walk on gated logging roads for Spruce Grouse
walk to small pond in woods for woodpeckers
North Fork Ahtanum Rd (paved)
Tampico

gate
gate
Eagle's Nest Viewpoint
North Fork Ahtanum Rd —bridge
tiny pond
Ahtanum Meadow Campground
Grey Rock Trail

Darland Mountain

Clover Flats Campground
Tree Phones Campground
Middle Fork Ahtanum Rd (gravel)
North Fork Ahtanum Rd (gravel)

South Fork Ahtanum Rd (paved)

To St. Joseph Mission at Ahtanum (5.3 miles) and Yakima (19 miles) via Ahtanum Rd

0   4
MILES

go right (west) in Tampico onto North Fork Ahtanum Road. In the breeding season, check the oak and riparian habitats, then dry conifer forest along the next 9.4 miles to the bridge at the end of the pavement. This is a very birdy drive. Especially notable are the many Veeries in the lower-elevation riparian habitat.

Just before the bridge, you have two options. For a try at Spruce Grouse, go right onto the gravel **North Fork Ahtanum Road**. In 6.5 miles, turn left to continue on the main North Fork Road. Cross the stream and park. In a few yards, head left (east) up a gated logging road. Spruce Grouse may be encountered anywhere up this and other roads on this north-facing slope but especially near streams or seeps. You can continue driving up the North Fork Road, poking about on as many of the side tracks as time allows. Take care in the hunting season; wearing hunter orange is advisable.

For woodpeckers and Boreal Owl, from the end of the pavement, keep straight ahead (south) onto the gravel **Middle Fork Ahtanum Road**. Park at a wide spot on the right in 1.5 miles, near a tiny pond. Another 100 feet up the road, find an old track on the right, blocked by a ditch and berm. Use this to guide yourself right cross country a few hundred yards, following the moist drainage to a small pond in the forest with a grove of aspens amid pines and firs. An impressive suite of woodpeckers has been noted here including Red-naped and Williamson's Sapsuckers, and Downy, Hairy, White-headed, and Pileated Woodpeckers.

Return to the road and continue uphill 4.3 miles to Tree Phones Campground, checking other aspen and willow groves along the way for songbirds, especially May and June. For Boreal Owl (best September and October before snow closes the road), do not enter the campground, but follow the main road right (west) and climb steadily three miles to **Eagle's Nest Viewpoint**, which offers fine views amid subalpine forest good for Gray Jay and Clark's Nutcracker. Raptors sail overhead in fall.

Return to the Middle Fork Ahtanum Road and continue uphill 0.4 mile to **Clover Flats Campground**. Boreal Owls are found in this mature forest of Engelmann Spruce and Subalpine Fir, best in fall from September until snow closes the road. In years when the spruce are laden with cones, crossbills (White-winged is irregular) can be common here. Check also for Pine Grosbeak.

The road deteriorates beyond Clover Flats Campground. Hike, or if equipped with a high-clearance vehicle, drive to the top of **Darland Mountain**, one of the highest points reached by road in Washington (elevation 6,981 feet). Besides glorious views of Mount Rainier and Mount Adams, look for Clark's Nutcrackers in the Whitebark Pines and Mountain Bluebirds in openings. In fall, this vantage is a good hawkwatch site. This road is in very poor condition, but in dry summer weather you can eventually connect to the North Fork Road.

SOUTH TO TOPPENISH CREEK

The **Toppenish National Wildlife Refuge** is a rich birding area situated in the Toppenish Creek bottomlands some 20 miles south of Yakima. Bobolinks (almost extirpated) and a variety of other species nest on the refuge, while migration and winter bring many waterfowl, raptors, sparrows, and blackbirds. To reach the refuge from Yakima, take I-82 southeast to Exit 50. Turn right onto SR-22 and proceed 3.2 miles to the second light in Toppenish. Go straight through this traffic light (you are now on US-97) to Pump House Road (4.7 miles), also marked Toppenish National Wildlife Refuge. Turn right here, then make an immediate sharp right into a parking lot with an information kiosk and short, paved path to a covered, raised observation platform. This is an excellent place in spring and early summer to study a variety of waterfowl, and later on, when waters recede, shorebirds such as Black-necked Stilt and American Avocet. Eastern Kingbird and Gray Catbird nest in riparian thickets in front of the platform.

A road leads from the parking lot to **refuge headquarters** (0.5 mile). Proceed by car if the gate is open; otherwise you may walk. Trees and brush about the headquarters may be teeming with migrants in spring and fall. Great Horned Owls nest in these trees, often mobbed by Black-billed Magpies. A trail goes north, shortly crossing a concrete bridge to seasonally flooded fields and marshes where birding is often good for waterfowl, raptors, shorebirds, Marsh Wren, and Common Yellowthroat, from February to June.

Return to Pump House Road and turn right (west). A good area for shrub-steppe species is reached in 0.7 mile. Park by the road and walk south into the sagelands along the base of Toppenish Ridge. Look for sparrows from

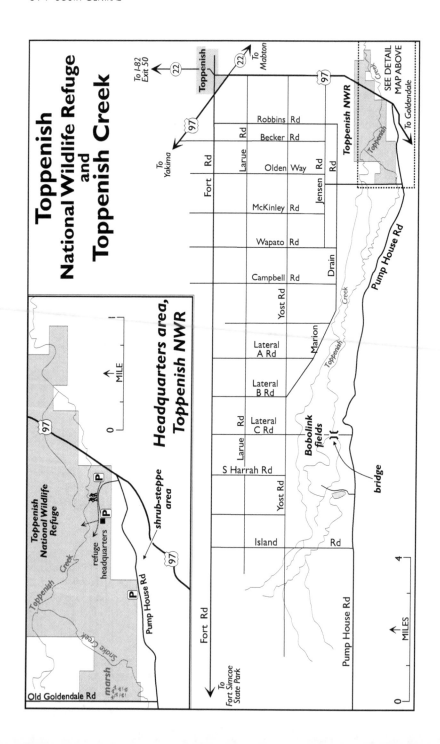

Toppenish
National Wildlife Refuge
and
Toppenish Creek

Headquarters area,
Toppenish NWR

April through early August—Sagebrush Sparrow in the densest tracts of Big Sagebrush, Lark Sparrow in the rocky and more arid places nearby, and Vesper Sparrow in areas of dense grass with few shrubs. Common Poorwills can be found at dusk from late April into September. Another patch of shrub-steppe habitat a short distance farther on (0.3 mile) offers similar possibilities.

Continue west on Pump House Road and turn right onto **Old Goldendale Road** (1.2 miles from the second sagebrush patch, 2.2 miles from the headquarters turnoff). A marsh on the right side of the road (0.5 mile) has Virginia Rail, Sora, Marsh Wren, and Common Yellowthroat. American Bitterns "pump" here on spring and summer nights.

Return to Pump House Road, turn right, and go 7.0 miles to **Lateral C Road**, checking flooded fields (mainly spring) along the way for waterfowl and shorebirds (especially Long-billed Curlew) and the Greasewood-dominated shrub-steppe for Loggerhead Shrike. Black-tailed Jack Rabbit, a declining species in Washington, is common here. At Lateral C, turn right and descend to the bridge over Toppenish Creek (0.4 mile), from which you often can see waterfowl and many swallows. Look, too, for Barn, Western Screech-, and Great Horned Owls. Another 0.4 mile on Lateral C brings you to an area of wet fields, site of a disjunct (nearly extirpated) Bobolink colony; look and listen for them from late May through July. The nearest other populations are in irrigated hayfields along the northern tier of counties east of the Cascades. Lateral C Road meets Fort Road 3.1 miles farther north. You may turn right here to join US-97 in Toppenish, or left to visit Fort Simcoe.

Fort Simcoe, a historic frontier outpost west of Toppenish and now a state park, is famous for its Lewis's Woodpeckers. Indeed, the planted Garry Oak groves around the grounds are probably the best place to observe this charismatic species in Washington. Most common from April through early September, the woodpeckers may winter in smaller numbers if acorns are available (some years the mast crop fails). Other birds of the Garry Oaks include California Quail, Northern Flicker, Steller's Jay (mainly winter), and White-breasted Nuthatch. Brushy growth by the creek south of the fort usually has a few pairs of Ash-throated Flycatchers in early summer. Migrants are occasionally numerous in both spring and fall in the thick brush, especially around the ranger's residence.

Fort Simcoe is reached by driving west from US-97 in Toppenish on Fort Road to Fort Extension Road (19.0 miles) and then 0.2 mile to Signal Peak Road. (From the intersection of Lateral C and Fort Road, it's 9.7 miles west to Fort Extension Road.) Turn left onto Signal Peak, go two miles, and turn right onto Fort Simcoe Road. The park entrance is on the left in five miles. Habitat on the approach to Fort Simcoe appears parched for much of the year, but is enlivened with many colorful wildflowers in early spring (March–April). Check shrub-steppe along the road for Loggerhead Shrike and Brewer's Sparrow.

WEST TO NACHES

Just west of Yakima is scenic, cliff-rimmed **Cowiche Canyon**, protected by a land trust. (See Wenas Creek map on page 292.) Take 40th Avenue south from US-12 to Summitview Avenue (1.5 miles). Turn right and go 7.1 miles to Weikel Road. Make a right here to the signed entrance (0.5 mile). A three-mile gravel trail follows the canyon bottom beside Cowiche Creek. Check the cliffs for Turkey Vulture, Red-tailed Hawk, Violet-green Swallow, and Rock and Canyon Wrens. The thick, brushy riparian vegetation has many resident Black-capped Chickadees. Flycatchers, vireos, and warblers can be numerous in migration. Cedar Waxwing, Yellow-breasted Chat, and Black-headed Grosbeak are a few of the summer residents.

Snow Mountain Ranch, showcasing riparian woodland, Garry Oak groves, and shrub-steppe-covered uplands, is another Cowiche Canyon Conservancy preserve. Return to Summitview and turn right (west). Go 1.75 miles to Cowiche Mill Road. Turn left (south) and drive 2.5 miles to parking. Walk the trail south to the Garry Oak Trail which traverses riparian habitat and oak groves. Western Scrub-Jays are resident. In summer, expect Yellow-breasted Chat and Lazuli Bunting.

Return on the trail the way you came and continue right (south again) to a bridge over Cowiche Creek South Fork to an information kiosk with map that depicts the trail system on Cowiche Mountain. A rewarding day can be had by heading up Cowiche Mountain. From the kiosk (bird-rich riparian woodland), climb the mountain, by crossing a grassy field to a brushy ravine (Ash-throated Flycatcher), then ascend up through shrub-steppe (Loggerhead Shrike, Sage Thrasher, Brewer's and Vesper Sparrows, and Western Meadowlark). The summit affords fine views and is ablaze with wildflowers in April and May. Horned Lark is common on these slopes.

Return to US-12 and head west, turning left onto Ackley Road (1.4 miles west of the 40th Avenue exit). A few hundred feet ahead is Powerhouse Road. Stop here to admire the petroglyphs at the **Painted Rocks**, up a short flight of steps, and to view nesting White-throated Swifts and Cliff Swallows (April through July). These imposing cliffs are the terminus of the Tieton Flow, a sinuous andesite lava flow that originated from the Goat Rocks volcano one to two million years ago.

Turn right (west) on Powerhouse Road and return to US-12 (0.9 mile). Turn left, passing Allan Road (7.0 miles), a southern access to the Wenas Creek region. Continue 1.2 miles on US-12 to the traffic light in the center of Naches (check your fuel if headed west to the mountain passes). From here it is 4.5 miles to the junction of US-12 and SR-410. Go right at this intersection onto the **Old Naches Road**. You will soon (0.1 mile) cross a canal where migrants can be thick in spring and fall. In summer, look for Yellow-breasted Chat and Lazuli Bunting. Continue on this road for another 0.5 mile to a

WDFW parking lot on your left, in the Oak Creek Wildlife Area. This is a winter feeding station for the Bighorn Sheep that reside on Cleman Mountain, to the north. A Golden Eagle nest—active for years, near the top of the cliffs directly across the river—can be scoped from here, and both eagle species often soar high above. Chukar and Rock Wren utilize the talus.

CHINOOK PASS HIGHWAY

by Andy Stepniewski and Hal Opperman
revised by Andy Stepniewski

Beginning 17 miles west of Yakima at an intersection with US-12, the seasonal Chinook Pass Highway (SR-410) ascends northwest, then west, following the Naches, Bumping, and American Rivers to beautiful Chinook Pass, an eastern access to Mount Rainier National Park. The highway is closed for the winter about five miles below the pass (from November through May in an average year). The full altitudinal range of Eastside habitats from Garry Oak and upper shrub-steppe to lower subalpine is present along this route and its many side branches, although lakes and marshes are in relatively short supply.

UPPER NACHES RIVER

Nile Road turns off left from SR-410 in 8.0 miles. In 1.4 miles, turn left from Nile Road onto Bethel Ridge Road (FR-1500), then left again in 1.0 mile onto Little Rattlesnake Road (FR-1501), which follows **Little Rattlesnake Creek** for the next 5.2 miles to a junction with FR-1503. Pacific-slope Flycatcher, Warbling Vireo, Veery, MacGillivray's and Yellow Warblers, and other riparian species are common along this stretch. At the junction, keep right onto FR-1503. A marsh-rimmed lake in 1.5 miles has many more birds of riparian and montane-forest habitats.

Return to **Nile Road** and turn left to a bridge over the Naches River (3.3 miles). Streamside vegetation and marsh along the road have many birds, including Black-chinned and Rufous Hummingbirds, Red-naped Sapsucker, Willow and Pacific-slope Flycatchers, Warbling Vireo, Black-capped Chickadee, House Wren, Veery, Gray Catbird, Cedar Waxwing, MacGillivray's and Yellow Warblers, Song Sparrow, Black-headed Grosbeak, Purple Finch, and Evening Grosbeak. Nile Road rejoins SR-410 in another 0.2 mile. Turn left toward Chinook Pass.

In 1.3 miles, **Bald Mountain Road** (aka Maloy Road and FR-1701) takes off uphill to the right, offering quick access to montane dry-forest habitats—excellent for Flammulated Owl in May and June. Drive up this road for 1.6 miles and turn right onto FR-1711. In another 0.8 mile, stop to listen for the owl. Good habitat for Flams continues for another quarter-mile. Several

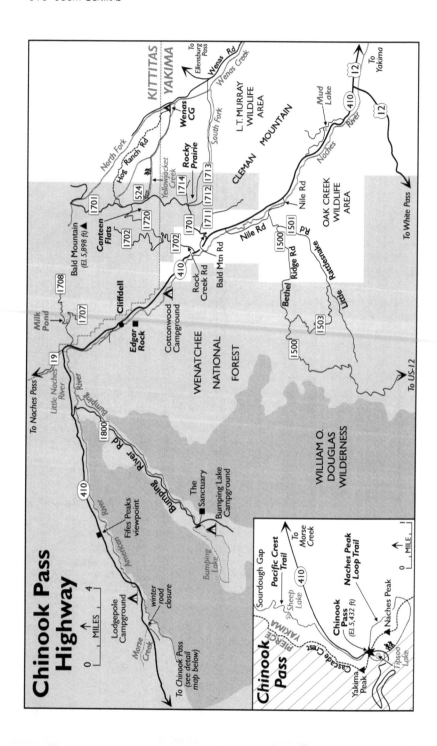

Chinook Pass Highway

miles farther on, the forest opens up with large patches of Bitterbrush, good for Common Poorwill.

For good daytime birding in open Ponderosa Pine and Douglas-fir forests at the head of the Wenas Creek drainage, return to FR-1701, turn right and travel uphill on FR-1701. Turn right in 2.2 miles onto FR-1712, go 0.1 mile, and bear left onto FR-1713. **Rocky Prairie** (elevation 3,800 feet) starts in 0.5 mile. Look here for White-headed Woodpecker, White-breasted and Pygmy Nuthatches, Western and Mountain Bluebirds, Townsend's Solitaire, and Cassin's Finch.

To reach **Canteen Flats** (elevation 4,400 feet), return to FR-1701 and continue three miles past the FR-1712 turnoff. The rocky meadows rimmed by open forest have birds similar to those of Rocky Prairie. A short spur road (FR-524; now closed to vehicular traffic, but you may walk it) descends eastward from Canteen Flats to a trailhead for Yellowjacket Creek. From here you may follow along Yellowjacket Creek and Dry Creek to Wenas Campground (hike described on page 296). Several miles farther north on FR-1701, wetter forests of Grand Fir and Western Larch are good for Williamson's Sapsucker, Hammond's Flycatcher, Ruby-crowned Kinglet, and MacGillivray's and Townsend's Warblers.

Nine-tenths of a mile farther up SR-410, a second road (FR-1702) turns off right and ascends **Rock Creek**. Begin checking for Flammulated Owls about five miles up, on a sidehill where Douglas-fir, Ponderosa Pine, and an undergrowth of Deerbrush and other shrubs make for a high density of moths, the owls' preferred food. In April, this area is good for Great Horned and Northern Saw-whet Owls.

Continue west along SR-410. In 5.4 miles, pull completely off the road opposite **Edgar Rock**, which towers above you across the Naches River. Turkey Vulture, Red-tailed Hawk, Peregrine Falcon, and numerous Violet-green Swallows may be seen overhead, while the riparian woodland by the roadside has Warbling Vireo, Veery, and Yellow Warbler. Cliffdell, in another 0.8 mile, offers the last reliable service station for 80 miles.

In 3.4 miles you reach FR-1708, a good owling road that leads to **Milk Pond**. Go two miles up the road to a ravine. By walking about 500 yards up this forested gulch, then ascending a slope to the left for another few hundred yards, you might encounter Northern Saw-whet or other owls. Hammond's Flycatcher, Hermit Thrush, Townsend's Warbler, and Evening Grosbeak are common in these woods.

LITTLE NACHES RIVER TO NACHES PASS

West again on SR-410, find FR-19, the **Little Naches Road**, on the right (0.7 mile). Near this corner the Bumping River and the Little Naches River unite to form the Naches River. The large Little Naches watershed—heavily clearcut in recent decades—now consists of a mosaic of meadows, gallery riparian woodland, and fir forests, favorable to Barred Owls, which have invaded the area. Stopping along the road at dawn or dusk, especially near openings in the forest, will often turn up one.

The historic Naches Trail—a wagon road to Puget Sound used by early settlers—followed the Little Naches River up across Naches Pass, then down the Greenwater and White River drainages on the Westside. FR-19, FR-1914, and FR-70 approximate its route. The actual pass, however, is now crossed by a deeply eroded, seven-mile jeep track. Despite the devastation from no-holds-barred logging and ATV traffic, patches of original forest in the wide vicinity of the 4,900-foot pass still harbor American Three-toed Woodpecker, Gray Jay, Ruby-crowned Kinglet, and other montane specialties. White-crowned Sparrow (*gambelii*) breeds at the pass, and there are even fall reports of Boreal Owl. Keen birders occasionally venture here to find Eastside species such as Calliope Hummingbird, Red-naped Sapsucker, Dusky Flycatcher, Mountain Bluebird, and Cassin's Finch at their western range limits. **Government Meadows**, a mile west of the summit, is generally a productive spot. Before setting out to explore this area, make sure you have up-to-date maps and road information and an America the Beautiful or Northwest Forest Pass. All of these are available at the USFS ranger district stations on SR-410 in Naches and Enumclaw.

BUMPING RIVER TO CHINOOK PASS

Continue west on SR-410 from the Little Naches Road intersection. In 3.7 miles, turn off left onto the Bumping River Road (FR-1800). Lands on both sides of the narrow valley corridor are protected in the William O. Douglas Wilderness, named for the late Supreme Court justice and noted conservationist, who made this area his second home. Look for Northern Goshawk and Pileated Woodpecker in the beautiful, mostly unlogged forest that lines the road, although the goshawk is remarkably elusive in the breeding season.

Stop off the highway in 6.5 miles to explore a meadow by the river. Spotted Sandpiper and American Dipper are expected here, while Vaux's Swifts zip by overhead. In another 4.6 miles you reach the dam for **Bumping Lake**, a reservoir with nesting Barrow's Goldeneye, Osprey, and Spotted Sandpiper. The picnic area at Bumping Lake Campground (USFS fee area), in 0.2 mile, provides an overlook of the lake.

At the dam, go east from FR-1800 onto an unmarked, sandy, but passable track. Follow the main track through thick Lodgepole Pine woods to its end (0.6 mile). Walk a hundred yards to **The Sanctuary**, a small grove of huge Western Redcedars forming a Westside-type forest—great for Barred Owl, Chestnut-backed Chickadee, and Varied Thrush. Put your identification skills to work sorting out the two species of pine, three true firs, a spruce, two hemlocks, two cedars, Western Larch, and Douglas-fir that occur here, along with Red Alder—almost exclusively a Westside tree.

From the Bumping River Road intersection, SR-410 follows the American River westward the rest of the way to Chinook Pass. Stop at the **Fifes Peaks Viewpoint** (7.0 miles). The forest here is quite moist, reflecting proximity to the Cascade Crest. Hammond's Flycatcher, Chestnut-backed Chickadee, Hermit and Varied Thrushes, and Townsend's Warbler are all common. Spy on the volcanic spires of the Fifes Peaks towering above; you may see a band of Mountain Goats. Stop again at **Lodgepole Campground** (4.8 miles). Williamson's Sapsucker is often found in the forest here—a mixture of Lodgepole Pine and Western Larch. The highway is closed for the winter at **Morse Creek** (2.0 miles). Near the winter-closure gate, a track leaves the highway on the left (downhill) side. Forest along this track has been a reliable spot to find Barred Owl and Chestnut-backed Chickadee, while the slopes on the right (uphill) side of the highway are excellent for Sooty Grouse.

It is 5.4 miles from Morse Creek to Chinook Pass (elevation 5,432 feet), in the subalpine along the eastern boundary of Mount Rainier National Park. Views of the mountain are superb, especially in early morning. The forest here is composed of Mountain Hemlock and spire-like Subalpine Fir, alternating with lush meadows (best flower display from mid-July through mid-August). Gray Jays and Clark's Nutcrackers panhandle shamelessly among the throngs of visitors. Sooty Grouse frequent the meadow edges. Migrant flycatchers, vireos, warblers, and sparrows can be numerous in the thickets in fall. In early evening, watch for a small flight of Black Swifts heading back to their nesting cliffs, presumably in the park. A modest showing of raptors appears over the ridges beginning in late August and continuing through mid-October.

Trails at the pass offer fine birding but are not fully open until the snow melts—usually by late July. The four-mile Naches Peak Loop is on the south side of the highway. Look for Mountain and Chestnut-backed Chickadees, Red-breasted Nuthatch, Pacific Wren, Townsend's Solitaire, Hermit and Varied Thrushes, American Pipit, Yellow-rumped and Townsend's Warblers, Chipping and Fox Sparrows, Pine Grosbeak (uncommon), Cassin's Finch, and Red and White-winged (irregular) Crossbills.

North from the pass, a two-mile trail leads to Sheep Lake, and in another mile to Sourdough Gap (elevation 6,400 feet). This trail opens earlier in summer than the Naches Peak Loop as it traverses a south-facing slope for the first 1.5 mile. Brushier patches on this initial stretch make for great habitat for migrating warblers and sparrows beginning in August. Both trails can be good for raptors from mid-August through October.

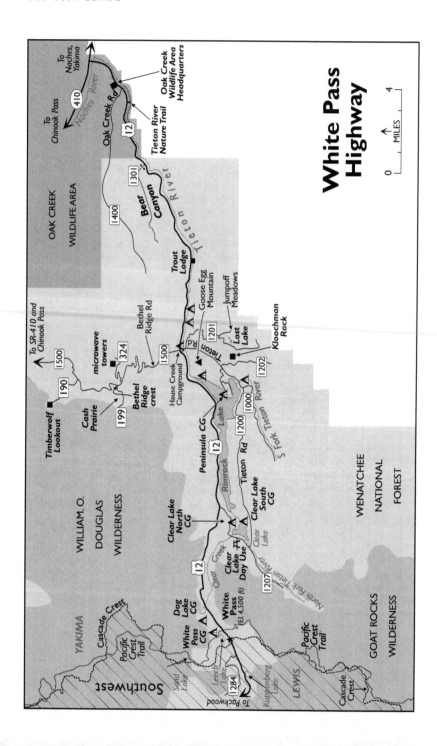

White Pass Highway

WHITE PASS HIGHWAY

by Andy Stepniewski

revised by Andy Stepniewski

One of the better Cascades birding routes is the 34-mile stretch of US-12 that ascends the Tieton River to 4,500-foot White Pass, along a transect from arid Garry Oak and shrub-steppe vegetation at the lower end to tall, wet subalpine forest at the Cascade Crest southeast of Mount Rainier.

OAK CREEK AND LOWER TIETON RIVER

Head south and west with US-12 at the junction with SR-410, about four miles west of Naches. Lewis's Woodpeckers and Bullock's Orioles frequent Garry Oaks at the **Oak Creek Wildlife Area headquarters** (2.0 miles). An extensive Elk-feeding program makes this a winter tourist attraction; several thousand animals can sometimes be observed. Nearby, an out-of-view carcass dump for road-killed animals attracts numbers of Turkey Vultures (summer) and Bald (winter) and Golden Eagles. Watch for them overhead.

West on US-12 in another 0.2 mile is **Oak Creek Road**, on the right. This gravel road runs uphill alongside the creek into the heart of the 42,000-acre wildlife area, passing through Garry Oaks, Ponderosa Pines, and riparian vegetation. For the first four miles, look for Golden Eagle, Common Poorwill, White-throated Swift, Lewis's Woodpecker, Western Wood-Pewee, Least Flycatcher (rare but regular in aspen groves), Rock and Canyon Wrens, Veery, Nashville Warbler, Yellow-breasted Chat, Western Tanager, Black-headed Grosbeak, Lazuli Bunting, and Bullock's Oriole. Western Gray Squirrels still occur here—one of the relatively few places in the state where this declining species may be seen.

Another access to the wildlife area is one mile farther along US-12, on the left. Park here (Discover Pass required) and take the path leading right toward the river. Cross the swinging bridge to the **Tieton River Nature Trail**, which follows the river beneath towering cliffs of andesite for several miles both up- and downstream. Habitats include riparian woodland, Garry Oak and Ponderosa Pine groves on slightly drier sites, and finally a zone of Bitterbrush on yet drier slopes. Look for Sooty Grouse, Lewis's Woodpecker, and Nashville Warbler, among many other species. At times in migration the trees here are filled with birds, especially on mornings following a storm.

Another 3.4 miles west on US-12—just beyond the Wenatchee National Forest boundary sign—turn off right onto gravel FR-1301 and park at the gate (America the Beautiful or Northwest Forest Pass required). A good walk goes uphill from here into cliff-rimmed **Bear Canyon**. The slopes are grown to picturesque Garry Oak, Ponderosa Pine, and Douglas-fir, while the canyon bottom has tall cottonwoods and willows. Bear Canyon is one of Washington's premier spots to observe butterflies (more than 60 species have been noted here) and is also good for bird species typical of the lower east slopes of the Cascades, such as Golden Eagle, Common Poorwill, White-throated Swift, Dusky Flycatcher, Cassin's Vireo, Violet-green Swallow, Canyon Wren, Townsend's Solitaire, Nashville Warbler, and Western Tanager.

Continuing west, US-12 parallels the rushing Tieton River. Check for Harlequin Duck (best mid-April–early June), Prairie Falcon (nesting on cliffs), and American Dipper. **Trout Lodge** (5.9 miles) has a small restaurant with several hummingbird feeders visible from the dining room, attracting Rufous and Calliope Hummingbirds. Please offer a word of thanks to the owners for providing this service. Between three and five miles west of the lodge on US-12, several forest service campgrounds are set in Ponderosa Pines, Black Cottonwoods, and willows along the Tieton River. All offer the chance to see White-headed Woodpecker.

BETHEL RIDGE

Continuing west on US-12, watch on the right for FR-1500, the **Bethel Ridge Road** (4.7 miles from Trout Lodge). This graded, though often washboarded, gravel road steeply ascends the south slopes of Bethel Ridge, the eroded remnant of an ancient volcano. After gaining over 3,500 feet in elevation and passing through various types of colorful volcanic rock (tuffs and breccias, mainly) and a succession of forested habitats (Ponderosa Pine to mixed-conifer to subalpine), the road tops out in 7.5 miles at over 6,000 feet elevation. It is open in summer only. Species to be found along the way include Flammulated and Northern Pygmy-Owls, Common Poorwill, Williamson's and Red-naped Sapsuckers, White-headed Woodpecker, Cassin's Vireo, Cassin's Finch, and Red Crossbill.

Check the Ponderosa Pine woods in the general vicinity of the fork at 0.3 mile from US-12 for White-headed Woodpecker. Two areas of wet montane meadow—the first 1.5 miles from the fork, the second in another half-mile—have Red-naped Sapsucker, Warbling Vireo, and MacGillivray's Warbler. Higher yet, FR-1500 leaves the Ponderosa Pine zone. Stop in 3.5 miles at a narrow band of mixed-conifer forest where Western Larch attracts Williamson's Sapsucker. Cold, snowy subalpine habitats with Subalpine Fir, Mountain Hemlock, and Lodgepole Pine begin abruptly in another 1.0 mile. Turn right here on FR-324 to reach the **microwave towers** atop Bethel Ridge. The dark, dense forests on the north aspects of the ridge harbor a few Spruce Grouse, although they are rarely seen. The promise of a tough slog through the nearly impenetrable vegetation is enough to deter all but the most sure-footed hikers. Easier to spot are Gray Jay and Clark's Nutcracker.

The Bethel Ridge crest is another 0.7 mile up FR-1500. At 0.2 mile from FR-324, turn left from FR-1500 onto FR-199 to reach **Cash Prairie** (1.1 miles), a beautiful subalpine meadow where Ruby-crowned Kinglet is common and the

Lincoln's Sparrow bubbly song emanates from the tall, corn-like False Helle-bore—a poisonous member of the lily family. Among the many raptors that soar over this meadow from late summer through fall, look especially for accipiters, Red-tailed and Rough-legged Hawks, Golden Eagle, American Kestrel, and Prairie Falcon.

The road ends in another 1.0 mile at a trailhead for the William O. Douglas Wilderness from which views extend to Mount Adams, the Goat Rocks, and the summit of Mount Rainier. The exposed, steep south-facing slopes have a few shrub-steppe plants such as Big Sagebrush and Scarlet Gilia; look for Rock Wren here. Only a few yards away are equally steep, north-facing slopes mantled in snow-forest species such as Mountain Hemlock, Subalpine Fir, and Lodgepole Pine, plus scattered Alaska Yellowcedar, Engelmann Spruce, and Whitebark Pine. Golden-crowned and Ruby-crowned Kinglets and Townsend's Warbler breed in these cold forests. Pine Grosbeak and White-winged Crossbill are rare wanderers.

Return to FR-1500 and turn left. Descend 3.5 miles to FR-190, turn left, and climb 2.6 miles to **Timberwolf Lookout**, at 6,400 feet. A small band of Mountain Goats is often seen on the nearby cliffs. Hawks sail by in the fall, most commonly accipiters and Red-taileds. Returning to FR-1500, you can take a left and go down FR-1500 to join SR-410, the Chinook Pass Highway, in about 16 miles (page 318). Otherwise, turn right and retrace your route up and over Bethel Ridge to US-12 in 11 miles.

AROUND RIMROCK LAKE

About three miles west of the FR-1500 intersection the Tieton River is dammed to form Rimrock Lake. US-12 follows the north shore of the reservoir closely. The deep, clear, cold waters are not inviting to birds, but you might see a few waterfowl, shorebirds, and gulls (and many swallows at the dam). Tieton Road goes around the south side of the lake through forest and wetland habitats, departing from US-12 about 2.5 miles below the dam and returning to it in 16 miles, near the west end of the lake. Although it is nine miles longer, this paved road is by far the better birding choice if you are not in a big hurry to get to the pass.

Three-tenths of a mile west of the FR-1500 intersection, turn left onto Tieton Road (FR-1200). Cross the Tieton River to a junction with FR-1201, on the left (0.2 mile). The wetlands on both sides of the road near this junction host a nice variety of forest birds. Red-naped Sapsucker and Willow Flycatcher are common. Look for Gray Catbird and warblers around the small pond. FR-1201 climbs steadily to a turnoff for **Jumpoff Meadows** in about 3.5 miles. Turn left onto FR-557 and travel 0.3 to the beginning of the meadows. The mixed Ponderosa Pine and Douglas-fir forest alternating with alder-and-willow-lined meadows offers good birding possibilities, including Barred Owl and Lincoln's Sparrow; Williamson's Sapsucker is reasonably common in areas with Western Larch.

Back on Tieton Road, travel uphill past Goose Egg Mountain on your right (nesting White-throated Swifts) and Kloochman Rock on your left, and turn left onto FR-1202 (2.5 miles). Go 0.3 mile to a swamp by the road. In the numerous snags, watch for woodpeckers (including White-headed) and swallows. Many forest species occur in the surrounding pines, alders, and willows.

The turnoff for **Peninsula Campground**, on Rimrock Lake, is 0.2 mile farther along Tieton Road on the right. A marsh with Virginia Rail, Sora, and many blackbirds is on the right (north) side of the entrance road. Red-naped and Red-breasted (scarce) Sapsuckers nest in the Quaking Aspen and Black Cottonwood groves. Flammulated Owl occurs, if not in the campground, then along the steep, south-facing slopes of Goose Egg Mountain grown to Ponderosa Pines with an understory of Deerbrush, at the campground entrance. Continue west on Tieton Road. At a fork in 1.6 miles, where FR-1000 goes left up the South Fork Tieton, stay right with FR-1200 (aka Tieton Road). A steady increase in precipitation is reflected in the changing habitats as you proceed westward to the entrance for Clear Lake South Campground (7.0 miles), including riparian areas with lush Mountain Alder and willow thickets, meadows, and tall, moist forests of Grand Fir and Engelmann Spruce. A stop at any of several pullouts or gravel lanes on your left may yield Ruffed Grouse, Calliope Hummingbird, Willow and Hammond's Flycatchers, Cassin's and Warbling Vireos, Chestnut-backed Chickadee, and Orange-crowned, Nashville, MacGillivray's, Yellow, Yellow-rumped, and Townsend's Warblers. Open, south-facing slopes on your right have Douglas-firs and Ponderosa Pines. There, look for Sooty Grouse, Clark's Nutcracker, Mountain Chickadee, Cassin's Finch, and Red Crossbill.

One mile past the Clear Lake South Campground turnoff, at the intersection with North Fork Tieton Road, keep right with FR-1200. In 0.6 mile, turn right into the **Clear Lake Day-Use Site** (USFS fee area). Take the paved nature walk through open forest of Douglas-fir and Grand Fir (Hammond's Flycatcher, Western Tanager, Cassin's Finch) to observation blinds at the edge of Clear Lake. During summer, look for nesting Ring-necked Duck, Barrow's Goldeneye, and Osprey. Diving ducks (including Surf and White-winged Scoters), loons, grebes, and Common Tern are regular, though uncommon, in fall migration.

Once again on Tieton Road, it is 0.7 mile to the bridge over **Clear Creek**. American Dippers often nest under the bridge. Snags and alder thickets have lots of Warbling Vireos and Yellow Warblers. American Redstarts, near the edge of their range, have been noted in the alders around the lake. **Clear Lake North Campground** (1.4 miles; USFS, primitive) is a fine spot to camp (you can scan Clear Lake from another vantage on the way there). Look for Northern Pygmy-Owl (uncommon) and Western Tanager in the surrounding forest.

Right from the campground, Tieton Road reaches US-12 in 0.4 mile. In September and October, head right (east) on US-12 for 1.7 miles to a historical pulloff with Rimrock Lake below. Nesting birds here include Common

Merganser, Osprey, Bald Eagle, Spotted Sandpiper, and American Dipper. Tens of thousands of land-locked Kokanee Salmon spawn along the creek in fall. Hundreds of gulls, mostly California but also a few Ring-billed, Herring, Thayer's, and Glaucous-winged, gather here for the fish feast. Bald Eagles also arrive, usually in November, to partake of this buffet, along with hundreds of Common Mergansers (sometimes a few Red-breasted). Sabine's Gull and Parasitic Jaeger are among the rarities noted here.

WHITE PASS AND VICINITY

West and steadily uphill, US-12 traverses a hazardous rockslide area (stopping not advised, although Peregrine Falcons have nested on the cliffs right above the highway). At **Dog Lake Campground** (5.5 miles), check for Barrow's Goldeneye on the lake, Williamson's and Red-naped Sapsuckers (Red-breasted also possible), and Gray Jay in the Western Larches.

Another 1.5 miles on US-12 brings you to the turnoff to White Pass Campground (USFS, primitive), on the shores of **Leech Lake**. Mountain species noted here in summer include Ring-necked Duck, Barrow's Goldeneye, Osprey, Northern Pygmy- and Barred Owls, Williamson's (east of the lake around corrals) and Red-breasted (lakeshore snags) Sapsuckers, Pileated Woodpecker, Rock Wren (talus slides north of the highway), and Hermit and Varied Thrushes. "Thick-billed Fox Sparrows," clearly disjunct from the Oregon population, have bred in brushy thickets near the corrals. Trails give access to extensive forests, subalpine meadows, and glacier-mantled peaks—for example, the Pacific Crest Trail south to the Goat Rocks Wilderness. The forest north up the Pacific Crest Trail may yield American Three-toed Woodpecker, and a hike of at least several miles reaches subalpine openings—good habitat for Pine Grosbeak (irregular). Boreal Owl has been found here in late summer.

West again on US-12 brings you to the 4,500-foot summit of **White Pass** (0.4 mile). The willow scrub and conifers around the lodge, and particularly north of the highway by the shores of Leech Lake, have yielded Rufous and Calliope Hummingbirds, Gray Jay, Clark's Nutcracker, many quite tame Common Ravens, Tree and Violet-green Swallows, and Lincoln's and White-crowned (*pugetensis*) Sparrows.

Continuing west, **Knuppenburg Lake** (0.8 mile) is worth a short stop; Barrow's Goldeneyes have nested here. Watch also for Gray Jays coming to beg for scraps. In 8.4 miles note a pullout to the left (south) for **Palisades Viewpoint**, overlooking a basalt cliff across the canyon. The lazy, wheezy song of Townsend's Warbler is easy to hear from this spot, but the birds often remain high in the tall Douglas-firs and can be difficult to spot. It is 2.3 miles to a major junction where you may turn north and ascend SR-123 along the Ohanapecosh River to Mount Rainier National Park (page 225), or continue southwestward with US-12, following the Cowlitz River to Packwood and birding sites in Southwestern Washington.

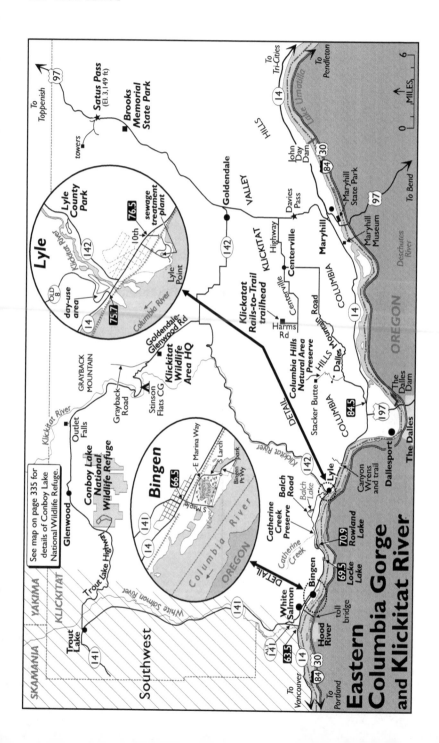

Eastern
Columbia Gorge
and Klickitat River

EASTERN COLUMBIA GORGE AND KLICKITAT RIVER

by Bill LaFramboise, Nancy LaFramboise, Wilson Cady, and Andy Stepniewski
revised by Catherine Flick , Stuart Johnston, and Roger Baker

East of Mount Adams, the Klickitat River drains a large basin southward, reaching the Columbia River gorge at Lyle. With its rolling hills, dry mixed Garry Oak/Ponderosa Pine forests with patches of Ceanothus and other shrubs, this country has habitats and some bird species similar to those of interior southern Oregon and northern California. Acorn Woodpecker and Lesser Goldfinch reach their northern range limits here (although Lesser Goldfinch is expanding its range within the state). Other breeding species with southern affinities are Anna's Hummingbird, Lewis's Woodpecker, Ash-throated Flycatcher, Western Scrub-Jay, and White-breasted Nuthatch.

Conboy Lake National Wildlife Refuge has the full complement of Eastside habitats, including Ponderosa Pine, pine/oak, mixed conifer, aspen groves, riparian, canals, grassy prairies, marsh, and wetland meadows. The small population of breeding Greater Sandhill Cranes at Conboy Lake is expanding into neighboring areas. Special bird encounters include Flammulated Owl, Red-naped Sapsucker, White-headed Woodpecker, Least and Gray Flycatchers, Eastern Kingbird, and Pygmy Nuthatch.

The Columbia Hills is designated by Washington Audubon as an Important Bird Area (IBA) for wintering raptors. During migration and winter, waterfowl are plentiful and diverse along the Columbia River sloughs, which always provide interesting sightings. The east end of the Columbia River Gorge includes basalt cliff habitats with breeding Golden Eagle, White-throated Swift, Peregrine and Prairie Falcons, and Rock and Canyon Wrens.

Be aware that Poison Oak is especially abundant in the woodland understory. Western Rattlesnakes are common throughout, particularly near rocky areas.

Site descriptions begin at the eastern Columbia Gorge, specifically in Bingen where the western Gorge leaves off (page 250). We proceed upriver to the eastern terminus of the Columbia River Gorge National Scenic Area near Maryhill. Mileposts markers along SR-14 serve as our reference points.

BINGEN

Driving east on SR-14, cross the White Salmon River bridge (milepost 63.5). In less than two miles is the turnoff for the toll bridge to Hood River, Oregon. Continue east on SR-14 into the town of Bingen. At milepost 66.5 (just east of the Shell station), turn right onto Maple Street at the sign for the Port of Klickitat and Bingen Marina. Cross the railroad tracks and continue straight ahead on South Maple, which ends just ahead at the Columbia River. From this street, there are clear views of **Bingen Pond** (east side) and the V-Cove (west side), surrounded by weedy thickets. Purple Martins nest within pylons along the water's edge.

The main attractions are waterfowl and winter sparrows. Fox, Song, Lincoln's, White-crowned, and Golden-crowned are common. Swamp Sparrow is rare but regular. Rarer still are the Sagebrush, Red Fox, White-throated, and Harris's Sparrows. Trumpeter and Tundra Swans, Northern Shoveler, Northern Pintail, Green-winged Teal, Canvasback, Redhead, Ring-necked Duck, and Greater and Lesser Scaups are regular in winter. A Tufted Duck wintered several years running. Lesser Goldfinch can be found here year round and has nested nearby. A trailhead from South Maple Street wraps around the south end of the pond. Willows and cottonwoods can hold an overwintering Red-shouldered Hawk, roosting owls, or migrant passerines in season.

Scan other Bingen Marina backwaters of the Columbia River by returning on South Maple and turning right onto East Marina Way, right again onto South Larch Street, and finally left (east) along East Bingen Point Way to a small park at Bingen Point.

Eastward on SR-14 at milepost 69.5, **Locke Lake** is divided in two by the highway. The southern half hosts flocks of ducks in winter. In migration, the oak forest here can be good for warblers and other passerines. Turkey Vultures soar in circles overhead, an occasional Golden Eagle may be seen overhead, Canyon Wrens sing from the cliff face, and nests of Bullock's Orioles dangle from the oaks. Courtney Road, at the west end of the lake, leads steeply up Burdoin Mountain through oak woodlands and eventually mixed conifer featuring Sooty Grouse near the junction of Atwood Road, Wild Turkey, Say's Phoebe, Western Bluebird, Nashville Warbler, and Lesser Goldfinch. Columbia River views from this road are breathtaking and worth the two-mile drive.

LYLE

At milepost 70.9, the highway bisects **Rowland Lake**, used by wintering waterfowl and loons as well as by breeding Osprey, Red-tailed Hawk, and Peregrine Falcon. California Quail, Lewis's Woodpecker, and Ash-throated Flycatcher frequent the oaks along the shore. Turn left onto Old Highway 8 and drive around the north side of Rowland Lake and east for 1.5 miles to parking for the Catherine Creek Trailhead. This is a paved, all-accessible trail on the north and south sides of the road through approximately 1,000 acres of oak/pine woods, cliffs, Poison Oak thickets, grasslands, basalt cliffs, and vernal ponds, owned by USFS. A trail heads uphill (north) across open slopes, which are ablaze in spring with colorful wildflowers, to a massive basalt arch providing a grand view of eastern Columbia Gorge. Turkey Vulture, Bald Eagle, Red-tailed Hawk, and American Kestrel are noted soarers over the cliffs. The grasslands are alive with Western Kingbirds, Tree Swallows, and Western Bluebirds vying for limited nesting cavities, the dry trill of Chipping Sparrows, the paired notes of Lazuli Buntings, and the melodic song of Western Meadowlarks.

Continue eastward on Old Highway 8, checking the oaks and fields for Lewis's Woodpecker, Western Scrub-Jay, and Lesser Goldfinch. In 1.8 miles, turn left onto Balch Road. Stop at the **Lyle-Balch Cemetery** in 0.4 mile; shrubbery outside the cemetery is prime habitat for Lesser Goldfinch. Also, find singing Lark Sparrows, Lazuli Buntings, and American Goldfinches. Watch Chipping Sparrows collect grass rootlets for its nest. After the cemetery, keep right at the fork in 0.2 mile. Visible from the road a short distance ahead on the right, **Balch Lake** is reliable for Wood Duck and Hooded Merganser. Ash-throated Flycatcher and Lesser Goldfinch nest in the surrounding oak and pine forest. This area is closed to the public to protect a small population of endangered Western Pond Turtles.

Continue about a half-mile back to Old Highway 8. Turn left (east) and stop at the second power pole, about 100 yards from the Balch Road corner (very narrow shoulder; parking on Balch Road is safer). Look one-quarter mile south for a lone Ponderosa Pine snag riddled with holes, an **Acorn Woodpecker granary**. The woodpeckers are often seen on or near the snag—if you are lucky, even flying between it and the woods to the north of Old Highway 8. A scope and patience are requisites for success.

Continue on Old Highway 8 east for 2.0 miles to **Balfour-Klickitat Day Use Area** (see Lyle inset map), a U.S. Forest Service park that is chock full of weedy grassland for hungry Lesser Goldfinches and oak/pine filled with Yellow-rumped Warblers in spring; Osage Orange and Sumac hedgerows block the wind. A trail heading northeast from the parking area leads to a wildlife-viewing nook above a small, protected cove of the Klickitat River, where Bald Eagles congregate in winter and an Anna's Hummingbird maintains a resident territory. During spring and fall migrations, see Cinnamon Teal, Spotted and Solitary Sandpipers, and Greater Yellowlegs at the cove. Near the parking lot and along the paved trail to the south, scope the Klickitat River delta to view large flocks of birds during migration: Common and Red-breasted Mergansers, Double-crested Cormorant, Semipalmated Plover, Sanderling, Baird's Sandpiper, California Gull mixed with other assorted gulls, and Caspian and Common Terns.

In 0.2 mile, Old Highway 8 rejoins SR-14 at milepost 75.7. Turn left, cross the Klickitat River, and in 0.1 mile turn left again onto SR-142. Drive 0.8 mile and turn left into **Lyle County Park** (unsigned). Take the one-lane dirt road that intersects with the Klickitat Walking Trail (signed) and leads down to an overlook of the Klickitat River. Year-round residents of woods and stream include Wild Turkey (most easily seen at dawn), Anna's Hummingbird, Lewis's Woodpecker, Western Scrub-Jay, Bushtit, and White-breasted Nuthatch, joined in summer by Osprey, Spotted Sandpiper, Vaux's Swift, Ash-throated Flycatcher, Nashville, MacGillivray's, and Black-throated Gray Warblers, Western Tanager, Black-headed Grosbeak, and Lesser Goldfinch. Common Goldeneye may be on the river in winter, and Bald Eagle is common at that season. Anna's Hummingbird can also be found by searching for feeders at residences in Lyle.

From the intersection with SR-142, take SR-14 east 0.6 mile and turn right onto 10th Street (milepost 76.5). Drive through the railroad underpass to the tiny **Lyle sewage treatment plant**. In winter, Lesser Goldfinches sometimes forage in weeds near the sewage lagoon, while blackberry thickets on either side of the railway embankment swarm with White-crowned and Golden-crowned Sparrows. West a few hundred yards beyond the lagoon is **Lyle Point** with weedy grassland and river frontage.

Dalles Mountain Road—a marvelous, 22-mile birding route up and over the Columbia Hills—starts near Dallesport and connects to US-97 about a mile north of Davies Pass. Grasslands and fields all along this route host many raptors—particularly in winter, when Northern Harrier, Red-tailed and Rough-legged Hawks, Golden Eagle, and Prairie Falcon are common. The breeding season brings Horned Larks, and Vesper, Savannah, and a few Grasshopper Sparrows to north flanks of the mountain. Try your luck with a Yellow-breasted Chat in the blackberries. Black-billed Magpie makes its first appearance in this part of the gorge.

Turn north onto Dalles Mountain Road from SR-14 at milepost 84.5. In 3.4 miles, turn left onto a steep gravel road, drive 1.4 miles, and park at a gate. Watch for Lewis's Woodpecker and Western Scrub-Jay in the pine/oak woods on the way up, and for sparrows and Lesser Goldfinch in the bramble thickets in winter. You are in the **Columbia Hills Natural Area Preserve** (DNR), set aside in 1993 to protect a 3,593-acre remnant of a type of grassland ecosystem rare in Washington, along with thriving populations of three rare plants (Obscure Buttercup, Douglas's Draba, Hot-rock Penstemon). You can continue up the road on foot to the top of 3,220-foot Stacker Butte (2.3 miles, 1,200 feet elevation gain). Enjoy a panoramic view and keep an eye out for raptors or spring migrants such as a singing Black-throated Sparrow in a Mock Orange shrub. The spring wildflower show is fantastic.

Dalles Mountain Road continues northeastward, slowly climbing the south flank of the Columbia Hills, crossing the crest, and descending toward the Klickitat Valley. In 11 miles, keep left on Dalles Mountain Road as it makes a 90-degree turn to the north, reaching **Centerville** in another 3.0 miles.

A side trip eight miles west on Centerville Highway, then north 0.5 mile on Harms Road to the **Klickitat Rails-to-Trailhead** is a treat, with spring views of Long-billed Curlew, Horned Lark, Vesper Sparrow, and Western Meadowlark. From Harms Road, the trail heads either west (along Swale Creek into Swale Canyon) or east (along Swale Creek toward Warwick).

A right turn onto Centerville Road gets you to US-97 in 4.3 miles. Swales in the Centerville area can hold temporary lakes in spring, excellent for migrant Canada Geese, Tundra Swans, American Wigeons, Mallards, Northern Pintails, and Green-winged Teals. In winter, agricultural fields hold numerous birds-of-prey including Short-eared Owl, especially on overcast or blustery, snowy days.

COLUMBIA HILLS

The Columbia Hills dominate the Washington side of the Gorge for nearly 50 miles, from the Klickitat River to Rock Creek. The river is less than 300 feet above sea level along this stretch, while the high point of the hills is above 3,000 feet. Goldendale and the Klickitat Valley, across the summit, are at an elevation of around 1,600 feet. Headed north on US-97, traction devices may be required in winter between the Gorge and Davies Pass.

SR-14 goes through a pair of tunnels on the eastern outskirts of Lyle. Stop at the small parking area 0.3 mile beyond the east portal of the east tunnel to look for Canyon Wren on the steep cliffs. In winter, Gray-crowned Rosy-Finches can sometimes be found along the railway tracks, feeding on waste wheat blown from the numerous passing trains. Hikers will enjoy the **Lyle Cherry Orchard Trail**, which begins here and climbs steeply more than 1,000 vertical feet to the ridge above the river—the western extremity of the Columbia Hills. Lesser Goldfinches are fairly common along the trail in the breeding season; look also for Western Scrub-Jays. Views of the Gorge are incredible.

The weedy fields around the Maryhill Museum (open March 15 to November 15) are a good place to look for Lesser Goldfinch. The entrance is on the south side of SR-14 at milepost 98.8, two miles west of the intersection with US-97. Still another possibility for this species is **Maryhill State Park** (Discover Pass required). From SR-14, take US-97 south toward Oregon (intersection half a mile east of the one for Goldendale). Turn left into the park in 1.6 miles, just before the Columbia River bridge. Go past the left turn onto Maryhill Highway, which parallels the park's north boundary, to the park entry booth. There are two places you can park from which to explore the park and its brushy surroundings: the graveled area near the entry booth and the day-use parking area 0.6 mile east. This area is a migrant trap in spring and fall. Late fall rarities have included Red-throated Loon, Black-legged Kittiwake, and Lesser Black-backed Gull. Goldfinches are often noted in the weedy growth and trees by the entrance kiosk or in surrounding fields. Look also for diving ducks on the river in winter, especially Barrow's Goldeneye.

Return toward the entry booth, turning right just before reaching it. Turn right onto Maryhill Highway. Drive slowly through the many orchards. This is private land, but you can park at fruit stands or at the historic church at one mile to scan the apricot and peach trees. At two miles, you will be entering U.S. Army Corps of Engineers land on a road that continues for five more miles (1.7 of which are gravel) with many places to stop. Scan the rocks for Rock Wren or the river for waterfowl, loons, and grebes in winter, and Bald Eagle and Osprey. The road follows the river closely until it reaches a copse at 4.8 miles. Trees and brush line the river for a quarter-mile here and are often productive. Pull in and park. Bullock's Orioles nest here, and it's a good place for small passerines in migration.

As you continue east, you will see an island below the dam on which Double-crested Cormorant, American White Pelican, and various gulls may be found when the water is low, summer or winter. Follow the road up the hill past the dismantled aluminum plant 2.2 miles to reach SR-14.

KLICKITAT RIVER

West of Goldendale is the **Klickitat Wildlife Area**, 14,000 acres of rugged canyons, Garry Oak groves, and park-like grasslands interspersed with Ponderosa Pine, Douglas-fir, and Quaking Aspen thickets. These diverse habitats support good populations of gallinaceous birds (California Quail, Chukar, Ruffed and Sooty Grouse, and Wild Turkey). Red-tailed Hawk, Golden Eagle, Lewis's Woodpecker, American Kestrel, American Dipper, Nashville Warbler, and Lark Sparrow are also common. A Discover Pass is required in the wildlife area.

To get there, travel west from US-97 in Goldendale on SR-142 for about 11.5 miles and turn right onto the Glenwood Highway. (Coming up the winding canyon from Lyle, this intersection is on the left in about 24 miles.) Four miles from the intersection, turn left onto Soda Springs Road—a gem and part of the wildlife area. The cottonwood, meadow, and oak/pine woodlands here provide excellent birding: Calliope Hummingbird, Gray and Dusky Flycatchers, Nashville, MacGillivray's, Yellow-rumped, and Wilson's Warblers, Spotted Towhee, Chipping and Golden-crowned Sparrows, Oregon Dark-eyed Junco, Black-headed Grosbeak, and Lazuli Bunting.

Back on the Glenwood Highway, drive 1.3 miles and turn right onto unmarked **Grayback Road** (5.6 miles from SR-142). You can drive north on this dirt road through grasslands and pine/oak groves for slightly more than two miles, where it abruptly deteriorates (keep left at the fork in 0.5 mile). Watch for Gray Flycatcher, especially in the first mile. Western and Mountain Bluebirds nest in boxes along the road, and all three nuthatches and Hermit Thrush can be found in the woodlands. Many other species are present in May and June, including Western Wood-Pewee, House Wren, and Vesper Sparrow. The views of nearby Mount Adams and of Mount Hood in Oregon are memorable, as is the spring wildflower display.

Proceeding westward, the Glenwood Highway soon begins a dramatic descent into the **Klickitat River Gorge**. Lazuli Bunting is common along this stretch as are raptors such as Bald and Golden Eagles and Cooper's and Red-tailed Hawks. Near the bottom of the descent (4.3 miles), turn left (south) onto a gravel road that drops down one mile through stately oaks to primitive **Stinson Flats Campground** (Discover Pass required), where lush growth and the Klickitat River attract diverse birds from Golden Eagle and Spotted Sandpiper to Yellow Warbler and Bullock's Oriole. The river, originating from melting glaciers and snowfields on Mount Adams, is famous for its Steelhead—an anadromous trout with a life cycle similar to that of most salmon.

Continuing toward Glenwood, the road soon crosses the Klickitat River (1.1 miles from the Stinson Flats turnoff). Leidl Campground at this bridge is also a good stop. Here begins the long ascent out of the gorge. An overlook of **Outlet Falls** is reached by driving right from the highway onto an unmarked dirt track (6.2 miles), then along this to another junction (0.2 mile) and right to a parking turnaround (0.1 mile). Walk several hundred feet down to a fenced observation point with spectacular views of the Klickitat River and Outlet Creek. Birds of cliffs and Douglas-fir forest can be found here, including Turkey Vulture, Vaux's Swift, Cassin's Vireo, Violet-green Swallow, Townsend's Warbler, and Western Tanager.

CONBOY LAKE NATIONAL WILDLIFE REFUGE

Conboy Lake National Wildlife Refuge, established in 1964, occupies over 6,500 acres of meadows, marshes, and woodlands in a high basin south of Glenwood. It can be reached via SR-142 and Goldendale-Glenwood Road or via SR-141 and the Trout Lake Highway. The small community of Glenwood sits about six miles west of Outlet Falls, described above. Drive west through Glenwood for about a mile and find Trout Lake Highway on the west side. Turn south here and drive 4.8 miles through Ponderosa Pine forest to the main refuge entrance, on the left at Wildlife Refuge Road. If coming from the west, you will find this entrance on your right about 10 miles east of Trout Lake.

Drive to the refuge headquarters parking lot (1.0 mile). An amazing variety of bird species is present along the two-mile **Willard Springs Nature Trail** loop, especially in May and June. The Ponderosa Pine forest here has White-headed Woodpecker, Gray Flycatcher (Wildlife Refuge Road), Cassin's Vireo, Mountain Chickadee, all three nuthatches, Brown Creeper, Chipping Sparrow, and House and Purple Finches. (Surprisingly, Cassin's Finch is scarce or absent.) Ruby-crowned Kinglet breeds in the Lodgepole Pine forest at the far northern end of the loop. Red-naped Sapsucker, Willow Flycatcher, and Eastern Kingbird are in riparian areas, while Virginia Rail, Sora, Wilson's Snipe, Marsh Wren, Common Yellowthroat, Yellow Warbler, and Savannah Sparrow inhabit the marsh, canal, and wet-grass habitats.

The refuge can be spectacular in spring when large numbers of migrant Canada Geese, Tundra Swans, Mallards, Northern Pintails, and other waterfowl stop to rest and feed in the flooded fields and shallow lakes. Nesting pairs of Greater Sandhill Cranes are a key attraction. Essentially extirpated from Washington as a breeder, cranes first returned to Conboy Lake in 1979—a testimony to the effectiveness of habitat restoration efforts. Look for them from the observation platform on the trail, or with a scope as they feed far out in the open fields. Black Terns may be present over the marsh and wetland fields in the breeding season during some years.

Fields and lakes can be viewed from an observation point at headquarters or by driving the roads that encircle the refuge. The most satisfying view may be from **Kreps Lane Road**. Leaving the headquarters road, turn left onto Trout Lake Highway. In one mile turn left on Laurel Road to Kreps Lane Road (1.4 miles). Turn left and drive about two miles to where it crosses Chapman Creek. Close studies of Greater Sandhill Crane are often possible in this vicinity. A visitor information kiosk provides a cottonwood and birch hotspot at milepost 15.95, BZ-Glenwood Highway to see close-up views of waterfowl, Northern Harrier, Red-breasted Sapsucker, and Tree and Cliff Swallows.

SATUS PASS

Birders connecting between Klickitat country and sites around Yakima will likely travel on US-97 across Satus Pass, situated on the ridge dividing the Columbia and Yakima River watersheds at an elevation of 3,149 feet. From the summit, it is 34 miles north to Toppenish, or 14 miles south to Goldendale. (See map on page 328.)

The combination of habitats on the drive up from Toppenish—from shrub-steppe to riparian to oaks, thence into Ponderosa Pine and finally mixed-conifer forests—boasts many birds. Most of the distance to the pass lies within the closed Yakama Indian Reservation. You must bird from the busy highway. Even so, a stop or two in strategically selected habitats should be productive. Lewis's Woodpecker, Ash-throated Flycatcher, Eastern Kingbird, Bushtit, and Bewick's Wren are among the many breeding species.

At the pass, an unimproved gravel road goes west and uphill. Take the second (larger) of two lefts at the fork in 0.1 mile, then keep right in 1.6 miles. In another 1.8 miles you reach communication towers at a ridgetop with spectacular views of the Cascade volcanoes. The north side of the ridge is forested, while the shallow-soiled south slopes are mostly open—great in spring and early summer for many wildflowers.

Birds possible along the road in summer include Sooty Grouse, Turkey Vulture, Northern Goshawk, Red-breasted and White-breasted Nuthatches, Rock Wren, Nashville, Yellow-rumped, and Townsend's Warblers, Fox Sparrow (especially in Deerbrush), Cassin's Finch, and Red Crossbill. Listen for

Flammulated Owl at night. Williamson's Sapsucker is fairly common, especially in the mixed-conifer forests past the communication towers. The road becomes very rough, however.

Brooks Memorial State Park and campground (Discover Pass required)—2.5 miles south of Satus Pass on US-97—is excellent for breeding birds in Ponderosa Pine forest, riparian groves, thickets, and shrubbery. Look for Cooper's Hawk, Red-naped Sapsucker (Red-breasted is rare), Western Wood-Pewee, Hammond's and Dusky Flycatchers, Cassin's and Warbling Vireos, Brown Creeper, House Wren, Orange-crowned, Nashville, MacGillivray's, Yellow, and Yellow-rumped Warblers, Black-headed Grosbeak, Purple Finch, and Red Crossbill. Gray Flycatcher is reported from the open pines near the power lines.

ROCK CREEK AND LAKE UMATILLA

by Bill LaFramboise and Nancy LaFramboise

revised by Roger Baker and Randy Robinson

Not far east of Maryhill, John Day Dam backs up the Columbia River for 70 miles to form Lake Umatilla (pronounced YOU-muh-TILL-uh). A long ridge known as the Horse Heaven Hills parallels the Columbia to the north, separating it from the Yakima River watershed. Several excellent birding sites in the bottomlands along Lake Umatilla swarm with migrating and wintering waterfowl, attendant Bald Eagles, and other birds of marshes, fields, open water, and brushy tangles. Away from the river, a road up Rock Creek, which drains the Horse Heaven Hills, provides a contrasting and productive habitat supporting Golden Eagle along the cliffs and Ash-throated Flycatcher, Yellow-breasted Chat, and other birds of riparian deciduous woodland and dry, rocky hillside. Be sure to have a full tank before starting up Rock Creek Road, as you will be entering an area with no gas stations.

ROCK CREEK AND HORSE HEAVEN HILLS

About 20 miles east of US-97, at milepost 121.1 on SR-14, turn north onto **Rock Creek Road**. Check the mouth of the creek for waterfowl in winter, Eared Grebe in summer. At 3.8 miles, stay left where Old Highway 8 goes right. Then in 0.4 mile turn right off the main road onto Rock Creek Road. Most of the road is bordered by private property; please respect the numerous signs. Stop to check promising areas of streamside vegetation. Lewis's Woodpecker, Red-eyed Vireo, Yellow-breasted Chat, Lazuli Bunting, and Bullock's Oriole are common during the breeding season. This is a good location for Ash-throated Flycatcher and one of the infrequent places Bushtits can be found east of the Cascades. Townsend's Solitaire is common during winter. Bald Eagle may be found in winter and Golden Eagle year round.

A side trip up Newell Road, on the right in 4.0 miles, provides similar habitats and birding opportunities. Continue north on Rock Creek Road 2.3 miles to a ranch driveway on the left. Just beyond it, Rock Creek Road parallels a particularly inviting half-mile stretch of riparian woodland dominated by White Alder—best birded on foot from the roadway.

Reaching the **Bickleton Highway** (3.1 miles from the ranch driveway), you can turn left for Goldendale (16 miles) and other points west or go right to begin the ascent of the south face of the Horse Heaven Hills to Bickleton. It's 20 miles to Bickleton on this paved road (high point 3,235 feet). Stop along the road at likely spots to inspect Garry Oak, Ponderosa Pine, and grassland habitats for Vaux's Swift, Calliope and Rufous Hummingbirds, Lewis's Wood-pecker, Red-naped Sapsucker and other woodpeckers, Western Wood-Pewee, Gray Flycatcher, Cassin's Vireo, White-breasted Nuthatch, warblers, Western Tanager, and Cassin's Finch. Open areas should have Western and Mountain Bluebirds and Vesper Sparrow. Explore side roads for more blue-bird-viewing possibilities. Additional stops can be made at the Box Springs Road junction in 12.4 miles, and at a bridge in another 6.6 miles where the road crosses Pine Creek; check here for riparian species.

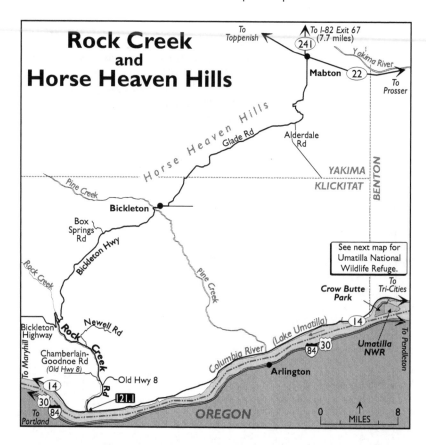

After passing through the small town of Bickleton (no gas, but a tavern serves food), the road makes a 90-degree left turn at the school. Wheat country begins in two miles. Birds to be found in these fields in winter include Rough-legged Hawk, Prairie Falcon, Gray Partridge, Northern Shrike, gobs of Horned Larks, and sometimes a few Lapland Longspurs and Snow Buntings. The road (now known as **Glade Road**) descends the north side of the Horse Heaven Hills, reaching Alderdale Road in 17.6 miles. Keep on Glade Road, descending steeply through vineyards and wheat fields with a few remnants of shrub-steppe and bunchgrass habitat. Be on the lookout for raptors such as Swainson's Hawk and Golden Eagle. Northern Shrikes winter along the route.

The floor of the lower Yakima Valley is reached at Mabton in 8.0 miles. To get to I-82, turn left onto SR-22, go 0.2 mile, then turn right onto SR-241, following it 6.3 miles to Alexander Road. Turn left here, then right in 1.0 mile onto Midvale Road. Find the I-82 interchange (Exit 67) in 0.2 mile.

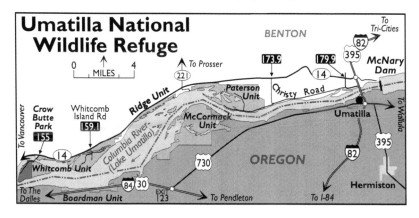

LAKE UMATILLA

The best birding along Lake Umatilla is in its eastern section—the 25 miles or so between Crow Butte Park and McNary Dam. Two outstanding Washington rarities—Magnificent Frigatebird from the tropics and Ross's Gull from the Arctic—were recorded here. The three sites described below are easily accessible and offer a good mix of birds in all seasons.

The entrance to **Crow Butte Park** is on the north side of SR-14 at milepost 155. In winter you may park at the closed gate and walk in. To bird the causeway, park at either end and walk; stopping your car on the causeway is not allowed. Great Egrets (Snowy has been seen), American White Pelicans, gulls, and terns may be present. Virginia Rail and Marsh Wren are here year round, and Swamp Sparrow has been found during the fall. Mudflats appear when the water is low, attracting migrating shorebirds. Raptors include Bald Eagle and an occasional Peregrine Falcon. The lagoon can harbor many waterfowl. An oasis of trees and shrubs, the park itself is an effective passerine migrant trap. Trees regularly host Barn, Great Horned, Long-eared, and (especially in migration) Northern Saw-whet Owls. Long-eareds nest in locusts along the river; be careful not to disturb or attract attention to them.

Umatilla National Wildlife Refuge, established in 1969 as mitigation for habitat lost to flooding when the John Day Dam was built, hosts thousands of ducks and geese in winter. The refuge is a mix of natural and managed wetlands and native shrub-steppe. Areas of the refuge are intensively farmed to provide food and cover for wildlife. Mallard counts reach 300,000, Canada Goose 30,000. Restrooms and drinking water are not available on most areas of the refuge.

To get to the **Whitcomb Unit** from Crow Butte Park, head farther east (right) on SR-14; at milepost 159.1, turn south onto Whitcomb Island Road. Cross the channel (at times mud-lined) to a fork (0.3 mile); explore both roads. Thousands of geese winter here—mostly Canada, but also a few Greater White-fronted and Snow (hundreds of the latter in recent years). Ross's Goose is rare, though perhaps increasing. This is a great place to view Bald Eagles in winter. From late March through June, the fields once hosted many Long-billed Curlews. Burrowing Owls have nested here and may still. Fall can be good for shorebirds along the channel just south of SR-14.

The refuge's **Paterson Unit** is farther east. Return to SR-14, turn right and at milepost 173.9, turn south onto Christy Road. In 3.7 miles, the road crosses the railroad tracks. Make an immediate right turn onto a gravel road. This bumpy (and for one mile very narrow) road parallels the Columbia River. Past the narrow portion, the road widens and there are numerous parking places. Watch for waterfowl, loons, grebes, American White Pelican, Osprey, Bald Eagle, and Caspian and Forster's Terns. In spring, Long-billed Curlews display in the fields to the north.

At 3.8 miles, take the fork to the right. Birds in these fields include Northern Harrier and Western Meadowlark; Mule Deer are common in the Bitterbrush. One mile from the fork, turn into a parking area on the left. A short walk brings you to a slough lined with marsh and riparian vegetation. Look for Greater White-fronted (especially fall) and Canada Geese, Blue-winged and Cinnamon Teal, Redhead, Ring-necked Duck, Lesser Scaup, Common Goldeneye, Ruddy Duck, Eared Grebe (summer and migration), Black-necked Stilt, American Avocet, Solitary and Stilt Sandpipers, Wilson's and Red-necked Phalaropes, and Bonaparte's Gull. The brush is good for Bewick's Wren. The road continues west for another 0.8 mile, ending at Paterson Slough.

Return to the railroad tracks to leave the refuge. If your final destination is west (back the way you came), turn left here; otherwise turn right. It is nearly six miles to Plymouth, where the road turns north, leading almost immediately to SR-14. Turn right and you will reach I-82 in less than a mile.

TRI-CITIES AND VICINITY

by Bill LaFramboise and Nancy LaFramboise
revised by Jane Abel and Keith Abel

The Tri-Cities (Richland, Kennewick, and Pasco) are three neighboring cities located near the confluence of the Columbia, Yakima, and Snake Rivers in a semi-arid region of southeastern Washington. The area receives an average of five to seven inches of precipitation a year and boasts over 300 sunny days. Shrub-steppe communities dominate the landscape and provide habitat for a host of birds, mammals, reptiles, and insects, while the immediate shoreline of the three rivers provides excellent riparian habitat. Together, these two differing habitats offer excellent opportunities for birdwatching in the Tri-Cities. For more Tri-City birding locations and information, visit: www.lowercolumbiabasinaudubon.org.

OUTLYING SITES NEAR THE TRI-CITIES

Rattlesnake Mountain is a treeless, east-west, subalpine ridge reaching 3,600 feet in elevation and is the dominant landform of the lower Columbia Basin. Much of the north face of the mountain is part of the Hanford Reach National Monument with restricted public access; however, the **south slope** is accessible by car on county roads. Although heavily farmed, pockets of shrub-steppe habitat remain, and during nesting season (April through July), you can find Loggerhead Shrike, Sage Thrasher, and Brewer's, Sagebrush, and Grasshopper Sparrows. In winter, search flocks of Horned Larks for Lapland Longspur and Snow Bunting. Rough-legged Hawk, American Kestrel, Merlin, Gyrfalcon (rare), Prairie Falcon, and Northern Shrike are also regular winter visitors.

A tour of the south slope begins near Prosser and returns to Benton City. Be aware that there are no services between Prosser and Benton City. Take Exit 80 from I-82 about 25 miles west of Richland or 45 miles southeast of Yakima. Proceed north on N Gap Road to Johnson Road (0.4 mile) and turn right. Continue for 2.4 miles to Bunn Road and turn left. The marshy areas along the road (0.2 mile) are often good for migrant waterfowl and shorebirds from early to mid-spring.

Continue north along Bunn Road for 0.7 mile and turn left onto King Tull Road. In 1.0 mile turn right onto **Crosby Road**, which begins the ascent of Rattlesnake Mountain. Look for Prairie Falcon, which can be found year round, Ferruginous and Swainson's Hawks, which are seen in spring and summer, and Rough-legged Hawk and Northern Shrike, found in winter. Continue north on paved Crosby Road, following its turns for 6.7 miles. When the pavement curves sharply right, continue straight on graveled Rotha Road to the top. The roadside at this point is flanked by Big Sagebrush; in April through late May, wildflowers such as Thompson's Paintbrush, Columbia Puccoon,

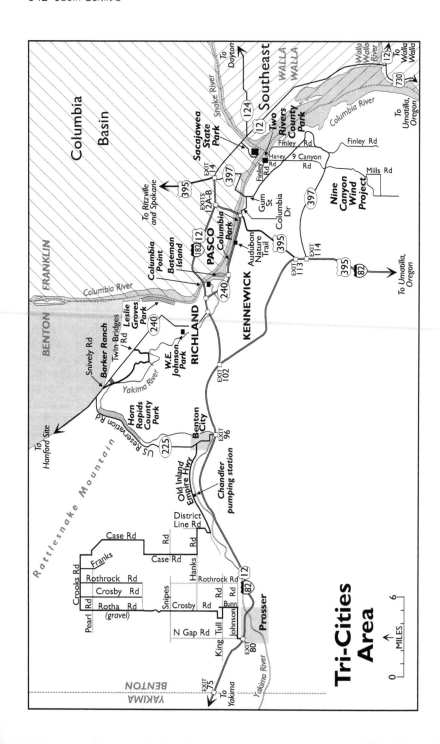

Carey's Balsamroot, Lupine, Fleabane, penstemon, and many others add a brief but colorful display to the shrub-steppe landscape. Look for Gray Partridge, Burrowing Owl, Loggerhead Shrike, Sage Thrasher, and Brewer's and Sagebrush Sparrows. Short-eared Owl and Common Poorwill are possible at dusk.

After passing Pearl Road in four miles, the terrain has more grasses attractive to Vesper and Grasshopper Sparrows. Continue for one mile on Rotha to Crooks Road and turn right. In winter, this is one of the better locations for Lapland Longspur and Snow Bunting, found among large flocks of Horned Larks that frequent the wheat fields. Side trips can be made down Crosby, Rothrock, or Franks Roads through similar habitat.

After traveling 4.0 miles from the junction of Rotha Road, Crooks Road bears to the right, becoming **Case Road**, and descends the mountain. In 10.7 miles, turn left onto Hanks Road. Travel this road for two miles to District Line Road and turn right. After 1.3 miles turn left, heading east, on Old Inland Empire Highway. Look for nesting Red-tailed Hawks, Barn and Great Horned Owls, Prairie Falcon, and Rock and Canyon Wrens on the basalt cliffs. Beware of fast-moving traffic. A good place to view the cliffs is at the **Chandler pumping station** 1.3 miles on the right after turning onto Old Inland Empire Highway. Virginia Rails are usually found in the marsh on the southwest side of the parking lot, and the hillside above the marsh is home to a large colony of Yellow-bellied Marmots.

Old Inland Empire Highway intersects SR-225 in 7.1 miles. Turn left to reach Horn Rapids Park (7.6 miles to entrance) or turn right, traveling through Benton City for two miles, to the I-82 interchange (Exit 96).

Horn Rapids County Park consists of nearly 800 acres of transitional river-to-upland shrub-steppe habitat, located along the Yakima River just west of Richland. After entering the park, take the first left turn and then a right turn to the day-use area. Some of the best birding is around the cottonwood trees near the day-use parking area; however, if time permits, visit the outer areas.

Often seen during spring migration (April–June) are Lewis's Woodpecker, multiple species of flycatchers and warblers, including Yellow-breasted Chat, kinglets, Swainson's and Hermit Thrushes, Gray Catbird, Northern Mockingbird (rare), migrating sparrows, Western Tanager, Lazuli Bunting, and Bullock's Oriole. Great Horned owls frequent the park, and from mid-May until July Common Nighthawks can be found roosting in cottonwood and locust trees. Long-billed Curlews nest (March–June) in the shrub-steppe areas near the park and are frequently seen and heard.

From Horn Rapids Park, take SR-225 north to SR-240 (0.8 mile). Turn right (east) on SR-240 and continue 1.4 miles to Snively Road on the right. Proceed on Snively (past the River Meadow Farm) as the road winds through Barker Ranch to Twin Bridges Road.

Barker Ranch is a private hunting ranch, but birding in this area can be enjoyed from the roadside. Increasing numbers of Sandhill Cranes use the fields as a stopover during spring migration and are often found along Snively or Twin Bridges Roads, from late February through April. The flooded fields and marshy areas also attract small numbers of migrating shorebirds, White-faced Ibis (rare), Wilson's Snipe, Swamp Sparrow (rare), and migrating passerines. Turn left onto Twin Bridges Road, which has narrow shoulders and few pullouts, so use caution. Proceed two miles to return to SR-240.

RIVERSIDE PARKS IN THE TRI-CITIES

Parks and natural areas near the rivers provide opportunities to observe a great diversity of waterfowl, shorebirds, gulls, and passerines. Waterfowl, uncommon inland, turn up here with regularity, including Surf and White-winged Scoters, Long-tailed Duck, and Red-breasted Merganser. The usual shorebirds are Black-necked Stilt, American Avocet, Killdeer, Greater and Lesser Yellowlegs, Dunlin, Spotted, Least, Pectoral, and Western Sandpipers, Long-billed Dowitcher, Wilson's Snipe, and Wilson's and Red-necked Phalaropes. Less common, but regular are Black-bellied, American Golden-, and Semipalmated Plovers, and Solitary, Stilt, Baird's, and Semipalmated Sandpipers. Larids are also seen in large numbers, with the possibility of Parasitic Jaeger and Black and Common Terns in migration.

Several flycatchers, Cassin's and Warbling Vireos, six swallow species, most of the western warblers, and Western Tanager are typical of the many passerine migrants. Birds of special interest seen regularly include Eurasian Wigeon, Barrow's Goldeneye, Clark's Grebe, Sabine's, Franklin's, and Glaucous Gulls, and Peregrine Falcon. The list of Washington rarities recorded in the Tri-Cities over the years is staggering: Garganey, Hudsonian Godwit, Lesser Black-backed Gull, Ovenbird, Northern Parula, Black-and-white, Prothonotary, Blackburnian, Chestnut-sided, Blackpoll, and Black-throated Blue Warblers, Le Conte's Sparrow, and Brambling.

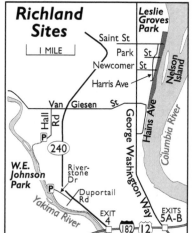

Richland Sites

Leslie Groves Park

1 MILE

Saint St
Park St
Newcomer St
Harris Ave
Van Giesen St
Hall Rd
240
W.E. Johnson Park
River-stone Dr
Duportail Rd
Yakima River
EXIT 4
182 12
George Washington Way
Nelson Island
Hains Ave
Columbia River
EXITS 5A-B

Richland's **W.E. Johnson Park** is a 236-acre undeveloped natural space along the Yakima River, used primarily for horseback riding and archery. The park's extensive wetland, riparian and shrub-steppe habitats offer good birding in all seasons.

There are two entrances to the park. First entrance: Exit SR-240 at Van Giesen Street heading west, travel 0.3

mile, then turn left onto Hall Road. Drive 0.4 mile and park in the archery range parking lot. Second entrance: Exit SR-240 at Duportail Road. Go west 0.1 mile to Riverstone Drive and turn right, then left on Banyon Street and right on Tanglewood Drive. The park entrance is a half-block farther on the left.

Habitats throughout the park attract migrating hummingbirds, flycatchers, vireos, kinglets, warblers, sparrows, and Western Tanagers. Marsh Wren, Wood Duck, and Virginia Rail can be found in marshy areas. Breeding species include Black-chinned Hummingbird, Bewick's Wren, Gray Catbird, Yellow Warbler, Yellow-breasted Chat, Black-headed Grosbeak, and Lazuli Bunting. In winter look for Pacific Wren, Hermit and Varied Thrushes, Bohemian (rare) and Cedar Waxwings, Orange-crowned and Yellow-rumped Warblers, Fox Sparrow, and Purple Finch (rare). The park is also a good place to search for owls: Barn, Western Screech-, Great Horned, Long-eared, and Northern Saw-whet have been found here.

Leslie Groves Park is a long and narrow park with multiple entrances that runs parallel with the Columbia River in north Richland. It is often an excellent place to study winter waterfowl and gulls.

To enter at Park Street, from SR-240 and Van Giesen Street head east on Van Giesen 1.5 miles to George Washington Way. Turn left and continue 0.7 mile to Newcomer Street. Turn right on Newcomer, travel 0.2 mile to Davison Avenue and turn left. In 0.3 mile turn right on Park Street and continue into the park. Additional entrances are at Snyder, Saint, Newcomer, and Hains Streets.

Over 25 species of waterfowl have been recorded in winter, including Canvasback, Redhead, Common and Barrow's Goldeneyes, and Hooded Merganser. Large concentrations of gulls can be found on the north end of nearby Nelson Island in winter, including the more uncommon Lesser Black-backed and Glaucous. Thickets of Russian Olive trees provide food for several species of woodpecker, kinglet, thrush, waxwing, warbler, and sparrow. Bald Eagles, Sharp-shinned, Cooper's, and Red-tailed Hawks, Merlin, and Northern Shrike are also common in winter. Spring and fall bring many passerine migrants.

Bateman Island is located at the confluence of the Yakima and Columbia Rivers. Access to Bateman Island is on foot over a causeway and continues with a very gentle circular trail system running through most of the island. Except in the midsummer heat, this is almost always an interesting place to bird.

From the junction of SR-240 and I-182 (Exit 5A) travel east on SR-240 and continue for 3.2 miles to the Columbia Center Boulevard. Turn left on N Columbia Center Boulevard. Continue 0.4 mile to Columbia Park Trail. Parking for Wye Park and Bateman Island is straight ahead.

Both spring and fall offer a great variety of passerine migrants. Wintering species include Pacific Wren, Hermit and Varied Thrushes, American Tree (rare), Fox, Song, Lincoln's, Harris's (rare), White-crowned, and Golden-crowned Sparrows, and Dark-eyed Juncos.

From the **Wye Park** boat launch (west of Bateman Island causeway), you can continue by foot or car over a very narrow and poorly maintained gravel road for about one mile. The road ends near the Ben Franklin Transit bus depot and the SR-240 bridge over the Yakima River, with plenty of room for vehicle turnaround. From this point, there is a reasonable view of the **Yakima Delta** and mudbars. Over 30 species of waterfowl and 32 species of shorebirds have been recorded here. Unfortunately, there is no predictable way to know if the water level (controlled by dams) will be high or low on any given day. Lower water levels expose mudbars for shorebirds. Sightings have included Marbled Godwit, Red Knot, Ruff, Sharp-tailed Sandpiper, and Red Phalarope—all highly unusual for this area of Washington.

Columbia Park is located east of Bateman Island on Columbia Park Trail and runs parallel with the Columbia River for several miles between Columbia Center Boulevard and US-395.

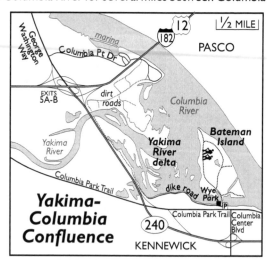

Many waterfowl and gull species, as well as loons and grebes, can be found here in fall and winter. Large flocks of Canada Geese sometimes contain a Greater White-fronted or Snow Goose. Brant and Eurasian Wigeon can often be found in flocks of American Wigeons. The **Dr. Rod Coler Audubon Nature Trail** (approximately two miles east of Bateman Island) is in woody habitat on the south side of the road and attracts many migrating and wintering passerines including Red-breasted Nuthatch, Brown Creeper, Pacific Wren, Golden-crowned Kinglet, Ruby-crowned Kinglet, and Hermit and Varied Thrushes. Bald Eagles frequently roost in the larger trees during winter.

Two Rivers County Park is located near the confluence of the Snake and Columbia Rivers directly opposite Sacajawea State Park and offers a large lagoon for easy waterfowl viewing.

From the junction of US-395 and SR-240, take Columbia Drive (through two traffic circles) into downtown Kennewick and continue east for 1.6 miles to Gum Street (SR-397). Turn right onto Gum Street, which becomes E Chemical Drive. In 1.7 miles turn left onto Finley Road. Two Rivers Park is on the left in 1.5 miles at Glynn Wheeler Lane.

Possibilities here include Greater White-fronted Goose, Eurasian Wigeon, and many species of diving ducks. Surf Scoter and Red-breasted Merganser are rare, but regular in late fall. Check the large groups of gulls for Mew, Thayer's, or Glaucous. The nature trail at the park's east end winds through nice riparian growth and is excellent in migration. Lewis's Woodpecker (spring migration), Brown Creeper, Pacific Wren, and a variety of sparrows have been seen along this trail.

Sacajawea State Park is a 284-acre park at the confluence of the Snake and Columbia Rivers. Although a very busy park in summer, it offers great river viewing, has many riparian areas and offers good year-round birding. Discover Pass required.

From Pasco, drive east on US-12 toward Walla Walla. Just before the Snake River, take a right on Sacajawea Park Road. Continue for one mile and cross the railroad tracks. The park is at the end of the road.

Spring migrants include many species of flycatchers and warblers, Black-headed Grosbeak, Lazuli Bunting, and Bullock's Oriole. Check flocks of American Goldfinches for Lesser Goldfinch. In winter, you can find Red-breasted Nuthatch, Brown Creeper, Pacific Wren, Hermit and Varied Thrushes, Orange-crowned and Yellow-rumped Warblers, and Fox Sparrow. Many species of loon, grebe, and waterfowl are also common in winter, and Bald Eagles roost here in that season. Though facilities are closed in winter, you may walk in.

NINE CANYON WIND PROJECT

The **Nine Canyon Wind Project** is located eight miles south of Two Rivers County Park and is worth the trip during winter months to see Snowy Owls and other interesting birds. At this writing, the road to Nine Canyon is closed for construction, but is expected to re-open in early 2016. Call 509-372-5860 for information.

From Two Rivers Park take E Finley Road west out of the park and turn left on S Haney Road. In 2.4 miles, Haney becomes Nine Canyon Road. Continue 5.7 miles to the top of the hill.

The owls are most often seen in the vicinity of Nine Canyon Road and Mills Road, at times perched directly on the road signs. If time permits, check the nearby fields for Gray Partridge, Lapland Longspur, Snow Bunting, and Gray-crowned Rosy-Finch. Rough-legged Hawk and Gyrfalcon (rare) have also been found in winter.

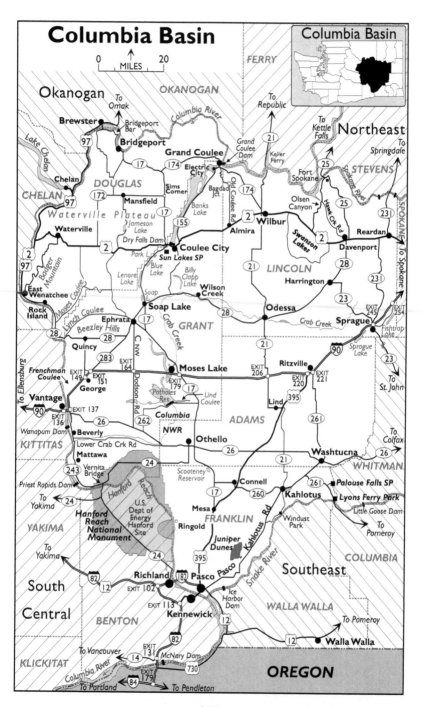

Columbia Basin

0 — MILES — 20

Columbia Basin

Okanogan

To Omak

Brewster

Bridgeport Bar

Bridgeport

97

Columbia River

Grand Coulee

Electric City

174

17

DOUGLAS

Chelan

Lake Chelan

CHELAN

97

172

Mansfield

Sims Corner

Bagdad Jct

Waterville Plateau

Jameson Lake

Waterville

2

Dry Falls Dam

Park Lake

Lenore Lake

Coulee City

Sun Lakes SP

Blue Lake

Billy Clapp Lake

Soap Lake

Wilson Creek

28

Ephrata

17

Beezley Hills

GRANT

Crab Creek

East Wenatchee

2 97

Badger Mountain

Rock Island

28

Moses Coulee

Lynch Coulee

28

Quincy

283

EXIT 164

C NW

Frenchman Coulee

EXIT 149

EXIT 151

George

EXIT 179

Moses Lake

17

Potholes Res.

Lind Coulee

Dodson Rd

To Ellensburg

90

Vantage

EXIT 137

EXIT 136

Wanapum Dam

Beverly

26

262

Columbia NWR

Othello

26

KITTITAS

Lower Crab Crk Rd

Mattawa

243

Vernita Bridge

24

Priest Rapids Dam

To Yakima

24

Scooteney Reservoir

Connell

17

260

YAKIMA

Hanford Reach National Monument

U.S. Dept of Energy Hanford Site

Mesa

Ringold

FRANKLIN

To Yakima

24

Juniper Dunes

Hanford Reach

395

Richland

82

12

EXIT 102

South Central

BENTON

182

Pasco

Pasco

EXIT 113

Kennewick

12

Ice Harbor Dam

82

EXIT 131

McNary Dam

To Vancouver

14

730

84

EXIT 179

To Portland

To Pendleton

Columbia River

KLICKITAT

OREGON

FERRY

To Republic

21

Grand Coulee Dam

Keller Ferry

To Kettle Falls

To **Northeast**

To Springdale

Fort Spokane

25

STEVENS

Olsen Canyon

174

2

Wilbur

Almira

25

Hawk Ck Rd

231

Reardan

Davenport

Swanson Lakes

28

231

LINCOLN

Harrington

21

23

Odessa

Crab Creek

Sprague

EXIT 245

EXIT 254

Fishtrap Lake

90

Sprague Lake

23

Ritzville

EXIT 206

EXIT 220

EXIT 221

395

To St. John

Lind

261

ADAMS

21

Washtucna

261

26

WHITMAN

To Colfax

Palouse Falls SP

Lyons Ferry Park

Little Goose Dam

Kahlotus

Kahlotus Rd

Windust Park

To Pomeroy

Snake River

COLUMBIA

Southeast

WALLA WALLA

To Pomeroy

12

Walla Walla

348

COLUMBIA BASIN

The Columbia Basin of Eastern Washington, as viewed from space, can be likened to the hole in a doughnut, with mountains ringing a roughly circular, generally low-lying plateau. In no other part of Washington is geologic history more evident, largely because so much of it is recent. Sixteen to thirteen million years ago, during the Miocene period, outpourings of lava spread from what is now southeastern Washington and northeastern Oregon to bury the region under multiple layers of dense basalt—the most striking feature of this landscape still today. Beginning about 10 million years ago, volcanic activity shifted westward and built the arc of High Cascades volcanoes, sporadically active to the present. The uplift of the Cascades caused a change in climate as the source of moisture from the ocean very slowly was shut off, determining the Basin's arid shrub-steppe environment. Still more recently—a mere 13,000 or so years ago—dozens of calamitous, southwestward-trending ice-age floods stripped the soils and gouged deep coulees, shaping the unique topography of bare rock and potholes now known as the Channeled Scablands.

Another transformative event has taken place within the lifetime of many readers of this book. In a triumph of engineering on a geologic scale, dams converted the Columbia and the Snake from free-flowing rivers into a series of lakes, and hundreds of thousands of acres of shrub-steppe habitat into irrigated farmlands. Today the Basin is a major producer of grains, hay, potatoes, vegetables, apples, pears, cherries, wine grapes, and hops. Irrigation runoff has raised water tables, filling many formerly dry potholes and creating extensive wetlands. A patchwork of the original shrub-steppe flora and fauna survives, although greatly reduced in extent.

The Columbia Basin is an outlier of the Great Basin ecoregion. Here one may find breeding birds typical of northern Nevada or southeastern Oregon—Greater Sage-Grouse, American White Pelican, Black-necked Stilt, American Avocet, Long-billed Curlew, Burrowing Owl, and Brewer's, Lark, and Sagebrush Sparrows. Wetlands and pothole lakes abound with marshbirds and waterfowl. Fall offers exciting shorebirding and the prospect of a few passerine vagrants at isolated riparian groves. Winter brings many raptors to bare agricultural fields, including Gyrfalcon and Snowy Owl.

The climate of the region is dry and continental. Temperatures climb to 90 degrees and above on 30–45 days in a typical summer and not uncommonly reach the low 100s. The southern Basin is the warmest and driest part. Pasco, at an elevation of 340 feet above sea level, has a July average maximum temperature of 90 degrees and receives just eight inches of precipitation annually. By contrast, Davenport—in the northern Basin at an elevation of 2,400 feet—has a July average maximum temperature of 83 degrees and receives 15 inches of precipitation annually. The north is colder in winter (January average low temperature 14 degrees in Davenport compared to 27 in Pasco) and receives much more snow (average 40 inches in Davenport, eight in Pasco). Wind sometimes makes birding difficult in open terrain in spring, especially in the afternoons. Blowing dust can be annoying. Winter days often are marred by oppressive low clouds and fog. Drifting snow can impede travel in winter in northern areas; elsewhere the roads are occasionally glazed with ice. On the whole, however, Basin roads are well-maintained and travel is trouble-free in any season.

Lodging and services are available in Pasco, Moses Lake, Ephrata, Soap Lake, Coulee City, Electric City, Grand Coulee, Othello, Connell, Wilbur, Davenport, Odessa, and Ritzville.

THE POTHOLES AND MOSES LAKE

by Mike Denny and Andy Stepniewski
revised by MerryLynn Denny

The western Columbia Basin has seen a wholesale conversion from dry shrub-steppe to irrigated cropland. Increased runoff has caused water tables to rise, flooding innumerable potholes and other low-lying spots and creating a diverse, bird-rich mix of habitats. From the Columbia River to Moses Lake, I-90 provides access to cliffs, marshes, lakes, and remnant patches of shrub-steppe, large areas of which are managed by state and federal fish and wildlife agencies. A Discover Pass is required to visit most of these sites.

FRENCHMAN COULEE AND DESERT WILDLIFE AREAS

From Vantage head east across the Columbia River, take Exit 143 from I-90, and turn west on Silica Road. Check marshes and trees around homes for vagrants during migration. Turn left at the first intersection onto Vantage Road SW and look for White-throated Swifts as you travel down into **Frenchman Coulee**. Gray-crowned Rosy-Finches come in to the cliffs to roost on winter afternoons. Say's Phoebes and Rock Wrens are common nesters here. Back at the intersection, turn left on Silica Road and look for Sagebrush Sparrows at 2.0 miles and at 2.5 miles.

Head back under I-90 and take Frontage Road east. In one mile turn right and check **Caliche Lakes** for waterfowl, terns and blackbirds. Continue east past George and turn right into **Martha Lake**, which can be full of waterfowl and terns in April and May. Another nine miles east are the rest area sewage ponds—across I-90 is the **Winchester Wasteway**, reached by crossing over I-90 at the next intersection and heading west on Frontage Road. Look for waterfowl and terns in spring and shorebirds in fall.

From the intersection, head south on Dodson Road about two miles, turn left onto Road I SW and take an immediate right onto the WDFW access road to the **Audubon Dodson Road Nature Trail**. The trail is best in April and May to see the waterfowl courtship displays. Drive another 1.4 miles south on Dodson Road to a large WDFW parking area on the left along Winchester Wasteway. If water levels are low enough, there may be shorebirds working the mudflats.

Proceed a little over six miles to **Frenchman Hills Road** and turn right to "Birder's Corner." Pull off at the small parking lot and check over the marsh. Blue-winged and Cinnamon Teal, Black-necked Stilt, American Avocet and Wilson's Phalarope nest here, and other shorebirds occur in migration.

Head back east on Frenchman Hills Road five miles, turn left on SR-262, and drive 5.6 miles to **Potholes State Park**. A variety of winter waterfowl such as Canada Goose, American Wigeon, Northern Pintail, Bufflehead, Common Goldeneye, Hooded and Common Mergansers, Pied-billed Grebe, and American Coot can be seen here, along with various raptors: Northern Harrier, Sharp-shinned, Cooper's, and Red-tailed Hawks, Bald Eagle, and Merlin. Shorebirds, including both Greater and Lesser Yellowlegs, and Baird's, Least, Pectoral, Semipalmated, and Western Sandpipers, as well as Long-billed Dowitchers, can be seen in August and September. In summer and fall, look for Bonaparte's, Franklin's, Ring-billed, California, and Herring (September–October) Gulls. Caspian and Forster's Terns appear in summer, and Common Terns in August and September. Black Terns may be seen in August and September, but are not common. Both the park and MarDon Resort a mile to the east are great migrant traps and can be good birding anytime of year. Vagrants include Red Knot, Brown Thrasher, Northern Parula, and Common Grackle.

POTHOLES WILDLIFE AREA

O'Sullivan Dam is the south end of Potholes Reservoir, which serves the irrigation needs of the central Columbia Basin. The reservoir and surrounding land comprise the **Potholes Wildlife Area**—32,500 acres of sand dunes, shrub-steppe, and riparian communities. The reservoir can be full of waterfowl fall through spring unless it freezes over. Western and Clark's Grebes nest here. There are only a couple pullouts along the dam. You need a scope to check Goose Island, although Caspian Terns, which used to nest there by the hundreds, have been driven out by wildlife officials seeking to protect salmon.

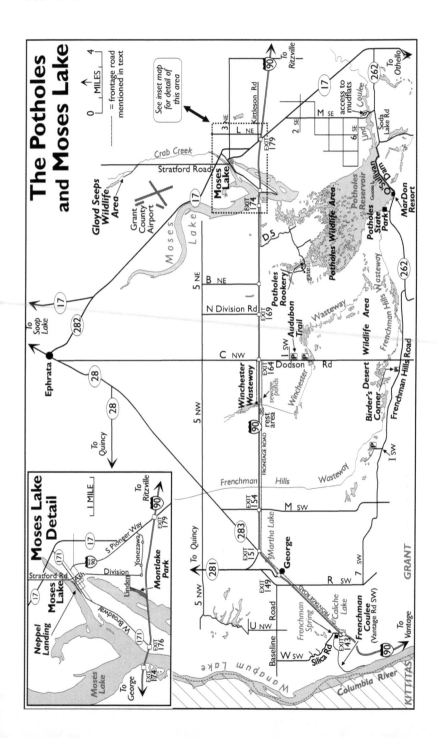

The Potholes and Moses Lake

0 MILES 4

------ = frontage road mentioned in text

See inset map for detail of this area

Gloyd Seeps Wildlife Area

Crab Creek

Stratford Road

Grant County Airport

Moses Lake

To Ritzville

Kittleson Rd

90

17

3 NE

L NE

EXIT 179

2 SE

M SE

access to mudflats

6 SE

Lind Coulee

262

To Othello

Soda Lake Rd

Sullivan Dam

Goose

MarDon Resort

Potholes Reservoir

Potholes State Park

Potholes Wildlife Area

D.5

17

To Soap Lake

282

28

Ephrata

28

To Quincy

5 NE

B NE

N Division Rd

EXIT 169

Potholes Rookery

gate

Wildlife Area

Wasteway

Frenchman Hills Road

262

C NW

Dodson Rd

EXIT 164

1 SW

Audubon Trail

P

P

Winchester Wasteway

sewage ponds

Winchester

Birder's Desert Corner

P

1 SW

Frenchman Hills Wasteway

5 NW

rest area

90

FRONTAGE ROAD

Frenchman Hills Wasteway

EXIT 154

M SW

P

1 SW

To Quincy

283

281

EXIT 151

EXIT 149

Martha Lake

George

R SW

7 SW

GRANT

5 NW

5 NW

U NW

Frenchman Spring

Caiiche Lake

Frenchman Coulee (Vantage Rd SW)

To Vantage

Baseline

W SW

Silica Rd

EXIT 143

90

FRONTAGE ROAD

Wanapum Lake

Columbia River

KITTITAS

Moses Lake Detail

1 MILE

To Ritzville

90

EXIT 179

17

S Pioneer Way

Yonezawa

Montlake Park

Stratford Rd

Division

Linden

Ash

171

Moses Lake

Neppel Landing

W Broadway

171

EXIT 176

EXIT 174

Moses Lake

To George

From MarDon, continue six miles east on SR-262, turn left onto M SE, and go 0.4 mile to **Lind Coulee**. If water levels are low in late summer or fall, this area can be full of shorebirds and waders; it's a good place for Stilt and Pectoral Sandpipers. There is a pullout on both left and right sides of the road (Discover Pass required at both). You can drive up and over the hill and through the riparian area. This is a great area to check any time of year for vagrants; also, winter sparrows may be found here. Just to the northeast is a private residence with many trees where Washington's first Eastern Wood-Pewee spent a few weeks in August 2013 and returned in 2014.

In winter, continue north on M SE and look for Rough-legged Hawk, Snowy Owl, Merlin, Gyrfalcon, Prairie Falcon, Northern Shrike, and, in snowy years, Lapland Longspur and Snow Bunting. From 6 SE up to 2 SE and to both sides of M SE, drive the roads and check the fields and farm implements for perched owls.

The **North Potholes Reserve** is accessed off I-90 Exit 174 just west of Moses Lake. Turn onto S Frontage Road and go west 2.5 miles to Road D.5 (look for green signs reading *Public Fishing* and *Public Hunting*). Turn left and wind through areas of sandy shrub-steppe looking for Burrowing Owl, Loggerhead Shrike, Sage Thrasher, and Lark and Black-throated Sparrows (rare). In the fall, hundreds of American White Pelicans congregate in this area. At a major fork in 2.6 miles, turn right for 1.1 miles to another fork. Angle right and traverse down a steep hill to the edge of the lake, which is lined with large willows. Park where the dike road makes its first turn to the left.

Potholes Rookery to the north is the state's largest wading-bird rookery—estimates include 600 pairs of Double-crested Cormorants, 50 pairs of Great Blue Herons, 60 of Great Egrets, and 300 of Black-crowned Night-Herons. Snowy Egrets have been observed (rare) but there are no breeding records. This area can be full of shorebirds in the fall, and during winter afternoons up to 60 Bald Eagles may come in to roost. Continue on the dike road to the gate, beyond which you can explore the area on foot. The interior race of Bushtit may be found here as well as at Potholes State Park. Make a right back up at the last fork and go south to several pullouts with excellent views of the islands and sloughs. Least Tern was found here in June 2012.

MOSES LAKE

Clark's Grebes (usually with Westerns) may be seen during the nesting season on **Moses Lake** from several waterfront locations including **Montlake Park**. Take Exit 179 from I-90 and go north 0.5 mile. Turn left onto Yonezowa Boulevard, then right at the third roundabout onto Division Street. Go 0.3 mile to Linden Avenue (street sign obscured by tree). The park is down the hill 0.2 mile. Many waterfowl can be seen here from fall through spring.

The **Gloyd Seeps Wildlife Area** can be birdy, especially in spring. At the north end of Moses Lake, head north on Stratford Road. Beginning at 3.5 miles north of SR-17, check for Long-billed Curlews in the shortgrass fields west of the highway; at 7.0 miles from SR-17, turn left to the wildlife area. Trails thread through the marsh and grasslands. Tricolored Blackbirds have been seen here.

Neppel (pronounced *Neh-PELL*) **Landing**, a narrow strip of prime waterfront viewing in downtown Moses Lake, is a good spot to scope waterfowl, including Wood Duck, Canvasback, Redhead, and mergansers. Also of special interest are nesting Western and Clark's Grebes. This city park is a good site for gulls, such as Ring-billed, California, and Herring and occasionally other species. Trees attract migrating warblers. Keep an eye and ear out for Belted Kingfisher and woodpeckers. In winter, the area functions virtually as a refuge, as birds from outlying areas stream in to avoid hunting pressure. Viewing is easy and close on this public walking and biking trail.

To reach Neppel Landing from I-90, take Exit 176 signed for Moses Lake. At the end of the freeway ramp, head north on SR-171 (aka West Broadway Avenue) 2.6 miles to S Ash Street. Turn left onto Ash; a parking lot is on the right a short distance ahead.

Leaving the park, you can retrace your steps to I-90 and head east for Spokane or west for Ellensburg and Seattle. Or you can continue north on SR-171 (Broadway) about a mile to a junction with SR-17. Turn left for Ephrata (18.6 miles), right for Othello (26 miles).

LOWER CRAB CREEK AND OTHELLO

by Randy Hill, Bob Flores, and Andy Stepniewski,
Bill LaFramboise, and Nancy LaFramboise
revised by Randy Hill

Crab Creek originates near the Spokane-Lincoln County line between Cheney and Davenport and merges into Moses Lake and the Potholes Reservoir. Formerly an intermittent stream, it now flows yearlong thanks to runoff from the Columbia Basin Irrigation Project. Lower Crab Creek—the stretch below O'Sullivan Dam—supports fall Chinook Salmon and Steelhead. Bending westward from the dam, the stream reaches the Columbia at Beverly, about eight miles south of the Vantage bridge. Lower Crab Creek Road follows the creek through rocky coulees, seep lakes and marshes, steppe-sagebrush, and encroaching irrigated fields and orchards. To the north are the low Frenchman Hills and to the south the Saddle Mountains—a basalt ridge system that rises abruptly some 2,000 feet above the surrounding plateau. Sizable chunks of wetland and shrub-steppe habitats along Lower Crab Creek are protected in state wildlife areas and a federal wildlife refuge. A good selection of Columbia Basin birds may be found here and in the agricultural lands around Othello *during the appropriate seasons. The spring migration of Sandhill Cranes is outstanding.*

VANTAGE BRIDGE TO BEVERLY

SR-26 heads south along the Columbia River from the I-90 interchange at the east end of the Vantage bridge. At the junction in 0.9 mile, where SR-26 heads east toward Othello, turn right onto SR-243 (marked Yakima/Richland). Several good birding stops await you on the short drive down to Beverly, where Lower Crab Creek Road turns off. The first is in 0.2 mile at a pullout on the right above **Wanapum Lake**. Sea ducks such as scoters or Long-tailed Duck have been seen here in migration, while waterfowl in fall and winter usually include many Greater Scaup. Winter flocks of Gray-crowned Rosy-Finches sometimes forage in weedy vegetation near the shoreline or across the highway to the east, below the cliffs.

Continue south on SR-243 to a road on the right at **Wanapum Dam** (3.5 miles). This road immediately doubles back 0.3 mile to a cove signed *Wanapum Dam Upper Boat Launch* (vault toilet); you may find bay ducks, loons, and grebes here. Return to SR-243, turn right, and in 0.3 mile turn off to the interpretive center below the dam. During July and August, Sockeye and Chinook Salmon pass through ladders and are visible at close range in the viewing room. Forster's Terns forage along the river.

Southbound once more on SR-243, turn right in 1.1 miles onto a gravel track (hard-packed and passable for ordinary vehicles). Park in 0.4 mile, where this track joins another that parallels the river. The strip of riparian growth in both directions is often filled with migrants. Waterfowl, loons, and Osprey frequent the river. Desert Buckwheat and various biscuitroots dominate the spring wildflower display on the cobbles and sandy terrain up from the riparian zone. Drive south (downstream) on the cobble track to rejoin SR-243 in 1.0 mile, a mile north of the old railroad bridge across the Columbia.

LOWER CRAB CREEK ROAD

Lower Crab Creek Road (aka Road 17 SW) turns east from SR-243 about a quarter-mile south of the railroad-bridge underpass at Beverly. Opposite this intersection, along the river, Townsend's Solitaires are regular from fall through spring in a small grove of Rocky Mountain Junipers. Burkett Lake Recreation Area (parking, toilet), on the south side of Lower Crab Creek Road 1.6 miles east of the intersection, often has diving ducks and waterbirds.

For the next 25 miles the road follows Crab Creek along a series of wide scabland channels at the base of the Saddle Mountains. This scenic route features wetlands, shrub-steppe, and cliff habitats, significant portions of which are set aside in the 17,000-acre **Lower Crab Creek Unit** of the Columbia

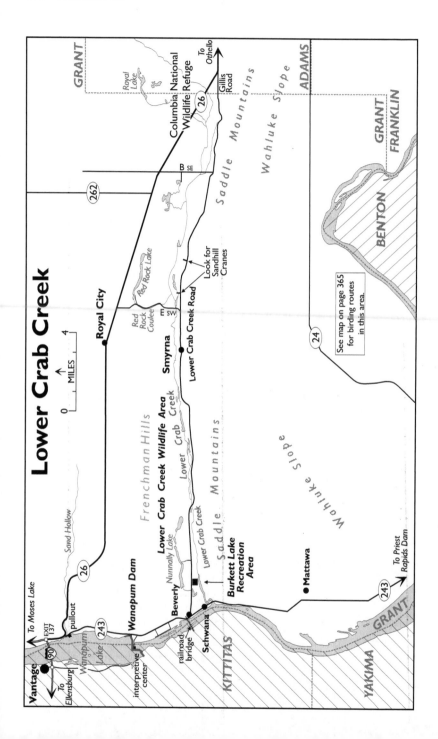

Lower Crab Creek

Basin Wildlife Area. A short spur on the left (north) side of the road, 2.8 miles from SR-243, leads to a small parking area (Discover Pass required) and trailhead for **Nunnally Lake**—a popular fly fishing and waterfowl hunting site within the wildlife area. The half-mile trail north to the lake passes through dense Russian Olive groves where Long-eared Owls roost in winter and nest in early spring. American Robins and Yellow-rumped Warblers can be abundant here in the same seasons. Look among them for a few individuals of less-common species (Townsend's Solitaire, Hermit and Varied Thrushes). Also check for wintering sparrows, especially at edges and openings where the grass is thick. The trail emerges from the thickets and crosses rocky ground with scant shrub-steppe vegetation, soon reaching an overlook of a chain of lakes set deep in an old coulee. Redheads and other diving ducks are common here, but skittish. Rails, orioles, and other marsh and riparian birds inhabit lake-edge vegetation in the nesting season. You may see a Prairie Falcon along the basalt cliffs or hunting over the open landscape.

Continue east on Lower Crab Creek Road, which quickly becomes gravel (0.2 mile). Power lines attract raptors all year long, including Golden Eagles. Migrant songbirds and breeding Eastern Kingbird, Lazuli Bunting, and Bullock's Oriole can be found at wet spots with willow growth. The road crosses Crab Creek (2.6 miles) and hugs the base of the Saddle Mountains. Check the cliffs for nesting Red-tailed Hawk, Great Horned Owl, White-throated Swift, American Kestrel, Prairie Falcon, and many Cliff Swallows. The bright green shrub along the valley floor is Greasewood, tolerant of alkaline soils. This is excellent habitat for Loggerhead Shrikes, which breed here rather commonly (uncommon in winter, when mostly replaced by Northern Shrikes).

At the community of **Smyrna** (7.8 miles), check the larger trees for migrants and wintering blackbirds. East of Smyrna look for shrub birds and for Barn and Great Horned Owls nesting in the low rock outcrops. In 1.5 miles, check the junipers and shrubs planted along the road. At the next junction (1.1 mile), turn east to stay on Lower Crab Creek Road. Two likely spots to look for Sandhill Cranes in late March and April are at 1.0 and 2.3 miles. In another 1.2 miles (3.5 miles from Road E SW), the road starts a steep climb through rocks where Great Horned Owl, Say's Phoebe, and Rock Wren are found.

From here to the next junction is a landscape of shrub-steppe (Loggerhead Shrike, Lark and Sagebrush Sparrows) alternating with open grasslands (Long-billed Curlew, Horned Lark). This stretch is excellent at night for Barn, Great Horned, and Long-eared Owls, Common Nighthawk, and Common Poorwill. At the fork in 3.8 miles, jog left on Road B SE (aka Corfu Road) to the Crab Creek crossing in 0.6 mile. Swales here can be profitable for waterfowl or shorebirds, depending on the season.

The next 2.4 miles of this road up to the intersection with SR-26 border the Corfu Unit of Columbia National Wildlife Refuge, a reliable winter location for Rough-legged Hawk, Prairie Falcon, Northern Shrike, and American

Tree Sparrow. Huge flocks of geese (sometimes five species), ducks, and Sandhill Cranes use the cropland in March and early April, and the activity at sunset can be spectacular. A willow woodland about 200 yards south of the intersection, to the east, is excellent for migrant songbirds (and often Lewis's Woodpecker) in May and for breeders such as Swainson's Hawk, Great Horned Owl, Eastern Kingbird, House Wren, Lazuli Bunting, and Bullock's Oriole. This unit is open to bird hunting October–January and closes during the spring crane migration.

Return to Lower Crab Creek Road and continue east; look for Chukar (upslope), Loggerhead Shrike, and Lark Sparrow in the first three miles of shrub-steppe habitats. Ferruginous Hawk and Prairie Falcon may be near a small colony of Washington Ground Squirrels that still survives in this vicinity. Irrigated pastures to the north have curlews and snipe in the nesting season, and other shorebirds during spring and fall migration. Cranes often use the area as a day roost in March and April.

Lower Crab Creek Road becomes **Gillis Road** at the Adams County line, where there is a cattle guard (4.6 miles from Road B SE). East along Gillis Road, cornfields and pastures have Sandhill Cranes in spring, and the cattail marsh to the north has Virginia Rail, Wilson's Snipe, Marsh Wren and blackbirds. Gillis Road ends in about a half-mile at an intersection with SR-26, eight miles west of Othello.

COLUMBIA NATIONAL WILDLIFE REFUGE

Extending nearly 10 miles south from Potholes Reservoir, the flood-carved **Drumheller Channels** offer some of the most rugged scablands terrain in the state. Seepage fills the lowest spots, creating innumerable lakes and small wetlands now mostly protected in a patchwork of public ownership—principally the 23,200-acre core area of Columbia National Wildlife Refuge and the WDFW's Seep Lakes/Goose Lakes units of the Columbia Basin Wildlife Area (8,423 acres). An excellent auto tour gives access to lake, shrub-steppe, cliff, and riparian habitats attractive to Columbia Basin birds. This route is especially good in spring when throngs of waterfowl are present. Certain areas are gated and closed during the winter months (October through February). Visit the web site *http://www.fws.gov/columbia* for current regulations.

To enter the refuge at the north entrance, turn south from O'Sullivan Dam Road onto Soda Lake Road (eventually becomes Morgan Lake Road). This turnoff is 5.0 miles east of the entrance to Potholes State Park and is opposite a WDFW parking area and boat ramp. As you travel south toward Soda Lake, keep an eye out for American Kestrel, Black-billed Magpie, and Western Meadowlark. Check the large patch of willows on the left (1.5 miles) for Great Horned and Long-eared Owls.

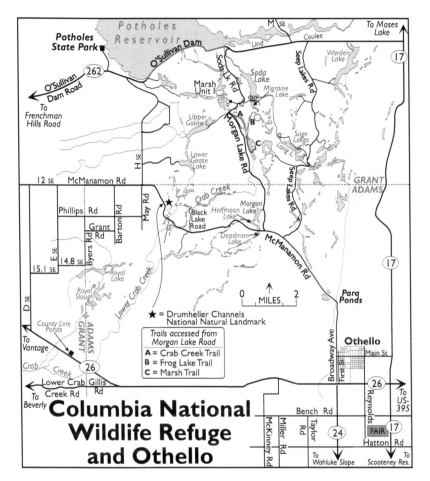

Continue to the **Soda Lake Dam** turnoff (0.7 mile), take a left, and drive onto the dam (0.2 mile). Look for Common Merganser, Common Loon, grebes, and American White Pelican. **Migraine Lake**, below the dam on the right, is part of the sanctuary closure, but it is easily viewed from the road. It often holds large numbers of American Wigeons (good chance for Eurasian in March) and diving ducks. Shorebirds can often be found along the lake edge, and Rock and Canyon Wrens on the rocks. Bonaparte's and occasionally Franklin's Gulls are here during summer and fall, and Sabine's Gull has appeared several years in September.

Go back to Soda Lake Road, turn left, then right at the next fork (0.2 mile). Stop at the parking area on the left just before the closed gate (0.2 mile). Scope **Marsh Unit 1** from this overlook, or take a short walk down to the wetlands for closer views of waterfowl, grebes, American Bittern, Great Blue

Heron, Great Egret, Black-crowned Night-Heron, and shorebirds. Greater White-fronted Goose and Sandhill Crane are likely in early spring, but entry to this crane roost area is closed from February to April. Rarities here have included Baikal Teal, Green Heron, and Sharp-tailed Sandpiper. The area is hunted October–January.

Return to the main road and turn right. Continue down the hill to the **Crab Creek Trail** (0.4 mile) and turn left into the parking area. This mile-long trail (winter closure) follows the floodplain through willows and shrub sandwiched between shrub-steppe and cliffs; it loops back, but an extension continues south to meet the two trails mentioned below. Birds expected include California Quail, Northern Flicker, Eastern Kingbird, five species of swallows, Rock, Marsh, and Bewick's Wrens, migrant kinglets and warblers, Yellow-breasted Chat, Song Sparrow, Lazuli Bunting, and Bullock's Oriole. American Tree Sparrow is often found in winter in shrubs along the creek.

Coming out of the parking area, turn left, cross Crab Creek, then follow the road to the left and continue 1.1 miles to the parking area for the Frog Lake and Marsh Trails, on the right. While driving, watch for Ferruginous Hawk and Violet-green, Northern Rough-winged, Cliff, and Barn Swallows. The trailhead and kiosk with map are across the road from the parking lot. **The Frog Lake Trail**—two miles (round trip) of spectacular scenery, plus a one-mile loop extension beyond Frog Lake (now dry) that is closed in winter—takes you through shrub-steppe, wetland, and riparian habitats, up to a plateau overlooking the Pillar-Wigeon chain of lakes. American Bittern might be heard along Crab Creek as you work your way to the top of the trail; look also for waterfowl, Common Nighthawk, Rock and Canyon Wrens, Lark and Savannah Sparrows, and Bullock's Oriole.

The 1.5-mile **Marsh Trail** (winter closure) turns right after crossing the creek and makes a loop through riparian and wetland habitats (the latter may dry up in summer). Birds noted on this trail include waterfowl, Great Blue Heron, Great Egret, White-faced Ibis (rare), Black-necked Stilt, American Avocet, other shorebirds, Eastern Kingbird, Song Sparrow, and blackbirds.

Continue south on this road (which soon becomes Morgan Lake Road) and stop at the north end of **Morgan Lake** in 2.8 miles. Listen for American Bittern (early and late in the day), Virginia Rail, and Rock and Canyon Wrens, and watch for Red-tailed Hawk, Barn Owl, Prairie Falcon, and Say's Phoebe. Wilson's Snipe often can be heard winnowing above the adjacent pasture in spring. The Columbia National Wildlife Refuge office and visitor center (51 N Morgan Lake Road) are east of the road and open weekdays when staff or volunteers are present.

At McManamon Road, you can turn left to reach Othello (route described in reverse, pages 362). If you turn right instead, in 0.2 mile you reach two deep lakes straddling the road: **Halfmoon Lake** (north) and **Deadman Lake** (south). Park east of the guard rail. Ring-necked Duck, Bufflehead, Common Goldeneye, and Hooded and Common Mergansers are some of the expected ducks on these lakes; look closely for Barrow's Goldeneye. Watch also for Virginia Rail and Marsh Wren around Halfmoon Lake and scan the surrounding cliffs for Prairie Falcon.

Continue west on McManamon Road, scanning for Long-billed Curlew, American Kestrel, Loggerhead Shrike, and Rock Wren. In 2.7 miles, look for unmarked **Black Lake Road** on the right (closed in winter). If the gate is open, drive through the coulees to the end of the road in one mile, admiring the spectacular columnar basalt. Take the footbridge across Crab Creek. Trails to the left (one mile long) and to the right (two miles long) through the narrow, rock-rimmed canyon offer a good variety of birds—some of them not found along McManamon Road. In the cliffs look for nesting Red-tailed Hawk, Barn and Great Horned Owls, American Kestrel, and Say's Phoebe, and listen for Rock and Canyon Wrens. Migrant warblers can be found in riparian habitat along Crab Creek, and Common Yellowthroat nests here. Eastern Kingbird, Marsh Wren, Spotted Towhee, Song and White-crowned (especially April and September) Sparrows also occur. All of the Columbia Basin swallows normally can be found flying around the canyon. The wetland impoundments and creek will produce a variety of waterfowl (including Wood Duck), Virginia Rail, Sora, and Belted Kingfisher.

Go back out to McManamon Road, turn right, cross over Crab Creek, and drive to the overlook at **Drumheller Channels National Natural Landmark** (1.7 miles). Look for Northern Harrier, Caspian Tern, various swallows, and Lazuli Bunting. Continue to May Road/Road H SE (1.1 miles); here the road signs display a letter/number grid for Grant County (north side of road) and family names for Adams County (south side of road). Turn right here to return to O'Sullivan Dam Road, at the west end of the dam, in about five miles. While en route, watch for Say's Phoebe, Western and Eastern Kingbirds, Horned Lark, Lark Sparrow, and Western Meadowlark in the shrub-steppe habitat. Or by continuing straight ahead on Road 12 SE, you can reach Royal Lake and other birding sites, connecting to SR-26 west of Othello.

OTHELLO AND VICINITY

Within a short distance of Othello one can find deep, shallow, and saline lakes and wetlands, riparian habitats, grasslands, shrub-steppe, rock outcrops, and irrigated agricultural fields—all with a complement of characteristic birds. In migration, birds find the town's urban habitats a good stop-off. Areas with conifers include Kiwanis Park (S Fifth and Sixth Avenues) and the cemetery (E Cemetery Street off 14th Avenue). The cemetery may have nesting Great Horned Owls and, sometimes, wintering Northern Saw-whet Owls.

Sandhill Cranes can be abundant in March and April, when thousands of birds pause to feed on waste corn in the fields south and west of Othello. This spectacle spawned the Sandhill Crane Festival, held annually at the end of March. Bus trips, other field trips, guest speakers, and exhibits draw thousands of visitors to this weekend event organized by the US Fish and Wildlife Service and local volunteers. Lesser numbers of cranes occur during fall migration.

McKinney and Bench Roads, which intersect about a mile south and two miles west of Othello, are a good place to look for Sandhill Cranes. About nine miles west of town SR-26 crosses Crab Creek. Pull off on the right side of the highway in another 0.7 mile before a guard rail. Saline County Line Ponds to the north have breeding shorebirds (Black-necked Stilt, American Avocet, Killdeer, Spotted Sandpiper, Wilson's Phalarope). When the ponds hold water, many migrant shorebirds can usually be found here from July into September, including Baird's and Semipalmated Sandpipers. The larger wetland south of the highway has fewer shorebirds but a greater variety of waterfowl, a crane roost some years, and occasionally a flock of American White Pelicans. A short distance west of the ponds, at milepost 30, another, larger crane roost is south of the highway. It is quite far out—you will need a scope. Be careful with traffic on SR-26!

Continue west on SR-26 to Road D SE (1.6 miles from the ponds) and turn right. Go north for two miles, watching for curlews, then turn right onto Road 15.1 SE. Sandhill Cranes and curlews are often found south of this road. In one mile, the road you are on curves north and becomes Road E SE. Check the refuge field to the east, where cranes and large flocks of geese (occasionally five species) feed from October to April. In 0.3 mile turn right (east) onto Road 14.8 SE. Stop at an overlook of **Royal Lake** (1.0 mile). Thousands of waterfowl winter on the lake, peaking at 40,000 to 50,000 birds in some years.

To connect to the Columbia National Wildlife Refuge auto tour or to loop back to Othello from the northwest, go north on Byers Road 1.7 miles, then right on Phillips Road to Barton Road (1.0 mile), watching for cranes and curlews. Both dark- and light-morph Harlan's Red-tailed Hawks have been seen here in winter. Continuing left for one mile, then right on McManamon Road (aka Road 12 SE) for one mile, brings you to the corner of Road H SE and McManamon Road. It's about 10 miles on McManamon to Othello.

Along the west edge of downtown Othello, Broadway heads north, becoming McManamon Road as it crosses the railroad tracks near potato-processing plants. Spilled grain from transport trucks attracts hordes of blackbirds along the shoulder before the road starts down the hill. Just beyond a couple of potato sheds at the bottom of the descent are the **Para Ponds** (2.5 miles from the corner of Broadway and Main in Othello), one of the great birding spots in the Columbia Basin. Traffic moves fast here; do not park or stand in traffic lanes. During winter and migration, one can find large numbers of waterfowl, including Trumpeter and Tundra Swans, Eurasian Wigeon, Greater Scaup, and Common and Barrow's Goldeneyes along with the commoner species. Thousands of Arctic-nesting geese fatten up in the fields to the north of the ponds during their late-winter and spring migration; scanning these flocks may produce five species. During spring and summer, this wetland is a showy place, with Blue-winged and Cinnamon Teal, Ruddy Duck, Black-necked Stilt, American Avocet, Marsh Wren, and four species of blackbirds including Tricolored (rarely breeding). American Bittern nests here, and this is one of the more reliable locations in Washington to see White-faced Ibis, usually in May. The fall shorebird migration typically has 10–12 species, with rarities that include Hudsonian Godwit, Sharp-tailed Sandpiper, and Ruff. Past the ponds, the cattle pens are the most reliable location in Washington to find wintering Tricolored Blackbirds. Heading west keep an eye out for Long-billed Curlew, Say's Phoebe, Common Raven, Lark Sparrow, and Western Meadowlark from spring through early summer in the surrounding shrub-steppe habitats. McManamon Road joins Morgan Lake Road and the Columbia National Wildlife Refuge auto tour in about three miles (page 359).

Ring-necked Pheasant, Northern Harrier, Swainson's and Red-tailed Hawks, Long-billed Curlew, American Kestrel, Black-billed Magpie, Horned Lark, Red-winged, Yellow-headed, and Brewer's Blackbirds, Western Meadowlark, Brown-headed Cowbird, House Finch, and American Goldfinch are common on the farmlands around Othello. Gyrfalcon is usually reported at least once each winter from the agricultural lands to the south and east of town, especially around the Adams County Fairgrounds. Burrowing Owls are traditionally found at the edges of fields north of SR-26 along Lemaster and Booker Roads (east of SR-17) and north of Sutton Road (west of SR-17) — more commonly in spring and summer, although a few overwinter. Short-eared Owls winter in this same area and are best found near dawn and dusk.

Scooteney Reservoir, southeast of Othello, can be a worthwhile stop, and offers one of the best viewing areas of a Sandhill Crane roost during the spring migration. Take SR-17 to Coyan Road (about nine miles south of SR-26 or four miles north of SR-260). Turn west onto Coyan Road, parking on the left just after crossing the Potholes Canal (0.5 mile). Walk along the dike to view waterfowl and shorebirds on the reservoir to your left and the field and marsh on your right. To reach the main reservoir access, return to SR-17 and turn right, then right (west) again in 1.4 miles at the sign. Waterfowl can be

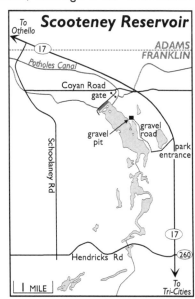

Scooteney Reservoir

abundant in winter. From late February through March, when low reservoir levels expose an extensive mudflat formed by decades of irrigation water delivery, several hundred to over 2,000 Sandhill Cranes visit the reservoir and the surrounding farmland (smaller numbers in fall). To view the roost, take the right fork (gravel) and continue another 0.5 mile beyond the residence to an old gravel pit. Trails west offer elevated views of the delta mudflat. The shorebird migration (stronger in fall) brings Black-bellied Plover, both yellowlegs, Dunlin, Least, Pectoral, and Western Sandpipers, and Long-billed Dowitcher. Great Egret and American Pipit are sometimes present in fall migration. For another birding opportunity, try the ponds 1.2 miles west of the SR-17/SR-260 intersection along Hendricks Road.

SOUTHERN COLUMBIA BASIN

by Bill LaFramboise, Nancy LaFramboise,
Mike Denny, MerryLynn Denny, and Bob Flores
revised by MerryLynn Denny

A significant expanse of Columbia Basin landscape survives in a near-natural state, from the crest of the Saddle Mountains south to the Hanford Reach—the last free-flowing stretch of the Columbia River between the Bonneville Dam and Canada. In this magnificent setting birders may find species characteristic of arid grasslands, steppe-sagebrush, and streambanks. By contrast, dams along the lower Snake River have eradicated the original canyon-bottom habitats. Nonetheless, there are several important birding sites along the Snake and especially a few miles farther north. Washtucna, Palouse Falls State Park, and Lyons Ferry Park are migration hotspots.

SADDLE MOUNTAINS AND HANFORD REACH

In 2000, the **Hanford Reach National Monument** (195,000 acres) was created to permanently protect the former buffer zone around the top-secret Hanford Site, which had remained in a relatively undisturbed state. Parts of the monument along the north and east shores of the scenic Hanford Reach are open to the public. Saddle Mountain National Wildlife Refuge, which was established in 1953 and has no public access, was incorporated into the Hanford Reach National Monument. The shrub-steppe community making up the refuge is one of only two large blocks of this habitat remaining in the state.

To explore the **Saddle Mountains**, northeast of Yakima, travel east on SR-24 from its junction with SR-243 for 16.5 miles and turn north onto the unsigned gravel road east of milepost 60. Look for Loggerhead Shrike and Lark and Sagebrush Sparrows in the shrub-steppe and Long-billed Curlews in

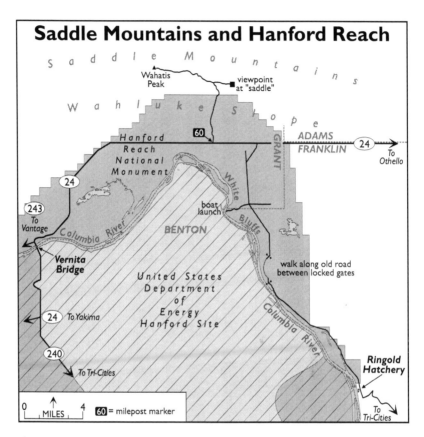

Saddle Mountains and Hanford Reach

S a d d l e M o u n t a i n s

Wahatis Peak

viewpoint at "saddle"

W a h l u k e S l o p e

Hanford Reach National Monument

60

GRANT

ADAMS

FRANKLIN

24

To Othello

243

To Vantage

Columbia River

Vernita Bridge

boat launch

White Bluffs

BENTON

walk along old road between locked gates

24 To Yakima

United States Department of Energy Hanford Site

Columbia River

240

To Tri-Cities

Ringold Hatchery

0 ↑ MILES 4   **60** = milepost marker

To Tri-Cities

the grassy areas. The road forks in 4.2 miles; turn right and drive along the crest of the ridge to a viewpoint (1.2 miles). Look for Chukar and Gray Partridge, raptors, Rock and Canyon Wrens, and Gray-crowned Rosy-Finch late fall through early spring. Prairie Falcon nests here most years.

Continue east on SR-24 for 2.8 miles and turn right onto an unsigned, partially paved road that gives access to the north portion of the **Hanford Reach**. Check riparian areas for vagrants during migration; Brown Thrasher has been seen here. Turn right at the four-way intersection and continue to the boat launch on the Columbia River. Check for waterfowl, gulls, and terns. Bank and Cliff Swallows nest in abundance on the **White Bluffs**.

Ringold and southern parts of the Hanford Reach are most easily visited from the Tri-Cities. In Pasco, take Road 68 north from I-182 (Exit 9) and bear right as it merges into Taylor Flats Road in 2.5 miles. Continue north 13.3 miles and turn left onto Ringold Road. In three miles, turn left again (sharply), following Ringold Road another 0.8 mile to a T-intersection. Turn right on Ringold River Road (gravel), then left onto one of three roads that lead to the

Ringold Fish Hatchery and Columbia River. Park and walk to observe hatchery ponds. Check the river (Snowy Egret was seen here). The Russian Olive trees can be very birdy during migration, and Bullock's Orioles nest here. Continue north on Ringold River Road, stopping at pullouts where you can reach the river. The road is closed by a gate in about eight miles—continue on foot.

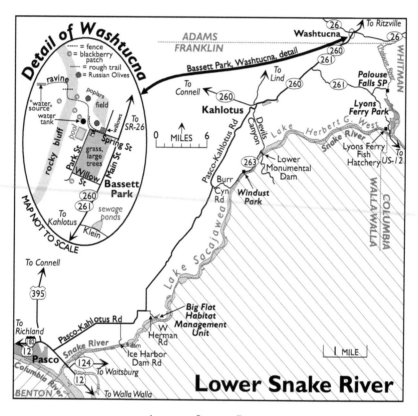

LOWER SNAKE RIVER

The lower Snake River—made famous in the annals of Lewis and Clark two centuries ago—has been tamed by four major dams, drowning the canyon bottoms beneath reservoirs over virtually its entire course. Although the canyon walls retain much of their natural character, most of the surrounding uplands are converted to agriculture. A number of birding sites are accessed by county roads and state highways paralleling the Snake River northeast from Pasco. Many other sites lie along the opposite bank of the river in the Southeast (page 498).

The Pasco-Kahlotus Road takes off to the northeast from US-12 just east of Pasco. In 13 miles turn right on W Herman Road (gravel) to **Big Flat Habitat Management Unit**. Park and walk across the causeway to explore 600 acres of plantings—mitigation for habitat destroyed by dams. Birding is best during migration and winter when many sparrows, thrushes, and possibly owls can be found. Use caution during hunting season.

Continuing northeast on Pasco-Kahlotus Road, turn right in 16.8 miles onto Burr Canyon Road and head down to **Windust Park** (five miles). This spot also stands out for migrants: Variegated Flycatcher found here in 2008, Yellow-bellied Flycatcher in 2009, and Black-and-white Warbler in 2007. In winter, it excels in owls. Watch for rattlesnakes May through September.

Continue east on SR-263 for 3.1 miles to Lower Monumental Dam; check for gulls any time of year. The highway turns and enters **Devils Canyon**. Here, look for Rock and Canyon Wrens; in winter Gray-crowned Rosy-Finches descend into holes in the cliffs in the afternoon. At the T, turn right with SR-263 into Kahlotus, another good migration spot.

Continue north, turn right onto SR-260, and head east 14 miles to **Washtucna**, an island of greenery in the midst of an arid hillscape that has proven to be one of the most consistent migrant traps in the Columbia Basin. The best birding is in and around **Bassett Park**, which can be swarming with passerines during spring and fall migrations. Cornell's eBird reports 189 species for Bassett Park, which features a variety of habitats. Among the birds commonly seen are California Quail, Red-tailed Hawk, American Kestrel, Olive-sided Flycatcher, Western Wood-Pewee, Willow, Hammond's, Dusky, Gray, and Pacific-slope Flycatchers, Say's Phoebe, Warbling and Red-eyed Vireos, kinglets, Townsend's Solitaire, Swainson's, Hermit, and Varied Thrushes, Gray Catbird, Orange-crowned, Yellow, Yellow-rumped, Townsend's, MacGillivray's, and Wilson's Warblers, Western Tanager, blackbirds, Bullock's Oriole, and Evening Grosbeak.

Uncommon or rare species seen at the park include: Broad-winged Hawk, Parasitic and Long-tailed Jaegers, Eastern Phoebe, Bell's, Blue-headed, and Philadelphia Vireos, Rose-breasted Grosbeak, and Indigo Bunting. Among the warblers seen here are Northern Waterthrush, Northern Parula, Black-and-white, Mourning, Magnolia, Chestnut-sided, Blackpoll, Black-throated Gray, and Black-throated Green. American Redstart and Gray and Least Flycatchers are regular.

The sewage ponds southeast of the park are always worth a look as well (off Klein/Portland Street).

Backtrack west on SR-260 and turn south onto SR-261 for 8.7 miles to **Palouse Falls State Park** (Discover Pass required), which deserves a stop at any season for birds and scenery. The few trees can be a magnet for birds during migration (Blue-headed Vireo, Chestnut-sided Warbler). Peregrine

Falcons and White-throated Swifts nest here, and in winter look for Gray-crowned Rosy-Finches on the cliff face.

Continue south five miles on SR-261 to **Lyons Ferry Fish Hatchery** on the right (heated restrooms open all winter). Check trees for sapsuckers in fall and winter. Just across the road is **Lyons Ferry Park**, where the Palouse River runs into the Snake. This is another migrant trap worth exploring anytime of year; a walk out to the island can be productive.

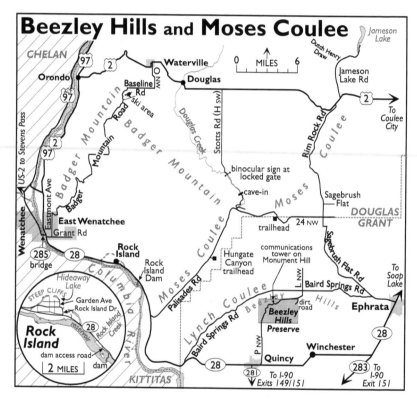

Beezley Hills and Moses Coulee

BEEZLEY HILLS AND MOSES COULEE

by Andy Stepniewski and Dan Stephens

revised by Andy Stepniewski and Dan Stephens

Across the Columbia River east of Wenatchee, a complex of ridges and coulees marks the transition between two broad, nearly level plateaus: the Potholes country on the south (elevation 1,100–1,300 feet) and the much higher Waterville Plateau to the north (elevation 2,300–2,600 feet). Moses Coulee, a deep gash incised by ice-age floods, skirts the edges of the higher plateau. The southern boundary of this area is defined by Lynch Coulee and the modest Beezley Hills. Rugged Badger Mountain lies to the west. The basalt cliffs and side canyons of Moses Coulee are populated by species such as Chukar, Golden Eagle, White-throated Swift, and Rock Wren. Some of the state's best shrub-steppe can be found on the coulee floor and in the Beezley Hills—home to Loggerhead Shrike, Mountain Bluebird, and Sagebrush Sparrow. There is dry montane forest (Badger Mountain) and fine riparian habitat for residents and migrants (especially along Douglas Creek). All of this plus a few ponds, lakes, and the deepwater Columbia River reservoir behind Rock Island Dam adds up to a series of habitats where it is easy to find 100 species of birds in a day during the breeding season. The sites have been described in such a way that you can readily link a selection of them into a loop starting from and returning to Ephrata or Wenatchee. Overall, early May offers the best birding, although March is better for waterfowl along the Columbia.

BEEZLEY HILLS

The Nature Conservancy's **Beezley Hills Preserve** (about 5,000 acres) shows off some of Washington's most pristine shrub-steppe habitat. Coming from the south, the most convenient approach is by turning north from SR-28 onto Road P NW (aka Columbia Way or Monument Hill Road), 0.8 mile east of the junction with SR-281 in Quincy. The road climbs steadily to a junction (7.1 miles). Turn left (west) onto a short spur and drive 0.1 mile to communication towers atop **Monument Hill** at 2,882 feet elevation. There are no facilities. Be careful; the gravel road can be slick if muddy or snowy. Directly across from the spur, wildflowers and Hedgehog Cactus, can be great in May.

Ice-age winds, by shifting and redepositing fine soils, played an important role in the development of the mosaic of shrub-steppe plant communities found on these slopes and ravines. The many south slopes with thin or rocky soil (lithosol) have a dazzling wildflower display in April and May. Horned Lark (common) and Mountain Bluebird are present in this habitat. Look for Loggerhead Shrike and Sagebrush Sparrow in deeper-soiled ravines below the summit where shrub cover is greater. In March and April and again from August through mid-October the top of Monument Hill makes a fine vantage to view migrating raptors.

To reach nearby north-facing habitats, with different birds, return to Monument Hill Road and drive left (east) along the ridgetop to a junction (2.1 miles). Pull over to the side of lightly-traveled Monument Hill Road and walk up the road to the right a couple of hundred yards. Relatively deep soils support a healthy growth of Big and Three-tip Sagebrush interspersed with Bluebunch Wheatgrass and a host of other interesting grasses and flowering plants. Common breeding birds here include Sage Thrasher, Brewer's Sparrow (areas of sagebrush and grasslands), and Vesper Sparrow (tracts of denser grasslands). Grasshopper Sparrow is uncommon and Western Meadowlark ubiquitous. From late March through April, keep a watch on the sky for migrating Sandhill Cranes—hundreds, even thousands exploit the thermals on these hills.

Back at Monument Hill Road, turn right and continue east a short distance; the road curves north and is now called Road L NW. At the first intersection with a stop sign, you have reached Baird Springs Road, though there is no road sign (1.1 miles). Ephrata (SR-28) is 9.7 miles east from this junction. There is some excellent sagebrush birding as you continue down this road to Ephrata. Westbound, Baird Springs Road descends Lynch Coulee beside an intermittent stream to join SR-28 seven miles west of Quincy. Birding can be rewarding along this route in shrub-steppe habitats and in riparian growth at springs and other wet spots at the edges of the deeply eroded streambed—especially in migration.

MOSES COULEE

Moses Coulee—a giant, basalt-lined, ice-age flood channel—slices southwestward some 40 miles from the high plateau near Mansfield down to the Columbia River. Cliffs provide excellent habitat for Chukar, Golden Eagle, Canyon Wren, and other rock-loving species. The broad coulee bottom—now mostly converted to hay farming—hosts many raptors, including the breeding species plus Rough-legged Hawk and Gyrfalcon (rare) in winter. Characteristic shrub-steppe birds can still be found in remnant parcels of habitat ranging in size from small pockets to large expanses.

Not far from the mouth of Moses Coulee, several waterbird sites in and near the small community of Rock Island are worth a visit. Rock Island Drive turns north from SR-28 about 12 miles east of the junction with US-2/US-97 in East Wenatchee (see inset map). A large truck stop is on the left just after the turn. Follow the main road into downtown Rock Island, staying with it as it turns left; in three or four blocks, turn right onto N Garden Avenue, across from the grocery store (0.3 mile). Drive to the end of this road (0.4 mile) and park at **Hideaway Lake**, an excellent waterfowl spot from November to April, when up to 20 species can been seen at one time (including Eurasian Wigeon most winters). A good location for setting up a scope is a few feet to the right along the trail that goes around the lake. Check trees near the water's edge for roosting Northern Saw-whet Owls in winter.

Return to SR-28 and turn left. Several more ponds beside the highway over the next mile are good for swans (early spring), other waterfowl, and gulls. Pull off to the right at the mouth of Rock Island Creek (2.1 miles from Rock Island Drive). Just across the railroad tracks are wetlands that once attracted a Snowy Egret. **Rock Island Reservoir**, visible from here, has many waterfowl in winter, including Greater Scaup. Deeper waters of the reservoir can be seen from the road to the dam, Rock Island Dam Road (0.3 mile farther along SR-28).

Continuing another 3.9 miles south along SR-28, **Palisades Road** turns off left and enters the lower end of Moses Coulee. Cliffs over the next several miles are especially attractive to Golden Eagle and Prairie Falcon—there is a safe pullout for scanning on the left in 1.5 miles. Other birds common along the coulee are Chukar and Lark Sparrow. An obscure gravel lane on the right (about nine miles from SR-28) leads to a trailhead parking lot for **Hungate Canyon** (BLM). A rough hike across sagebrush into a narrow side canyon with a tiny stream flanked by clumps of Water Birch and willow may reward you with Rock and Canyon Wrens and Lazuli Bunting.

Farther along Palisades Road, in 5.3 miles you come to the south access for **Douglas Creek** (turn left), especially known for its spring wildflowers but also for birds of the riparian zone and cliffs. The road is blocked by a cave-in in the lower part of the canyon, but you can walk the rest of the way in or drive around to the north access (next page); the approach from the north is the best way to explore Douglas Creek at this time. Birding possibilities are similar in both parts. Back on Palisades Road, another parking area and trail through shrub-steppe and along the base of cliffs is found on the right in 4.5 miles.

Palisades changes names and continues to an intersection in 5.0 miles. The intersecting road, which goes north to join US-2 in about 11 miles (or south and east to Ephrata in about 12 miles), is variously called Sagebrush Flat(s) Road, Road J NW, B-SE Road, Rim Rock Road, Moses Coulee Road SE, and Coulee Meadows Road—depending on which signs or maps you happen to be consulting. Turn left (north). Off to your right is **Sagebrush Flat**, managed by WDFW primarily for endangered Pygmy Rabbits. The disjunct Washington population of this Great Basin species was virtually extirpated due to widespread conversion to agriculture of the deep, loose soils it requires for burrows, and the concomitant removal of sagebrush (the main component of its diet). But a reintroduction effort at Sagebrush Flat has shown some success.

Proceed north 1.8 miles to a dirt track going off to the right in Rimrock Estates. Walk this area of Big Sagebrush to find Sage Thrasher and Brewer's and Sagebrush Sparrow. Mountain Bluebirds are also common here, thanks to numerous nest boxes. Continue north on the main road and descend into Moses Coulee. Cliffs in 6.1 miles are good for White-throated Swift and Canyon Wren. Reach US-2 in 3.2 miles.

Go right (east) 1.1 miles on US-2 to Jameson Lake Road and turn left. The road goes north on the floor of Moses Coulee, dead-ending in about seven miles at the south end of **Jameson Lake**. Significant (22,400 acres) parcels of the shrub-steppe ecosystem here and at nearby McCartney Creek are protected by The Nature Conservancy. Cliffs and talus line the route, home to Chukar, Red-tailed Hawk, Golden Eagle, White-throated Swift, American Kestrel, Prairie Falcon, and Rock and Canyon Wrens. Look for Mountain Bluebird (in boxes) and Sagebrush Sparrow, particularly in the first two miles.

At 3.9 miles from US-2, park at a trailhead on the left for **Dutch Henry Draw**. This interesting 15-minute walk brings you to the base of the cliffs and a dry waterfall, passing through brushy terrain that is good for Common Poorwill and Lazuli Bunting. As one continues toward Jameson Lake, the embankments by the road are actually giant ripple marks laid down by ice-age floods. Shrub-steppe habitat here has more native bunchgrasses than along the first part of the road, and hosts Sage Thrasher and Brewer's and Vesper Sparrows. The lake has been growing for the last few decades, making for some productive wetlands. Numerous waterfowl breed here, including all three teal species, Barrow's Goldeneye, and Ruddy Duck. Look also for Pied-billed and Eared Grebes and a colony of California Gulls. A small group of Franklin's Gulls has been seen here.

DOUGLAS CREEK

For the north approach to Douglas Creek, turn south from US-2 onto Road H SW (Stotts Road). The intersection is about 13 miles west of Jameson Lake Road and eight miles east of Waterville. Proceed south, watching for Short-eared Owl and Loggerhead Shrike along the way. This county road eventually descends Slack Canyon, reaching Douglas Creek in about eight miles. Turn right here, drive a short distance, and park by the binocular sign at a locked gate. You may walk up this unroaded part of the canyon for about eight miles for a true wilderness experience.

More of Douglas Creek can be explored by returning to the main gravel road and going downstream for about a mile. Several primitive campsites are off to the side of the road. Park at the third campsite—the center of the Douglas Creek bird-banding station. Over 100 species of birds have been seen in this section of the canyon. Common breeding species include Chukar, Red-tailed Hawk, Common Poorwill, American Kestrel, Western Wood-Pewee, Eastern Kingbird, Cliff Swallow, Rock and Canyon Wrens, Cedar Waxwing, Yellow-breasted Chat, Lark Sparrow, Black-headed Grosbeak, and Lazuli Bunting. During migration the canyon is jumping with most of the common transient flycatchers, vireos, warblers, and sparrows. Interesting passage species, among them a few rarities, are Least and Gray Flycatchers, Cassin's Vireo, Veery, Hermit Thrush, Black-and-white, Nashville, and Townsend's Warblers, Northern Waterthrush, American Redstart, Wilson's Warbler, and Lincoln's and Golden-crowned Sparrows. The county road is closed south of here due to a cave-in; if and when it reopens, you will again be able to drive down the rest of the canyon to join Palisades Road in Moses Coulee. In the meantime, you can walk.

BADGER MOUNTAIN

Badger Mountain lies between the Columbia River and Moses Coulee, northeast of Wenatchee. Its upper elevations support the most extensive conifer forest in the western Columbia Basin. Badger Mountain Road goes up and over this large ridge system to Waterville in about 25 miles. In East Wenatchee, turn east from SR-28 onto Grant Road (first intersection south of the SR-285 bridge), then left (north) in one long block onto Eastmont Avenue, which becomes Badger Mountain Road as it leaves town and begins climbing. Look for bluebirds at lower elevations and for Spotted Towhee, Chipping Sparrow, and Cassin's Finch higher up, in brushy terrain on south-facing slopes. The road crosses the crest in about six miles, then remains at an elevation of 3,000–3,500 feet as it contours along the southeast face of Badger Mountain until reaching a ski area about 20 miles from East Wenatchee. Along the way, stop in several places in the Ponderosa Pine and Douglas-fir forest to look and listen for Hairy Woodpecker, Dusky Flycatcher, Cassin's Vireo, White-breasted Nuthatch, Swainson's Thrush, and Western Tanager. Northern Goshawk has been seen here in May. Take the main road (now called Baseline Road) east from the ski area for two-plus miles, then turn north on Road O NW (also called Waterville Road) and drive another 2.5 miles to US-2 in Waterville. If you are driving this route in reverse from Waterville, go south from US-2 a block south of the Catholic church onto S Chelan Avenue, which becomes Road O NW/Waterville Road upon leaving town.

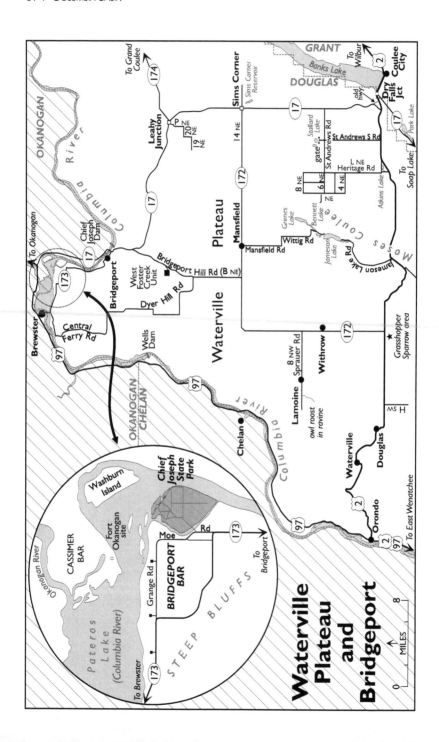

Waterville
Plateau
and
Bridgeport

WATERVILLE PLATEAU AND BRIDGEPORT

by Andy Stepniewski
revised by Andy Stepniewski

The northwest corner of the Columbia Basin is a high plateau bordered by the deep gorge of the Columbia River on the west and north, the Grand Coulee on the east and southeast, and Badger Mountain on the southwest. Technically, the name Waterville Plateau is reserved for a relatively small section north of Waterville, but by tradition birders employ this term to designate the whole 30-by-40-mile area described here.

Ice-age floods gouged out Moses Coulee, a north-south gash that bisects the plateau for more than half its length. The Withrow Moraine, which marks the southern extent of glaciation in the last ice age, crosses the southern part of the plateau in a southeasterly direction, from near Chelan to Coulee City. Monotonous wheat fields extend for miles on the unglaciated land to the south, providing little habitat for birds other than the many Horned Larks. Northward, the plateau bears abundant evidence of glaciation—large "haystack" rocks and piles of glacial debris, kettle lakes, and generally uneven, stony ground. Because of this rough landscape, farming has proved marginal, despite near-heroic attempts over the past century. Significant areas of former farmland are now set aside in the USDA Conservation Reserve Program, and shrub-steppe habitats are slowly returning to some of these. Bird species such as Gray Partridge, Greater Sage-Grouse, Swainson's Hawk, Short-eared Owl, American Kestrel, and Vesper Sparrow benefit from the enhanced habitat. Federal budget cutbacks to this program, however, threaten many of these areas of "recovering shrub-steppe." Many thousands of acres have reverted to active farmland in recent years. Awareness of the conservation value for birds of these government set-asides is growing, though. It is hoped the program will continue to protect these valuable habitats.

The plateau is known for northern, open-country specialties in winter, including raptors such as Rough-legged Hawk and Gyrfalcon. Horned Lark (arcticola), Lapland Longspur, and Snow Bunting are usually findable among large flocks of the resident Horned Larks (merrilli). Raptors and shrub-steppe birds provide interest in the breeding season. Chukar, White-throated Swift (summer), and Gray-crowned Rosy-Finch (winter) can be found on cliffs and rockslides in upper Moses Coulee. Waterfowl, rails, and shorebirds are present seasonally at several lakes. A small population of Sharp-tailed Grouse inhabits brushy draws on the north slopes of the plateau, which descend toward the Columbia River. Orchards and ornamental plantings in and around Bridgeport support winter flocks of Bohemian Waxwings and finches. The Bridgeport Bar in the Columbia bottomlands is a great place in winter to sort through sparrow flocks and view waterbirds on the river.

Birding on the high plateau can be difficult in winter, even hazardous. Always check the weather first. Avoid storms. Blowing snow obscures vision and quickly buries roads, and it may be miles to the nearest human habitation. Even in fair weather you may find dense fog atop the plateau. Stick to the main, plowed roads. During thaws, beware of soft shoulders and ungraded secondary roads, or you may find your vehicle up to its axles in mud. It is advisable to bring tire chains, a shovel, extra clothing, emergency food and water, cell phone, and sleeping bags on any winter trip.

There is no single best way to bird the plateau. Much of it is served by a grid of gravel section-line roads, and the more you explore, the more birds you will see. Several consistently productive areas are described below, loosely grouped for convenience of presentation.

WATERVILLE PLATEAU (SOUTH)

Amidst the wheat fields 13 miles east of Waterville on US-2 is an intersection with SR-172. From May to July, pull off the highway about a quarter-mile west of this junction and walk to the south through grassland habitat with scattered Big Sagebrush, looking for Grasshopper Sparrow—a local species on the plateau. In winter, you'll find an interesting roost for Great Horned and Long-eared Owls near **Lamoine** by driving north on SR-172 8.0 miles to Road 8 NW (Sprauer Road). But on your way, stop in Withrow to check the Withrow grain elevators for Gray Partridge and attendant Gyrfalcon or Prairie Falcon. Turn west onto Road 8 NW and travel 6.0 miles to a ravine, on the left, flanked by dense pines in the wheat fields. Walk along the pines to search for owls and Gray Partridge. Continue north, then east, on SR-172 to reach Mansfield.

Eastward from the SR-172 junction, US-2 soon drops down to cross Moses Coulee, reaching the Jameson Lake turnoff in about eight miles. After climbing back out of the coulee, look for the junction with Heritage Road (aka Road L NE) in about nine more miles (coming from the east, this is about eight miles west of Dry Falls Junction). Turn north here and go 0.7 mile to an unmarked dirt road on the right leading to **Atkins Lake**. In periods of normal precipitation, this large swale in the wheat fields is a shallow lake that may have water for most of the year. During one of the irregular droughts, however, the lake may be entirely dry and not worth a stop. It can be a fabulous place for waterbirds, except in winter when frozen. Thousands of geese, dabbling and diving ducks, and Sandhill Cranes are present in spring if conditions are right. Raptors can also be conspicuous—look for Northern Harrier, Red-tailed Hawk, and Prairie Falcon year round. Swainson's Hawk is fairly common in summer. Winter possibilities include Northern Goshawk, Rough-legged Hawk, Golden Eagle, and Gyrfalcon. Bald Eagle and Peregrine Falcon occur mainly in migration. Late summer can prove attractive for shorebirds—many species uncommon or rare in the interior have been observed when suitable mud is exposed. Winter often brings Horned Larks, Lapland Longspurs, and Snow Buntings to the lake edges.

Greater Sage-Grouse can be found, with luck, at any season in patches of the original Big Sagebrush habitat about four to eight miles north of Atkins

Lake. In the early morning, drive the grid of roads within the rectangle formed by Road 4 NE on the south, Road 8 NE on the north, Road L NE on the east, and Road J NE on the west.

Haynes Canyon is a good place for shrub-steppe birds, right off US-2. About six miles east of the Road L NE corner (1.6 miles west of Dry Falls Junction), go north on SR-17 toward Bridgeport; keep an eye out for Chukar in road cuts and for Gray Partridge in grassier stretches. A section of old highway—not driveable, but walkable—projects south from SR-17 on the right, 1.1 miles north of US-2. Sagebrush Sparrow is regular along this old road, which parallels the canyon, from April to July. Stop again 2.0 miles farther north on SR-17, where the shrub-steppe habitat has more native bunchgrasses and may produce Sage Thrasher and Brewer's Sparrow.

Continue north 2.8 miles on SR-17 to Saint Andrews E Road (aka Road 6 NE). Turn left here and go west three miles to the intersection with Road O NE (also reachable by driving east three miles from Road L NE). Turn north onto Road O NE and go half a mile to scope Stallard Lake from behind a closed gate. Waterfowl, Sandhill Crane (mainly April), Black-necked Stilt, American Avocet, and phalaropes are the attraction here. This is a good place for shrikes (Northern in winter and Loggerhead in the breeding season). In winter, look for American Tree Sparrows in brush near the gate.

WATERVILLE PLATEAU (NORTH)

Sims Corner marks the intersection of SR-17 and SR-172, 7.6 miles north of Saint Andrews E Road (aka Road 6 NE). **Sims Corner Reservoir** lies just out of view to the southeast. In spring, large numbers of Sandhill Cranes may be seen from the road as they come in to or depart from this water body. The reservoir is on private property; do not enter without permission (ask at the only farmhouse at this corner).

The largest remaining population of Greater Sage-Grouse in the state—about 700 birds—persists on the northern part of the Waterville Plateau. A good area for finding these birds lekking (peak season March–April) is near **Leahy Junction**. From Sims Corner, go north eight miles on SR-17 to the SR-174 intersection, then left on SR-17 to Road P NE (0.1 mile). Turn left and wind southward on a gravel road through hills covered with Big Sagebrush and Bluebunch Wheatgrass, watching for Loggerhead Shrike, Sage Thrasher, and Brewer's and Vesper Sparrows from April through August. This is all private property: do not trespass. Take time to admire the views of the Cascade Range, particularly beautiful in early morning light.

The 12.5 miles of SR-172 between Sims Corner and Mansfield can be good in winter for Gray Partridge, Rough-legged Hawk, Gyrfalcon, Lapland Longspur, and Snow Bunting. In summer these fields may have Northern Harrier, Swainson's and Red-tailed Hawks, and American Kestrel. You will also hear and see many Horned Larks—doubtless the commonest breeding bird on the Waterville Plateau.

Approaching Mansfield from the east, SR-172 veers left into town. Check the grain elevators in town for Gray Partridge (dawn or dusk best) and Eurasian Collared-Dove and the surrounding utility poles for raptors such as Northern Goshawk, Gyrfalcon, and Prairie Falcon, especially in winter. Residential plantings in town might have Bohemian Waxwing or Common Redpoll. Check the tall spruce trees in the cemetery on the west side of Mansfield for Great Horned Owl and crossbills, White-winged in some winters.

Where SR-172 goes right (northwest) in town, stay straight on Railroad Avenue to visit **Bennett Lake** and **Grimes Lake** in upper Moses Coulee. Turn left onto Mansfield Road (0.3 mile). Follow Mansfield Road south 3.3 miles, where it curves left (east) and becomes Wittig Road, reaching Bennett Lake in another 4.6 miles. A dirt road that turns off to the left here, open only July through October, leads in half a mile to Grimes Lake. These lakes have produced many Tundra Swans, a variety of dabbling and diving ducks, Virginia Rail and Sora, both yellowlegs, Stilt, Baird's, Pectoral, and Semipalmated Sandpipers, and other shorebird species. The cliffs and talus slopes have Chukar, Common Poorwill, White-throated Swift, Say's Phoebe, thousands of Cliff Swallows, Rock and Canyon Wrens, and in winter many roosting Gray-crowned Rosy-Finches that forage in the fields between these lakes and **Jameson Lake** (1.3 miles farther south on the main road). From the dilapidated resort at the road's end scan the waters of Jameson Lake for waterfowl—especially in migration.

WELLS WILDLIFE AREA AND BRIDGEPORT

Bridgeport Hill Road (Road B NE) goes north from SR-172 about three miles west of Mansfield. Note the intersection in 4.7 miles where Dyer Hill Road turns left. Continuing straight ahead, Bridgeport Hill Road descends along West Foster Creek. The poorly-signed entrance to the Wells Wildlife Area's **West Foster Creek Unit** (1,050 acres) is on the left in 2.4 miles. The access road (impassable if wet or snowy) doubles back sharply and descends steeply to a few parking spots (Discover Pass required). Small numbers of Sharp-tailed Grouse are sometimes found in Water Birches and brush near the stream, but California Quail are far more common. Take the rough trail downstream a couple of hundred yards to a feeder. In winter, look for American Tree Sparrows here or in the nearby cattails.

Another place for Sharp-tailed Grouse in winter is along Foster Creek on the right (east) side of Bridgeport Hill Road, beginning about three miles farther downhill. Look for them "budding" in the Water Birches by the roadside from here down to the SR-17 intersection in another mile or so, and on the east side of SR-17 after you turn left and drop down toward Bridgeport. The grouse will feed at any time of day but are sensitive to disturbance, so early morning is usually the best time to find them. Common Redpolls—irregular winter visitors—may feed in the Water Birches.

In 2.2 miles from the intersection make a left from SR-17 onto SR-173 and keep on it through **Bridgeport**, on the Columbia River. In winter, check residential streets for Merlins and flocks of Bohemian Waxwings and other winter songbirds. A Northern Hawk Owl wintered here once, too. Continuing west on SR-173, turn right onto Moe Road (5.6 miles), which runs north, then west, becoming Grange Road. In 1.4 miles, turn right into a parking area for the **Bridgeport Bar Unit** (502 acres) of the Wells Wildlife Area (Discover Pass required). A second parking area is 1.1 miles farther along Grange Road. The short walk from these access points down to the Columbia River can be productive for waterfowl, Bald Eagle, and scads of coots in winter. Rarities such as Yellow-billed Loon have shown up here. The scrubby growth can have loads of sparrows.

Grange Road rejoins SR-173 in 0.1 mile. Turn right. Abundant brush and trees at a third WDFW access, on the right in 0.7 mile, attract passerines (Bohemian Waxwing in winter). This access also offers good waterbird viewing on the river, as do several pullouts on the right for the next two miles. SR-173 then turns right and crosses the Columbia to Brewster and close-by Okanogan birding sites (page 432).

Do not turn here with SR-173, but stay straight ahead onto Crane Orchard Road. In 2.4 miles, where Crane Orchard Road peels off to the right, stay left on Central Ferry Canyon Road, which turns to gravel, begins to climb through Central Ferry Canyon, and soon enters the **Central Ferry Unit** (1,538 acres) of the Wells Wildlife Area. Riparian vegetation all the way up can have good birding in winter. In four miles after leaving Crane Orchard Road, park on the right and walk the gravel road downhill on the left side of the road to a nice riparian area dominated by Water Birches and thickets of wild rose and Red-osier Dogwood, which attracts Townsend's Solitaire, Varied Thrush, Bohemian Waxwing, and Common Redpoll in winter. Sparrows can be numerous. Sharp-tailed Grouse, though present in modest numbers, are secretive and seldom seen.

Continue up Central Ferry Road and turn left onto a dirt lane marked *Packwood Cemetery* (0.8 mile). Park and walk this quarter-mile spur through open Ponderosa Pine forest. A fire swept the forest but habitat for birds persists. Watch for Northern Pygmy-Owl, Hairy Woodpecker, Steller's Jay, Clark's Nutcracker, Mountain Chickadee, White-breasted and Pygmy Nuthatches, Cassin's Finch, and Red Crossbill. Continuing uphill, the road soon breaks out onto the Waterville Plateau. With a good map and a bit of care, you can bird your way in 15 miles or less to the Dyer Hill Road/Bridgeport Hill Road intersection.

Grand Coulee

by Andy Stepniewski and Donald Haley
revised by Andy Stepniewski and Matt Yawney

Some 13,000 years ago, a lobe of the continental ice sheet dammed the Columbia River about where Grand Coulee Dam now stands. Diverted to flow south along a zone of weakness in the plateau basalts, the river gouged away rock and sediments, forming the ancestral Grand Coulee. This chasm was further enlarged by the numerous Spokane Floods that swept across the landscape in the waning years of the last ice age. When the ice sheets receded, the Columbia recaptured its prior course. The abandoned channel now has the form of a wide valley flanked by basalt cliffs. Its upper (northern) end is occupied by a large reservoir, Banks Lake. The floor of the lower (southern) part has lakes—some of them alkaline because there is little or no drainage—marshes, patches of shrub-steppe habitat, and riparian groves.

This landscape supports a rich and interesting fauna, including some birds that are unusual away from the coast. Birding is best from spring through early winter. In a normal winter most of the lakes are frozen by January, and birds are few. Even then, of interest are the winter roosts of Gray-crowned Rosy-Finch on the cliffs and northern visitors such as Gyrfalcon and Snow Bunting atop the adjacent plateaus. Our itinerary proceeds from south to north, starting from near Ephrata (pronounced ee-FRAY-tuh). In spring and early summer, birders may also wish to visit the state's only nesting colony (so far) of Tricolored Blackbirds near Wilson Creek.

Ephrata

From the junction of SR-28/SR-283 (14.7 miles north of I-90 Exit 151), go north toward Ephrata on SR-28, 2.4 miles to Martin Road NW. Go left (west) here 0.4 mile to a parking area on the left (south side of Martin Road NW). Walk downhill on a dirt track to the treed area, where berry-laden Russian Olive trees attract loads of birds in winter: accipiters, Hermit and Varied Thrushes, American Robins, both waxwings, Yellow-rumped Warblers, and sparrows. Spring and fall, these trees attract migrants. Check the irrigation canal, where American Dipper has been noted. Both Barn and Great Horned Owls are regular, and Barred, Long-eared, and Northern Saw-whet have been seen.

After birding this fine area, head back to SR-28 and turn left (north) 0.2 mile to **Oasis Park**, on the left. Best birding is early morning to avoid highway noise. The park has an RV area and a day-use area, but birders should head for the patches of deciduous trees and main pond south of the parking lot. The pond which can be good for a variety of waterfowl in early spring, including Wood Duck, especially in early morning. Vagrant landbirds have been found around the last week of May. Check the large willow tree by the main pond for nesting Great Horned Owl.

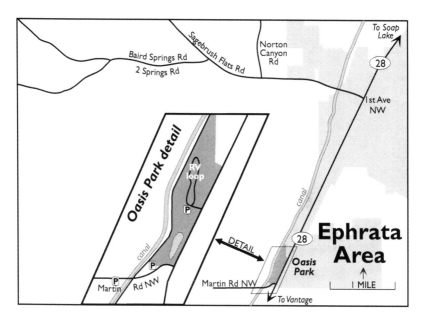

Excellent shrub-steppe habitat is close by Ephrata. From Oasis Park, go north (left) on SR-28 through Ephrata 2.8 miles to 1st Avenue NW. Go left here (the road becomes Sagebrush Flats Road) 1.5 miles to Norton Canyon Road. Turn right to the grasslands along this road, which are excellent for Grasshopper Sparrow. Lazuli Buntings frequent the brushy draw. American Tree Sparrow can be found along this road in the winter.

Travel back to Sagebrush Flats Road and go right 0.9 mile . Turn left (south) on Baird Springs Road (aka 2 Springs Road) for some excellent birding in sagebrush habitat over at least the next three miles. Look and listen for Loggerhead Shrike, Sage Thrasher, and Brewer's and Vesper Sparrows. Sagebrush Sparrow can be readily found here from mid-June through July and may nest nearby. Though much quieter in winter, American Tree Sparrow can be found.

Return to SR-28 in Ephrata, go left (north) toward Soap Lake, and in 5.3 miles find the junction with SR-17.

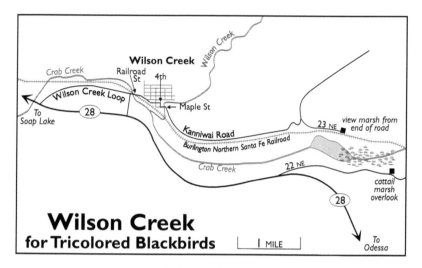

Wilson Creek
for Tricolored Blackbirds

WILSON CREEK

The discovery in 1998 of a colony of Tricolored Blackbirds—the first state record for this species—put the town of Wilson Creek on the birding map. In the same vicinity, the seasonally inundated Crab Creek bottomlands attract many waterfowl, shorebirds, gulls, and terns. Cliffs, talus slopes, and brushy terrain provide nesting sites for raptors, including Ferruginous Hawk, and for a variety of shrub-steppe specialists.

There are two turnoffs for Wilson Creek on the north side of SR-28. The west turnoff is about 16 miles east of the intersection with SR-17 at Soap Lake and the other is a mile and a half farther east (24 miles west of Odessa). Use whichever one is more convenient; either way you will be on Wilson Creek Loop. Continue to an intersection and take Railroad Street into town (straight ahead in 1.5 miles if coming from the west exit, or right at a stop sign in 0.3 mile if coming from the east exit). Follow Railroad Street through a couple of bends and turn right onto Fourth Street (0.5 mile). In 0.1 mile turn left onto Maple Street, which shortly crosses a bridge and reaches an intersection with Kanniwai Road, where you turn right.

For about two and one-half miles, the road runs through farmlands in a coulee with cliffs on the left, where Ferruginous Hawks have nested, and marshes on the right in places (across the railway track). Tricolored Blackbirds are often noted in mixed-species blackbird flocks in fields along this road, away from their nesting sites in the Crab Creek marshes. Turn right onto Road 23 NE and drive to its end in 0.7 mile at the railroad crossing, again looking for blackbirds and waterbirds in the marshes. Respect private property signs.

To observe the nesting marsh, return to SR-28 at the east Wilson Creek Loop exit, turn left, and go 2.8 miles to Road 22 NE. Bear left here, stopping to scope the shallow seasonal lake on the left for swans (Tundra is abundant in spring), geese, ducks, shorebirds, gulls, and terns. In 1.9 miles pull off to the left and walk a few yards (watch out for rattlesnakes) to an overlook of the large cattail marshes where many Red-winged, Tricolored, and Yellow-headed Blackbirds nest.

If you have not found Tricolored Blackbird so far, try Road 22NE all the way to Marlin, checking blackbird flocks in agricultural fields along the way.

Several sites along SR-28 between Wilson Creek and Soap Lake are worth a stop. (See map on next page.) **Brook Lake** (aka Stratford Lake) can be scoped from a gravel pullout on the right side of the highway 3.8 miles past the west Wilson Creek Loop turnoff. In fall, this lake hosts upwards of 55,000 Canada Geese. Usually a few Greater White-fronted and Snow Geese are present in this huge throng. Rarities such as Ross's Goose and Brant have been seen here, too. Look also for Western Grebe and American White Pelican.

Continuing west on SR-28, you come to an intersection with Pinto Ridge Road on the right (3.8 miles). If you are visiting during spring or fall migration, you might want to check the oasis at **Summer Falls**, reached by going 6.1 miles north on this road to the Summer Falls day-use area (closed seasonally). Look for warblers at a willow-lined seep.

Continuing west on SR-28, a dirt track turns off left in 4.2 miles. Go a short distance into a patch of Big Sagebrush and Bitterbrush, where Sage Thrasher and Lark Sparrow may be found. It is another 4.1 miles west on SR-28 to the junction with SR-17 at the south edge of Soap Lake.

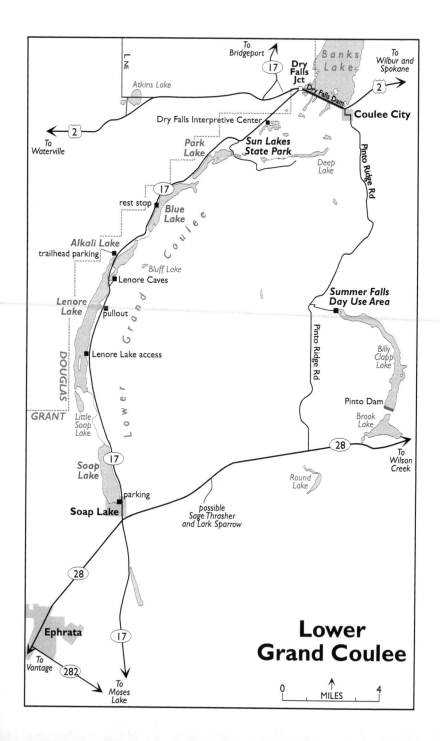

Lower
Grand Coulee

LOWER GRAND COULEE

From the intersection with SR-28, take SR-17 north 0.7 mile through the town of Soap Lake to the parking area at the south end of the lake, on the left. **Soap Lake** is slightly saltier than the ocean and distinctly alkaline—chemically akin to a salty solution of sodium bicarbonate. The reputed curative properties of these waters continue to draw vacationers, while Northern Shoveler, Ruddy Duck, Eared Grebe, and Ring-billed Gull are attracted by the copepods and other tiny invertebrates that swarm just below the lake's surface in the warmer months. Soap Lake is one of the better spots in Eastern Washington to look for scoters, Long-tailed Duck, and Sabine's and Franklin's Gulls (mainly fall). Shorebirds (Sanderling and Pectoral Sandpiper in fall) can be found on this beach as well as on the one at the north end of the lake. Pullouts along the way provide other opportunities for bird-viewing.

Much of the valley bottom to the north is occupied by four large lakes within the Sun Lakes Wildlife Area (9,140 acres; Discover Pass required). The southernmost, and largest, is **Lenore Lake**. Turn off left from SR-17 to a fishing access 6.0 miles north of the south parking area at Soap Lake. Many species of freshwater ducks use the lake, except in mid-winter when it is frozen. Marine ducks such as scoters and Long-tailed Duck are regular. Look for Golden Eagles, which nest in the cliffs across the lake from here.

A roadside pullout 1.8 miles farther north, on the right, allows more views of the lake. Several Barrow's Goldeneyes nest here, an unusual location for this species. The cliffs close by are a reliable winter roost location for Gray-crowned Rosy-Finches. Look for them beginning in late afternoon as they check out the crevices (and perhaps Cliff Swallow nests). Canyon Wren is fairly common here, though often difficult to spot.

Another 1.1 miles farther north on SR-17, at a sign marked Lenore Caves, turn left into a parking area. A short asphalt path leads north to a small spawning channel constructed for the Lahontan Cutthroat Trout that were stocked in Lenore Lake. Look for them in the channel from late March through June. Across the highway, take the Lenore Caves turnoff (parking lot in 0.4 mile); you will have a great overlook of **Alkali Lake**, the next lake in the chain. During spring and fall, large numbers of ducks, coots, and other waterbirds can be observed here. Red-necked Grebes have nested here. A short hike (about one-quarter mile, in places a bit rough) leads to the Lenore Caves—which have been used by humans for at least 5,000 years—and another beautiful view. Some of the species you may observe are Golden Eagle, Say's Phoebe, and Canyon and Rock Wrens.

Continue north on SR-17 to a parking lot, on the left, on the north side of Lenore Lake (1.1 miles). Here, a footpath passes through a fence opening and heads up through a rocky cleft to shrub-steppe habitat and the talus apron at the base of the tallest cliffs. In addition to shrub-steppe species such as Logger-

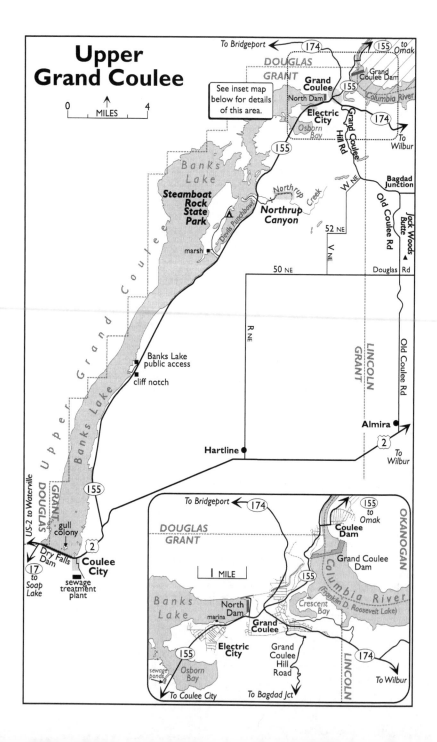

Upper Grand Coulee

0 |___ MILES ___| 4

See inset map below for details of this area.

To Bridgeport ← 174

155 to Omak

DOUGLAS

GRANT

Grand Coulee

Grand Coulee Dam

Columbia River

North Dam

155

Electric City

Osborn Bay

Grand Coulee Hill Rd

174

To Wilbur

155

Banks Lake

Steamboat Rock State Park

Devils Punchbowl

Northrup Creek

Northrup Canyon

W NE

Bagdad Junction

Jack Woods Butte

52 NE

V NE

50 NE

Old Coulee Rd

Douglas Rd

marsh

Upper Grand Coulee

R NE

LINCOLN GRANT

Banks Lake public access

cliff notch

Old Coulee Rd

Almira

2

To Wilbur

Hartline

Banks Lake

155

US-2 to Waterville

DOUGLAS GRANT

gull colony

Dry Falls Dam

17 to Soap Lake

2

Coulee City

sewage treatment plant

Inset map

To Bridgeport ← 174

155 to Omak

Coulee Dam

OKANOGAN

DOUGLAS GRANT

1 MILE

Grand Coulee Dam

155

Columbia River (Franklin D. Roosevelt Lake)

Banks Lake

North Dam

marina

Crescent Bay

Grand Coulee

155

Electric City

Osborn Bay

Grand Coulee Hill Road

LINCOLN

174

To Wilbur

sewage ponds

155

To Coulee City

To Bagdad Jct

head Shrike and Brewer's Sparrow, check for Chukar, Golden Eagle, Prairie Falcon, and Canyon Wren. Rattlesnakes are abundant here.

Blue Lake (1.8 miles) can be an excellent inland site for loons in migration. Commons are often present in large numbers, especially in fall, along with a few Pacifics in October. Yellow-billed has occurred. Red-necked Grebe has nested at the south end of the lake in recent years. Scope from the rest stop on the right in another 1.8 miles or from any of the pullouts along the highway.

Birds are abundant in the lakes, marshes, and riparian habitats of **Sun Lakes State Park** (3.1 miles). For a fine morning birdwalk from mid-May to mid-June, park in the lot (1.3 miles) beyond the campground entrance and walk the first mile or so of the 2.5-mile road to Deep Lake. The road follows a stream lined with Water Birch, Red-osier Dogwood, and wild rose. Look for waterfowl, Red-tailed Hawk, Black-billed Magpie, Common Raven, swallows, Rock Wren, Yellow-breasted Chat, Lark Sparrow, Lazuli Bunting, Yellow-headed Blackbird, and Bullock's Oriole. Peregrine Falcon may nest on the cliffs.

Dry Falls is one of the geologic marvels of the state. Stop at the overlook and interpretive display 1.9 miles farther north on SR-17, on the right. In summer, you can often go eyeball to eyeball with White-throated Swifts as they slice the sky right before you. Look for Chukar here, too. In winter, rosy-finches roost in the cliffs below the overlook. The lakes far below often have waterfowl. Scan the skies for both Prairie and Peregrine Falcons.

The Lower Grand Coulee ends at Dry Falls Junction, where SR-17 meets US-2 (2.0 miles). Turn left for birding sites on the Waterville Plateau or right to continue to the Upper Grand Coulee.

UPPER GRAND COULEE

North from the Dry Falls Dam at Coulee City lies the huge Upper Grand Coulee, now mostly flooded by artificial Banks Lake. Filled with water pumped up from Franklin D. Roosevelt Lake with 12 of the world's largest pumps, Banks Lake constitutes the headworks of the Columbia Basin Irrigation Project. About 2,360 miles of canals and laterals thread their way downslope from Dry Falls Dam to irrigate 640,000 acres of productive farmland throughout the southern Columbia Basin. The lake and most of the shoreline are included in the Banks Lake Wildlife Area.

Banks Lake may host birds more often seen along the coast, especially during fall migration. Sea ducks are regular, including inland Washington's largest congregation of Red-breasted Mergansers (late fall; a few winter). Jaegers are possible. Large numbers of Herring Gulls winter on the lake if areas of open water persist, and Glaucous Gulls are sometimes seen with them.

From Dry Falls Junction, drive east across **Dry Falls Dam** on US-2, checking the waters north of the dam for diving ducks, loons, and grebes. A pullout partway across (1.2 miles from the junction) provides a vantage for an extensive area of lake, mudflat and marsh on the south side of the dam. Blue-winged and Cinnamon Teal, Black-necked Stilt, American Avocet, and Wilson's Phalarope can often be scoped from here. Swivel your scope 180 degrees across the dam to a rocky island in Banks Lake that supports a large colony of Ring-billed and California Gulls and a few Double-crested Cormorants and Caspian Terns, along with some Great Blue Herons and Black-crowned Night-Herons nesting in dwarf Hackberry trees.

Once across the dam, in 0.7 mile, turn right (south) onto 4th Street. Go 0.3 mile to Main Street. Turn left (east) and go 0.2 mile to McEntee Street. Go right (south) 0.7 miles **to Coulee City Sewage Treatment Plant**. Scan the ponds from the berm on the right for waterfowl (Eurasian Wigeon has occurred) shorebirds, and gulls (Franklin's noted).

Back on US-2, go east 2.3 miles from Coulee City to a junction with SR-155, where US-2 goes right. Keep straight here and head north on SR-155 along the east shore of Banks Lake. A pullout and overlook at a large notch in the cliff (7.8 miles) is a great place to see nesting White-throated Swift, Violet-green Swallow, Canyon Wren, and occasionally Peregrine Falcon. In fall, check for Common Loon and flotillas of Red-breasted Mergansers on the waters far below. Banks Lake Public Access (1.0 mile) goes to the lake, passing a dense patch of Big Sagebrush filled with Brewer's Sparrows (April through July).

SR-155 parallels the lakeshore to the turnoff to **Steamboat Rock State Park** (6.7 miles). On the way, stop at as many pullouts as time permits. Greater Scaup, mergansers, Common Loon, and Horned Grebe may be found in fall and spring. Note the large Cliff Swallow colonies on cliffs beside the highway. After turning into the park, a dirt road goes off to the left in 0.4 mile. Walk this road to a grove of Russian Olives beside a cattail marsh. Check the trees for Barn and Long-eared Owl, American Robin, Varied Thrush, and American Tree Sparrow (winter). The park has a developed campground with ornamental plantings that attract migrants in season. Chukar and Gray Partridge occur here. Berry-consuming birds such as California Quail, American Robin, Varied Thrush, and Townsend's Solitaire are especially common. The ready prey attracts accipiters; Northern Goshawk is regular in winter.

For the hardy, a steep trail ascends to the top of mesa-like Steamboat Rock. Although not particularly good for birds, the rock is famous for its display of Bitteroot (May and June). Bald and Golden Eagles and Prairie Falcon nest here. Bats roost in the cliffs, including the rare Spotted Bat. North from the park entrance on SR-155, a bay known as Devils Punchbowl hosts Western Grebe families in summer and hundreds of mergansers in fall, including many Hooded and Red-breasted. Scan for these from one of the many pullouts.

The gravel road into **Northrup Canyon** turns off right in 3.4 miles and ends at a gate (0.6 mile). The park is in a natural state, with no facilities other than a wide trail along a canyon lined by towering granitic rocks. These witnesses of the older rocks that underlie much of the Columbia Basin protrude up into the otherwise widespread, and recent, Columbia Plateau basalts. The canyon has scattered forests of Ponderosa Pine and Douglas-fir and a riparian corridor lined with Water Birch and dense brush. Resident bird species include Chukar, Golden Eagle, Great Horned Owl, Northern Pygmy-Owl, Downy and Hairy Woodpeckers, Northern Flicker, Black-capped and Mountain Chickadees (may hybridize here), Red-breasted Nuthatch, Canyon Wren, Song Sparrow, and Red Crossbill (irregular). Spring brings many migrants and summer visitors, including Long-eared and Northern Saw-whet Owls (possibly year round), Common Poorwill, White-throated Swift, Calliope Hummingbird, Lewis's Woodpecker, Red-naped Sapsucker, Western Wood-Pewee, Say's Phoebe, many House Wrens, Lazuli Bunting, Bullock's Oriole, and Cassin's Finch.

During the warm months, the parking lot by the gate is a good place to find Spotted Bats—identifiable at night by their clearly audible clicking. In late fall and early winter, dozens of Bald Eagles fly into the tall conifers in late afternoon to roost. Their cacklings and wild aerobatics against the backdrop of the cliffs are an exciting spectacle. This is one of the largest roosts in interior Washington, with over 100 birds in some years. Numbers decline when arctic air masses arrive in late December or January, and Banks Lake freezes.

If you follow the trail all the way to the old homestead, you can then turn left (north) and go higher up into the canyon to a more challenging single-track trail uphill to beautiful Northrup Lake—actually more of a pond. Species to look for there include: Osprey, Virginia Rail, Mountain Bluebird, and Cassin's Finch.

Returning to SR-155, turn right, passing small Jones Bay at 1.7 miles, then crossing larger **Osborn Bay** (2.4 miles). On both, look for Western and Clark's Grebes, which nest. Fall and early winter see the arrival of thousands of waterfowl of many species.

In **Electric City** the small boat launch and marina (1.6 miles) often has many diving ducks, and the booms in the bay attract gulls in late fall and early winter. Ring-billed, California, Herring, and Glaucous-winged are the regular species. Rarer species include Sabine's, Bonaparte's, Thayer's, Iceland (once, November), and Glaucous. In 0.5 mile turn left from SR-155, park, and walk onto **North Dam**. Scan this end of the lake for waterfowl (especially Common Goldeneye in the colder months), loons, grebes, and gulls (especially Herring). Cruising the residential streets in Electric City and the nearby towns of Grand Coulee and Coulee Dam can yield Bohemian Waxwing and Common Redpoll in winter.

The plateau above Grand Coulee is known in winter for Gray Partridge, Rough-legged Hawk, Snowy and Short-eared Owls, Gyrfalcon, Prairie Falcon, Northern Shrike, Horned Lark (abundant), Bohemian Waxwing (junipers around the isolated farmhouses), Lapland Longspur, Snow Bunting, and Gray-crowned Rosy-Finch. However, it is best avoided when conditions of fog or drifting snow prevail.

From the North Dam approach road, continue east on SR-155 to its junction with SR-174 (0.4 mile). Turn right (south) onto SR-174 and go 0.5 mile to Spokane Way (keep an eye out for Wild Turkeys). Turn right onto Spokane Way (becomes Grand Coulee Hill Road) and climb steeply to a junction (4.7 miles). Bear left (east) here (road name changes to Old Coulee Road at the Lincoln County line) to **Bagdad Junction** (2.2 miles). This expansive plateau country is grown to wheat. The best strategy is to drive the main, plowed section roads, looking for birds.

The highest part of the plateau, and possibly the best for birds, is reached by continuing south on Old Coulee Road from Bagdad Junction to **Jack Woods Butte** (elevation 2,818 feet), just northeast of the junction with Douglas Road (4.0 miles). From here you can bird graveled Douglas Road westward for the next eight miles (road changes name to Road 50 NE at the Grant County line) to the intersection with Road R NE. From here, you can either proceed south on Road R nine miles to US-2, at Hartline just east of Coulee City, or you can return to Grand Coulee.

To reach **Grand Coulee Dam**, take SR-155 two miles north from Grand Coulee. The mile-wide dam, completed in 1941, backs up the Columbia River more than 150 miles. Tours are offered into the innards of this gigantic structure, where a cavernous room is lined with 24 enormous turbines that generate enough power to supply the needs of two cities the size of Seattle. The dam has also been a salmon exterminator; no fish ladders were constructed to surmount this monumental barrier. Check the roiling waters below the dam from fall through spring for Common Merganser, gulls, and dippers. In winter, protected waters behind the dam may have diving ducks, loons, grebes, Bald Eagle, and loafing gulls.

NORTHEASTERN COLUMBIA BASIN

by Jim Acton, Mark Houston, and Andy Stepniewski
revised by Jon Isacoff

Endless wheat fields flank US-2 as it crosses the northern Columbia Basin east from Coulee City, interrupted only when the highway dips into scablands where soils scoured away by ice-age floods have been slow to redevelop. Shrub-steppe, scattered Ponderosa Pine forests, riparian vegetation, marshes, and pothole lakes are found in these unfarmable places. Because of elevation and proximity to the Selkirk Mountains, precipitation is higher than in most other parts of the Columbia Basin. The increased moisture sustains verdant grasslands with much Idaho Fescue—a snow- and cold-tolerant bunchgrass—and Quaking Aspen copses. Similar scablands habitats are found near Sprague, 25 miles farther south.

SWANSON LAKES

Nine miles east of Wilbur on US-2, Creston is the gateway to the **Swanson Lakes Wildlife Area**—20,000 acres of shrub-steppe, lake, marsh, riparian, and scattered Ponderosa Pine habitats. Taken together with close to 20,000 acres of adjacent BLM lands, this constitutes one of the most significant Channeled Scablands tracts in public ownership in Washington. Lakes in this wildlife area host high numbers of swans, geese, and ducks in spring and again in fall. Shorebirding can be exciting, particularly in late summer. Shrub-steppe denizens include Loggerhead Shrike, Sage Thrasher, and Brewer's Sparrow in Big Sagebrush, and Vesper and Grasshopper Sparrows in bunchgrass with less shrub cover. A primary habitat-management focus for Swanson Lakes is a remnant population of Sharp-tailed Grouse and a recently reintroduced population of Greater Sage-Grouse. They are seldom seen from publicly accessible locations, so time is probably better spent searching for other species.

The following circuit visits the major habitats, returning to US-2 east of Creston. Swanson Lakes Road turns south from US-2 just east of the grain elevators in Creston. Drive south through wheat farms and in 8.0 miles stop to scan steppe habitats on both sides of the road—excellent for Burrowing and Short-eared Owls, Horned Lark, and Vesper, Savannah, and Grasshopper Sparrows. Continue two miles to Swanson School Road. The old one-room schoolhouse on the left is plastered with Cliff Swallow nests.

Just south of the schoolhouse, the road crosses a narrow neck separating the two Swanson Lakes. When water levels are favorable, scoping the lakes from this vantage can yield most of the expected Columbia Basin waterbirds in spring and early summer, including Blue-winged and Cinnamon Teal, Northern Shoveler, Canvasback (a few), Redhead, Lesser Scaup, Ruddy Duck, Black-necked Stilt, American Avocet, and Wilson's Phalarope. Interesting

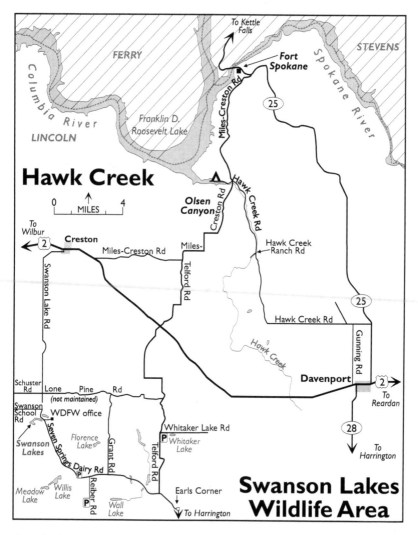

Hawk Creek

Swanson Lakes
Wildlife Area

shorebirds observed here from July through September include Black-bellied Plover, American Golden-Plover, Willet, Marbled Godwit, Red Knot, and Stilt, Baird's, Pectoral, and Semipalmated Sandpipers, in addition to the common species.

Just south of the lake (0.5 mile), note the road going left (east) to the WDFW office (information, restrooms). Take the right fork at this intersection, continuing south on Seven Springs Dairy Road. In 4.4 miles search for Sage Thrasher and Brewer's Sparrow in shrub-steppe habitat accessible from a parking area on the left. Turn right onto Reiber Road (0.3 mile) and go south

1.3 miles to a BLM parking area. If you walk the grasslands here, you might encounter Sharp-tailed Grouse.

Return to Seven Springs Dairy Road, turn right, and drive 4.3 miles to an intersection. Turn left and go north on Telford Road to Whitaker Lake Road (3.7 miles). If you are interested in searching for Sharp-tailed Grouse, park in the lot at this corner and explore the shrub-steppe terrain. Otherwise, drive to **Whitaker Lake** 0.7 mile east, where you may find waterfowl, shorebirds, and Black Tern. Starting about two miles farther north on Telford Road, an area of lake and marsh followed by an aspen copse may be worth some stops. Continue north on Telford Road to reach US-2 in a bit less than six miles.

HAWK CREEK

For a quick change of scenery and birdlife, go straight across US-2 on Telford Road to visit Hawk Creek—rich in breeding birds, particularly in May and June. This 45-mile circuit takes you down **Olsen Canyon** to Lake Roosevelt and Fort Spokane, returning via Hawk Creek to US-2 in Davenport.

Go north on Telford Road 4.6 miles and turn right onto Miles-Creston Road. Follow this road 3.6 miles across rolling uplands interspersed with Ponderosa Pine stands to the top of Olsen Canyon. Stop in the open pine woods anywhere along Telford or Miles-Creston Roads to listen for the harsh, two-part song of Gray Flycatcher—the only breeding *Empidonax* in this habitat. You should also expect Lewis's Woodpecker, Mountain Chickadee, Pygmy Nuthatch, and Red Crossbill. It is about three miles down Olsen Canyon to Hawk Creek Road. Partial logging of Douglas-fir stands along this stretch has fostered new deciduous undergrowth providing habitat for a nice diversity of species. The breeding empid of this quite different habitat is Dusky Flycatcher, which has a more spirited song than Gray. Several old logging tracks lead off to the left, allowing you to search for this species and many other birds.

At the intersection with Hawk Creek Road, you may turn left and drive half a mile to Hawk Creek Campground (hookups, fee) in the Franklin D. Roosevelt National Recreation Area. Or continue straight ahead on Miles-Creston Road for 7.2 miles, then left on SR-25 for half a mile to historic **Fort Spokane** (campground, hookups, fee). The Ponderosa Pine forest here has all three nuthatches, Cassin's Finch, and possibly White-headed Woodpecker.

Hawk Creek Road follows **Hawk Creek** uphill from the intersection with Miles-Creston Road. In 4.6 miles, turn right onto Hawk Creek Ranch Road and park. A small parcel of state land with riparian vegetation along the creek offers a nice assortment of birds. Common breeding species include Ruffed Grouse, Calliope Hummingbird, Belted Kingfisher, Red-naped Sapsucker, Veery, MacGillivray's Warbler, Yellow-breasted Chat, Black-headed

Grosbeak, and Lazuli Bunting. There are several reports of Least Flycatcher from this area.

Once again winding up Hawk Creek Road to the upper reaches of the canyon, check the stands of mixed Douglas-fir and Ponderosa Pine for Wild Turkey, Northern Saw-whet Owl, Lewis's Woodpecker, Steller's Jay, Clark's Nutcracker, and Townsend's Solitaire. On the plateau, be alert for Mountain Bluebird and Lark Sparrow. Hawk Creek Road turns left in 4.1 miles and goes east to an intersection with Gunning Road in five more miles. Turn right here to reach US-2 on the western outskirts of Davenport in 3.3 miles.

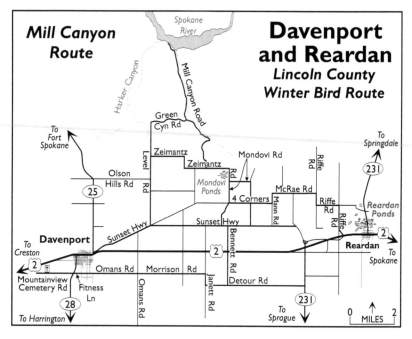

MILL CANYON

Mill Canyon is one of the most bird-diverse spots in the Columbia Basin, with nearly 200 species having been seen between the top of the canyon and its terminus, where Mill Creek meets the Spokane River. Locally- and regionally-rare birds documented here include Pacific Loon, Northern Goshawk, Ferruginous Hawk, Williamson's Sapsucker, Black-throated Blue Warbler, White-throated and Golden-crowned Sparrows, and Gray-crowned Rosy-Finch.

From Davenport, proceed north on SR-25 and take an immediate right onto Sunset Highway. Go approximately three miles and turn left onto Level Road. Head north 4.8 miles on Level, turn right onto Green Canyon Road, and you are now in the Mill Canyon system. During breeding season, look for Western Wood-Pewee, Gray Flycatcher, Yellow-rumped Warbler, and Lark Sparrow in the Ponderosa Pine section at the top of the canyon. In the evening, this is also a good spot to look for Common Nighthawk and Common Poorwill.

As you proceed down Green Canyon Road, which merges into Mill Canyon Road and the canyon proper, you may encounter all of the Lincoln County canyon breeding birds of interest, including Ruffed Grouse, Black-chinned and Calliope Hummingbirds, Red-naped Sapsucker, Dusky Flycatcher, Say's Phoebe, Cassin's and Warbling Vireos, Veery, Orange-crowned, MacGillivray's and Yellow Warblers, Yellow-breasted Chat, Black-headed Grosbeak, and Lazuli Bunting. Most of these species nest throughout the canyon from top to bottom. Mill Canyon is also the most likely place in Lincoln County to encounter Pileated Woodpecker, which is seen more from fall through spring but may nest periodically. During winter irruptive years, Mill Canyon is an excellent spot for Bohemian Waxwing, Pine Grosbeak, and Common Redpoll.

In the lower portion of the canyon, Lewis's and White-headed Woodpeckers have nested in some years, though they are intermittent. In the tall cottonwoods near the mouth of Mill Creek, Western Screech-Owls have nested. Unfortunately, the water level of the Spokane River at this location is highly irregular. When conditions are right during spring and fall migration, shorebirds may be present, including American Avocet, Semipalmated Plover, and Baird's and Pectoral Sandpipers.

Winter birding in the Spokane River at the bottom of Mill Canyon can be excellent. Surf and White-winged Scoters, Long-tailed Duck (rare), Red-breasted Merganser, Pacific (rare) and Common Loon, and all grebe species save Clark's are attracted to the food-rich waters here. Herring Gull can be regular in winter and Bonaparte's, Thayer's, and Glaucous Gulls have occurred here seasonally.

You can retrace your route to Davenport, or, to proceed southeast toward Reardan, follow Mill Canyon Road 6.8 miles from the bottom of the canyon to the top, staying on Mill Canyon Road. (Bear left at the intersection with Green Canyon Road.) Turn left onto Zeimantz Road E and proceed 1.5 miles. Continue onto Mondovi Road N and go two miles. Turn left onto Sunset Highway for 0.3 mile and then right onto Bennett Road N for 1.0 mile. Turn left onto US-2 and head east for 6.4 miles into Reardan.

DAVENPORT AND REARDAN

In birding circles, the **Davenport cemetery** is well known as a migrant trap. Near the west edge of town, turn south from US-2 onto SR-28, drive 0.9 mile, and turn right onto Mountainview Cemetery Road, reaching the cemetery in 0.7 mile. In spring and fall, this isolated patch of tall spruces, firs, and pines can be full of migrant flycatchers, vireos, Ruby-crowned Kinglets, thrushes, warblers, sparrows, Western Tanagers, Bullock's Orioles, and finches. Vagrants seen here over the years include Ovenbird and Black-and-white, Tennessee, Chestnut-sided, Blackpoll, and Palm Warblers. Fall and winter bring an influx of Red and White-winged (irregular) Crossbills, Common Redpolls (irregular), and Pine Siskins.

Reardan is the next town east of Davenport, 13 wheat-field-lined miles on US-2. The **Reardan Ponds** are 0.4 miles north of US-2 on both sides of SR-231. Public access areas (Discover Pass required) are found on both the north and south sides of the ponds. Generally, most species of shorebirds and marshbirds are best seen from the south access. To reach that parking area, proceed north from US-2 on SR-231 for three blocks. Turn right onto Railroad Avenue, go 0.2 miles and turn left onto Audubon Way. The parking area will be visible on the left. The ponds are good for many species of ducks and marshbirds, including Black Terns from April to August. This is one of the best spots in Eastern Washington for shorebirds, especially in late summer after the water level has fallen off to expose mud. Less-common species such as Solitary, Baird's, and Semipalmated Sandpipers, occur regularly. Rarities such as Piping Plover (the only Washington record), Whimbrel (two records), Ruff, Sharp-tailed Sandpiper, White-rumped Sandpiper (three of the five state records), and Red Phalarope have turned up here.

From December to February, try the 32-mile **Lincoln County Winter Bird Route** that loops around the high wheat fields north and south of US-2 between Reardan and Davenport. Rough-legged Hawks can be common along this route. Snowy and Short-eared Owls are seen regularly, as are Gray Partridge, Northern Harrier, Prairie Falcon, large numbers of Horned Larks (including side-by-side studies of the pale arcticola race and much yellower resident merrilli race), Snow Bunting, and American Tree Sparrow. Lapland Longspur and Gray-crowned Rosy-Finch are less common but annual; Gyrfalcon is rare but annual. Most years, early spring finds some of the deeper swales in the wheat fields filled with snowmelt water. These temporary lakes can attract migrating Tundra Swans and clouds of geese and dabbling ducks.

Use these directions and the accompanying map (page 392) to find your way along the loop. Begin in Reardan at the junction of SR-231 and US-2. Go west on US-2 to Riffe Road (1.1 miles). Turn right and follow Riffe Road as it winds north and west. In 2.8 miles, turn left onto McRae Road. Wind west and south for 2.4 miles, then turn right onto Four Corners Road. Keep straight west for two miles and turn right onto Mondovi Road.

In one mile, keep straight as paved Mondovi Road swings to the right. You are now on Zeimantz Road (gravel). Go a half-mile, then swing left with Zeimantz Road. Waterfowl may be present in the shallow Mondovi Ponds on the left. Continue west and north 3.9 miles to Level Road. Turn left here and go three miles to Sunset Highway. Go right 2.8 miles to SR-25. Here, go left for 0.1 mile to US-2.

Turn right and go through Davenport (mind the speed limits); in 0.8 mile turn left onto SR-28. In another 0.9 mile turn left onto Fitness Lane, which becomes Omans Road. In 2.9 miles keep straight as Omans Road turns right. You are now on Morrison Road. In 2.9 miles turn right onto Janett Road. Turn left in 0.5 mile onto Detour Road. The knolls along this road are a good bet for Snowy Owl. Turn left onto SR-231 in 4.5 miles, rejoining US-2 in 1.7 miles. Reardan is about three miles east of this intersection and Davenport about 10 miles west.

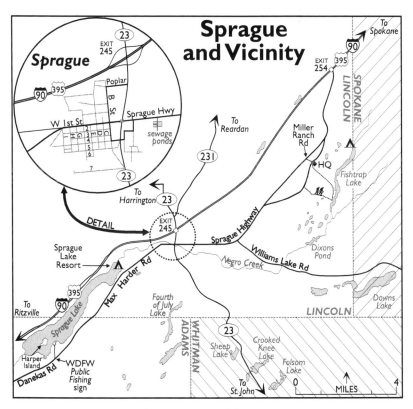

SPRAGUE AND VICINITY

The area around Sprague, about 36 miles southwest of Spokane, has emerged during recent years as one of the top birding destinations in Eastern Washington. The habitats here are varied and include deep-water **Sprague Lake**, several shallow lakes and ponds (some with marshy edges and mudflats), sewage lagoons, deciduous and riparian areas, productive grasslands, and Ponderosa Pine groves.

Leave I-90 at Exit 245 and go south on SR-23 to Poplar Street (0.2 mile). Turn right and go 0.2 mile to B Street. Turn left (south) and go 0.2 mile. Turn right onto First Street (becomes Max Harder Road) and drive west out of Sprague.

One stop many birders enjoy during migration is the Sprague Lake Resort (fees apply). To reach the resort, proceed as above and at 1.6 miles, turn right onto Sprague Resort Road. Go 0.3 mile to the end. The trees and shrubs at the resort form one of the finest migrant traps in Eastern Washington. Every regularly occurring migrant flycatcher, vireo, warbler, and sparrow has been observed here. Rarities seen include Least Flycatcher, Great-tailed Grackle, Tennessee Warbler (three records), Blackpoll Warbler, Eastern Blue Jay, Clay-colored Sparrow and nearly annual White-throated and Golden-crowned Sparrows. The marsh behind the resort is now thought to be the new home to the now defunct Tricolored Blackbird colony formerly at Texas Lake. Singing birds in counts up to 14 individuals have been seen during recent years. Be sure to obey private property signs at the edge of the resort.

To continue birding Sprague Lake, return to Max Harder Road and turn right. Proceed to the WDFW Public Fishing area at 4.4 miles (Max Harder becomes Danekas Road when crossing into Adams County). Turn right and drive north 0.3 mile to a fork, then left to an overlook of Harper Island, where Ring-billed and California Gulls nest in large numbers. In past years, American White Pelicans and Caspian Terns also have nested, though their status is intermittent. A scope is mandatory at this location to see the thousands of waterfowl that congregate in fall and spring. A number of local and regional rarities have shown up here over the years including Tufted Duck, Surf and White-winged Scoters, Long-tailed Duck, Pacific Loon, Sabine's Gull (September), Franklin's Gull (spring and early summer), and Common Tern (September).

Return to Sprague on Max Harder Road and drive straight east through town on First Street, which becomes Sprague Highway Road. You will pass under SR-23 on the east side of town; continue 0.4 mile to the **Sprague sewage ponds**, on the right. Scoping from the road should yield a variety of ducks and gulls (including Bonaparte's on occasion). If water levels are not too high, the eastern pond can have shorebirds, especially in August and September. Look for Black-necked Stilt, American Avocet, both yellowlegs, Stilt, Baird's, Least, Pectoral, Semipalmated, and Western Sandpipers, Long-billed Dowitcher, and Wilson's and Red-necked Phalaropes.

Continuing east on Sprague Highway another 3.6 miles brings you to the southern access to 8,000 acres of federal land at **Fishtrap Lake**. Habitat diversity is high for such a relatively small area—Palouse steppe, shrub-steppe, Ponderosa Pine forests, riparian thickets, and marsh-lined lakes. Turn right at the BLM entrance sign. Birding can be excellent in spring and early summer along this gravel road for the next three miles to BLM headquarters at Miller Ranch Road. En route you will find the trailhead for Fishtrap Lake, on the right. A 3.5-mile trail starts here and visits all the major habitats, including deeper waters of the lake, looping back to end at headquarters.

You can also bird quite effectively by making frequent stops along the road to sample the different habitats, most of which can be found close by. Shallow ponds and wetlands attract marsh species, including scads of waterfowl (Blue-winged and Cinnamon Teal, Northern Shoveler, Redhead, Ruddy Duck), Virginia Rail, Sora, Wilson's Phalarope, Black Tern, Marsh Wren, and Yellow-headed Blackbird. Grasslands and shrub-steppe have Gray Partridge, Northern Harrier, Swainson's Hawk, Common Nighthawk, American Kestrel, Horned Lark, and Vesper, Savannah, and Grasshopper Sparrows. Redtailed Hawk, Great Horned Owl, Downy Woodpecker, Black-capped Chickadee, House Wren, Western Bluebird, and Lazuli Bunting nest in aspen and riparian habitats. Look for Lewis's Woodpecker, Pygmy Nuthatch, and Red Crossbill in the pines.

The road forks at headquarters. Take the right branch, reaching Sprague Highway in 1.3 miles. Turn right here to reach I-90 (Exit 254) in 2.3 miles.

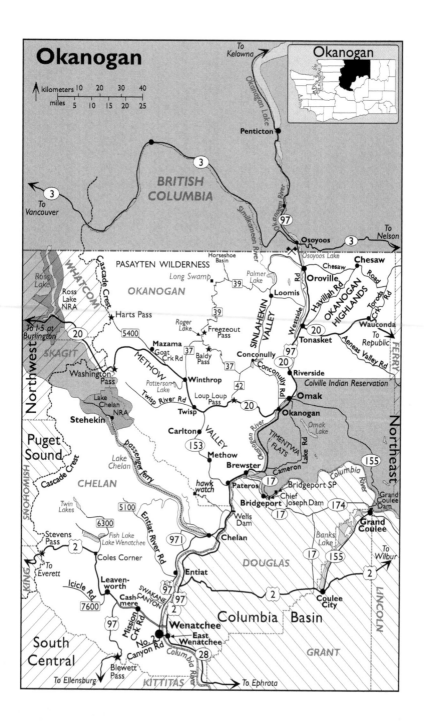

Okanogan

kilometers 10 20 30 40

miles 5 10 15 20 25

To Kelowna

Okanogan

Penticton

BRITISH COLUMBIA

③

③ To Vancouver

Okanogan Lake

Similkameen River

97

Osoyoos

To Nelson

③

Osoyoos Lake

PASAYTEN WILDERNESS

Horseshoe Basin

Chesaw

Chesaw

Chesaw Road

WHATCOM

Cascade Crest

Ross Lake

Ross Lake NRA

OKANOGAN

Long Swamp

Palmer Lake

39

Loomis

Oroville

Havillah Rd

OKANOGAN HIGHLANDS

Toroda Crk Rd

Harts Pass

Roger Lake

Freezeout Pass

39

SINLAHEKIN VALLEY

Westside Rd

20

Wauconda

To Republic

FERRY

To I-5 at Burlington

20

5400

Mazama

Goat Crk Rd

37

Baldy Pass

37

Tonasket

97

20

Aeneas Valley Rd

SKAGIT

Washington Pass

METHOW

Patterson Lake

Winthrop

Conconully

Conconully Rd

Riverside

Colville Indian Reservation

Northwest

Lake Chelan NRA

42

Loup Loup Pass

20

Omak

Stehekin

Twisp River Rd

Twisp

Carlton

VALLEY

Okanogan

Okanogan River

TIMENTWA FLATS

Omak Lake

Northeast

Puget Sound

Cascade Crest

Lake Chelan

153

Methow

Brewster

Cameron Lake Rd

155

SNOHOMISH

CHELAN

passenger ferry

hawk watch

Pateros

17

Bridgeport SP

Columbia River

Grand Coulee Dam

Twin Lakes

5100

Bridgeport

Chief Joseph Dam

174

Stevens Pass

6300

Fish Lake

Lake Wenatchee

Entiat River Rd

97

Wells Dam

17

Grand Coulee

2

To Everett

Coles Corner

Chelan

Banks Lake

To Wilbur

KING

Icicle Rd

Leavenworth

Entiat

DOUGLAS

17

155

Cashmere

7600

SWAKANE CANYON

AH 97

97

2

Coulee City

2

LINCOLN

97

Mission Crk Rd

Wenatchee

East Wenatchee

Columbia Basin

GRANT

South Central

No. 2

Canyon Rd

28

To Ellensburg

Blewett Pass

Columbia River

KITTITAS

To Ephrata

OKANOGAN

If you like birding in wide open spaces, give north central Washington a try. This vast area stretches more than half the distance from the Cascade Crest to the Idaho line, and more than half the distance from British Columbia to Oregon. Composed of just two counties, Okanogan and Chelan—largest and third largest in Washington, respectively—the region accounts for less than 2 percent of the state's population. Of people, that is. When it comes to birds, few other places in North America have as many breeding species (about 200). Migration and winter bring yet more birds; in all, more than 300 species occur in the region.

The geography is simple enough: mountains to the east (Okanogan Highlands) and to the west (northeastern Cascades), separated by the broad valley of the Okanogan River that gives the region its name. All three of these zones continue north, oblivious of the U.S.-Canada border. The Okanogan River flows south to join the Columbia River, which forms the southern boundary of the region. The Columbia channel marks the point where the recent basalt flows that inundated the Columbia Basin stopped abruptly upon contact with the much older rocks of the Okanogan country. West and south from the Okanogan River mouth, high ridges of the Cascades come right to the Columbia, side by side with the Methow, Stehekin/Chelan, Entiat, and Wenatchee River valleys.

Elevational differences produce a great variety of habitats. At 6,000–7,000 feet, the subalpine and alpine zones at Harts Pass and in the Okanogan Cascades offer superb opportunities to search for species such as White-tailed Ptarmigan and Boreal Chickadee. At the lower extreme (700–2,500 feet elevation), shrub-steppe habitats on the drier slopes of the river valleys and on the Timentwa Flats support Great Basin species such as Sage Thrasher and Brewer's Sparrow. Well-watered sites in river bottoms—e.g., the Sinlahekin, the Similkameen, and the Okanogan near Oroville—sustain a bonanza of bird species of riparian, marsh, wet-meadow, and lacustrine habitats. Extensive Ponderosa Pine and mixed-conifer forests mantle the middle elevations between these extremes. The Okanogan Highlands offer a quite special landscape of grasslands, Ponderosa Pine, Douglas-fir and mixed-conifer forests, and extensive riparian areas, interspersed with lakes and marshes. A small population of Great Gray Owls appears to be established in this mid-elevation mosaic of habitats, which is also excellent for Flammulated, Northern Pygmy-, and Northern Saw-whet Owls.

Summers are generally warm in the valleys (July average high temperature 87 degrees in Omak, 86 degrees in Winthrop) but cooler in the mountains (July average high 76 degrees in Chesaw, 66 degrees at Stevens Pass). If camping, be aware that nights are cold (even freezing) at 6,000 feet. Winters are cold in the lowlands (January average low temperature 22 degrees in Wenatchee, 17 degrees in Omak) and colder still in the mountains (January average low 11 degrees in Chesaw and Winthrop). Storms along the Cascade Crest are frequent and often prolonged, bringing heavy precipitation (494 inches annual snowfall and 81 inches total precipitation at Stevens Pass). To the east, precipitation is uniformly low, ranging from 9 inches annually at Wenatchee to 14 in Winthrop and Chesaw. The amount that comes as snowfall is much more variable, however—annual average 26 inches at Omak, 28 at Wenatchee, 50 at Chesaw, and a perfect 72 inches at Winthrop, making for famed cross-country skiing. Except for SR-20 (closed for the winter above Mazama), all state and federal highways are plowed and sanded, as are many secondary roads. With reasonable precautions, and allowance made for occasional severe conditions, winter driving in the Okanogan poses few or no difficulties.

Wenatchee—with 32,000 inhabitants, the largest city in Eastern Washington north of the Columbia Basin—offers a full range of accommodations and all essential services. Leavenworth, Cashmere, Chelan, Stehekin, Twisp, Winthrop, Mazama, and Pateros cater to travelers and vacationers in the Cascades. Along the Okanogan Valley on US-97, motels, restaurants, provisions, and gas stations can be found at Brewster, Okanogan, Omak, Tonasket, and Oroville. The region has many USFS and other campgrounds.

STEVENS PASS TO WENATCHEE

by Dave Beaudette, Lee Cain, Dan Stephens, and Andy Stepniewski
revised by Dan Stephens

From Puget Sound at Everett, US-2 follows the Snohomish and Skykomish River valleys to the Cascade Crest at Stevens Pass, then descends along the Wenatchee River drainage to the Columbia River at Wenatchee. The highway is open all year, except for temporary winter closures for avalanche control. Eastward from the summit, it is only a one-hour drive from moist lower-subalpine forests to dry Eastside woodlands and semi-arid shrub-steppe habitats. To the south, hundreds of glacial lakes nestle beneath serrated granite ridges in the rugged, sparsely timbered Alpine Lakes Wilderness.

STEVENS PASS

The **Old Cascade Highway**—closed to through traffic—offers about the same mix of species as the far busier Stevens Pass. This road turns north from US-2 about a quarter-mile west of the summit. The habitat at the top end is a thick forest of Silver Fir, Mountain Hemlock, and some Alaska Yellowcedar. A good birding spot is at the first switchback (1.5 miles). The forest is more open here, with Noble Fir, Douglas-fir, and heavy brush. Sooty Grouse hoot along the road in spring and early summer, and Golden Eagles sometimes fly along the ridge to the north. Forest and openings can have Gray Jay, Clark's Nutcracker, Hermit and Varied Thrushes, MacGillivray's, Yellow-rumped, and Wilson's Warblers, Red Crossbill, Pine Siskin, and Evening Grosbeak. Dusky Flycatcher and Nashville Warbler sometimes can be found in brushy places. The Wellington Trailhead (Iron Goat Trail #1074—America the Beautiful or Northwest Forest Pass required) is at the end of a short spur road one mile beyond the switchbacks. Look for American Dipper from the footbridge over the Tye River at the road's end (2.3 miles).

The Silver Fir forest at Stevens Pass (elevation 4,061 feet) has been opened to make the **Stevens Pass Ski Area**, creating an abundance of brushy habitats easily accessible from US-2. Walk along any of the roads around the ski slopes. Breeding birds include Rufous Hummingbird, Olive-sided and Willow Flycatchers, Violet-green and Barn Swallows, Hermit and Varied Thrushes, MacGillivray's, Yellow, Yellow-rumped, Townsend's, and Wilson's Warblers, Slate-colored Fox, Lincoln's, and White-crowned (*pugetensis*) Sparrows, Dark-eyed Junco, and Pine Siskin. Purple and Cassin's Finches occur in fall; later, a few Common Redpolls may appear among the more numerous siskins. White-winged Crossbills are regular here in irruption years. The Pacific Crest Trail crosses Stevens Pass, providing access to the Alpine Lakes Wilderness to the south and the Henry M. Jackson Wilderness to the north.

Perhaps the easiest way to reach upper-subalpine parkland habitats is on the trail above **Union Gap**. From Stevens Pass, drive about four miles east and downhill on US-2, turning left onto Smithbrook Road (FR-6700). In 2.7 miles, park at the Smithbrook Trailhead (America the Beautiful or Northwest Forest Pass required) and walk the one-mile trail to Union Gap. The trail passes through brushy slopes, old-growth forest (where Northern Pygmy-Owl and other birds typical of moist forest can be expected), and a small sedge meadow (check for Lincoln's Sparrow). At the crest (elevation 4,680 feet), turn left and take the Pacific Crest Trail to Lake Valhalla (1.5 miles). You encounter mature Silver Fir and Mountain Hemlock forest first, then parkland with lots of Mountain Ash and huckleberries. From the ridge above the lake, climb right (west) on an unmarked footpath up a small peak, reaching open slopes with huckleberry pastures and views south to Mount Rainier and north to Glacier Peak. This habitat is especially good for migrants in late summer and fall: Sharp-shinned, Cooper's, and Red-tailed Hawks, American Kestrel, Prairie Falcon, Bohemian Waxwing (after mid-October), and a variety of warblers and sparrows.

Continue east on US-2 for 1.6 miles to the Stevens Pass Nordic Center and the Upper Mill Creek Road. The open areas about 2.5 miles up this road

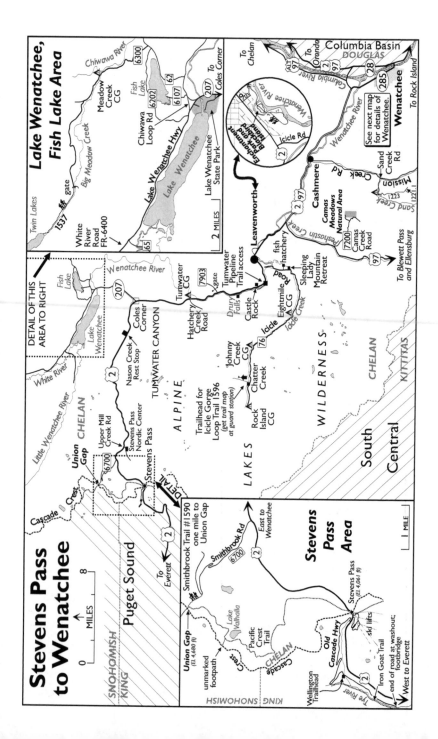

are good for both subspecies of White-crowned Sparrow (*pugetensis* and possibly *gambelii*) as well as Slate-colored Fox Sparrow. Another 11 miles down US-2, the Nason Creek Rest Stop is good for Ponderosa Pine species; White-headed Woodpecker has been seen here.

LAKE WENATCHEE

Five miles long and a mile wide, Lake Wenatchee enjoys a spectacular setting in a glacial trench between two high mountain ridges. The state park at the outlet (east) end of the lake is often crowded and noisy, and much of the shoreline is private. Better birding can usually be had at the inlet end. Turn north from US-2 onto SR-207 at Coles Corner, 2.7 miles east of Nason Creek Rest Stop and 14 miles north of Leavenworth. At a fork in 4.3 miles—0.8 mile past the entrance to Lake Wenatchee State Park South (camping, picnicking)—bear left onto Lake Wenatchee Highway, passing the north park entrance in 0.3 mile. Continue 5.8 miles on the highway to a junction with White River Road. Keep left here onto FR-65 (aka Little Wenatchee River Road). In another half-mile stop at the large meadow to look for Wilson's Snipe and Common Yellowthroat. Cross the bridge over the **White River** and bird the riparian groves and conifer forest for the next half-mile from the road and on a couple of dirt tracks that lead off into the forest. Birds to look for include Common Merganser, Ruffed Grouse, Osprey, Black and Vaux's Swifts, Calliope Hummingbird, Red-naped Sapsucker, Western Wood-Pewee, Willow, Hammond's, and Pacific-slope Flycatchers, Warbling and Red-eyed Vireos, Steller's Jay, Common Raven, many Tree, Violet-green, and Cliff Swallows, Mountain and Chestnut-backed Chickadees, Red-breasted Nuthatch, American Dipper, Veery, Swainson's and Hermit Thrushes, Nashville, MacGillivray's, Yellow, and Townsend's Warblers, Western Tanager, Lazuli Bunting, Purple and Cassin's Finches, and Red Crossbill.

Smaller, quieter **Fish Lake**—just northeast of Lake Wenatchee—is worth a look. If coming from the preceding site, drive east on Lake Wenatchee Highway 5.6 miles from the White River Road intersection, then make a left onto Chiwawa Loop Road (this turn is 0.2 mile west of the Lake Wenatchee State Park North entrance). In 0.6 mile, turn left onto FR-6107 (aka FR-6401 and Cove Resort Road).

If coming from the south, turn right at the fork 0.8 mile after the Lake Wenatchee State Park South entrance (just after crossing the Wenatchee River). Keep right in 0.4 mile at the next intersection. You are now on Chiwawa Loop Road, from which FR-6107 (aka FR-6401 and Cove Resort Road) turns left in 0.1 mile (*Fish Lake* sign). Drive north 0.8 mile on this road, park on the left just before a crowded resort area, and take the forest trail that winds along the southwest edge of Fish Lake. Look for geese and ducks, Red-necked Grebe, Osprey, Bald Eagle, and a variety of swallows, including Bank as this short trail nears the marshy west end of the lake.

FR-62 goes northwestward from Fish Lake deep into the Cascades, offering many USFS campgrounds along the Chiwawa River and trailheads for wilderness hiking and backpacking. For a quick sample of the lower part of these forest habitats, continue east on Chiwawa Loop Road from the FR-6107 turnoff, and in 0.7 mile turn left onto FR-62 (aka Chiwawa River Road). At an intersection in 2.2 miles, where FR-62 goes straight, turn left onto FR-6300. In 2.5 miles, note Meadow Creek Campground (fee) on the right. At a fork in another 0.4 mile, keep left on FR-6300, which traverses moist forest for the most part. In 3.5 miles, a small stretch of Deerbrush hugs the steep south-facing slopes. Breeding birds in this habitat are Calliope Hummingbird, Dusky Flycatcher, Orange-crowned and Nashville Warblers, and Slate-colored Fox Sparrow. Continue driving up the road another 1.2 miles and park near a locked gate. Just before the gate, walk left along FR-6309 for 30 yards over a creek to explore riparian habitat dominated by alders.

From the gate, Trail 1537 heads into the Glacier Peak Wilderness, reaching the Twin Lakes (elevation 2,822 feet) in two miles. Barrow's Goldeneye and Spotted Sandpiper nest here. Birding riparian and conifer habitats near the gate and along the trail might yield Vaux's Swift, Rufous Hummingbird, Red-naped and Red-breasted Sapsuckers (and hybrids), Olive-sided Flycatcher, Warbling Vireo, Chestnut-backed Chickadee, Pacific Wren, Swainson's and Varied Thrushes, Nashville, MacGillivray's, Yellow, and Townsend's Warblers, Western Tanager, and Black-headed Grosbeak.

LEAVENWORTH AND ICICLE CREEK

US-2 follows the Wenatchee River as it tumbles down the **Tumwater Canyon**, flanked by towering granitic peaks. Tumwater Campground (USFS, fee, closed through 2015 because of flood damage) is on the left side of the highway at the head of the canyon, 5.6 miles south of the SR-207 junction. To the right is Hatchery Creek Road, FR-7905. This road is good for Ruffed Grouse and, at 1.9 miles, a riparian area is excellent birding with Black-throated Gray Warbler often seen.

Return to US-2 and pull off at the blocked FR-7903 road on the left in another 2.1 miles. This road/trail meanders through a variety of habitats for several miles with good chances for Sooty Grouse, plus a great variety of eastside forest species. Continue down the highway toward Leavenworth for 1.3 miles to a pullout just below the Wall Rapids. Here, scan to the west across the river into the Drury Falls cliff complex for Peregrine Falcon. At least one pair has successfully nested here for the last 15 years. Early morning and evening are the best times to see birds at the nests, as the adults hunt the Wenatchee River drainage during the day. Look in and above the white cliffs. The active nest sites change frequently and are not always visible from the highway.

Proceed 2.3 miles downcanyon and turn left into a parking area where a steep trail leads to Castle Rock. Hike around Castle Rock where, from the top of the trail, you can view a complex of cliffs where Peregrine Falcon has consistently nested. One mile farther down US-2 turn right into a parking lot (not marked and easy to miss). Take the Tumwater Pipeline Trail across the steel bridge that once supported water pipes leading to generators that powered Great Northern electric locomotives through the eight-mile Cascade Tunnel, where coal-burning engines could not operate. The power plant was abandoned decades ago when diesel replaced steam. Walk upstream on the smooth path. Look among the giant boulders in the torrent below for Harlequin Duck, Common Merganser, and American Dipper. Trailside thickets of Bigleaf Maple and Ocean Spray, interspersed with Douglas-fir and Ponderosa Pine, have breeding Pacific-slope Flycatcher, Cassin's Vireo, Nashville Warbler, and Western Tanager. An Osprey nest is on the highway side about a mile upstream from the Pipeline Bridge.

Continue down US-2 and turn right in 1.6 miles onto Icicle Road, on the western outskirts of Leavenworth. In 2.1 miles turn left on Hatchery Road to reach **Leavenworth National Fish Hatchery**. If the gate is closed, park outside and walk in. Cross the dam to the east side of the hatchery to find a natural area that features a one-mile loop trail where over 120 bird species have been recorded. Breeding season and migration are the best times for birding. The habitat is primarily deciduous forest and brush, with a few conifers. Wood Duck, Harlequin Duck, and Common Merganser nest along the waterways; other nesting species include Osprey, Western Screech-Owl, Black-chinned and Rufous Hummingbirds, Red-naped and Red-breasted Sapsuckers (and hybrids), White-headed (pines) and Pileated Woodpeckers, Pacific-slope Flycatcher, Red-eyed Vireo, all three nuthatches, American Dipper (dam), Veery, Swainson's Thrush, Gray Catbird, several species of warblers, and Purple and Cassin's Finches. Black Swift is often seen overhead and evidently breeds somewhere in these mountains. In migration, check for Fox and Golden-crowned Sparrows. Winter brings a few Pine Grosbeaks.

The turnoff to **Sleeping Lady Mountain Retreat** is 0.3 mile farther along Icicle Road. Many environmental conferences are held here, along with music festivals and other events open to the public. Birders are free to wander the grounds: look for White-headed Woodpecker, Lazuli Bunting, and Cassin's Finch, among many others, and for Harlequin Duck and American Dipper in the creek.

Icicle Road (becomes FR-7600) continues up Icicle Creek for more than 15 miles, serving a number of campgrounds (USFS). Check Lower Johnny Creek and Eight Mile campgrounds for Harlequin Duck in the spring and early summer. The blacktop ends in 10 miles; continue on the gravel road for another 2.3 miles to the USFS Chatter Creek Guard Station (maps, information). Half a mile farther on is parking (America the Beautiful Pass or Northwest Forest Pass required) for the **Icicle Gorge Loop Trail 1596**, a four-mile loop on a smooth, gentle trail that follows alongside boulder-strewn Icicle Creek. Walk left to cross the creek on a bridge. The trail goes upstream and then veers away from the noisy creek into moist forest, followed by a dry forest of Ponderosa Pine and Douglas-fir; then, the trail comes back to Icicle Creek and follows it for about 100 yards, where Harlequin Duck can be seen in late spring and summer. Continue on the trail as it leaves Icicle Creek and soon crosses Jack Creek; continue for another 0.2 mile to FR-7600. Turn right and cross Icicle Creek into Rock Island Campground (0.1 mile), picking up the trail again on the opposite bank. Walk downstream on this trail to return to the parking lot. Species to look for at various places along the loop include Harlequin Duck, Common Merganser, Rufous and Calliope Hummingbirds, Belted Kingfisher, Red-naped Sapsucker, Hairy Woodpecker, Olive-sided, Hammond's, and Pacific-slope Flycatchers, Chestnut-backed Chickadee, Hermit Thrush, Townsend's Warbler, Red Crossbill, and Pine Siskin. To reach drier habitats and vistas of Icicle Canyon, take View Trail.

From the same parking lot, walk 50 yards back toward the guard station and head uphill on a moderately steep trail for about three-quarters of a mile to a prominence overlooking the valley, passing through Douglas-fir and Deerbrush forest—good habitat for Cassin's Vireo and Western Tanager.

Trailheads along FR-7600 give access to the **Alpine Lakes Wilderness Area** (393,000 acres), renowned for its picturesque lakes set in glacially polished basins and framed by Alpine Larches that turn blazing yellow in fall. White-tailed Ptarmigan, American Pipit, and other alpine species occur above treeline, but getting into their habitat demands lengthy hiking or backpacking on steep, rocky trails, which few birders undertake.

Just past the Icicle Road intersection, US-2 enters **Leavenworth**. Made up as a Bavarian village, this friendly community offers many shops, restaurants, and motels, as well as prime riparian birding practically in the middle of town. Turn right onto Ninth Street (0.9 mile from Icicle Road) and go downhill three blocks to an intersection. Turn left here onto a gravel lane to parking for Enchantment Park (0.1 mile). A short trail goes upstream along the Wenatchee River to a bridge over a slough to **Blackbird Island**. This luxuriant riparian community, created a century ago by a logging mill pond (breached in 1932), is home to many birds. In May and June, look for Common Merganser, Osprey, Vaux's Swift, Western Wood-Pewee, Warbling and Red-eyed Vireos, a variety of swallows, House Wren, Veery, Gray Catbird, MacGillivray's and Yellow Warblers, and Black-headed and Evening Grosbeaks. Downy Woodpecker, Northern Flicker, and Black-capped Chickadee are here year round, joined by Bald Eagle in winter. This place can be hopping in migration, too.

PESHASTIN CREEK AND MISSION CREEK

About four miles east of Leavenworth, US-97 turns south from US-2 and ascends the Peshastin Creek drainage for 21 miles to Blewett Pass (aka Swauk Pass) (page 404). Take this highway, and in 5.2 miles from US-2 turn left (east) onto Camas Creek Road (FR-7200). Go uphill 3.0 miles to an intersection with a minor road on the left. Turn left and then park in the small parking lot on the right. This large, tree-rimmed meadow is the 1,300-acre **Camas Meadows Natural Area** (DNR), dedicated to preserving a number of rare plants. It is also a great place for birds and butterflies. Walk into the meadow for about a quarter-mile to an aspen stand taking care to stay on the narrow trail.

Return to the parking lot and walk the minor road to the northeast for a half-mile through a disturbed Ponderosa Pine area; stay left at a road that leads to private property. Hairy, White-headed, and Black-backed Woodpeckers have all been noted in the vicinity as have a variety of passerines. Return to FR-7200 and proceed on this easement through private property (bird only from the road) to a junction in 0.7 mile. FR-7200 runs through riparian habitat for another half-mile; walk or stop frequently along this birdy riparian area. Continue for another 1.5 miles along FR-7200 through mixed forest and Ponderosa Pine woodland to a large logged-over area. Species in this area include Sooty Grouse, Northern Goshawk, Northern Pygmy-Owl, Williamson's and Red-naped Sapsuckers, Hairy and White-headed Woodpeckers, Dusky Flycatcher, all three nuthatches, Western Bluebird, Veery, Swainson's Thrush, Nashville Warbler, Chipping Sparrow, Cassin's Finch, and Red Crossbill.

Return to US-2 (now combined with US-97) and head east. In 6.4 miles, turn right onto Aplets Way in the town of Cashmere, noted for a fruit confection called "Aplets and Cotlets" that can be purchased in any of the innumerable shops. The road soon changes name to Division Street. Bend right onto Pioneer Avenue in 0.6 mile, and, in about 0.1 mile, turn left onto **Mission Creek Road**. In 0.5 mile, the road jogs right, then left, and runs south along Mission Creek—initially through orchards, then through a mosaic of riparian and coniferous habitats. Birding is especially productive in May and June along this road, where you can expect Ruffed Grouse, Cooper's Hawk, Red-naped Sapsucker, Hammond's and Pacific-slope Flycatchers, Cassin's and Warbling Vireos, Black-capped and Mountain Chickadees, Veery, Swainson's Thrush, Gray Catbird, MacGillivray's, Yellow-rumped, Black-throated Gray, and Wilson's Warblers, Black-headed Grosbeak, Lazuli Bunting, Bullock's Oriole, and Purple Finch. There are good pullouts at 2.7, 3.4, and 4.7 miles; otherwise this is all private property.

In 6.4 miles, turn right onto Sand Creek Road, which ends in one mile at a primitive campground (USFS, fee) and trailhead for **Red Hill Mountain**. Calliope Hummingbird, Hammond's Flycatcher, and Nashville and MacGillivray's Warblers can be found near the parking lot. The surrounding slopes are part of the Devil's Gulch Roadless Area (25,000 acres), known for its old-growth Ponderosa Pine, an increasingly rare habitat type in Washington. Surveys have been conducted here for several years; the list of breeding species includes Sharp-shinned Hawk, Northern Goshawk, Flammulated, Northern Pygmy-, and six other species of owls, Common Poorwill, Vaux's Swift, Rufous Hummingbird, Williamson's Sapsucker, Hairy, White-headed, Black-backed, and Pileated Woodpeckers, Gray, Dusky, and Pacific-slope Flycatchers, Cassin's Vireo, White-breasted and Pygmy Nuthatches, Swainson's and Hermit Thrushes, and Purple and Cassin's Finches.

Red Hill Mountain Trail #1223 provides an excellent birding route. You will share it with dirt- and mountain-bikers, but they are generally not out in the early morning, when birding is at its best. The trail begins at the restroom, crosses Sand Creek, and gently switchbacks up through open Douglas-fir on a moist, north-facing slope to meet a ridgeline where Ponderosa Pines dominate. You arrive at a small logged-over area, now in a brushy state (Dusky Flycatcher). In 3.8 miles, you reach a saddle among still more imposing pines. Go left about a quarter-mile on Trail #1223.1 for great views of the Stuart Range.

WENATCHEE

From the Aplets Way junction in Cashmere, continue east on US-2/US-97 toward Wenatchee for 7.7 miles and take the exit signed *East US-2* and *North US-97*. In another 0.6 mile, take the exit signed *WA Apple Visitor Ctr* and *State Patrol*. At the end of the long exit ramp (0.3 mile), turn right onto Euclid Avenue. In 0.4 mile, where the road makes its second curve to the right, Euclid becomes Penny Road. Turn left here to stay on Euclid. Go 0.4 mile, turn left into the **Wenatchee Confluence State Park**, then right into the first parking lot (Discover Pass required). This popular park (camping, picnicking) at the confluence of the Wenatchee and Columbia Rivers has the best riparian birding in Wenatchee. It is also a proven site for local

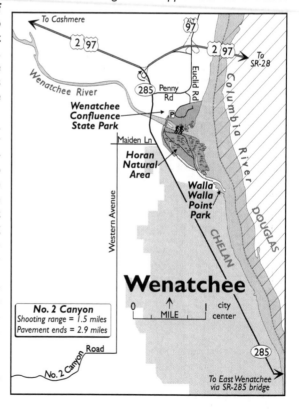

and even state rarities, with records for Brant, Eurasian Wigeon (regular), Long-tailed Duck, Red-breasted Merganser, Great Egret, Green Heron, Yellow-crowned Night-Heron, Parasitic Jaeger, Little, Laughing, Mew, Western, and Thayer's Gulls, Arctic Tern, Gyrfalcon, Purple Martin, and Magnolia and Blackburnian Warblers, to name a few. Some 235 species have been recorded in the Confluence Park/Walla Walla Park complex.

A paved path leads from the parking lot to a footbridge over the Wenatchee River. From the bridge, search for Harlequin Duck (migration), Common Merganser, Great Blue Heron, Black-crowned Night-Heron, Spotted Sandpiper, Vaux's Swift, and Northern Rough-winged Swallow, among many others. Ospreys nest on the neighboring railway span. Just south of the footbridge, leave the paved path at the entrance to the **Horan Natural Area** (interpretive signage and trail map, on the left), a 97-acre, undeveloped part of the park. Birding in the open, weedy spaces and riparian habitat with a dense grove of Black Cottonwoods can be good at any season but is especially fine in spring and early summer. Birds seen regularly include California Quail, Ring-necked Pheasant, Mourning Dove, Western Screech-Owl, Eastern Kingbird, Gray Catbird, Spotted Towhee, and Purple Finch. Sparrows are often abundant in migration and winter—among the many White-crowneds, look for Lincoln's, Swamp, White-throated, Harris's, and Golden-crowned. Wood Duck is a common nester in the sloughs and ponds. Overhead, look for Black Swifts in summer (occasional). Bald Eagles are common, especially in winter.

Trails through the natural area eventually rejoin the paved path. From here, you can continue along the Columbia River to Walla Walla Point Park. Stop at the first bench inside this park to scope the river edge for waterfowl, gulls, and terns and to admire the fine views of the river and surrounding hills. Birds often seen here include Canada Goose, Great Blue Heron, Spotted Sandpiper, Caspian Tern, and, in migration, small numbers of Baird's, Least, Pectoral, and Western Sandpipers, as well as Long-billed Dowitchers. Black, Common, and Forster's Terns occur uncommonly. Arctic Tern has been recorded. Water levels fluctuate frequently due to dam operations. When water levels are high, inspect the lawns in both parks for gulls and shorebirds.

A very different spot on the outskirts of Wenatchee is **No. 2 Canyon**. Leaving Confluence State Park, retrace your route on Euclid to the T-intersection where Euclid changes names to Penny Road. Turn left here onto Penny Road. Travel 0.6 mile and turn left onto SR-285. Go 0.8 mile, turn right onto Maiden Lane, and continue uphill 0.5 mile to Western Avenue. Make a left here and go 2.8 miles to No. 2 Canyon Road. Turn right onto this road. In 1.5 miles, note a shooting range on your right. Scattered tall serviceberry bushes, on the left at the base of a steep, rocky slope, are attractive to Ash-throated Flycatcher, here at the northern extreme of its breeding range.

From this point forward, the road hugs a verdant strip of riparian vegetation, inviting many stops (private property: please bird from the road). An early-morning walk through the steep-walled canyon in spring or early summer may yield Chukar, Red-tailed Hawk, Golden Eagle, Common Poorwill, American Kestrel, Western Wood-Pewee, Dusky Flycatcher, Warbling Vireo, Black-billed Magpie, Common Raven, Violet-green Swallow, Townsend's Solitaire (especially migration), Veery, Yellow-breasted Chat, Black-headed Grosbeak, Lazuli Bunting, and Bullock's Oriole. The pavement ends in 2.8 miles, but you can go farther on a primitive road (summer only) into Douglas-fir and Ponderosa Pine habitat. At 0.5 mile past the end of the pavement is a large gate and a primitive road or trail to the right. Park here and hike through riparian and Ponderosa Pine woodland and eventually into an extremely birdy basin. Species to look for include Northern Goshawk, Northern Pygmy- and Northern Saw-whet Owls, Calliope Hummingbird, White-headed Woodpecker, Gray Flycatcher, Dusky Flycatcher, all three nuthatches, Nashville and MacGillivray's Warblers, Chipping Sparrow, Cassin's Finch, and Red Crossbill.

ENTIAT MOUNTAINS TO LAKE CHELAN

by Jim Alt, Bob Kuntz, Kraig Kemper, and Andy Stepniewski
revised by Dan Stephens

North of Wenatchee, several rugged, southeastward-trending ridges and valleys dissect the eastern slopes of the Cascade Range, from the crest down to the Columbia River. In succession from the Wenatchee River, these are the Entiat Mountains, the Entiat River, the Chelan Mountains, Lake Chelan, and finally Sawtooth Ridge, whose northeast face drains to the Methow River. Alternate US-97 and US-97 follow the Columbia from Wenatchee to Pateros. For almost the whole 50-mile distance, the river is actually Lake Entiat, created by Rocky Reach Dam—a reservoir with impoverished habitat and limited birding access. Birding can be excellent, however, along the deep canyons that penetrate into the Cascades, accessible from the highway on a number of side roads. Typically, these canyons are grown to semi-arid shrub-steppe habitats at lower elevations, transitioning to dry Ponderosa Pine and Douglas-fir and then to moist forests at upper elevations.

SWAKANE CANYON

Swakane Creek drains the south end of the Entiat Mountains to the Columbia. The rough and rocky track that follows this minor stream is worth enduring not only for birds, but also for scenery, wildflowers, and butterflies. From the combined US-2/US-97 just north of Wenatchee, go north on Alt US-97 to a primitive road (FR-7415) marked *Swakane Canyon Rd* (5.3 miles). Turn left to enter this spectacular canyon, known for its diversity of migrants and breeding birds, and even for its winter birding possibilities. Much of the lower canyon is within the Swakane Wildlife Area (19,200 acres).

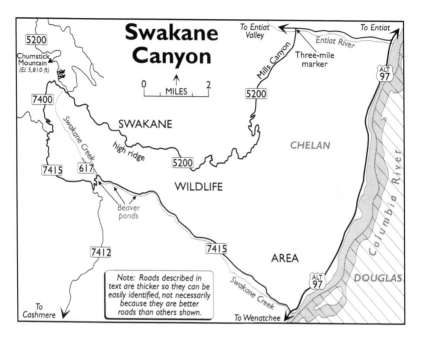

In 0.1 mile, stop below a cliff (Chukar, Black-billed Magpie, Rock and Canyon Wrens). Check Water Birch and other riparian growth for Yellow-breasted Chat, Black-headed Grosbeak, Lazuli Bunting, and Bullock's Oriole. Continue up for four more miles to the lower limit of Ponderosa Pine forest and patches of serviceberry shrubs. Watch for California Quail, Red-tailed Hawk, Golden Eagle, Mourning Dove, Calliope Hummingbird, Lewis's Woodpecker, Dusky Flycatcher, Western Kingbird, Violet-green Swallow, Mountain Chickadee, all three nuthatches, House Wren, Nashville Warbler, and American Goldfinch. The first of several Beaver ponds is reached in another three miles, then excellent riparian habitat and a series of larger ponds by the road—great habitat for Black-chinned Hummingbird, Red-naped Sapsucker, Downy and Hairy Woodpeckers, Western Wood-Pewee, Willow and Pacific-slope Flycatchers, Cassin's and Warbling Vireos, Tree and Violet-green Swallows, Black-capped Chickadee, Veery, Cedar Waxwing, Orange-crowned, Nashville, MacGillivray's, and Yellow Warblers, and Black-headed Grosbeak. In winter, the alders in these swamps attract Pine Siskins.

In 1.5 miles, the road turns left and crosses Swakane Creek to a lush aspen grove and meadow where you can expect Calliope Hummingbird, Willow and Dusky Flycatchers, Cassin's Vireo, Nashville and MacGillivray's Warblers, and Chipping Sparrow. Or walk upstream on the opposite bank for a half-mile on FR-617 through forest, riparian, and meadow habitats. It is possible to see all three *Carpodacus* finches (House, Purple, Cassin's) in this part of the canyon.

From here the adventurous can embark on a summer-only high-country trek that emerges onto the Entiat River Road. Continue up FR-7415 for 3.6 miles to an intersection with FR-7400. Turn right onto this road, and in 3.0 miles stop at the intersection with FR-5200. To the left, a one-mile hike up FR-5200 brings you to the top of **Chumstick Mountain** (elevation 5,810 feet)—a fine hawkwatching vantage in fall. Turning right from the FR-7400 intersection, FR-5200 follows a high ridge dominated by late-successional Western Larch for about five miles; continue down FR-5200 into Mills Canyon, which hits the Entiat River Road at the three-mile marker. Mixed-conifer forests with Western Larch (Williamson's Sapsucker, Hammond's Flycatcher, Ruby-crowned Kinglet), burns (woodpeckers, Dusky Flycatcher), Ponderosa Pine forests (nuthatches, crossbills), and finally open bunchgrass slopes (Common Poorwill at dusk, Vesper Sparrow) feature along this route.

ENTIAT RIVER

The Entiat River basin reaches far into the heart of the Cascades, giving access to the Glacier Peak Wilderness (576,865 acres), one of Washington's largest expanses of wild country. The Entiat River Road turns left from Alt US-97 less than 10 miles north of the mouth of Swakane Canyon. The road proceeds first through open farmland with orchards and some riparian habitats. Check the thickets near the Entiat River mouth on the left in a half-mile. (The old highway that follows the edge of the riparian zone downstream makes a good birding trail.) Hooded Merganser, Bald Eagle, Western Wood-Pewee, Black-headed Grosbeak, and Bullock's Oriole occur here. Flycatchers, warblers, Western Tanager, and sparrows can be thick in migration, particularly during inclement weather.

Upriver, in another 5.5 miles, find the **Entiat National Fish Hatchery**. Tall Black Cottonwoods here have Red-eyed Vireo. Look for Veery, Gray Catbird, and many other species in the lush understory. Continuing along Entiat River Road, habitats in the lower reaches of the basin are always in transition due to recurring fires. Characteristic species of brushy lower elevations include Chukar, Golden Eagle, Calliope Hummingbird, and White-headed and Black-backed (in recently burned timber) Woodpeckers. Riparian areas have Red-naped Sapsucker, MacGillivray's and Yellow Warblers, and Yellow-breasted Chat.

Turn right in 4.9 miles from the hatchery onto FR-5300 (aka Mud Creek Road). Driving this road for 12 miles to its junction with SR-971 at Navarre Coulee, just south of Lake Chelan State Park, you'll see Ponderosa Pine forest including areas of burned timber. Brushy slopes with some snags attract Common Poorwill, Western Wood-Pewee, Dusky Flycatcher, and Orange-crowned and Nashville Warblers. Vegetation along **Mud Creek**, on the way up to the ridgeline, has Calliope Hummingbird, Black-headed Grosbeak, Lazuli Bunting, Bullock's Oriole, and other typical riparian species. The

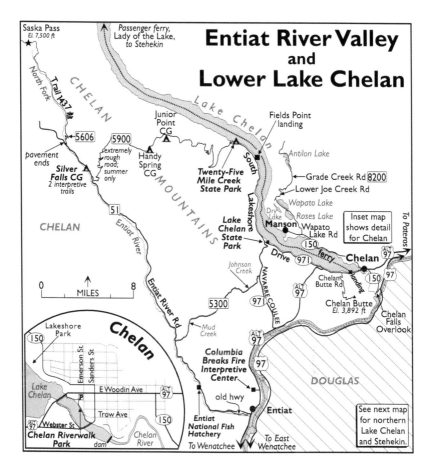

downslope segment along **Johnson Creek** is good for woodpeckers (Lewis's, White-headed, Black-backed, Pileated).

Continue up Entiat River Road (becomes FR-51) to an intersection with FR-5900 in 17.8 miles. Here you may turn right and begin a summer-only, 28-mile tour up and over the Chelan Mountains (high point 6,600 feet) to Twenty-Five Mile Creek State Park on Lake Chelan. *WARNING:* This is an extremely rough road that requires a high-clearance four-wheel drive truck even in summer, and is generally not open until July. Boreal Owl and Pine Grosbeak have been noted at Handy Spring Campground 13 miles along this road. The Handy Spring and Junior Point campground areas are more easily accessed from the Lake Chelan side, but a four-wheel drive vehicle is still recommended. This area is generally not open until sometime in early July. Vast areas of old burns characterize the area from Junior Point to the lake via FR-59.

Silver Falls Campground, a bit less than a mile farther up FR-51 (Entiat River Road) from the FR-5900 intersection, is worth a stop. Beginning in the campground, the 1.2-mile Riverside Trail features tall, moist forest where you can expect Harlequin Duck (spring and early summer), Hammond's Flycatcher, Pacific Wren, and Townsend's Warbler. Areas of alder have MacGillivray's and Yellow Warblers, and American Dippers can be seen from the several river overlooks. From the parking lot, the falls can be seen to the north. Black Swift nest at the falls but are best viewed from below in the early morning and evening. The trail to the falls is moderately difficult and has Western Tanager and Cassin's Vireo.

The paved road ends about three miles above Silver Falls Campground, at an intersection with FR-5606. Moist forests in this vicinity have Gray Jay, Clark's Nutcracker, Mountain Bluebird, Veery, and Hermit Thrush. Northern Goshawk is regular along the **North Fork** of the Entiat River, in some of Washington's largest stands of ancient forest outside designated wilderness areas. Northern Spotted Owl was found here in the past. Take FR-5606 about four miles to a trailhead. From here Trail #1437 follows the North Fork for some nine miles, reaching the boundary of the Glacier Peak Wilderness at Saska Pass (elevation 7,500 feet). *WARNING:* FR-5606 can be treacherous due to mud and rutting, and a high-clearance four-wheel drive vehicle is required. This road is generally not open until early July.

As you head north on Alt US-97 toward Chelan, turn left into the **Columbia Breaks Fire Interpretive Center** (2.7 miles from Entiat River Road). A half-mile trail winds through Ponderosa Pine, Bitterbrush, and Big Sagebrush, abutting tall granite cliffs. Look for Bald and Golden Eagles, Common Poorwill, Lewis's Woodpecker, Say's Phoebe, Clark's Nutcracker, Canyon Wren, and Bullock's Oriole. Migration brings many other birds; Golden-crowned and other sparrows may be found in winter.

CHELAN AND VICINITY

A popular destination for vacationers and outdoor recreationists, the community of Chelan (year-round population 4,000) sits at the southeast tip of Lake Chelan, two miles inland from the Columbia River and about 40 road miles north of Wenatchee. Numerous nearby sites offer dry-forest habitats as well as opportunities to scope the lake for waterbirds.

The ornamental plantings and forest of Ponderosa Pine, Douglas-fir, and Bigleaf Maple at **Lake Chelan State Park** can be rewarding in migration and the early part of the nesting season. Look for forest species such as White-headed Woodpecker, Red-breasted and White-breasted Nuthatches, and Brown Creeper. American Dipper can often be found by walking upstream along a well-beaten trail from the far end of the boat launch. Diving ducks, loons, and grebes are seen on the lake from fall through spring. Winter birds include Hermit Thrush and Pine Grosbeak as good possibilities. Birding is frustrating in summer, however, when the park is crowded with campers and powerboaters. The park is located about nine miles west of Chelan on South Lakeshore Drive (Alt US-97 for the first three miles, then right onto SR-971). If coming from the south on Alt US-97, turn left onto SR-971 about nine miles north of the Entiat River Road intersection and drive north for about nine more miles through Navarre Coulee to the park entrance.

Views of Lake Chelan, the Columbia River, and the wheat fields on the Waterville Plateau to the east are well worth the nerve-wracking drive to the top of **Chelan Butte**. About a mile and a half west of Chelan, turn left from South Lakeshore Drive (Alt US-97) onto Millard Street (also signed Chelan Butte Road), which soon changes to dirt. Dusty in spring and summer, super-steep in places, slick and often impassable after a rain, the 4.7-mile road to the summit is usually closed by snow in winter. Varied habitats along the way—deciduous thickets, Ponderosa Pines, steep slopes with bunchgrass and some sagebrush—all attract interesting birds. Park where you can and walk over the hillsides, particularly near the summit (watch out for rattlesnakes in rocky areas). In spring and summer look for California Quail, Swainson's Hawk, Golden Eagle, White-throated Swift, Lewis's and White-headed Woodpeckers, Say's Phoebe, Western and Eastern Kingbirds, Clark's Nutcracker, all three nuthatches, Brewer's and Vesper Sparrows, and many others. Fall and winter possibilities include accipiters, Red-tailed and Rough-legged Hawks, Northern Pygmy-Owl, Gray-crowned Rosy-Finch, and Pine Grosbeak.

If you are stopping in Chelan, paved **Chelan Riverwalk Park** makes a fine diversion right in the center of downtown. Park on Emerson Street about 200 yards south of East Woodin Avenue. Walk southeast along the water, cross the narrow neck of the lake on the bridge, then continue northwest to the West Woodin Avenue bridge to return to the starting point. In winter, check for a sprinkling of waterfowl, Common Loon, Pied-billed and Western Grebes, and Belted Kingfisher. In migration, Yellow-rumped Warblers flit in the trees. Four species of swallows are common in summer.

Scan the cliffs at the **Chelan Falls Overlook** to see Golden Eagle, White-throated Swift, and Canyon Wren. Take SR-150 south 2.4 miles from Alt US-97 in Chelan.

In the opposite direction, SR-150 leaves Alt US-97 in Chelan and winds along the north shore of Lake Chelan. Stop at any of the pullouts to watch for Redhead, Greater Scaup, Bufflehead, and Common Goldeneye, Common Loon, and Horned, Red-necked, and Western Grebes. In 6.7 miles, turn right on Wapato Lake Road and climb through apple and pear orchards alternating with new development, passing Roses and Wapato Lakes (waterbirds, especially in fall and spring). After a peek at the marsh just beyond Wapato Lake, proceed to Lower Joe Creek Road (4.1 miles from SR-150). Turn right here, then left in 1.9 miles onto Grade Creek Road (becomes FR-8200), which passes through mixed pine and riparian habitat to **Antilon Lake** (2.0 miles), nestled in a rocky gorge with Ponderosa Pines (Pygmy Nuthatch, Cassin's Finch, Red Crossbill). Beyond the lake, the landscape is one of scattered pines with thick patches of shrubby Deerbrush—the result of past fires. This habitat has many Common Poorwills, easily seen on an evening drive.

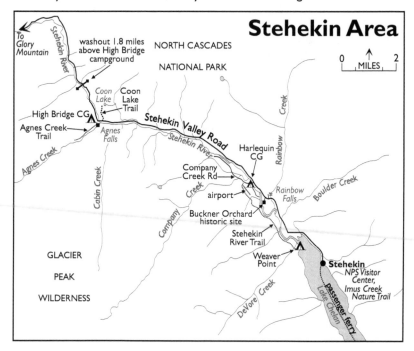

LAKE CHELAN AND STEHEKIN

A narrow, glacier-forged trench, Lake Chelan probes 50 miles into the North Cascades. While the eastern end is developed, the rest is wild and scenic. To experience the lake, it is well worth taking the boat trip to Stehekin, a resort village at the upper end in the heart of the **Lake Chelan National Recreation Area**. Beyond is the vast North Cascades National Park and trail access to various USFS wilderness areas, making this the largest contiguous expanse of wild country in Washington.

The parking lot and docks for the ***Lady of the Lake*** are on Alt US-97 (South Lakeshore Drive) a half-mile west of downtown Chelan; a second boarding point is at Fields Point, 16 miles northwest of Chelan on South Lakeshore Drive. Frequency of service, duration of the trip, and fare vary according to the season and/or which of three boats you take. The most leisurely one-way cruise requires four hours, while the fastest boat makes the same run in an hour and a quarter. Contact the Lake Chelan Boat Company for full information (509-682-4584, *www.ladyofthelake.com*).

Lake Chelan is the third-deepest lake in the United States (1,528 feet). At one place its bottom is over 400 feet below sea level. Fed by 27 glaciers and 59 streams, the lake is cold and relatively unproductive for birds. Nonetheless, you might see a few diving ducks, Common Loons, Red-necked or Western Grebes, Ospreys, and Bald and Golden Eagles, especially around the small shallows and marsh on the approach to Stehekin. The bordering vegetation changes from semi-arid shrub-steppe and Ponderosa Pine to moist conifer forests as the boat travels deeper into the mountains, bringing a good possibility of seeing Mountain Goats or Black Bears on the cliffs and steep slopes.

Stehekin is a wonderful place to relax in an unhurried atmosphere. Plan on staying one or two days to extract the most from the birding possibilities. There are several primitive campgrounds in the area plus a number of homes or cabins available to rent. Three lodges provide more complete services. For information, contact the Lake Chelan Chamber of Commerce (800-424-3526, *www.visitlakechelan.com*) or stop by the National Park Service's Golden West Visitor Center in Stehekin.

Try to allow at least a few hours before reboarding the boat to see species near the boat landing, including, commonly, Rufous and Calliope Hummingbirds, Olive-sided and Hammond's Flycatchers, swallows (including Violet-green), Nashville Warbler, Western Tanager, and Cassin's Finch. Just behind the visitor center is the three-quarter-mile **Imus Creek Nature Trail**, which climbs a hill with views. In spring, American Dippers forage along the lakeshore at the creek mouth, and Veeries often sing beside the creek. You can also take the narrated bus tour to 312-foot Rainbow Falls, 3.5 miles up Stehekin Valley Road. Black Swifts may nest behind these falls. Train your eyes skyward on occasion to look for them anywhere in the Stehekin area.

Most visitors travel up-valley by the National Park Service shuttle bus, which goes to High Bridge (11 miles). Alternatives to the bus include renting bicycles and riding up the road to the birding spots or renting a canoe and paddling around the head of the lake.

For the first 1.5 miles the Stehekin Valley Road parallels the east shore of Lake Chelan. In recent years, Horned Grebes have attempted to nest at the head of the lake. Trumpeter Swan, Harlequin Duck, and Osprey are occasionally observed near the mouth of the Stehekin River. Check the marsh, willows, and cottonwoods for owls (Great Horned and Barred), woodpeckers (particularly Red-naped Sapsucker), and breeding passerines such as Veery, Gray Catbird, Nashville and Yellow Warblers, and American Redstart.

A few hundred yards after passing the turnoff to Rainbow Falls (3.5 miles), take a dirt road left into **Buckner Orchard**, a pioneer homestead site. Look here in spring and summer for hummingbirds (Rufous and Calliope), flycatchers, warblers, Western Tanager, Bullock's Oriole, and Cassin's Finch. Harlequin Bridge and Campground are another three-quarters of a mile up Stehekin Valley Road (yes, Harlequin Ducks are sometimes seen here from mid-April through August). A couple of hundred yards past the campground, take Company Creek Road left to the National Park Service maintenance yard and check the pond area for Wood Duck and passerines. Birding is excellent along the **Stehekin River Trail**, which starts at the maintenance yard and meanders southward four miles through marsh (Beaver ponds) and riparian forest to Weaver Point at the northwest edge of the lake. Western Screech-Owls have nested near the south end of the Stehekin Airport, and a pair of Bald Eagles has nested near Weaver Point.

From Harlequin Bridge continue up Stehekin Valley Road another six miles to **High Bridge**, a major trailhead for North Cascades National Park. Of interest to birders is the 1.2-mile trail to Coon Lake, a swampy lake with waterfowl (Barrow's Goldeneyes nest here) and excellent also for passerines. Northern Goshawk has been observed on the Old Wagon Trail from near Coon Lake and also along the first two miles of Agnes Creek Trail (trailhead 0.3 mile past High Bridge). Northern Spotted Owl was seen in this general area in the past. Stehekin makes a great base camp for hiking or backpacking into the wilderness. Free permits are required for overnight trips and may be obtained at the visitor center on a first-come, first-served basis.

COOPER RIDGE

Cooper Ridge forms the eastern end of the Sawtooth Ridge system that divides the Chelan and Methow watersheds. The high point, Cooper Mountain (5,867 feet), is 10 straight-line miles north and a bit west of Chelan. The driving distance is 25 miles, however—much of it over steep, twisting roads. Allow at least an hour for the trip. The main attraction for birders is the fall hawk migration (late August–late October). Typical bird species of farms, streams, cliffs, Ponderosa Pine forest, and shrub-steppe may be found at several places on the way up.

In Chelan, from the junction where SR-150 turns south to the Chelan Falls overlook, head east on Alt US-97. Travel 2.9 miles and turn left (north) onto **Apple Acres Road**. In 3.5 miles, stop by the roadside below impressive cliffs of gneiss to scan for Golden Eagle and other raptors and to listen for Canyon Wren. Peer downward from the west side of the highway to a kettle lake, an erosional feature remaining from the withdrawal of the Okanogan Ice Lobe at the close of the Pleistocene. Check the Ponderosa Pine forest for Pygmy Nuthatch.

Continue another 1.2 miles, turn left (west) onto Antoine Creek Road, and drive through farmlands. In late fall, Pine Grosbeaks have been found in the last orchard (2.6 miles) and at scattered sites in the dense riparian vegetation along Antoine Creek for the next three miles. The pavement ends in another 1.2 miles. Continue steeply uphill (west) on the main gravel road. Antoine Creek Road becomes FR-8140 (1.9 miles); the Okanogan National Forest boundary is in another 1.9 miles. From here to the intersection at the crest of Cooper Ridge (8.0 miles), nearly the entire landscape is of Ponderosa Pines, grown back in the wake of a huge fire in 1970. Bitterbrush covers many slopes, providing critical winter forage for a large Mule Deer herd. A small area of Lodgepole Pine and Engelmann Spruce forest may be found at the crest. This entire area is fire-dependent with stands of various ages displaying a mosaic pattern. Fires vary in intensity and size and will continue to affect this area into the future.

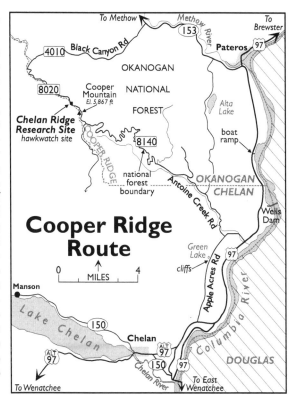

Under proper weather conditions, hawkwatching can be memorable at the Chelan Ridge Research Site, a cooperative project begun in 1997 by the (now combined) Okanogan and Wenatchee National Forests and HawkWatch International. It has been documented as the best fall hawkwatching site so far discovered in Eastern Washington. Even though tens of thousands of raptors pass through the Cascades in migration, there are so many ridges that movement is widely dispersed across a broad front. Defying the general pattern, the Chelan Ridge site may see more than 100 individuals on a good day; 2000–3000 are tallied annually. The station is active from the last days of August to the end of October unless closed earlier by snow. Visitors are welcome.

From the T-intersection with FR-8140 at the crest of Cooper Ridge turn right onto FR-8020, which contours around the east side of Cooper Mountain. After 1.5 miles, park just beyond a cattle guard; the Forest Service has placed two portable toilets here. Find the rough, steep trail marked by ribbons on the west side of the road and hike about three-quarters of a mile across a sagebrush-covered, south-facing sidehill to the hawkwatching station, located on a promontory at an elevation of 5,100 feet. The ridge crest here is narrow; level sites for spotting scopes are limited. The view in all directions is fabulous—west to the high peaks of the North Cascades, north across the Methow Valley to the Tiffany Mountain area, east to the wheatlands of the northern Columbia Basin, and south to a sliver of Lake Chelan about 4,000 feet below. Bring all provisions; there is no water anywhere in the area. Sun protection may be important. Be prepared for wind and cold. Please pack out all garbage.

Favored hawk flight paths change with wind direction and during the course of the day; you will need to determine which quadrants of the landscape and the sky are most productive at the time of your visit. Sharp-shinned Hawk is the species most frequently spotted, followed (in descending order) by Red-tailed Hawk, Cooper's Hawk, Golden Eagle, Northern Harrier, American Kestrel, Osprey, Northern Goshawk, and Merlin. Seven other species occur in lesser numbers, including five or six Broad-winged Hawks each year—the great majority of the Washington records. In October 2000, a passing Northern Hawk Owl caused a stir.

For the shortest route to the Methow Valley, continue north on FR-8020 for 3.5 miles, turn right, and descend on FR-4010 (Black Canyon Road) for nine miles to join SR-153 above Pateros. If you are instead going back the way you came along Antoine Creek Road, keep left at Apple Acres Road and go 1.9 miles to US-97 above the Columbia River. Turn left and travel 4.4 miles to a boat ramp on the right. Ospreys nest nearby and are usually easy to spot. From fall through spring, scope the waters of the Columbia anywhere in this area for diving birds. Pacific Loons, though scarce, are seen regularly—particularly in stretches where the river is flowing (above reservoir levels). The junction with SR-153 in Pateros, gateway to the Methow Valley, is another 4.6 miles north.

METHOW VALLEY

by Andy Stepniewski

revised by Andy Stepniewski

The Methow River drains a broad slice of the North Cascades, much of it wild and remote. Near the crest, dense, somber conifer forests mantle the glacially overdeepened valleys, cut through by alder-choked avalance chutes. The maritime climate dumps immense, wet winter snowfalls. A few miles east from the crest, however, a rainshadow effect sets in, allowing a steady transition to drier, more open forests. Just 30 miles downslope, rangelands occupy the valley bottoms, and Bitterbrush and other shrub-steppe flora cover the south-facing hillsides—prime winter range for a Mule Deer herd numbering over 20,000 animals.

About 75 species of birds breed in the varied habitats of the lower parts of the valley. Killdeer, Western Kingbird, Black-billed Magpie, American Crow, swallows, Western Meadowlark, and Brewer's Blackbird can be abundant in farm fields.

Several species of "eastern" affinity—Eastern Kingbird, Red-eyed Vireo, Veery, Gray Catbird, American Redstart (uncommon)—occur in cottonwoods. Typical dry-forest species such as Lewis's Woodpecker, Western Wood-Pewee, Yellow-rumped Warbler, and Cassin's Finch can be found in the pines. White-tailed Ptarmigan, American Pipit, Gray-crowned Rosy-Finch, and Pine Grosbeak may repay a summer foray to the Cascade Crest at Harts Pass and Slate Peak. Winter brings Bohemian Waxwings and Common Redpolls to the valley; Bald and a few Golden Eagles are drawn to spawned salmon in the Methow River.

After a brief gold-mining boom in the late 1800s, the Methow went the way of many another Eastside mountain economy, getting by on logging, grazing, and limited tourism (much of it tied to the fall deer-hunting season). A swelling Washington population, and the opening of the North Cascades Highway (SR-20) in 1972, have stimulated residential and tourism development. The Methow is now a year-round destination with many resorts in all price ranges offering fishing, hiking, whitewater rafting, horseback riding, and golf in summer, and cross-country skiing, snowshoeing, and snowmobiling in winter. Snowfall forces the winter closure of SR-20 west from Mazama (typically November or December to April); during those months the sole approach to the Methow country is from the east. Winthrop is the main town and a fine base of operations for birders, summer or winter.

PATEROS TO TWISP

The huge Carlton Complex Fire ravaged more than a quarter-million acres in the lower Methow Valley, including Pateros, and surrounding areas in the summer of 2014. The fire destroyed huge swaths of Bitterbrush and other wildlife habitat. WDFW biologists said the fire would have major effects on deer, other mammals such as squirrels and bears, and on birds. Regrowth in most burned areas was expected in four or five years.

Year-round access to the Methow Valley begins at the junction of US-97 and SR-153 in Pateros on the Columbia River. Heading west on SR-153, you'll drive along impounded Columbia River waters for the first mile, full of waterfowl in spring and fall—American Wigeon, Redhead, and many other species. At 1.7 miles from US-97, turn left onto Alta Lake Road. From here it is 1.6 miles to **Alta Lake State Park**. The park is crowded at times; nonetheless, an early-morning exploration of the pine forest and other habitats should yield a good representative bird list. Species to look for in the campground and on the trail uphill toward the steep, rocky bluffs include Chukar, Rock Pigeon (nesting on the cliffs), Common Poorwill, White-throated Swift, Calliope Hummingbird, Olive-sided Flycatcher, Western Wood-Pewee, Clark's Nutcracker, Mountain Chickadee, Red-breasted Nuthatch, Western Bluebird, Gray Catbird (in riparian growth near the end of the lake), Nashville Warbler, Western Tanager, Black-headed Grosbeak, and Cassin's Finch. (Note: The 2014 fire likely destroyed habitat for some of these birds for a few years.)

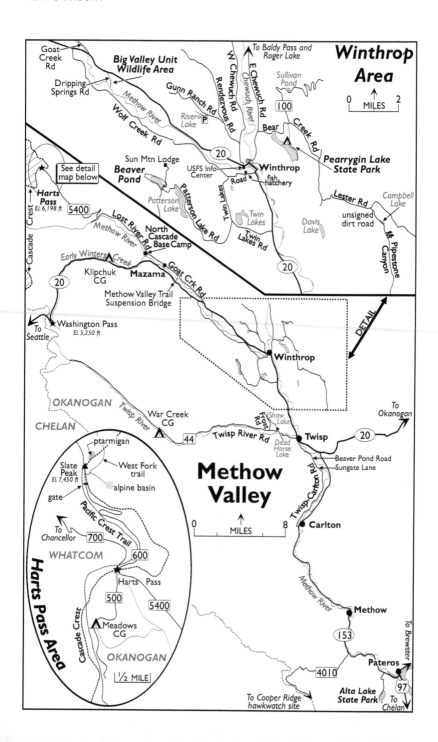

As you continue up SR-153 beside the Methow River, keep an eye out for American Dipper and for Bald and Golden Eagles in winter. In 5.0 miles, Black Canyon Road (FR-4010) provides access to the Chelan Ridge hawkwatching site (page 421). In another 15.8 miles, just before Carlton, turn left from SR-153 onto the **Twisp-Carlton Road**. This quiet alternative to SR-153 passes orchards, hay fields, pine woods, and excellent riparian habitat. The first couple miles are productive for Lewis's Woodpecker. A particularly good one-mile stretch with a tall Black Cottonwood overstory and a lush shrub layer begins in 6.7 miles. To explore this span, park on the left just after Sungate Lane (0.4 mile) and bird on foot along the main road for the next 0.6 mile to Beaver Pond Road, looking and listening for Least Flycatcher (uncommon), Red-eyed Vireo, Veery (common), Gray Catbird, and Black-headed Grosbeak, among others. Black Swifts often join the many swallows overhead, especially in periods of cool or stormy weather. In 2.6 miles, the road meets SR-20. Turn left into Twisp.

Twisp River Road reaches deep into the Cascades, with fine birding of dry and wet habitats. In 0.2 mile, turn left onto this road (Second Avenue in Twisp), drive 2.8 miles, and turn right onto Frost Road (poorly signed). In 1.4 miles, reach **Shaw Lake** in the Big Buck Unit (5,600 acres) of the Methow Wildlife Area. Habitats here include several shallow lakes, dense riparian thickets, and Bitterbrush-dominated shrub-steppe. Waterfowl, shorebirds, and Yellow-headed Blackbird are possibilities from this overlook. Mountain Bluebirds, Yellow-breasted Chats, Lazuli Buntings, and Black-headed Grosbeaks are just a few of the likely birds. From Shaw Lake, return 0.2 mile on Frost Road. Park and walk the dirt track going off to the left (east) toward **Dead Horse Lake**. Groves of Quaking Aspen and Black Cottonwood with shrubby thickets, alternating with bunchgrass-covered hillsides, provide habitat for many breeding birds including Red-naped Sapsucker, Gray Catbird, and Bullock's Oriole. The lake should have waterfowl or shorebirds, depending on the water level. Dry forests and brushy hillsides as you proceed along Twisp River Road have Flammulated Owl, White-headed Woodpecker, Pygmy Nuthatch, Red Crossbill, and Cassin's Finch. Harlequin Ducks breed along the river. Look for this striking waterfowl when the river comes into view.

Farther upriver, the road becomes FR-44 upon entering the Okanogan National Forest. In 12 miles, wetter forest in and around War Creek Campground has Barred Owl, Hammond's Flycatcher, Red-breasted Nuthatch, Hermit Thrush, and MacGillivray's and Townsend's Warblers.

WINTHROP AND VICINITY

Winthrop, on SR-20 nine miles north of Twisp at the confluence of the Methow and Chewuch Rivers, is an agreeable community with a made-over Western theme and fine year-round birding. Summer has the greatest diversity of birds, especially in riparian habitats. Harlequin Duck can be found then along the Methow River right in town. American Dipper is common in the colder months. Winter also brings roving flocks of Bohemian Waxwings and Common Redpolls (irregular) along with a few Pine Grosbeaks. The best strategy for winter songbirding is to drive the streets of Winthrop, checking feeders and yard plantings. Five sites offering good spring and early-summer birding close to Winthrop are outlined below. Directions are given from the main intersection in the heart of the Winthrop business district, where SR-20 westbound makes a 90-degree left turn to cross the Chewuch River. Zero your trip-odometer here.

Twin Lakes and **Beaver Pond** are fine birding spots southwest of Winthrop. Drive south on SR-20 for 3.1 miles to an intersection with Twin Lakes Road, signed to Sun Mountain. (Coming from Twisp, this intersection is 5.6 miles north of the Second Avenue/Twisp River Road junction.) Turn west onto Twin Lakes Road, go 1.1 miles, and turn right onto a road signed *Fishing Access*. Follow signs to the fishing access parking lot (0.5 mile), overlooking Little Twin Lake. Depending on water levels, both this and Big Twin Lake can be excellent shorebird viewing spots from late July through August. Upwards of 20 species have been tallied in recent years.

To reach Beaver Pond, return to Twin Lakes Road and go right (west) 0.8 mile to Patterson Lake Road. Make a left (south) here and go 5.3 miles to a public parking area and trailhead on the left. Take the trail around Beaver Pond and other ponds nearby, a prime birding spot with open water, marsh, riparian vegetation, and coniferous forest. Look for nesting Wood Duck, Ring-necked Duck, Barrow's Goldeneye, Hooded Merganser, Ruffed Grouse, Virginia Rail, Sora, Spotted Sandpiper, Rufous Hummingbird, Belted Kingfisher, Red-naped Sapsucker, Downy and Pileated Woodpeckers, Willow Flycatcher, Eastern Kingbird, Cassin's (parking-lot pines) and Warbling Vireos, Tree Swallow, Veery, Orange-crowned, Yellow, and Townsend's Warblers, American Redstart (uncommon), Song Sparrow, Western Tanager, Black-headed Grosbeak, Lazuli Bunting, and Red-winged Blackbird. Mammal viewing can be super here. Frequently observed species include Black Bear, Moose, Beaver, Muskrat, Marten, several weasels, Coyote, and Mule Deer. Mountain Lion and Bobcat are seldom seen but possible.

To reach **Pearrygin Lake State Park** from downtown Winthrop, take the continuation of the main street north from SR-20 through the end of the business district. Curving to the right, this street becomes Bluff Street, then East Chewuch Road as it heads north out of town, reaching an intersection with Bear Creek Road in 1.6 miles. (Continuing straight with East Chewuch Road will take you to Baldy Pass and Roger Lake.) Turn right; the park entrance is on the right in 1.7 miles. Park in the main parking area, walk past the restrooms to the far southeast corner of the tent-camping loop, and continue south along a gravel lane signed *No Unauthorized Vehicles*, quickly leaving the commotion of the campground behind. Vesper Sparrows nest on the bunchgrass- and Bitterbrush-grown slopes on the left, while the lakeshore on the right offers marsh and riparian habitats where you may find Hooded Merganser, Pied-billed Grebe, Mourning Dove, various owls including Great Horned, Northern Pygmy-, Long-eared, and Northern Saw-whet, Common Poorwill, Red-naped Sapsucker, Lewis's and Downy Woodpeckers, Willow Flycatcher, Eastern Kingbird, Gray Catbird, Black-capped Chickadee, House Wren, Veery, American Redstart (occasional), Yellow Warbler, Spotted Towhee, Black-headed Grosbeak, Lazuli Bunting, Red-winged Blackbird, Western Meadowlark, Brewer's Blackbird, Brown-headed Cowbird, and Bullock's Oriole. Ospreys are often seen around the lake, and Common Nighthawks over the surrounding hills. Persistent seeds and fruits on lakeside trees and brush attract waxwings, finches, and other birds in winter.

Bear Creek Road (now gravel) continues 0.2 mile past the park entrance to an intersection with FR-100. **Sullivan Pond** is reached by turning left onto FR-100, which climbs steeply to the pond in 2.0 miles (check boxes along the way for Western and Mountain Bluebirds). Nestled on a broad ledge, this small lake, some years merely a marsh, has wonderful views of the Methow Valley below. Enjoy the cacophany of nesting Pied-billed Grebes and Yellow-headed Blackbirds; Ring-necked and Ruddy Ducks are also here in summer. Open, mixed forest and riparian growth have Common Nighthawks and Common Poorwill, Red-naped Sapsucker, Dusky Flycatcher, Warbling Vireo, and Vesper Sparrow. All three nuthatches may be found in Ponderosa Pines throughout the area. White-headed Woodpecker is fairly common above the pond in the Ponderosa Pines.

Backtrack along FR-100 and take Bear Creek Road in the other direction (left if coming from Sullivan Pond, straight ahead if coming from the state park). Stay right at the T-intersection in 2.0 miles, and in another 1.6 miles turn left and follow Lester Road for 2.4 miles to an unsigned dirt road. Turn right and drive past Campbell Lake, ending in 1.3 miles at the trailhead for **Pipestone Canyon** in the Methow Unit (16,775 acres) of the Methow Wildlife Area (Discover Pass required). Walk a half-mile on the wide trail along the canyon floor through habitats of cliffs, talus slopes, Bitterbrush, fruiting shrubs, and Douglas-fir forest with a Douglas Maple understory. A great diversity of birds can be found here including Dusky Grouse, Golden Eagle, White-throated Swift, Northern Flicker, American Kestrel, Prairie Falcon, Western Wood-Pewee, Dusky Flycatcher, Say's Phoebe, both shrikes (seasonally), Cassin's and Warbling Vireos, Violet-green Swallow, Red-breasted and White-breasted Nuthatches, Rock and Canyon Wrens, Gray Catbird, Cedar Waxwing, Nashville Warbler, Spotted Towhee, Lazuli Bunting, and Red Crossbill. It is a good low elevation site for Clark's Nutcrackers. Owling can be good here. Listen for Great Horned, Northern Pygmy-, Short-eared, and Northern Saw-whet Owls.

From the main intersection in downtown Winthrop take SR-20 westbound across the Chewuch River bridge. In 0.2 mile, on the opposite side of the highway from the USFS Methow Valley Information Center, turn right onto West Chewuch Road. Drive north 0.9 mile to Rendezvous Road. Turn left, proceed 1.1 miles, and make another left onto Gunn Ranch Road. In 0.8 mile, stop at a parking area off to the left for the Rendezvous Lake Unit (3,180 acres) of the Methow Wildlife Area (Discover Pass required). Except in the fall hunting season, the riparian thickets and open fields around **Riser Lake**, a short walk ahead, make an excellent birding site. Look for Cinnamon Teal, Barrow's Goldeneye, Pied-billed Grebe, Spotted Sandpiper, Eastern Kingbird, Tree Swallow, House Wren, Western Bluebird, and Bullock's Oriole.

UPPER METHOW VALLEY

Wolf Creek Road offers an easygoing route upvalley on the opposite bank of the Methow River from the highway. Headed southeast from the main intersection in the Winthrop business district, SR-20 bends right and crosses the Methow River (0.5 mile). Take a right 0.1 mile after the bridge onto Twin Lakes Road, passing the Winthrop National Fish Hatchery (short trail with good riparian birding) and reaching the intersection with Wolf Creek Road in 1.3 miles. Turn right onto this road, paved the first four miles, then gravel, which runs beside riparian areas (Purple Finch) and pine and Douglas-fir forest. Look for Black Swifts overhead (easier to spot when foraging low in cool and cloudy weather). Reach SR-20 in nine miles.

An access to **Big Valley Unit** (847 acres) of the Methow Wildlife Area is not far downstream from this intersection. Turn right onto SR-20, travel 1.6 miles, and turn right onto Dripping Springs Road (known on some on-line maps as Big Valley Ranch Trail). Park in 0.3 mile. Choose the trail that takes off directly behind the restrooms. It is about a quarter-mile walk to the Methow River. Pines and Douglas-firs en route should have Western Wood-Pewee, Hammond's Flycatcher, Red-breasted Nuthatch, and Yellow-rumped Warbler. Riparian growth nearer the river may produce Red-naped Sapsucker, Northern Flicker, Red-eyed Vireo, Veery, American Robin, Cedar Waxwing, and Nashville, MacGillivray's, and Yellow Warblers, and American Redstart. Bald Eagle and American Dipper are found along the river, especially in winter. Irrigated and dryland pastures in other parts of the wildlife area are managed for Mule and White-tailed Deer. Golden Eagles hunt over these fields in winter. At night, listen for Great Horned, Barred, and Northern Saw-whet Owls.

Turn left from Dripping Springs Road and backtrack northwestward on SR-20, then go right in 1.1 miles onto Goat Creek Road. In 3.5 miles, an obscure, unmarked gravel spur on the left leads to parking for the **Methow Community Trail**. Follow the old roadbed for one mile to an impressive suspension bridge over the Methow River, passing coniferous and riparian habitats. Look for Harlequin Duck, Common Merganser, Rufous and Calliope Hummingbirds, Red-naped Sapsucker, Hammond's Flycatcher, Mountain Chickadee, Red-breasted and White-breasted Nuthatches, American Dipper, Veery, Yellow Warbler, American Redstart, Black-headed Grosbeak, Cassin's Finch, and Red Crossbill. The riparian woodland and sloughs beyond the suspension bridge are especially good for "eastern" species such as Least Flycatcher, Red-eyed Vireo, Veery, Gray Catbird, Northern Waterthrush, and American Redstart. For a much shorter hike to this superb area, go west on SR-20 from Goat Creek Road one mile to milepost 183. There is very limited parking here by the highway. Walk west on the trail which parallels the highway as it crosses the first driveway and swings to the right (north).

Mazama (limited services) is 1.7 miles ahead on Goat Creek Road. A short connector on the left leads to SR-20 (0.4 mile). From here SR-20 (closed in winter) begins its ascent of the North Cascades along Early Winters Creek, reaching Western Washington via Washington Pass (17.5 miles; page 124). On the way up, **Klipchuk Campground** (4.3 miles) is a fine place to study birds of the upper forest, including Sooty Grouse, Williamson's Sapsucker (uncommon), Hammond's Flycatcher, and Varied Thrush.

In Mazama, Goat Creek Road changes name to Lost River Road and continues straight ahead up the Methow Valley. In 2.1 miles, find **North Cascade Base Camp** (866-996-2334, *http://www.northcascadesbasecamp.com/*), a rustic lodge set in forest. Birders are welcome to walk the grounds, but be quiet in the early morning to avoid disturbing guests. The Tractor and Beaver Trails can be walked as a loop (about a mile) past a number of Beaver ponds lined with riparian vegetation, and areas of wet coniferous forest with giant Western Redcedars. Typical birds in summer include Ruffed Grouse, Barred Owl, Red-naped Sapsucker, Downy, Hairy, and Pileated Woodpeckers, Hammond's Flycatcher, Warbling and Red-eyed Vireos, Veery, Swainson's Thrush, MacGillivray's and Townsend's Warblers, and Red Crossbill. Rufous and Calliope Hummingbirds visit the feeders outside the dining-room windows. Winter birders on cross-country skis might encounter Northern Pygmy-Owl, Brown Creeper, and Pine Grosbeak.

HARTS PASS

Famous for mountain scenery, backcountry trails, and subalpine meadows with an extravagant summer wildflower display (160 species), the Cascade crest around Harts Pass is an exceptional site for high-country and boreal bird species. Extensive wildfires have changed much of the higher elevation subalpine forest on this route, causing a marked reduction in birds tied to mature forests such as Spruce Grouse, Boreal Owl, Boreal Chickadee, and Pine Grosbeak but attracting another cast such as Northern Hawk Owl to the sea of burnt snags.

The first rocky wagon track to the gold mines west of the crest at Chancellor and Barron was engineered by Colonel W. Thomas Hart in 1900. The road was widened (to 36 inches!) in 1903 and a second time in 1936. Although well maintained and easily travelable by any passenger auto, it is too narrow in some places for two cars to pass. The main complication is not there, however, but on the rest of the road where the smooth surface may give drivers a false sense of security and tempt them to go too fast, leading to hair-raising close encounters at the many blind curves and dips. Nor is this a place for long, wide vehicles; trailers are expressly forbidden.

Continue west on Lost River Road (becomes FR-5400), staying right at a fork seven miles past North Cascade Base Camp. The steep gravel road cut into the side of the mountain continues steadily uphill through a variety of forested habitats harboring bird species such as Sooty Grouse, Rufous Hummingbird, Western Wood-Pewee, Hammond's Flycatcher, Cassin's and Warbling Vireos, Swainson's and Hermit Thrushes, Nashville, Yellow, Yellow-rumped, MacGillivray's and Townsend's Warblers, Chipping Sparrow, Western Tanager, Dark-eyed Junco, Lazuli Bunting, and Pine Siskin. A half-mile section, known as Deadhorse Point (about three miles past the fork), is subject to rockslides and washouts and must be negotiated carefully. Park beyond the steepest portion and look below to a natural salt lick that attracts Mountain Goats, up to 50 on occasion, especially in early summer.

A sea of blackened snags covers much of the landscape beyond Deadhorse Point. These remain from several big forest fires. Mountain Bluebirds and Chipping Sparrows are common. Woodpeckers and Northern Hawk Owl are about, too At a junction 9.8 miles from the fork, just before Harts Pass, turn left onto FR-500 to reach **Meadows Campground** (primitive) in one mile and the road's end at the Pacific Crest Trail a mile beyond that. The subalpine forest, formerly good for boreal species, is now in a regenerating state. Northern Hawk Owls have nested amid the burned snags nearby.

To try for boreal forest birds, head back to Harts Pass, which escaped the fire. Return to the junction with FR-5400 and turn left for 0.1 mile to reach Harts Pass (elevation 6,198 feet) and another small USFS campground. These meadows and lichen-festooned forests of Engelmann Spruce, Subalpine Fir, and Subalpine Larch can be excellent for boreal specialties such as Spruce Grouse, Boreal Owl, American Three-toed Woodpecker, Boreal Chickadee, Pine Grosbeak, and White-winged Crossbill (irregular). Other inhabitants include Rufous Hummingbird, Gray Jay, Clark's Nutcracker, Common Raven, Mountain Chickadee, Red-breasted Nuthatch, Pacific Wren, Golden-crowned and Ruby-crowned Kinglets, Mountain Bluebird, Hermit Thrush, American Robin, Varied Thrush, Yellow-rumped and Townsend's Warblers, Chipping and Fox Sparrows, Cassin's Finch, and Red Crossbill.

The road forks again; go right onto FR-600 and continue past a trailhead parking area for the Pacific Crest Trail to another parking lot where the road is gated (2.4 miles). You are at the highest point reached by road in Washington (elevation 7,200 feet). Walk up the road for a few hundred yards beyond the gate to a trailhead for the **West Fork Pasayten River Trail**. Often closed by lingering snow until well into July, the trail switchbacks down through the meadows into a cirque. At the first fork, go left with the main trail a few hundred yards onto the rocky north slopes of Slate Peak, or right into a compact basin that contains examples of most of the upper subalpine and alpine plant communities found in the North Cascades. Fox Sparrows are numerous in trees at timberline, joined by a few White-crowned Sparrows (*gambelii* race); the adjacent forb meadows have Savannah Sparrows. Above treeline, American Pipits perform their flight song and aerial display. Search the snowbank edges and mats of alpine vegetation for Gray-crowned Rosy-Finch. White-tailed Ptarmigans are here, but luck and hard work are usually needed to find one. Males seem tied to boulder-strewn slopes with scattered heather patches: you might even spy one by looking down from the parking lot. Females with broods are most often noted in seep habitats with high insect availability, just below the snowbanks.

The summit of **Slate Peak** is another few minutes' walk up the road. In good weather, beginning in August and continuing through mid-October, the summit can be a decent hawkwatching platform. Expect Sharp-shinned and Red-tailed Hawks in modest numbers, with a sprinkling of other species. The peak's north ridge is another possibility for ptarmigan.

OKANOGAN VALLEY

by Andy Stepniewski
revised by Penny Rose and Shep Thorp

The Okanogan River winds along the broad trench of the Okanogan Valley through irrigated orchards and hay fields, open rangeland and areas of riparian habitat. Bold, rounded domes of granitic and metamorphic rocks (gneiss) provide a dramatic backdrop in many places. Glacial terraces, formed when a large trunk glacier partially filled the valley, are conspicuous along the sides. Common species throughout the valley in May and June, when birding possibilities peak, include California Quail, Ring-necked Pheasant, Red-tailed Hawk, Killdeer, Mourning Dove, Common Nighthawk, Downy Woodpecker, Northern Flicker, American Kestrel, Western Kingbird, Black-billed Magpie, American Crow, Violet-green, Northern Rough-winged, Bank, Cliff, and Barn Swallows, Black-capped Chickadee, House Wren, American Robin, Cedar Waxwing, Black-headed Grosbeak, Brewer's Blackbird, Bullock's Oriole, and House Finch. In winter, flocks of Bohemian Waxwings rove about the orchards and brushy draws. Some years there are also flocks of Common Redpolls; look for these in areas of Water Birch and alders, or in ornamental birches in the towns, where a few Pine Grosbeaks may also turn up. Bald Eagle roost along the river, and both Red-tailed and Rough-legged Hawks also may be seen. Agriculture, grazing, and urbanization have diminished the natural qualities of the landscape close to US-97. However, towns along the highway serve as good jump-off points for birding sites away from the valley bottom.

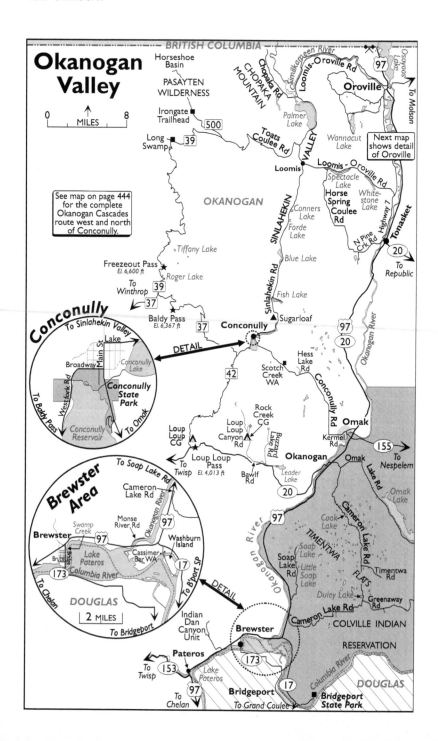

Okanogan Valley

0 — MILES — 8

See map on page 444 for the complete Okanogan Cascades route west and north of Conconully.

BRITISH COLUMBIA

Horseshoe Basin

PASAYTEN WILDERNESS

CHOPAKA MOUNTAIN

Chopaka Rd

Similkameen River

Loomis-Oroville Rd

Oroville

Osoyoos Lake

To Molson

97

Irongate Trailhead

500

Palmer Lake

Toats Coulee Rd

Wannacut Lake

Next map shows detail of Oroville

Long Swamp

39

Loomis

Loomis - Oroville Rd

Spectacle Lake

OKANOGAN

SINLAHEKIN VALLEY

Horse Spring Coulee Rd

White-stone Lake

Highway 7

Tonasket

Conners Lake

Forde Lake

N Pine Crk Rd

Tiffany Lake

Blue Lake

20

To Republic

Freezeout Pass El. 6,600 ft

Roger Lake

Sinlahekin Rd

Fish Lake

To Winthrop

39

37

Baldy Pass El. 6,367 ft

37

Conconully

Sugarloaf

Okanogan River

Conconully

To Sinlahekin Valley

Lake

Main St

Broadway

Conconully Lake

DETAIL

Hess Lake Rd

97

20

Westfork Rd

To Baldy Pass

Conconully State Park

42

Scotch Creek WA

Conconully Rd

Omak

Conconully Reservoir

To Omak

Rock Creek CG

Loup Loup CG

Loup Loup Canyon Rd

Buzzard Lake Rd

Kermel Rd

155 To Nespelem

Okanogan

Omak

Omak Lake

Brewster Area

To Soap Lake Rd

Cameron Lake Rd

Loup Loup Pass El. 4,013 ft

To Twisp

Bawlf Rd

Leader Lake

20

Lake Rd

Cameron Lake Rd

Cook Lake

Cameron Lake Rd

Monse River Rd

Okanogan River

97

97

TIMENTWA

Soap Lake Rd

Timentwa Rd

Brewster

Swamp Creek

97

Washburn Island

River

Soap Lake

Bruce

Lake Pateros

Cassimer Bar WA

17

Okanogan

Little Soap Lake

FLATS

173

Columbia River

To B 'port Spr

Duley Lake

Greenaway Rd

To Chelan

DOUGLAS

2 MILES

To Bridgeport

Indian Dan Canyon Unit

DETAIL

Cameron Lake Rd

COLVILLE INDIAN

Brewster

RESERVATION

Pateros

173

To Twisp

153

Lake Pateros

Columbia River

DOUGLAS

97

To Chelan

Bridgeport

17

Bridgeport State Park

To Grand Coulee

BREWSTER AND VICINITY

The small community of Brewster — gateway to the Okanogan Valley — is located on the north shore of the Columbia River (actually Lake Pateros, the reservoir behind Wells Dam) about seven miles above Pateros and three miles below the mouth of the Okanogan River. In winter, drive the town's residential streets, where ornamental plantings and feeders often attract House Finch, Black-capped Chickadee, Bewick's Wren, Downy Wood-pecker, and the occasional accipiter and Merlin. Before heading off to explore the several birding routes that converge in Brewster, visit some excellent birding sites close by. One is the spot where Swamp Creek empties eastward into Lake Pateros. From US-97, drive south on SR-173 (aka Bridge Street N) one block to Lakeview Way and turn left. You'll be just north of Swamp Creek.

You can also view the lake and shoreline by turning into the parking lot just south of Swamp Creek (0.2 mile south of US-97). Check for wintering gulls, including Ring-billed, California, Herring, and, rarely, Glaucous Gull. Continu-ing south on Bridge Street, head west (right) on Bruce Street (0.7 mile) to ac-cess waterfront at a local dock and boat launch. This is a terrific area to scope ducks, grebes, and loons. Bald Eagles frequent the area.

Return to US-97, turn left (southwest) and drive 2.5 miles to to Indian Dan Canyon Road. Turn right onto this gravel road and go 1.4 miles to the **Indian Dan Canyon Unit** of the Wells Wildlife Area (8,200 acres total, of which the Indian Dan Canyon Unit is 4,412 acres). (*Note:* the entire Indian Dan Canyon Unit was burned by the massive 2014 Carlton Complex wildfire. Biologists expect regrowth in the next four to five years.) Slopes are covered with Bitterbrush and Big Sagebrush, while ravines have riparian habitats with clumps of aspen. Birding these habitats in spring and summer should yield many of the usual Eastside breeding birds including Lark Sparrow. Northern Goshawk occurs fairly regularly in winter. In another mile, turn left on Getz Road and pass a small, marshy lake in the valley bottom; look for Ruddy Ducks, Marsh Wren, and Yellow-breasted Chat. Sharp-tailed Grouse is a remote possibility.

From SR-173 and US-97 in Brewster, travel east 3.4 miles and stop at a wide pullout on the right to survey **Cassimer Bar** and the mouth of the Okanogan River. Scope for Wood Duck, loons, grebes, Double-crested Cormorant, and American White Pelican, and listen for booming American Bittern. Continue east on US-97 0.1 mile and turn left onto Monse River Road for views of Northern Rough-winged and Cliff Swallow colonies under the Okanogan River Bridge. Return to US-97, turn left and cross the bridge 0.1 mile to an unmarked gravel road on the right. Follow this to a Douglas County PUD fishing access for a better view of this rich birding area, where groves of introduced Russian Olives and other trees alternate with ponds and marshes. Spring and fall can be excellent for migrant passerines. Summer residents include Osprey, Virginia Rail, Forster's Tern, Western Wood-Pewee, Willow Flycatcher, numerous swallows, and Marsh Wren.

The intersection of US-97 and SR-17 is 1.2 miles farther east. Turn right and go south on SR-17 for 0.2 mile. Turn right onto an unmarked road that ends in a half-mile at a causeway to **Washburn Island**. Park and scan the water and marshlands from here or walk across to the island. Depending on the season, this embayment may be filled with waterbirds. Osprey, Marsh Wren, and Yellow-headed Blackbird are a few of the many species that nest here. In winter, scope the lake for diving ducks (Long-tailed Duck rarely), loons and grebes. As the causeway enters onto Washburn Island, to the west and east is a line of mixed bramble and deciduous trees leading to grain feeders one-quarter mile in either direction. This is an excellent area to view sparrows and the occasional Northern Harrier, accipiter, Great Horned Owl, and Merlin. Rarely, American Tree Sparrows have been seen along the edge of the agricultural fields and bramble. Western Meadowlarks occasionally are present.

Go south another 7.9 miles on SR-17 and turn left for 2.7 miles to **Bridgeport State Park**. Rock Wrens inhabit rocky ravines uphill from the campground. Adjacent deeper-soiled slopes have a well-developed shrub-steppe habitat (Sage Thrasher, Lark Sparrow). In winter, check the small evergreen trees for evidence of whitewash and roosting Northern Saw-whet Owls. Great Horned Owls breed in the large conifers in the center of the park and are present year round. Northern Goshawk has also been reported. Northern Flicker, American Robin, Varied Thrush, and House Finch frequent the park, which borders the north shore of the Columbia River. Redheads are often seen near the swimming beach.

TIMENTWA FLATS

East of the southern Okanogan Valley, on the Colville Indian Reservation, is a high plateau sometimes called the Timentwa Flats. Birders must abide by Colville regulations, which forbid harassing wildlife and bird species, including using calls or sound recordings to attract birds. Although not included in the regulations, the Colville tribes ask that bird species found on the reservation by individuals not be recorded in digital format—for example, eBird. (Many species on the reservation are classified as sensitive and also are culturally significant; the tribes strive to protect their exact locations.) The wide-open, rolling upland Timentwa Flats, dotted with monstrous glacial erratics, has the same terrain as the adjacent Waterville Plateau across the Columbia River to the south, but is wilder, with no towns and far fewer signs of habitation. Shrub-steppe, Ponderosa Pine forests, small lakes, riparian groves with Quaking Aspen and Water Birch, and dryland wheat farms are the principal habitats. One main gravel road and a few offshoots permit easy, safe exploration of this remote region, but be especially careful during winter and the spring thaw when roads here can become difficult or impossible to negotiate.

From the junction with SR-17 east of Brewster, go north 2.6 miles on US-97 to **Cameron Lake Road** (aka Wakefield-Cameron Lake Road), an excellent year-round birding route that crosses the heart of the Timentwa Flats to end in Okanogan. Downy Woodpecker, Black-billed Magpie, and Black-capped Chickadees are resident in copses along wetland edges. Breeding species include Calliope Hummingbird, Red-naped Sapsucker, House Wren, Western Bluebird, and Bullock's Oriole. The many small lakes attract waterfowl and migrant shorebirds. Northern species such as Rough-legged Hawk, Snowy Owl, Gyrfalcon, Horned Lark, Snow Bunting, and American Tree Sparrow await those properly equipped for winter birding. Cameron Lake Road ascends 6.3 miles to the edge of the plateau. Once on the rim, look for Loggerhead Shrike, Horned Lark, and Brewer's, Vesper, Savannah, and Grasshopper Sparrows. Continue east, then north to an intersection with **Greenaway Road** (5.7 miles). This is raptor country with good numbers of Red-tailed and Rough-legged Hawks. Other raptors include Golden Eagle, Snowy Owl (rare), Gyrfalcon (rare), and Prairie Falcon. Check ponds and lakes for shorebirds. Baird's, Pectoral, and Semipalmated Sandpipers are regular in fall migration. Sandhill Cranes can be common in wheat-field stubble and wet swales from late March to mid-April. If road conditions permit, head east on Greenaway Road to a wildlife area (2.0 mile) rich in Grasshopper and Savannah Sparrows.

Continue north on Cameron Lake Road for 0.7 mile to **Duley Lake**. Except when frozen, this lake attracts numerous waterfowl including nesting Redhead and Eared Grebes, American Wigeon, and Ruddy Ducks. Unusual records include Thayer's Gull and Forster's Tern. Depending on water levels, shorebird diversity and numbers can be good beginning in late July and continuing through August. Red-tailed Hawks have nested on the cliffs at the north end of the lake. Turn right onto **Timentwa Road** (3.2 miles) and drive 1.5 miles through wheat field, ponds, and weedy swales. This higher-elevation portion of the plateau (above 2,700 feet) has proven excellent in winter and early spring for Horned Lark, Lapland Longspur, Snow Bunting, and American Tree Sparrow. Fantastic numbers of Snow Buntings (2,000–3,000) have been observed in late February and early March, particularly near the cattle ranch just east of Snyder Lake. The cattle disturb the frozen ponds and earth, providing these agriculture-loving species an opportunity to forage.

Once more headed north on Cameron Lake Road, stop in 0.6 mile to check dense riparian habitat for sparrows and game birds, especially in winter —most recently Gray Partridge, American Tree Sparrow, and White-crowned Sparrow. In another 2.1 miles lies a dirt lane to the west, giving access to three small lakes amidst wheat fields that sometimes have waterfowl and shorebirds. The main road winds north for 2.4 miles through shrub-steppe (Common Raven and Horned Lark year round, Sage Thrasher and Brewer's Sparrow in summer). Here begins the descent, gradual at first, through pines alternating with riparian groves. Continue north 0.9 mile to

Cook Lake, on the right, particularly good for Greater Scaup and other diving ducks in spring. Penley Lake (0.8 mile), a small alkaline lake, has nesting American Avocets and Black-necked Stilts. For the next two-plus miles, up to where the Ponderosa Pine forest abruptly ends, make a number of stops to look for Northern Pygmy-Owl, White-headed Woodpecker, Gray Flycatcher (May– July), Mountain Chickadee, White-breasted and Pygmy Nuthatches, and Red Crossbill. An area of denser brushland by the road (1.1 mile from the last pines) attracts Brewer's, Vesper, and Grasshopper Sparrows and Lazuli Bunting. At the intersection with Cameron Lake-Omak Lake Road (1.7 mile), stay left on Cameron Lake Road and proceed west, inspecting the shrub-steppe habitats with Bitterbrush and Big Sagebrush for Loggerhead Shrike (uncommon) and Lark Sparrow from April through July. In 1.4 miles, reach the combined US-97/SR-20 a mile north of Okanogan.

The **Soap Lake** area, on the western slope of the Timentwa Flats, is good for waterbirds from spring through fall. From the junction of US-97 and SR-17 east of Brewster, go north 4.1 miles on US-97 and turn right onto Soap Lake Road, which climbs the flanks of a glacial terrace into rangelands with scattered alkaline lakes. On the terrace (1.5 miles), in open areas, look for Red-tailed Hawk, Loggerhead Shrike, and Brewer's and Lark Sparrows. For the next three miles you pass three alkaline lakes: Little Soap Lake, an even smaller unnamed lake, and finally mile-long Soap Lake. Look here in nesting season for teals (all three) and other puddle ducks, Barrow's Goldeneye, Eared Grebe, Wilson's Phalarope, and Yellow-headed Blackbird. Shorebirds occur in migration, especially yellowlegs, Baird's Sandpiper, and other peeps.

CONCONULLY AND SINLAHEKIN VALLEY

US-97 offers little in the way of birding between Omak and Oroville. Better to seek out the Sinlahekin Valley. Sinlahekin Creek threads its way along a glaciated valley for 17 miles, from Blue Lake (elevation 1,686 feet) north to Palmer Lake (elevation 1,145 feet). This broad trench probably holds a greater diversity of breeding birds than any other area of comparable size in Washington. On both sides, steep slopes with rock outcrops and cliffs ascend abruptly to an elevation of more than 5,000 feet. Ponderosa Pine forest and various bunchgrasses alternate with large areas of Bitterbrush, serviceberry, chokecherry, and snowberry. The valley floor has tangled, dense stands of Water Birch, willow, and aspen, with numerous Beaver ponds and several other impoundments. Two interesting routes lead from US-97 to the Sinlahekin Valley. One takes off from Omak, proceeds northwest through Conconully and then north to Loomis; the other heads north from Tonasket and then west toward Loomis.

To reach **Conconully**, an excellent birding destination and route in its own right, begin in Omak (north end) at the junction of US-97 and Riverside Drive. Proceed west on Riverside 1.0 mile and turn right onto Cherry Avenue (becomes Kermel Road), following signs for Conconully Lake. Go 2.1 miles to a stop sign, then right (north) onto Conconully Road. For about half the 15-mile distance from here to Conconully, the road passes through orchards and grazing country (Red-tailed Hawk, American Kestrel, Western Kingbird, Black-billed Magpie, Western Meadowlark, Brewer's Blackbird, House Finch, American Goldfinch). For the remainder, rangelands alternate with shrub-steppe habitats where Chukar, Vesper and Lark Sparrows, and Western Meadowlark are common. From Kermel Road, travel northwest 8.2 miles on Conconully Road to Hess Lake Road and turn right. Hess Lake, on the left in 0.2 mile, supports breeding Ruddy Ducks and Yellow-headed Blackbirds; a marshy area beyond the lake has Virginia Rail and Common Yellowthroat. The road ends at a WDFW area set aside for Sharp-tailed Grouse.

Returning to Conconully Road, turn right and continue 2.7 miles to a parking area for the **Scotch Creek Wildlife Area**, where a small number of Sharp-tailed Grouse can be seen in winter eating catkins from Water Birches, most reliably in the area north of the Conconully Road where it is intersected by Happy Hill Road. Other winter species include Gray Partridge, Northern Harrier, Northern Goshawk, Red-tailed and Rough-legged Hawks, Golden Eagle, Prairie Falcon, and Northern Shrike.

Continue northwest on Conconully Road. On the left in four miles is the first entrance for **Conconully State Park** (not well signed), which affords a good view of Conconully Reservoir. Scan for waterfowl and gulls. Return to Conconully Road and turn left. Go 0.4 mile, turn left, then left again in one block into the main park entrance (Discover Pass required). The trees here are worth checking in migration, as is the open area west of the campground.

Farther west along Broadway from the park entrance, curve left (now proceeding south on West Fork Road), to find forest birds typical of Ponderosa Pine forests, which are fairly common between the road and the reservoir. These include Northern Pygmy-Owl, Calliope Hummingbird (feeders at cabins), all three nuthatches, Cassin's Finch, and Evening Grosbeak. In winter, listen for Red Crossbills. Rarely, White-winged Crossbills are heard or seen here and in town. After leaving Conconully Reservoir, West Fork Road enters a riparian area and then begins ascending West Fork Salmon Creek through forests of Douglas-fir, Western Larch, and Ponderosa Pine. Baldy Pass and Roger Lake lie ahead.

Back in town, check winter feeders for passerines. Nice finds include Northern Goshawk, Golden Eagle, White-headed Woodpecker, Clark's Nutcracker, Townsend's Solitaire, and Pine Grosbeak.

To reach the Sinlahekin Valley from Conconully, go north on Main Street and in 0.2 mile turn right onto Lake Street, which becomes **Sinlahekin Road**, running east, then north along the shore of Conconully Lake before contouring around Sugarloaf and descending toward Fish Lake. In 5.3 miles, stop in the Douglas-fir forest to look and listen for Hairy Woodpecker,

Hammond's Flycatcher, Cassin's Vireo, and Nashville Warbler, among many other breeding species. In winter, check open areas for Northern Goshawk. Between here and Loomis, the route passes through the **Sinlahekin Wildlife Area** (22,840 acres), Washington's oldest state wildlife area. When purchased, these lands were intended primarily to provide habitat for the large Mule Deer herd. Today they are managed—including controlled burns—for a diversity of wildlife.

At an intersection with Fish Lake Road (1.4 miles), stay left with Sinlahekin Road to a view of Blue Lake (3.4 miles), where Hooded Merganser and Common Loon are regular. Shallower Forde Lake, 5.1 miles farther north, has Pied-billed Grebe, a variety of waterfowl, and many Willow Flycatchers and Common Yellowthroats. Red-necked Grebes have nested here. Marshfringed **Connors Lake** is an exceptional birding site. Turn off right from Sinlahekin Road in 1.5 miles, go a few yards, then turn right again to find the lake in 0.4 mile. The many nesting waterbirds include Canada Goose, Wood Duck, Gadwall, Mallard, Blue-winged and Cinnamon Teal, Barrow's Goldeneye, and Spotted Sandpiper. Surrounding riparian zone and marsh habitats are great for Ruffed Grouse, Black-chinned and Calliope Hummingbird, Red-naped Sapsucker, Willow Flycatcher, Eastern Kingbird, Warbling Vireo, Tree, Northern Rough-winged, and Barn Swallows, Marsh Wren, Veery, Gray Catbird, Cedar Waxwing, Nashville Warbler, MacGillivray's Warbler, Common Yellowthroat, Yellow Warbler, Yellow-breasted Chat, and Bullock's Oriole. Rarities such as Rose-breasted Grosbeak have been recorded here.

The riparian zone is best accessed on foot from headquarters along the Dave Brittell Memorial Trail that extends south to Hunter's Camp, south of Forde Lake. Northern Harrier, Short-eared Owl and Western Screech-Owl have nested near headquarters. On forested and brushy slopes away from water, look for Chukar, Cooper's and Red-tailed Hawks, Golden Eagle, Common Nighthawk, Common Poorwill, Lewis's, Hairy, and Pileated Woodpeckers, Merlin (particularly in fall), Western Wood-Pewee, Dusky Flycatcher, Western Kingbird, Red-eyed Vireo, Clark's Nutcracker, Mountain Chickadee, White-breasted Nuthatch, Rock, Canyon, and House Wrens, Western Bluebird, Townsend's Solitaire, Spotted Towhee, Chipping Sparrow, Western Tanager, Lazuli Bunting, and Cassin's Finch.

About five miles farther north, Sinlahekin Road enters Loomis and becomes Palmer Avenue. At the fork, turn left onto northbound Loomis-Oroville Road. (If you wish to connect to US-97 or SR-20 in Tonasket, turn right here and head east 11.6 miles to an intersection with Westside Road; turn right to reach Tonasket in another five miles.) Northward 4.3 miles on the Loomis-Oroville Road lies **Palmer Lake**, nestled in a trough. Between Loomis and Palmer Lake, scan hay fields for Bobolink and rocky faces for Chukar. American Bittern, Virginia Rail, Sora, Spotted Sandpiper, Wilson's Snipe, Willow Flycatcher, several swallow species and

Common Yellowthroat should be looked for in the marshes at the southern and northern end of Palmer Lake. Good viewing access can be found at the Split Rock Day Area (BLM) at the southern end. A few Common Mergansers, Common Loons, and Western Grebes can sometimes be scoped on the deep waters of the lake; White-winged Scoter and other sea ducks occur rarely. A Ross's Gull was recorded here. A better bet for waterbirds usually is to continue around the lake 4.4 miles to its north end. Sandbars may have resting gulls or Caspian Terns.

The second approach to the Sinlahekin Valley from US-97 begins in Tonasket, about 22 miles north of Omak. In Tonasket, turn left on Fourth Street, go 0.3 mile and turn right onto Highway 7 (following signs to the Many Lakes Recreation Area). After five miles, the road curves left and becomes the Loomis-Oroville Road. In three miles, find a Public Fishing Access on the left at **Whitestone Lake**. Redheads and Red-necked Grebes nest here. Continue west on Loomis-Oroville Road 3.1 miles to an unmarked access on the left to view the east end of **Spectacle Lake** for Redhead, Red-necked Grebe, Killdeer, and Belted Kingfisher. It is 5.5 miles west to Loomis and the Sinlahekin Valley.

For a side trip featuring high-plateau birding, continue west 3.4 miles on Loomis-Oroville Road and turn left onto **Horse Spring Coulee Road**. The road climbs steeply 0.7 mile to a sage and grassland area. Continue south another 0.7 mile and stop at a fork for Brewer's, Vesper, and Lark Sparrows and Sage Thrasher. Continue until the sage ends in wide expanse of grassland at the Double R Ranch in 1.2 miles. Bird from the road for Grasshopper Sparrow and nesting Long-billed Curlews. From here, you may either return to Loomis-Oroville Road or continue 9.6 miles to an intersection with North Pine Creek Road. This route proceeds through homesteads, Ponderosa Pine, riparian areas, and a few ponds. Go left on North Pine Creek Road to return to US-97 and Tonasket (3.8 miles); turn right to reach Fish Lake and the Sinlahekin Wildlife Refuge.

SIMILKAMEEN RIVER

The outlet creek of Palmer Lake meanders north for a couple of miles to reach the Similkameen River and outstanding birding. A little over a half-mile north of the north end of the lake, turn left from the Loomis-Oroville Road onto **Chopaka Road**, which leads up the Similkameen Valley for 6.5 miles to a closed gate a short distance before the U.S.-Canada border (not a port of entry). Here, you'll find riparian habitat and river views, where you can see Wilson's Snipe, Yellow Warbler, and Bullock's Oriole. Most of the land along Chopaka Road is private, but interesting habitats reach the road. In the first mile are meadows, areas of brush, fields (many flooded in the spring) featuring Eastern Kingbird, Savannah Sparrow, Lazuli Bunting, Bobolink, and a variety of waterfowl. Sloughs lined with riparian vegetation lie ahead—great for

Black-chinned Hummingbird, Red-naped Sapsucker, Willow Flycatcher, War-bling Vireo, Veery, Gray Catbird, and MacGillivray's and Yellow Warblers. To the west, Chopaka Mountain sweeps precipitously down from its summit for more than 6,000 feet in one unbroken slope. The cliffs have Chukar, Golden Eagle, White-throated Swift, Violet-green Swallow, and Rock and Canyon Wrens. Farther along, look for Calliope Hummingbird, Pileated Wood-pecker, Dusky Flycatcher, Cassin's Vireo, House Wren, and Nashville War-bler on the open, brushy slopes and in Douglas-fir forest at the base of the mountain. A few areas of open water expand the possibilities. At 4.3 miles from the Loomis-Oroville Road is a parking area on the right for WDFW's **Similkameen-Chopaka Wildlife Area.** This spot affords close views of the Similkameen as well as pedestrian access through cottonwood and snowberry to a rich riparian area on an old railroad bed, where you can see Warbling and Red-eyed Vireos, as well as Least Flycatcher.

Return to the Loomis-Oroville Road and turn left. In 0.5 mile, pull out to the right at an overlook of **Champney Slough**, (recent habitation and shrinking roadsides make this less than ideal but worth the effort), in the heart of an area of exceptional diversity of breeding birds. More than 100 species have been documented here, including Chukar, Osprey, Bald Eagle, Cooper's Hawk, Western Screech-Owl, Common Poorwill, Lewis's Woodpecker, Red-naped Sapsucker, Least Flycatcher (calling from riparian vegetation on the island) Warbling and Red-eyed Vireos, Northern Rough-winged Swallow, Rock and Canyon Wrens, Veery, Gray Catbird, American Redstart(uncom-mon), Yellow Warbler, Yellow-breasted Chat, Black-headed Grosbeak, and Bullock's Oriole. For the faint of heart, many of these species can be found along Chopaka Road.

Continuing north, then east, the Loomis-Oroville Road follows the Similkameen River downstream to Oroville (15.7 miles). Various unmarked accesses to the stream allow you to see Lewis's Woodpecker, Eastern and Western Kingbirds, and Bullock's Oriole. At four miles from Champney Slough, turn left (north) onto Similkameen Road for a side trip to good sage habitat with Brewer's, Vesper and Lark Sparrows. As you travel along Loomis-Oroville Road, check the steep slopes and cliffs for Chukar, Golden Eagle, and Common Poorwill.

OROVILLE AND VICINITY

The small farming and ranching community of Oroville, just below the U.S.-Canada border, is a crossroads of excellent birding routes, west to the Similkameen Valley, east to the Okanogan Highlands (page 448) or north on US-97 to the Okanagan Valley of British Columbia.

Driscoll Island Unit-Sinlahekin Wildlife Area (350 acres) is south of Oroville near the confluence of the Okanogan and Similkameen Rivers. Cur-rently, access to the island is by boat. However, observing the island from a

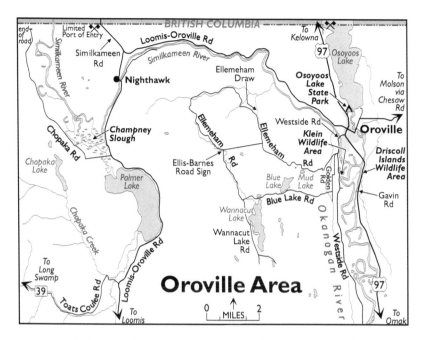

Oroville Area

concrete platform on the shore offers good birding, especially early on a May or June morning. Drive south 2.9 miles on US-97 (Main Street) from Central Avenue in Oroville; turn right onto Gavin Road. The lush streambank habitats host Spotted Sandpiper, Rufous Hummingbird, Belted Kingfisher, Willow Fly-catcher, Eastern Kingbird, Gray Catbird, Northern Waterthrush, American Redstart, Yellow Warbler, Black-headed Grosbeak, and Bullock's Oriole. Another access 0.8 mile farther north on US-97 (closer to Oroville) signed *Public Fishing Access* has similar possibilities.

To begin a 20-mile loop through an old mining district southwest of Oroville, head 0.3 mile south of Central Avenue on US-97 (Main Street), turn west on 12th Avenue, and cross the Similkameen River, curving left onto Westside Road (aka Highway 7 and Janis-Oroville Road). In 1.0 mile from US-97, turn right at a sign for **Ellemeham Mountain**. The many bird-rich habitats here include steep, barren slopes and rocky outcrops, shrub-steppe, aspen-lined watercourses, grasslands, and a few areas of marsh and lakes. This route is especially good during the breeding season. At the fork in 0.1 mile, keep right on Ellemeham Road, which climbs steeply out of the Okanogan Val-ley. In 2.0 miles, look for ducks such as nesting Blue-winged and Green-winged Teal and shorebirds at **Mud Lake**. Over the next 10 miles as the road leaves the lake, drops down into Ellemeham Draw (3.8 miles), climbs out of the draw and then starts down a canyon, look for Clay-colored Sparrow (rare), espe-cially in early June. Their preferred habitat is patches of snowberry and wild rose that contrast strongly with the silver-hued Big Sagebrush. Also look for

Sage Thrasher (uncommon), and Brewer's, Vesper, and Grasshopper Sparrows in areas of shrub-steppe.

As you continue down the canyon, the riparian vegetation hosts Red-naped Sapsucker, Dusky Flycatcher, Warbling Vireo, House Wren, Veery, and Orange-crowned and Yellow Warblers. Edges of riparian and sagebrush can be rich with sparrows such as Lark and White-crowned. About 10 miles past Mud Lake, you reach a sign for Ellis-Barnes Road; turn right (south). Proceeding down the canyon, in 2.5 miles past the Ellis-Barnes sign, you reach the intersection of Wannacut Lake Road and **Blue Lake Road**. Continue straight east on Blue Lake Road 4.1 miles, stopping at a couple of other lake viewpoints. Turn left onto Golden Road, then right in 1.6 miles to reach the starting place on Westside Road in another 0.1 mile. Turn left to return to Oroville.

Klein Wildlife Area, a Bureau of Reclamation site, is 0.7 mile south of the Ellemeham Mountain intersection on Westside Road. Park at a pullout on the left and take the trail (often flooded in the spring) across a slough (Wood Duck, Spotted Sandpiper, Gray Catbird) and through weedy fields to tall riparian habitat flanking the Okanogan River. Expect the same assortment of birds as at Driscoll Island, including Yellow-breasted Chat. Here, however, you can immerse yourself in their habitat.

The entrance to **Osoyoos Lake State Park** is east of US-97, 0.6 mile north of the Main Street-Central Avenue corner in Oroville. The park is busy in summer but worth a stop at other seasons. Osoyoos Lake is a good bet for Osprey, and the marsh near the lake's outlet has Virginia Rail, Marsh Wren, and Yellow-headed Blackbird. Ornamental plantings and riparian vegetation can be productive for passerines in migration, especially during inclement weather. Migration and winter also attract a sprinkling of diving ducks, loons (mostly Common, but Yellow-billed has occurred), and grebes. Greater Scaup and Red-breasted Merganser often winter in small numbers.

OKANOGAN CASCADES

by Andy Stepniewski

revised by Teri Pieper and Andy Stepniewski

Some 20–25 miles west of Omak and Oroville a high divide separates the Methow and Okanogan drainage basins. Loup Loup Pass, on the crest of the divide at 4,020 feet elevation, is in the mixed-conifer belt with interesting forest species. Farther north, the peaks, valleys, ridges, and meadows of the Cascade Range along and east of the divide are justly famous for their boreal habitats and avian specialties such as Spruce Grouse, Boreal Owl, American Three-toed Woodpecker, Boreal Chickadee, Pine Grosbeak, and White-winged Crossbill. FR-39 provides ready summer access to this country; a map of the Okanogan National Forest, obtainable at headquarters in Okanogan or at most USFS ranger stations, is a useful aid.

LOUP LOUP PASS

Loup Loup Pass, on SR-20 toward the south end of the Methow-Okanogan divide, is an especially good place to observe species of the mid-elevation forests. (Map on page 432.) From the intersection of US-97 and SR-20, turn west with SR-20, cross the river to Okanogan, and turn left with SR-20 to climb out of the Okanogan Valley. In 9.0 miles from US-97, turn right to check the Ponderosa Pines around **Leader Lake**, a popular camping spot. Pygmy Nuthatch and Cassin's Finch are common here. Four-tenths of a mile farther along SR-20, turn right onto Buzzard Lake Road. Look and listen for Common Poorwill at dusk during the warmer months. Bear left in 0.4 mile onto Bawlf Road, keeping straight where a connector from SR-20 comes in from the left. The road (aka Loup Loup Canyon Road) from here to **Rock Creek Campground** is good for Flammulated Owl, especially along the mountainside about 3.5 miles from SR-20.

Take the connector back to SR-20 and travel west 8.3 miles to the turnoff for **Loup Loup Campground** (USFS, fee). Go right on FR-42 for 0.5 mile, then right another 0.5 mile to the campground. Birding at Loup Loup is especially good in May and June. The camping area is usually uncrowded then, but nights can be cold at 4,000 feet elevation. Great Horned, Northern Pygmy-, and Barred Owls, Williamson's Sapsucker, Olive-sided Flycatcher, Western Wood-Pewee, Hammond's Flycatcher, Mountain Chickadee, Brown Creeper, Ruby-crowned Kinglet, Swainson's and Hermit Thrushes, Yellow-rumped and Townsend's Warblers, Western Tanager, Cassin's Finch, and Red Crossbill are some of the species found in this forest of Douglas-fir, Grand Fir, and Western Larch. A small wet meadow adds many other species. Snowshoe Hare, Northern Flying Squirrel, and Black Bear are among the mammals observed here.

Descending west from Loup Loup Pass, SR-20 reaches the Methow Valley and a junction with SR-153 in about 11 miles (page 424). Going north 16 miles on FR-42 from the Loup Loup Campground takes you to a junction with FR-37 between Conconully and Baldy Pass—a shortcut to the route described in the following section.

BALDY PASS TO TIFFANY SPRING

Taken consecutively, this and the two following sections form a 75-mile loop through more high-elevation habitats than any other birding route in the state, beginning in the Okanogan Valley at Conconully and returning to it near Loomis (no services available between these two points). The road is usually snow-free from June through early November.

This route used to traverse miles and miles of mixed-conifer and boreal forests. However, in 2006, 175,000 acres of this area burned in the lightning-caused Tripod wildfire. Some areas burned in a mosaic pattern leaving

Okanogan Cascades

BRITISH COLUMBIA

Horseshoe
Basin
Sunny Pass

PASAYTEN
WILDERNESS

vista overlook

CHOPAKA MTN

Cold Springs CG

Fourteen Mile Rd

Iron Gate Trailhead

Long Swamp CG

300

Long

Swamp

500

Toats Coulee Rd

375

39

To Loomis

Coulee Creek Rd

South Fork Toats

Corral Butte
El. 6,849 ft

To Sinlahekin Rd

Thirtymile Meadows

view

39

North Twentymile Meadows

150

LOOMIS STATE FOREST

Smarty Creek Trail

South Twentymile Meadows

Tiffany Spring CG

3810

Lone Frank Pass

Tiffany Lake

39

Middle Tiffany Mountain
El. 7,967 ft

Tiffany Mountain
El. 8,245 ft

Roger Lake

Freezeout Pass
El. 6,600 ft

OKANOGAN

FR-37 to Winthrop

Baldy Pass
El. 6,367 ft

McCay Creek crossing

Sinlahekin Road to Loomis

Conconully

Detail map of Conconully on page 432

37

West Fork Rd

Conconully Road to Omak

0 ____ 4
MILES

To Loup Loup Pass

42

patches of live trees while other areas burned completely leaving vast swaths of standing dead trees. Lynx numbers are down, while more Moose are being observed in newly open areas. This landscape will continue to change in the near future, producing different habitats as regeneration occurs. Some of the sought-after boreal species such as Spruce Grouse, Boreal Chickadee, and Pine Grosbeak, which contributed to make this a once extraordinary route, are more difficult to find. On the other hand, Northern Hawk Owls are using the dead trees for nesting. As the forest returns, we can expect these owls to decline again. Other species using the burned forest include various woodpeckers, Mountain Bluebird, and Chipping Sparrow. Trailheads continue to provide access to the alpine areas such as Tiffany Mountain. Nearby are riparian habitats, lakes, and marshes.

From Conconully Road (Main Street) in Conconully, go west on Broadway to West Fork Road, continuing past the entrance to the state park (page 437). After you leave Conconully Reservoir, bird the riparian area and begin ascending the South Fork of Salmon Creek through forests of Douglas-fir, Western Larch, and Ponderosa Pine.

At the next junction (3.1 miles from Conconully Road), keep right on FR-37 (marked Winthrop) and continue uphill. Look for Williamson's Sapsucker, especially as you enter the Okanogan National Forest where Western Larches are numerous (2.4 miles). The road continues steadily up to **McCay Creek** (10.5 miles), where Engelmann Spruce and Subalpine Fir furnish the first suitable habitat on the route for Spruce Grouse and Boreal Owl.

Views of the many granite peaks become spectacular as you approach **Baldy Pass** and enter into the area burned in 2006 (1.8 miles, elevation 6,367 feet). Stop before you arrive at the pass and walk around to look for Spruce Grouse, Boreal Owl, American Three-toed Woodpecker, Gray Jay, Clark's Nutcracker, Boreal Chickadee, Pacific Wren, Ruby-crowned Kinglet, Hermit and Varied Thrushes, and Slate-colored Fox Sparrow. From the pass, the road winds west down the mountain and through a vast burned forest for 5.6 miles to a junction with FR-39. (Continuing straight ahead on FR-37 from this junction for 12 miles, then turning left onto East Chewuch Road, will bring you down the Chewuch River drainage to Winthrop (page 425) in 20 miles total.)

Go right (north) on FR-39 for 1.5 miles to the **Roger Lake** spur, on the right (may not be well marked). The wet fen surrounding the lake, previously rimmed by a dense Engelmann Spruce forest, is recognized as an area of many unusual boreal plants. A walk around the lake, though not easy (littered with fallen logs and boggy in places; wear rubber boots), is an excellent way to observe many species in an interesting setting. American Three-toed Woodpecker, Gray Jay, Clark's Nutcracker, Wilson's Snipe, and Lincoln's Sparrow all breed in the area. The forest service has designated Roger Lake, as well as nearby Tiffany Mountain, as Research Natural Areas.

Continuing north on FR-39 from Roger Lake, the road climbs steeply to **Freezeout Pass** (1.8 miles, elevation 6,600 feet). A worthwhile two-mile hike to the 8,245-foot summit of **Tiffany Mountain** begins here. Species to look for include Dusky Grouse (along the trail), White-tailed Ptarmigan (scarce, above treeline), Clark's Nutcracker (often near Whitebark Pines), Common Raven, Horned Lark, Mountain Bluebird, Townsend's Solitaire, American Pipit (wet swales), Bohemian Waxwing (feeds on Common Juniper berries above treeline, especially late October), Lapland Longspur (fall), Snow Bunting (mainly November), and Gray-crowned Rosy-Finch. The fall raptor migration (August through October) can often be exciting from these slopes. In October, a magnificent display of color from the scattered Subalpine Larches is an added treat.

From the pass, descend 4.0 miles to **Tiffany Spring Campground** (USFS, primitive). Along the way watch for Northern Hawk Owls, reported to be breeding in the forest of snags. From the campground, a trail climbs past Tiffany Lake to Middle Tiffany Mountain (elevation 7,967 feet), another good fall raptor lookout. White-tailed Ptarmigan are perhaps easier to find on Middle Tiffany than on Tiffany Mountain. In late fall, look for flocks of Gray-crowned Rosy-Finches in the cirque basin north of the peak.

TWENTYMILE AND THIRTYMILE MEADOWS

North from Tiffany Spring, FR-39 traverses a band of high-elevation Lodgepole Pine, Engelmann Spruce, and Subalpine Fir forest with meadows and boggy areas in valley bottoms. Vast swaths of these forests were burned. Many of the boreal species that were tied to mature Engelmann Spruce, such as Boreal Owl and Boreal Chickadee, have nearly disappeared. Birds that thrive on sunlight and forest openings, such as Olive-sided Flycatcher, Mountain Bluebird, and Chipping Sparrow have flourished after the 2006 fire. At 3.3 miles, Smarty Creek Trail leads downstream (north), reaching the first of the **South Twentymile Meadows** in a short distance. Spruce Grouse hens and their broods frequent bottomlands along the trail, beginning in July. Keep left on FR-39 at the junction with FR-3820 to Lone Frank Pass (1.3 miles).

In 4.4 miles, go right onto FR-150 (becomes South Fork Toats Coulee Creek Road) into the Loomis State Forest. Bottomlands along this primitive road are excellent Spruce Grouse habitat, and there are several enticing meadows along the way; unfortunately, the area has been affected by poor logging practices.

Return to FR-39 and continue north, stopping in 1.4 miles to enjoy the view of Twentymile Meadows and the rugged crest of the Cascades off to the west. In another 3.2 miles you reach **Thirtymile Meadows**. Forests in this area were burned in the 1996 Thunder Mountain burn. Although the initial boom in woodpecker numbers has ended, American Three-toeds remain fairly common. The Dwarf Willow patches attract Mule Deer and the occasional Moose. In 4.0 miles, park at a pass and take the half-mile hike up **Corral Butte** (400 feet elevation gain) for another outstanding view of the entire region. Open slopes may have Dusky Grouse and Townsend's Solitaire.

LONG SWAMP TO CHOPAKA MOUNTAIN

Ever northward, look for Spruce Grouse, Boreal Owl, and Boreal Chickadee as FR-39 descends steadily. Townsend's Warblers are common in ravines with tall spruces. Continue to **Long Swamp** (4.2 miles), an extensive area of bog and willow-grown marsh hemmed in by Engelmann Spruce and Subalpine Fir. Boreal Owl, Boreal Chickadee, Ruby-crowned Kinglet, Wilson's Warbler, and Lincoln's Sparrow are regular here, as are Moose and Lynx; the latter may occasionally be seen when driving the road at night. A few hundred yards after the tiny campground, a spur road on the left (FR-300) parallels the north side of the wetland for two miles. The main road (FR-39) goes right from this intersection, following the swamp toward the east. A dirt spur (FR-375) on the right in 1.9 miles gives access to lower reaches of Long Swamp (Willow Flycatcher, Northern Waterthrush).

Keep east on FR-39 (becomes Toats Coulee Road), descending until reaching a junction marked *Iron Gate Trailhead* (5.0 miles). This spur (FR-500) leads north to a trailhead (5.7 miles) offering a fabulous 4.5-mile hike to Sunny Pass, gateway to the **Horseshoe Basin** region of the eastern Pasayten Wilderness Area (530,000 acres). This trip is best done as a backpack. Outfitters are available in any of the surrounding towns to facilitate travel to this remarkable region, considered by many naturalists the crown jewel of Washington's alpine. Once at the pass, it is another mile into the heart of the meadows and two or three miles farther still to various alpine summits—all straightforward rambles on tundra and sketchy trails. These high, rounded summits—markedly different from the jagged peaks of the North Cascades some 35 miles to the west—were enveloped in ice and smoothed over during the Pleistocene. Alpine-zone vegetation is better developed in the Horseshoe Basin than anywhere else in Washington, bringing to mind that of many Colorado alpine areas; a number of unusual plants have been documented here. Spruce Grouse, White-tailed Ptarmigan, Boreal Owl, American Three-toed Woodpecker, Boreal Chickadee, American Pipit, Gray-crowned Rosy-Finch, Pine Grosbeak, and White-winged Crossbill (irregular) are all expected. Other interesting species include Northern Harrier(may breed), Golden Eagle, Wilson's Snipe, Prairie Falcon, Olive-sided Flycatcher, Gray Jay, Clark's Nutcracker, Common Raven, Horned Lark, Mountain Chickadee, Red-breasted Nuthatch, Rock and Pacific Wrens, Golden-crowned and Ruby-crowned Kinglets, Mountain Bluebird, Townsend's Solitaire, Hermit and Varied Thrushes, Yellow-rumped and Townsend's Warblers, Vesper (uncommon), Savannah, Fox, Lincoln's, and White-crowned Sparrows, Cassin's Finch, and Red Crossbill.

Farther down Toats Coulee Road is an intersection with Fourteen Mile Road (5.8 miles from FR-500). Turn left (north). Keep right at 0.4 mile, left in another 3.8 miles and again left at 1.2 miles. In another 1.1 miles is the Cold Springs Campground. Beyond, in 0.2 mile, turn right into the parking at the trailhead for **Chopaka Mountain Natural Area Preserve** (2,764 acres), which protects 11 state-listed plant species, including Few-flowered Shooting Star and a number of rare sedges, gentians, moonworts, and cinquefoils. A four-mile hike on an old mining track leads to the summit (7,800 feet). Palmer Lake lies nearly 6,600 feet below, straight down the escarpment. White-tailed Ptarmigan are found with some regularity on alpine meadows on the north side of the summit, and Horned Lark is reliable. If you are not in a hiking mood, drive past the trail turnoff for 0.4 mile to **Vista Overlook**. Expansive views of the Pasayten country to the west are your reward after a short stroll on this wheelchair-accessible trail. In the forest nearby, look for Spruce and Dusky Grouse and Boreal Chickadee.

From Fourteen Mile Road, Toats Coulee Road descends in 7.4 miles to irrigated hay fields on the Sinlahekin Valley floor, where a large colony of Bobolinks can be seen (best late May through mid-July). In another half-mile reach the Loomis-Oroville Road, two miles north of Loomis (page 441).

OKANOGAN HIGHLANDS

by Andy Stepniewski

revised by Andy Stepniewski

East of the Okanogan River lies a terrain of ancient gneiss, schist, and granitic bedrock smoothed over by glaciation. Once a large island—the Okanogan subcontinent—this territory became embedded in the North American continent that moved westward and collided with it some 100 million years ago. Kettle Falls is about on the east coast of the former island; the Columbia River flows through a trench where the two plates engaged. Tonasket is on the island's other coast—the west coast of the North American landmass until 70–50 million years ago when another subcontinent, the North Cascades, collided and docked. The Okanogan Valley is the remnant of the trench on the ocean floor where these two plates met. Coincident with the latter event, a massive magma flow pushed up the older continental crust of gneiss many miles east of the trench. The resultant Okanogan Dome—a granite intrusion some 20 miles across—forms the core of the Okanogan Highlands.

Habitats are varied in this scenic region: shrub-steppe and Ponderosa Pine forests at valley-bottom elevations; open grasslands and Douglas-fir/Western Larch forests at higher and moister elevations, interrupted by marshes and glacial lakes; and higher still, stands of Engelmann Spruce and alder and willow thickets in cold swales. Of the many breeding birds, some have boreal affinities (e.g., Common Loon, Great Gray Owl); non-breeding visitors of interest to birders include Snow Bunting, White-winged Crossbill (irregular), and Common Redpoll.

The most productive birding areas extend north from SR-20 to the U.S.-Canada border. This is a remote region; once you leave US-97 in the Okanogan Valley, services are few. The main roads are kept open in winter and are usually well sanded. Nonetheless, make sure you are properly equipped if contemplating a winter visit. Carry chains, a shovel, and cold-weather survival supplies (extra clothing, extra food, sleeping bags). Four-wheel drive, though not absolutely necessary, may be reassuring.

TONASKET TO MOLSON

At the north end of Tonasket on US-97, bear east onto Whitcomb Avenue, which merges into Jonathan Street, then becomes **Havillah Road** (Tonasket-Havillah Road on some maps) as it leaves town and begins climbing out of the Okanogan Valley. In early summer, check for Bobolinks in the irrigated fields on the left side of the road (3.6 miles). Ahead, while ascending a long slope, begin looking for Western Bluebirds as you enter a scattered forest of Ponderosa Pine (3.5 miles). Still farther, a denser stand of pines on the right side of road at 5.9 miles can be good for White-breasted and Pygmy Nuthatches and Red Crossbill. Open fields from here up—and throughout the region—are excellent for raptors. In summer, check for Northern Harrier, Swainson's and Red-tailed Hawks, Golden Eagle, and American Kestrel, and in winter for Rough-legged Hawk and the occasional Gyrfalcon.

At the **Highland Sno-Park** sign (2.2 miles), turn right onto FR-3230, a gravel road that winds south through a mosaic of fields and forests—excellent Great Gray Owl habitat. Begin looking at the end of the meadow beyond the third cattle guard (0.5 mile), especially at dawn and dusk. A particularly good area for this rare, highly local breeding species has been the selectively logged Douglas-fir and Western Larch forest south of the fourth cattle guard (0.4 mile). Walk south from here on the old logging roads (cross-country ski trails in winter). Watch also for Williamson's Sapsucker (early April through September), Hairy, American Three-toed, Black-backed (uncommon), and Pileated Woodpeckers, and Northern Flicker. Continue driving uphill on FR-3230. Turn right onto FR-260, signed Highland Sno-Park (0.4 mile), and park at the gate (0.1 mile). Great Gray Owls have been seen here regularly. Listen for Barred and Northern Saw-whet Owls after dark. (Boreal Owl was heard here one cold March night.)

Return to Havillah Road and turn right, passing the village of Havillah (0.6 mile) with its imposing Lutheran church, testimony to the hardy settlers who farmed this area in the late 1800s. Beyond Havillah is another area of grass-lands, excellent in winter for Rough-legged Hawk and Gray-crowned Rosy-Finch. At the next junction (2.7 miles), turn left (north) toward Chesaw on Havillah Road (Kipling Road on some maps). Beyond the **Sitzmark Ski Area** (1.1 miles), turn right (east) onto Hungry Hollow Road and go 0.2 mile to a dense grove of Engelmann Spruce and Quaking Aspen, a fine place to find White-winged Crossbills in invasion years (typically late July through winter). Listen for their loud, staccato *chif...chif...chif* call with an inflective quality quite different from the strident, harder notes of most Red Crossbills. Search also for Northern Pygmy-Owl and Pine Grosbeak, especially in winter. Great Gray Owls have nested nearby on fenced, private land (no access, but birds are sometimes seen from the road). Willow Flycatcher and Northern Waterthrush nest in an alder swamp on the downhill side of the road.

Return to Havillah Road and turn right, stopping at an overlook above **Muskrat Lake** (0.6 mile) with a beautiful view of the Okanogan Highlands. Scope the lake (drier in recent years, but water may return) and margins for nesting waterfowl, Red-necked and Eared Grebes, Tree Swallow, Mountain Bluebird, and Vesper Sparrow. In winter, the snowy fields attract Rough-legged Hawks and Snow Buntings. Continuing north on Havillah Road, in winter check the vicinity of several cattle feedlots beginning in 1.4 miles for Northern Goshawk, Rough-legged Hawk, Golden Eagle, American Tree Sparrow (roadside weeds), Snow Bunting, and Gray-crowned Rosy-Finch.

In 1.6 miles, Havillah Road meets Chesaw Road (aka Oroville-Toroda Creek Road; turning left here will bring you to Oroville and US-97 in a dozen miles, page 441). Continue ahead on Davies Road to reach **Teal Lake** (2.0 miles). Ring-necked Duck, Red-necked Grebe, Gray Jay, and Ruby-crowned Kinglet are representative of the many species found on and around the lake. North of Teal Lake, turn left (west) onto Fletcher Road (0.7 mile) and go steeply down to Molson Road (2.0 miles), passing another area of grasslands. Turn right to the all-but-abandoned mining town of Molson (1.5 miles). During its brief heyday in the early 1900s, Molson was the terminus for a railway, at that time the highest in the state. The open fields around town are excellent in summer for Swainson's Hawk, Say's Phoebe, and Mountain Bluebird, and in winter for Snow Bunting and Common Redpoll (weedy areas).

Continuing northwest out of town, Molson Road becomes Ninemile Road (the former railroad grade). For the next two miles, a string of shallow lakes known as the **Molson Lakes** hosts Common Loon (apparently non-breeders), Red-necked Grebe, many waterfowl (including Canvasback), and Yel-low-headed Blackbird in the warmer months. The lakes are usually frozen in winter except for a small patch of open water at the west end of the western-most lake that sometimes attracts Bufflehead and Common Goldeneye. Within the following two miles, the road turns west and follows a fenceline on the U.S.-Canada border where you may find Northern Pygmy-Owl and Pygmy Nuthatch in the pines.

CHESAW TO BONAPARTE LAKE

On the southern outskirts of Molson, turn east toward Chesaw on Mary Ann Creek Road (aka Molson Summit Road and County Road 4839). Keep left with this road at a fork in 2.9 miles, passing through a region of Engelmann Spruce and Quaking Aspen on north slopes and valley bottoms, and Douglas-fir on south-facing slopes. The spruces have breeding Ruby-crowned Kinglet, the deciduous bottomlands, Ruffed Grouse. Beginning in 3.0 miles and continuing for the next 2.0 miles to the intersection with Chesaw Road (aka Oroville-Toroda Creek Road), the 2,480-acre **Chesaw Wildlife Area** protects habitat for a remnant population of Sharp-tailed Grouse (but Gray Partridge and Ruffed Grouse are more common here). Grasslands on the left (east) side of the road are nesting habitat; wintering habitat is in the riparian growth on the right. Sharp-taileds are especially fond of the buds of Water Birch, identifiable from its distinctive copper-colored bark; seed cones of this tall shrub also attract Common Redpolls (Hoary has been recorded) some winters.

Before continuing to Chesaw, explore other roads in the area, such as Nealy, Hungry Hollow, Davies and Fields Roads (see map, page 448). Turning back west on Chesaw Road, in 2.2 miles, turn right onto Fields Road. In 0.5 mile, you'll find Fields Lake on your right, with many nesting ducks and Black Terns. Davies Road connects in another 0.6 mile. Continuing on Fields Road, you travel through a gully with habitat for Clay-colored Sparrow. In 1.4 miles, connect again with MaryAnn Creek Road, and turn right five miles (east) to loop back to Chesaw Road.

Turn left at the intersection; it is 2.1 miles east to the center of the village of Chesaw. Keep straight ahead onto Bolster Road. For the next three miles, the road parallels alder- and willow-lined **Myers Creek**, an excellent place in late spring and early summer for Northern Waterthrush, American Redstart, Common Yellowthroat, and Lincoln's Sparrow. Ruby-crowned Kinglets are common in patches of Engelmann Spruce. This is all private land, so you must bird from the road; creek noise is an added challenge. In winter, check the Mountain Alder and Water Birch thickets around Chesaw for Common Redpoll (erratic).

Return to Chesaw, turn left onto Chesaw Road, and travel 2.3 miles to an intersection on the right with Myers Creek Road (aka Lost Lake Road). This road (closed by snow in winter) follows Myers Creek upstream, becoming FR-34 as it enters the Okanogan National Forest (3.1 miles). At a four-way intersection (1.7 miles), take FR-050, following signs to Lost Lake. In 0.4 mile, just before the Lost Lake Campground entrance, turn left (south) with FR-050, proceed 0.5 mile, and park at a slight rise overlooking **Lost Lake** and adjacent marsh, where Common Loon and Black Tern usually nest. Williamson's Sapsucker can be found in the campground; watch also for American Three-toed Woodpecker.

Return to Chesaw Road and turn right. For the next 7.2 miles to Beaver Lake Campground, the road passes through a succession of interesting habitats. First comes a forest-rimmed meadow (Great Gray Owl has been seen here), followed by a mature forest of Douglas-fir and Engelmann Spruce in a deep gorge (Northern Goshawk, Northern Pygmy-Owl, Barred Owl). Finally, **Beth Lake** and **Beaver Lake** have nesting Barrow's Goldeneye, Red-necked Grebe, Black Tern, and many other wetland birds. From Beaver Lake Campground at night, listen for Flammulated Owl "booting" from the steep, south-facing slopes north of the campground and Barred Owl hooting from the dense, old-growth forests on the steep ridges to the south.

FR-32 turns right at a fork next to the campground. In summer, you may drive this road south from Beaver Lake to Bonaparte Lake (following paragraph). When winter snow closes the gravel forest roads, continue instead on Chesaw Road to its end in about four miles at a T-intersection with Toroda Creek Road. Go right here and ascend the Toroda Creek valley to reach SR-20 at Wauconda in about 14 miles. Great Gray and Northern Pygmy-Owls have been seen in fields and forest edges at various places along this route. Northern Saw-whet Owls call from the hillsides in late winter, and flocks of Common Redpolls sometimes feed along the weedy roadsides. From Wauconda, it is 3.5 miles west on SR-20 to the intersection with Bonaparte Lake Road.

Except in winter, you may turn right (southwest) onto FR-32 at Beaver Lake Campground and drive south to Bonaparte Lake. Stay left with FR-32 at the fork with FR-33 in 3.2 miles. In another 1.4 miles, turn left (east) onto FR-3240, marked **Virginia Lilly Nature Trail**. Drive this road slowly at dawn or dusk, watching for Great Gray Owl. Park at the nature trail parking lot (spur on the left in 6.6 miles). The loop trail (may be overgrown in places) goes through Douglas-fir and Engelmann Spruce forests, with marsh and pond habitats. Black-backed Woodpeckers have been seen here.

Bonaparte Lake Campground, another 1.3 miles down FR-32, is a good base for exploring this part of the Okanogan country. Bonaparte Lake itself is usually not too productive, but the surrounding forests have Flammulated Owl. South from the campground, FR-32 becomes Bonaparte Lake Road (open year round) and continues past peat bogs with Virginia Rail, Sora, and Wilson's Snipe, reaching SR-20 in five-plus miles. From this corner, it is 20 miles west to Tonasket or 20 miles east to Republic (page 457).

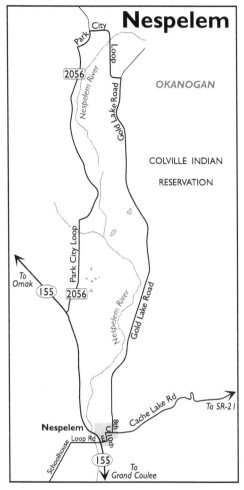

Nespelem

To Omak

155

To SR-21

To Grand Coulee

NESPELEM

A great area for "eastern" species such as Least Flycatcher, Red-eyed Vireo, Veery, Northern Waterthrush, and American Redstart is at Nespelem on the Colville Indian Reservation, 19 miles north of Grand Coulee on SR-155. Start in town on SR-155 at the highway's intersection with Videoquest Boulevard (aka Schoolhouse Loop Road). First, check the riparian habitat along the west side of the highway. For quieter birding, go west 0.1 mile from the intersection and park on the west side of the creek. Walk upstream (north) along the track here. Look also for Black-chinned Hummingbird and many other species tied to riparian habitat. Bewick's Wren, spreading north from the Columbia Basin, has been noted here.

Nearby, Park City Loop Road offers excellent low-elevation Okanogan birding hitting a variety of habitats: riparian, fields and pastures, and Ponderosa Pine woodland. Go north two miles from Nespelem on SR-155 to Park City Loop Road. Go right (east) and stop as you please along this lightly travelled road. Check aspen copses for Least Flycatcher and Ponderosa Pine woods for White-breasted Nuthatch, Cassin's Finch, and Red Crossbill. In 4.7 miles, keep right (south) on the loop. In this area, stop by the Nespelem River and explore the expansive stretch of riparian habitat, a good bet for all the expected "eastern" birds. In 0.8 mile, turn right onto Gold Lake Road. Continue south 5.3 miles into Nespelem, where the road becomes 8th Street. At C Street, turn right (west) and go 0.1 mile to 10th Street. Go left (south) 0.1 mile to E Street (aka Jackson Boulevard and Videoquest Boulevard). Turn right (west) and reach SR-155 in 0.1 mile.

The Northeast

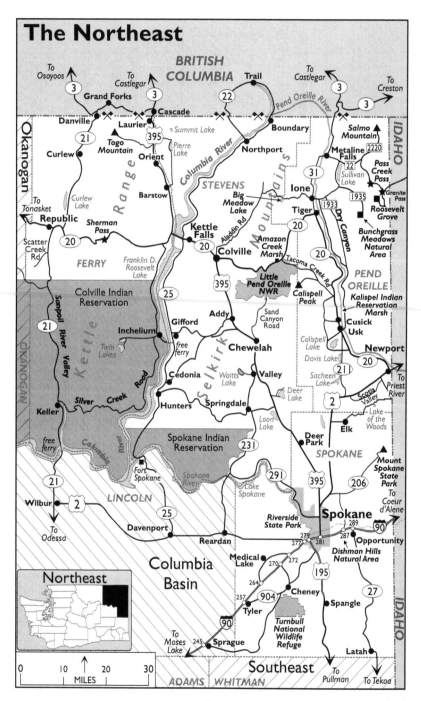

NORTHEAST

Northeast of the Columbia Basin lies a dramatically different landscape. Whereas the Basin is an arid shrub-steppe resting atop a geologically young basalt plateau, the Northeast takes birders into a green, wet region that rests at the intersection of three distinctive eco-zones: the Pacific Northwestern, the Northern Rocky Mountain, and the Canadian Boreal. Sage, potholes, and Ponderosa give way to lush wet meadows, wet-belt Douglas-fir and cedar forests, and remote subalpine zones. Birding on a glorious summer day in Calispell Lake or Bunchgrass Meadows, one might get the air of being in the Adirondack region of northern New York State rather than in Washington. North from the Sanpoil, Kettle, Columbia, and Pend Oreille Rivers, three main north-south-trending ridge systems composed of much older metamorphic and granitic rocks rise to a little over 7,000 feet. Glacially carved valleys that provide some of the finest, most intact riparian corridors in Washington separate these mountains—from west to east, the Kettle Range and two ridges of the Selkirk Mountains—and provide unparalleled birding opportunities too.

Precipitation in the region increases sharply with gain in elevation from the Columbia Basin, and also on a southwest-to-northeast gradient. Spokane, for example, gets about 18 inches annually, Ione in the northeast corner about twice as much. The higher peaks get upwards of 60 inches, much of it in the form of snow that lingers into July in an average year. Parts of the Selkirks in the extreme northeast corner are moist enough that forest communities resemble those of the west slopes of the Cascades. The lower foothills, and the scablands around Spokane, have open stands of Ponderosa Pine. Forests of Douglas-fir and Western Larch are typical at mid-elevations, joined or replaced by Engelmann Spruce, and Grand and Subalpine Firs on the higher peaks.

Compared to the rest of the state, the Northeast has a long, cold winter, less moderated by mild Pacific weather systems. Outbreaks of arctic air from north and east of the Rocky Mountains spill into the region with greater frequency and intensity, bringing sub-zero temperatures. January average low temperatures are 22 degrees at Republic and 29 degrees at Spokane. The mostly dry snow comes in moderate quantities. Main highways are well plowed and sanded; indeed, winter driving is quite often easier here than in milder parts of the state. If traveling in winter, it is always advisable to have emergency food, extra clothing, and a sleeping bag stashed in your vehicle.

Summer is characterized by more rainfall than elsewhere in Eastern Washington; violent thunderstorms do occur. July and August see a good number of bothersome insects anywhere near standing water or in forests. Summer days are hot (average July high temperatures 81 degrees in Republic, 86 in Spokane) but nights are cooler, especially in the mountains.

Services and accommodations are available in the Spokane metropolitan area, and also in the smaller communities of Cheney, Chewelah, Colville, Ione, Kettle Falls, Metaline Falls, Newport, Republic, and Usk.

KETTLE RANGE

by Andy Stepniewski

revised by Randy Robinson

Republic, an old mining town, provides the jumpoff for several birding routes. South along SR-21 through the Sanpoil River valley, one encounters exceptional riparian habitats that support several "eastern" bird species. Near the south end of this route you can go east for 50 miles on the Silver Creek Road, a superb birding trail through a mosaic of habitats. East from Republic, SR-20 crosses the Kettle Range at Sherman Pass, with opportunities for boreal species. The descent of the east slope is also good for birds of riparian habitats. From the Columbia River, other options abound, including the Kettle River valley and Togo Mountain to the north, or east across the Columbia to Colville and the Little Pend Oreille (page 470).

SANPOIL RIVER VALLEY

SR-21 runs down the Sanpoil River valley some 50 miles from Republic to Keller Ferry. This relatively lightly-traveled route offers outstanding birding during the breeding season (May–July), when a morning's effort should net 85 or 90 species. Extensive riparian habitats alternate with dry, open Ponderosa Pine forests and wetter forests of Douglas-fir; short side trips lead to mountain lakes. Some of the northern part of the route lies within the Colville National Forest. The southern four-fifths is in the Colville Indian Reservation, 1.4 million acres of forested mountains, rangeland, and lakes. This reservation is home to 12 different tribes, all shoehorned together in 1872 by President Grant in an executive order. Birders may visit the reservation freely, but Colville regulations forbid using calls or sound recordings to attract birds. Camping, fishing, or hunting require permits.

The Sanpoil River winds through a dramatic valley known in geologic parlance as a graben—an elongate, depressed block between the raised Okanogan Highlands mountain block on the west and the Kettle Dome on the east. In places, tall cliffs loom over the highway. Everywhere, the landscape reveals the recent action of ice-age glaciers that overrode the mountaintops and molded the valleys into broad, U-shaped troughs. This is gold-

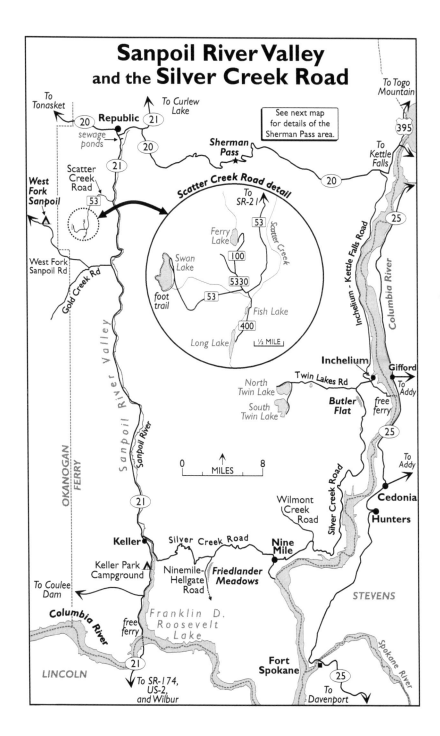

Sanpoil River Valley
and the Silver Creek Road

To Togo Mountain

To Tonasket

To Curlew Lake

See next map for details of the Sherman Pass area.

20 Republic 21

sewage ponds

20

21

Sherman Pass

To Kettle Falls

395

20

25

West Fork Sanpoil

Scatter Creek Road

53

Scatter Creek Road detail

To SR-21

53

Scatter Creek

West Fork Sanpoil Rd

Gold Creek Rd

Ferry Lake

Swan Lake

100

5330

foot trail

53

Fish Lake

400

Long Lake

½ MILE

Inchelium - Kettle Falls Road

Columbia River

Inchelium

Gifford

Twin Lakes Rd

To Addy

Sanpoil River Valley

Sanpoil River

North Twin Lake

South Twin Lake

Butler Flat

free ferry

25

OKANOGAN FERRY

0 MILES 8

Wilmont Creek Road

Silver Creek Road

To Addy

Cedonia

Hunters

21

Keller

Silver Creek Road

Nine Mile

Keller Park Campground

Ninemile-Hellgate Road

Friedlander Meadows

STEVENS

To Coulee Dam

Columbia River

free ferry

Franklin D. Roosevelt Lake

Spokane River

LINCOLN

21

To SR-174, US-2, and Wilbur

Fort Spokane

25

To Davenport

and silver-mining country. Since the late 1800s, various mines have yielded over 2.5 million ounces of gold and 14 million ounces of silver. A few mines are still producing, and others are proposed.

Begin at the junction of SR-20 and SR-21 on the southern outskirts of Republic. (Alert: the gas stations and convenience marts at this junction are the last dependable services until Wilbur, nearly 70 miles south.) Go south on SR-21 for 0.4 mile and make a sharp left, then take the first right in a few hundred feet to the **Republic sewage ponds,** which lie 0.2 mile along this gravel road. You must scope the ponds from the road. Expect dabbling and diving ducks, and sometimes phalaropes.

Return to SR-21, turn left, and go 6.5 miles to **Scatter Creek Road** (FR-53). Turn right here for a series of small mountain lakes with primitive campgrounds in a forested setting. The rich riparian zone along Scatter Creek is worth checking en route if traffic is not too heavy, especially early in the morning. Swainson's Thrush is common, and many other birds of the moist coniferous forest should be found. Turn left in 5.6 miles onto FR-400 to reach Fish and Long Lakes. From where the road ends in about a mile, take the hiking trail to look for nesting Barrow's Goldeneyes on **Long Lake.** Return to FR-53 and turn left. Turn right in 0.1 mile onto FR-5330. In another 0.3 mile, bear right onto FR-100 to the access to **Ferry Lake** (1.2 miles), which has hosted nesting Common Loons. These birds are sensitive to human encroachment; please avoid disturbing them. Return again to FR-53 and turn right to **Swan Lake** (1.6 miles). Here, waterfowl and Osprey can be found, as well as birds of the moist forest. Take time to walk the mile-and-a-half trail that encircles this pretty mountain lake, birding marshy edges, alder thickets, and moist conifer forest. The trail begins a few hundred yards before the boat launch and ends at the far end of the campground.

Return to SR-21, turn right, and go 7.6 miles to Gold Creek Road, on the right. Park here and scan the high cliffs on the east side of the highway for Golden Eagle, White-throated Swift, and Clark's Nutcracker. A detour along forest roads leads to an old campground known locally as **West Fork Sanpoil.** To reach it, take Gold Creek Road 2.5 miles to a fork just before a bridge, then go right onto unmarked West Fork Sanpoil Road. In another 6.6 miles, FR-205, on the right, goes into the primitive campground. Look for Northern Waterthrush, American Redstart, and other birds of wet-forest habitats in the alder-dominated, boggy terrain along the creek. If you want to head across into the Okanogan country, the West Fork Sanpoil Road connects northwest from here via the Aeneas Valley Road to SR-20 in about 23 miles. The hay field just before the SR-20 intersection is excellent for Bobolinks (June and July). The Bonaparte Lake Road turnoff (page 452) is 7.6 miles east on SR-20 and Tonasket (page 448) about 12 miles west.

The riparian habitat along the **Sanpoil River valley** for the next 20 miles or so south on SR-21 from the Gold Creek Road intersection is probably unmatched in Eastern Washington for both extent and quality. In the summer of

2014, a wildfire burned large areas of the yellow pine forest in the valley and on the rocky hillsides. However, the riparian habitat was largely spared.

Birding beside the road is a sound strategy to experience this habitat. There are a number of obvious access points on abandoned gravel lanes and on side roads with bridges that cross the river. Traffic is usually light, but do take care to find a safe pullout. Dominated by Black Cottonwood, various willows, and Quaking Aspen as overstory trees, the riparian zone boasts a species-rich shrub-and-herb layer. There is probably more habitat here for "eastern" passerines than anywhere else in the state. Indeed, Eastern Kingbird, Red-eyed Vireo, Veery, Gray Catbird, and Northern Waterthrush are all common breeding species. Least Flycatcher and American Redstart, though far less common, can often be found as well. Other interesting species include Red-naped Sapsucker, Pileated Woodpecker, Willow, Hammond's, and Dusky Flycatchers, Warbling Vireo, Clark's Nutcracker (pines near cliffs), Violet-green Swallow, Pygmy Nuthatch (pines), Cedar Waxwing, Orange-crowned, Nashville, MacGillivray's, and Yellow Warblers, Common Yellowthroat, Yellow-breasted Chat, Black-headed Grosbeak, Lazuli Bunting, and Bullock's Oriole. The forested slopes away from the river have Calliope Hummingbird (easiest at feeders scattered about the residential areas of Republic), Hairy Woodpecker, Western Wood-Pewee, Steller's Jay, Mountain Chickadee, Nashville, Yellow-rumped, and Townsend's Warblers, and Western Tanager. Fields of hay along the road have many Savannah Sparrows and Red-winged and Brewer's Blackbirds. In 19 miles, one area of wet, grassy fields on the left (east) side of the highway may have a few Bobolinks.

From Gold Creek Road, it is about 29 miles to the intersection with Silver Creek Road at the north edge of Keller; birding possibilities along this road are described in the following section. Keeping south on SR-21 will bring you in 3.4 miles to **Keller Park Campground** in the national recreation area along what used to be the lower reach of the Sanpoil River, but is now an arm of Franklin D. Roosevelt Lake. Ospreys nest south of here and can often be seen cruising the shoreline. It is about seven more miles to **Keller Ferry** (free; operates 6AM to 11:45PM). Bald and Golden Eagles are often noted from the ferry, and a loon or two might be about. Once across the lake, it is about 14 miles on SR-21 to a junction with SR-174. Turn left here to reach Wilbur and US-2 in less than a mile.

SILVER CREEK ROAD

This splendid gradient winds for about 50 miles across the Colville Indian Reservation to Inchelium, passing through a variety of habitats: Ponderosa Pine, Douglas-fir, riparian, and mountain meadows. The road surface is good: graveled, sealed, or paved in various sections. There are no services, and you will encounter few if any other vehicles. The starting point is from SR-21 at Keller. For about nine miles, the road climbs out of the Sanpoil River valley, eventually reaching an old burned area near the top of a series of switchbacks. Look for woodpeckers, including Hairy and White-headed, here. Turn right down Ninemile-Hellgate Road (13.7 miles from SR-21). **Friedlander Meadows** stretch along the east side for more than two miles. Northern Goshawk, Great Gray Owl (two records, May–June), Williamson's Sapsucker, and Gray Jay are just a few of the tantalizing prospects in and around these beautiful, wet mountain meadows.

Back at Silver Creek Road, turn right and continue the descent into the drainage basin of South Fork Ninemile Creek. Riparian habitats here attract species such as Red-naped Sapsucker, Olive-sided, Hammond's, and Pacific-slope Flycatchers, Brown Creeper, Veery, Swainson's Thrush, American Redstart, and Yellow-breasted Chat. In 13.2 miles, stop at the **Wilmont Creek Road** junction. Ponderosa Pine forest and grasslands around this corner and for a mile or so south have many birds, including Mourning Dove, White-headed Woodpecker, American Kestrel, Western Wood-Pewee, Dusky Flycatcher, Western Kingbird, Cassin's Vireo, Black-capped Chickadee, Red-breasted and Pygmy Nuthatches, House Wren, Western Bluebird, Spotted Towhee, Chipping Sparrow, Western Tanager, Lazuli Bunting, Western Meadowlark, and Cassin's Finch. Black Swifts have sometimes been seen in June in this general vicinity, suggesting the possibility of nearby nesting.

Continuing along Silver Creek Road, through yet more open Ponderosa Pine forest, where Wild Turkeys should be looked for, you soon come into view of Franklin D. Roosevelt Lake. **Butler Flat**, a large sedge-and-cattail wetland (open water in wet seasons) is visible west of the road at about 22 miles from the Wilmont Creek Road corner. Depending on water levels and the season, look for Tundra Swan, geese, scads of dabbling ducks, Northern Harrier, Bald Eagle, other raptors, Virginia Rail, Sora, Savannah Sparrow, and blackbirds.

The intersection with Twin Lakes Road is about two miles ahead. If you go left (west), you will reach the turnoff to North and South Twin Lakes in about eight miles. Common Loons nest on these lakes. Turning right onto Twin Lakes Road brings you 1.6 miles to Inchelium. South from Inchelium, it is 2.7 miles to the free ferry to Gifford and SR-25 on the east shore of Franklin D. Roosevelt Lake. Alternatively, one can go north on the Inchelium-Kettle Falls Road to join SR-20 a few miles west of the US-395 junction and the Kettle Falls bridge.

SHERMAN PASS AND SHERMAN CREEK

The next route picks up once more in Republic. East from here, SR-20 ascends to Sherman Pass at the crest of the granitic Kettle Range, en route passing an impressive old burn, then winds its way down Sherman Creek toward the Columbia River and Colville. Sherman Pass reaches subalpine elevations and some boreal birding possibilities. Typical species of riparian and coniferous forest are definite attractions of this route. Where SR-20/SR-21 divides, three miles east of Republic, turn right with SR-20 and begin the long climb to Sherman Pass. Somewhat more than halfway to the summit the road enters the 20,000-acre, lightning-caused **White Mountain Burn**. An interpretive display (12.4 miles) explains the 1988 fire and its aftermath. Willow Flycatcher, Orange-crowned and MacGillivray's Warblers, and Fox Sparrow are common. Pine Grosbeak might be present in winter.

The road surmounts **Sherman Pass** (elevation 5,575 feet) in another 1.8 miles amidst a forest of Lodgepole Pine, Subalpine Fir, and Engelmann Spruce. To explore boreal habitats around the pass, continue east downhill 0.8 mile to Sherman Pass Overlook, on the left. In 2013, the Forest Service closed the overlook (and campground) to remove hazard trees that had been killed by pine beetles. As of September, 2014, they did not have a schedule for reopening the facility.

It's possible to park at the campground gate and walk in to Trail 96 at the west end of the campground loop. Trail 96 contours west from here, reaching a junction with Trail 82 in about a half-mile. Turn right to explore more of this forest, or left to reach the Kettle Crest Trail and Sherman Pass in about another half-mile. These trails, especially Trail 96 near and in the campground, pass through typical boreal plant communities with abundant huckleberries and other members of the heath family and a rich assemblage of forbs. This is prime habitat for Spruce Grouse. However, this species can be maddeningly difficult to find. An early morning or evening walk might be the best strategy to stumble upon one. This habitat is also excellent for Boreal Owl. Sherman Pass provides the only all-year road access to this species' habitat in Washington, but your best bet for finding one is probably September–October. Other common species here include Hairy Woodpecker, Gray Jay, Mountain Chickadee, Pacific Wren, Golden-crowned and Ruby-crowned Kinglets, Townsend's Solitaire, Hermit and Varied Thrushes, Yellow-rumped and Townsend's Warblers, Red and White-winged (erratic) Crossbills, and Pine Siskin. Look for American Three-toed Woodpecker, too. Boreal Chickadee has been noted on Sherman Pass, but is not common.

Headed downhill again on SR-20, in 3.2 miles you reach **Albian Hill Road** (FR-2030), on the left. If you've just struck out on Spruce Grouse at the pass trails and really want to see one, try exploring this high route north along North Fork Sherman Creek, then, about 12 miles in on FR-2030, east onto FR-6110 along South Fork Boulder Creek. (A Colville National Forest map is helpful.) Hens with chicks are often noted at wet areas in July and August. The nearby drier, huckleberry-grown slopes harbor mostly males.

Back on SR-20, continue down another 7.7 miles to **Camp Growden CCC** on the right, a fine, birdy place with Beaver ponds, wet meadow, riparian vegetation, and nearby conifer stands. Species noted here include Common Merganser, Willow and Hammond's Flycatchers, Cassin's Vireo,

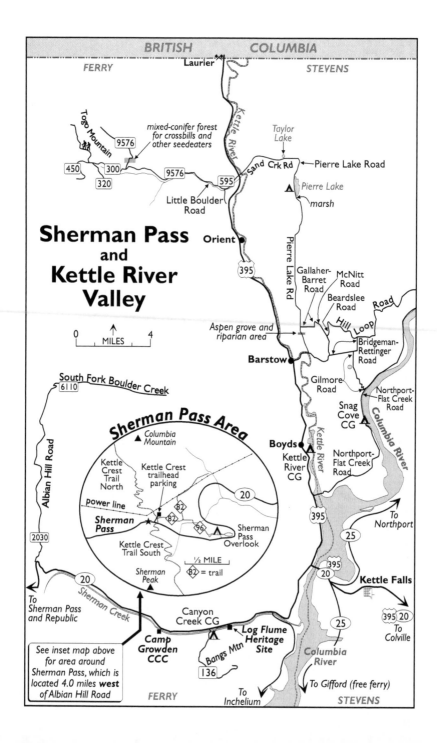

BRITISH COLUMBIA

FERRY   Laurier   STEVENS

Togo Mountain

mixed-conifer forest
for crossbills and
other seedeaters

Taylor
Lake

9576

450   300   9576

320

595

Little Boulder
Road

Sand Crk Rd ← Pierre Lake Road

Pierre Lake

marsh

Sherman Pass
and
Kettle River
Valley

Orient

395

Pierre Lake Rd

Gallaher-
Barret
Road

McNitt
Road

Beardslee
Road

Hill Loop Road

0   MILES   4

Aspen grove and
riparian area

Bridgeman-
Rettinger
Road

Barstow

Gilmore
Road

Northport-
Flat Creek
Road

South Fork Boulder Creek

6110

Sherman Pass Area

Columbia
Mountain

Snag
Cove
CG

Columbia River

Kettle
Crest
Trail
North

Kettle Crest
trailhead
parking

20

Boyds

Kettle
River
CG

Northport-
Flat Creek
Road

Albian Hill Road

power line

**Sherman
Pass**

82

82

96

Sherman
Pass
Overlook

Kettle River

395

2030

Kettle Crest
Trail South

To
Northport

25

½ MILE

82 = trail

Sherman
Peak

395
20

20

Kettle Falls

To
Sherman Pass
and Republic

Sherman Creek

Canyon
Creek CG

**Camp
Growden
CCC**

Log Flume
Heritage
Site

Bangs Mtn

136

395 20
To
Colville

25

Columbia
River

See inset map above
for area around
Sherman Pass, which is
located 4.0 miles **west**
of Albian Hill Road

FERRY

To
Inchelium

To Gifford (free ferry)

STEVENS

Northern Rough-winged Swallow, American Dipper, Swainson's Thrush, MacGillivray's and Yellow Warblers, and Song Sparrow.

From **Canyon Creek Campground**, on the right in 2.8 miles, an easy, one-mile trail follows Sherman Creek downstream. Cross the creek and look for the trail on the left, emanating from the alders not far from the south bank. Hammond's Flycatcher (common), Veery, Swainson's Thrush, and Orange-crowned and Yellow Warblers are to be expected. The other end of the trail is at the parking area for the Log Flume Heritage Site along Sherman Creek (one mile farther east on SR-20). **Bangs Mountain Road** (FR-136) goes right at a fork at the entrance to Canyon Creek Campground, a short distance past the creek crossing. This road climbs 5.0 miles through moist, mixed-conifer forest with abundant deciduous growth—excellent owl habitat. Great Horned, Northern Pygmy-, Barred, Great Gray, and Northern Saw-whet Owls are recorded here. At a pond at 3.0 miles, look for nesting Hooded Mergansers. Ruffed Grouse are common, from the bottom of the road to the top. The open, brushy terrain where the road ends is reputed to be good for Dusky Grouse.

The road to Inchelium turns off to the right 2.9 miles past the Log Flume Heritage Site, giving access to the Silver Creek Road. It is a further 4.1 miles on SR-20 to US-395. Follow the combined highways across the Columbia to Kettle Falls (USFS district ranger station) and Colville (page 470).

KETTLE RIVER AND TOGO MOUNTAIN

Before crossing the Columbia, you might want to explore birding possibilities to the north, along the Kettle River. A tour through this area offers impressive breeding-bird diversity and opportunities for mountain species, such as Spruce Grouse and crossbills. From the SR-20 intersection, go north on US-395 for 6.2 miles to the **Kettle River Campground**, on the right along the flooded lower end of the river (now part of Roosevelt Lake). A surprising mix of habitats is found in or adjacent to this campground, including brushy fields, lake and river shore, and Ponderosa Pine woodland. Birds to look for include Spotted Sandpiper, Western Wood-Pewee, Eastern Kingbird, Cassin's Vireo, Red-breasted and Pygmy Nuthatches, Western Bluebird, Chipping Sparrow, and Red Crossbill.

To visit **Togo Mountain**, long known for Spruce and Dusky Grouse, continue north 16.0 miles on US-395 and turn left onto Little Boulder Road (3.6 miles north of the village of Orient). At 1.1 miles, stay right at a fork, then left at another fork in 2.7 miles (just past a cattle guard). You are on FR-9576. The next main fork is at 3.5 miles, where FR-300 goes straight ahead. Go right here on FR-9576, and make a stop (0.4 mile) in the towering, mixed-conifer forest of Western Larch, Lodgepole Pine, and Engelmann Spruce. This forest provides ample seed for crossbills and other seedeaters. Both Red and White-winged Crossbills have been noted here. Return to the last fork and turn right onto FR-300. In 2.0 miles, just before a cattle guard, FR-320 turns off left, marked by a battered wooden sign indicating *Verdant Ridge Road* and *End of Road 1.5 Miles*. Continue straight here on FR-300. In 0.2 mile is another fork. The branch straight ahead is signed FR-450; take the one on the right. This is a rough old mining track that goes north three miles toward the summit of Togo Mountain (elevation 6,043 feet). In the ravines, dense Engelmann Spruce and Subalpine Fir offer good habitat for Spruce Grouse, American Three-toed Woodpecker, Pacific Wren, Hermit and Varied Thrushes, and Yellow-rumped and Townsend's Warblers. Boreal Owl might be present. Farther, the track swings out onto exposed, south-facing slopes and a more open forest where Douglas-firs host Townsend's Solitaires.

Return to US-395. Armed with a Colville National Forest map or DeLorme Washington Atlas (and forewarned that road names and numbers on these maps don't always match reality), you can explore many roads east of here, across the Kettle River, searching a variety of habitats.

One option after coming back out from Togo Mountain is to cross directly over US-395 onto Rock Cut Road. In 0.3 mile, after crossing the bridge, Rock Cut Road goes right. Stay straight on Sand Creek Road. After passing Taylor Lake, with views from the road of lake and marsh, bend right; the road is now Pierre Lake Road (four miles from the bridge). In a half-mile is the first view of **Pierre Lake**. This is a picture-perfect scene, with buttressed cliffs, forested slopes, and a marsh-fringed lake. Habitats are diverse, as a sampling of the bird species attests: Barrow's Goldeneye, Common Merganser, Pileated Woodpecker, Willow Flycatcher, Swainson's Thrush, and Common Yellowthroat. Farther down the road, you pass the USFS campground, then the marsh at the south end of the lake.

In 9.0 miles from the intersection of Sand Creek Road and Pierre Lake Road, note the intersection where Gallaher-Barrett Road comes in from the left. Keep straight here, then stop to check the aspen grove and riparian habitat on both sides of the road a half-mile ahead. Least Flycatcher is just one possibility, among many other riparian species.

Turn around, drive back north, and turn right onto Gallaher-Barrett Road (which becomes McNitt Road). In 2.2 miles, turn left onto graveled **Beardslee Road**. Check brush patches along this stretch for Clay-colored Sparrow, especially after the hairpin turn where the road changes names to Hill Loop Road. In three miles, turn right at an aspen grove and follow it around a 90-degree bend; here the road is named Bridgeman-Rettinger Road. In 0.7 mile, the road jogs right. In another 0.3 mile, turn left onto **Gilmore Road**. You can only glimpse a lake on the right, but roadside birding is good, with dry scrub on the hillsides alternating with riparian habitats. Check for Black-chinned Hummingbird, Red-naped Sapsucker, Hairy and Pileated Woodpeckers, Western Wood-Pewee, Least and Dusky Flycatchers, Eastern Kingbird, Warbling and Red-eyed Vireos, Veery, Swainson's Thrush, Gray Catbird, Orange-crowned, Yellow, and Wilson's Warblers, Common

Yellowthroat, Western Tanager, Spotted Towhee, Chipping and Clay-colored Sparrows, Black-headed Grosbeak, and Lazuli Bunting. From this delightful spot the road descends to the Columbia River. Turn right in 2.7 miles onto Northport-Flat Creek Road. In 1.8 miles is **Snag Cove Campground**. To reach interesting brushy and pine habitats, walk about 1,000 feet north of the camp and hike uphill on a faint track just before (south of) an old fence. Continue along Northport-Flat Creek Road 6.8 miles from the campground, across the Kettle River, to reach US-395. Turn left 3.5 miles to the junction with SR-20.

FROM THE COLUMBIA TO THE PEND OREILLE

by Hal Opperman and Andy Stepniewski
revised by Terry Little

SPOKANE INDIAN RESERVATION AND LAKE SPOKANE

Lincoln and Stevens Counties are separated by the Spokane River at SR-231. Southern Stevens County hosts some nice birding habitat featuring a few species that are easier to find here than in the northern parts of the region. White-throated Swift (there's a colony in the bluffs above the Long Lake Dam), are often joined by one or two Vaux's Swifts early and late in breeding season. Gray Flycatchers and Western Bluebirds are found in stands of medium or larger Ponderosa Pines on level ground. White-headed Woodpeckers are scarce but seen in these areas from time to time. Rock and Canyon Wrens are in the Basalt cliffs and scree along the Spokane River. Calliope and Black-chinned Hummingbirds, Veery, and Yellow-breasted Chat are found in the riparian habitat along creeks near their intersection with the Spokane River.

To reach the **Spokane Indian Reservation**, begin at the intersection of SR-231 and SR-291, travel about 100 yards south, and turn right (west) onto Martha Boardman Road. Drive 0.6 mile to Chamokane Creek. This is an excellent spot to find Willow Flycatcher, Red-eyed Vireo, Bewick's Wren, American Dipper (winter), Veery, Gray Catbird, MacGillivray's Warbler, Yellow-breasted Chat, and Bullock's Oriole. Ponderosa Pine forest above the creek hosts Gray Flycatcher, Clark's Nutcracker (irruptive), White-breasted and Pygmy Nuthatches, Western and Mountain Bluebirds, Chipping, Vesper, and Lark Sparrows, Cassin's Finch, Red Crossbill, and occasionally White-headed Woodpecker. Because the roads are poorly marked, it is best to backtrack to SR-231 to leave the area.

The intersection of SR-291 and SR-231 also provides the starting point to reach Lake Spokane (aka Long Lake), a boating and fishing reservoir that is drawn down in winter months. Go east on SR-291 one mile to the Dam Over-

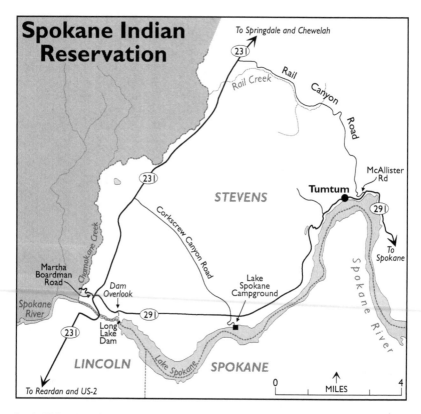

Spokane Indian Reservation

To Springdale and Chewelah

231

Rail Creek

Rail Canyon Road

231

STEVENS

McAllister Rd

Tumtum

291

To Spokane

Corkscrew Canyon Road

Spokane River

Chamokane Creek

Martha Boardman Road

Dam Overlook

Lake Spokane Campground

Spokane River

231

291

Long Lake Dam

LINCOLN

Lake Spokane

SPOKANE

To Reardan and US-2

0   MILES   4

look. Take the short trail out to the overlook, where you cannot miss the Osprey nest right along the trail. In spring and summer, this is a reliable place to find White-throated Swifts, (Vaux's occasional), flying with the numerous Violet-green Swallows. Rock and Canyon Wrens can be found along the cliffs. Peregrine Falcons sometimes make an appearance. Bald Eagles can be found near the dam in winter.

Continue east along SR-291 for 3.5 miles to the **Lake Spokane Campground** (Discover Pass required; gate closed in winter). The fenceline along the entrance hosts Say's Phoebe, Western and Eastern Kingbirds, Western and Mountain Bluebirds, and Vesper and Lark Sparrows. The campground itself can produce Gray Flycatcher, all three nuthatches, and Cassin's Finch. The cliffs across SR-291 from the campground have Golden Eagle, Clark's Nutcracker, and Canyon and Rock Wrens. White-headed Woodpecker has been seen in the area (rare).

About six miles farther east on SR-291 is the little community of Tumtum, where you can look over Lake Spokane. While the lake is not great for waterfowl, the far eastern end attracts a rather large nesting colony of Western Grebes, which can be found easily anywhere on the lake in summer. Also present are Double-crested Cormorants, which can be otherwise difficult to find in Stevens County. In late fall, a number of gulls gather on the lake, including Bonaparte's, California, and Herring—all three uncommon in the area. In winter, look for goldeneyes and mergansers.

Rail Canyon Road offers a variety of habitats and species. A mile or so after you enter Tumtum, take McAllister Road (paved) north off of SR-291. McAllister becomes Rail Canyon Road (gravel). In the first four miles, you pass through dry Ponderosa Pine and Douglas-fir with birds typical of the habitat. About three miles from SR-291, Flammulated Owls have been found. Great Horned, Northern Pygmy-, and Northern Saw-whet Owls are also seen in the area, joined by Common Nighthawks and Common Poorwills in summer. Continuing on Rail Canyon Road, the habitat changes and species related to a wetter climate begin to appear. Orange-crowned, Nashville, MacGillivray's, Yellow, Yellow-rumped, and Townsend's Warblers all nest here along with Cassin's and Warbling Vireos, Veery, and Swainson's Thrush. The road joins SR-231 in 7.6 miles.

CHEWELAH TO VALLEY

The seven-mile stretch between the small towns of Chewelah and Valley can produce a staggering number of species almost any time of year. The wealth and diversity of habitat make this an exciting area to bird. Before beginning the route in Chewelah, check the city park (US-395 and Lincoln), which has hosted a pair of Merlins for years. Pygmy Nuthatches are common here, as well. The route begins south of the park at the intersection of Main Street and US-395. Travel south on US-395 for 3.2 miles, turn right (west) on **Farm to Market Road**, and go 0.7 mile to the intersection with Heine Road. A Prairie Falcon wintered near this intersection for two years. Behind two dark-blue silos here, a tiny wet area surrounded by weeds and brush is a sparrow magnet in the fall. In amongst the common Song and White-crowned Sparrows, this spot has yielded, over the years, American Tree, Fox, Lincoln's, White-throated, Harris's, and Golden-crowned Sparrows. As you continue south on Farm to Market Road, you may find Golden Eagle, Clark's Nutcracker, and Canyon Wren in 1.7 miles on cliffs on the west side of the road, although pine forest obscures the view. Lazuli Buntings are common in the summer.

In another 0.3 mile, is **Newton Road**, a short road that reconnects with US-395 and that should be checked in fall, winter, and spring. In spring, when the Colville River floods the adjacent fields, an impressive variety of waterfowl can be present. Greater White-fronted and Snow Geese occasionally join the abundant Canada Geese. Large flocks of Tundra Swans sometimes include a few Trumpeters. With a little patience, Eurasian Wigeon are found annually. In mid-April, Black-necked Stilt, American Avocet, Greater Yellowlegs, and, rarely, Bonaparte's Gull appear. Lewis's Woodpeckers have been spotted on three occasions in the few trees along the road. In fall and early winter, Northern Shrikes

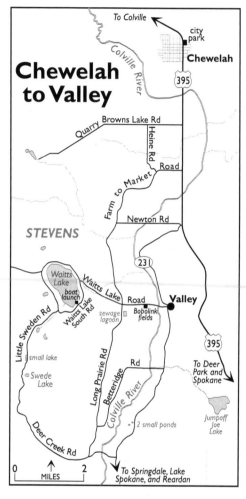

Chewelah to Valley

To Colville

city park

Chewelah

Colville River

395

Browns Lake Rd

Quarry

Heine Rd

Road

Farm to Market

Newton Rd

STEVENS

231

Waitts Lake

boat launch

Waitts Lake

Waitts Lake Road

Waitts Lake South Rd

sewage lagoon

Bobolink fields

Valley

Little Sweden Rd

small lake

Swede Lake

Long Prairie Rd

Betteridge Rd

Colville River

395

To Deer Park and Spokane

2 small ponds

Jumpoff Joe Lake

Deer Creek Rd

0   2
MILES

To Springdale, Lake Spokane, and Reardan

sit on the wires and small bushes, and Horned Larks and Snow Buntings are sometimes seen. In winter, numerous raptors, including Bald Eagles, Northern Harriers, Red-tailed and Rough-legged Hawks, and Merlins (uncommon) visit the area.

At the intersection of Newton and SR-231 (at US-395), turn south and follow SR-231 to the small town of **Valley**. At Waitts Lake Road, turn right (west). In 0.5 mile, you will find an old unused metal corral. The fields across the road host an increasing nesting colony of Bobolinks. When water levels are adequate, the surrounding wet fields can yield shorebirds in spring and Black Terns in summer. In another 0.7 mile, is the intersection of Waitts Lake Road and Farm to Market Road (called Long Prairie Road south of here). The sewage treatment lagoons just south of the intersection are worth checking for waterfowl and shorebirds. Barrow's Goldeneyes occur in spring and fall, Wilson's Phalaropes nest here, and Red-necked Phalaropes are seen in August and September.

From the intersection, continue west on Waitts Lake Road. In 1.3 miles, veer left onto Waitts Lake South Road and continue 0.6 mile to the public boat launch ramp (*Public Fishing* sign and guard rail). Red-necked Grebes nest on **Waitts Lake**. The best birding on the lake itself is in the fall. Scoters sometimes join the rafts of the more common species: Bufflehead, goldeneyes, Common Loon, and Horned and Western Grebes.

Back on Waitts Lake South Road, continue south and west for another 0.3 mile to a riparian area filled with aspen and willows. There is a spot to pull over, but you'll need to bird carefully from the road. Willow Flycatcher,

Warbling and Red-eyed Vireos, Gray Catbird, and American Redstart are easy to find here. Common Redpolls occasionally can be found in winter. Soras and Wilson's Snipes call from the grassy marsh across the road.

Continue again on Waitt's Lake South Road. In another 0.4 mile, turn left onto **Little Sweden Road**, a 3-mile-long road that can be very productive. Residents include all three chickadees and all three nuthatches along with Brown Creeper, Pacific Wren, and kinglets. Also present are Ruffed Grouse, Western Screech-, Great Horned, Northern Pygmy-, and Northern Saw-whet Owls, Hairy and Pileated Woodpeckers, Gray and Steller's Jays, and Clark's Nutcracker. In winter, Northern Goshawk, Bohemian Waxwing, Pine Grosbeak, Cassin's Finch, Common Redpoll, and Evening Grosbeak can occur. Summer brings a whole different set of species that includes Calliope Hummingbird, Red-naped Sapsucker, Hammond's Flycatcher, Cassin's, Warbling, and Red-eyed Vireos, Swainson's and Varied Thrushes, Orange-crowned, Nashville, MacGillivray's, Yellow, Yellow-rumped, and Townsend's Warblers, American Redstart, Western Tanager, and Black-headed Grosbeak. On the right side, two miles up Little Sweden Road, a small lake has Wood, Ring-necked, and Ruddy Ducks, Red-necked Grebe, Virginia Rail, and Common Yellowthroat.

Back in Valley, be sure to check all the treetops in winter, as Sharp-shinned and Cooper's Hawks and Merlins can often be found pursuing the many House Finches and House Sparrows. Where Waitt's Lake Road intersects SR-231, head south on SR-231. In 1.7 miles, turn right (west) on **Betteridge Road**. The first mile of Betteridge Road crosses the Colville River and passes through hay fields that abound with raptors, especially in winter. Red-tailed Hawks are common, joined by numerous Bald Eagles, Northern Harriers, and Rough-legged Hawks. Northern Shrikes are present in winter, as well. In September and early October, Western and Mountain Bluebirds and American Pipits line the fences and power lines. Where Betteridge Road takes a 90-degree turn to the left, a pair of Say's Phoebes often hangs out at the farmhouse on your left. Black-chinned and Calliope Hummingbirds frequent the feeder there. Along Betteridge Road, you can find House and Bewick's (rare) Wrens, Gray Catbird, Cedar Waxwing, Orange-crowned, Nashville, and MacGillivray's Warblers, Black-headed Grosbeak, Lazuli Bunting (numerous), and Bullock's Oriole. Sparrows gather in large flocks along this road in the fall, and Western and Eastern Kingbirds are common. Dusky Flycatchers call from the forest. The small seasonal lake has Blue-winged and Cinnamon Teal, Wilson's Phalarope, and sometimes Black Tern. Tundra Swans are present in the spring.

Backtrack on Betteridge Road to SR-231 and head south 1.6 miles to milepost 68. Two small ponds on the west side of the highway are always worth a look (scope). Trumpeter and Tundra Swans (rare) favor the larger pond. Marsh Wrens can be heard fussing from the reeds. An American Bittern was spotted here once. The pond is a favorite in summer for Black Terns.

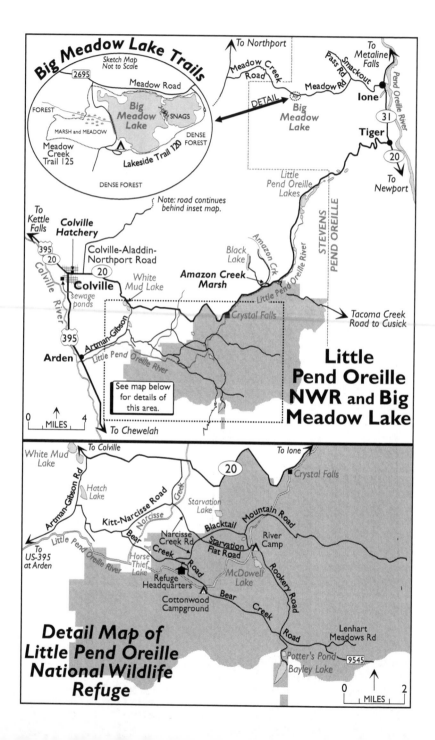

Big Meadow Lake Trails

Sketch Map Not to Scale

2695

Meadow Road

FOREST

Big Meadow Lake

SNAGS

MARSH and MEADOW

Meadow Creek Trail 125

DENSE FOREST

Lakeside Trail 120

DENSE FOREST

To Northport

Meadow Creek Road

Pass Rd

Smackout

To Metaline Falls

Meadow Rd

DETAIL

Big Meadow Lake

Ione

Pend Oreille River

31

Tiger

20

To Newport

Little Pend Oreille Lakes

STEVENS

PEND OREILLE

Note: road continues behind inset map.

To Kettle Falls

Colville Hatchery

395

20

Colville River

Colville-Aladdin-Northport Road

20

Colville

White Mud Lake

Sewage ponds

Artman-Gibson

395

Arden

Little Pend Oreille River

Black Lake

Amazon Crk

Amazon Creek Marsh

Little Pend Oreille River

Crystal Falls

Tacoma Creek Road to Cusick

See map below for details of this area.

0 MILES 4

To Chewelah

Little Pend Oreille NWR and Big Meadow Lake

White Mud Lake

To Colville

Artman-Gibson Rd

Hatch Lake

Kitt-Narcisse Road

Narcisse

Narcisse Creek

Little Pend Oreille River

To US-395 at Arden

Bear Creek

Horse Thief Lake

Narcisse Creek Rd

Road

Refuge Headquarters

Cottonwood Campground

20

Crystal Falls

To Ione

Starvation Lake

Blacktail

Mountain Road

Starvation Flat Road

River Camp

McDowell Lake

Bear Creek

Rookery Road

Road

Lenhart Meadows Rd

Potter's Pond

Bayley Lake

9545

0 MILES 2

Detail Map of Little Pend Oreille National Wildlife Refuge

LITTLE PEND OREILLE

East of Colville lies an extensive forested plateau and mountain complex, crisscrossed by old logging roads and with many lakes, marshes, and streams. The forests on drier uplands are mainly composed of Ponderosa Pine and Douglas-fir. Poorly drained, wetter sites have Engelmann Spruce, Lodgepole Pine, and Western Larch.

To reach this area, go east on SR-20 from the intersection with US-395 in Colville. In 0.4 mile (Hoffstetter Street), you might want to check the woods and brush around a county hatchery used for vocational education on the left, a patch of habitat with Pacific-slope Flycatcher, Red-eyed Vireo, and Gray Catbird. About five miles east of the hatchery is **White Mud Lake**, on the south side of SR-20 (limited parking). Look here for a variety of waterfowl, including nesting Common Goldeneyes. In another half-mile, turn right onto Artman-Gibson Road (brown sign for *Little Pend Oreille NWR*). In 1.6 miles, look for Mountain Bluebirds at the intersection with Kitt-Narcisse Road; then turn left onto this road, which meanders southeastward. In 2.2 miles, turn right (south) onto Bear Creek Road (gravel). Check Horse Thief Lake and marsh on the left in 1.0 mile for Ring-necked Duck, Pied-billed Grebe, Osprey, Bald Eagle, rails, American Coot, and Yellow-headed Blackbird.

The 40,200-acre **Little Pend Oreille National Wildlife Refuge**, established in 1939, is one of the largest in the state—and one of the least birded. Given the diversity, extent, and quality of its habitats, this site should be a first-class birding destination. Large areas of unfragmented forest are interspersed with streams, lakes, wetlands, and meadows. Forest composition ranges from Ponderosa Pine at 1,800 feet elevation up to Subalpine Fir at 5,600 feet. Birding is most productive from the nesting season through fall migration (late May–early September). Hunting season runs from September through December. The road to headquarters is open year round. The rest of the refuge is closed off by gates from January 1 to April 14, but you may walk or ski in.

Refuge headquarters is on the right, 2.2 miles from the Horse Thief Lake stop. Wild Turkey, Wilson's Snipe, Black-chinned Hummingbird, White-headed Woodpecker, and five species of swallows are regular in this vicinity. In winter, you may see Pine Grosbeak, Cassin's Finch (uncommon), Red Crossbill, Pine Siskin, and Evening Grosbeak; Common Redpoll occurs erratically.

Continue east 0.8 mile along Bear Creek Road to **Cottonwood Campground**, on the right. Excellent riparian, marsh, and wet-meadow habitats make this one of the birdiest spots on the refuge. Breeding species include Olive-sided Flycatcher, Western Wood-Pewee, Willow and Dusky Flycatchers, Eastern Kingbird, Cassin's and Red-eyed Vireos, House Wren, American Dipper, Veery, Varied Thrush, Cedar Waxwing, MacGillivray's Warbler, Common Yellowthroat, American Redstart, Yellow, Yellow-rumped, and

Townsend's Warblers, Song Sparrow, Black-headed Grosbeak, Lazuli Bunting, and Bullock's Oriole.

Continue on Bear Creek Road for three miles, then veer off to the right onto a dirt road (Bayley Lake Road) that leads in 0.9 mile to an observation platform and interpretive display at **Potter's Pond**. Marsh and pond are home to many birds, among them Ring-necked Duck, Common Goldeneye, Ruddy Duck, Willow Flycatcher, Warbling Vireo, Tree Swallow, Marsh Wren, Common Yellowthroat, Yellow Warbler, and Yellow-headed Blackbird. A few shorebirds sometimes appear here in fall migration. Moose also like this spot. The road continues another 0.2 mile to the north end of a large wetland and **Bayley Lake**, a good place for Common Goldeneye and other waterfowl. Ospreys and Bald Eagles nest at the south end of the lake. Bear Creek Road continues east from the Potter's Pond turnoff, becoming FR-9545. In 2.5 to three miles, south of Lenhart Meadows and Bear Creek, listen for Flammulated Owl at night.

Refuge headquarters is also the departure point to reach another rewarding birding road: **Blacktail Mountain Road**. From headquarters, turn back west along Bear Creek Road, then go right in 0.6 mile onto Narcisse Creek Road. Travel 1.1 miles and turn right through a green gate (closed in winter). The road forks immediately ahead. Starvation Flat Road (the right branch) leads to River Camp and McDowell Lake. The left branch is Blacktail Mountain Road. This dirt road should be passable to most vehicles, but watch out for soft sand and for wet and muddy spots. The road starts in dry Ponderosa Pine woodland, then proceeds eastward through areas that have been logged at various times, providing an interesting succession of habitats. At 7.6 miles, you reach moist, uncut forest of Engelmann Spruce, Western Redcedar, Western Larch, and Lodgepole Pine at about 3,600 feet elevation. Breeding species along this route include Spruce Grouse, American Three-toed Woodpecker, Hammond's Flycatcher, Cassin's and Warbling Vireos, Mountain and Chestnut-backed Chickadees, Red-breasted Nuthatch, Brown Creeper, Pacific Wren, Golden-crowned Kinglet, Swainson's and Varied Thrushes, Nashville (in brushy clearcuts), Yellow-rumped, and Townsend's Warblers, Chipping Sparrow, Dark-eyed Junco, Western Tanager, and Red Crossbill. You can drive this road eastward for several more miles, eventually reaching a divide at 4,900 feet elevation, where Dusky Grouse and Boreal Chickadee (rare) can be found.

Back at Narcisse Creek Road, a right turn brings you to Kitt-Narcisse Road in 1.7 miles. Turn right again to reach SR-20 in 1.4 miles. From this intersection you can turn left to reach Colville in about nine miles. If you wish to go east toward Tiger, turn right from Kitt-Narcisse Road onto SR-20. Travel 8.9 miles and turn left onto Black Lake Road. Then make an immediate right onto Spruce Canyon Road, which follows the north side of Amazon Creek Marsh, at the confluence of Amazon Creek and the Little Pend Oreille River. At the fork in 0.3 mile, bear right to loop back to SR-20 in 0.4 mile. The extensive alder-and-willow marsh is excellent for American Bittern, Wilson's Snipe, Vaux's Swift, Willow Flycatcher, Red-eyed Vireo, Ruby-crowned Kinglet (spruces at the marsh edge), Gray Catbird, Northern Waterthrush, MacGillivray's Warbler, Common Yellowthroat, American Redstart, and Fox Sparrow.

Continuing east and north, SR-20 follows the Little Pend Oreille River, eventually joining SR-31 at Tiger (17.5 miles); turn left here to reach Ione in about three miles. For much of this distance, SR-20 runs past the **Little Pend Oreille Lakes**, a chain of lakes given over to resorts and recreational activities. The large surrounding area, served by numerous roads and trails, is managed by the state Department of Natural Resources and the U.S. Forest Service for off-road-vehicle use. Depending on your (and their) tolerance for noise, dust, and hurtling ATVs, you may find Spruce Grouse, Flammulated and Barred Owls, and American Three-toed and Black-backed Woodpeckers nearly anywhere. Ospreys nest near some of the many small lakes, and Red-necked Grebes and a few waterfowl may nest on quieter waters.

BIG MEADOW LAKE

One of the birding jewels of the Northeast, Big Meadow Lake is also a popular weekend destination for local residents, so you may find it quieter on weekdays. Coming from Colville, turn north from SR-20 onto Colville-Aladdin-Northport Road (signed *Aladdin Road*) on the east edge of town, across from the airport. Look for Wild Turkeys in the fields as you drive up the picturesque valley for about 20 miles to the intersection with Meadow Creek Road (brown sign for *Meadow Lake*). Turn right and follow this gravel road to the entrance to **Big Meadow Lake Campground**, on the right in 6.2 miles. Coming from Ione, go west from SR-31 in the middle of town on Houghton Street. In 0.4 mile, turn left onto Eighth Avenue and go 0.1 mile to Smackout Pass Road (aka Blackwell Street). Turn right and head west out of town. In 2.7 miles is an intersection with Meadow Road, on the left (sign to Meadow Lake). Follow this road south and west 5.0 miles to your first view of Big Meadow Lake, a trailhead pullout on the left. A variety of waterbirds should be present. The entrance to Big Meadow Lake campground is 0.4 mile farther, also on the left.

Big Meadow Lake enjoys a beautiful setting with a variety of habitats and a high diversity of breeding birds. In the low and boggy terrain are Engelmann Spruce-dominated forests with a diverse shrub-and-moss understory, very boreal in character. Uplands have Lodgepole Pine and Douglas-fir, Mountain Alder, and willow thickets. Nearby are extensive grass-and-sedge meadows. An island toward the east end of the lake is studded with snags, ideal for nesting ducks, woodpeckers, and swallows. This is one of the few sites in Washington where Buffleheads and Common Goldeneyes regularly breed; Barrow's Goldeneyes also breed here. The wails, grunts, and cries of Red-necked

Grebes break the peaceful atmosphere in summer. Common Loons are also frequently seen, though breeding here is rare, probably on account of human disturbance. At the alder-dominated swampy lake edges, especially near the campground, the staccato song of Northern Waterthrush is frequently heard. American Redstart is a less-common summer visitor. Trails around the lake and at the west end of the lake provide opportunities to find a plethora of species including Spruce Grouse, Barred Owl, American Three-toed Woodpecker, Olive-sided and Willow Flycatchers, and Lincoln's Sparrow.

COLVILLE SEWAGE LAGOONS

The Colville Sewage Lagoons are one of the best shorebird hotspots in Eastern Washington. The lagoons are located on the west end of Colville. From downtown Colville, head west on First Street, cross the railroad tracks, turn left onto Louis Perras Road, and continue south past Oakshott Road. Chances are you will find the gates to the facility locked. At this time, the very friendly staff at the office are willing to open the gates between 8AM and 3PM, Monday through Friday. Besides the shorebirds, the lagoons also attract a number of waterfowl, Black Tern, Merlin, and Peregrine Falcon. In spring, the flooded fields along Oakshott Road draw waterfowl (including Eurasian Wigeon) and shorebirds, including American Avocets and Black-necked Stilts.

NORTHEAST CORNER

by Andy Stepniewski
revised by Jon Isacoff

The Northeast Corner, though remote, is among the finest in the state for sought-after boreal species. This region rests at the intersection of three distinct eco-zones: Pacific Northwestern, Rocky Mountain, and Canadian Boreal. Reflecting the diversity of ecosystems here, four species of chickadees can be found in this region in a single day: Black-capped, generally in lowland deciduous growth; Chestnut-backed in conifer forests, especially those with Douglas-fir and Western Redcedar; Mountain in the montane forest stands; and Boreal in the higher spruce and Subalpine Fir stands. It is not uncommon to find mixed flocks of Mountain and Chestnut-backed or Mountain and Boreal while birding in this area. Good roads into the subalpine zone make the Northeast Corner one of the best places in the state to look for boreal bird species.

SULLIVAN LAKE

Access to the Northeast Corner is either from Ione or from Metaline Falls, 10 miles farther north on SR-31. A good way to begin your visit is by following Sullivan Lake Road, which loops between these towns along the west shore of Sullivan Lake (elevation 2,600 feet). Here you will find four Colville National Forest campgrounds and good forest and lake birding possibilities. Other birding routes branch off from this road into the backcountry to the northeast, east, southeast, and south.

Coming from Ione, find the intersection with Sullivan Lake Road, on the east side of SR-31 at the south edge of town (about a mile from the downtown business district). Turn east here and cross the Pend Oreille River. Note the intersection with Dry Canyon Road (FR-1933) on the right in 4.6 miles; this is the turnoff for Dry Canyon, described below (page 479). In another 1.9 miles Harvey Creek Road (FR-1935) turns off on the right toward Bunchgrass Meadows (page 478). It is an additional 1.8 miles to the south end of Sullivan Lake and **Noisy Creek Campground**, an excellent place for Red-eyed Vireos and other riparian woodland birds. American Dippers periodically nest at the bridge where Noisy Creek enters Sullivan Lake. Check the lake for nesting Common Mergansers and Red-necked Grebes. Migrant Horned Grebes are somewhat common, and scoters occasionally make an appearance here in October and November before freezeout.

The road follows the shoreline 4.1 miles to the small dam at the north end of the lake. One-tenth mile ahead is the entrance to **West Sullivan Lake Campground**, on the right, opposite the Sullivan Lake Ranger District office (509-446-7500, maps, information). The combination of coniferous and deciduous habitats in the campground and nearby is attractive to a wide array of breeding species, including woodpeckers, flycatchers, vireos, thrushes, and warblers (Nashville, Yellow, Wilson's, American Redstart, and Northern Waterthrush). Black-chinned Hummingbirds have been seen here, too. Rarities have occurred at Sullivan Lake, among them Broad-winged Hawk, Magnolia Warbler, and Nelson's Sharp-tailed Sparrow.

Four-tenths of a mile farther north, Sullivan Creek Road (FR-22) turns off to the right, providing access to high-mountain birding at Salmo Pass and Pass Creek Pass. Continuing ahead on Sullivan Lake Road, one reaches Mill Pond Campground in one mile, and the Mill Pond Historic Site half a mile beyond that. Both are linked into a system of trails around **Mill Pond**. Recommended are Trails 520 and 550 from the historic site. Look for Harlequin Duck (especially near the inlet of the pond), Red-necked Grebe, Osprey, and Bald Eagle. Sullivan Lake Road ends in 3.3 miles at a junction with SR-31. Turn left; the foot of the bridge over the Pend Oreille River at Metaline Falls is 2.2 miles ahead. Follow SR-31 across the bridge to return up the Pend Oreille Canyon to Ione.

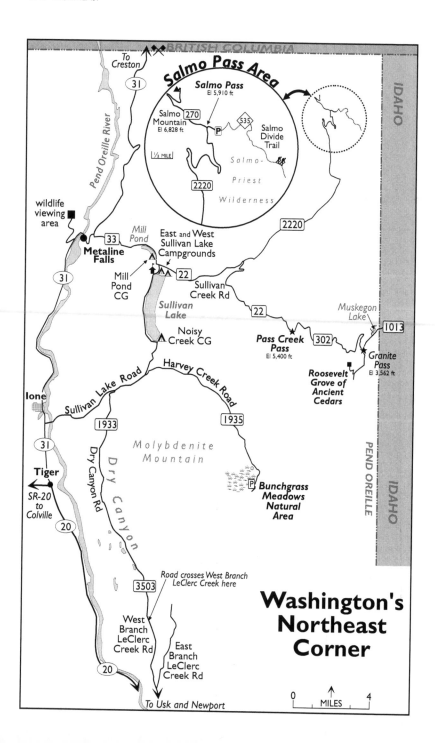

BRITISH COLUMBIA

IDAHO

To Creston

31

Salmo Pass Area

Salmo Pass
El 5,910 ft

Salmo Mountain
El 6,828 ft

270

535

P

Salmo Divide Trail

½ MILE

Salmo-Priest Wilderness

2220

Pend Oreille River

wildlife viewing area

2220

33

Mill Pond

East and West Sullivan Lake Campgrounds

Metaline Falls

31

Mill Pond CG

22

Sullivan Creek Rd

Sullivan Lake

22

Muskegon Lake

1013

Noisy Creek CG

Harvey Creek Road

Pass Creek Pass
El 5,400 ft

302

Granite Pass
El 3,562 ft

Roosevelt Grove of Ancient Cedars

Ione

Sullivan Lake Road

1933

1935

Molybdenite Mountain

P

Bunchgrass Meadows Natural Area

31

Tiger

SR-20 to Colville

20

Dry Canyon Rd

Dry Canyon

PEND OREILLE

IDAHO

Road crosses West Branch LeClerc Creek here

3503

West Branch LeClerc Creek Rd

East Branch LeClerc Creek Rd

Washington's Northeast Corner

20

To Usk and Newport

0 MILES 4

SALMO PASS

Doubtless, the main attraction of the Northeast Corner is the boreal birding possibilities. Ready access to some fine high-country sites bordering the roadless, 39,937-acre Salmo-Priest Wilderness Area, is via FR-22 at the north end of Sullivan Lake. Turn east from Sullivan Lake Road about 700 yards north of the ranger station. **East Sullivan Lake Campground** is on the right one-half mile or so ahead. Check Sullivan Creek at established pullouts for Harlequin Duck (uncommon) and near bridge overpasses for nesting American Dipper. In six miles from Sullivan Lake Road, where FR-22 turns right toward Pass Creek Pass, bear left onto FR-2220. After 12.6 miles of steady climbing through mostly old-growth Western Hemlock, Engelmann Spruce, Western White Pine, and Western Redcedar (Interior Wet Belt species), you reach a fork at **Salmo Pass** (elevation 5,910 feet). Park here to bird the immediate area; then walk or drive along the right branch to a parking lot in 0.4 mile, where the road ends. Walk along the Salmo Divide Trail 535, which starts here and continues for three miles. The surrounding subalpine forest of Engelmann Spruce, Subalpine Fir, and Whitebark Pine has a diverse layer of boreal shrubs, including Sitka Mountain Ash, several types of huckleberries, and a dense cover of False Azalea and White Rhododendron— prime habitat for Spruce Grouse, Northern Goshawk, American Three-toed Woodpecker, Boreal Chickadee, Slate-colored Fox Sparrow, Pine Grosbeak, and White-winged Crossbill. The steep slopes on your left are probably the best easily accessible site in the Northeast to search for Boreal Owl. Common mammals include Hoary Marmot, Pika, Red Squirrel, and Red-tailed Chipmunk. This is also prime habitat for Fisher and Wolverine, though they are almost never seen. Grizzly Bears are very rare, but apparently some still survive, and the Salmo Priest Wilderness is an established federal Grizzly management area. Since 2000, several packs of Gray Wolves have repopulated the general area.

Return to the fork at the pass. The other branch, FR-270, is a spur climbing 2.2 miles to the summit of **Salmo Mountain** (elevation 6,828 feet). The views extend far into British Columbia—the Selkirks to the north, the Purcells to the northeast—and east to the Idaho Selkirks. The scrubby vegetation here has had a small breeding population of White-crowned Sparrows of the *oriantha* subspecies. All of the species listed above may be seen on this branch road. Other species to look and listen for include Dusky Grouse (late summer), Northern Pygmy-Owl, Rufous Hummingbird, Gray Jay, Clark's Nutcracker, Mountain Bluebird, Townsend's Solitaire, Nashville, Yellow-rumped, and Townsend's Warblers, and both crossbill species (White-winged in late summer and fall).

PASS CREEK PASS

From the intersection with FR-2220 (the road to Salmo Pass), FR-22 turns south and in seven and one-half miles reaches Pass Creek Pass (elevation 5,400 feet). This vicinity has proven particularly good for Boreal Owl, especially in fall. Across the pass, the road number changes to FR-302 upon entering the Idaho Panhandle National Forest. You'll reach Granite Pass (elevation 3,562 feet) in 7.4 miles. Stay right at an intersection; it is another 1.8 miles along FR-302 to the parking lot for the **Roosevelt Grove of Ancient Cedars**, on the right (trails to cedars and waterfalls). This area shows off what is perhaps Washington's finest remaining Interior Wet Belt forest, with magnificent stands of Western Hemlock, Western Redcedar, and Engelmann Spruce. The list of birds to look for resembles one for the coastal habitats of Western Washington: Vaux's Swift, Pileated Woodpecker, Hammond's Flycatcher, Chestnut-backed Chickadee, Pacific Wren, and Swainson's and Varied Thrushes.

Return to Granite Pass. At the intersection where FR-302 goes left, stay straight onto FR-1013. Just ahead, a small Beaver pond and alder and boggy habitats lie next to the road—worth checking for Ruffed Grouse, vireos, and warblers. Nine-tenths of a mile from Granite Pass, walk north on closed FR-656. There is an intriguing June sight record of a Great Gray Owl along this road. Continue 0.3 mile on FR-1013 and look on your left for a small pullout, barely inside the Idaho line. A trail leads from here to **Muskegon Lake** (elevation 3,441 feet) in a few hundred yards. Barrow's Goldeneyes and many Swainson's Thrushes nest here.

BUNCHGRASS MEADOWS

Another jewel of the Northeast corner is Bunchgrass Meadows to the southeast of Sullivan Lake. Turn east from Sullivan Lake Road onto Harvey Creek Road (FR-1935) and begin winding up along the creek through a steep-sided chasm, densely grown to Interior Wet Belt forests. The road is rugged but should be passable to ordinary vehicles. Go a little over 10 miles until you come to a large parking area on the right. Here, the road sits on a divide, with the meadow below you to the right, draining westward to the Pend Oreille River. To the left, the Granite Creek drainage slopes east toward Idaho. Here is an open spruce-and-fir forest, with a tall shrub layer of White Rhododendron, False Azalea, Big-leaf Huckleberry, and Beargrass. Birds of this habitat include American Three-toed Woodpecker (watch for scaled-off bark on spruce trees), Chestnut-backed, Mountain, and Boreal Chickadees, Red-breasted Nuthatch, Pacific Wren, Golden-crowned and Ruby-crowned Kinglets, Swainson's, Hermit, and Varied Thrushes, Nashville, Orange-crowned, Yellow-rumped, Townsend's, and Wilson's Warblers, and Pine Grosbeak. White-winged Crossbills are irregularly common, usually from late July through the fall until snow blocks access to the area in late October or November.

From the parking area walk a short distance to the Bunchgrass Meadows Natural Area, a 795-acre boreal sedge meadow and sphagnum bog (elevation 4,961 feet) set in a subalpine basin rimmed by Engelmann Spruce, Subalpine Fir, and Lodgepole Pine. This area can be extremely wet and muddy throughout the summer due to the natural springs and bogs. Mosquitoes in June and July can be fierce. High waterproof boots are recommended. A number of warbler and sparrow species nest and feed in and around this area as well as species not commonly associated with 5,000-foot meadows. These include Mallard, Great Blue Heron, Wilson's Snipe, MacGillivray's and Yellow Warblers, and Song Sparrow, among others. Bunchgrass is among the best places in Washington to find breeding Lincoln's Sparrow. It is also is a good spot for Moose. Rare mammals here include Masked Shrew and Northern Bog Lemming.

DRY CANYON

A quiet route south toward Usk, Dry Canyon offers lower-elevation woodland and riparian birding even when the high country of the Salmo-Priest Wilderness is inaccessible or unproductive due to inclement weather or the earliness of the season. This is also a fine choice as an entrance or exit route between the Northeast Corner and points south. Turn south from Sullivan Lake Road onto Dry Canyon Road (FR-1933). In 0.5 mile, at a junction with FR-4536, stay right on FR-1933. Soon you enter Dry Canyon, with Dry Canyon Ridge on the right and an area of boggy terrain on the left. There is excellent birding along this good gravel road for about the next six miles, up to a fair-sized lake on the left (look for Barrow's Goldeneyes). The songbird mix along this narrow canyon is interesting, with Red-eyed Vireo, Swainson's Thrush, and Northern Waterthrush in the valley bottom forest, and Nashville Warbler in brush along the exposed talus slopes to the west.

Upon leaving the national forest about a mile past the lake (sign and cattle guard), the road surface is poor for about another half-mile, then improves. You are now on CR-3503. Clearcuts start to appear. In 5.6 miles from the cattle guard, the road crosses the West Branch of LeClerc Creek. Extensive willow-and-alder riparian habitat here has Willow Flycatcher (numerous), Warbling Vireo, Gray Catbird, Northern Waterthrush, American Redstart, Yellow Warbler, Fox Sparrow, and Evening Grosbeak. In another 2.1 miles is a large meadow with Vesper Sparrows. Pavement starts in two miles as you reach a T-intersection with LeClerc Creek Road. Turn right and travel another mile to a T-intersection with LeClerc Road (CR-9325). Turn left here to reach Usk (17 miles), Newport (33 miles), and birding sites of the Pend Oreille Valley described in the following section. Or turn right and head north to cross the Pend Oreille River and reach Ione in 18 miles.

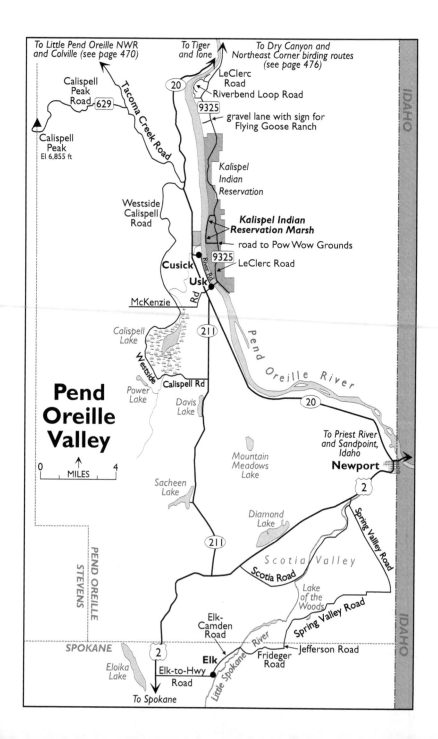

To Little Pend Oreille NWR and Colville (see page 470)

To Tiger and Ione

To Dry Canyon and Northeast Corner birding routes (see page 476)

Calispell Peak Road 629

Tacoma Creek Road

20

LeClerc Road

Riverbend Loop Road

9325

gravel lane with sign for Flying Goose Ranch

Calispell Peak El 6,855 ft

Kalispel Indian Reservation

Westside Calispell Road

Kalispel Indian Reservation Marsh

road to Pow Wow Grounds

Cusick

River Rd

9325

LeClerc Road

Usk

Rd

McKenzie

Calispell Lake

211

Pend Oreille River

Westside

Calispell Rd

Power Lake

Davis Lake

Pend Oreille Valley

0 MILES 4

Sacheen Lake

Mountain Meadows Lake

20

To Priest River and Sandpoint, Idaho

Newport

2

Diamond Lake

211

Scotia Valley

Spring Valley Road

Scotia Road

Lake of the Woods

PEND OREILLE

STEVENS

Elk-Camden Road

Spring Valley Road

SPOKANE

2

Elk

Little Spokane River

Frideger Road

Jefferson Road

Eloika Lake

Elk-to-Hwy Road

To Spokane

IDAHO

PEND OREILLE VALLEY

by Andy Stepniewski and Jim Acton
revised by Jon Isacoff

The Pend Oreille River flows west from Idaho into Washington at Newport, then bends north toward British Columbia, where it empties into the Columbia River. The southern Pend Oreille Valley sits in a depression known as the Newport Fault, which also marks the southern edge of the last glaciation. As the glaciers began to recede at the end of the ice age, ice dammed the streams, flooding the valleys to the south and leaving behind a landscape of glacial debris and lakes. Today, this area and the glaciated land along the Pend Oreille just north of it have a number of notable birding sites in riparian and wetland habitats.

SOUTHERN PEND OREILLE VALLEY

Coming from the junction of US-2 and US-395 at the north edge of Spokane, take US-2 north toward Newport. For some good owling and other birding possibilities, turn right in about 21 miles onto Elk-to-Highway Road and travel eastward to Elk. In 3.4 miles, just after the Elk post office, turn left onto Elk-Camden Road, which follows the Little Spokane River northeastward. Turn right in 2.3 miles onto Frideger Road, cross the river, and climb out of the valley. The road soon becomes gravel; look for Wild Turkeys where it crosses Ponderosa Pines with brushy understory. In 3.1 miles, turn left onto Jefferson Road. Drive 0.5 mile, bear left at a junction onto paved Spring Valley Road, and continue to **Lake of the Woods**, set in a deep, forested valley. Stop at a pullout bordered by large rocks, on the right (2.3 miles). Summer finds Willow Flycatchers, Gray Catbirds, and Common Yellowthroats conspicuous about the large marsh at the east end of the lake, below the pullout. Douglas-fir forest by the road should yield Olive-sided Flycatcher, Cassin's Vireo, and Western Tanager. Searching for Barred and Northern Saw-whet Owls can be profitable in late winter and spring.

The best spot is about one-half to one mile east of the lake, up the hill along Spring Valley Road. This is timber company land; bird from the road. Barred Owls are in dense, swampy forest to the south along with Warbling and Red-eyed Vireos, Black-capped, Mountain, and Chestnut-backed Chickadees, Swainson's Thrush, Northern Waterthrush, MacGillivray's Warbler, and American Redstart.

Continue east, then north, on Spring Valley Road for about nine miles to the intersection with Scotia Road. (Continuing straight, then turning right onto US-2—just ahead—brings you to Newport in about three miles.) Turn left onto Scotia Road, which follows the Little Spokane River down the Scotia Valley (all private property; bird from the road). Alder and Water Birch thickets along the river may have Common Redpoll and Pine Siskin in winter. In 10 miles, turn left onto US-2, drive west 1.7 miles, then turn right onto SR-211.

Follow SR-211 for 4.1 miles to **Sacheen Lake**. Turn left onto Sacheen Terrace Drive (the second of two roads next to each other on the left), which immediately curves to the right and passes a fire station (unmarked). Stop to view the moist grasslands across the road to the south. Three-tenths of a mile from SR-211, turn left at a *Public Fishing Access* sign (Discover Pass required). Park near the boat ramp. This is one of the most reliable locations in Eastern Washington to hear American Bitterns in the early hours of day. Look for Ospreys and Vaux's Swifts. You might see a Hooded or Common Merganser or other waterbirds on the lake.

Return to SR-211 and turn left. In 4.3 miles is a turnout on the right (east) side, about half a mile south of **Davis Lake**. Opposite, a paved road crosses private land to Camp Spaulding. Although traffic noise can be bothersome, birds that may be found on either side of the highway include Virginia Rail, Willow Flycatcher, Warbling and Red-eyed Vireos, Swainson's Thrush, Gray Catbird, Cedar Waxwing, MacGillivray's Warbler, Common Yellowthroat, American Redstart, and Yellow Warbler. A public boat ramp (1.4 miles) provides access to the shoreline at the other end of the lake. You may see a few Red-necked Grebes in the breeding season and a small number of ducks in migration.

CALISPELL LAKE

Calispell Lake is among the most diverse breeding bird areas in Eastern Washington. Over 200 species have been documented here with local and regional rarities including: Ross's Goose, Franklin's Gull, Black Swift, Lewis's Woodpecker, Least Flycatcher (nearly annual), Eastern Phoebe, and American Tree Sparrow. Continuing north on SR-211, in 1.1 miles go left onto Westside Calispell Road. Here begins a loop around Calispell Lake. Birding in the moist woodlands, forested hillsides, wet meadows, marshes, and open waters along this road can be excellent. However, all bordering land is private property, and you must bird from the road. Stop to investigate marshy areas for American Bittern, Virginia Rail, Sora, and winnowing Wilson's Snipe.

All of the typical non-sage-steppe breeding passerines of Eastern Washington have been documented at Calispell Lake, some in abundance. This is among the best places in Washington to find specialty birds of the wet interior forests, including healthy breeding populations of Red-eyed Vireo, Northern Waterthrush, American Redstart, and Bobolink, the latter of which seem to have proliferated a bit in recent years. For the first part of the loop, you are distant from Calispell Lake; the road draws nearer between seven and eight miles, allowing reasonable scope views.

Calispell Lake can produce breathtaking numbers of birds. In March, it is a well-known stopover for large numbers of Tundra Swans (up to 2,000) and many thousands of geese and ducks. All the atypical geese of interior Washington have been documented here, including Greater White-fronted, Snow,

Ross's, and Cackling. Wood Duck counts in late spring can be upwards of 50 birds. Nearly all the regular breeding waterfowl in Eastern Washington breed or have bred at Calispell Lake. In spring, locally rare shorebirds including Black-necked Stilt and American Avocet can be seen wading the edge of the lake. Beginning in May, large numbers of Black Terns nest and feed in the lake, typically in the dozens, but occasionally up to 100 birds are seen. Bonaparte's Gulls are also annual in May in small numbers.

On the south-facing slopes north of the lake, one will encounter dry Ponderosa Pine/Douglas-fir forest that provides some of the only local habitat for specialty birds of this ecosystem including healthy breeding populations of all three nuthatch species, Brown Creeper, House Wren, Yellow-rumped Warbler, and Red Crossbill. Check aspen groves for boisterous Red-naped Sapsuckers and singing Least Flycatchers during breeding season. Beginning in July, look for shorebirds in the shallows, especially yellowlegs. In 9.1 miles from SR-211, turn right onto McKenzie Road. Go east across a slough, the outlet of Calispell Lake, checking fields to the north for Bobolinks. Turn left at a junction in 1.1 miles, keeping on McKenzie Road until reaching the stop sign at SR-20 (1.2 miles). Fifth Street, the entrance to Usk, is directly across the highway.

USK AND VICINITY

Take Fifth Street east from SR-20 into the tiny mill town of **Usk**, home of the Ponderay Newsprint plant. Continue ahead over the railroad track to the Pend Oreille River bridge (0.5 mile). The numerous pilings in the river here were used to corral logs as they floated downstream to local sawmills. Today they provide nesting platforms for a growing colony of Double-crested Cormorants (recently more than 200 birds) and numerous Ospreys. There are many places for close-up views along River Road (turn north one block before the bridge). Ruffed Grouse and Gray Catbirds frequent the bushes near the shore.

Continue north approximately two miles to the town of Cusick where a small public meadow is adjacent to the public boat launch. This is another excellent spot to scope the river and check for interesting birds in the meadow trails. Bewick's Wren, locally rare, has been documented singing here in recent years. Cusick is also an excellent place to look for Pine Grosbeak and Common Redpoll during irruptive years.

Several excellent birding sites along the opposite bank of the Pend Oreille River are easily reached from Usk. Cross the bridge, turn left onto LeClerc Road (CR-9325) on the other side, and drive north to the Kalispell Indian Reservation. Access to some areas may be restricted; check at the tribal headquarters (1981 Leclerc Road, Cusick, WA 99119; 509-445-1147). In 2.1 miles, turn left onto a road marked by a sign for the Qualispe Pow Wow Grounds. Continue 0.7 mile and turn right onto a dike road at the edge of the river. This gravel lane goes north along the river through the **Kalispell Indian Reser-**

vation Marsh, returning to LeClerc Road in 1.8 miles. In fall and winter, this is among the best places in Northeastern Washington to see specialty birds of the open country, including Lapland Longspur (rare), Snow Bunting, and American Tree Sparrow. Common Redpolls will also use the open fields to feed. In late summer, if the Pend Oreille river is low, mudflats are exposed adjacent to the dike road and can produce good shorebirding.

Continue north on LeClerc Road. In 5.6 miles, turn left onto a gravel lane marked by a sign for the **Flying Goose Ranch.** The gravel lane goes west from here about one-half mile to the Pend Oreille River. Along the way are broadleaf trees, grasslands, and marsh and river habitats, a combination offering excellent birding potential. Look for American Bittern (rare), Osprey, Northern Harrier, and abundant Virginia Rails and Soras. Here also, in years when the Pend Oreille is drawn down in late summer, the mudflats at the end of the gravel lane are excellent for shorebirds, including records of Black-bellied and Semipalmated Plovers among the more typical species. Bonaparte's and Franklin's Gulls have also been documented here. Be sure to check the deciduous trees along the river for interesting species, including a Northern Pygmy-Owl that occasionally visits in late fall and winter.

Continue again north onto LeClerc Road for approximately 1.2 miles and turn left onto Riverbend Loop Road, an approximately two-mile-long spur that loops back to LeClerc Road. This is all private property, so be sure to bird from the road. The forested areas along this road are excellent for Chestnut-backed Chickadee, Pacific Wren (abundant), Red Crossbill, and Evening Grosbeak. Black Swift and Merlin (locally rare) have also been documented here. At approximately 1.5 miles, a defunct airfield forms a small seasonal lake. In most years in July and August, this is a premier shorebird spot, though conditions can be highly variable. When there is good late summer mud, up to 100 shorebirds may be present. Solitary and Semipalmated Sandpiper are annual, sometimes in good numbers. Stilt and Buff-breasted (one record) have been documented here.

Continue again onto LeClerc Road. To return to the Usk Bridge, turn right (south). To proceed to the jump-off point for the Northeast Corner via the Dry Canyon route (pages 479), turn left (north) for approximately 4.4 miles and bear right onto LeClerc Creek Road.

TACOMA CREEK AND CALISPELL PEAK

About 3.5 miles north of Cusick, just after the intersection with Westside Calispell Road, SR-20 crosses the Tacoma Creek bridge (Cliff Swallow colony). In another 0.3 mile, turn left from SR-20 onto **Tacoma Creek Road**. For the next few miles, the gravel road follows the creek through marshy riparian habitat with Red-eyed Vireo, American Dipper, Northern Waterthrush, American Redstart, and many other species. **Sportsman Pond**, on the right in 4.2 miles (just after the USAF Survival School), can be good for Ring-necked Duck, Common Goldeneye, Hooded Merganser, and Tree and Northern Rough-winged Swallows. Vaux's Swifts skim the water when the weather is overcast, allowing you to look down on them to observe their brown rumps and tails.

The turnoff for **Calispell Peak Road** (FR-629) is on the left in another 2.1 miles. In years past, this road had a great reputation for boreal bird specialties. However, a once-productive Beaver swamp has been drained, and many of these species are more readily found at other locations such as Abercrombie Mountain, Salmo Pass, or Bunchgrass Meadows. However, the area is ripe for exploring. A high-clearance vehicle is recommended; exercise judgment if you decide to proceed, as you may encounter deep mudholes or water over the road, especially early in the season. The road climbs through a number of cut-over areas where the forest has been opened. The remnant Western Larch and invading brush are fine habitat for Red-naped Sapsucker, Cassin's and Warbling Vireos, Gray Jay, Mountain and Chestnut-backed Chickadees, Red-breasted Nuthatch, Swainson's and Varied Thrushes, Orange-crowned, MacGillivray's, Yellow-rumped, Townsend's, and Wilson's Warblers, and Red Crossbill.

Look for a cattle guard 4.6 miles in. Continue to a clearing on the left side of the road a few hundred yards past the cattle guard, at about 4,100 feet elevation. Spruce Grouse, Northern Pygmy-Owl, Barred Owl, American Three-toed and Black-backed Woodpeckers, Black-capped, Mountain, and Chestnut-backed Chickadees, Townsend's Solitaire, Northern Waterthrush, and Moose have all been found in this vicinity. If you have time on your hands and an adventuresome spirit, you may be able to keep driving the remaining six miles to enjoy the view and good fall hawkwatching from the 6,855-foot summit of Calispell Peak.

Continuing west, Tacoma Creek Road climbs for 8.8 miles to a 4,200-foot crest, then descends the Olson Creek drainage along one edge of the Little Pend Oreille National Wildlife Refuge, reaching SR-20 in another 4.9 miles (page 470). This road is far better maintained than Calispell Peak Road and passes through similar habitats where you can expect to find most of the same birds.

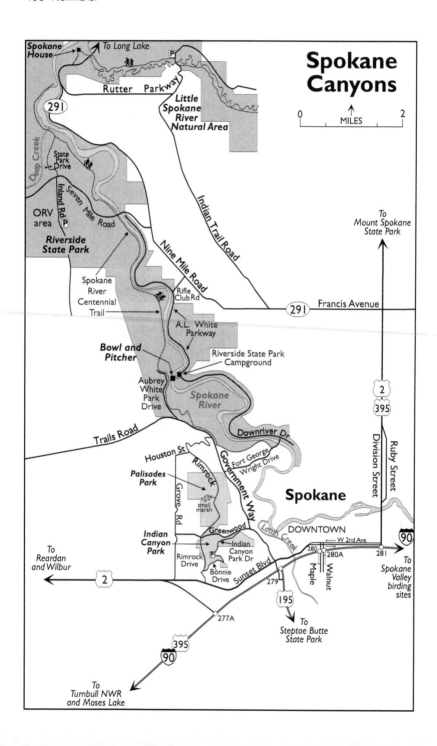

Spokane Canyons

0 — MILES — 2

To Long Lake

Spokane House

Rutter Parkway

Little Spokane River Natural Area

291

Deep Creek

State Park Drive

Inland Rd.

Seven Mile Road

ORV area

Riverside State Park

Nine Mile Road

Spokane River Centennial Trail

Indian Trail Road

Rifle Club Rd

A.L. White Parkway

Bowl and Pitcher

Riverside State Park Campground

Aubrey White Park Drive

Spokane River

Trails Road

Downriver Dr.

To Mount Spokane State Park

291 Francis Avenue

2 395

Division Street

Ruby Street

Houston St

Rimrock

Fort George Wright Drive

Government Way

Spokane

Palisades Park

Grove Rd.

small marsh

Indian Canyon Park

Greenwood

Lorah Creek

DOWNTOWN

W 2nd Ave

90

Rimrock Drive

Indian Canyon Park Dr

280

280A

281

Bonnie Drive

Sunset Blvd

279

Maple

Walnut

To Spokane Valley birding sites

To Reardan and Wilbur

2

277A

195

To Steptoe Butte State Park

395

90

To Turnbull NWR and Moses Lake

SPOKANE AND VICINITY

by Andy Stepniewski and Jim Acton
revised by Kim Thorburn

The southern end of Washington's Northeast belongs to the Columbia Basin. Rolling plateaus—originally grown to steppe and scattered shrub-steppe, and groves of Ponderosa Pine—are interrupted by Channeled Scablands topography of lakes and marshes. Much of the deeper-soiled terrain is now given over to dryland wheat farming. This is, on average, the warmest and driest part of the Northeast and holds the bulk of the human population, mainly in the Spokane River Valley. The Spokane metropolitan area has numerous sites for finding birds of dry forest, grassland, and riparian habitats, especially in late spring and early summer when breeding activity is at a peak. These same sites can also be excellent in spring and fall migration. Notable Spokane vagrant records include Broad-winged Hawk (September), Tennessee Warbler (August), Black-throated Green Warbler (July), Blackpoll Warbler (May), Ovenbird (November), Indigo Bunting (September), and Rose-breasted Grosbeak (June, October). Less than an hour from the city, Mount Spokane State Park offers mountain birding with a flavor of the Selkirks, while Turnbull National Wildlife Refuge is a fine Channeled Scablands birding site.

SPOKANE CANYONS

If you find yourself in Spokane with a half-day or less at your disposal, your best bet for seeing both typical birds and possible vagrants is the canyons of the Spokane River and tributaries, in the western part of the city. The following itinerary visits several of the most productive sites.

To reach the **Little Spokane River Natural Area**, leave I-90 at Exit 281 and go north on US-2/US-395 (Division Street) 4.4 miles to the intersection with Francis Avenue. Turn left (west) here onto SR-291. In 2.2 miles swing right onto Indian Trail Road, which ends in 4.8 miles at Rutter Parkway. Bear right onto Rutter and continue 0.9 mile to a parking lot on the left, just across the Little Spokane River bridge (Discover Pass required).

A two-mile trail goes west from here, ending at a parking lot on SR-291 not far from the Spokane House Interpretive Center in Riverside State Park. If you walk the first half-mile, you will encounter a variety of habitats, including river, marsh, a fine riparian zone (Black Cottonwood, Quaking Aspen, willows, Red-osier Dogwood), brushy slopes, Ponderosa Pine woodland, and granitic cliffs. Species expected on this trail include Hooded Merganser, Great Blue Heron, Osprey, Bald Eagle, Northern Pygmy-Owl, Red-naped Sapsucker, Downy, Hairy, and Pileated Woodpeckers, Western Wood-Pewee, Willow Flycatcher, Eastern Kingbird, Cassin's, Warbling, and Red-eyed Vireos, a variety of swallows; Black-capped and Mountain Chickadees, all three nuthatches, Rock, Canyon, House, Pacific and Bewick's Wrens, Veery,

Gray Catbird, Yellow Warbler, Yellow-breasted Chat (infrequent), Black-headed Grosbeak, Red-winged Blackbird, Bullock's Oriole, Cassin's Finch, and Red Crossbill.

Back at the parking lot and across the bridge, another trail runs upstream (eastward) on the opposite bank, through Douglas-fir habitats on shady, north-facing slopes.

Turn right (south) out of the parking lot, re-cross the Little Spokane River, and keep right on Rutter Parkway to SR-291 (3.1 miles from the parking lot). Turn left, travel 3.5 miles, and turn right onto Seven Mile Road, which soon crosses the Spokane River. Look for a sign for the **Riverside Park ORV Area** in 2.2 miles. Turn left (south) onto Inland Road and drive through dry Ponderosa Pine woodlands, continuing past the parking lot where ORVs load and unload. In about 1.1 miles, you reach the beginning of an area of open grasslands where you may encounter a few hikers, bicyclists, or horseback riders, but no ORVs. For the next half-mile, grasslands and bordering pines are home to White-headed Woodpecker (rare), Gray Flycatcher, Red-breasted and Pygmy Nuthatches, Western Bluebird, and Chipping, Vesper, and Lark Sparrows. Turkey Vultures fly around the dry basalt cliffs to the west.

Return to Seven Mile Road and cross over the pavement onto State Park Drive, about 75 feet to the right. The road is gated in 0.3 mile (Discover Pass required), but you may walk in past the gate and look down into the forested basalt canyons along Deep Creek, on the left. Listen for Rock and Canyon Wrens. During breeding season, Townsend's Solitaires are common. Northern Goshawks have been seen on snags here. From the Deep Creek Overlook, a Bald Eagle's nest can be seen in a snag across the canyon.

Retrace your route along Seven Mile Road back across the Spokane River to SR-291 (Nine Mile Road), and turn right. In 1.4 miles, turn right onto Rifle Club Road (brown sign for *Riverside State Park*), then left in 0.4 mile onto Aubrey L. White Parkway. After 1.6 miles, turn into the parking lot on the right for the **Riverside State Park Campground** (Discover Pass required). A short trail affords great views of the Spokane River in a gorge with the **Bowl and Pitcher** and other dramatic rock formations as a backdrop. Check for Osprey and Bald Eagle. White-throated Swifts nest on the high basalt cliffs to the west, and an impressive Cliff Swallow colony resides just below the viewpoint. Pygmy Nuthatch, Western Bluebird, and Red Crossbill are also common in this part of the park and in the old burn in the Ponderosa Pine woodland to the north.

Continuing along the parkway (becomes Downriver Drive), exit left in 3.4 miles, before the underpass, and circle right, crossing a bridge over the Spokane River onto Fort George Wright Drive. In 1.4 miles, turn right onto Government Way and, in another 1.4 miles, reach Aubrey L. White Parkway (aka Aubrey White Park Drive and Riverside State Park Drive), an access to

Riverside State Park and the **Spokane River Centennial Trail**. At this junction, extensive areas of brush mantle the hillside to the south, very attractive to Nashville Warbler, Spotted Towhee, Lazuli Bunting, and many other species. Drive in one mile to a parking area that overlooks the Bowl and Pitcher from the other side of the river (Discover Pass required). If you continue on foot past the gate and down toward the river, you will reach a recent burn with woodpecker potential. Pacific-slope Flycatcher, Cassin's Vireo, and Lark Sparrow also reside in this area.

Turn around and follow Government Way back the way you came. At the traffic light where Fort George Wright Drive goes left, stay straight on Government Way for 1.2 miles, then turn right onto Greenwood Road. Bear right where the roadway splits (0.3 mile) and go uphill into **Indian Canyon Park**. The dense riparian growth along the creek on your left is filled with vireos and warblers, including a few Yellow-breasted Chats. There are a few places to park and walk trails.

As you reach the top of the hill along Greenwood, the roadway splits again (0.7 mile). Take Rimrock Drive to the right (north) through **Palisades Park**. This overlooks the city and has large-rock borders to prevent off-road activities. The length of the road all the way to Houston Street (2.0 miles) can be especially good for passerines in fall migration (late August–September), when you might see Olive-sided Flycatcher, Western Wood-Pewee, and Chipping, Lark, and White-crowned Sparrows, among other species. Look for accipiters here, also, including Northern Goshawk during winter. Midway along this route, a sketchy path follows a small creek westward for 150 yards along the forest edge to a marsh (may dry up in summer); here you may find Downy and Hairy Woodpeckers, all three nuthatches, and Red Crossbill.

Double back along Rimrock Drive, continuing past the Greenwood Road intersection 0.6 mile to the junction with **Bonnie Drive**. Turn left onto Bonnie, drive 200 yards or so, and stop anyplace suitable. Walk left to the canyon edge. You are at the narrow upper end of a forested funnel through which a small creek flows down to Latah Creek. In fall migration, birds work their way up the canyon to this spot and can often be seen at or below eye level as you look out onto the Douglas-firs. Eastern Kingbirds stay for days; small numbers of Hammond's, Gray, Dusky, and Pacific-slope Flycatchers may be seen. Cassin's, Warbling, and Red-eyed (scarce) Vireos pass through. Cedar Waxwings and Western Tanagers are interested in the many berry-producing shrubs. Fall warblers found here include Orange-crowned, Nashville, MacGillivray's, Yellow, Palm (rare), Yellow-rumped, Townsend's, and Wilson's Warblers, Yellow-breasted Chat, and sometimes even a Common Yellowthroat. Sparrows are everywhere in September, with White-crowned most numerous, Chipping and Lincoln's in moderate numbers, Golden-crowned uncommon, and Clay-colored, White-throated, and Harris's appearing once in a while. Cooper's Hawks breed in the canyon, and Sharp-shinneds and Northern Goshawks are possibilities during later fall and in winter.

Continue east on Bonnie Drive, turn left at **Indian Canyon Park Drive** (0.4 mile), and go downhill to a small parking place on a hairpin curve (0.2 mile), another good fall migration spot for vireos, warblers, and some sparrows. Below the cliff is a small waterfall. This middle part of the canyon is breeding territory for Pacific-slope Flycatcher, Cassin's Vireo, Dark-eyed Junco, and Western Tanager. Calliope Hummingbirds breed throughout the canyon—Black-chinneds too, although they are not as numerous. Other possibilities are Vaux's Swift, Black-capped and Mountain Chickadees, Rock, Canyon, House, Pacific, and Bewick's Wrens, Golden-crowned (winter) and Ruby-crowned Kinglets (migration), Gray Catbird, and Black-headed and Evening (fall and winter) Grosbeaks.

To reach I-90, proceed down Indian Canyon Park Drive to rejoin Greenwood Road (0.6 mile) and continue 0.3 mile to Government Way. Turn right onto Government Way and, in 0.8 mile, turn left onto Sunset Boulevard. Continue 1.1 miles to Maple Street, then turn right and follow the signs a few blocks to the onramps.

SPOKANE VALLEY

The Spokane Valley, now much of it incorporated as the cities of Spokane Valley and Liberty Lake, stretches east from the city of Spokane to the Idaho line. The small population of Upland Sandpipers that once nested here was extirpated several decades ago, but remnant patches of habitat still support a few Grasshopper Sparrows, Western Meadowlarks, and other grassland birds. Also of interest to birders are some forested preserves in the hills at the valley's south edge.

The **Dishman Hills Natural Area** consists of 562 rugged acres of dry forest, brushland, small seasonal springs and ponds, and rocky cliffs. Over 100 species of birds, nearly 400 of plants, and more than 50 of butterflies have been found here. The best time to visit is May or June; bird activity is much diminished in the hot summer months. Birds to expect include Western Wood-Pewee, Pacific-slope Flycatcher, Cassin's and Warbling Vireos, Violet-green Swallow, Black-capped and Mountain Chickadees, all three nuthatches, Rock Wren, Yellow-rumped Warbler, Chipping Sparrow, and Red Crossbill.

To reach this natural island in the midst of urban development, go east from downtown Spokane on I-90 to Exit 285 (Sprague Avenue), which dumps you directly onto Appleway Boulevard, the eastbound lanes of Sprague. In 1.4 miles, turn right onto Sargent Road and go two blocks to the north parking lot and entrance at Camp Caro. (A sign at the entrance reads *Ina Hughes Johnston Natural Area*.)

The preserve has an extensive network of trails. The Pinecliff Loop Trail visits the main habitats in a one-mile loop, starting just behind the environmental

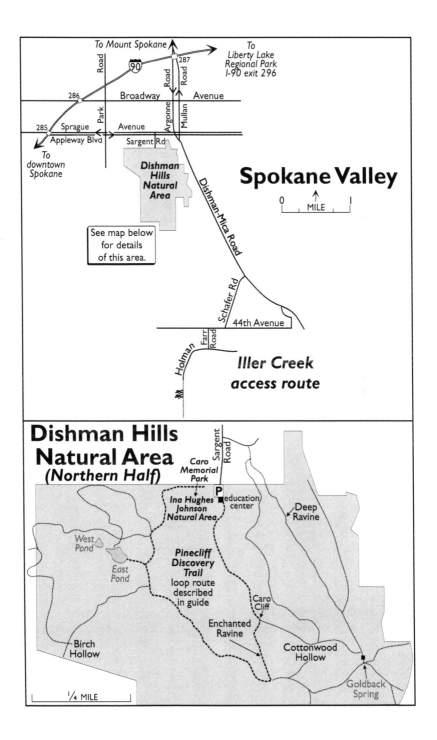

education center. Walk south through Ponderosa Pine woodland and patches of brushland. In about 500 yards, note granitic Caro Cliff to your left. Just beyond the cliff, take the right branch of the trail to Enchanted Ravine. Dense vegetation has developed in the shade of the gorge, dominated by Douglas-firs. From the ravine, the trail ascends to a high, forested plateau. Here and there, openings afford good views of the Spokane Valley. A spur trail leads to East and West Ponds—potholes that fill with water from winter and spring rains. Although they dry out in summer, the depressions are moist enough year round to maintain wetland vegetation, a magnet to many birds. The trail returns to the parking lot in about one-quarter mile.

Iller Creek Conservation Area is a 1400-acre tract at the southern end of the envisioned Dishman Hills Conservancy. A coalition is working to create the conservancy by establishing a corridor connecting the Iller Creek Conservation Area to the Dishman Hills Natural Area. Iller Creek has a number of different habitat types, including riparian, brushy, and forested slopes. A walk up the trail offers some of the best passerine birding in the Spokane area. Of the regularly occurring Eastern Washington vireos, thrushes, and warblers, all but Northern Waterthrush and Common Yellowthroat can be found here, and even these two have been recorded. Although best from mid-May through June, birding holds up quite well through the heat of summer.

From Camp Caro, return to Appleway, turn right, and go 0.4 mile to Dishman-Mica Road. Turn right, go 2.3 miles, and turn right onto Schafer Road. In 0.9 mile, turn right onto 44th Avenue, left in 0.2 mile onto Farr Road, and right in 0.3 mile onto Holman Road, which ends in 0.8 mile at a turn-around where the trail starts. Look for Calliope Hummingbird, Orange-crowned Warbler, and Yellow-breasted Chat in the Buckbrush on the west side of the road, and Lazuli Bunting and perhaps Black-headed Grosbeak along the slopes of the creek below. The lower part of the trail follows Iller Creek closely in a riparian zone of Mountain Alder, Douglas Maple, willows, and Black Cottonwood. Ponderosa Pines grow on the exposed sunny slopes of the gorge. Look for Red-naped Sapsucker, Willow and Dusky Flycatchers, Warbling and Red-eyed (uncommon) Vireos, Black-capped Chickadee, House Wren, Veery, Swainson's Thrush, Gray Catbird, Nashville, MacGillivray's, Yellow, and Wilson's Warblers, American Redstart, Spotted Towhee, and Chipping, Fox, and Song Sparrows.

As one works upstream, Ponderosa Pine and Black Cottonwood are replaced by Western Hemlock, Douglas-fir, Grand Fir, and Western Larch. Birds common along this portion include Ruffed Grouse, Olive-sided (along the ridge) and Hammond's Flycatchers, Mountain Chickadee, Red-breasted Nuthatch, Pacific Wren, Golden-crowned Kinglet, Nashville, Yellow-rumped, and Townsend's Warblers, Western Tanager, and Red Crossbill. Ruby-crowned Kinglet and Hermit Thrush are conspicuous in migration. The trail loops at Big Rock, the site of an old burn. (There is also access to this portion of the trail from Stevens Creek Road off of the Palouse Highway to the south.) Lewis's and Pileated Woodpeckers, American Kestrel, and Brown Creeper have nested in the burn area, and Rock Wrens are regularly found in the rocky outcrop to the east. The usual raptors along the drainage are Northern Harrier, Sharp-shinned and Red-tailed Hawks, and sometimes Barred Owl.

Returning from Iller Creek, go back on Dishman-Mica to Sprague. Here, two one-way streets face you across Sprague: Mullan Road (northbound) and Argonne Road (southbound), connecting to and from I-90 at Exit 287 in 1.2 miles.

Liberty Lake Regional Park is 3,600 acres of wetland, riparian, and mountain-forest habitats. From I-90, take Exit 296 and follow Liberty Lake Road 0.2 mile south. Turn left at East County Vista Drive, travel 0.8 mile to North Molter Road, and turn right. Proceed 0.3 mile and turn left onto East Valleyway Avenue, which curves right and becomes North Lakeside Road. In 2.3 miles from Molter, turn right onto South Zephyr Road, which leads in 0.3 mile to parking (fee May to September).

An extensive trail system climbs from the Liberty Lake marsh to a cedar grove conservation area through Ponderosa Pine then Douglas-fir, Western Larch, and Western Redcedar. Wood Duck, Virginia Rail, Sora, and Red-winged Blackbird inhabit the marsh. The trail follows Liberty Creek where Red-naped Sapsucker, Willow, Least, and Pacific-slope Flycatchers, Red-eyed and Warbling Vireos, and MacGillivray's and Yellow Warblers breed. At higher elevations, there are Ruffed Grouse, Chestnut-backed Chickadee, Red-breasted and Pygmy Nuthatches, Varied Thrush, and Cassin's Finch.

MOUNT SPOKANE STATE PARK

Mount Spokane, about 25 miles northeast of Spokane, is part of the southern Selkirk Mountains. Upper-elevation forests offer a chance of finding Dusky Grouse and Hermit Thrush. Gray Jays are common and conspicuous. Sought-after boreal species such as Pine Grosbeak and White-winged Crossbill occur erratically in winter. Moose and Mountain Lions are possible.

From Exit 281 on I-90, go north on US-2 (city streets a good part of the way) for 10.4 miles to SR-206 (aka East Mount Spokane Park Drive), and turn right. Proceed on SR-206 for 2.3 miles to a traffic circle, where you take the second exit and continue 13.3 miles to the entrance to Mount Spokane State Park. Alternatively, from I-90 take Exit 287, go north on Argonne Road (later Bruce Road) 8.5 miles to the traffic circle at SR-206, and take the first exit (right) onto SR-206. Continue 13.3 miles to the park. (Discover Pass is required; Sno-Park permit required from December 1–May 1.)

Dense forest on the initial stretch of park road has resident Barred Owls. On reaching the pass (3.2 miles), turn right and park by **Selkirk Lodge** (0.3 mile). Enjoy the views extending to the mountains of the Northeast Corner and east into Idaho. Wet-forest habitats with abundant Douglas Maple, alder thickets, and Western Hemlock make this probably the best area for birds in the park. Walk (or ski) the trails south and east of the lodge during winter for Northern Pygmy-Owl, Gray and Steller's Jays, Common Raven, Chestnut-backed Chickadee, Pine Grosbeak, Cassin's Finch, Red and White-winged (irregular) Crossbills, and Common Redpoll (irregular). During the breeding season, look for Ruffed and Dusky Grouse, Vaux's Swift (inclement weather), American Three-toed Woodpecker, Cassin's and Warbling Vireos, Pacific Wren, Ruby-crowned Kinglet, Swainson's, Hermit (more common higher up), and Varied Thrushes, Orange-crowned, MacGillivray's, Townsend's, and Wilson's Warblers, Fox Sparrow, Lazuli Bunting, and Pine Siskin. During migration, large numbers of Yellow-rumped Warblers and White-crowned Sparrows can be present. Always be on the watch for Northern Goshawk and Golden Eagle.

The road from Selkirk Lodge north to the downhill ski area passes through more stands of mature Interior Wet Belt forest—especially good for Chestnut-backed Chickadee and crossbills—although this stretch can be a human zoo, especially on weekends. The four-mile road to the summit (elevation 5,883 feet) offers a different set of habitats. The road is closed to vehicles during the winter, but open to foot or ski traffic. Montane forests of Subalpine Fir, Douglas-fir, Lodgepole and Western White Pines, and Western Larch, encountered first, are home to Dusky Grouse, Olive-sided Flycatcher, Mountain Chickadee, and Hermit Thrush. High south slopes with grasslands and lichen-covered rocks have Horned Larks, Mountain Bluebirds, and American Pipits. Check this area in fall for migrating raptors. Bohemian Waxwings, Lapland Longspurs, and Snow Buntings may be around at times in fall and early spring. Gray-crowned Rosy-Finches have been seen along the road.

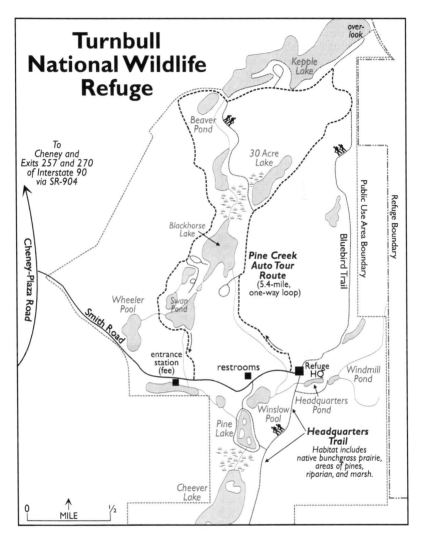

TURNBULL NATIONAL WILDLIFE REFUGE

The 18,200-acre refuge, situated about 20 miles southwest of Spokane, is one of the area's prime birding sites, with over 200 species recorded. Coming from Spokane, go west on I-90 to Exit 270, then south on SR-904 to Cheney-Plaza Road in Cheney (6.4 miles). Coming from the west, take I-90 Exit 257 and follow SR-904 to Cheney and the intersection with Cheney-Plaza Road on the right (10.4 miles), marked with a brown refuge sign. Go south 4.3 miles on Cheney-Plaza Road to the main visitor entrance (Smith Road), on the left.

Roads inside the refuge are well signed. Drive to an interpretive display at the entrance station (fee or America the Beautiful Pass required), where you can pick up a refuge brochure with a map. Maps and birdfinding information can also be obtained at refuge headquarters during weekday business hours. June is the best month overall, when nesting is at its peak, but May and September are good for landbird migrants, and April, October, and November for waterfowl migration. Rare vagrants recorded on the refuge include Mountain Plover (May), Golden-winged Warbler (August), Rose-breasted Grosbeak, and Rusty Blackbird (October).

Most of the refuge is closed to the public, but a large visitor-use area permits sampling of all of the habitats. The 5.4-mile Pine Creek Auto Tour Route is the most convenient way to do this. The tour starts just before refuge headquarters, on the left, and runs one way counterclockwise, ending near the entrance station. Three main habitats are encountered on this drive.

In the open Ponderosa Pine parkland, look for many bird species characteristic of the dry coniferous forest, including Hairy Woodpecker, Western Wood-Pewee, Mountain Chickadee, Red-breasted and Pygmy (common) Nuthatches, Western Bluebird, Chipping Sparrow, Cassin's Finch, and Red Crossbill.

In the scattered groves of Quaking Aspen, Water Birch, Douglas Hawthorn, and alder, with understory thickets of wild rose, Red-osier Dogwood, serviceberry, and other shrubs, expect Ruffed Grouse, Northern Saw-whet Owl, Red-naped Sapsucker, Downy Woodpecker, Willow and occasional Least Flycatchers, Warbling and Red-eyed (uncommon) Vireos, Black-capped Chickadee, White-breasted Nuthatch, House Wren, Veery, Gray Catbird, Yellow Warbler, and more.

Most of the common waterfowl species of the West nest in Turnbull's marshes and lakes, including Canada Goose, Trumpeter Swan, Mallard, Blue-winged, Cinnamon, and Green-winged Teal, Redhead, and Ruddy Duck. Small flocks of Tundra Swans, and many other species of waterfowl, come through the refuge during migration. Other marshbirds include Pied-billed Grebe, American Bittern, Virginia Rail, Sora, American Coot, Spotted Sandpiper, Wilson's Snipe, Black Tern, Marsh Wren, Common Yellowthroat, and Yellow-headed and Red-winged Blackbirds.

To reach areas of native bunchgrass prairie, another habitat on the refuge, take the hike south along Headquarters Trail, which runs east of Winslow Pool and Pine Lake about 1.5 miles to the far end of Cheever Lake. Areas of pines and riparian and marsh habitats, are also met with on this trail, making this probably the most species-rich area open to the public on the refuge. In the grasslands, look for Gray Partridge, Red-tailed Hawk, American Kestrel, Say's Phoebe, Western Bluebird, Vesper and Grasshopper Sparrows, and Western Meadowlark.

The refuge is also good habitat for mammals, including Columbian Ground Squirrel, Red Squirrel, Least Chipmunk, Elk, White-tailed Deer, Coyote, Badger, River Otter, and Long-tailed Weasel. In May and June, the open spaces among the pines are carpeted with an astonishing collection of wildflowers. Take precautions against Wood Ticks, which are especially plentiful from March through May.

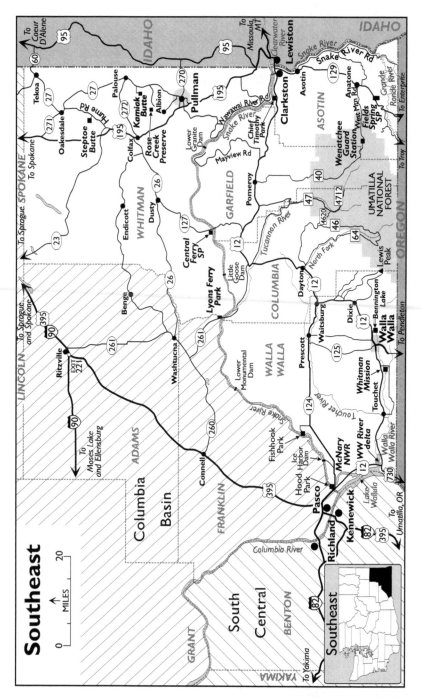

Southeast

0 — MILES — 20

498

SOUTHEAST

If the Selkirk Mountains of the Northeast put one in mind of the Canadian Rockies, with species such as Spruce Grouse, Boreal Chickadee, and White-winged Crossbill, then birders visiting the Blue Mountains of the Southeast might think they were in Utah. Here the ranges of species of the Middle Rockies—Broad-tailed Hummingbird, Cordilleran Flycatcher, Green-tailed Towhee—flirt with the corner of the state.

Remote and uninhabited, the rugged Blues rise as a forested rampart above a sea of former steppe habitats, now virtually all converted to cropland. The Columbia River borders the region on the west; the Snake River forms its eastern and part of its northern boundary. Many who live here are dependent on a resource-based economy, with wheat farming, cattle grazing, and logging as primary industries, though Walla Walla's wine industry exploded in the first decade of this century. The Walla Walla Valley today is home to more than 100 wineries.

Tamed by four large dams, the Snake has become the region's economic lifeline. Each year tugs push countless barges laden with millions of tons of grain, lumber, and other goods through the Snake River locks and along the Columbia River waterway. The once-legendary Snake River runs of salmon and Steelhead are now listed as endangered, an environmental cost of the dams.

The Southeast is divided into four subregions, each with its own distinctive topography, habitats, and birdlife.

The *western lowlands* provide typical Columbia Basin birding in the irrigated agricultural lands of the Walla Walla River drainage and along the shoreline of Lake Wallula, the reservoir at the region's western edge. In particular, the Walla Walla delta is renowned as one of Eastern Washington's consistently best sites for shorebirds, gulls, and waterfowl, with numerous records of rarities.

The deeply eroded *Blue Mountains* of Washington's southeast corner and adjacent Oregon are home to owls, woodpeckers, and other forest birds in good variety and numbers. Forest types are transitional to those of the Rockies to the east, while brush associations have affinities with the Great Basin to the south. Far too seldom visited, the surprising Blues are one of the birding frontiers of the state.

The Grande Ronde volcano—source of the basalt flows that engulfed the Columbia Basin—forms the backside of the Blues, above a high plateau. Arid steppe habitats extend along the Snake and *Grande Ronde River gorges*. Very lightly birded, this remote and scenic region at the eastern edge of the state is great for birds of bare rock, high cliffs, open fields, and riparian vegetation in canyon bottoms.

North of the Snake River, the *Palouse* is an arresting landscape of great mounds of windblown silt from prehistoric floods, now given over to dryland wheat farming. Birds still thrive in the few remaining pockets of original grassland habitats. The highest spots are pre-Cambrian rocks of the ancient North American continent. Islands of trees and brush in the surrounding wheat barrens, these eminences offer good vagrant potential.

The climate of the Southeast varies considerably but predictably. Lake Wallula—in the lowest part of the Columbia Basin, just 340 feet above sea level—is hot in summer (temperatures exceeding 90 degrees on about 40 days during a typical year), fairly mild in winter (January average low 28 degrees), and dry (eight inches average annual precipitation). Thirty miles east and 1,000 feet above sea level, Walla Walla experiences similar temperatures but receives twice as much precipitation (18 inches). Although winter temperatures remain about the same as one moves toward the Idaho line, summers are cooler. Pullman (2,400 feet above sea level) sees 15 days above 90 degrees, while at Anatone, in the shadow of the eastern Blues at 3,570 feet, the thermometer climbs above 90 degrees only eight days per year. Precipitation increases slightly (22 inches at Pullman, 20 at Anatone).

The highlands are another story. Data are meager, but the Blues are much cooler and wetter than the rest of the region. Average annual precipitation in the highest parts (above 5,500 feet) is 8–10 times greater than at the Columbia River. Summer thunderstorms, though infrequent, may be severe; be alert for washouts. Most gravel roads in the high Blues are closed throughout the winter and may not be entirely snow-free until mid-June or even later.

Snowfall is generally light in the lowlands (19 inches annually at Walla Walla, 29 at Pullman, but 66 at Anatone). Highways and most secondary roads are kept plowed; nonetheless, watch for blowing and drifting snow. Be cautious if traveling off the main roads at this season.

Services, including accommodations, may be found in Walla Walla, Waitsburg, Dayton, Pomeroy, Clarkston, Pullman, and Colfax.

WESTERN LOWLANDS

by Mike Denny and MerryLynn Denny

revised by MerryLynn Denny

The western part of the region, extending to the base of the Blue Mountains, occupies the lowest and some of the driest parts of the Columbia Basin. Notable topographic features include the confluence of the Snake and Columbia Rivers, the Walla Walla River valley, and Wallula Gap, where basalt lava flows laid down 17 million years ago and since exposed by erosion are visible. Irrigation has dramatically changed the landscape. Shrub-steppe habitats are now mostly only a memory, replaced with productive farmland grown to wheat, potatoes, orchards, vineyards, alfalfa and hay, onions (the famous Walla Walla Sweets), and other crops. Open country is devoted mainly to cattle grazing. The following sites are accessed from US-12, the main highway across southeastern Washington.

LOWER SNAKE RIVER

Heading southeast from Pasco, US-12 crosses the Snake River to Burbank. Take the first exit and head east on SR-124. **Hood Park** is the first left after the roundabout. Many migrants can be found here in spring and fall; check the park and wildlife area for owls, sapsuckers and sparrows in winter. Scan the waterfowl on the river; scoters are sometimes present. A trail under the highway allows access for scoping the waterfowl on the other side.

Continue east on SR-124, turn left onto Monument Drive in 5.2 miles, and continue to **Ice Harbor Dam**. Drive west along the shoreline below the dam. Late fall and winter produce close views of waterfowl, American White Pelicans and gulls. Thayer's, Lesser Black-backed, and Glaucous Gulls have been seen on the mid-river island. Heading back upstream, take Shoreline Drive over the hill where there are pullouts from which to view the lake behind the dam. Keep going to a T-intersection at Charbonneau Drive. Turn left to reach **Charbonneau Park**, another migrant spot, and check for sparrows and owls (winter).

Head south on Charbonneau Drive to a T-intersection with Harbor Boulevard. Turn right and go 1.6 miles through the unincorporated village of Sun Harbor to SR-124. Turn left onto SR-124, continue 7.5 miles east, and turn left onto Fishhook Park Road. Follow this road through several curves to **Fishhook Park** in 4.4 miles. You'll be driving through one of the country's largest privately owned orchards at over 6,000 acres. Park at the gate in winter and walk in. Look for waterfowl, owls, winter finches, and mountain birds. Spring and fall can produce rare migrants: Gray-cheeked Thrush, Magnolia and Chestnut-sided Warblers, Rusty Blackbird, and White-winged Crossbill have been seen here.

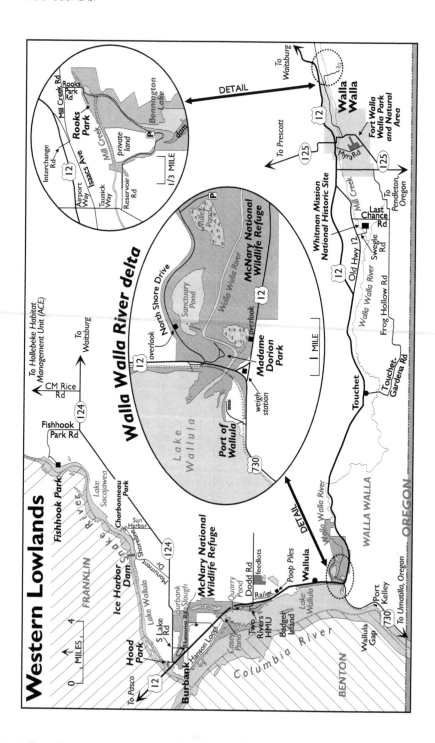

Continue east on SR-124 four miles and turn left onto C M Rice Road for eight miles to **Hollebeke Habitat Management Unit**, a U.S. Army Corps of Engineers mitigation site. These 247 acres are covered with plantings that attract many species of birds every month of the year. Be very cautious during hunting season. Winter birds that may be found here include Swamp, White-throated, Harris's, Golden-crowned, and many White-crowned Sparrows. Bohemian and Cedar Waxwings feast on the berries. Owls can be found in the dense overgrown areas.

LAKE WALLULA

Lake Wallula is the name given to the huge impoundment of Columbia River waters behind McNary Dam. The east bank of the reservoir from the mouth of the Snake River to the Oregon line is one of the most productive areas in Washington for birds associated with water and shorelines; the shallows are an important nursery for fall Chinook Salmon. Most of the best birding spots are in the McNary National Wildlife Refuge—15,894 acres of river islands, backwater sloughs, seasonal wetlands, delta mudflats, riparian area, and shrub-steppe uplands set aside for wildlife in 1954 in mitigation for bottomlands drowned by the dam.

Coming west into Burbank on SR-124, about a mile east of the intersection with US-12, take South Lake Road 0.7 mile to **McNary National Wildlife Refuge headquarters** (64 Maple Street), where refuge information is available. There is a deck with scopes, and a paved walk leads to a blind for closer looks. Just up from the blind is the "birding spur," where Canada and Prothonotary Warblers were found. In winter, **Burbank Slough** may have over 100,000 geese, including 8,000 Snow Geese.

Continue south from the headquarters on South Lake Road and turn left on East Humorist Road for 2.6 miles to a pullout on the right where you can scan the slough for geese, swans, and eagles. Backtrack 1.1 miles to Hanson Loop Road to check the fields on both sides for geese. Continue on Hanson Loop 2.2 miles, crossing US-12 to an unmarked gravel road going left before the right curve. Drive down to **Casey Pond**, where many waterfowl, shorebirds, and gulls can be found fall to spring.

Return to US-12, turn right, and continue east three miles, turning right at Dodd Road to **Two Rivers Habitat Management Unit**. At the end of the paved road, go straight ahead 0.5 mile to Quarry Pond, veering left to the parking area. From fall to spring, many hundreds of waterfowl can be seen, and when the pond turns to ice, the Bald Eagles and gulls gather. Red-breasted Mergansers winter here. Back just before the pavement, turn right onto the dirt road and stay left 0.8 mile to the parking area. Walk down Old Highway 12 to the trees, then right on a trail out to the river where you need a scope to see terns (Caspian, Common, Arctic, and Forster's), gulls, shorebirds (Ruff), and waterfowl. This spot is best in fall with low water before hunting season begins; be careful during hunting season. Riparian areas can be good for passerines. A Red-shouldered Hawk was seen here in 2014.

Cross over US-12 and proceed past the Tyson slaughterhouse on **Dodd Road**. On the right are many feedlots where blackbirds gather, and on the left are the "blood ponds" that may have shorebirds. Pacific Golden-Plover, Ruddy Turnstone, Red Knot, Buff-breasted Sandpiper, and Sabine's Gull have all been seen here. Backtrack west on Dodd Road and turn left on Railex Road 1.5 miles to the famous "poop piles." Thousands of gulls and blackbirds can be present from October to April, if there is a fresh dumping of waste from the slaughterhouse. Park off-road and stay clear of trucks and equipment. Tricolored, Yellow-headed, and Rusty may join the thousands of Red-winged and Brewer's Blackbirds and European Starlings. Gulls include Mew, Ring-billed, California, Herring, Thayer's, Glaucous-winged, Glaucous, and, occasionally, Franklin's or Lesser Black-backed. Across US-12 to the west is **Badger Island**, one of the few places in the state where American White Pelicans nest. A no-hunting island, this area can attract up to 60,000 waterfowl in winter.

Heading south on US-12 from Dodd Road for 5.4 miles, you arrive at North Shore Road and Madame Dorion Park (currently closed but may open in future). Across the road to the west is the access to the **Walla Walla River delta**. Go right (north) on the dirt road parallel to the railroad tracks to a small parking lot. Watching for trains, cross the tracks and follow the trail either down to the shoreline or up to the bluff on the right. You will need a scope to bird this area. About 200 species have been recorded here, including Brant, Garganey, Steller's Eider (the only interior Lower 48 record), Brown Pelican, Snowy Egret, White-faced Ibis, American and Pacific Golden-Plovers, Snowy Plover, Whimbrel, Hudsonian Godwit, Sharp-tailed Sandpiper, Sabine's Gull, Black-tailed Gull, and the state's first Lesser Black-backed Gull in 2000, Snow Bunting, and Northern Waterthrush.

Water levels on Lake Wallula fluctuate as reservoir control officials respond to competing demands for power generation, barge traffic, irrigation, recreation, movement of salmon and various other wildlife considerations. The level can be checked on-line; search for "McNary Pool Level." If the forebay level is above 339, there will be little mud for shorebirds. This area is heavily hunted from October to January. In February, the waterfowl come in by the thousands, and shorebirds are always present if there is exposed mud. Eight species of gulls may be present, especially in winter.

Take North Shore Road east up the hill to the overlook (0.4 mile). **Sanctuary Pond** (aka Smith's Harbor) is not hunted and can be full of waterfowl in the winter. Continue on east for 1.2 miles to the **Millet Pond**, heavily hunted but often great for waterfowl and shorebirds February through May. A Black-and-white Warbler was seen here. You can go past the ponds and down to a parking area and walk the dike trails. Many passerines are present during migration. Snowy Egret and White-faced Ibis have been seen here.

Backtrack to US-12, turn left (south), cross over the Walla Walla River, then turn right on US-730 and go two miles down into Wallula Gap. In another two miles, turn right into Port Kelley (large grain elevators) and check the river for waterfowl, gulls, and passerines in migration. Continue west 1.5 miles to a large pulloff on the left. Look for White-throated Swift, Prairie Falcon, Say's Phoebe, Canyon Wren, and passerines in the willows and sage during migration.

WALLA WALLA VALLEY

Going east on US-12 you will come to Touchet (pronounced *Too-she*). From here, you can either head north on Touchet River Road and explore the riparian areas along the river or head south and look over the alfalfa and hay field for raptors, including Swainson's Hawks that sometimes gather by the dozens in September. Continue east on US-12 past unincorporated Lowden for three miles, turn right onto Old Highway 12, proceed east 2.3 miles to Swegle Road, and turn right. **Whitman Mission National Historic Site** will be the next left (0.5 mile). A walk around the grounds can be especially good during migration; in winter look for sparrows and owls. Many summer birds nest here, including Western and Eastern Kingbirds, Cedar Waxwings, and Bullock's Orioles.

In Walla Walla, take Myra Road south from US-12 1.6 miles to **Fort Walla Walla Park and Natural Area**. There are trails around both that can be birdy anytime of year. Look for Wood Duck (April), California Quail, Wild Turkey, Red-tailed Hawk, Downy Woodpecker, Black-billed Magpie, and Lesser and American Goldfinches, among other species. A Brown Thrasher was found here in 2008. A Northern Parula also was seen here.

East of Walla Walla on US-12, take Airport Way south (turns into North Tausick Way) 0.6 mile and turn left (east) onto Reservoir Road. Follow it to **Bennington Lake**. You'll find several trails around the lake and groves of juniper and pine to explore for owls in winter. Northern Shrike and Townsend's Solitaire also are found in winter. Summer nesting species include Tree Swallow, Yellow-breasted Chat, Bullock's Oriole, and many more. A Broad-winged Hawk and a Wilson's Plover were found here in 2012.

Rooks Park is another U.S. Army Corps of Engineers site with trails. Backtrack to North Tausick Way, turn right (north), go 0.3 mile to East Isaacs Avenue, turn right (east), go 1.5 miles, and turn right to Rooks Park. There are over two miles of paved trails along Mill Creek east and west of the park; if the park gate is locked, you can park outside and walk in.

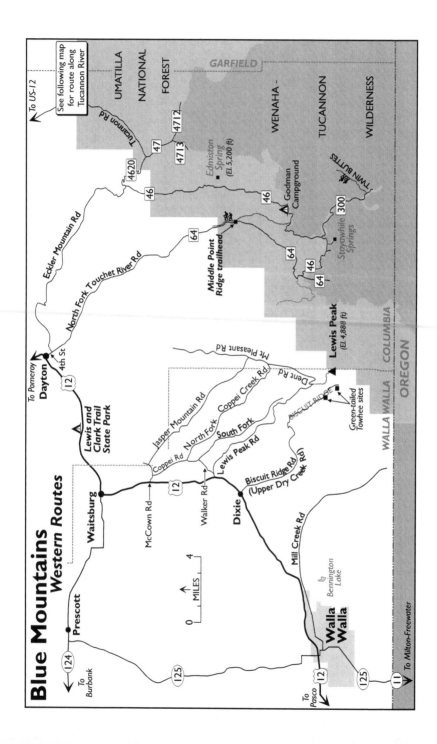

Blue Mountains
Western Routes

See following map for route along Tucannon River

To US-12

UMATILLA
NATIONAL
FOREST

GARFIELD

Tucannon Rd

4712

4620   47   4713   Edmiston Spring (El. 5,200 ft)

46   WENAHA -

Eckler Mountain Rd

64   46   Godman Campground

TUCANNON

Middle Point Ridge trailhead   64   300   TWIN BUTTES

North Fork Touchet River Rd   46   Stentz white Springs

WILDERNESS

64   64

To Pomeroy   4th St

Dayton   Mt Pleasant Rd

12   Lewis Peak (El. 4,888 ft)

Lewis and Clark Trail State Park   Dent Rd   Coppei Creek Rd

Jasper Mountain Rd

North Fork

South Fork   BISCUIT RIDGE

Coppei Rd   Green-tailed Towhee sites

WALLA WALLA

COLUMBIA

Waitsburg   Lewis Peak Rd   OREGON

McCown Rd   12   Walker Rd   Biscuit Ridge Rd (Upper Dry Creek Rd)

Dixie

Prescott   Mill Creek Rd

MILES

Bennington Lake

0   4

124   Walla Walla

To Burbank   125   12

125

To Pasco   125   11

To Milton-Freewater

BLUE MOUNTAINS

by Mike Denny, MerryLynn Denny, Andy Stepniewski
revised by MerryLynn Denny

Encompassed by the Umatilla National Forest, the Blue Mountains rise abruptly to the east of Walla Walla, peaking above 6,000 feet. Precipitation increases dramatically as you ascend the western slopes; mountain streams cascade down to the Walla Walla and Tucannon River basins. Erosional forces have produced steep-sided canyons and rocky escarpments, home to raptors and other birds of the cliffs. At lower elevations, wheat- and rangelands reach up to the lower forest zone. Lush riparian growth along the drainages is filled with birds in spring and early summer. At middle elevations, brushy patches clinging to steep valley sides host Washington's only breeding Green-tailed Towhees. A mosaic of forest communities (low, high, wet, dry) ranges from Ponderosa Pine, Douglas-fir, and Grand Fir up to Subalpine Fir, Engelmann Spruce, and Western Larch, with bird species appropriate to these habitat types. Some call the Blue Mountains Washington's Woodpecker Heaven; as more and more birders are discovering, the same might be said for owls. Elk, Mule Deer, Bighorn Sheep, and Black Bear are also common.

A good strategy to bird the Blues is to begin at low elevations in the morning and work to higher, forested habitats toward mid-day. Or, during periods of inclement weather (which can be frequent in the high mountains), one might be advised to take refuge low down all day. Birding is best from mid-June to early October, after which the higher roads begin to drift over with snow.

US-12 traces the western and northern base of the Blue Mountains on its way from Walla Walla to Clarkston, passing through Dixie, Waitsburg, Dayton, and Pomeroy—well-preserved towns established in the 1870s on lumbering, wheat farming, and supplying Idaho-bound miners. The core of the high Washington Blues is set aside in the roadless Wenaha-Tucannon Wilderness Area (177,469 acres, partly in Oregon). Access by road is thus mostly an in-and-out affair from US-12 along various ridgelines and drainages. An exception is the up-and-over route via the Wenatchee Guard Station, providing an excellent connection between Pomeroy and the canyonlands east of the mountains.

BISCUIT RIDGE

To look for Green-tailed Towhee, head east on US-12 from Walla Walla eight miles to the town of Dixie and turn south at the school onto Biscuit Ridge Road. After 6.5 miles the road does a hairpin turn, becomes gravel and is steep, but OK for passenger cars. In another 3.7 miles, you are on a ridge along a south-facing slope. From mid-May to mid-August, in the brushy areas on the slopes for the next mile, you can usually hear the Green-tailed Towhees, with a little patience. This is all private property, so you want to stay on or near the road. In May and June especially, the paved section of this road is very birdy. Pacific-slope Flycatchers are abundant along here, nesting in the banks and cliffs along the creek. Veery, MacGillivray's Warbler, Fox Sparrow, Western Tanager, and Lazuli Bunting are also abundant.

LEWIS PEAK AND COPPEI CREEK

Back on US-12, head north two miles from the Biscuit Ridge Road turnoff to **Lewis Peak Road**. It's passable to the top (elevation 4,888 feet) except in winter, when you can walk up to look for Northern Goshawk, Pine Grosbeak, crossbills, and Common Redpolls. Again, this land is all private property, but there are pullouts; birding can be rewarding here any time of year.

To reach Coppei (pronounced COP-eye) Creek, after you exit US-12 onto Lewis Peak Road, veer left at the fork in 0.2 mile onto Walker Road. Go up over Walker Hill, then down to a T-intersection. You can park here and walk either direction or drive up six miles south along **South Fork Coppei Creek Road**. All the riparian areas along Coppei Creek are passerine heaven from late April through mid-July and again in August–September during migration. Willow Flycatcher, Veery, Gray Catbird, Yellow-breasted Chat, and Lazuli Bunting are common. Least Flycatcher has nested up South Fork Road. High-mountain bird species may be present in winter.

From the intersection, go left (downstream), cross the two forks of the creek, and turn right to **North Fork Coppei Creek Road**. In 3.2 miles you will come to a steep grade. Park and walk uphill along this birdy area. Indigo Bunting was found over halfway to the top in 2008. MacGillivray's Warblers and Lazuli Buntings are abundant; Dusky Flycatcher, Cassin's Vireo, and Pacific Wren are found in lesser numbers. Northern Pygmy-Owl is present year round.

There are two ways to return to US-12. You can continue driving up to the top and merge left onto Mount Pleasant Road, heading 2.2 miles east to a fork. Take the left fork onto Jasper Mountain Road and follow it down to McCown Road. Go left onto McCown; it is a little over a mile to US-12. (Blue Mountain Audubon maintains many bluebird boxes along Jasper Mountain Road, and Western Bluebirds are common from April–July.)

Or you can backtrack on North Fork Coppei Creek Road to the point where you earlier crossed the two forks of the creek. Instead of turning left across the creeks, continue straight ahead onto Coppei Road, which intersects with McCown in 2.5 miles. Take a left onto McCown and go a half-mile to US-12.

Once you are back on US-12, continue north 3.3 miles into Waitsburg, where the highway makes a right-angle turn to the east. **Lewis and Clark Trail State Park** (campground) is 4.4 miles farther east on US-12. Many birds inhabit the dense riparian woodland along the Touchet River here, including Western Screech-Owl, Eastern Kingbird, Warbling and Red-eyed (uncommon) Vireos, Black-billed Magpie, Veery, Gray Catbird, Yellow Warbler, Yellow-breasted Chat, Black-headed Grosbeak, and Bullock's Oriole.

NORTH FORK TOUCHET RIVER

An excellent loop into the high Blue Mountains follows a ridgeline south from Dayton above the North Fork Touchet River, returning via the river valley. Turn right onto Fourth Street in Dayton (5.5 miles from Lewis and Clark Trail State Park), then left in 0.5 mile onto Eckler Mountain Road (aka Mustard Street, Mustard Hollow Road, and Kendall Skyline Road). Follow this road (summer only) for about 16 miles to an intersection on the left with FR-4620 (connects in about four miles to Tucannon Road). Keep on Eckler Mountain Road, which becomes FR-46 upon entering the Umatilla National Forest in another 0.8 mile. **Edmiston Spring** (6.0 miles, elevation 5,200 feet) offers a fine sample of the higher-elevation birdlife (Wild Turkey, Williamson's Sapsucker, Ruby-crowned Kinglet).

Another 5.1 miles uphill is **Godman Campground**, on the high Blue Mountain divide (north slope draining to the Touchet River, south slope to the Wenaha River in Oregon). These forests of Subalpine Fir and Western Larch are inhabited by Northern Goshawk and by Williamson's Sapsucker and other woodpeckers, including American Three-toed (uncommon). Five miles farther, FR-300 turns off left from FR-46, leading in about six miles to the trailhead for the short hike to Twin Buttes. These high-altitude forests should be checked in September and October for Boreal Owl.

Return to FR-46 and turn left. The road snakes along the ridgetop, mostly in subalpine forest (good for Boreal Owl). In about two-thirds of a mile park at the trailhead on the left and make the short hike to **Stayawhile Springs**. Flammulated Owls have been noted in the dense, long, narrow stand of trees and woody shrubs to the west and south of this spot; forests to the east and north are prime habitat for Boreal Owl.

At the junction with FR-64 (5.1 miles from FR-300), turn right and head down the North Fork Touchet River. In 6.9 miles, park at the **Middle Point Ridge Trailhead**. Cross the rushing stream on a footbridge. As you walk downstream on the trail through old-growth forest of Grand Fir, Engelmann Spruce, and Western Larch, with abundant Western Yew in the understory, look for Hammond's and Pacific-slope Flycatchers, Chestnut-backed Chickadee, Pacific Wren, and Townsend's Warbler. From the trailhead, it is about 17 miles downhill via FR-64 (becomes North Fork Touchet River Road, then Fourth Street) to US-12 in Dayton.

TUCANNON RIVER

The Tucannon River drains the large midsection of the Washington Blues northward to the Snake River. US-12 crosses the Tucannon 13 miles north of Dayton. Turn east (right) at the north end of the bridge onto Tucannon River Road and follow the beautiful Tucannon Valley, a mosaic of farms and riparian vegetation rimmed with basalt cliffs. In 1.1 miles look toward the river for the

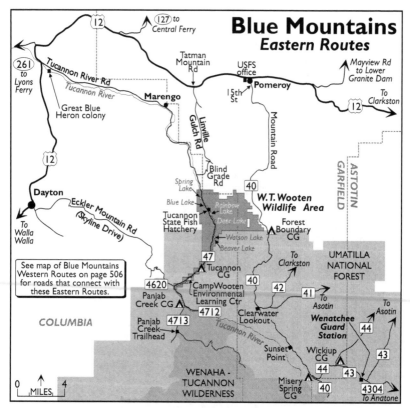

large Great Blue Heron colony in the Black Cottonwoods. Also watch for Spotted Sandpiper, Belted Kingfisher, and Eastern Kingbird in summer. In the fields, watch for Wild Turkey and White-tailed Deer early in the morning or in the evening. Good bets on the way to tiny Marengo (10 miles from the heronry viewpoint) include many Red-tailed Hawks (nesting on the cliffs north of the road, especially along the first few miles), Chukar, Great Horned and Short-eared Owls, Common Nighthawk, and Rock Wren. Ferruginous Hawk is also possible.

Beyond Marengo the road bends to run more or less south. After entering the **William T. Wooten Wildlife Area** (11,778 acres), you reach the first of five artificial impoundments at Spring Lake (10.1 miles). This is a rugged area of valleys and ridges with conifers and brush on the high, steep slopes. Look for Red-naped Sapsucker, Red-eyed Vireo, and Gray Catbird in streamside vegetation on the valley floor. Park at the **Tucannon State Fish Hatchery** (1.0 mile) and walk south to Rainbow Lake, watching for Pacific-slope Flycatchers, Cassin's and Red-eyed Vireos, Gray Catbirds, and huge numbers of butterflies in spring. In August and early September, Solitary Sandpipers (as many as eight at once) occur at the hatchery ponds and Rainbow Lake.

Continuing south, the road soon enters the Umatilla National Forest and becomes FR-47. **Camp Wooten Environmental Learning Center** (6.1 miles from the hatchery) is good for most of the middle-elevation birds of the Blue Mountains. Northern Pygmy-, Barred, and Northern Saw-whet Owls are present in March and April; in summer, Flammulated Owl can be found another 1.3 miles south on FR-47. Watch for woodpeckers and American Dipper along this portion of the river. In another 0.7 mile (2.0 miles from Camp Wooten), you will come to FR-4620, on the right, which connects to the North Fork Touchet River loop (page 506).

Continuing south on FR-47, Panjab Creek Campground is reached in 1.8 miles (USFS, primitive, fee). The road divides here; take the right fork (FR-4713) to the **Panjab Creek Trailhead** (3.0 miles). This trail traverses a superb example of a moist Eastside forest (elevation about 4,000 feet). Look for Northern Goshawk, Pileated Woodpecker, Chestnut-backed Chickadee, Hermit and Varied Thrushes, and Western Tanager.

As you return to US-12, ff you will next be heading east on US-12 toward Pomeroy, a shortcut (weather permitting) can be made by turning right from Tucannon Road onto Blind Grade Road, 2.0 miles downstream (north) from Spring Lake. This appropriately-named gravel road switchbacks steeply up to a four-way junction (2.4 miles). From here, take the paved Linville Gulch Road (becomes Tatman Mountain Road) for 6.5 miles down to US-12. Turn right to reach Pomeroy in about five miles.

WENATCHEE GUARD STATION

Wenatchee Guard Station, on the crest of the Washington Blues at an elevation of about 5,200 feet, may be approached either from the north (US-12 at Pomeroy) or from the east (SR-129 at Anatone). Time and other considerations allowing, the 40-mile drive between these two towns—over the top and down again, in either direction—is a perfect way to experience the birds of this remote corner of Washington. Breathtaking vistas of deep gorges and into three states are an added inducement.

On the east side of Pomeroy, turn south from US-12 onto 15th Street. (You can obtain maps, road and trail information, and a Northwest Forest or America the Beautiful Pass at the USFS ranger district office on US-12 a mile west of this corner.) At 7.8 miles south of US-12, you reach an intersection, with SR-128 splitting off to the left; continue straight ahead onto Mountain Road, which eventually becomes FR-40. In another 7.4 miles, you reach **Forest Boundary Campground**, just within the national forest boundary. Ponderosa Pine dominates; look for White-headed Woodpecker, Pygmy Nuthatch, Yellow-rumped Warbler, and Cassin's Finch. In another 7.9 miles south, at Clearwater Lookout, you enter the eastern Blue Mountains. From this point forward, the slopes to the left of the road drain to Asotin Creek, which reaches the Snake River at Asotin. **Sunset Point** (4.0 miles) affords spectacular views of the upper Tucannon Basin on the south side of the road. Although this is not officially designated wilderness, no sign of humankind is visible below—a rare experience nowadays.

In another 3.7 miles is the turnoff to **Misery Spring Campground**. Here, at 6,200 feet, the trees are Subalpine Fir, Engelmann Spruce, and Western Larch. Ruby-crowned Kinglets are abundant. Look also for American Three-toed Woodpecker, Gray Jay, Pacific Wren, Townsend's Warbler, and Fox and White-crowned (*oriantha*) Sparrows. The road forks; go left on FR-44 to **Wickiup Campground** (3.2 miles). These high forests have been good for Northern Goshawk, Dusky Grouse, and Williamson's Sapsucker.

The road forks again by the campground; stay right with FR-43 and enjoy the dramatic vistas on your way to **Wenatchee Guard Station** (3.2 miles). You are at the crest of the Blue Mountains, a broad anticlinal arch (inverted U) of Columbia Plateau basalts. South from this vantage the terrain has been deeply incised by stream erosion, to the point that virtually none of the original plateau remains. Some of the northernmost Mountain Mahogany, a gnarled and grayish-hued small tree, clings to these rocky, south-facing ridges. Cool, moist forests blanket the north slopes, which have yet to be chewed away by erosion. Green-tailed Towhee was first documented as a breeder in Washington in a canyon near the guard station in 1923. Since then, however, records from this area have been few. If you're in an exploratory mood, try hiking about the south-facing slopes, checking shrub patches.

To join the Grande Ronde country, continue east on FR-43 along the ridgeline, then stay right onto FR-4304 at a fork in 0.6 mile. (Switch to map on page 510.) In another 6.9 miles the road changes name to West Mountain Road as you leave the Umatilla National Forest. In 5.6 miles, merge right onto Mill Road, reaching SR-129 in Anatone in 1.8 miles. Turn right here for Fields Spring State Park (page 514).

SNAKE AND GRANDE RONDE RIVER CANYONS

by Mike Denny, MerryLynn Denny, Andy Stepniewski

revised by Keith Carlson

The extreme southeast corner of Washington is a paradise for those who love arid, hot slopes and grand scenery. This may be the Golden Eagle capital of the state. Other birds of cliffs and rocky slopes are well represented as are birds of prey. In the breeding season, riparian corridors host many neotropical visitors, especially along tributary streams of the main rivers. Geology buffs and rockhounds will find much of interest, too. A swarm of feeder dikes (fissures formed as the earth's crust stretched) here and in nearby Oregon was the source of the succession of intermittent lava flows that covered the entire Columbia Basin with layers of basalt, ending around 13 million years ago. More recent uplift of the Blue and Wallowa Mountains resulted in Hells Canyon—one of the deepest gorges in North America (8,000 feet), carved by the

Snake River a few miles south in Oregon. The depth of the Snake and Grande Ronde canyons in Washington is only modestly less. Both rivers retained their courses, downcutting through the thousands of feet of Columbia Platrau basalts as the mountains gradually rose. The incised meanders of the lower Grande Ronde River are a particularly striking testimony to its origins as a slow-moving stream on a level plain.

SNAKE RIVER CORRIDOR

Begin this all-day trip on US-12 at 23 miles east of Pomeroy. Look for **Chief Timothy Park** as you reach the Snake River at the bottom of Alpowa Grade. The park is operated by a concessionaire offering camping, boating, and picnic sites May 1–October 31. Along with the bay at the mouth of Alpowa Creek, the sheltered waters attract waterfowl, loons, grebes, and Bald Eagles in winter. During the closed season, you can enter the park on foot. It's worth a hike to look for Great Horned, Barn, and Northern Saw-whet Owls.

Continuing east on US-12 for 1.7 miles, find the entrance to **Chief Timothy Habitat Management Unit** (HMU) on the north side. There is an easy walking trail of about a half-mile past a Great Blue Heron rookery and a riparian area that is home to Bewick's Wren, Gray Catbird, Cedar Waxwing, nesting Yellow Warbler and Yellow-breasted Chat. Western Tanager, Black-headed Grosbeak, Lazuli Bunting, and Lesser Goldfinch are common. Continue east on US-12 toward Clarkston. In three miles, at Evans Road, a small pond and marsh east of the road is worth a check for Virginia Rail, Wilson's Snipe, and Marsh Wrens. In another three-quarters of a mile, check the cliffs for nesting Peregrine Falcons and, in winter, roosting Gray-crowned Rosy-Finches.

In a half-mile, turn left at the traffic light at SR-128 and then left to Hells Canyon Resort Marina, where there are often good looks at waterfowl, grebes, and gulls. Leaving the marina, turn left onto Port Drive; turn left on 13th Street, then right on Port Way, and continue to Granite Lake Park (parking and restrooms). The park offers good winter viewing for waterfowl. Wood Duck, Ring-necked Duck, both scaups, Common and Barrow's Goldeneyes, all three mergansers (Red-breasted is uncommon), and rarely, but annually, Surf and White-winged Scoters and Long-tailed Ducks may be seen.

The Clarkston Greenbelt Trail starts here and offers great birding for those who want to walk, jog, or bike. The trail continues up the Snake River to Asotin (11 miles). The birding is best in migration and winter, when waterfowl and gulls gather. To reach **Swallows Park**, go left on Ninth Street to Port Drive and turn left. Port Drive merges into Fifth Street; continue south on Fifth a half-mile to Diagonal Street. Veer right one block to Sixth Street (SR-129), taking it south 2.3 miles to the park entrance. There are public restrooms at the north and south parking areas. Check the lawns near the

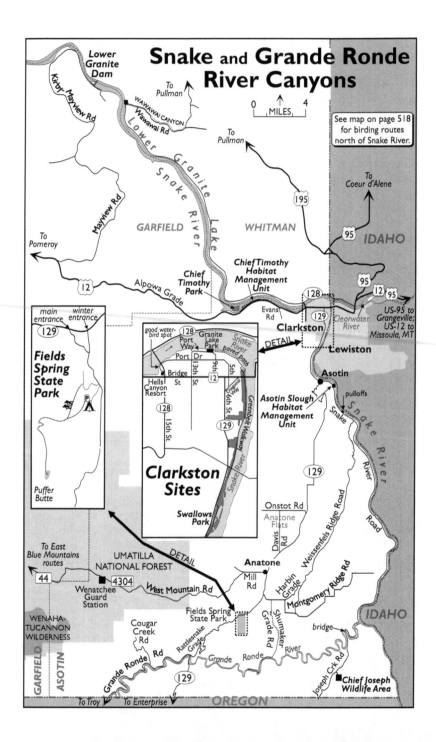

Snake and Grande Ronde River Canyons

north parking area for Eurasian Wigeon among the many American Wigeons. During migration, check the ever-present flocks of Canada Geese for Greater White-fronted, Snow, Ross's, and Cackling Geese. At the south parking area near the boat launch, scope the mud and sand islands for resting gulls. During winter, one may find unusual gulls among the many Ring-billed, California, and Herrings. Mew, Thayer's, Iceland, Lesser Black-backed, Glaucous-winged, and Glaucous Gulls are seen annually. The mud islands also provide the area's only reliable shorebird habitat during migration. Willet, Marbled Godwit, and Ruddy Turnstone have been seen.

Continue south from Swallows Park on SR-129 for 4.2 miles. Here, SR-129 bends 90 degrees right, but you should continue straight through Asotin on First Street, curving onto **Snake River Road** (Asotin CR-2090). A patch of riparian woodland along Snake River Road 0.9 mile south of the SR-129 junction, the **Asotin Slough Habitat Management Unit**, is attractive mainly during migration. Three miles from Asotin, two pulloffs to the left overlook gravel bars in the river that often hold resting gulls. Check the trees for kinglets and Lesser Goldfinches. Continuing south, look for Bald and Golden Eagles and Peregrine and Prairie Falcons.

Travel 20 miles south along Snake River Road to the bridge over the Grande Ronde River. Here, go left, crossing to Joseph Creek Road on the other bank of the winding Grande Ronde. In 3.1 miles, turn left into 9,735-acre **Chief Joseph Wildlife Area** (Discover Pass required). Park at the closed, gated road. Look for Wild Turkeys, particularly in morning or late afternoon. Say's Phoebes and Western Bluebirds nest here. Scan the surrounding cliffs for Bald Eagle (winter), Red-tailed Hawk, Golden Eagle, and Prairie Falcon. Bighorn Sheep, Elk, and Mule Deer are seen regularly. Spring and summer are particularly good in riparian areas along Joseph Creek.

Bird from the road as you continue two miles upstream to the Oregon state line. Warbling and Red-eyed Vireos, Yellow and MacGillivray's Warblers, Black-headed Grosbeak, Lazuli Bunting, and Bullock's Oriole are common. Winter brings Common Redpolls (irregular) and Pine Siskins. In fall and winter, many Townsend's Solitaires, Hermit Thrushes, American Robins, Varied Thrushes, and Evening Grosbeaks come to feed on the fruits of the gnarled hackberry trees.

ASOTIN-ANATONE LOOP

Start this wonderful half-day loop at either Asotin or Weissenfels Ridge Road, 4.4 miles south of Asotin, depending on the season. In spring and summer, the loop is best started from Weissenfels Ridge Road to take advantage of the morning sun at your back. In winter, take SR-129 from Asotin toward Anatone (pronounced *Anna-tone*).

Weissenfels Ridge Road leaves Snake River Road and follows Ten Mile Creek for 1.2 miles through riparian habitat that hosts nesting accipiters,

Red-tailed Hawks, and Great Horned Owls along with Warbling and Red-eyed Vireos and warblers. As the road leaves the creek, it climbs quickly through sage, rock, and grass, offering splendid views of the Snake River Canyon. Look for Chukar and Rock and Canyon Wrens. After a long three miles, the road tops off at a corral and fencelines, where there are Horned Larks and Western Meadowlarks. Near the ranch at the top (10km sign), a long stretch of utility poles and fenceposts have served as perches for Gyrfalcon in winter. This also is a good area for Golden Eagles and Prairie Falcons.

The next 4.5 miles of mixed stubble, grass, and grazing land is very productive. Western and Mountain Bluebirds nest in the boxes along the road, and Sage Thrashers have been seen here. In early morning and late afternoon, look for Short-eared Owls. Vesper, Lark, Savannah, and Grasshopper Sparrows are regular. In about eight miles, Harbin Grade Road joins from the right. This road is called Kiesecker Gulch Road on some maps, but the road signs read Harbin Grade. This road goes through riparian areas with House Wrens, a variety of warblers and Chipping Sparrows. Avoid this road in winter or when the temperature is below freezing: it can be treacherous. Both Harbin Grade and Weissenfels Ridge Road intersect with Montgomery Ridge Road, where you should turn right.

On Montgomery Ridge Road, you can either continue ahead to connect with SR-129, or you can take an interesting side trip onto **Shumaker Grade Road**, a graded, gravel road that switchbacks 3,000 feet down to the Grande Ronde River. Check for Common Poorwill, Warbling Vireo, Nashville, MacGillivray's, Yellow, and Yellow-rumped Warblers, and Western Tanager on the upper canyon sides, and for Chukar, Golden Eagle, Cliff Swallows, and Yellow-breasted Chat lower.

Return to Montgomery Ridge Road and turn left to reach SR-129, where you can turn left to go two miles to Fields Spring State Park or turn right to continue the loop (see below) back through Anatone to Asotin.

A mile after leaving Anatone, turn left onto Davis Road and proceed four miles north to Onstot Road, turning right to return to SR-129 in two miles. Known locally as **Anatone Flats**, this area is excellent in winter for Northern Harrier, Rough-legged Hawk, Prairie Falcon, and Northern Shrike. During irruption years, it's been very good for Snowy Owls. Sort through flocks of Horned Larks for Lapland Longspurs (rare) and Snow Buntings. When Onstot Road intersects with SR-129, turn left to return to Asotin in 13 miles. You may see Short-eared Owls in the fields and on the fenceposts. On the way down the steep, curving grade to Asotin, watch for Chukars.

FIELDS SPRING STATE PARK TO THE GRANDE RONDE RIVER

If you are arriving from the Blue Mountains via West Mountain and Mill Roads, watch the nest boxes along the road for Mountain Bluebirds. In the town of Anatone, turn right (south) onto SR-129, go 3.7 miles, and turn left onto Park Road. It is a half-mile to the entrance to **Fields Spring State Park** (Discover Pass required).

Perched near the rim of the Grande Ronde Canyon at the base of the Blue Mountains, the 445-acre park offers up a long list of birds in the relatively open forests of Douglas-fir, Grand Fir, Ponderosa Pine, and Western Larch. Look for Ruffed and Dusky Grouse, Great Horned Owl, Northern Pygmy-Owl, Rufous Hummingbird, Williamson's Sapsucker, Hairy, White-headed (uncommon), American Three-toed, and Pileated Woodpeckers, Olive-sided Flycatcher, Western Wood-Pewee, Hammond's, Dusky, and Pacific-slope Flycatchers, Cassin's Vireo, Mountain and Chestnut-backed Chickadees, Red-breasted, White-breasted, and Pygmy Nuthatches, Brown Creeper, Golden-crowned Kinglet, Swainson's and Hermit Thrushes, Orange-crowned, MacGillivray's, Yellow, Yellow-rumped, and Townsend's Warblers, Western Tanager, Lazuli Bunting, and Cassin's Finch.

A mile-long trail to **Puffer Butte** (elevation 4,500 feet) yields a spectacular view of Oregon, Idaho, and the Grand Ronde River. The trailhead is a few yards west of the main bathrooms in the campground. The trail climbs through a moist forest with an understory of shrubs and wildflowers to the broad, forested summit. Hike south on a rocky trail into the steppe vegetation below, where the birdlife includes Gray Partridge and Vesper and Lark Sparrows. Check for raptors such as Red-tailed Hawk, American Kestrel, and Prairie Falcon.

Beyond the state park, SR-129 twists down Rattlesnake Grade to the **Grande Ronde River**, losing 2,700 feet of elevation in nine miles. Look for Golden Eagle, Rock and Canyon Wrens, and Brewer's Sparrow on the way down. Elk may be seen on the far ridges. As one goes lower, Warbling and Red-eyed Vireos and Yellow Warblers are common in the riparian woodland of White Alder along Rattlesnake Creek. Everywhere in this region, Lazuli Buntings can be heard in brush patches on the dry, rocky slopes.

Where SR-129 crosses the river, Boggan's Oasis offers food, lodging, and restrooms, but no fuel. A WDFW launch site (Discover Pass required) by the bridge is a good spot for Western Tanager and Bullock's Oriole. Back across the bridge, turn left (west) onto Grande Ronde Road. In 4.6 miles, take Cougar Creek Road to the right. Red-eyed Vireos are present in the streamside to the creek crossing (1.7 miles). Return to Grande Ronde Road and continue birding west, looking for Bald Eagle nests along the way. Stop at the bridge over Menatchee Creek to look for American Dippers nesting under the bridge. Retrace the route, returning on SR-129 to Anatone. The road continues on to Asotin and then to US-12 in Clarkston. (See the side trip to Anatone Flats on page 515.)

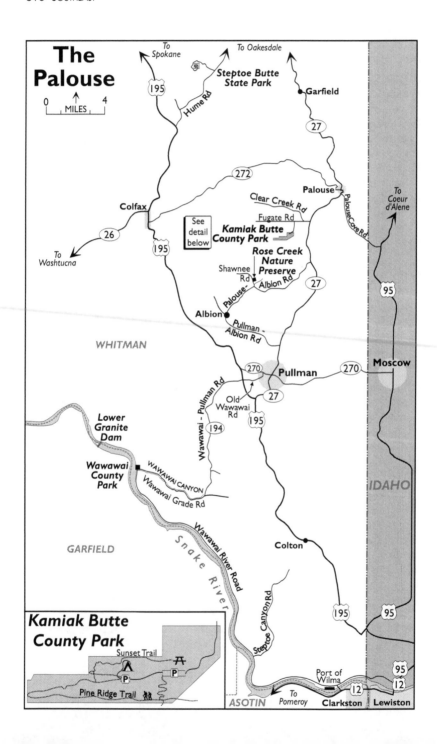

THE PALOUSE

by Joe Lipar and John Roberson
revised by Mike Clarke

The Palouse (pronounced puh-LOOSE) is a 3,000-square-mile district covered by piles of windblown, yellowish-brown silt called loess (rhymes with muss). Each successive ice-age flood deposited thick layers of sediment in the lowest parts of the Columbia Basin to the southwest. Later, as the waters retreated, silt was carried by the prevailing southwest winds and dropped here, forming the Palouse Hills. In some places, the underlying basalt is covered by as much as 200 feet of loess. The rolling hills that the French-Canadian explorers and fur traders called la pelouse (grassland) were once a realm of bunchgrass with a high forb component. Ravines had dense stringers of Douglas Hawthorn and scattered Ponderosa Pine. North slopes were clothed in snowberry, serviceberry, and Woods Rose. This landscape has virtually all been converted to one of Washington's most bountiful agricultural regions. Wheat is king. Only a few remnant tracts of native vegetation survive. Gone, too, are the huge numbers of Sharp-tailed Grouse, replaced by introduced Gray Partridge and Ring-necked Pheasant.

Pullman is home to Washington State University. Exploring the extensive mature plantings of conifers and deciduous trees in the older residential districts and on campus is worthwhile during migration. Winter brings flocks of Bohemian Waxwings and, in some years, Red and White-winged Crossbills and Pine Grosbeaks. Black-billed Magpies are a common but showy presence. Away from Pullman, the following sites, though relatively small, have some of the best remaining patches of natural Palouse brush and grassland habitat.

An outstanding site close to Pullman is **Rose Creek Nature Preserve**, a 22-acre property of the Palouse-Clearwater Environmental Institute. Take SR-27 (Grand Avenue) 2.2 miles north from SR-270 to Pullman-Albion Road. Turn left, go five miles to Albion, and turn right on Main Street. Go 2.8 miles on Palouse-Albion Road (Old Albion Road on some maps) to Shawnee Road (aka Four Mile Road). Turn left, make another left in 0.1 mile to stay on Shawnee Road, and continue 0.3 mile to the tiny parking area on the right at the entrance of the preserve. Look for the trailhead just west of the parking area. The trail winds through a remnant of Palouse riparian vegetation, featuring thickets of hawthorn, Bitter Cherry, and Cow Parsnip. More than 250 species of plants are recorded here, attracting mammals such as White-tailed Deer, Porcupine, and Coyote. Birds are abundant and varied. Permanent residents include California Quail, Gray Partridge, Northern Harrier, Barn Owl, Great Horned Owl, American Kestrel, and Bewick's Wren. The riparian area comes alive in spring and summer— look then for Calliope Hummingbird, Western Wood-Pewee, Willow Flycatcher, Eastern Kingbird, Warbling and Red-eyed Vireos (migrant only), Ruby-crowned Kinglet (migrant), Western Bluebird, Veery (scarce), Gray Catbird, and MacGillivray's and Yellow Warblers.

After birding the streamside woodland and scrub of Rose Creek, walk along Shawnee Road for birds of the open country and pine forests. The 750-acre tract west for the next mile is the university's **Hudson Biological Reserve**. A mosaic of Ponderosa Pine forests, riparian areas, and steppe makes this a very birdy place, especially in spring and summer. In addition to the list for Rose Creek, look for Swainson's (summer) and Rough-legged Hawks (winter), Hairy Woodpecker, Dusky Flycatcher, Pygmy Nuthatch, and Townsend's Solitaire (winter, in junipers). Taken together, the Hudson Biological Reserve and Rose Creek make up one of the largest contiguous parcels of the Palouse ecosystem still in a natural or near-natural state.

Kamiak Butte is just northeast of Rose Creek. To get there, go back to Palouse-Albion Road, turn left, and go 5.1 miles to SR-27. Turn left and go 2.9 miles to Clear Creek Road. (If coming from Pullman, this is 11.8 miles north on SR-27 from its intersection with SR-270.) Turn left, keeping left again at the first junction (0.3 mile). You are now on Fugate Road. Go another 0.7 mile to the Kamiak Butte County Park entrance and turn left; parking is a mile up the hill. Park hours are dawn to dusk. A three-mile loop trail goes uphill from the parking area to the top of the butte, then along the crest and down to the upper parking area. At the top are magnificent views of the surrounding Palouse. Shorter hikes on a network of trails near the parking area are also possible.

Interesting resident species in the Ponderosa Pine and Douglas-fir forests and extensive brushy understory include Mountain Chickadee, Red-breasted, White-breasted, and Pygmy Nuthatches, Brown Creeper, Pacific Wren, Bewick's Wren, and Red and White-winged (during irruptions) Crossbills. Summer visitors of note are Red-naped Sapsucker, Olive-sided, Pacific-slope, and Cordilleran (not as yet incontrovertibly documented in Washington, but this site is a good bet) Flycatchers, Cassin's Vireo, Western Bluebird, Swainson's and Hermit Thrushes, MacGillivray's Warbler, Western Tanager, Black-headed Grosbeak, and Cassin's Finch. Owling can be very good (best in March and April), mainly for Great Horned, Northern Pygmy-, Barred, and Northern Saw-whet Owls. As an isolated stand of trees in an otherwise mostly unforested landscape, Kamiak Butte offers the possibility of rare strays in migration. Black-billed Cuckoo and Hooded Warbler are two examples of vagrants that have been noted here.

A similar eminence is **Steptoe Butte**, an isolated, 3,612-foot hill of 400-million-year-old quartzite. From the junction of US-195 and SR-270 (two miles west of Pullman), go north 14.2 miles on US-195 to the junction with SR-26 in Colfax. Continue north on US-195 and in 6.6 miles turn right onto Hume Road. Stay right with Hume where it meets Scholz Road (1.2 miles); another 3.9 miles brings you to the Steptoe Butte State Park, on the left. The terrain is mostly open, lacking the forest cover of Kamiak Butte. However, deciduous trees and brush around the picnic area at the base of the butte provide habitat for a number of species including Northern Flicker, Western Wood-Pewee, Bewick's Wren, and Bullock's Oriole.

As you wind your way to the top and a spectacular overlook of the Palouse (4.2 miles), look for Gray Partridge, Western and Eastern Kingbirds, Brewer's, Vesper, Savannah, and Grasshopper Sparrows, Black-headed Grosbeak, and Lazuli Bunting. A few Black-throated Sparrows have been found here in summer with increasing frequency in recent years. Raptors are conspicuous, especially in March–April and again in September–October. Late fall through early spring can bring Common Redpolls to the base of the butte and Snow Buntings to the grassy slopes. Gray-crowned Rosy-Finches are regularly seen near the peak.

South of Pullman is **Wawawai Canyon**, which descends 2,000 feet to the Snake River. To reach it, take Davis Way (SR-270) west from Grand Avenue (SR-27) in Pullman 0.6 mile, turn left onto Old Wawawai Road, and continue 1.7 miles to US-195. Go straight across the highway (becomes Wawawai-Pullman Road) and continue to a T-intersection in 10 miles. Turn right into Wawawai Canyon on Wawawai Grade Road. Birding the riparian habitat along the creek and on brushy hillsides to the south can be profitable in spring and early summer. Near brushy terrain in particular, pull safely off the road and look for Willow Flycatcher, Say's Phoebe, Eastern Kingbird, Black-capped Chickadee, Gray Catbird, Yellow Warbler, Yellow-breasted Chat, Spotted Towhee, Black-headed Grosbeak, and Lazuli Bunting. In about 2.5 miles, before crossing to the north side of canyon, check the Mount Mazama ash deposit (from the violent explosion 6,600 years ago that led to the formation of Oregon's Crater Lake) on the north side of the creek for nesting Bank Swallows. Continuing on another 2.5 miles, you will reach **Wawawai County Park** on the Snake River (Lower Granite Lake). Here you may find Bewick's Wren in the brush, Yellow-breasted Chat, and Bullock's Oriole nesting in the campground, or migrants in the ornamental plantings.

South from here, Wawawai River Road follows the Snake River through a gorge; various pullouts allow safe stops. Chukar, Red-tailed Hawk, Say's Phoebe, and Rock and Canyon Wrens are common on the high cliffs. Bald (winter) and Golden Eagles and Prairie Falcons might be seen. In 16.8 miles, pass Steptoe Canyon Road and continue to follow the river along Wawawai River Road. As you approach Clarkston, scan the water for American White Pelicans in summer and waterfowl, including Barrow's Goldeneye, in winter. Checking brushy areas along the road in early spring can produce White-throated and Golden-crowned Sparrows, difficult to find in the region. A range expansion of Lesser Goldfinches in recent years has made them now relatively common here. Gulls roost along this section of the river in the winter, and occasionally Iceland (Kumlien's), Thayer's, Lesser Black-backed, Glaucous, and Glaucous-winged Gulls can be found amongst the more common Ring-billed, California, and Herring. The Port of Wilma, 8.0 miles from Steptoe Canyon Road, is a good spot to view gulls coming in to roost in the evening. From here, continue travelling east for 4.5 miles and turn left onto US-12. Follow signs for US-95 to US-195 north to return to Pullman.

BIRDS OF WASHINGTON BAR GRAPHS

by Tom Aversa
revised by Ryan Merrill

Included here are all the species of annual occurrence in Washington—i.e., rare or better as determined by the abundance definitions on the facing page. Westside (W) and Eastside (E) have separate graphs if status differs; otherwise they are combined (WE). The Cascade Crest is the division. Species graphed on one side of the state but not on the other are no more than Accidental in occurrence on the side where they are not graphed—i.e., a species must attain the frequency of Casual or better on a second side of the state in order to be graphed there. The status of *all* species recorded in the state, graphed or not, is discussed in the Annotated Checklist. The status of each species has been updated as needed from the first edition of this guide to reflect changes during the past decade.

Most species have pronounced habitat associations; some occur quite locally. For example, Black Oystercatcher is shown as Uncommon in Western Washington but in fact can be found only along rocky saltwater shorelines. For a more complete picture, the bar graphs should be used in conjunction with the Annotated Checklist. These two sections were reviewed and revised conjointly, and complement one another. A primary source of information in the preparation of both has been the database of records maintained since 1993 by the Washington Field Notes compilers (Russell Rogers, succeeded in 2001 by Tom Aversa, and in 2009 by Ryan Merrill), derived from reports submitted to them by field observers.

Abundance definitions strike a balance between the probability of finding (seeing or hearing) the bird and its actual abundance. Certain retiring species or those in hard-to-cover habitats may be numerically more abundant yet more difficult to detect than certain other, numerically scarcer ones with exhibitionist tendencies, or that frequent exposed habitats.

In 2000, ABA's Checklist Committee drafted a set of standard definitions for the bar graphs used in the ABA Birdfinding Guide series. Their aim was to create a set of sensible, easily understandable definitions for the terminology used to denote the abundance and findability of birds, which would be useful not only within ABA, but also for the birding community continent-wide. It is

ABA's hope that, over time, those persons or groups publishing field checklists, annotated checklists, and other compilations dealing with abundance of bird species will adopt these definitions. When standardized terms gain widespread acceptance, disparities between the various meanings of terms such as *fairly common* and *casual* will disappear, giving birders a realistic understanding of a species' actual abundance as well as a good idea of how likely finding it might be. ABA encourages widespread adoption of these abundance definitions; no specific permission is necessary.

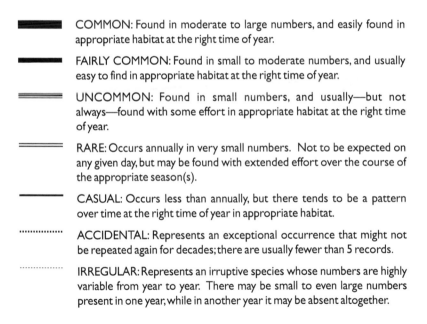

COMMON: Found in moderate to large numbers, and easily found in appropriate habitat at the right time of year.

FAIRLY COMMON: Found in small to moderate numbers, and usually easy to find in appropriate habitat at the right time of year.

UNCOMMON: Found in small numbers, and usually—but not always—found with some effort in appropriate habitat at the right time of year.

RARE: Occurs annually in very small numbers. Not to be expected on any given day, but may be found with extended effort over the course of the appropriate season(s).

CASUAL: Occurs less than annually, but there tends to be a pattern over time at the right time of year in appropriate habitat.

ACCIDENTAL: Represents an exceptional occurrence that might not be repeated again for decades; there are usually fewer than 5 records.

IRREGULAR: Represents an irruptive species whose numbers are highly variable from year to year. There may be small to even large numbers present in one year, while in another year it may be absent altogether.

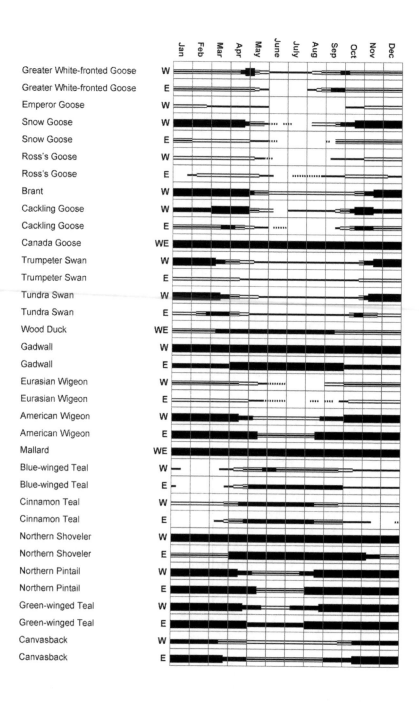

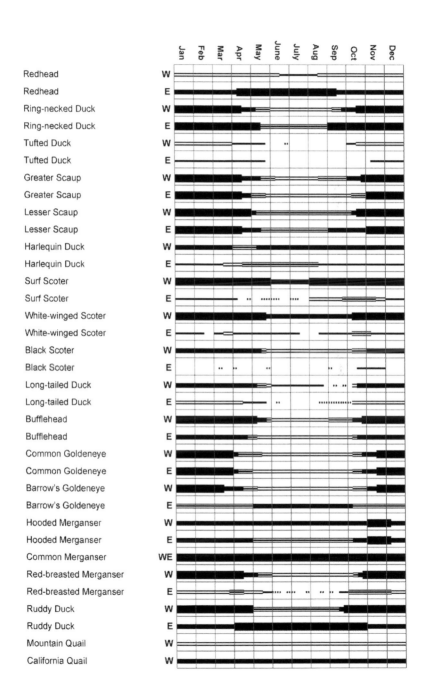

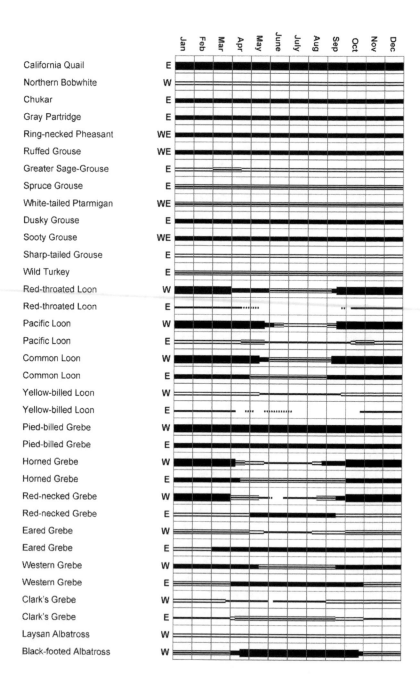

		Jan	Feb	Mar	Apr	May	June	July	Aug	Sep	Oct	Nov	Dec
California Quail	E												
Northern Bobwhite	W												
Chukar	E												
Gray Partridge	E												
Ring-necked Pheasant	WE												
Ruffed Grouse	WE												
Greater Sage-Grouse	E												
Spruce Grouse	E												
White-tailed Ptarmigan	WE												
Dusky Grouse	E												
Sooty Grouse	WE												
Sharp-tailed Grouse	E												
Wild Turkey	E												
Red-throated Loon	W												
Red-throated Loon	E												
Pacific Loon	W												
Pacific Loon	E												
Common Loon	W												
Common Loon	E												
Yellow-billed Loon	W												
Yellow-billed Loon	E												
Pied-billed Grebe	W												
Pied-billed Grebe	E												
Horned Grebe	W												
Horned Grebe	E												
Red-necked Grebe	W												
Red-necked Grebe	E												
Eared Grebe	W												
Eared Grebe	E												
Western Grebe	W												
Western Grebe	E												
Clark's Grebe	W												
Clark's Grebe	E												
Laysan Albatross	W												
Black-footed Albatross	W												

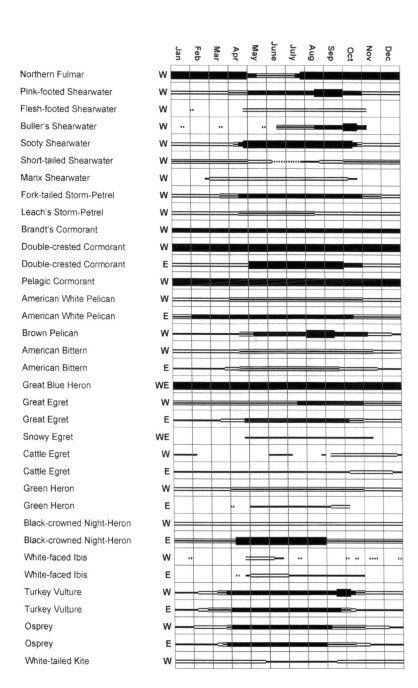

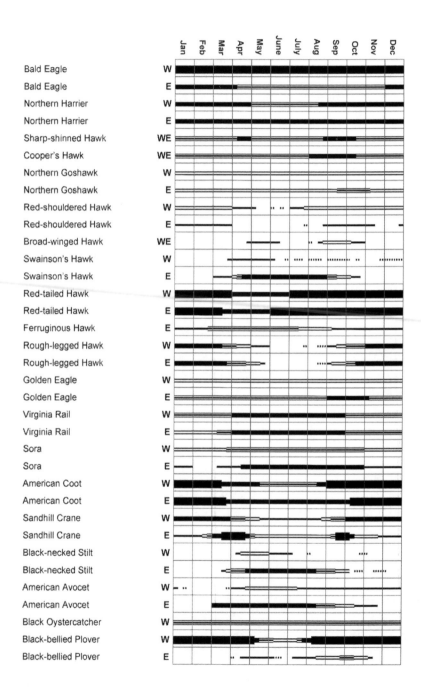

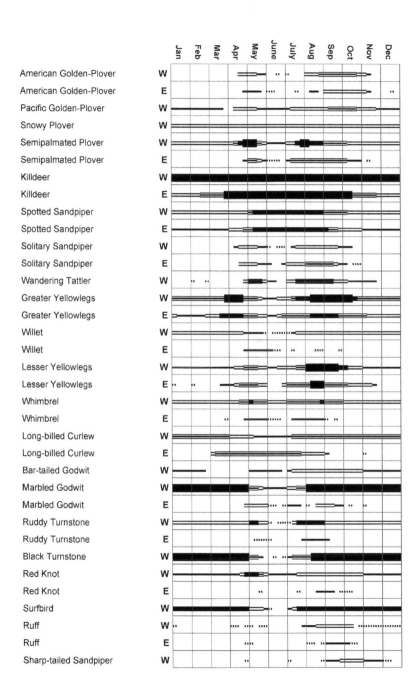

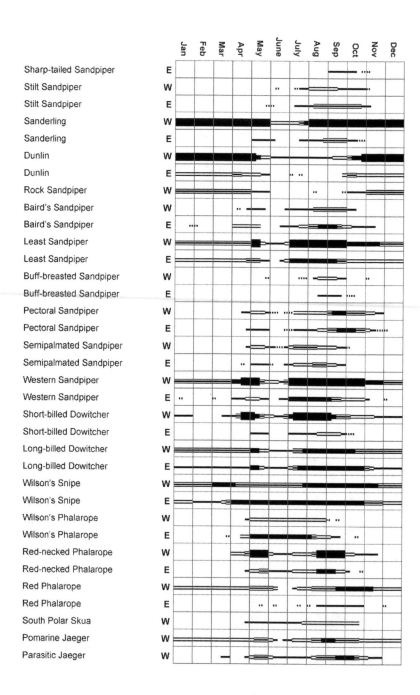

		Jan	Feb	Mar	Apr	May	June	July	Aug	Sep	Oct	Nov	Dec
Sharp-tailed Sandpiper	E												
Stilt Sandpiper	W												
Stilt Sandpiper	E												
Sanderling	W												
Sanderling	E												
Dunlin	W												
Dunlin	E												
Rock Sandpiper	W												
Baird's Sandpiper	W												
Baird's Sandpiper	E												
Least Sandpiper	W												
Least Sandpiper	E												
Buff-breasted Sandpiper	W												
Buff-breasted Sandpiper	E												
Pectoral Sandpiper	W												
Pectoral Sandpiper	E												
Semipalmated Sandpiper	W												
Semipalmated Sandpiper	E												
Western Sandpiper	W												
Western Sandpiper	E												
Short-billed Dowitcher	W												
Short-billed Dowitcher	E												
Long-billed Dowitcher	W												
Long-billed Dowitcher	E												
Wilson's Snipe	W												
Wilson's Snipe	E												
Wilson's Phalarope	W												
Wilson's Phalarope	E												
Red-necked Phalarope	W												
Red-necked Phalarope	E												
Red Phalarope	W												
Red Phalarope	E												
South Polar Skua	W												
Pomarine Jaeger	W												
Parasitic Jaeger	W												

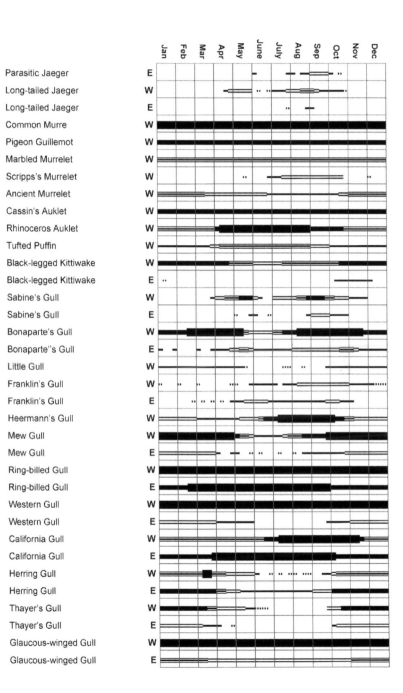

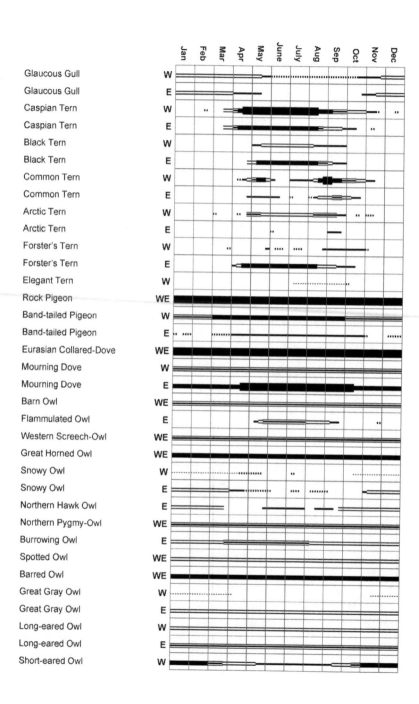

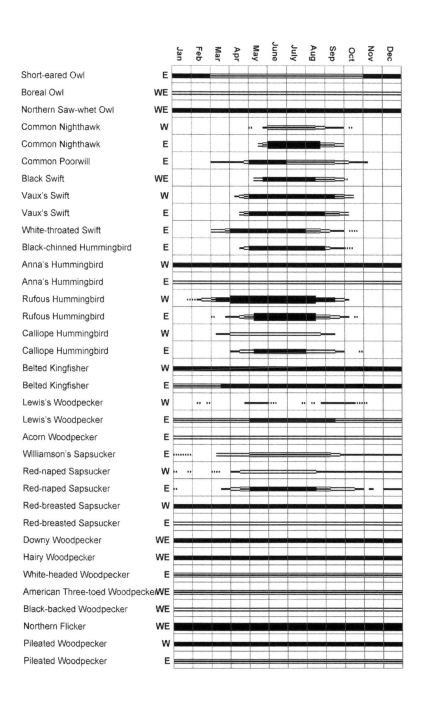

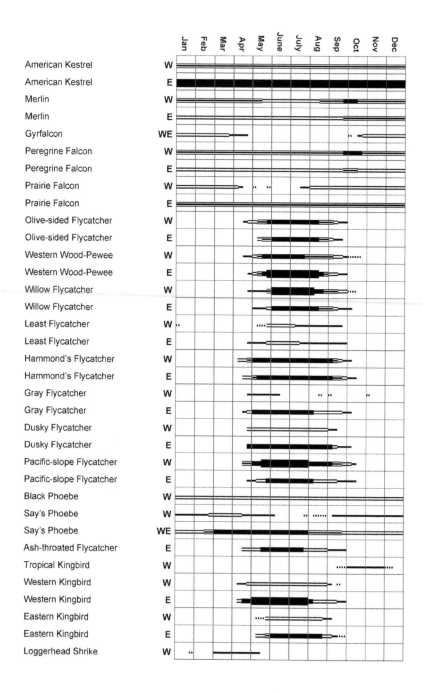

		Jan	Feb	Mar	Apr	May	June	July	Aug	Sep	Oct	Nov	Dec
American Kestrel	W												
American Kestrel	E												
Merlin	W												
Merlin	E												
Gyrfalcon	WE												
Peregrine Falcon	W												
Peregrine Falcon	E												
Prairie Falcon	W												
Prairie Falcon	E												
Olive-sided Flycatcher	W												
Olive-sided Flycatcher	E												
Western Wood-Pewee	W												
Western Wood-Pewee	E												
Willow Flycatcher	W												
Willow Flycatcher	E												
Least Flycatcher	W												
Least Flycatcher	E												
Hammond's Flycatcher	W												
Hammond's Flycatcher	E												
Gray Flycatcher	W												
Gray Flycatcher	E												
Dusky Flycatcher	W												
Dusky Flycatcher	E												
Pacific-slope Flycatcher	W												
Pacific-slope Flycatcher	E												
Black Phoebe	W												
Say's Phoebe	W												
Say's Phoebe	WE												
Ash-throated Flycatcher	E												
Tropical Kingbird	W												
Western Kingbird	W												
Western Kingbird	E												
Eastern Kingbird	W												
Eastern Kingbird	E												
Loggerhead Shrike	W												

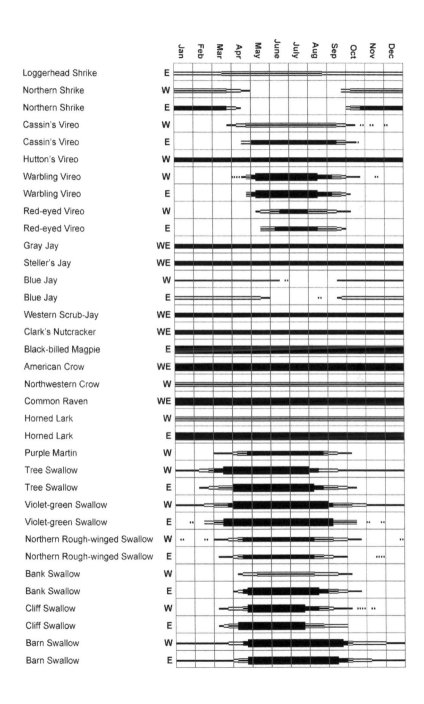

	Jan	Feb	Mar	Apr	May	June	July	Aug	Sep	Oct	Nov	Dec
Loggerhead Shrike	E											
Northern Shrike	W											
Northern Shrike	E											
Cassin's Vireo	W											
Cassin's Vireo	E											
Hutton's Vireo	W											
Warbling Vireo	W											
Warbling Vireo	E											
Red-eyed Vireo	W											
Red-eyed Vireo	E											
Gray Jay	WE											
Steller's Jay	WE											
Blue Jay	W											
Blue Jay	E											
Western Scrub-Jay	WE											
Clark's Nutcracker	WE											
Black-billed Magpie	E											
American Crow	WE											
Northwestern Crow	W											
Common Raven	WE											
Horned Lark	W											
Horned Lark	E											
Purple Martin	W											
Tree Swallow	W											
Tree Swallow	E											
Violet-green Swallow	W											
Violet-green Swallow	E											
Northern Rough-winged Swallow	W											
Northern Rough-winged Swallow	E											
Bank Swallow	W											
Bank Swallow	E											
Cliff Swallow	W											
Cliff Swallow	E											
Barn Swallow	W											
Barn Swallow	E											

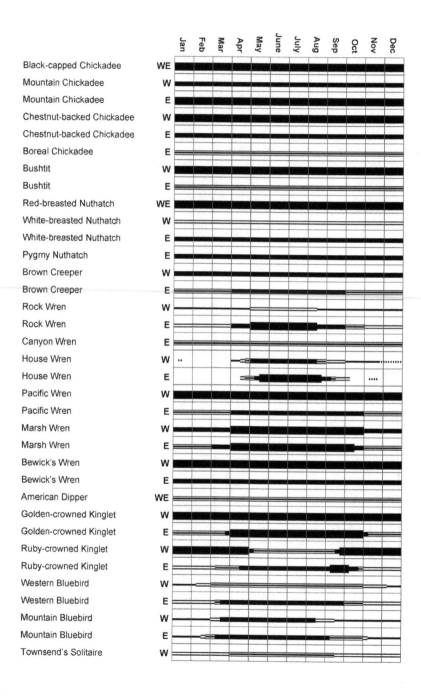

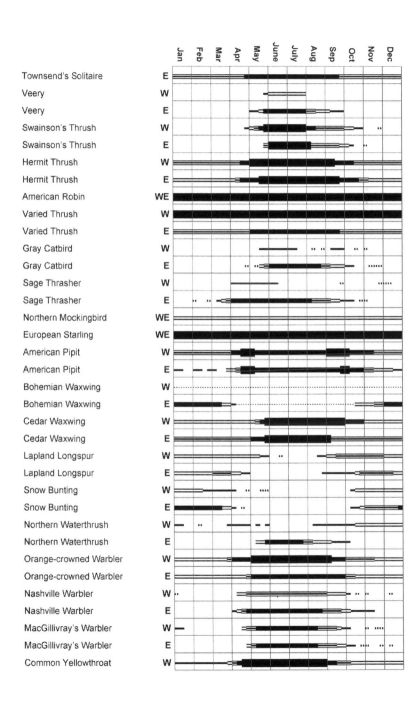

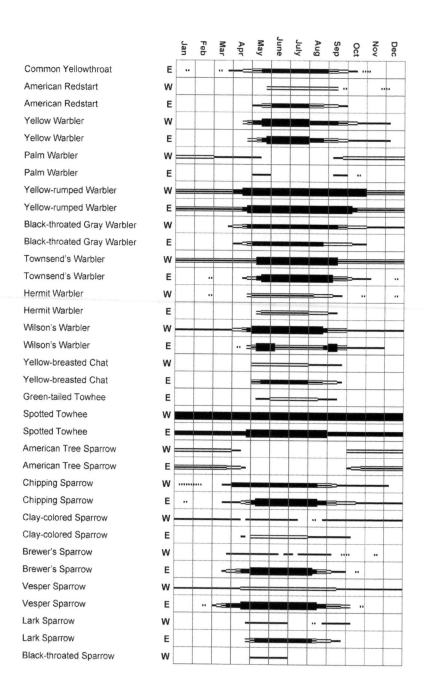

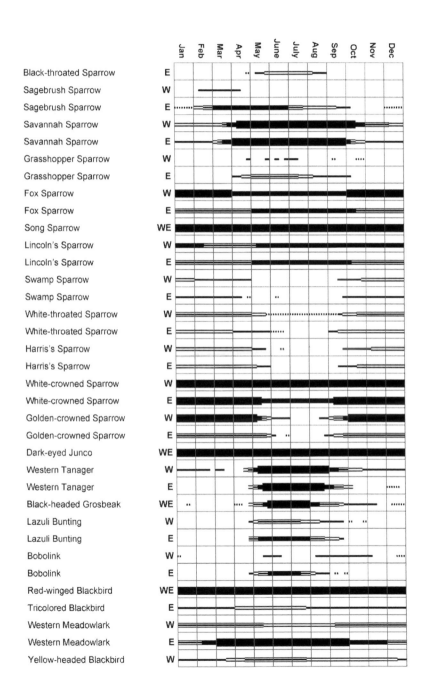

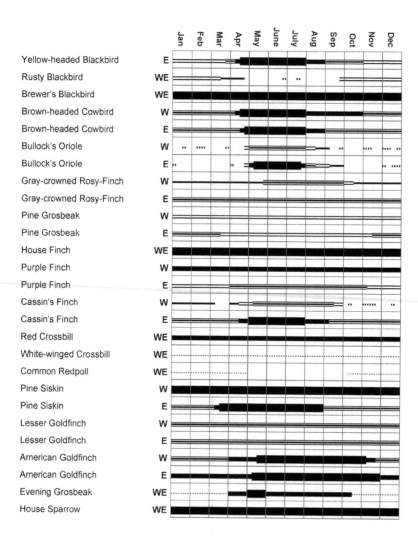

ANNOTATED CHECKLIST

by Andy Stepniewski and Hal Opperman
revised by Matt Bartels

The 510 species listed here have been recorded at least once in Washington. Italicized common names indicate species on the Review List of the Washington Bird Records Committee (WBRC). Observations of any of these species, or of species not on this list, should be reported to the WBRC with written details and any supporting evidence such as photographs and sound recordings. (Submit a report on-line at *http://wos.org/*) Reports of the WBRC are the authority for records of rarities used in the compilation of this list. Abundance terms (common, fairly common, etc.) are employed here in a manner consistent with those for the bar graphs of seasonal occurrence—see page 522 for definitions.

Fulvous Whistling-Duck *Dendrocygna bicolor* — One bird shot from flock of 10 at Grays Harbor in October 1905.

Taiga Bean-Goose *Anser fabalis* — One bird observed at Hoquiam over 12-day period in December 2002. In addition, a 1993 Bean Goose (also in Hoquiam) was not described thoroughly enough to distinguish Taiga from Tundra Bean-Goose.

Greater White-fronted Goose *Anser albifrons* — Uncommon winter resident, usually with Canada Geese. Fairly common to common in migration. Impressive migration along outer coast in late April. Large flocks of migrants occasionally noted August–September, taking direct overwater route from breeding grounds in southwestern Alaska to coastal Washington, thence across Cascades to staging area in Klamath Basin en route to central California for winter. Many stop briefly at McNary NWR.

Emperor Goose *Chen canagica* — Casual visitor along tidewater shorelines in Western Washington. Most records from sheltered waters along Pacific, North Olympic Coasts, smaller number from Puget Sound, Vancouver Lowlands.

Snow Goose *Chen caerulescens* — Common winter resident on Skagit, Stillaguamish River deltas, nearby farmlands. These birds comprise genetically distinct portion of Wrangel Island breeding population that migrates south along Pacific Flyway, winters mainly from Fraser River delta south to Port Susan. Birds noted in small numbers in Eastern Washington (principally fall, but hundreds now winter at Umatilla NWR) belong to breeding populations in northeast Siberia, Alaska, western Canadian Arctic that utilize Central Flyway to winter mostly in southern Oregon, Central Valley of California. Blue-morph birds uncommon in the Skagit River delta and rare elsewhere in Washington.

Ross's Goose *Chen rossii* — Rare (almost uncommon), probably increasing migrant in Eastern Washington, predominantly spring. Most frequent, numerous in Southeast where sometimes seen in small flocks. Rarer on Westside in winter or spring (usually singles). Most migrants take direct route from Klamath Basin northeast into Saskatchewan in April, back again in fall, passing east of Washington; off-course birds expected April, occasionally other seasons. Blue form accidental in Washington.

Brant *Branta bernicla* — Alaska-breeding **Black Brant** (subspecies *nigricans*) common migrant, local winter resident on saltwater bays, closely tied to beds of Eelgrass. Large numbers at Dungeness, Willapa NWRs, usually a few at Alki Beach, West Point in Seattle. Accidental fall–winter in Eastern Washington. **Gray-bellied Brant** (thought to be distinct taxon but not yet described), from Melville Island in Canadian High Arctic, winters on Padilla Bay.

Cackling Goose *Branta hutchinsii* — Smaller form of group previously classified as part of Canada Goose, with three subspecies regularly occurring in migration and winter. More common in western Washington in winter, but all subspecies have been found in the east. **Taverner's Cackling Goose** (subspecies *taverneri*): on average, largest Cackling Goose subspecies in Washington (slightly smaller than Lesser Canada Goose). Breeds northern, western Alaska, winters mostly in Willamette and Lower Columbia River valleys and Columbia Basin with smaller but growing numbers in Puget Trough. **Aleutian Cackling Goose** (subspecies *leucopareia*): small, darkish, with fairly prominent white neck ring. Between Taverner's and Minima in size but slightly paler than either. Breeds on a few Aleutian Islands, winters mostly in California and Oregon. Once near extinction; protection has aided recovery in recent years—now uncommon at Willapa NWR, on the coast, and even in Puget Sound in fall migration, with a few wintering. Casual in eastern Washington. **Ridgway's Cackling Goose** (subspecies *minima*): tiny (half again larger than Mallard), dark-breasted, short-necked, with characteristic yelping call. Most have indistinct neck ring. Migrates from breeding grounds in western Alaska to wintering sites from Puget Sound through Willamette and Lower Columbia River valley. Uncommon in Eastern Washington. Wintering grounds have shifted dramatically north in recent decades from central California to our state. Population small, protected; appears stable. **Richardson's Cackling Goose** (subspecies *hutchinsii*) accidental in winter with only a few records from the Columbia Basin.

Canada Goose *Branta canadensis* — Larger forms of group previously given this name. Common year round as migrant, breeder, wintering resident. Four subspecies present and abundant. **Moffitt's** (Western) **Canada Goose** (subspecies *moffitti*): largest, palest of light-breasted forms. Year-round resident statewide; numbers greatly augmented in winter with British Columbia breeders. Canada Geese did not breed in Western Washington until transplanted birds of this race established sedentary populations beginning in 1950s. Now widespread, common. **Lesser Canada Goose** (subspecies *parvipes*): medium-sized, difficult to distinguish from Taverner's Cackling Goose. Nests from eastern Alaska across Yukon, Northwest Territories; common migrant in Washington on way to wintering sites in Willamette Valley, Lower Columbia River Valley. Common wintering subspecies in Columbia Basin, less common Westside. **Dusky Canada Goose** (subspecies *occidentalis*): dark-breasted form (close to Moffitt's in size), usually lacks neck ring. Breeds in relatively small numbers on Copper River delta in Alaska, winters primarily in southwestern Washington (e.g., Julia Butler Hansen, Ridgefield, Steigerwald NWRs), Willamette Valley of Oregon. **Vancouver Canada Goose** (subspecies *fulva*): often considered inseparable from Dusky, but slightly larger. Breeds in coastal rainforest zone from southeast Alaska to northern Vancouver Island; some southward movement in winter through western Washington to Willamette Valley.

Trumpeter Swan *Cygnus buccinator* — Once close to extinction, essentially disappeared from Washington. Began to winter again locally in Mount Vernon area in early 1970s, spread as numbers increased. Now common in winter in northwestern

Washington lowlands. Readily found on farm fields on Skagit/Samish Flats, also Snohomish River valley, Chehalis River floodplain. Regular in smaller numbers on lakes elsewhere in Western Washington, especially on outer coast. Still rare east of Cascades; reintroduction at Turnbull NWR came close to failing, but a persistent small group now breeds annually. Small numbers sometimes winter on ponds near Ellensburg. Lead pollution from fishing, hunting continues as major danger.

Tundra Swan *Cygnus columbianus* — Common migrant, winter resident on Westside. Many winter on Skagit/Samish Flats (with Trumpeters), also Ridgefield, Franz Lake NWRs in Southwest. East of Cascades in spring, impressive flocks often noted high in sky flying northeastward over broad front: Blue Mountains, Palouse, Northeast. Fairly common spring at stopover sites (e.g., McNary NWR, Atkins Lake, Turnbull NWR, Calispell Lake), less numerous fall. In addition to our regular subspecies, "Whistling" (subspecies *columbianus*), the Siberian breeding Bewick's Tundra Swan (subspecies *bewickii*) rare in winter, usually mixed with other Whistling Tundra Swans.

Whooper Swan *Cygnus cygnus* – One bird observed in Snohomish and Skagit Counties from December 2006–January 2007, and then in Whatcom County in February 2007.

Wood Duck *Aix sponsa* — Fairly common resident statewide. Numbers dwindle in winter, especially east.

Gadwall *Anas strepera* — Common resident statewide, especially numerous around Puget Sound. Much less common on Eastside in winter.

Falcated Duck *Anas falcata* — Four records, all from near coast: January 1979 from Naselle River, July 1993 at Sequim, February–March 2002 and February 2005, both at Samish Island.

Eurasian Wigeon *Anas penelope* — Uncommon to locally fairly common winter resident west of Cascades—more winter in Western Washington than anyplace else in Lower 48. Especially numerous near Samish, Dungeness River estuaries. Can often be picked out in American Wigeon flocks in city parks. Rare but regular winter resident east of Cascades (usually not difficult to find in Tri-Cities), more often noted in spring. Eurasian X American hybrids occur regularly, at rate of about five percent of Eurasians.

American Wigeon *Anas americana* — Common winter resident, migrant statewide. Uncommon breeder east of Cascades; rare, local west.

Mallard *Anas platyrhynchos* — Common resident statewide, winter numbers higher east than west until waters freeze. Astronomical numbers on Columbia River during hunting season.

Blue-winged Teal *Anas discors* — Fairly common summer resident in Eastern Washington, uncommon in Puget Trough. Fairly common in migration. Casual early-winter resident.

Cinnamon Teal *Anas cyanoptera* — Fairly common summer resident of ponds, marshes, sloughs in Eastern Washington, less common in Western Washington. Rare winter on Westside.

Northern Shoveler *Anas clypeata* — Common summer resident, principally in Columbia Basin, Puget Trough. Common migrant. Common winter resident west, uncommon east (locally fairly common in warmer parts of Columbia Basin).

Northern Pintail *Anas acuta* — Uncommon summer resident, much more local west of Cascade Crest. Common migrant statewide. Common winter resident in Western Washington lowlands, especially Puget Trough; common to uncommon on Eastside, with numbers, wintering localities varying greatly year to year.

Garganey *Anas querquedula* — Three records: Skagit Flats (April 1961), Chehalis River floodplain near Satsop (April–May 1991), Richland (December 1994).

Baikal Teal *Anas formosa* – Four records: Kent, King County (December 2004–April 2005); Grant County (May 2008); Ridgefield NWR, Clark County (January 2009); Ferndale, Whatcom County (March 2009).

Green-winged Teal *Anas crecca* — Continental North American subspecies *carolinensis* fairly common but local summer resident east; rare, local west. Common migrant, winter resident on both sides of Cascades. **Common Teal** (Eurasian-breeding subspecies *crecca*) rare winter visitor (mainly Western Washington), usually with flocks of *carolinensis*.

Canvasback *Aythya valisineria* — Uncommon summer resident on lakes in Eastern Washington; rare west. Fairly common (west) to common (east), but local, winter resident. Can be abundant in vicinity of grain terminals on Columbia, Snake River reservoirs. East of Cascades many gather in early spring migration in large numbers at places such as the Walla Walla River delta.

Redhead *Aythya americana* — East of Cascades, common summer, fairly common winter resident. Rare on Westside, largely restricted to fresh water.

Ring-necked Duck *Aythya collaris* — Uncommon summer resident on Eastside (most numerous in Northeast), uncommon to rare on Westside. Common migrant, winter visitor statewide. Largely restricted to fresh water.

Tufted Duck *Aythya fuligula* — Rare winter resident (mostly November–April) in lowlands, usually with flocks of scaups or Ring-necked Ducks. Dependable stakeout occasionally found, sometimes returning for successive winters. Several interior records, but great majority from west of Cascades. Most reliable places probably around Grays Harbor, Everett, Columbia River from gorge to mouth, around Priest Rapids Dam—but records widely scattered. Several records of hybrids, presumably with undetermined scaup species.

Greater Scaup *Aythya marila* — Common migrant, winter resident in Western Washington, especially on sheltered marine waters. In Eastern Washington, locally common migrant, winter resident on Columbia, Snake River reservoirs, especially near grain terminals.

Lesser Scaup *Aythya affinis* — Uncommon, local summer resident east (especially Northeast), west (especially Ridgefield NWR). Common migrant, winter resident on low-elevation fresh-, saltwater bodies statewide.

Steller's Eider *Polysticta stelleri* — Three records: one bird stayed at Port Townsend for nearly four months (October 1986–February 1987); another at Walla Walla River delta in September 1995; one found in Edmonds for only one day in September 2006.

King Eider *Somateria spectabilis* — Sixteen records extend from late October to July, all on the Westside and all but three on inland marine waters. Exceptions include two in Clallam County (December 1988 and July 2014) and one in Grays Harbor County seen for three winters beginning in 2009.

Common Eider *Somateria mollissima* — Three records: Port Angeles (August 2004); Tatoosh Island (April 2005); Westport (October 2012).

Harlequin Duck *Histrionicus histrionicus* — Fairly common winter resident of coastal waters with rocky substrates. Good sites include Salt Creek County Park, Ediz Hook, Sequim Bay, Fort Worden, Fort Flagler, west side of Whidbey Island, Alki Beach in West Seattle. Scarce on coast for only short period in spring, as many males return to salt water soon after breeding. Uncommon summer resident on rivers at low to middle elevations in Olympic, Cascade, Selkirk Mountains. Good sites include

Stehekin River upstream from Stehekin, Methow River near Winthrop, Tieton River below Rimrock Lake, Naches River above Cliffdell, Sullivan Creek above Sullivan Lake.

Surf Scoter *Melanitta perspicillata* — Common winter resident of coastal waters, in sheltered bays as well as rougher waters just off breakers. Non-breeding flocks local in summer, especially Penn Cove, Drayton Harbor. Uncommon in Eastern Washington—mostly fall on Columbia, Snake River reservoirs, Grand Coulee lakes.

White-winged Scoter *Melanitta fusca* — Similar to Surf Scoter in status, distribution, except rare in Eastern Washington in fall.

Black Scoter *Melanitta americana* — Fairly common but local winter resident on marine waters with rocky bottom, rare in summer. Good sites include Ocean Shores, Ediz Hook, Fort Worden, Fort Flagler, Lummi Bay, Alki Beach in West Seattle. Casual in Eastern Washington fall.

Long-tailed Duck *Clangula hyemalis* — Fairly common but local winter resident on sheltered marine waters. Good sites include Ediz Hook, Dungeness Spit, Sequim Bay, Protection Island, Fort Worden, Fort Flagler, Point Roberts, Birch Bay, west side of Whidbey Island, deepwater sounds off Orcas Island. Rare in Eastern Washington—mostly fall on Columbia, Snake River reservoirs, Grand Coulee lakes.

Bufflehead *Bucephala albeola* — Common winter resident, migrant west, fairly common east; found on fresh, salt water. Breeds on a few lakes in Northeast, most reliable site Big Meadow Lake.

Common Goldeneye *Bucephala clangula* — Common winter resident on fresh, salt water statewide. Rare breeder east of Cascades in northern part of state, e.g., lakes in Sinlahekin Valley, Soap, Beth Lakes in Okanogan, Big Meadow Lake in Northeast (probably most reliable site). Rare summer on Westside, mainly at sewage ponds. Identification confusion with female Barrow's Goldeneye clouds true status as breeding species.

Barrow's Goldeneye *Bucephala islandica* — In Western Washington, common but local winter resident on sheltered saltwater bays, to much lesser extent freshwater lakes (usually with rocky bottoms, shores). Highly associated with pilings—e.g., on parts of Hood Canal. Uncommon winter resident in Eastern Washington, most at grain ports on Columbia, Snake Rivers, a few on flowing rivers (especially Columbia within Hanford Reach). Fairly common summer resident at mid-elevations on forested lakes (nesting in tree cavities near lakeshore) in Cascades, Okanogan Highlands, Selkirks. Colonies nest in cliff cavities in treeless areas at Lenore Lake in Grand Coulee, Jameson Lake in Moses Coulee, thus akin to Iceland, Labrador breeders.

Smew Mergellus albellus — Two records of adult males near Columbia River in Skamania County in successive winters (December 1989, January–February 1991), considered to be same individual. Another at McKenna (Pierce County) in March 1993.

Hooded Merganser *Lophodytes cucullatus* — Fairly common summer resident in Western Washington lowlands, mainly around Puget Trough. On Eastside, uncommon summer resident, mostly in Northeast. Fairly common (briefly common fall) in migration, winter across state, although numbers fall off on Eastside when freezing reduces available habitat.

Common Merganser *Mergus merganser* — Common resident year round, nesting in tree cavities along lowland rivers, lakes. In winter, also found on deep, clear saltwater bodies, larger lakes, lower Columbia River.

Red-breasted Merganser *Mergus serrator* — Common winter resident on inland marine waters, protected coastal bays. Uncommon fall migrant and casual winter resident in Eastern Washington along the Columbia River, Snake River, and Banks Lake.

Ruddy Duck *Oxyura jamaicensis* — Fairly common to locally common summer resident in Eastern Washington, highest concentration around Potholes; also breeds uncommonly in southern Puget Trough. Common winter resident of freshwater habitats in Western Washington lowlands, especially around Puget Sound; local on salt water, mostly in mud-bottomed bays. Fairly common winter resident in Eastern Washington.

Mountain Quail *Oreortyx pictus* — Rare, local year-round resident. Native population in Skamania, Klickitat Counties apparently extirpated. Possibly native population in Snake River drainage close to extirpation—a few coveys still reported occasionally along Grande Ronde River, aided by recent reintroductions. Widely introduced in Western Washington late 19th–early 20th centuries, thrived on logged-over land in early successional stages as forests were left to regenerate unaided. Modern industrial forests inhospitable, quail now reduced to scattered populations from Kitsap Peninsula southwest to Mason, northwestern Thurston, southeastern Grays Harbor Counties. Secretive, unpredictable.

California Quail *Callipepla californica* — Introduced from California. Common, conspicuous (east), fairly common, local (west) at lower elevations except in dense forests—especially farmlands, brushy places, parks, lightly developed residential areas. Absent from dryland wheat fields, where replaced by Gray Partridge. Present populations firmly established on Eastside, perhaps declining on Westside.

Northern Bobwhite *Colinus virginianus* — Introduced from eastern U.S. Rare year-round resident of South Sound Prairies, where populations probably not self-sustaining. Frequently released in small numbers in other parts of state but rarely survives for more than one or two seasons.

Chukar *Alectoris chukar* — Introduced from Near East. Fairly common year-round resident on rocky slopes of Eastern Washington lowlands, especially near cliffs. Often difficult to find. Best looked for near dawn, dusk when calling most intense, comes to roadsides for grit. Good sites include Huntzinger Road south of Vantage, Lower Grand Coulee (especially slopes north of Sun Lakes State Park), SR 129, between Asotin and Anatone.

Gray Partridge *Perdix perdix* — Introduced from Europe. Fairly common year-round resident of Eastern Washington, mostly in wheat fields, nearby brushy areas but also on native steppe on higher plateaus, ridges. Elusive. One good strategy: cruise wheat-field roads near dawn, dusk for birds gathering roadside grit, listen for peculiar, scratchy call. Also check around grain elevators.

Ring-necked Pheasant *Phasianus colchicus* — Introduced from Old World. Fairly common year-round resident of wheat fields, brushy edges, shrub-steppe, parks, similar open landscapes at lower elevations on east of Cascades. Uncommon, declining, west of Cascades. Presumably securely established in many parts of state but continuing releases make true status difficult to determine.

Ruffed Grouse *Bonasa umbellus* — Fairly common year-round resident of deciduous woodlands statewide, mostly at lower elevations. Absent from Columbia Basin below Ponderosa Pine zone. Best looked for in spring when drumming.

Greater Sage-Grouse *Centrocercus urophasianus* — Rare, local, year-round resident of Big Sagebrush habitats with good cover of native grass, difficult to find except at lek sites. Two populations survive—about 900 birds in central Douglas County (especially south, west of Leahy Junction, around Jameson Lake), estimated 200 birds on Yakima Training Center. A WDFW project to establish a third population in Lincoln County is ongoing.

Spruce Grouse *Falcipennis canadensis* — Uncommon year-round resident of subalpine forests in Northeast, Okanogan, barely west across Cascade Crest in Mountain

Hemlock in Whatcom County. Small, disjunct population on mid- to upper Cascades slopes in northwestern Yakima County and Skamania County near Mount Adams. Often difficult to find due to elusive behavior—definitely an asset for survival of this tame-as-a-barnyard-chicken species. Best looked for along gravel roads in September–October as birds gather grit, especially early or late in day, or in late July–August along streams as hens lead broods to insect-rich foraging areas. Harts Pass good bet, also Salmo Pass, FR-39 from Roger Lake to Long Swamp.

White-tailed Ptarmigan *Lagopus leucura* — Uncommon, local summer resident in alpine areas of Cascades. Highly cryptic, sits tight, hence usually missed. Best odds: mossy, herb-rich seeps above treeline in late July–August where hens lead chicks to forage for insects. Good sites include Mount Rainier (Panorama Point, Burroughs Mountain, Fremont Peak), Slate Peak, Chopaka Mountain. Wintering sites unknown, but probably wanders downslope in fall, especially to thickets of Sitka Alder.

Dusky Grouse *Dendragapus obscurus* — Interior breeding species of the pair split from Blue Grouse. Prefers more open areas in and near forests than Sooty Grouse. Fairly common, mostly at mid-to-high altitude from central Okanogan county east through Selkirks and south into the Blue Mountains. Birds show characteristics of hybridization when range meets with range of Sooty Grouse.

Sooty Grouse *Dendragapus fuliginosus* — Coastal breeding species of the pair split from Blue Grouse. Prefers denser, wetter forests. Fairly common throughout Western Washington (mostly at altitude but present in forests from sea level to alpine) and across the Cascade Crest until meeting apparent hybrid zone with Dusky. Never a sure thing, but Hurricane Ridge (Clallam County) comes close.

Sharp-tailed Grouse *Tympanuchus phasianellus* — Rare year-round resident in grassy shrub-steppe habitats in northern Columbia Basin, Okanogan (Douglas, Lincoln, Okanogan Counties). Once widely distributed throughout Eastern Washington grasslands, now close to extirpation. Remaining sites largely on private property; information on whereabouts difficult to obtain. Colville Indian Reservation has most remaining birds. Seen occasionally in winter at Swanson Lakes Wildlife Area (Lincoln County), West Foster Creek Unit of Wells Wildlife Area, along Bridgeport Hill Road (Douglas County), and at the Scotch Creek Wildlife Area outside Conconully (Okanogan County).

Wild Turkey *Meleagris gallopavo* — Introduced from eastern North America. Uncommon to locally fairly common year-round resident of open forests, farmlands east of Cascades, usually near streams. Populations fluctuate with fresh releases. In Western Washington probably increasing but difficult to evaluate wild status.

Red-throated Loon *Gavia stellata* — Common migrant, winter resident on protected marine waters, sometimes close to shore in shallow water. High numbers winter at Bowman Bay/Deception Pass. Tokeland, Grays Harbor (especially Ocean Shores), Hood Canal Bridge area, Sequim Bay, Dungeness NWR, Padilla Bay also excellent sites. Rare migrant, winter resident on Westside lowland lakes, lower Columbia River. Casual on Eastside reservoirs in winter.

Arctic Loon *Gavia arctica* — Four records: Priest Rapids Lake, January–March 2000; Edmonds, December 2000–January 2001; Point-No-Point, April 2007; Tokeland, May 2014.

Pacific Loon *Gavia pacifica* — Common spring, fall migrant along outer coast, often in impressive numbers—especially May, late September–October. Common winter resident on deeper inland marine waters; attracted in large numbers to tidal rips, e.g., at Deception Pass, Rosario Strait, Spieden Channel, Cattle Pass, Obstruction Pass, Admiralty Inlet, Point No Point. Uncommon migrant, rare winter resident in Eastern Washington, mainly on Columbia River reservoirs.

Common Loon *Gavia immer* — Common migrant, winter resident on sheltered coastal waters; fairly common migrant, winter resident on Columbia River reservoirs. Uncommon, local summer resident of secluded lakes in northern half of state on both sides of Cascades.

Yellow-billed Loon *Gavia adamsii* — Rare migrant, winter resident in Western Washington, usually on sheltered coastal waters, frequently in fairly shallow bays. Elusive, often not staying in any one location for extended periods. Semi-regular at Westport, Ocean Shores, Neah Bay, John Wayne Marina on Sequim Bay, various spots in north Puget Trough. Casual winter resident in Eastern Washington along Columbia River. Casual west in summer.

Pied-billed Grebe *Podilymbus podiceps* — Common (west) to fairly common (east) summer resident in marshes, wetlands, shallow lakes with emergent vegetation; absent from mountains, heavily forested zones. Migrant statewide, including mountain lakes. In winter, common resident in western lowlands, less common, local east. Strong preference for freshwater habitats, rarely in saltwater bays.

Horned Grebe *Podiceps auritus* — Common winter resident west of Cascades on protected marine waters, occurring singly or in small groups; small numbers on large freshwater lakes. Uncommon to locally fairly common on Columbia River reservoirs in winter. Uncommon summer resident on Eastside, nests rarely in Okanogan, Northeast.

Red-necked Grebe *Podiceps grisegena* — Common winter resident west of Cascades on protected marine waters, highest abundance in Port Townsend area; a few also on large freshwater lakes. Fairly common breeder on forested lakes in Okanogan, Northeast (e.g., Sinlahekin Valley, Molson Lake, Big Meadow Lake, Sullivan Lake).

Eared Grebe *Podiceps nigricollis* — Fairly common summer resident in shallow Eastern Washington alkaline ponds, pothole lakes with emergent vegetation. Known sites include Turnbull NWR, Molson Lake, Muskrat Lake, Big Goose Lake, Fishtrap Lake. Large numbers congregate in fall, a few birds winter, on Soap Lake (Grant County). Uncommon, local winter resident on Westside, mostly on sheltered marine waters.

Western Grebe *Aechmophorus occidentalis* — Fairly common but local summer resident on large lakes in Eastern Washington. Nests on Moses Lake, Potholes Reservoir, Banks Lake (Steamboat Rock State Park). Spectacular courtship display peaks late April–early May. Uncommon winter resident on Columbia River reservoirs. Common winter resident on marine waters, occupying variety of habitats from sheltered bays to rough waters just beyond breakers. Local winter resident on large Western Washington lowland lakes (e.g., Lake Washington). Wintering numbers declining.

Clark's Grebe *Aechmophorus clarkii* — Uncommon, local summer resident in Columbia Basin, invariably with Westerns. Nests on Moses Lake, Potholes Reservoir, Banks Lake (Steamboat Rock State Park). Rare migrant, winter resident on lakes, protected marine waters elsewhere in state.

White-capped Albatross *Thalassarche cauta* — First North American record collected 35 miles off Quillayute River mouth in September 1951. Second Washington record, on pelagic trip off Westport in January 2000.

Laysan Albatross *Phoebastria immutabilis* — Rare pelagic visitor, best October–April. Numbers steadily increasing in Northeastern Pacific since 1990s, including recent establishment of breeding colony off northwestern Mexico.

Black-footed Albatross *Phoebastria nigripes* — Year-round pelagic visitor, uncommon only in winter when most are nesting in mid-subtropical Pacific. Hundreds often recorded on summer–fall trips off Westport—best way to see this species in Lower 48.

Short-tailed Albatross *Phoebastria albatrus* — Once common off Pacific Coast, disappeared from Washington waters before 1900. With partial recovery of breeding population in Western Pacific in recent years, has become rare offshore, with 13 records in the past 20 years, annual in last seven years.

Northern Fulmar *Fulmarus glacialis* — Fairly common to common pelagic visitor, usually well offshore, with definite peak in fall (beginning August). Numbers vary year to year. Both color morphs occur, with lightest birds representing about 10 percent of total. In winter, recorded on inland marine waters (Straits of Juan de Fuca, Georgia), also often as beached birds on outer coast.

Providence Petrel *Pterodroma solandri* – Only Washington record—and one of only a few for North America—observed in September 1983 off Westport.

Murphy's Petrel *Pterodroma ultima* — Seen mostly far offshore, with seven records for Washington, most in April and May. Probably more regular in seldom-visited waters.

Mottled Petrel *Pterodroma inexpectata* — Observations increasing, probably regular early spring and late fall visitor off outer coast. One record from the Puget Sound in November 2009 is the only sighting on inland marine waters. Several records of birds found dead on Pacific beaches.

Hawaiian Petrel *Pterodroma sandwichensis* — Two records, one from offshore in Grays Harbor County, September 2008, and one from offshore in Pacific County May 2014.

Cook's Petrel *Pterodroma cookii* — One bird found dead on Pacific beach December 1995.

Pink-footed Shearwater *Puffinus creatopus* — Fairly common to common pelagic visitor May–October, rare winter.

Flesh-footed Shearwater *Puffinus carneipes* — Rare pelagic visitor, most likely late July–October but scattered records in other warm months. Almost always seen near shrimp trawlers.

Great Shearwater *Puffinus gravis* — Six records, all off coast, and all in August, September, and October.

Wedge-tailed Shearwater *Puffinus pacificus* — Two records, both of them found dead on Ocean Shores beaches, one, September 1999, and one, January 2011.

Buller's Shearwater *Puffinus bulleri* — Fairly common to common pelagic visitor August–October.

Sooty Shearwater *Puffinus griseus* — Common offshore visitor in warmer months, from just beyond breakers to pelagic waters. Rare winter. Most commonly seen shearwater from shore. Immense numbers pass by August–September, sometimes thousands entering Grays Harbor, Willapa Bay. Uncommon in Strait of Juan de Fuca, rare in Puget Sound, particularly during, after fall storms.

Short-tailed Shearwater *Puffinus tenuirostris* — Uncommon late summer–winter pelagic visitor, numbers variable year to year. Rare in inland marine waters during, after fall storms (particularly late October–November), where records outnumber Sooty Shearwater.

Manx Shearwater *Puffinus puffinus* — First securely documented records in North Pacific Ocean from Westport, Ocean Shores in September of 1990. Since then, records have multiplied rapidly along North American Pacific Coast. Manx Shearwater now annual in small numbers in Washington. Most records from outer coastline, with only a few well offshore, and a few from inland marine waters. Reliably found near Destruction and Anderson Islands in summer. Dates range February–October with peak in June–July.

Wilson's Storm-Petrel *Oceanites oceanicus* — Four records, all in pelagic waters in the summer months (July 1984, September 2001, July 2003, August 2005).

Fork-tailed Storm-Petrel *Oceanodroma furcata* — Southern subspecies *plumbea* nests on islets off Outer Olympic Coast but rarely seen from shore. Fairly common spring through early fall on pelagic trips. Seen almost annually on inland marine waters east to Admiralty Inlet, most likely after storms. Aleutian-breeding subspecies *furcata* known from a few specimens.

Leach's Storm-Petrel *Oceanodroma leucorhoa* — Common breeder on islets off Outer Olympic Coast but virtually never noted from shore. Leaves breeding sites under cover of darkness, heads out to deeper, warmer waters than those reached by most pelagic boats. On Westport pelagic trip found fairly regularly late July–early August, hit-or-miss late April–early May. Occasionally seen on inland marine waters, usually after storms.

Ashy Storm-Petrel *Oceanodroma homochroa* – Two records, both seen in pelagic waters: June 2006 and April 2008.

Red-billed Tropicbird *Phaethon aethereus* — One bird collected off Westport in June 1941.

Magnificent Frigatebird *Fregata magnificens* — One Eastside record, from Umatilla NWR in July 1975. One Westside record, bird seen at several locations on Puget Sound, South Coast, mouth of Columbia River for much of October 1988.

Blue-footed Booby *Sula nebouxii* — Two records: One bird collected in Puget Sound off Everett in September 1935; one seen over Samish Island, Skagit County in August 2006.

Brown Booby *Sula leucogaster* — Ten records in the state, all since 1997. Records spread across all seasons and divided evenly between marine waters (on pelagic trips) and inland marine waters.

Brandt's Cormorant *Phalacrocorax penicillatus* — Large numbers of non-breeders in summer along North Olympic Coast, in San Juans, northern Puget Trough. Breeding records from small number of rocks and promontories on Outer Olympic Coast, also at Cape Disappointment. Fairly common to locally common winter resident on marine waters (uncommon in southern Puget Trough). Good winter sites include Point No Point, Possession Bar, Port Susan, Hale Passage, deeper channels in San Juans. Frequents deeper water, more tidal rips than Double-crested or Pelagic.

Double-crested Cormorant *Phalacrocorax auritus* — Common summer resident along saltwater coastlines including inland marine waters, locally in Columbia Basin, Pend Oreille River valley. Large numbers winter in Western Washington, much smaller numbers east. Only cormorant seen in freshwater habitats.

Red-faced Cormorant *Phalacrocorax urile* — One bird seen at mouth of Elwha River in May 1999.

Pelagic Cormorant *Phalacrocorax pelagicus* — Common year-round resident on marine waters. Prefers deep, clear waters to shallow bays.

American White Pelican *Pelecanus erythrorhynchos* — Fairly common year-round resident along Columbia River, nearby reservoirs, lakes in South Central Washington—most numerous late summer–early fall, least numerous winter. Increasing, spreading; noted regularly east along Snake River to Clarkston north to Bridgeport, Banks Lake. In 1994, resumed breeding near Wallula after 60-year hiatus in state. Strays to Western Washington regularly, in small numbers, at any season. Recently, a breeding colony has appeared on Miller Sands Island, just outside Wahkiakum County, in the Oregon portion of the mouth of the Columbia River.

Brown Pelican *Pelecanus occidentalis* — Common, apparently increasing post-breeding summer–fall visitor along outer coast, particularly conspicuous at Westport, Ocean Shores. Has made remarkable recovery since 1970s, when populations crashed. In fall, uncommon in Strait of Juan de Fuca, casual in Puget Sound—a very few have persisted well into winter. Recorded east.

American Bittern *Botaurus lentiginosus* — Uncommon, local, possibly declining summer resident in extensive marshes statewide. Rare winter. Good bet at Ridgefield, Steigerwald, and Nisqually NWRs in Western Washington, Toppenish NWR east of Cascades.

Great Blue Heron *Ardea herodias* — Common year-round resident statewide. Nesting colonies declining in some areas due to habitat loss, nest predation by burgeoning Bald Eagle population.

Great Egret *Ardea alba* — Fairly common summer resident at Potholes Reservoir. Uncommon elsewhere in Columbia Basin, but breeding colonies appearing at new sites such as Toppenish NWR and Hanford Reach. Fairly common late-summer–fall visitor, uncommon winter resident in Southwest, also along outer coast north to Grays Harbor.

Snowy Egret *Egretta thula* — Casual to rare visitor to Eastern, Western Washington, less frequent in recent years after being near-annual during the 1980s and 1990s. Records from late April to early December, with most in spring (peak May).

Little Blue Heron *Egretta caerulea* — Six records: Three westside records of immatures: October 1974–January 1975 (Whatcom), October 1989 (Whidbey Island), and September 2014 (Skagit). Three eastside records: One adult near Ellensburg in June 2002, one adult in Douglas County, August 2010, and one immature in Spokane County in November 2014.

Cattle Egret *Bubulcus ibis* — Casual to rare (irregularly uncommon) late-fall post-breeding visitor to lowlands on both sides of Cascades, mainly in fields. Most disappear in cold winter weather. Casual spring–summer. Decreasing in recent years, with only about five reports in the last five years.

Green Heron *Butorides virescens* — Once casual (first nested 1939), now uncommon summer resident of sloughs, swamps in lowland Western Washington; rare winter. Rare in Eastern Washington.

Black-crowned Night-Heron *Nycticorax nycticorax* — Common but local breeding resident of Columbia Basin; winters in small numbers. Rare and local on Westside.

Yellow-crowned Night-Heron *Nycticorax violacea* — Two records: Walla Walla May–June 1993, Wenatchee September 2001.

White Ibis *Eudocimus albus* — One record, from Pacific County in late December 2000–January 2001.

Glossy Ibis *Plegadis falcinellus* – One record, from Nisqually NWR in May 2005.

White-faced Ibis *Plegadis chihi* — Rare and irregular visitor on both sides of Cascades, mostly May–June. Sometimes appears in large flocks. Several pairs attempted nesting at Lake Kahlotus in 2001.

Turkey Vulture *Cathartes aura* — Fairly common summer resident of open country in Westside lowlands, along lower east slopes of Cascades. Uncommon, local in Southeast; nearly absent from much of Columbia Basin. Common migrant across Strait of Juan de Fuca in fall, many arriving in vicinity of Salt Creek County Park after passage south from Vancouver Island.

California Condor *Gymnogyps californianus* — Noted along Columbia River by Lewis-Clark Expedition in 1805, from Wind River to ocean. Many other reports from various parts of state across 19th century, last from September 1897 at Coulee City. Large numbers of condors once came to Columbia to feast on salmon carcasses in fall spawning season. Nesting, though hypothesized, not demonstrated north of California.

Osprey *Pandion haliaetus* — Fairly common, increasing migrant, summer resident statewide. Large numbers nest semi-colonially at mouth of Snohomish River in Everett, along Pend Oreille River at Usk. Casual winter.

White-tailed Kite *Elanus leucurus* — Rare, local winter resident in Southwest. Recently nearly absent from state. After steady increase in population through mid-2000s, population has largely disappeared by mid-2010s and long-term trends are unclear. Occupies bottomlands, open fields, rank grasslands as far north at maximum range as Chehalis River drainage in Lewis, Thurston, Grays Harbor counties. Rare in summer (first nesting record Raymond 1988). Traditionally most easily found in Wahkiakum County near Julia Butler Hansen NWR. Casual wanderer northward in western lowlands, especially late winter–spring.

Bald Eagle *Haliaeetus leucocephalus* — Common year-round resident in Western Washington lowlands, mostly along coasts. Breeding numbers increased dramatically in last decades. Densest breeding population on San Juan Islands. Famous early-winter concentration on Skagit River near Marblemount, attracted to spawning salmon. High numbers also winter on Samish, Skagit, Stillaguamish River deltas. In Eastern Washington, uncommon breeder in Okanogan, Northeast (mostly along Okanogan, Sanpoil, Kettle, Columbia, Colville, Pend Oreille Rivers). Numbers east of Cascades highest in winter as Canadian lakes freeze, forcing many birds south.

Northern Harrier *Circus cyaneus* — Fairly common (east), uncommon, local (west) summer resident in grassland habitats; fairly common to locally common winter resident in similar habitats statewide when free of deep snow.

Sharp-shinned Hawk *Accipiter striatus* — Uncommon year-round resident in conifer-forest landscapes statewide. Most nest in relatively remote localities where can be secretive, difficult to find. In winter, descend from higher elevations (or farther north), concentrate near sources of songbird prey such as feeders in towns. Fairly common migrant, especially fall.

Cooper's Hawk *Accipiter cooperii* — Uncommon, probably increasing year-round resident in open forests (conifer, mixed, deciduous) throughout state, especially in riparian settings. In nesting season, outnumbers Sharp-shinned in lowlands, around towns; reverse true in winter. Fairly common migrant, especially fall.

Northern Goshawk *Accipiter gentilis* — Rare summer resident in mountains wherever mature forests occur. Declining due to loss of habitat. Probably rarest in Olympic Mountains, Southwest; most common at mid-elevations along east slopes of Cascades, in Okanogan Highlands, Selkirk, Blue Mountains. Difficult to locate in breeding season—occasionally chanced upon soaring over nesting territory, particularly mid-morning. Uncommon fall migrant along high mountain ridges. Rare to locally uncommon winter resident in lowlands, mainly east of Cascades—especially wooded areas close to waterfowl or pheasant concentrations.

Red-shouldered Hawk *Buteo lineatus* — Rare winter resident of lowland riparian forests in Southwest; expanding northward from Oregon. Regular (1–2 birds) each winter in recent years at Ridgefield NWR, probably increasing elsewhere along lower Columbia River. Recent records northward to Kent Valley, Skagit Game Range, Neah Bay, eastward to riparian bottomlands in South Central.

Broad-winged Hawk *Buteo platypterus* — Rare migrant statewide; much more frequent fall (annual in recent years). Most fall sightings from hawk observatory at Chelan Ridge. A few seen regularly each fall from observatory at Rocky Point on southern tip of Vancouver Island, headed south across Strait of Juan de Fuca—indicating largely undetected southbound migration through Western Washington.

Swainson's Hawk *Buteo swainsoni* — Fairly common summer resident in Eastern Washington, occupying agricultural fields, moister shrub-steppe grasslands; uncommon in lowermost, driest portions of southern Columbia Basin. Formerly widespread in prairies with scattered trees for nesting. Has adapted to irrigated alfalfa, hay farming, dryland wheat fields, nesting wherever windbreaks or clumps of trees available nearby. Several hundred pairs nest in Columbia Basin, future seems reasonably secure. Casual in spring migration west.

Red-tailed Hawk *Buteo jamaicensis* — Common year-round resident in most habitats statewide, except dense forest. Numbers augmented in migration, winter with visitors from north, interior of continent, including uncommon **Harlan's Hawk** (*harlani*) and possibly **Krider's Hawk** (*krideri*), though reports of the latter are hard to distinguish from other, more likely, subspecies.

Ferruginous Hawk *Buteo regalis* — Uncommon, local summer resident in Columbia Basin, typically nesting on coulee walls in most arid portions. Winters casually in Walla Walla region. Declining due to loss of habitat. Fewer than 50 pairs remain in state. Some may be adapting to forage on irrigated fields with high rodent populations, if disturbance-free nest sites available nearby. Hanford Site best, but much of it off-limits to birders. Other known sites: Juniper Dunes Wilderness Area, Palouse Falls, Sprague Lake, Crab Creek east of town of Wilson Creek. Recorded west.

Rough-legged Hawk *Buteo lagopus* — Fairly common winter resident. Local west of Cascades, most likely on Samish/Skagit Flats. In Eastern Washington, especially in dryland wheat fields, Kittitas Valley.

Golden Eagle *Aquila chrysaetos* — Uncommon, declining, year-round resident of cliffs, rugged terrain from low to mid-elevations on Cascades east slopes, Okanogan Highlands, Selkirks, Snake River Canyon, Blues. Rare resident in San Juan Islands, Olympics, locally on west slopes of Cascades. Fairly common migrant along alpine ridges fall. In winter, some descend to open country in lowlands.

Yellow Rail *Coturnicops noveboracensis* — Three records: Skagit River delta in November 1935, Columbia Basin (Adams County) in April 1969, and Ridgefield NWR (Clark County) in May 2007.

Virginia Rail *Rallus limicola* — Year-round resident of freshwater, brackish marshes. Fairly common summer; numbers lower in winter, especially east of Cascades.

Sora *Porzana carolina* — Uncommon (west) to fairly common (east) summer resident of freshwater (rarely saltwater) marshes, wet fields, ranging up to mid-elevation sedge meadows on Eastside. Rare west in winter.

American Coot *Fulica americana* — Winter resident in huge numbers on lowland lakes, ponds, reservoirs; much smaller numbers on protected marine waters. Fairly common but local summer resident of lakes, ponds statewide.

Sandhill Crane *Grus canadensis* — In March–April, again September, Lesser Sandhill Crane (subspecies *canadensis*) passes through Eastern Washington by thousands—especially conspicuous west of Othello in corn stubble, on Waterville Plateau. In Western Washington, fairly common migrant in Woodland Bottoms, Vancouver Lowlands; hundreds winter. Also sometimes seen in spring passage along outer coast. Greater Sandhill Crane (subspecies *tabida*) formerly widespread summer resident on both sides of Cascades, now virtually extirpated. A few still nest at

Conboy Lake NWR, also near Signal Peak on Yakama Indian Reservation (closed to public). Rare migrant, mixed in with Lessers.

Black-necked Stilt *Himantopus mexicanus* — Locally fairly common summer resident in Columbia Basin, lower Yakima River valley—especially Potholes, Toppenish NWR, Satus Wildlife Area. Recent arrival in Washington, first nested 1973. Rare migrant, summer resident in Western Washington; nested 2001 at Ridgefield NWR.

American Avocet *Recurvirostra americana* — Locally fairly common summer resident in Columbia Basin, nesting around pond edges, other wet habitats (especially alkaline). Migrants may be seen as early as March, as late as November. Rare migrant, summer resident in Western Washington. Has nested at Crockett Lake (successfully 2000, attempted 2002).

Black Oystercatcher *Haematopus bachmani* — Uncommon year-round resident on rocky coastlines. Paired in nesting season, often concentrates into localized flocks (up to 40 birds) in winter. Most numerous in Northwest—especially Cape Flattery, San Juans, Fidalgo Island, northern Whidbey Island. Virtually absent from Puget Sound proper, very local along South Coast. A few often noted on log booms at Ediz Hook. Recorded east.

Black-bellied Plover *Pluvialis squatarola* — Common migrant, winter resident in or near marine habitats; casual spring, uncommon fall migrant east of Cascades. Often seen in plowed, wet fields.

American Golden-Plover *Pluvialis dominica* — Rare spring, uncommon fall migrant on coasts—Damon Point at Ocean Shores reliable site. Rare fall migrant in Eastern Washington, casual spring.

Pacific Golden-Plover *Pluvialis fulva* — Rare spring, uncommon fall migrant along outer coast; recorded east. Casual in winter west. Best sites Damon Point at Ocean Shores, Leadbetter Point, Dungeness NWR. Often occurs side-by-side with American Golden-Plover; separation challenging but brightest golden juvenile Pacifics readily identifiable.

Lesser Sand-Plover *Charadrius mongolus* — Four records, all recent, all seen between last week of August and first week of September. Three records (2010, 2012, 2013) from Ocean Shores, one record (2013) from Bottle Beach.

Snowy Plover *Charadrius nivosus* — Uncommon, local year-round resident along South Coast beaches north to Grays Harbor county line, most on Leadbetter Point, Midway Beach (Grayland). Recorded east.

Wilson's Plover *Charadrius wilsonia* — Two records, both from 2012. One east, in Walla Walla County (August–September 2012); one west, Grays Harbor County (October–November 2012).

Common Ringed Plover *Charadrius hiaticula* — One record, Port Susan Bay (Snohomish County), September 2006.

Semipalmated Plover *Charadrius semipalmatus* — Common migrant, rare winter resident on saltwater beaches, tideflats. Uncommon migrant in interior. Has nested at Ocean Shores.

Piping Plover *Charadrius melodus* — One record, at Reardan Ponds for four days in July 1990.

Killdeer *Charadrius vociferus* — Common year-round resident, except uncommon to rare in winter east of Cascades. Open-country bird, most often seen on lawns, fields, gravel roads/parking lots, beaches, tideflats, bare ground.

Mountain Plover *Charadrius montanus* — Five winter records from outer coast (three from Pacific County, two from Grays Harbor County) in November 1964, December 2000, February 2005, January 2011, November 2014; one from Turnbull NWR (Spokane), May 1968.

Eurasian Dotterel *Charadrius morinellus* — Four fall records (September 3–November 4), three from Ocean Shores, in 1934, 1979, 1999, one from Pacific County in 2007. One bird remained for over two weeks.

Spotted Sandpiper *Actitis macularius* — Fairly common, widespread summer resident; nests close to water on both sides of Cascades, from sea level to alpine lakes. A few winter in western lowlands.

Solitary Sandpiper *Tringa solitaria* — Uncommon fall, rare spring migrant, generally more numerous east. Almost always seen at ponds, other freshwater sites from lowlands up to forested mountain lakes.

Gray-tailed Tattler *Tringa brevipes* — One record, in October 1975 at Leadbetter Point.

Wandering Tattler *Tringa incana* — Fairly common migrant on rocky shores, jetties on outer coast; local in appropriate saltwater habitats elsewhere. Best sites include Westport, Ocean Shores jetties. Accidental in winter. Recorded east.

Spotted Redshank *Tringa erythropus* — One record, from late November to early December 2014 in Skagit County.

Greater Yellowlegs *Tringa melanoleuca* — Common (west) to fairly common (east) in migration, uncommon (west) to rare (east) winter resident, in both freshwater, saltwater habitats.

Willet *Tringa semipalmata* — Rare to locally uncommon winter resident of coastal estuaries, salt marshes, north to Drayton Harbor; most often noted at Tokeland, nearby New River mouth, Ediz Hook, Dungeness NWR. Casual spring migrant through interior.

Lesser Yellowlegs *Tringa flavipes* — Uncommon spring, common fall migrant statewide; casual in winter west. Favors same habitats as Greater Yellowlegs (mudflats, shorelines, shallow marshes).

Wood Sandpiper *Tringa glareola* — One record from Samish Flats (Skagit County) in August 2011.

Upland Sandpiper *Bartramia longicauda* — Formerly uncommon summer resident in Spokane Valley between Spokane, Idaho line; no breeding records there since 1993. Probably extirpated as breeder in state, although one 2002 summer record from former breeding area is intriguing. Casual fall, accidental spring migrant east, west.

Little Curlew *Numenius minutus* — One record, at Leadbetter Point in May 2001.

Whimbrel *Numenius phaeopus* — American subspecies *hudsonicus* fairly common migrant, rare, local winter resident in various wet habitats west of Cascades. Casual migrant (mostly fall) in Eastern Washington. Two May records of white-rumped Siberian subspecies *variegatus*, both from Ocean Shores.

Bristle-thighed Curlew *Numenius tahitiensis* — Up to 10 individuals observed length of outer coast, from Leadbetter Point to Tatoosh Island, in May 1998. One prior record from Leadbetter Point in May 1982.

Long-billed Curlew *Numenius americanus* — Uncommon spring, early-summer resident in Columbia Basin grasslands, agricultural fields. Winters at Tokeland, rare elsewhere; most migrate to California, Mexico. Migrants occasionally noted on outer coast, along Columbia River, even in mountain meadows.

Hudsonian Godwit *Limosa haemastica* — Rare fall migrant. Most records juveniles from Pacific Coast, Semiahmoo Bay, Columbia Basin, late August to mid-October. Casual in spring.

Bar-tailed Godwit *Limosa lapponica* — Rare fall, casual spring migrant, mostly on outer coast; one bird stayed into winter. Best places Willapa Bay (especially Tokeland), Grays Harbor (especially Westport, Ocean Shores). Scattered records from other saltwater bays, shorelines such as Dungeness area, southern Puget Sound.

Marbled Godwit *Limosa fedoa* — Common winter resident at Tokeland, uncommon migrant, winter resident elsewhere on coastal mudflats. Rare migrant in Columbia Basin (e.g., Columbia River, Potholes Reservoir).

Ruddy Turnstone *Arenaria interpres* — In Western Washington, fairly common migrant, rare winter resident on saltwater shorelines; also on plowed fields in spring (e.g., Chehalis River floodplain). Casual fall migrant east of Cascades.

Black Turnstone *Arenaria melanocephala* — Common migrant, winter resident on rocky coasts. Best sites include Penn Cove, Fort Flagler, jetties at Ocean Shores, Westport, West Seattle. Roosts on log booms (e.g., Ediz Hook), piers, boats, rafts. Accidental in Columbia Basin in migration.

Great Knot *Calidris tenuirostris* — One record, from early September 1979 at La Push.

Red Knot *Calidris canutus* — Uncommon to rare migrant on outer coast, except briefly fairly common in Grays Harbor (Bottle Beach, Bowerman Basin) late April–early May. Casual migrant in Puget Sound region (mostly spring). Winters rarely on coast. Casual fall migrant in Eastern Washington.

Surfbird *Calidris virgata* — Fairly common but local migrant, winter resident on rocky saltwater shorelines. Some favored sites include Fort Flagler, Ediz Hook, Neah Bay, jetties at Ocean Shores, Westport, West Seattle.

Ruff *Calidris pugnax* — Rare fall migrant in Western Washington, peak August–September. Most records juveniles along outer coast—Grays Harbor (especially Ocean Shores), Willapa Bay best. Accidental in spring. Casual fall in Columbia Basin.

Sharp-tailed Sandpiper *Calidris acuminata* — Rare, irregular fall migrant, often in company of Pectoral Sandpiper, mostly on outer coast. Favored sites include Ocean Shores, Leadbetter Point, Fir Island (Skagit County). Casual in Eastern Washington (Potholes, Walla Walla River delta). Records almost all of juveniles. Very few summer records of adults.

Stilt Sandpiper *Calidris himantopus* — Rare fall migrant in Western Washington; uncommon fall, accidental spring east of Cascades.

Curlew Sandpiper *Calidris ferruginea* — Accidental spring (one record each from Potholes, Leadbetter Point, Ocean City), casual fall migrant. Fall records all but two from coasts (mid-July–early October).

Temminck's Stint *Calidris temminckii* — One record, from Ocean Shores in November 2005.

Red-necked Stint *Calidris ruficollis* — Five records, all from late-June through July: Whidbey Island (July 1993); Dungeness (July 2005) Snohomish County (June 2007); Ocean Shores (July 2009); Bottle Beach (July 2013).

Sanderling *Calidris alba* — Common migrant, winter resident along sandy beaches of outer coast; fairly common but local in similar situations around Puget Trough. Casual spring, uncommon fall migrant east of Cascades.

Dunlin *Calidris alpina* — Commonest wintering shorebird at this latitude. Common migrant, winter resident on coastal bays, flocks numbering in tens of thousands at favored sites such as Samish/Skagit Flats, Grays Harbor, Willapa Bay. Uncommon migrant, rare winter resident in Columbia Basin.

Rock Sandpiper *Calidris ptilocnemis* — Uncommon, declining migrant, winter resident on Pacific, North Olympic Coasts, rare along marine waters farther inland. Favored sites jetties at Ocean Shores, Westport, mouth of Columbia River. One or two records of distinctive Pribilofs subspecies *ptilocnemis*. Question of which other subspecies reach Washington not fully resolved, although most birds likely *tschuktschorum*.

Baird's Sandpiper *Calidris bairdii* — Uncommon to locally fairly common fall migrant east of Cascades, including at high-mountain lakes August–early September; uncommon, local on coasts, inland Puget Sound (especially Damon Point at Ocean Shores, Crockett Lake). Casual west, rare east in spring.

Little Stint *Calidris minuta* — One record of an adult at the Yakima River confluence (Benton County), in August 2004.

Least Sandpiper *Calidris minutilla* — On Westside, common spring, fall migrant; on Eastside, uncommon (spring) to fairly common (fall). Uncommon (west) to rare (east) winter resident. Forages on muddy borders of ponds, estuaries, saltwater mudflats, also in shallow freshwater, saltwater marshes. Typically seen in small groups rather than large flocks.

White-rumped Sandpiper *Calidris fuscicollis* — Seven records, four from eastern Washington (May–June), three from western Washington (July–August).

Buff-breasted Sandpiper *Tryngites subruficollis* — Rare fall migrant. Juveniles occur most years along coast from mid-August to mid-September; Damon Point at Ocean Shores most reliable place. A few fall records from Puget Trough, Eastern Washington; one late-May record from Leadbetter Point.

Pectoral Sandpiper *Calidris melanotos* — Fairly common fall migrant statewide; rare (west) to casual (east) in spring.

Semipalmated Sandpiper *Calidris pusilla* — Uncommon fall migrant, rare in spring. Most Western Washington reports come from Northwest (especially Crockett Lake).

Western Sandpiper *Calidris mauri* — Common spring, fall migrant west, uncommon winter resident on saltwater shorelines. Greatest numbers along outer coast in spring, especially Bowerman Basin, where upwards of 500,000 birds may stop in a single day. Rare spring, fairly common fall migrant east.

Short-billed Dowitcher *Limnodromus griseus* — Common migrant on outer coast—mostly in bays but occasionally on beaches. Impressive spring concentrations in Grays Harbor (Bowerman Basin, Bottle Beach). Much more frequent than Long-billed on saltwater, estuarine habitats. Rare fall, casual spring migrant in Eastern Washington. Most adults migrating through Washington belong to subspecies *caurinus*, less extensively red beneath in alternate plumage, hence fairly readily separable from Long-billed, especially in spring. Subspecies *hendersoni* casual migrant east.

Long-billed Dowitcher *Limnodromus scolopaceus* — Fairly common migrant statewide, usually on fresh water; uncommon winter on coastal bays.

Jack Snipe *Lymnocryptes minimus* — One record, from Skagit Game Range in September 1993.

Wilson's Snipe *Gallinago delicata* — Fairly common migrant statewide. Fairly common summer resident east; uncommon, local west. Fairly common west, uncommon to rare east in winter. Found in many types of wet habitats, from lowland fields to mountain meadows.

Wilson's Phalarope *Phalaropus tricolor*— Locally fairly common migrant, summer resident of marshes, wet meadows, pond edges in Eastern Washington. Rare migrant in similar freshwater habitats on Westside (mostly spring); a few breeding records. Rare migrant on salt water.

Red-necked Phalarope *Phalaropus lobatus* — Common spring, fall migrant west, often abundant in pelagic waters. In Eastern Washington, uncommon spring migrant, fairly common fall (sometimes locally abundant at sewage ponds).

Red Phalarope *Phalaropus fulicarius*— Mainly noted on Westport pelagic trips where uncommon spring, fairly common fall. Occasionally wrecks along outer coast after severe October–November storms. Casual migrant east of Cascades.

South Polar Skua *Stercorarius maccormicki* — Rare spring–summer, uncommon fall pelagic visitor. Usually seen as quick flyby or with concentrations of shearwaters, gulls at fishing trawlers, well off Westport.

Pomarine Jaeger *Stercorarius pomarinus* — Fairly common pelagic visitor, numbers higher during migration than mid-winter, mid-summer. Rarely seen from shore, then usually distant, making identification difficult. Casual on inland marine waters; recorded east.

Parasitic Jaeger *Stercorarius parasiticus* — Fairly common (spring) to common (fall) pelagic migrant; substantial numbers also on inland marine waters, coastal bays in fall, apparently tracking Common Tern migration. Rare fall migrant along Columbia River east of Cascades.

Long-tailed Jaeger *Stercorarius longicaudus* — Uncommon fall (peak August), rare spring pelagic visitor well offshore, quite scarce some years. Casual on inland marine waters. Casual fall in Eastern Washington, mainly along Columbia River.

Common Murre *Uria aalge* — Fairly common to common year round on pelagic waters, Pacific Coast. Breeds in summer on islets along Outer Olympic Coast; numbers, nesting success vary greatly, depending on water temperature, food availability. Numbers increase in summer, early autumn from individuals moving north for winter. On inland marine waters, fairly common to common in winter (especially northern parts), uncommon to absent in summer.

Thick-billed Murre *Uria lomvia* — Casual fall–winter visitor on outer coast, pelagic waters; accidental in inland marine waters. Dates range from late September to March with strong peak in December. One June record from 2014 at Hobuck Beach, Clallam.

Pigeon Guillemot *Cepphus columba* — Fairly common year-round resident of deep coastal waters, nesting in rocky bluffs, jetties, sandbank burrows, locally on pilings. Largest numbers around Protection Island. Not pelagic. Withdraws from outer coast in winter. Numbers increase on protected waters in winter, from California breeding populations that move north.

Long-billed Murrelet *Brachyramphus perdix* — Ten accepted records, all since 1993: most from outer coast, most between August and November, with one March and one July record. One Eastern Washington record from Garfield County in August, 2001.

Marbled Murrelet *Brachyramphus marmoratus* — Declining but still fairly common year-round resident of deep, protected coastal waters. Nests in old-growth coastal forests, especially on Olympic Peninsula, fewer on west slopes of Cascades. Usually easy to see at Salt Creek County Park, also tidal rips such as at Point No Point, Fort Flagler, off southern ends of Orcas, San Juan Islands. Decline due primarily to loss of nesting habitat, but other factors may contribute.

Kittlitz's Murrelet *Brachyramphus brevirostris* — Single record, from Friday Harbor (San Juan Island) in January 1974.

Scripps's Murrelet *Synthliboramphus scrippsi* — Previously considered conspecific with Guadalupe Murrelet, (as "Xantus's Murrelet"), Scripps's average one or more records a year on Westport pelagic trips, most in fall (August–September), with several summer records and one winter record.

Guadalupe Murrelet *Synthliboramphus hypoleucus* — One accepted record from July 2003 on Westport pelagic trip. Several other plausible off-shore reports remain undocumented.

Ancient Murrelet *Synthliboramphus antiquus* — Uncommon to locally fairly common late-fall–early-winter resident of marine waters—mostly in deeper waters of eastern Strait of Juan de Fuca, northern Puget Sound. Usually arrives after strong November storms, becomes decidedly uncommon by January. Most easily found at tidal rips at Point No Point, Fort Worden, and Fort Flagler, or from Port Townsend-Coupeville Ferry. Sometimes seen on pelagic trips from Westport, mostly in winter as distant flyby. Probably breeds intermittently in tiny numbers in seabird colonies along Outer Olympic Coast. Recorded east.

Cassin's Auklet *Ptychoramphus aleuticus* — Once most abundant breeding non-gull seabird in Washington, now fairly common, seriously declining. Nests on islets off Outer Olympic Coast but infrequently seen from shore. Regular on Westport pelagic trips. Rare on inland marine waters.

Parakeet Auklet *Aethia psittacula* — Rarely observed on pelagic trips and found dead on beaches, but apparently regular off-shore, especially in winter. Over 1500 seen at Grays Canyon in early March 2013, indicating greater abundance than expected in spring.

Whiskered Auklet *Aethia pygmaea* — One record, at Penn Cove two days in May 1999.

Rhinoceros Auklet *Cerorhinca monocerata* — Common summer resident in deeper coastal waters, though scarcer in southern Puget Sound. Thousands nest on Protection Island. Large numbers often seen at entrance to Grays Harbor on pelagic boat trips. Less common in winter.

Horned Puffin *Fratercula corniculata* —Rare visitor on outer coast and accidentally in inland marine waters. More regular off-shore presence indicated by occasional large die-offs observed by beach surveys.

Tufted Puffin *Fratercula cirrhata* — Locally uncommon summer resident on islands along Outer Olympic, North Olympic coasts. Infrequent on Westport pelagic trips. Easiest to see at Cape Flattery, La Push; also Diamond Point, Protection Island boat trip.

Black-legged Kittiwake *Rissa tridactyla* — Fairly common on pelagic waters, except uncommon summer. Numbers vary from one year to the next. Often seen from shore at Westport jetty, north jetty of Columbia River, less often at Neah Bay, Cape Flattery. Occurs eastward in small numbers along Strait of Juan de Fuca in late fall, particularly just after major storms; casual at same time on marine waters farther inland, as well as along Columbia River in Eastern Washington.

Red-legged Kittiwake *Rissa brevirostris* — Casual along or off Pacific Coast. Most records in winter (December–March). One bird stayed for a week at Tatoosh Island late June–early July. Another found on Westport pelagic trip in mid-August 2000, and one offshore near the mouth of the Columbia in September 2013.

Ivory Gull *Pagophila eburnea* — Two records, from Ocean Shores in December 1975, one from Yakima River confluence (Benton County) in January 2008.

Sabine's Gull *Xema sabini* — Fairly common to sometimes common spring, fall pelagic migrant; rare in Puget Sound, other protected marine waters. In Eastern Washington, rare fall migrant along Columbia River, Grand Coulee lakes, mainly September.

Bonaparte's Gull *Chroicocephalus philadelphia* — Common spring, fall migrant in Western Washington lowlands, fairly common but local winter resident; sometimes impressive concentrations at sewage lagoons, tidal rips. Uncommon migrant in Eastern Washington.

Black-headed Gull *Chroicocephalus ridibundus* — Casual fall migrant, winter resident mostly on inland marine waters. Records mostly from winter but stretch from mid-August to April. One from outer coast (Ocean Shores, November 1972), one from eastern Washington (Grant County, December 2007).

Little Gull *Hydrocoloeus minutus* — Casual migrant, winter resident west of Cascades, most often with Bonaparte's Gulls and mostly on inland marine waters. Formerly annual at Point No Point in migration, recent records very sparse. Recorded east.

Ross's Gull *Rhodostethia rosea* — Two records: McNary Dam (Benton County) for five days in November–December 1994; Palmer Lake (Okanogan County) for 12 days in December 2011.

Laughing Gull *Leucophaeus atricilla* — Seven records, all between May and September: five from outer coast, one from Point No Point and one from eastern Washington, in Wenatchee.

Franklin's Gull *Leucophaeus pipixcan* — Uncommon fall migrant east, west—mostly juveniles. Rare (east) to casual (west) spring migrant and winter resident. Best sites include Grand Coulee lakes, Sprague Lake, Walla Walla River delta.

Black-tailed Gull *Larus crassirostris* – Seven records, all since 2004 all from March to October. Locations diverse: three on outer coast/pelagic waters; two in inland marine waters; two in eastern Washington.

Heermann's Gull *Larus heermanni* — Common post-breeding visitor to outer coastal waters, Strait of Juan de Fuca; rare into winter. Progressively less frequent on marine waters farther inland. Easy to see August–October at Grays Harbor, Tokeland. Recorded along Columbia River east.

Mew Gull *Larus canus* — Common winter resident of coastal waters, near-coastal freshwater lakes, lowland agricultural fields west of Cascades; rare late-fall migrant, winter resident in Eastern Washington, mainly along Columbia, Snake Rivers.

Ring-billed Gull *Larus delawarensis* — Locally common summer resident in Eastern Washington, nesting colonially on sand, gravel islands in lakes, rivers; has also nested on dredge-spoil islands in Grays Harbor, Willapa Bay. Non-breeders abundant, widespread in Western Washington in summer. Common migrant west. Locally uncommon to variably common winter resident on both sides of Cascades, with good numbers most years around Tri-Cities, Walla Walla, Skagit River deltas. Often roosts, forages in agricultural fields.

Western Gull *Larus occidentalis* — Common resident on South Coast, where it breeds; fairly common on northern coasts, uncommon on inland marine waters. Washington birds represent lighter-mantled northern (nominate) subspecies. Hybridizes readily with Glaucous-winged Gull ("**Olympic Gull**"), complicating identification. Rare winter resident in Eastern Washington, most likely just below Columbia, Snake River dams.

California Gull *Larus californicus* — Common but local spring, summer resident in Eastern Washington. Breeding sites include Potholes Reservoir, Banks Lake, Columbia River north of Richland and Snake River. Common summer, fall along coasts, even well offshore to pelagic waters. In winter, common along Columbia and Snake Rivers, uncommon in coastal Western Washington.

Herring Gull *Larus argentatus* — Winter resident. Locally fairly common in Eastern Washington along Columbia, Snake Rivers, Grand Coulee lakes. In Western Washington, uncommon except locally common at late-winter smelt runs on Columbia River. Higher numbers on outer coast than on inland marine waters; more common in fresh water than salt water around Puget Trough. Casual in summer. Asian *vegae* race recorded four times since 2012.

Thayer's Gull *Larus thayeri* — Uncommon to locally common winter resident of coastal waters; most abundant along North Olympic Coast (Elwha River mouth, Ediz Hook), south Puget Sound (Tukwila, Gog-Le-Hi-Te Wetlands), least common on outer coast where outnumbered by Herring Gull. Rare in winter on Grand Coulee lakes, along Columbia, Snake Rivers in Eastern Washington. Use caution in separating from Western X Glaucous-winged hybrids.

Iceland Gull Larus glaucoides — Casual winter visitor (November–April) around marine waters (pelagic, Strait of Juan de Fuca, Puget Sound), Columbia, Snake Rivers. Separation from Thayer's Gull tricky, controversial. Most, if not all, records identifying the subspecies have been of the subspecies *kumlieni*.

Lesser Black-backed Gull *Larus fuscus* — After first record at Walla Walla River delta in 2000, has become a rare winter visitor with a few records every year. Most from Eastern Washington, but at least three records from Western Washington.

Slaty-backed Gull Larus schistisagus — Casual winter visitor (October–mid-March) to inland marine waters. Majority of records come from lower Puget Sound.

Glaucous-winged Gull *Larus glaucescens* — Common year-round resident on all coastal waters, wandering short distance inland to forage, loaf, roost on agricultural fields, freshwater lakes. Many Washington birds (in some areas, most) hybridizes with Western Gull ("**Olympic Gull**"), generally exhibiting shade or two darker mantle than pure Glaucous-wingeds, primary tips darker than mantle. In Eastern Washington, uncommon winter resident along Columbia, Snake Rivers, Grand Coulee lakes. A few breed.

Glaucous Gull *Larus hyperboreus* — Rare to locally uncommon winter resident. First- and second-cycle birds predominate. Favored Westside sites include Elwha River mouth, Ediz Hook, Cedar River mouth in Renton. East of Cascades, mainly along Columbia River (especially Tri-Cities, Walla Walla River delta), semi-regular on Grand Coulee lakes.

Great Black-backed Gull *Larus marinus* — One record, January–February 2004 in Renton (King County).

Least Tern *Sternula antillarum* — Six records, three from Ocean Shores, two from inland marine waters, and one from eastern Washington. All records occurred between May and August.

Caspian Tern *Hydroprogne caspia* — Non-breeders abundant summer residents in coastal bays, inland marine waters; breeding colonies local, erratic, partly due to human persecution. Fairly common summer resident in Eastern Washington on a few major lakes, Columbia and Snake Rivers.

Black Tern *Chlidonias niger* — Fairly common but local summer resident of Eastern Washington marshes, shallow lakes. Good sites include Muskrat, Beth Lakes in Okanogan County, Turnbull NWR, Calispell Lake. Rare migrant in Western Washington. Has nested at Ridgefield NWR.

Common Tern *Sterna hirundo* — Fairly common spring, fall migrant on outer coast, smaller numbers on pelagic waters. Virtually absent spring, uncommon fall on inland marine waters. Recently has become less regular in inland marine waters. Uncommon fall migrant along Columbia River to coast.

Arctic Tern *Sterna paradisaea* — Uncommon pelagic migrant, easiest to see in August–September. Formerly bred on Jetty Island in Everett. Casual east in fall.

Forster's Tern *Sterna forsteri* — Fairly common but local summer resident from Potholes south along Columbia River to Tri-Cities; uncommon north to mouth of Okanogan River, west to Columbia Gorge. Nests on gravel islands, also in marshes. Casual west, mostly fall.

Elegant Tern *Thalasseus elegans* — Irregular post-breeding visitor to outer-coastal beaches, bays in El Niño years, rarely to Puget Sound. Typically arrives in July or August.

Rock Pigeon *Columba livia* — Native to Old World; domesticated birds introduced to North America by early European settlers. Common year-round resident around farms, towns, cites. Naturalized Rock Pigeons breed on basalt cliffs in Eastern Washington.

Band-tailed Pigeon *Patagioenas fasciata* — Fairly common (summer) to uncommon (winter) resident of forests, well-treed residential areas in lowland Western Washington. Requires large conifers for nesting; core populations may be declining. Nests in smaller numbers upward to subalpine, spilling across Cascade Crest at Snoqualmie Pass; accidental reports east to Walla Walla, Spokane. Noted to gather at mineral springs.

Eurasian Collared-Dove *Streptopelia decaocto* — Introduced to New World from Eurasia. After arriving in Washington in Walla Walla County in 1996 and not being seen again until 2000 in Spokane, then spread rapidly across state and now have been observed in every county. Appear to favor smaller towns, farms over urban sites.

White-winged Dove *Zenaida asiatica* — Ten accepted records, mostly from western Washington and mostly from the summer (May–July). Two from Eastern Washington, three from fall (August–November).

Mourning Dove *Zenaida macroura* — Common summer resident east of Cascades, from Columbia Basin up into lower forest zones. Winters locally in smaller numbers, mainly near feedlots. Uncommon to locally fairly common year-round resident in Western Washington lowlands, mostly in open forests, agricultural areas, towns.

Yellow-billed Cuckoo *Coccyzus americanus* — Formerly rare, local summer resident in lowland hardwood, riparian forests in Western Washington, extirpated by 1940. Now casual, with seven spring–summer records (four west, three east), two fall records (both from eastern Washington), all since 1974. Decline illustrated by recent trend: only five records in the 1990s and one record since 2000.

Black-billed Cuckoo *Coccyzus erythropthalmus* — Accidental. Four records in narrow window June 19–July 1—three from eastern edge of state, one from Puget Sound.

Barn Owl *Tyto alba* — Uncommon to locally fairly common year-round resident of open agricultural areas in lowlands on both sides of Cascades. Often nests in haystacks, cliffs, human structures. Probably declining in Western Washington due to urban encroachment, retirement of pasturelands. Populations east of Cascades suffer in severe winters.

Flammulated Owl *Psiloscops flammeolus* — Uncommon, local summer resident in Ponderosa Pine, mixed pine and Douglas-fir forests in Eastern Washington. Some good sites include Old Blewett Pass, Bonaparte Lake, Rock Creek west of

Okanogan, Bethel Ridge. Often near brushy terrain (especially Deerbrush), where an abundance of moths is possibly an attraction. Recorded west.

Western Screech-Owl *Megascops kennicottii* — Uncommon to locally fairly common year-round resident in lowland deciduous groves on both sides of state, but absent from many parts of central Columbia Basin. Western Washington populations declining, likely due to Barred Owl increase.

Great Horned Owl *Bubo virginianus* — Fairly common year-round resident at all elevations up to treeline in wide array of habitats, but usually absent from intact, moist conifer forests.

Snowy Owl *Bubo scandiacus* — Irruptive winter resident. In invasion years, easily found at coastal sites such as Skagit and Samish Flats (salt marshes, nearby fields), Ocean Shores (Damon Point), Dungeness NWR. Also in croplands across northern Columbia Basin. In non-flight years, when absent on Westside, a few usually present near Moses Lake, Davenport, Reardan.

Northern Hawk Owl *Surnia ulula* — Rare winter visitor, far more frequent east of Cascades than west, often in recent burns. Records in most winters, usually just 1–2 birds but sometimes up to 4–5 per season. Breeding confirmed in Okanogan County in 2007.

Northern Pygmy-Owl *Glaucidium gnoma* — Uncommon year-round resident of conifer, mixed forests at low to mid-elevations; some upslope movement to treeline in fall. Perhaps most numerous at mid-elevations on east slopes of Cascades. At least some move downslope in winter in Eastern Washington, where they can reach valley bottoms, though usually not far from mountains. Most active at dawn, dusk.

Burrowing Owl *Athene cunicularia* — Uncommon, local, declining summer resident of steppe habitats in Columbia Basin, rare north to Okanogan County. A few winter. Most readily found in Tri-Cities area. Accidental migrant west, formerly bred at Grays Harbor.

Spotted Owl *Strix occidentalis* — Rare and declining year-round resident of extensive mature forests of Cascades, Olympics. Good numbers east of Cascade Crest in forests much different in structure than colossal old growth they inhabit on Westside. Information on whereabouts difficult to obtain due to sensitive nature of national debate concerning ancient forests; inescapable fact: these owls are indeed declining.

Barred Owl *Strix varia* — Fairly common resident in moist, mixed forests statewide. Recent arrival in state, first noted 1965 in Pend Oreille County. Has spread, increased phenomenally; now found even in well-treed large cities, for example in Seattle's Discovery Park. Some evidence that it is replacing Spotted Owl (with which it occasionally hybridizes) and possibly Western Screech-Owl.

Great Gray Owl *Strix nebulosa* — Rare, local, perhaps irregular year-round resident of mid-elevation mixed-conifer forests adjacent to openings, meadows in Okanogan County and Blue Mountains. Recent nesting documented from near Havillah, Bonaparte Lake, Colville Indian Reservation, Blue Mountains. Rare winter resident, possible breeder in Northeast. On Westside, casual, irregular winter resident in lowlands of northern Puget Trough, presumably birds coming coastward from east of Coast Mountains in British Columbia via Fraser River.

Long-eared Owl *Asio otus* — Uncommon summer resident in copses in shrub-steppe, lower-conifer habitats east of Cascade Crest. In winter, gathers at roosts, often in densely treed parks. Rare west of Cascades in any season; has nested.

Short-eared Owl *Asio flammeus* — Uncommon, local summer resident in Eastern Washington, declining due to loss of suitable grassland habitat. Most numerous in wetter, northern portions of Columbia Basin. Formerly nested locally in Western

Washington grasslands but now apparently extirpated. Fairly common but local winter resident, often seen on Samish, Skagit, Stillaguamish Flats, Vancouver Lowlands, at Nisqually NWR, in open country east of Cascades (e.g., Kittitas Valley).

Boreal Owl *Aegolius funereus* — Rare year-round resident of Engelmann Spruce/Subalpine Fir forests at or east of Cascade Crest, also Mount Rainier. Distribution poorly understood. Some known sites include Harts Pass, Long Swamp, Salmo Pass, Upper Ahtanum drainage west of Yakima, Sunrise (Mount Rainier), higher Blue Mountains. Most easily detected in fall when birds answer taped calls with piercing *skiew!* Primary call given in spring, rarely heard in Washington due to deep snow making owls' habitat inaccessible at that season.

Northern Saw-whet Owl *Aegolius acadicus* — Fairly common resident of mature conifer, mixed forests at low to middle elevations statewide, withdrawing from snowy parts of range in winter. Winter roost sites often frequented for long periods, marked by pellets, whitewash on ground. Active calling begins in winter but declines greatly by May, making detection much more difficult later in spring.

Common Nighthawk *Chordeiles minor* — Common summer resident of open country, lower forest zones east of Cascade Crest. Once common west of Cascades, now uncommon, local, declining in open lowland habitats. Still fairly common in San Juans, also seen regularly on upper west slopes of Cascades along rocky, logged-off ridges. Arrives late in spring (late May).

Common Poorwill *Phalaenoptilus nuttallii* — Fairly common summer resident in rocky portions of shrub-steppe habitats, brushy terrain of Ponderosa Pine zone in Eastern Washington. Sits on gravel roads at dusk, fluttering up to hawk for moths; most easily found by red eyeshine. Accidental west.

Black Swift *Cypseloides niger* — Fairly common but local summer resident of cliffs in Cascades, mostly from Snoqualmie Pass north; smaller numbers in Olympics. Inclement weather pushes birds into lowland foraging sites where they may be seen low to ground—often over water. Sometimes observed along Outer Olympic Coast. Nesting confirmed in North Cascades at Gorge Creek east of Newhalem. Probable nesting sites include other waterfalls in North Cascades in the vicinity of Darrington, Index (Snohomish County); Cle Elum River valley north of Cle Elum Lake; Stehekin at north end of Lake Chelan. Reports from Pend Oreille indicate Selkirks may be another possible breeding location.

Vaux's Swift *Chaetura vauxi* — Fairly common summer resident in moist forests statewide, also cities in forest zones (e.g., Seattle, Walla Walla). Probably declining due to loss of large trees with cavities for nesting; has not made wholesale adaptation to chimneys, although occasionally nests in them. Away from moist forests, noted in breeding season in areas of mature Garry Oaks. In fall migration, gathers in large numbers at favorite roosts such as smokestacks, abandoned icehouses.

White-throated Swift *Aeronautes saxatalis* — Fairly common summer resident on cliffs in Columbia Basin, Okanogan Valley. Easily seen in Grand Coulee, Frenchman Coulee. Recorded west.

Ruby-throated Hummingbird *Archilochus colubris* — One record, on east slope of Cascades in June 1992.

Black-chinned Hummingbird *Archilochus alexandri* — Uncommon to locally common summer resident in lowland, lower-elevation mountain riparian habitats bordering Columbia Basin, Okanogan Valley. Often visits wells drilled by Red-naped Sapsucker. Recorded west.

Anna's Hummingbird *Calypte anna* — Recent arrival from south. First Washington record Seattle 1964, first nesting record Tacoma 1972. Now fairly common to locally common year-round resident in lowland residential areas, parks in Western Washington, east along Columbia River to about Lyle. Humans undoubtedly aiding spread (year-round feeding, winter-blooming ornamental plantings). East of Cascades, rare but increasing, now occasionally attempting to winter and confirmed breeding.

Costa's Hummingbird *Calypte costae* — Fourteen accepted records, twelve since 2000. Most from spring migration but stretching from April to December. Most records from Puget lowlands and Klickitat County.

Broad-tailed Hummingbird *Selasphorus platycercus* — Four records, August 2000 in Asotin County, June 2002, May 2005, and May–July 2005 in Walla Walla County.

Rufous Hummingbird *Selasphorus rufus* — Common summer resident in forest zones statewide, including brushy clearcuts. Arrives early spring, coincident with first flowering Salmonberries and currrants. Especially conspicuous, widespread in summer when postbreeders take to mountain meadows. Sometimes noted zooming southward along barren alpine ridges in fall migration. Casual to rare in winter.

Allen's Hummingbird *Selasphorus sasin* — Only state record collected in Seattle in May 1894.

Calliope Hummingbird *Selasphorus calliope* — Fairly common summer resident in brushlands of lower forests of Eastern Washington mountains; majority in Ponderosa Pine zone. Regular in western Columbia Gorge, locally in small numbers in upper Skagit Valley (may breed). Rare migrant elsewhere in Western Washington.

Broad-billed Hummingbird *Cynanthus latirostris* — One record from October 2014 in Skamania County.

Belted Kingfisher *Megaceryle alcyon* — Fairly common year-round resident of streambanks, shorelines (freshwater, saltwater) statewide. Numbers much lower east of Cascades after winter freezeup.

Lewis's Woodpecker *Melanerpes lewis* — Fairly common but local summer resident in Eastern Washington, most depart in winter. Favors Garry Oak groves, large Ponderosa Pine snags, cottonwood-lined river valleys. Declining due to loss of cavities for nesting (including competition with European Starlings), human encroachment, degradation of understory in otherwise good nesting areas. Largest numbers at Fort Simcoe; winters there some years. Lyle also good bet year round. Formerly fairly common resident locally west of Cascades—extirpated as consequence of management practices that changed forest structure, suppressed nesting snags. Now casual migrant on Westside.

Acorn Woodpecker *Melanerpes formicivorus* — Resident in tiny numbers in Klickitat County—most consistent sites near Balch Lake and Grayback Road. Accidental in other locations including a notable surge north on both sides of the Cascades in the winter of 2014–2015.

Williamson's Sapsucker *Sphyrapicus thyroideus* — Uncommon summer resident in mixed-conifer forests at middle elevations of east slopes of Cascades, Okanogan Highlands, Blue Mountains. Birds in Washington strongly associated with Western Larch. Good sites include Havillah, Loup Loup Campground, Lodgepole Campground (on SR-410 east of Chinook Pass), many sites above 5,000 feet in Blue Mountains. Also Swauk Basin, Table Mountain, Manastash highlands.

Yellow-bellied Sapsucker *Sphyrapicus varius* — Eleven accepted records. Accidental in winter east, west. One summer record from Okanogan County. Reports increasing.

Red-naped Sapsucker *Sphyrapicus nuchalis* — Fairly common summer resident in Eastern Washington in relatively open forests (except oaks)—especially riparian corridors. Usually easy to find at Wenas Campground. Hybridizes with

Red-breasted Sapsucker near Cascade Crest, mostly along east slope. Highly migratory; winter reports more likely involve hybrids. Rare during migration in western lowlands.

Red-breasted Sapsucker *Sphyrapicus ruber* — Fairly common year-round resident in conifer, mixed forests west of Cascade Crest, including less-developed parts of Puget Lowlands with sufficient remaining trees. Becomes more conspicuous in city parks, other marginal habitats when severe winter weather forces birds downslope. Spills over onto east slopes of Cascades (dominant sapsucker species in moist forests for many miles eastward from Snoqualmie Pass). Hybrizes with Red-naped in broad zone at upper edge of drier Eastside forest habitats.

Downy Woodpecker *Picoides pubescens* — Fairly common year-round resident in lower-elevation deciduous, mixed forests (especially riparian), windbreaks, woodlots, ornamental plantings around farms, towns, parks. Local in conifer forests east of Cascade Crest. Underparts, center of back dusky in Westside populations, white in birds from Eastern Washington.

Hairy Woodpecker *Picoides villosus* — Fairly common year-round resident of conifer forests statewide, at all elevations. Interior breeding populations brightly contrasting black-and-white; Westside breeding race dingier.

White-headed Woodpecker *Picoides albolarvatus* — Uncommon, local year-round resident east of Cascades in Ponderosa Pine zone. Seldom easy to find. Declining due to loss of mature pines, now nearly extirpated in Spokane region, Blue Mountains. Fairly dependable at Wenas Campground, along lower White Pass Highway, at Little Pend Oreille NWR, along Silver Creek Road in Colville Indian Reservation. Recorded west.

American Three-toed Woodpecker *Picoides dorsalis* — Uncommon year-round resident in higher forests from Cascade Crest east, locally on upper west slopes of Cascades. Favors Engelmann Spruce, to lesser extent Lodgepole Pine. Attracted to recent burns; locations thus vary. Wanders down to mid-elevation burns but core range higher than that of Black-backed. Perhaps most easily found along FR-39 between Roger Lake, Long Swamp. Very rare breeder in Olympics.

Black-backed Woodpecker *Picoides arcticus* — Rare, nomadic year-round resident of mid- to high-elevation conifer forests east of Cascade Crest (barely west). Frequents lower elevations, drier forests than American Three-toed. To find one, look for recent burns, as post-burn explosion of insects concentrates populations for several years. Absent productive burns, birds spread out thinly over large areas.

Northern Flicker *Colaptes auratus* — Commonest woodpecker statewide, year-round resident from sea level to subalpine. Breeding form **Red-shafted Flicker** (subspecies *cafer*); populations augmented in winter by large influx from north. **Yellow-shafted Flicker** (subspecies *auratus*) rare winter resident. Red-shafted X Yellow-shafted intergrades numerous in winter; a few also noted in breeding population.

Pileated Woodpecker *Dryocopus pileatus* — Fairly common year-round resident in mature conifer forests, woodlots in Western Washington; much less common on Eastside in similar habitats. Requires large territories with ample decaying snags, downed logs for nesting, foraging. Declines in forests where development, forest-management practices suppress these, but otherwise tolerant of human encroachment, breeding successfully in wooded city parks, suburbs, semi-rural residential areas.

Crested Caracara *Polyborus plancus* — Three accepted records: Two from Grays Harbor County (Ocean Shores, August 1983 and Oakville, May 2006), one from Clallam County (Neah Bay, January–February 1998).

Eurasian Kestrel *Falco tinnunculus* — One bird discovered late October 1999 on Samish Flats, seen irregularly into November.

American Kestrel *Falco sparverius* — Common summer resident in Eastern Washington open habitats—farmlands, meadows, shrub-steppe, clearcuts, alpine parklands. In winter, withdraws from higher elevations, shrub-steppe; numbers increase in farmlands. Uncommon (summer) to fairly common (winter) resident locally in similar habitats in Southwest, uncommon elsewhere on Westside except rare to absent along outer coast.

Merlin *Falco columbarius* — Fairly common migrant, uncommon winter resident along outer coast, margins of inland marine waters, especially where swarms of Dunlins occur. Usually fairly easy to find at Nisqually, Dungeness NWRs, Ocean Shores, Leadbetter Point, Skagit and Samish Flats. Uncommon to rare winter resident statewide around towns, cities, farms. A few pairs of coastal **Black Merlin** (subspecies *suckleyi*) breed in forests of Olympic Peninsula, Puget Trough (also in cities). **Taiga Merlin** (subspecies *columbarius*) suspected to breed (rarely) in Eastern Washington forests. Prairie Merlin (subspecies *richardsoni*) rare in migration, winter.

Eurasian Hobby *Falco subbuteo* — Two records, one from Discovery Park, Seattle, in October 2001, one from Neah Bay, Clallam in October–November 2014.

Gyrfalcon *Falco rusticolus* — West of Cascades, rare winter resident on Skagit and Samish Flats, coastal marshes, beaches (e.g., Ocean Shores), other open lowland landscapes frequented by large flocks of dabbling ducks. East of Cascades, rare winter resident on higher plateaus—most reports from Waterville Plateau, Davenport-Reardan region, Anatone Flats (Asotin County). Drawn to waterfowl concentrations, also wheat fields bordered by brushy or grassy terrain where Gray Partridge, Ring-necked Pheasant likely targets.

Peregrine Falcon *Falco peregrinus* — Three races. **Peale's Peregrine** (subspecies *pealei*) increasing but still uncommon summer resident along cliffs of Outer Olympic Coast, San Juan Islands—particularly in vicinity of seabird colonies. Fairly common fall migrant, uncommon winter resident of marshes, open country, coastlines. **Continental Peregrine** (subspecies *anatum*) formerly widely distributed in Eastern Washington, mostly extirpated as breeder in decades after World War II. Now found statewide as migrant, winter resident (much less common east), especially near waterfowl, shorebird concentrations. **Tundra Peregrine** (subspecies *tundrius*) found in migration, mostly along outer coast. Reintroduced birds (subspecies uncertain) successfully established, increasing locally in Cascades, along Columbia River; a few pairs now nest on tall buildings, bridges in Seattle, Tacoma, Spokane.

Prairie Falcon *Falco mexicanus* — Uncommon year-round resident in Eastern Washington lowlands, breeding mostly on basalt cliffs in southern half of Columbia Basin, rare north to Okanogan County. In winter, often in open agricultural country. Widespread wanderer late summer, fall over subalpine meadows, ridges east of Cascade Crest, locally west (especially Mount Rainier). Rare winter on Westside, most reliable site Samish Flats.

Olive-sided Flycatcher *Contopus cooperi* — Fairly common summer resident in conifer forests, especially with openings, tall snags. Vocalizes, hawks insects from high, exposed perches.

Greater Pewee *Contopus pertinax* – One record from Edmonds (Snohomish County) in November 2008.

Western Wood-Pewee *Contopus sordidulus* — Common summer resident in riparian woodlands, dry conifer forests east of Cascade Crest. Avoids wet, closed conifer forests, hence much less common, local in Western Washington, where confined mostly to lowland riparian situations.

Eastern Wood-Pewee *Contopus virens* — One record from Grant County, August 2013. Returned in 2014.

Yellow-bellied Flycatcher *Empidonax flaviventris* — One record from Franklin County, August 2009.

Alder Flycatcher *Empidonax alnorum* — Four records: two from Okanogan County, June 2002 and 2006; one from Skagit County, June 2004; one from Pend Oreille County, June 2014.

Willow Flycatcher *Empidonax traillii* — Common summer resident of Western Washington wetland habitats, shrubby areas, including clearcuts. Less common, local east of Cascades, except widespread, common in Northeast. Absent as breeder from Columbia Basin. Arrives late in spring, becoming conspicuous only late May when calling begins.

Least Flycatcher *Empidonax minimus* — Rare, increasing migrant, summer resident. Most likely in aspen copses, cottonwood stands in Okanogan, Walla Walla County, but has occurred widely in hardwood groves on both sides of Cascades. Has nested in Puget Lowlands. Fall migrants found regularly at migrant traps such as Washtucna.

Hammond's Flycatcher *Empidonax hammondii* — Fairly common summer resident of denser conifer forests—sometimes with deciduous component—statewide. Although favors upper portions of taller trees, may also perch, forage low, in open, especially on migration.

Gray Flycatcher *Empidonax wrightii* — Recent arrival in Washington (first nested 1972), now fairly common but local summer resident of open, brush-free understories of Ponderosa Pine forests, especially along driest, easternmost slopes of Cascades, northern Columbia Basin. Repeated selective logging may be responsible for creating microhabitat structurally similar to its customary Great Basin habitats. Easy to find in upper Wenas Creek region. Accidental west, mostly spring.

Dusky Flycatcher *Empidonax oberholseri* — Fairly common migrant, summer resident of brushy openings of forests east of Cascade Crest. Also in higher-elevation aspen clumps, recent lava flows (Mount Adams). Generally favors drier, sunnier, more open habitats than Hammond's. Rare in clearcuts in early successional stages on upper west slopes of Cascades. Rare migrant west.

Pacific-slope Flycatcher *Empidonax difficilis* — Common summer resident of moist forest understories in Western Washington; fairly common east of Cascades, mostly in riparian habitat. **Cordilleran Flycatcher** *Empidonax occidentalis* may occur in Southeast, but evidence contradictory, incomplete. Best to call all Washington birds Pacific-slope or "Western" until status of this recently-split species pair can be resolved.

Black Phoebe *Sayornis nigricans* — Increasing in western Washington. Rare, now regular resident in southwest Washington, north to Skagit County. Breeding confirmed at Ridgefield NWR. One eastern Washington record from Clear Lake, Yakima County.

Eastern Phoebe *Sayornis phoebe* — Casual spring visitor (late May–July). Twelve accepted records, nine east, three west. Two December records, and one from September.

Say's Phoebe *Sayornis saya* — Fairly common summer resident in open terrain of lowland Eastern Washington, particularly in shrub-steppe zone; uncommon in openings in Garry Oak, Ponderosa Pine zones. For nesting, favors eaves of ranch buildings, rocky outcroppings. Hardy; some may attempt wintering in warmest parts of Columbia Basin. Rare but regular in spring migration west of Cascades, casual in winter.

Vermilion Flycatcher *Pyrocephalus rubinus* — Six fall–winter records, all from Western Washington lowlands.

Ash-throated Flycatcher *Myiarchus cinerascens* — Fairly common summer resident in Garry Oak zone along Columbia River from White Salmon east to about Rock Creek. Easy to find in oaks near Lyle or along Rock Creek. Less frequent northward, e.g., Satus Creek, Fort Simcoe. Rare, local breeder east base of Cascades north to Wenatchee. Not as conspicuous as many flycatchers, often perching within tree canopy. Easiest to detect in early morning when calling most intense. Recorded west.

Variegated Flycatcher *Empidonomus varius* – One record from Franklin County, September 2008.

Tropical Kingbird *Tyrannus melancholicus* — Rare fall visitor (late September to mid-December) to Western Washington lowlands, usually near salt water, mostly along outer coast. Grays Harbor, Willapa Bay best bets for finding one. Silent birds difficult-to-impossible to separate from Couch's Kingbird (not recorded in Washington).

Western Kingbird *Tyrannus verticalis* — Common summer resident in open habitats in Eastern Washington. Characteristic, easily found species along roadsides in farming, ranch country, often building nest on utility-pole insulators. In Western Washington, breeds in small numbers; rare in migration.

Eastern Kingbird *Tyrannus tyrannus* — Fairly common summer resident in lowland Eastern Washington in riparian habitats, particularly with dense, tall shrub layer. Rare migrant and local breeder in Western Washington.

Scissor-tailed Flycatcher *Tyrannus forficatus* — Twelve records, all between May and October, all since 1983. Five records from eastern Washington, mostly in the Potholes area. Seven records from western Washington, most found on outer coast and in upper Skagit.

Fork-tailed Flycatcher *Tyrannus savana* — One record, from Chinook River valley in September 1995.

Loggerhead Shrike *Lanius ludovicianus* — Uncommon summer, rare winter resident in shrub-steppe landscapes, declining due to habitat loss. Good sites include Crab Creek in Grant County, Pumphouse Road west of Toppenish NWR. Casual in Western Washington lowlands in spring migration.

Northern Shrike *Lanius excubitor* — Fairly common (east) to uncommon, local (west) winter resident in open habitats with some brushy terrain. Many good sites on Eastside—e.g., Waterville Plateau. Skagit/Samish Flats typical of Westside sites.

White-eyed Vireo *Vireo griseus* — One record, from Vashon Island (King County) in July 1981.

Bell's Vireo *Vireo bellii* — Four records: Skagit County, September 2007; Adams County, September 2008, Grant County, May 2009; Douglas County, June 2010.

Yellow-throated Vireo *Vireo flavifrons* — One record, from Spencer Island in October 1995.

Cassin's Vireo *Vireo cassinii* — Fairly common (east) to uncommon (west) summer resident in drier forests at low to middle elevations. Commonest in open Eastside forests with tall shrub or alder component—especially Douglas-fir, less often Ponderosa Pine. Also fairly easy to find in drier, open Douglas-fir forests in Western Washington, especially in rainshadowed northeastern Olympics, San Juan Islands.

Blue-headed Vireo *Vireo solitarius* — Seven records, all from August and September, six from eastern Washington migrant traps and one from Seattle.

Hutton's Vireo *Vireo huttoni* — Fairly common year-round resident of lowland hardwood or mixed forests, woodlands in Western Washington. Generally frustrating to locate except when singing (begins February, frequency tapers off into spring). Not usually found in small patches of woods such as gardens or small city parks, but occurs in large parks (e.g., Discovery Park in Seattle). In winter, often joins roving, mixed-species flocks of chickadees, nuthatches, creepers, kinglets, other small passerines. Recorded east slopes of Cascades.

Warbling Vireo *Vireo gilvus* — Common migrant, summer resident in deciduous woodlands statewide. Washington's commonest vireo, often breeding in tiny patches of willows, aspens, alders in otherwise conifer-dominated landscapes.

Philadelphia Vireo *Vireo philadelphicus* — Five records: Grant County in September 1991; Lincoln County in June 2002; Kittitas County in May 2004; Adams County in August 2005; Whitman County in June 2007.

Red-eyed Vireo *Vireo olivaceus* — Fairly common but local summer resident in tall Black Cottonwood stands along major river valleys. Good sites include Skagit, Nooksack Valleys, Snoqualmie Valley from North Bend to Fall City, floodplain forests along Columbia River (Clark, Skamania, western Klickitat Counties). Probably most numerous, widespread in Northeast—especially valleys of Pend Oreille (easy to find at Sullivan Lake), Sanpoil, Kettle, Colville Rivers. Rarely noted in migration.

Gray Jay *Perisoreus canadensis* — Fairly common year-round resident in mature conifer forests of higher mountains throughout state. Uncommon, local at lower elevations in southwestern Washington. Usually easy to find at Paradise on Mount Rainier, Hurricane Ridge, picnic areas or campgrounds along upper portions of North Cascades Highway. Populations inhabiting Okanogan Highlands, mountains of Northeast, Southeast characterized by dark-gray underparts, contrasting, nearly all-white head. Birds from Cascades west have smaller white forehead area, extensive, dusky crown, auricular patch, nape; light-gray underparts appear almost white.

Pinyon Jay *Gymnorhinus cyanocephalus* — Captain Charles Bendire found this species "quite numerous" in oak openings at Fort Simcoe in June 1881. Only other state record: small flock near Goldendale in April 1967 (one bird collected).

Steller's Jay *Cyanocitta stelleri* — Fairly common year-round resident of coniferous forests virtually statewide, mostly at low to middle elevations; post-breeding wandering up to subalpine habitats, down to Garry Oak zone. Coastal movements in fall may be striking.

Blue Jay *Cyanocitta cristata* — Rare but regular winter resident in Eastern Washington towns and cities, especially along eastern edge of state (e.g., Spokane, Pullman, Walla Walla). Casual winter resident in western lowlands, mostly in residential areas.

Western Scrub-Jay *Aphelocoma californica* — Fairly common year-round resident in lowlands of Southwest. Species on the move, with now breeding north to Bellingham, west to Raymond, east to Goldendale and Yakima. Most common in habitats dominated by Garry Oak, as well as in towns and cities. Resident Washington birds belong to coastal form of species (dark upperparts contrast vividly with white underparts). Individual of distinctive interior population (more muted in coloration) observed at Chief Timothy State Park (Asotin County) in February 2002.

Clark's Nutcracker *Nucifraga columbiana* — Fairly common year-round resident in drier subalpine forests in Cascades, Selkirks, Blue Mountains. Small numbers in Olympics (northeastern rainshadow), Blues. Whitebark Pine major food source. Also found in Ponderosa Pine forests, especially if rugged terrain nearby for seed caching. Easily seen at Mount Rainier (Paradise, Sunrise), Chinook Pass, where it seeks handouts. Occasionally wanders to lowlands.

Black-billed Magpie *Pica hudsonia* — Common, conspicuous year-round resident throughout unforested Eastern Washington, about ranches, farms, riparian edges, shrub-steppe habitats up to lower Ponderosa Pine zone. Generally shuns highly built-up cities. Post-breeding wanderers reach subalpine habitats, especially in Okanogan Highlands, Blue Mountains. Recorded west in winter.

American Crow *Corvus brachyrhynchos* — Common, prodigiously increasing year-round resident of Western Washington, from lowlands up into middle elevations of mountains, especially about farms, cities, suburbs, recently logged areas. In Eastern Washington, common summer resident, uncommon to locally fairly common winter resident in Okanogan, Columbia, Yakima, Walla Walla River valleys. Not found in dense, contiguous conifer forests. Perhaps still absent from San Juan Islands, Outer Olympic Coast (see Northwestern Crow).

Northwestern Crow *Corvus caurinus* — "After lengthy discussion it is pretty well settled that the Crow of the northwestern sea-coasts is merely a dwarfed race of [American Crow], and that it shades perfectly into the prevailing western type whenever that species occupies adjacent regions" (William Leon Dawson, *The Birds of Washington*, 1909). True a hundred years ago, still true today. Northwestern Crow originally inhabited Puget Trough shoreline, outer coast from Grays Harbor north, isolated by uncut, deep forests from American Crow populations along streams in Eastern, southwestern Washington. Deforestation by settlers, commercial loggers fostered interbreeding along south Puget Sound by late 1800s, with result that Dawson found it "impossible to pronounce with certainty upon the subspecific identity of crows seen near shore in Mason, Thurston, Pierce, or even King County." With continuing development, American Crow invaded whole Puget Trough, swamping indigenous Northwestern population. Phenotypically pure Northwestern Crows arguably recognizable along Outer Olympic Coast (e.g., La Push), in San Juan Islands.

Common Raven *Corvus corax* — Widespread, conspicuous, year-round resident in most terrestrial habitats except cities, towns. Mostly lacking from main urban corridor Everett–Tacoma. Amazingly adaptable, found from sea level to alpine elevations, even in winter. May form sizable winter flocks in lowlands.

Sky Lark *Alauda arvensis* — Now accidental in state. Formerly bred in small numbers at American Camp on southern San Juan Island. Strayed there from introduced, non-migratory population established on southeastern Vancouver Island since early 1900s (subspecies *arvensis* from western Europe). First recorded on San Juan Island 1960, first documented nesting 1970, apparently extirpated as breeder by mid-1990s. Subspecific identity of two birds seen across Strait of Juan de Fuca near Sequim, in winter 1998–1999, not determined. Perhaps wanderers from introduced population, perhaps migrants from Asia (subspecies *pekinensis*).

Horned Lark *Eremophila alpestris* — Common, widespread, year-round resident, especially in open areas of Eastern Washington. Three breeding races, at least one more as winter resident. Subspecies *strigata* uncommon year-round resident in lowlands west of Cascades. Seriously declining on account of habitat loss, now confined as breeder to prairies on Joint Base Lewis-McChord, beach dunes at Ocean Shores, sandbars in Columbia River (Wahkiakum, Pacific Counties). Subspecies *alpina* fairly common but local during nesting season in alpine communities—Olympics, high volcanoes, elsewhere in Cascades (especially east side of crest). Burroughs Mountain on Mount Rainier one fairly accessible site. Subspecies *merrilli* common year round in most open, low-elevation habitats in Eastern Washington—especially wheat fields, shallow-soiled portions of shrub-steppe zone. Characteristic, conspicuous bird of Columbia Basin, beginning breeding cycle early in spring (February some years), raising as many as three broods. Forms large, roving flocks in winter, especially over wheat fields. Pale subspecies—including **arcticola** from interior British Columbia as well as *alpina*—common winter residents, especially in northern parts of Columbia Basin. Good numbers on Waterville Plateau, Timentwa Flats mixed in with *merrilli* flocks.

Purple Martin *Progne subis* — Fairly common, increasing, but still local summer resident of Western Washington lowlands, mainly around Puget Sound, lower Columbia River. Historically rare in Washington, increased with Euro-American development until late 1950s when European Starlings began appropriating nesting cavities. Martin numbers crashed to point of near-extirpation by early 1990s; numerous nest-box schemes have greatly aided recovery. Currently, most nest on pilings over water, shunned by starlings. Recorded east.

Tree Swallow *Tachycineta bicolor* — Common summer resident near open country (where forages, often over water) with cavities (where nests, usually in stubs, snags), at low to mid-elevations; absent from dense forests, central Columbia Basin. Casual winter west. Earliest swallow to return in spring (first birds usually February).

Violet-green Swallow *Tachycineta thalassina* — Common summer resident throughout Washington, including cities, agricultural areas, open forests of all ages, around open water. In Columbia Basin, local in towns, around farm buildings; uncommon on high cliffs (Yakima Canyon, Columbia River south of Vantage). Nests in cavities in trees, cliffs, buildings, also in nest boxes. Casual winter west. Early migrant, appearing in March (even February in south).

Northern Rough-winged Swallow *Stelgidopteryx serripennis* — Fairly common summer resident along streams, other water bodies with sandy banks, where nests.

Bank Swallow *Riparia riparia* — Locally common summer resident in Eastern Washington, mostly near rivers, irrigation canals. Nests colonially, absent from some areas, abundant in others. Especially numerous along Hanford Reach (one colony may contain 10,000 nests some years), parts of lower Yakima River valley. Sometimes forms large roosting or staging flocks during fall migration. Nests locally in Western Washington, perhaps increasing; colonies discovered recently along Toutle River (Cowlitz County), Green River (King County), Skagit River near Concrete and Marblemount (Skagit County). Rare migrant elsewhere on Westside.

Cliff Swallow *Petrochelidon pyrrhonota* — Common summer resident in lowlands throughout state, often nesting in large colonies under bridges. Abundant locally in Eastern Washington—e.g., on cliffs of Grand Coulee, Yakima Canyon, Hanford Reach, Snake River.

Barn Swallow *Hirundo rustica* — Common summer resident statewide at all but highest elevations—wherever open habitat for foraging exists in proximity to suitable nest-building sites (almost always man-made structures such as buildings, bridges). Casual winter west.

Black-capped Chickadee *Poecile atricapillus* — Common year-round resident nearly statewide in habitats with deciduous vegetation, mostly at lower elevations. Distinctly less common with westward progression on Olympic Peninsula. Mostly absent from San Juan Islands, also from some areas in central Columbia Basin that appear to contain suitable habitat.

Mountain Chickadee *Poecile gambeli* — Common year-round resident of coniferous forests throughout Eastern Washington. Spills west over Cascade Crest into higher subalpine forests in a few places—fairly common around Mount Rainier. Also fairly common in drier forests southwest of Mount Adams. Casual in lowlands outside nesting season, irregularly into western Washington.

Chestnut-backed Chickadee *Poecile rufescens* — Common year-round resident of coniferous forests in Western Washington. Main chickadee on San Juan Islands, where found in all forested habitats. In Eastern Washington, fairly common in wetter forest habitats along east slopes of Cascades (above Ponderosa Pine zone), in Northeast (Mount Spokane north), uncommon in Blue Mountains.

Boreal Chickadee *Poecile hudsonicus* — Uncommon year-round resident of dense, high-elevation forests along northern tier of counties in Eastern Washington. Favors Engelmann Spruce, Subalpine Fir forests, occasionally nearby Lodgepole Pines. Harts Pass, Tiffany Mountain area, Salmo Pass good bets. Hardest to find in June, when nesting. Inhabits some of the remotest parts of Washington; one of the last of state's regular resident species to be discovered (1920).

Bushtit *Psaltriparus minimus* — Brown-crowned Pacific form (subspecies *minimus*, *saturatus*) common year-round resident in shrubby growth in mixed-forest openings, parks, gardens throughout Puget Lowlands. Scarce on outer coast. East through Columbia Gorge at least to Rock Creek, also locally along base of east slopes of Cascades in south central Washington (Satus Creek south of Toppenish, Yakima River near Cle Elum). "Interior" form (subspecies group *plumbeus*) extremely local in eastern Washington. In addition to an unreviewed earlier report from Yakima County, recently confirmed breeding in a small flock at Potholes Reservoir (Grant County).

Red-breasted Nuthatch *Sitta canadensis* — Common year-round resident in all forested zones, from city parks, suburban gardens to treeline. Winter populations in lowlands—particularly east—include migrants from higher latitudes or elevations.

White-breasted Nuthatch *Sitta carolinensis* — In Eastern Washington, subspecies *tenuissima* uncommon to locally fairly common year-round resident in Ponderosa Pine forests and mixed Garry Oak/Ponderosa Pine woodlands ringing Columbia Basin. Coastal subspecies *aculeata* once locally fairly common in mixed Garry Oak/Douglas-fir woodlands of Western Washington but now virtually extirpated; Ridgefield NWR most important remaining site.

Pygmy Nuthatch *Sitta pygmaea* — Fairly common but local year-round resident of Eastern Washington Ponderosa Pine forests. Easy to find at Kamiak Butte, Turnbull NWR, forests around Spokane. Recorded west.

Brown Creeper *Certhia americana* — Fairly common summer resident of moist forest habitats statewide. In winter, fairly common resident of Western Washington lowlands, foothills. In Eastern Washington, fairly common in migration, uncommon to rare winter resident at lower elevations.

Rock Wren *Salpinctes obsoletus* — Common summer resident of rocky canyons, coulees, talus slopes in Eastern Washington. Uncommon to rare in winter in southern parts of Columbia Basin. A few on west slopes of Cascades—e.g., has colonized blast area of Mount Saint Helens. Otherwise, casual in Western Washington lowlands in migration, winter.

Canyon Wren *Catherpes mexicanus* — Uncommon year-round resident of cliffs in Eastern Washington, usually best detected by vocalizations. Recorded west near Cascade Crest.

House Wren *Troglodytes aedon* — Common summer resident of relatively open, brushy habitats at low elevations in Eastern Washington, especially around edges of lower forest zones, in towns. Fairly common to common but highly local summer resident of similar habitats in Western Washington, notably dry prairies, forests of South Sound, Whidbey Island, San Juans, other areas of recent clearcuts.

Pacific Wren *Troglodytes pacificus* — Common year-round resident of coniferous forest west of Cascade Crest, mostly withdrawing downslope to escape heavy snows in winter. In Eastern Washington, summer resident of wetter habitats at higher elevations, fairly common migrant at lower elevations; winters sparingly in well-vegetated lowland stream bottoms.

Marsh Wren *Cistothorus palustris* — Common summer resident of low-elevation marshes with cattails or other emergent vegetation suitable for nest sites. In winter, fairly common resident in variety of wetland habitats, but Eastside populations thin out or disappear when subfreezing temperatures settle in. In all seasons, widely distributed west, much more local east (Potholes, Toppenish NWR, Turnbull NWR, major Eastside population centers).

Bewick's Wren *Thryomanes bewickii* — Common year-round resident in Western Washington lowlands, including urban environments. In Eastern Washington, until recently confined to Columbia River from Gorge east to about Tri-Cities, lower Yakima River (especially around Satus Creek south of Toppenish). Recent dramatic range expansion; now fairly common to locally common length of Snake River into Idaho, north through Palouse to Spokane area, uncommon up into Okanogan County and some parts of northeast. May die back in severe winters.

Blue-gray Gnatcatcher *Polioptila caerulea* — Fourteen records statewide. Casual in fall–winter (October–February) at low elevations, mostly in Western Washington. Most records from westside. Summer records from a territorial male in Hardy Canyon (Yakima County) in 2002 and 2003, and from Clark County in 2011.

American Dipper *Cinclus mexicanus* — Uncommon year-round resident on rushing streams mostly in forested mountainous areas, throughout state. As higher-elevation streams freeze either partially or wholly in winter, many descend to lower elevations. Also gather in fall, early winter in streams where salmon spawn, to dip for eggs.

Golden-crowned Kinglet *Regulus satrapa* — Common, widespread summer resident of coniferous forests, nesting even in well-treed city neighborhoods. Common outside nesting season in lowland Western Washington, important component of mixed-species foraging flocks. Common migrant, uncommon local winterer in lowlands of Eastern Washington.

Ruby-crowned Kinglet *Regulus calendula* — Common migrant, winter resident in Westside lowland habitats. Uncommon spring, common fall migrant east. Fairly common summer resident in drier, higher Eastern Washington subalpine forests, also west on rainshadowed northeastern slopes of Olympics, and just west of Cascade Crest. Stays late in lowlands in spring until breeding grounds open up, often heard singing then.

Northern Wheatear *Oenanthe oenanthe* — Three records: Nisqually NWR (Thurston County) in September 2004; Westport (Grays Harbor County) late October–early November 2012; Vashon Island (King County) October 2014.

Western Bluebird *Sialia mexicana* — Fairly common summer resident in Eastern Washington, primarily in lower portions of Ponderosa Pine, upper shrub-steppe zones. Favors openings in drier forests. Easy to find in suitable habitat in Okanogan Valley, also on bluebird nest-box trails (e.g., Bickleton area, Umptanum/Wenas Road). In Western Washington, uncommon in Joint Base Lewis-McChord area; rare, local in forest clearings, around farmlands elsewhere in Puget Trough. Usually findable somewhere in state in any month. Returns early in spring (first birds back by February). Strong numbers winter most years at Lyle in Columbia Gorge, a few others in Columbia Basin, Puget Trough.

Mountain Bluebird *Sialia currucoides* — Fairly common summer resident, mostly eastside in open terrain from upper shrub-steppe habitats upslope to alpine. Easy to find on bluebird trails (Umptanum/Wenas Road, Bickleton area). On Westside, fairly common on Mount Rainier (easy to see at Sunrise), Mount Saint Helens. Uncommon on upper west slopes of Cascades, especially in wind-blasted, open forest near crest, descending lower very locally in clearcuts. Rare spring migrant, casual winter resident east, west.

Townsend's Solitaire *Myadestes townsendi* — Fairly common (east) to uncommon (west) summer resident of forest openings in mountains, except apparently absent from wet west side of Olympics. Usually near steep, rugged terrain, occupying wide range of elevations from lower forest line (Eastside), middle elevations (Westside) up to alpine. Often nests under overhanging roots or near rock crevices on steep roadcuts. Uncommon spring migrant statewide. Uncommon (east) to rare (west) in winter in berry-rich habitats (riparian areas, ornamental plantings, groves of junipers).

Veery *Catharus fuscescens* — Fairly common summer resident of dense riparian habitats in lower forest zones (especially Ponderosa Pine) of Eastern Washington, with small, disjunct population in Skagit River drainage in Whatcom County. Easy to find along Wenas Creek. Arrives relatively late in spring (singing after about May 25).

Gray-cheeked Thrush *Catharus minimus* — One record, from McNary NWR in October 1990.

Swainson's Thrush *Catharus ustulatus* — Common summer resident in moist, leafy understory of mixed or hardwood forests at low to middle (occasionally higher) elevations virtually statewide. Especially widespread, conspicuous in lowlands west of Cascades—even in parks, small woodlots. Two well-marked races breed in state—**Russet-backed Thrush** (subspecies *ustulatus*) of Western Washington, southeastern Cascades, **Olive-backed Thrush** (subspecies *swainsoni*) of northeastern Cascades, Northeast, Southeast.

Hermit Thrush *Catharus guttatus* — Fairly common to common summer resident in most mid-, upper-elevation mountain forests. Favors habitats with sparser shrub understory than Swainson's Thrush, at higher elevations, although elevational overlap substantial. Uncommon or absent in moistest forests. Washington's hardiest *Catharus* thrush, only one in winter when occurs in small numbers in western lowlands, milder parts east.

Dusky Thrush *Turdus naumanni* — One record, from Mount Vernon (Skagit County) in June 2002.

Redwing *Turdus iliacus* – One record from Olympia (Thurston County) from December 2004–March 2005.

American Robin *Turdus migratorius* — Most common, widely distributed Washington thrush in all seasons. Nests wherever there are trees or heavy brush (but not in dense, wet forests), forages in nearly every conceivable habitat. Large post-breeding flocks congregate in mountains in summer. Wintering numbers in lowlands apparently swelled by birds arriving from mountains or farther north. Spring, fall movements often impressive, but migration patterns, various populations involved not worked out.

Varied Thrush *Ixoreus naevius* — Common summer resident in mature, moist, relatively intact Westside forests, from sea level to lower subalpine. Generally descends below zone of heavy snow in winter. Now largely absent as breeding bird from Puget Lowlands due to forest fragmentation, urbanization, but fairly common there as winter resident, attracted to native, exotic food sources. Common in winter in forests along outer coast. East of Cascade Crest, fairly common to locally common summer resident in lower, closed subalpine, upper mixed-conifer forests—lower along stream courses—but mostly absent in drier Douglas-fir and Ponderosa Pine forests. Descends to low elevations where uncommon in winter. Like other retiring woodland thrushes, stays close to cover, can be difficult to see; haunting song, given especially in early morning, betrays its presence.

Gray Catbird *Dumetella carolinensis* — Fairly common but skulking summer resident along streams in Eastern Washington in dense, shrubby vegetation (willows, Red-osier Dogwood, wild rose, Blue Elderberry). Most common in major river valleys of Okanogan, Northeast (e.g., Pend Oreille, Colville, Kettle, Sanpoil, Okanogan). Less common, local south to Yakima area along east base of Cascades; disjunct population near Trout Lake. Casual west.

Brown Thrasher *Toxostoma rufum* — Casual vagrant. Fifteen records: 10 in spring/summer, four in fall and one in winter. Also little pattern to location, spread evenly on each side of state, from Clallam County to Spokane County.

Sage Thrasher *Oreoscoptes montanus* — Fairly common summer resident in Eastern Washington in areas of extensive Big Sagebrush with associated vigorous cover of perennial grasses. Mostly absent where ground cover is introduced Cheatgrass, hence from southern Columbia Basin except on a few high-elevation or north-facing ridges (Rattlesnake Mountain, Horse Heaven Hills east of Bickleton). Easy sites include Quilomene Wildlife Area, Umptanum Road. Casual spring migrant in western lowlands.

Northern Mockingbird *Mimus polyglottos* — Rare wanderer from south to lowlands on both sides of state, mostly fall–winter. Sometimes appears in urban settings. Several recent breeding records eastside.

European Starling *Sturnus vulgaris* — Common statewide in lowland habitats. Absent from relatively intact forest, also higher elevations except around developed sites. Introduced to North America from Europe. Reached Washington from east by early 1950s, abundant statewide only 20 years later. Implicated in significant declines of cavity-dependent species in Washington such as Lewis's Woodpecker, Purple Martin, Western Bluebird. Forms huge flocks in winter.

Siberian Accentor *Prunella montanella* — Two records: the first, a first for Western Hemisphere outside Alaska at Indian Island (Jefferson County) in October 1983; another on Orcas Island (San Juan County) in January 1991.

Eastern Yellow Wagtail *Motacilla tschutschensis* — Two records from Ocean Shores: late July 1992, mid-September 2000.

White Wagtail *Motacilla alba* — Nine accepted records, three of the white form, four black-backed, and two not distinguished to subspecies group. Three from winter, six from April–May. All from Western Washington.

Red-throated Pipit *Anthus cervinus* — Two records: One from San Juan Island in September 1979; one from Bainbridge Island (Kitsap County) in May 2004.

American Pipit *Anthus rubescens* — Common migrant (April–May, September–October) in open areas of lowlands virtually statewide, especially along coast (shores, dunes), agricultural fields; often detected calling overhead. Fairly common but local summer resident at high elevations of Cascades, Olympics, occupying moist seeps where alpine vegetation well developed. Easy to find on trails above Paradise at Mount Rainier (especially from Panorama Point up), Hurricane Ridge, Deer Park, high passes in North Cascades. Uncommon winter on shorelines, open farmlands in lowland Western Washington.

Bohemian Waxwing *Bombycilla garrulus* — Fairly common to irregularly common winter resident in orchards, vineyards, residential areas of Eastern Washington, usually in large flocks. Rare, irregular west of Cascades. Probably easiest to find from Lake Chelan north to Methow, Okanogan River valleys, also Spokane, urban areas in Southeast (Pullman, Walla Walla). Once regular south to Yakima but scarcer recently. Handful of confirmed breeding records from North Cascades. Sometimes found in fall in upper subalpine (Cascades, Northeast), feeding on Common Juniper berries and Mountain Ash.

Cedar Waxwing *Bombycilla cedrorum* — Common summer resident of open forests, orchards, residential areas with mature ornamental plantings, usually at low to mid-elevations. Irregular winter resident in lowlands; numbers, locations vary year to year. Most consistent in winter in Columbia Basin; lesser numbers around Puget Sound.

Phainopepla *Phainopepla nitens* — One record, from Seattle in September 1994.

Lapland Longspur *Calcarius lapponicus* — In Western Washington, uncommon fall migrant, rare winter resident, rare spring migrant in open terrain along outer coast, locally in Puget Trough. Uncommon fall migrant along alpine ridges in Cascades. Most easily found late September–November in open habitats at Ocean Shores Game Range, Damon Point, outer portions of Dungeness Spit. In Eastern Washington, uncommon migrant, rare winter resident in northern parts of Columbia Basin, over higher ridges southward. Flocks on Waterville Plateau, Timentwa Flats late March–April may contain birds in breeding plumage.

Chestnut-collared Longspur *Calcarius ornatus* — Eight records: Five in spring/summer (late May–early July), three in fall (October–mid-December). Five from outer coast, two from Puget Sound lowlands, one in Okanogan County.

Smith's Longspur *Calcarius pictus* — Two records: One in August 2006 at Marymoor Park (King County); one in late-August to early–September 2013 at Ocean Shores (Grays Harbor County).

McCown's Longspur *Calcarius mccownii* — One record, Montlake Fill, Seattle, June 2013.

Snow Bunting *Plectrophenax nivalis* — Local, somewhat irregular fall migrant, winter resident on open terrain. Rare at best in Western Washington, most often found late fall along Pacific, North Olympic Coasts (Ocean Shores, Dungeness Spit), occasionally on beaches elsewhere. Numbers much higher in Eastern Washington. Often fairly common on high Columbia Plateau (Waterville Plateau, Timentwa Flats, Davenport/Reardan area). Highest numbers there in February, perhaps bottled up awaiting snowmelt farther north.

McKay's Bunting *Plectrophenax hyperboreus* — Four records: three records of birds wintering with Snow Buntings at Ocean Shores (December 1978–March 1979, January–February 1988, and December 2011–February 2012); another bird seen for two days in November 1993 on Lummi Flats (Whatcom County).

Ovenbird *Seiurus aurocapilla* — Casual migrant. Fifteen Westside records: 10 from June and one each month from July through November. Eleven Eastside records, eight mid-May to mid-July (two September, one November). Seasonal imbalance may be artifact of easier detection when birds singing.

Northern Waterthrush *Parkesia noveboracensis* — Fairly common summer resident of wetlands lined with alder and willow, swamps of Okanogan, Northeast. Good sites include Amazon Creek Marsh, Little Pend Oreille Lakes, Myers Creek north of Chesaw, Big Meadow Lake. Rare fall migrant, winter visitor to sloughs in lowland Western Washington.

Golden-winged Warbler *Vermivora chrysoptera* — Two records: one, banded at Turnbull NWR (Spokane County) in August 1998; one on Bainbridge Island (Kitsap County) September 2003.

Blue-winged Warbler *Vermivora cyanoptera* — Four records: Skagit County, September 1990; Douglas County, August 2006; Clallam County, June 2011; Walla Walla County, August 2012.

Black-and-white Warbler *Mniotilta varia* — Casual migrant, occurs almost annually. Records scattered across calendar, map; largest concentration in Eastern Washington in spring (May–June).

Prothonotary Warbler *Protonotaria citrea* — Three records, all from Tri-Cities area: Richland (Benton County) in September 1970; McNary NWR (Walla Walla County), October 2005; Richland again, August 2007.

Tennessee Warbler *Oreothlypis peregrina* — Casual fall, accidental spring migrant east, west. One long-staying winter record from Satsop (Grays Harbor County).

Orange-crowned Warbler *Oreothlypis celata* — Common (west) to fairly common (east) migrant, rare winter resident in lowlands. Two subspecies breed. Relatively bright *lutescens* common summer resident of deciduous forests, brushy places in Western Washington lowlands, becoming less common, local at higher elevations; decidedly uncommon, spottily distributed in forest zones on east slope of Cascades. Duller *orestera* fairly common summer resident in mountains of Northeast, Southeast. Third subspecies, *celata*, rare migrant.

Lucy's Warbler *Oreothlypis luciae* — One record from November 2014 in Neah Bay, Clallam County.

Nashville Warbler *Oreothlypis ruficapilla* — Fairly common summer resident in forested zones of Eastern Washington, extending west in Columbia Gorge to around Mount Adams. Inhabits brushy, open habitats, often along streams, at forest edges, in regenerating clearcuts, near rock slides, road cuts. Small numbers drift down upper west slope of Cascades to nest in similar habitats. Uncommon spring, fall migrant through lowlands on east side of Cascades, rare in fall west of the Cascades. Eastern subspecies *ruficapilla* recorded once (Stevens County, July 2012).

MacGillivray's Warbler *Geothlypis tolmiei* — Fairly common summer resident of shrubby tangles almost statewide, easiest to find in regenerating clearcuts, rank vegetation along roadsides, avalanche chutes, from middle elevations to subalpine. Typical of riparian vegetation through much of Eastern Washington conifer zone. Quite uncommon in Puget Lowlands except locally (e.g., South Sound Prairies). Absent from dense, wet forests, Columbia Basin. Uncommon to fairly common migrant in lowlands virtually statewide.

Mourning Warbler *Geothlypis philadelphia* —Two records: Lyons Ferry (Franklin County), May 2001; Washtucna (Adams County), August 2007.

Kentucky Warbler *Geothlypis formosa* — One record, near Darrington (Snohomish County) in June 1992.

Common Yellowthroat *Geothlypis trichas* — Common summer resident of wetlands, brushy fields at mostly lower elevations in Western Washington; a few winter. Fairly common but local summer resident east of Cascades, where more characteristic of cattail marshes.

Hooded Warbler *Setophaga citrina* — Six records, four from sping/summer, two from winter. First record wintered at Discovery Park in Seattle (December 1975–April 1976). Three records from Whitman County (June 1986, December 1989, May 2014), each of several days duration. One from Grant County (June 2004). One from Skamania County (July–August 2013).

American Redstart *Setophaga ruticilla* — Uncommon to locally fairly common summer resident of dense alder- and willow-dominated wetlands in Okanogan, Northeast. Good sites include Myers Creek north of Chesaw, Sullivan Lake, West Fork Sanpoil Campground, Big Meadow Lake. Rare to locally uncommon west of Cascade Crest, most dependable site County Line Ponds in Skagit River valley. Rare migrant anywhere away from breeding grounds.

Cape May Warbler *Setophaga tigrina* — Two records: one in Bellingham in September 1974; one in Spokane, January–April 2005.

Northern Parula Setophaga americana — Casual (west) to accidental (east), mostly in summer. All but one record from end of May through mid-September. Exception was the first state record from January–February 1975 in Richland (Benton County).

Magnolia Warbler Setophaga magnolia — Casual fall migrant on both sides of Cascades. Nineteen fall records (nine from westside, 10 from eastside). Five spring records (four on eastside, one on westside).

Bay-breasted Warbler Setophaga castanea — Three state records, all since 2002: near Moses Lake (Grant County), September 2002; near Chehalis (Lewis County), June 2006; Vantage (Kittitas County), September 2010.

Blackburnian Warbler Setophaga fusca —Six records: three spring records (late May, June), all from Eastern Washington; three fall records (August, September, December), two from Western Washington and one from Eastern Washington.

Yellow Warbler Setophaga petechia — Common summer resident statewide. Nests in riparian areas, similar places where willows, other deciduous trees grow near water (ponds, ditches, mountain streamlets).

Chestnut-sided Warbler Setophaga pensylvanica — Casual migrant, more frequent June-July than fall. Overall, Eastside records outnumber Westside records by about 2-to-1, and spring/summer records outnumber fall records by the same margin.

Blackpoll Warbler Setophaga striata — Casual fall migrant (late August–September) in Eastern Washington. About 27 fall records, only two from Western Washington. Five spring records (May and June), four from Eastern Washington, one from Western Washington.

Black-throated Blue Warbler Setophaga caerulescens — Accidental fall migrant east, west; accidental winter visitor west. Nine of eleven records between late September and December. One spring record from Olympia (Thurston County), March–April 1995. One summer record from King County, June 2012.

Palm Warbler Setophaga palmarum — In Western Washington, rare fall migrant, winter resident. Easiest to find on outer coast (especially in Scot's Broom thickets at Ocean Shores). Casual spring migrant east, west; accidental east in fall.

Yellow-rumped Warbler Setophaga coronata — Breeding form **Audubon's Warbler** (subspecies auduboni)—common summer resident in open coniferous forests of Eastern Washington, somewhat less numerous but still widespread, common in open forests of Western Washington (northeastern Olympics, subalpine parkland, old-growth Douglas-fir on upper west-slope Cascades), though mostly shunning tree farms, moist forests of outer coast, dense Silver Fir forests of Cascades. Common migrant statewide. **Myrtle Warbler** (subspecies coronata) common (west) to uncommon (east) migrant in lowlands. Both subspecies uncommon in western lowlands in winter, mostly around Puget Trough (Myrtle fairly common on South Coast). In Eastern Washington, Audubon's uncommon winter resident in Columbia Basin (fairly common in southern portion), especially attracted to Russian Olive; Myrtle, though scarcer, also occurs, especially in willows.

Yellow-throated Warbler Setophaga dominica — Two records, one in Twisp (Okanogan County) December 2001–January 2002; one in Asotin County, October 2003.

Prairie Warbler Setophaga discolor — One record, from Wallula (Walla Walla County) in December 1989.

Black-throated Gray Warbler Setophaga nigrescens— Fairly common summer resident in mixed deciduous/conifer woodlands at low elevations west of Cascade Crest. On Eastside, fairly common summer resident locally in similar habitats along

Yakima, lower Cle Elum Rivers in western Kittitas County, also a few in mixed woodlands in western Klickitat County; rare migrant elsewhere.

Townsend's Warbler *Setophaga townsendi* — Common summer resident of conifer forests (especially fir-dominated) almost statewide; now local in Puget Lowlands due to fragmentation of habitat. In Eastern Washington, largely absent from Ponderosa Pine zone, uncommon in subalpine parkland. Many individuals in southwestern Cascades, eastern Olympics show signs of hybridization with Hermit Warbler (see discussion on page 232). Uncommon winter resident of Westside lowlands.

Hermit Warbler *Setophaga occidentalis* — Uncommon, local summer resident of conifer forests on south, east slopes of Olympic Mountains, in Southwest. Local on upper east slopes of Cascades from White Pass south. Not on outer coast. Recent research reveals two narrow zones of hybridization with Townsend's Warbler: one in eastern Olympics, other along west slope of Cascades from about Mount Adams north to White Pass (see discussion on page 232). Many individuals in or near these zones not safely separable.

Black-throated Green Warbler *Setophaga virens* — Three records: Dishman (Spokane County) in July 1975; Wanapum State Park (Kittitas County) in June 2003; Washtucna (Adams County) in November 2004.

Canada Warbler *Cardellina Canadensis* – One record, McNary NWR (Walla Walla County), September 2010.

Wilson's Warbler *Cardellina pusilla* — Brighter-golden subspecies *chryseola* common summer resident west of Cascade Crest in variety of moist, wooded habitats with well-developed understory vegetation; arrives on breeding territory late April–early May. Casual in winter. East of crest, duller *pileolata* subspecies common spring, fall migrant, most passing through late in late May or early June; uncommon, local summer resident of moist, shrubby places in open mountain forests, particularly in Northeast.

Yellow-breasted Chat *Icteria virens* — Fairly common to locally common summer resident of lower-elevation, open, brushy streamside habitats in Eastern Washington, mostly at the margins between Ponderosa Pine forests and shrub-steppe around edges of Columbia Basin. Scattered records from Western Washington in migration, nesting season.

Green-tailed Towhee *Pipilo chlorurus* — Rare, local summer resident of brushy habitats on steep hillsides in Blue Mountains, often requiring time, physical commitment to reach. Good sites include Lewis Peak, Biscuit Ridge, Wenatchee Guard Station. Accidental in Puget Lowlands in winter.

Spotted Towhee *Pipilo maculatus* — Common summer resident statewide, except in high mountains, dense forest, Columbia Basin. Mostly in low to mid-elevation shrubby habitats, including urban areas, open forests, clearcuts, margins of wetlands, brush-filled ravines. Common west, fairly common east in winter; withdraws from snowy areas.

American Tree Sparrow *Spizella arborea* — Uncommon (east) to rare (west) winter resident of cattail-marsh edges, brushy habitats. Most frequent November–December around Molson, West Foster Creek, Potholes, Big Flat HMU. West of Cascades, most reports from mixed-species sparrow flocks at Skagit Game Range, Snoqualmie Valley.

Chipping Sparrow *Spizella passerina* — Common summer resident of open conifer forests in Eastern Washington, especially Ponderosa Pine zone, subalpine. Fairly common but local in dry-forest habitats of Western Washington—e.g., northeastern Olympics (Hurricane Ridge to Sequim), Mount Constitution on Orcas Island,

Joint Base Lewis-McChord prairies, Mount Rainier (especially rainshadow side). Uncommon elsewhere in migration.

Clay-colored Sparrow *Spizella pallida* — Rare, local summer resident and occasional breeder in Spokane Valley, Okanogan, Northeast. Mostly reported on hillsides with dense brush. Scattered summer records elsewhere in Eastern Washington. Casual in Western Washington in any season, perhaps increasing.

Brewer's Sparrow *Spizella breweri* — Nominate subspecies common summer resident of Big Sagebrush communities with healthy understory of native bunchgrasses (not Cheatgrass). Good sites include Quilomene Wildlife Area (Kittitas County), Beezley Hills (Grant County), Tule Road south of Toppenish NWR (Yakima County), northern Timentwa Flats (Okanogan County). Casual (spring) to accidental (fall) on Westside in migration. Slightly larger, darker, longer-tailed **Timberline Sparrow** (subspecies *taverneri*) recorded a few times in migration, mostly April–early May. Best chance brushy ravines east of Cascades away from sagebrush; field identification perilous.

Vesper Sparrow *Pooecetes gramineus* — Coastal subspecies *affinis* rare, local, declining summer resident of lowland prairies in Western Washington—remnant populations in prairies of lower Puget Trough (especially at Joint Base Lewis-McChord) and on San Juan Island. Casual in winter. Widespread interior subspecies *confinis* common summer resident east of Cascades in flourishing stands of native grasses, often with scattered sagebrush—particularly in wetter, higher elevations of northern Columbia Basin. In South Central, mainly on north aspects of higher east-west trending ridges (Rattlesnake Mountain, Horse Heaven Hills). Also found near small trees, brush around edges of agricultural lands.

Lark Sparrow *Chondestes grammacus* — Fairly common but local summer resident in several distinct shrub-steppe habitats. Most frequent in lowest, hottest parts of Columbia Basin in variety of shrubs (Big Sagebrush, rabbitbrush) with dense Cheatgrass groundcover. Less common, but still regular, in agricultural settings near shrub-steppe. Uncommon on dry ridges, agricultural edge settings in Ponderosa Pine zone. Casual spring, fall migrant west of Cascades.

Black-throated Sparrow *Amphispiza bilineata* — Rare summer resident in lowest, rockiest, driest parts of Columbia Basin. May not occur annually. Best bet May–June in Vantage area, particularly along Recreation Road north of Vantage and east edge of Yakima Training Center along Huntzinger Road. Casual spring migrant west.

Sagebrush Sparrow *Artemisiospiza nevadensis* — Fairly common but local summer resident of mature Big Sagebrush stands with less grass cover than those favored by Brewer's Sparrow. Easy to find in Moses Coulee, Quilomene Wildlife Area, south slopes of Rattlesnake Mountain in Benton County, Hanford Reach National Monument, Yakima Training Center (widespread at lower elevations), lowermost sagebrush habitats on SR-17 just north of Dry Falls in Douglas County. Casual early-spring migrant west.

Lark Bunting *Calamospiza melanocorys* — Casual spring, fall migrant. Three records from southeastern Washington, one from Columbia Basin, six from near North Olympic, Pacific coasts, one from Puget Trough (first-year male at Joint Base Lewis-McChord in mid-July).

Savannah Sparrow *Passerculus sandwichensis* — Common summer resident of low-elevation grasslands, seaside dunes, farmlands statewide, mostly in human-influenced landscapes—even weedy vacant lots in cities. Also found in high-elevation meadows of Okanogan, Northeast (e.g., Harts Pass, Horseshoe Basin, Rainy Pass, Bunchgrass Meadows). In winter, rare west, casual east in same habitats—numbers vary from year to year. Westside breeding populations belong to coastal subspecies *brooksi*, Eastside to widespread interior subspecies *nevadensis*. Other subspecies can be common in migration, but differentiation difficult in the field.

Grasshopper Sparrow *Ammodramus savannarum* — Uncommon, local, summer resident of grasslands in Eastern Washington; one breeding-season record west. Sensitive to changes in vegetation—here one year, gone the next. Secretive nature, high-pitched song (often barely audible above frequent winds in this habitat) make it difficult to detect. Soap Lake Road (Okanogan County) seems dependable. Fairly common in northeastern Columbia Basin, on boulder-strewn plains northwest of Moses Lake toward Soap Lake (Grant County). Grasslands at Swanson Lakes, Turnbull NWR, Snake River in southeast also good. Casual west.

Le Conte's Sparrow *Ammodramus leconteii* — Five records, four from late May through June, one from November: Kennewick (Benton County), May 1964; Willapa Bay (Pacific County), November 1982; Deep Lake (Stevens County), June 1993; Lake Wenatchee (Chelan County), June 1996; Marblemount (Skagit County), June 2014.

Nelson's Sparrow *Ammodramus nelsoni* — One record, Sullivan Lake in September 1986.

Fox Sparrow *Passerella iliaca* — Several subspecies in Washington, assignable to four groups. **Sooty Fox Sparrow** (subspecies group *unalaschensis*) rare summer resident in dense brush on Outer Olympic Coast, Dungeness prairies (formerly), some smaller San Juan Islands. Common (west) to uncommon (east) winter resident in lowlands, augmented by other subspecies of Sooty group from farther north. **Slate-colored Fox Sparrow** (subspecies group *schistacea*) fairly common but local summer resident in brushy forest habitats from moderate elevations to subalpine, in Blue Mountains, Selkirks, Kettle Range, Okanogan Highlands, both slopes of Cascades. Local breeders winter south of Washington. Another subspecies (*altivagans*) intermediate between Slate-colored and Red groups, from farther north, uncommon (east) to rare (west) fall migrant, rare winter resident. **Red Fox Sparrow** (subspecies group *iliaca*) likely annual in winter, on passage. **Thick-billed Fox Sparrow** (subspecies group *megarhyncha*) apparently present at least some years around White Pass and possibly other sites in the far south Cascades in summer, with only one or two accepted records in the state.

Song Sparrow *Melospiza melodia* — Common year-round resident at low to mid-elevations statewide, at home in all but most arid, barren, or densely forested habitats. Local in Columbia Basin. Prefers brushy places with water easily available. Populations from Cascades west have dark brown backs and strongly-marked underparts compared to paler populations breeding from Columbia Basin eastward. Other forms of this highly variable species, sometimes found in winter, not yet systematically tracked, sorted out.

Lincoln's Sparrow *Melospiza lincolnii* — Secretive migrant statewide, in numbers much greater than generally appreciated. Uncommon to locally fairly common winter resident in dense brush in lowlands west of Cascades, uncommon east. Fairly common summer resident of mid-elevation wetlands in Cascades, mountains of Northeast.

Swamp Sparrow *Melospiza georgiana* — Rare migrant, winter resident, mostly west of Cascades in marshes, other wetland habitats. Secretive. Often observed in dense growth of introduced Reed Canary Grass.

White-throated Sparrow *Zonotrichia albicollis* — Uncommon migrant, winter resident in dense lowland brush. Increasing. Rare, perhaps increasing, in summer.

Harris's Sparrow *Zonotrichia querula* — Uncommon winter resident of lowland, relatively open, brushy habitats, more frequent east of Cascades.

White-crowned Sparrow *Zonotrichia leucophrys* — Three forms. Subspecies *pugetensis* common summer resident throughout Western Washington, in shrubby habitats in cities, farmland, clearcuts, young forests, extending up to Cascade Crest in recently logged sites. Fairly common summer resident in Eastern Washington in brushy habitats along Yakima River drainage from vicinity of Snoqualmie, Stampede, White Passes down to lower edge of Ponderosa Pine zone. Uncommon in winter in western lowlands, rare east. Subspecies *gambelii* uncommon, local summer resident in Cascades, from Slate Peak, Horseshoe Basin south to White Pass. Common migrant in Columbia Basin, especially April when wave upon wave move through shrub-steppe. Fairly common migrant in Western Washington (but uncommon on outer coast). Large numbers winter locally in southern Columbia Basin. Uncommon to locally fairly common in winter in Western Washington (more common than *pugetensis*). Song distinctive, allowing easy separation from *pugetensis* where breeding ranges come into contact in Cascade passes—both forms also sing in late winter, on spring passage. Subspecies *oriantha* uncommon summer resident locally on high peaks in Northeast (e.g., Salmo Mountain), Blue Mountains. Accidental in North Cascades, and dark-lored birds recorded west of the Cascades in winter and spring migration. Main wintering range probably south of Washington.

Golden-crowned Sparrow *Zonotrichia atricapilla* — Common migrant, winter resident of shrubby cover in lowlands of Western Washington, east in Columbia Gorge to about Maryhill. Uncommon to irregularly fairly common migrant, uncommon winter resident east of Cascades. Has nested in subalpine in northernmost Cascades (fairly common summer resident in mountains just north of Fraser River in British Columbia).

Dark-eyed Junco *Junco hyemalis* — One of commonest, most widespread species in state. Two forms, formerly considered separate species are regular in state. **Oregon Junco** common year-round resident of brushy edges, open forests in conifer-dominated habitats at all elevations statewide, though spottily distributed through heavily populated portions of Puget Trough in summer. In winter, numbers increase on both sides of Cascades—particularly at lower elevations, including Columbia Basin where absent in breeding season. **Slate-colored Junco** uncommon winter resident, usually noted among flocks of Oregons. Some winter birds intermediate (females often impossible to separate). One record of a third form, **Gray-headed Junco**, in King County (December 2006).

Rustic Bunting Emberiza rustica —Three records: immature stayed at former Kent sewage ponds (King County) for winter of 1986–1987; adult male wintered two years later at same spot—possibly same bird; another individual visited feeders at Leavenworth, November 1998–January 1999.

Summer Tanager Piranga rubra — Seven records, four from winter and three from late spring/summer: One bird visited Skagit County feeder, December 1997–January 1998; one at Ridgefield NWR (Clark County), May 2001; one in Chimacum (Jefferson County), June 2004; one in Ilwaco (Pacific County), December 2012; one in Seattle (King County), also December 2012; one in West Seattle (King County), November 2013; one in Olympia (Thurston County), June 2014.

Western Tanager *Piranga ludoviciana* — Common summer resident statewide in conifer forests (except coastal rain forests). Now largely absent as breeder from developed areas of Puget Trough. Most common in Eastern Washington; Douglas-fir forests favored breeding habitat there. Fairly common migrant nearly statewide. Casual in winter west.

Rose-breasted Grosbeak *Pheucticus ludovicianus* — Casual statewide in spring, summer (May–July)—occurs almost annually. Accidental fall, winter (September–January).

Black-headed Grosbeak *Pheucticus melanocephalus* — Common summer resident of mature lowland broadleaf forests (especially riparian) statewide. Can occur with scattered conifers, but absent where conifers dominate.

Lazuli Bunting *Passerina amoena* — Fairly common summer resident of brushy habitats in Eastern Washington, mostly at lower elevations but extending higher in recently logged sites; uncommon, local on subalpine ridges. In lowlands west of Cascades, uncommon spring migrant, possibly increasing but still uncommon local summer resident.

Indigo Bunting *Passerina cyanea* — Casual to rare in late-spring, summer on both sides of state. Most records (29 records) from May – July. Accidental (four records) in fall (September–November): one record from March in Snohomish County. About three-quarters of records from Western Washington.

Painted Bunting *Passerina ciris* — Three records: A well-photographed male visited Seattle feeders in February–March 2002. A similarly cooperative adult male near Tonasket (Okanogan County) in July–August 2012. An immature was found at Neah Bay (Clallam County) in September 2013.

Dickcissel *Spiza americana* — Nine records: three from May–June, six from October–February. Seven from Western Washington, two from Eastern Washington.

Bobolink *Dolichonyx oryzivorus* — Fairly common but local summer resident of irrigated hay fields in Okanogan, Northeast; outpost colony near Toppenish in Yakima County. Casual in migration in other parts of state when most often detected calling in flight. First noted in Washington in hay fields at Valley (Stevens County) in 1907, about same time invaded similar irrigated habitats in neighboring parts of Idaho, British Columbia.

Red-winged Blackbird *Agelaius phoeniceus* — Common summer resident statewide in wetland habitats of all types, sizes. Also common in winter, when birds move away from frozen-over sites to forage in fields, feedlots in large flocks, frequently with other blackbirds, starlings. Males establish, advertise territories early. Females frequently remain in segregated flocks prior to pair formation.

Tricolored Blackbird *Agelaius tricolor* — Uncommon, extremely local summer resident in Eastern Washington, first found in small breeding colony discovered in 1998 in wetlands along Crab Creek east of town of Wilson Creek. Also breeding near Othello (Adams County), near Texas Lake (Whitman County), possibly elsewhere. Casual in winter in Columbia Basin—usually one or a few birds among larger flocks of other blackbird species. Also a few fall, winter reports from Vancouver Lowlands.

Eastern Meadowlark *Sturnella magna* – One record, Marblemount (Skagit County) in June 2012.

Western Meadowlark *Sturnella neglecta* — Common summer resident in open, low-elevation landscapes of Eastern Washington—shrub-steppe, agricultural fields, ranchland. Once locally common breeder on Western Washington prairies but now rare, seriously declining due to habitat loss; can still be found on South Sound Prairies (Weir Prairie, Mima Mounds), has colonized blast zone on northwest side of Mount Saint Helens. Uncommon to locally fairly common winter resident west of Cascades, mostly in agricultural fields or near coasts. Uncommon, quite local in winter east, mostly on bare, snow-free fields (rarely in shrub-steppe).

Yellow-headed Blackbird *Xanthocephalus xanthocephalus* — Common summer resident of cattail, tule marshes in Eastern Washington, mostly in lowlands but locally up into forest zones (as at Molson). Uncommon to rare in winter in Columbia Basin, mostly at feedlots or in corn stubble. In Western Washington nests regularly at a few places including Ridgefield NWR; rare elsewhere or in other seasons, especially during spring migration (late April to late May).

Rusty Blackbird *Euphagus carolinus* — Rare statewide at lower elevations in fall–winter, usually among flocks of Brewer's and Red-winged Blackbirds. Usually more than one every winter on Skagit or Samish Flats or in Snohomish County.

Brewer's Blackbird *Euphagus cyanocephalus* — Widespread, common resident summer (east), year round (west) at low- to mid-elevations. Mostly found around agricultural lands but also in shrub-steppe, open forest, cities. Forms large foraging flocks in winter, often with other blackbird species. Very locally common east in winter, mostly in feedlots, but absent from vast majority of summer range.

Common Grackle *Quiscalus quiscula* — Casual, nearly annual since 1995. Eastside records outnumber Westside records by about 2-to-1. Most records concentrated late April to early July, rest scattered August to March. First breeding record Ephrata 2002.

Great-tailed Grackle *Quiscalus mexicanus* — Ten records split evenly between east and west. Seven from summer (May–August), two from winter (January–March and March–May), one in Puyallup (Pierce County) from August 2013 into 2014.

Brown-headed Cowbird *Molothrus ater* — Common migrant, summer resident statewide, except in closed forests or at high elevations; small numbers in mixed flocks winter at feedlots on both sides of Cascades. Originally local in Eastern Washington grasslands, increased with Euro-American settlement. On Westside, occurred only casually until first breeding record (Seattle 1955), spread explosively after that. Strongly implicated in decline of many vireos, warblers, other passerines, although specific data for Washington are meager.

Orchard Oriole *Icterus spurius* — Eight records: seven from Western Washington, all from October and through winter; one from Eastern Washington, Grant County in June 2005.

Hooded Oriole *Icterus cucullatus* — Ten records, nine from late April to early August, one from November. Casual spring–summer visitor to Western Washington lowlands; one June record from Eastern Washington, Walla Walla County July 2008.

Bullock's Oriole *Icterus bullockii* — Common summer resident of lowland riparian habitats, farmlands, orchards in Eastern Washington. Once rare in Western Washington, expanded into lowlands there after about 1970—now uncommon to locally fairly common in farmlands, parks, suburbs, riparian areas of lower Puget Trough, where often associated with cottonwoods.

Baltimore Oriole *Icterus galbula* —Six records, four from summer (May–June), one late fall (November) and one early spring (March). Three records from King County, three from Eastern Washington (Kittitas, Chelan, Benton Counties).

Scott's Oriole *Icterus parisorum* — Two records: one in Chehalis (Lewis County), February–April 1980; one in Selah (Yakima County), April 2007.

Brambling *Fringilla montifringilla* — Casual west (16 records) to accidental east (three records) winter visitor. Dates range from late October to mid-April. Prolonged stays typical—over four months, in one case. Records tend to bunch up. Two to three records each in winters of 1990–1991, 1991–1992, 1992–1993, 2012-2013, 2014–2015. Absent most other winters.

Gray-crowned Rosy-Finch *Leucosticte tephrocotis* — Uncommon summer resident in alpine zone of Cascades, small population in Olympics. Often seen above Paradise (Panorama Point), Sunrise (Burroughs Mountain) on Mount Rainier. Nests in rocky areas, forages among rocks or on snow or icefields. In fall, gradually descends through mountains to winter in open country in Eastern Washington, especially northern parts (locally in Southeast). Usually easier to find than in summer, but still uncommon; frequented sites include Lenore Lake, Lower Monumental Dam, Lower Granite Dam, among many others. Often roosts at night in abandoned nests of Cliff Swallows or crevices in cliffs, dispersing by day to weedy areas in open fields or along roads where it feeds on grain spilled from passing trucks. Casual in winter west of Cascade Crest. Washington breeders, most winterers belong to gray-cheeked subspecies *littoralis*, **Hepburn's Rosy-Finch**. Small numbers of brown-cheeked subspecies *tephrocotis* (nominate form, breeding in Rocky Mountains) occur among winter flocks of *littoralis*, particularly in Southeast.

Pine Grosbeak *Pinicola enucleator* — Uncommon summer resident of subalpine in high Olympics, Cascades (around Mount Rainier, from Snoqualmie Pass north), Selkirks, rare in Blues. Most suitable breeding habitat accessible only by hiking or backpacking. By auto, seems most reliable at Harts Pass, Rainy Pass, Washington Pass in North Cascades. Descends to lower levels in winter when locally uncommon in Eastern Washington, particularly in drainages with abundance of berry-producing shrubs or seed-laden conifers, towns with Mountain Ash trees, apple orchards with persistent fruit. Check especially northern Okanogan, Methow River valleys. Rare wanderer in western lowlands in winter.

House Finch *Haemorhous mexicanus* — Common year-round resident in variety of relatively open lowland habitats throughout state, especially cities, towns, agricultural areas, wandering in non-breeding season to weedy fields in shrub-steppe zone. First reported in Eastern Washington in 1885, apparently self-introduced from Idaho or Oregon. By 1920s spread through non-forested eastern parts of state. Casual in Western Washington until first nesting, Christmas Bird Count records (both in 1952), expanded rapidly after that.

Purple Finch *Haemorhous purpureus* — In Western Washington lowlands, foothills, fairly common but apparently declining year-round resident of mixed forests, particularly near openings. Uncommon to locally fairly common summer resident of forest zones along lower east slopes of Cascades (especially drainages of Methow River in Okanogan County, Wenatchee River in Chelan County, Yakima River in Kittitas County, Wenas Creek in Yakima County). Rare in winter in Eastern Washington. Eastern subspecies, *purpureus*, recorded three times, once in Okanogan County (2009), once in Pierce County (2012), and once in Kitsap County (2014).

Cassin's Finch *Haemorhous cassinii* — In Eastern Washington, common summer, uncommon winter resident in Ponderosa Pine zone. Summer resident in open subalpine forests along both slopes of Cascade Crest (uncommon), on Mount Rainier (fairly common). Otherwise, accidental west in any season.

Red Crossbill *Loxia curvirostra* — Fairly common but often irregular year-round resident of most conifer-forest zones in state. Of 10 types of Red Crossbill described in North America (potential species splits), seven occur in Washington (Types I, II, III, IV, V, VII, X). Although call-notes distinctive, types difficult to separate in field (may intermingle). Understanding of Washington status a work in progress.

White-winged Crossbill *Loxia leucoptera* — Erratic visitor at any season, mainly to higher mountains in Okanogan, Northeast, especially in forests of Engelmann Spruce. Often absent for extended periods (even years). Invades from north in major flight years, typically in July or August, spreading through mountains, sometimes lowlands. Singing conspicuous in these years; breeding suspected but never confirmed. Harts Pass, Salmo Pass good bets even in non-invasion years.

Common Redpoll *Acanthis flammea* — Irregular winter visitor, extremely rare some years to irruptively uncommon others. Most often noted in Okanogan, Northeast in alders, birches at mid-elevations of major river valleys, ornamental birches in towns—Winthrop, Chesaw good sites.

Hoary Redpoll Acanthis hornemanni — Irruptive winter visitor, casual at best; not reported every year. Experience of invasion of 2001–2002 suggests minute but fixed proportion of redpolls reaching Washington will be Hoary Redpolls (subspecies *exilipes*). Of 20 accepted records, half from Okanogan or Ferry Counties, only two from Western Washington (Whatcom and Skagit Counties), the remaining eight from across Eastern Washington. Separation from Common Redpolls and documentation remains difficult.

Pine Siskin *Spinus pinus* — Usually Washington's most abundant, ubiquitous finch. Common summer resident of conifer forest, mixed forest with important conifer component, statewide; found at all elevations, even in small conifer stands in cities. Presumably most descend from higher elevations in winter, when fairly common to irregularly common in western lowlands—numbers vary from year to year, even largely absent in winter of 2013–2014. Uncommon (irregularly fairly common), local winter resident in Columbia Basin.

Lesser Goldfinch *Spinus psaltria* — Uncommon but increasing year-round resident in agricultural or weedy habitats along Columbia River in southern Klickitat County and along Snake River. Usually in open areas not far from Garry Oaks. Recent years have seen a likely range expansion through the Snake River and up the westside lowlands, nearly reaching the Puget Trough.

Lawrence's Goldfinch Spinus lawrencei – Two records, both recent: May 2011 in Friday Harbor (San Juan County); May 2013 in Keyport (Kitsap County).

American Goldfinch *Spinus tristis* — Fairly common to common statewide in variety of lowland habitats in all seasons. Numbers drop in winter, especially west. Often commences nesting in June or July, well after most other birds.

Evening Grosbeak *Coccothraustes vespertinus* — Fairly common summer resident in low- to mid-elevation conifer forests statewide (except wettest forests on coast), somewhat irregular in winter but usually uncommon. On the move in spring, when it is a common visitor to deciduous trees (for buds), bird feeders. Seeks areas of insect concentrations such as Spruce Budworm outbreaks; thus numbers at any given locality can vary from year to year. Perhaps most readily detected calling high overhead.

House Sparrow *Passer domesticus* — Locally common at lower elevations, mostly around cities, farms; more confined to urban areas west. Introduced to North America from Europe. Moved west with railroads, reaching Spokane in 1895, Seattle by 1897.

REFERENCES

Alden, P.C., and Paulson, D.R. 1998. *National Audubon Society Field Guide to the Pacific Northwest.* Knopf, New York.

Alt, D.D., and D.W. Hyndman. 1984. *Roadside Geology of Washington.* Mountain Press, Missoula, Montana.

American Birding Association. 2014. *ABA Checklist: Birds of the Continental United States and Canada.* Version 7.7. American Birding Association, Colorado Springs.

American Ornithologists' Union. 1998. *Check-list of North American Birds.* 7th ed. American Ornithologists' Union, Washington, DC. Supplements appear annually in the July *Auk.*

Bell, B.H., and G. Kennedy. 2006. *Birds of Washington State.* Distributed by Lone Pine Publishing, Auburn, Washington.

Cannings, R., and R. Cannings. 2013. *Birdfinding in British Columbia.* Greystone Books, Vancouver. (With the publication of this excellent book, our Washington guide now no longer covers British Columbia sites adjacent to the Washington border.)

Cassidy, K.M. 1997. *Land Cover of Washington State: Description and Management.* Vol. I in Washington State Gap Analysis—Final Report (K.M. Cassidy, C.E. Grue, M.R. Smith, and K.M. Dvornic, eds.). Washington Cooperative Fish and Wildlife Research Unit, University of Washington, Seattle.

Cullinan, T. (compiler). 2001. *Important Bird Areas of Washington.* Audubon Washington, Olympia.

Dawson, W.L. 1909. *The Birds of Washington.* 2 vols. Occidental Publishing Company, Seattle.

eBird.org. *View and Explore Data.* 2015. (Online sightings data for locations, seasons and species).

Franklin, J.F., and C.T. Dyrness. 1973. *Natural Vegetation of Oregon and Washington.* Pacific Northwest Forest and Range Experiment Station, Forest Service, U.S. Department of Agriculture, Portland.

Freelan, S. "Map of the Salish Sea (Mer des Salish) & Surrounding Basin." Web. Stefan Freelan, Western Washington University, Department of Environmental Studies, Huxley College of the Environment. April 25, 2015. *http://staff.wwu.edu/stefan/salish_sea.shtml.*

The Great Washington State Birding Trail. Cascade Loop (2002), Coulee Corridor Scenic Byway (2003), Southwest Loop (2005), Olympic Loop (2006),

Palouse to Pines Loop (2009), Sun and Sage Loop (2009), Puget Loop (2011), Audubon Washington, Olympia. (Large folding maps.)

Hunn, E.S. 2012. *Birding in Seattle and King County* (2nd ed.). Seattle Audubon Society, Seattle.

Jewett, S.A., W.P. Taylor, W.T. Shaw, and J.W. Aldrich. 1953. *Birds of Washington State*. University of Washington Press, Seattle.

Krosby, M., and Rohwer, S. 2010. "Ongoing Movement of the Hermit Warbler X Townsend's Warbler Hybrid Zone." *PLoS ONE*, 5(11), e14164. doi:10.1371/journal.pone.0014164

Kruckeberg, A.R. 1991. *The Natural History of Puget Sound Country*. University of Washington Press, Seattle and London.

Lewis, M.G., and F.A. Sharpe. 1987. *Birding in the San Juan Islands*. Mountaineers, Seattle.

Marshall, D.B., M.G. Hunter, and A.L. Contreras (eds.). 2003. *Birds of Oregon: A General Reference*. Oregon State University Press, Corvallis.

Morse, B. 2001. *A Birder's Guide to Coastal Washington*. R.W. Morse Company, Olympia.

Morse, B., T. Aversa, and H. Opperman. 2015. *Birds of the Puget Sound Region*. (14th printing revised). R.W. Morse Company, Olympia.

Nehls, H., M. Denny, and D. Trochlell. 2008. *Birds of Inland Northwest and Northern Rockies*. R.W. Morse Company, Olympia.

O'Connor, G., and K. Wieda. 2001. *Northwest Arid Lands: An Introduction to the Columbia Basin Shrub-Steppe*. Battelle Press, Columbus, Ohio; distributed by University of Washington Press, Seattle.

Online Guide to the Birds of Washington State. Web. BirdWeb.org. 2005. Seattle Audubon Society.

Paulson, D. 1993. *Shorebirds of the Pacific Northwest*. University of Washington Press, Seattle and London, and Seattle Audubon Society, Seattle.

Smith, M.R., P.W. Mattocks, Jr., and K.M. Cassidy. 1997. *Breeding Birds of Washington State: Location Data and Predicted Distributions*. Volume 4 in Washington State Gap Analysis—Final Report (K.M. Cassidy, C.E. Grue, M.R. Smith, and K.M. Dvornic, eds.). Seattle Audubon Society, Seattle.

Stepniewski, A. 1999. *The Birds of Yakima County, Washington*. Distributed by Yakima Valley Audubon Society, Yakima.

Stepniewski, A. 2011. "The 'Meadows Area' of the Northeastern Cascades." *WOS News* (Issue 135, Oct-Nov 2011):1. wos.org. Washington Ornithology Society bimonthly newsletter, Seattle.

Swan, Ed. 2014 *The Birds of Vashon Island A Natural History of Habitat and Population Transformation*. (2nd ed.). The Swan Company, Vashon, Washington.

Wahl, T.R. 1995. *Birds of Whatcom County Status and Distribution*. T.R. Wahl, Bellingham.

Wahl, T.R., B. Tweit, and S.G. Mlodinow (eds.). 2005. *Birds of Washington Status and Distribution*. Oregon State University Press, Corvallis.

Washington Bird Records Committee. "Sixth Report." Mlodinow, S. and Aanerud, K. (2002), *Washington Birds* 8:1-18. "Seventh Report." Mlodinow, S. and Aanerud, K. (2008), *Washington Birds* 10:21-47. "Eighth Report." Aanerud, K. (2011) *Washington Birds* 11:35-55. Reports are available at http://wos.org/records.html.

Washington Birder. *County Checklist*. 2015. Web. http://wabirder.com

Washington Department of Fish and Wildlife. "Pygmy Rabbits in Washington." Conservation Program. August 2013. Web. Dec 17, 2014. http://wdfw.wa.gov/conservation/pygmy_rabbit/

Washington Department of Natural Resources. 2003. *State of Washington Natural Heritage Plan*. Washington State Department of Natural Resources, Olympia.

Zalesky, P.H. 2001. *Birding in Snohomish County*. rev. ed. Pilchuck Audubon Society, Everett.

WASHINGTON ORNITHOLOGICAL SOCIETY

The Washington Ornithological Society was chartered in 1988
to increase knowledge of the birds of Washington
and to enhance communication among all persons interested in those birds.

The Washington Ornithological Society (WOS) provides a forum for birders from throughout the state to meet and share information on bird identification, biology, population status, and birding sites. Over 400 enthusiastic birders—from backyard feeder watchers to professional ornithologists—belong to WOS. Membership is open to all persons interested in birds and birding.

WHAT WOS HAS TO OFFER:

• A bimonthly electronic newsletter with news and information about the society, birds, birders, habitat, sightings, and other topics.

• Washington Birds, our scholarly journal, previously mailed to all members upon publication, now published online. Several earlier printed versions are available online at our website.

• Washington Field Notes, a regular report on noteworthy sightings from around the state.

• WOS sponsors the Patrick Sullivan Young Birders Fund, which gives grants to young birders for birding activities or study.

• WOS meetings are held on the first Monday of each month (except July, August, and September) at the Center for Urban Horticulture on the University of Washington Seattle campus. Meetings feature refreshment, socializing, and interesting programs.

• WOS Annual Conference, open to all members, is held in a different part of the state each year. It includes speakers, workshops, identification contests, and field trips.

• Field trips for members are held throughout the year to all areas of the state.

• WOS sponsors the Washington Bird Records Committee, which maintains the official state bird list and birding records that substantiate it. The committee decides whether to accept reported sightings of rarely seen species or new species and publishes reports on its decisions.

• The state checklist of birds, prepared by WOS, is offered in various convenient formats for carrying in the field, downloading, or printing out.

• The WOS website provides photos, information about upcoming field trips, good birding locations, information about Christmas Bird Counts around the state, checklists, avian research in the region, and WOS merchandise. A growing number of WOS publications are available on the website. Sightings of rare birds can be submitted to the Washington Bird Records Committee at the website: *http://wos.org/records*

• Dues are $25 for an Individual, $30 for a Family, $15 for a Student, and $500 for a Lifetime membership.

WOS is a non-profit organization under section 501(c)(3) of the Internal Revenue Code.

Washington Ornithological Society
12345 Lake City Way NE #215 , Seattle, Washington 98125

WASHINGTON BIRD RECORDS COMMITTEE

Observations of species on the Washington Review List (common names italicized on the Annotated Checklist in this guide or not listed there at all) should be reported to the WBRC with written details and any supporting evidence such as photographs and sound recordings. Complete your report on-line or submit it to the WBRC at the address below. Documentation should include:

Species name.

Number of individuals seen.

Location.

Date.

Time and duration of sighting.

Observer's contact information.

Description of size, shape, and plumage. Describe in detail all parts of the bird, including the beak and feet. Mention more than just the diagnostic characters, yet include only what was actually observed in the field.

Description of voice or call, if heard.

Description of behavior.

Habitat—general and specific.

Distance from you to the bird.

Optical equipment used (including binoculars, telescopes, cameras)
Light (sky condition, amount of light on bird, position of sun)

Similar-appearing species which were eliminated by description, call or behavior (7, 8, and 9 above). Explain.

Previous experience with this species and similar-appearing species.

Other observers.

Field guides, other books, articles, and advice consulted, and how these influenced your description.

Were field notes about the observation written during observation, immediately after, later, or not at all?

If you were able to take photos, make sound recordings, or draw sketches of the bird you observed, send them by postal mail or by email to:

Washington Ornithological Society
Washington Bird Records Committee

12345 Lake City Way NE #215
Seattle, WA 98125
http://wos.org/records
email: *wbrc@wos.org*

American Birding
A S S O C I A T I O N

Join the American Birding Association

*When you become a member of the American Birding Association,
you join thousands of birders
who are eager to improve their knowledge and skills
to get the most out of their birding experiences.*

- ✔ **Network** with friends and share the passion of birding.

- ✔ **Learn** more about birds and birding.

- ✔ **Sharpen** and augment your birding skills.

- ✔ **Participate** in workshops, conferences, and tours.

- ✔ **Receive** our full-color magazine, *Birding*, and our quarterly
  magazine, *Birder's Guide*.

You don't have to be an expert birder to be a member of
the American Birding Association. You're qualified
simply by having a desire to learn more about birds,
their habitats, and how to protect them.

ABA membership offers you the opportunity to meet and
learn from experts and to improve your skills through
our internationally attended conferences and
conventions, Institute for Field Ornithology workshops,
specialized tours, and volunteer opportunities. It is
great way to get to know others who share your
interests.

ABA Membership
PO Box 3070, Colorado Springs, CO 80934
Phone: 800-850-2473
www.aba.org/join

ABA Birdfinding Guide Series

A Birder's Guide to Alaska
George C West
*

A Birder's Guide to Belize
Bert Frenz
*

A Birder's Guide to Florida
Bill Pranty
*

A Birder's Guide to Louisiana
Richard Gibbons, Roger Breedlove, Charles Lyon
*

A Birder's Guide to Metropolitan Areas of North America
Paul Lehman
*

A Birder's Guide to Michigan
Allen T Chartier and Jerry Ziarno
*

A Birder's Guide to the Rio Grande Valley
Mark W Lockwood, William B McKinney, James N Paton, Barry R Zimmer
*

A Birder's Guide to Southeastern Arizona *Richard Cachor Taylor*
*

A Birder's Guide to Southern California *Brad Schram*
*

A Birder's Guide to the Texas Coast
Mel Cooksey and Ron Weeks
*

A Birder's Guide to Virginia
David Johnston
*

A Birder's Guide to Washington, Second Edition
Members of the Washington Ornithological Society

ABA SALES
www.aba.org/abasales

AMERICAN BIRDING ASSOCIATION

PRINCIPLES OF BIRDING ETHICS

Everyone who enjoys birds and birding must always respect wildlife, its environment, and the rights of others. In any conflict of interest between birds and birders, the welfare of the birds and their environment comes first.

CODE OF BIRDING ETHICS

1. Promote the welfare of birds and their environment.

1(a) Support the protection of important bird habitat.

1(b) To avoid stressing birds or exposing them to danger, exercise restraint and caution during observation, photography, sound recording, or filming.

Limit the use of recordings and other methods of attracting birds, and never use such methods in heavily birded areas or for attracting any species that is Threatened, Endangered, or of Special Concern, or is rare in your local area.

Keep well back from nests and nesting colonies, roosts, display areas, and important feeding sites. In such sensitive areas, if there is a need for extended observation, photography, filming, or recording, try to use a blind or hide, and take advantage of natural cover.

Use artificial light sparingly for filming or photography, especially for close-ups.

1(c) Before advertising the presence of a rare bird, evaluate the potential for disturbance to the bird, its surroundings, and other people in the area, and proceed only if access can be controlled, disturbance can be minimized, and permission has been obtained from private land-owners. The sites of rare nesting birds should be divulged only to the proper conservation authorities.

1(d) Stay on roads, trails, and paths where they exist; otherwise keep habitat disturbance to a minimum.

2. Respect the law and the rights of others.

2(a) Do not enter private property without the owner's explicit permission.

2(b) Follow all laws, rules, and regulations governing use of roads and public areas, both at home and abroad.

2(c) Practice common courtesy in contacts with other people. Your exemplary behavior will generate goodwill with birders and non-birders alike.

3. Ensure that feeders, nest structures, and other artificial bird environments are safe.

3(a) Keep dispensers, water, and food clean and free of decay or disease. It is important to feed birds continually during harsh weather.

3(b) Maintain and clean nest structures regularly.

3(c) If you are attracting birds to an area, ensure the birds are not exposed to predation from cats and other domestic animals, or dangers posed by artificial hazards.

4. Group birding, whether organized or impromptu, requires special care.

Each individual in the group, in addition to the obligations spelled out in Items #1 and #2, has responsibilities as a Group Member.

4(a) Respect the interests, rights, and skills of fellow birders, as well as those of people participating in other legitimate outdoor activities. Freely share your knowledge and experience, except where code 1(c) applies. Be especially helpful to beginning birders.

4(b) If you witness unethical birding behavior, assess the situation and intervene if you think it prudent. When interceding, inform the person(s) of the inappropriate action and attempt, within reason, to have it stopped. If the behavior continues, document it and notify appropriate individuals or organizations.

Group Leader Responsibilities [amateur and professional trips and tours].

4(c) Be an exemplary ethical role model for the group. Teach through word and example.

4(d) Keep groups to a size that limits impact on the environment and does not interfere with others using the same area.

4(e) Ensure everyone in the group knows of and practices this code.

4(f) Learn and inform the group of any special circumstances applicable to the areas being visited (e.g., no tape recorders allowed).

4(g) Acknowledge that professional tour companies bear a special responsibility to place the welfare of birds and the benefits of public knowledge ahead of the company's commercial interests. Ideally, leaders should keep track of tour sightings, document unusual occurrences, and submit records to appropriate organizations.

PLEASE FOLLOW THIS CODE— DISTRIBUTE IT AND TEACH IT TO OTHERS.

Additional copies of the Code of Birding Ethics can be obtained from:
ABA, P.O. Box 744, Delaware City, DE 19706.
Phone 800-850-2473 or 302-838-3650;
www.aba.org; e-mail: info@aba.org

7/1/96

INDEX

Rather than being listed alphabetically by name, several categories of index entries are grouped by type of site or facility: Dam; Ferry; Indian Reservation; Mountain passes; Park (includes private, municipal, county, state, and national); Sewage treatment facilities; Wilderness Areas; Wildlife Area. If you can't find a site indexed under its proper name, look for it in one of these groups.

*The **Abbreviated Table of Contents** boxes let you find the chapter location of any numeric index entry. For example, if you are on the Pacific Coast and wonder whether you can expect to find Brewer's Blackbird, you can quickly ascertain—by comparing the Abbreviated Table of Contents page-number range with the page numbers of the index entries—that this species is not mentioned in the text for this region. All ABA Birdfinding Guides use this time-saving feature.*

W